*A big thank you to John Christopher and Christine Marie,
who, with their joint efforts in vision and literary ideas
came up with a promotional page for the book.*

*You can go to the promotional link about this book at:
www.myspace.com/Imagine1989
Enjoy!*

*Chief Editor: "Tiffany S. Teofilo is Sandusky native, a youth
media scholar and an accountant. She enjoys long walks on the beach,
teaching and editing exceptional books like this one!"*

*I'd like to thank my father, who unknowingly gave me the idea for a
title.
The same man who taught me not to expect anything
And to always be prepared.
Thanks for all your help in all these years.
You're the best and
The wisest person I know!*

*I'd also like to thank all my kids who kept their cool
while I worked so patiently to get this book
completed.
Thanks, Lisa, Stacey, Tommy, Julie and Chrissy!*

*In loving memory of my mother. I'd like to thank her
for turning me on to the classic movies and the classical music.
I will always miss you and your laughter, and allowing me to be me.*

*Also, in loving memory of Dr. Joseph Buder who
was always there with a kind word and
could always put me at ease just being Doc'!
He helped me through most of the
Toughest times in my life
And I got through the most of
them because of him!*

And of Course in Loving memory of "Sir John Lennon."
Bigger than life "Mr. Lennon"!
You touched my heart and my mind and my soul. You'll always forever
will be missed, and loved ... !
There will never be another like you John!

And "The Beatles" could not have been, if not for the gentle
Soul of "Sir George Harrison". You too shall be missed
And loved always ... !

"... Now it's past my bed I know, and I'd really like to go.
Soon will be the break of day, sitting here in Blue Jay Way ..."

"Blue Jay Way - (Fog Upon L.A.)"
"The Beatles"
From: "The Magical Mystery Tour"

Dedications? To whom? For what? And then it came to me in great suffering.

"... Timothy James Smith..."

"DO YOU THINK BEFORE YOU SPEAK?
CAN SOMEONE CATCH YOU OFF GUARD?
DO YOU NEED TO MANIFEST STRANGE
PEOPLE IN THE YARD?

DID A THOUGHT OCCUR BEFORE YOU SPOKE?
TAKE IT EASY, SEE I AM RESTING.
TALK AND TELL TOO MUCH YOU
HELP WITH THE INVESTING.

FOR CRYING OUT LOUD! YOU'RE THERE!
SMOKING, THINKING, WON'T LET GO.
TOUGH JOB WAS MINE
IS YOURS YOU KNOW.

HAVE YOU TALKED WHEN YOU FOUND
OUT THAT I WAS YOUR MENTOR TIM?
HEARD YOU THINKING, BEFORE YOUR TALKING,
YOU'RE RIGHT AND I STILL AM."

This I dedicate to the man, the title, Timothy James Smith on this morning of September 16th, 2:04 A.M. 2000.

We had a common bond as far as minds go. And we were out there knowing we were granted a Higher Permission to be.

Tim instructed me on destinations. Imagine them all. Can you? Life is complicated if you spend too much time thinking that. Doesn't it lay right in front of you?

It's a different world every day. A change takes place quick in ways. Life was much too much for Tim to take.

One cold and rainy December morning, after I had sent out Christmas cards, I received a phone call from Tim's mother. I was in total denial when she said that he had died on October 5th that year in 1999.

My mind wondered into the spirit of the holidays ahead clouded, knowing it couldn't be true. In January of 2000, a long time friend came to see me. Dennis, who had met Tim, said not to worry. Tim was probably out on a mission somewhere hiding out. Sure, I thought. That's it! A secret mission. A mission for G.O.D.! For two months this book was laid to rest. Was Tim? I went back in time again...

...It was 1998, it was June when I drove to Toledo to pop in on him. Why didn't I hug him when our eyes met? Our last words still have me very upset. "Are ya working for God?" I wanted reactions. Tim held back the tears, "Talk's over. Time to take action."

Something didn't feel right. Something is wrong! Pot wasn't giving me the answers so I called a place with a question. Vital Statistics. Timothy had indeed died. The cause of his death would come to me in the mail on a certificate that I had to see for myself. Both his birth and death certificate arrived on February 7th, 2000. Tim had committed suicide. My eyes swelled with questions. Why? Was it me?

For I was the lady in the hold land in which every where he looked. I was the one he loved up until he breathed the last breath he took. If only I complied and warmed your cheek as you wished so, would it have made a difference? Would it have kept you from wanting to go? Here's the hug I wanted to give you, the one I give you now. I love you Tim. You are my friend where ever you are and this isn't the end.

This is not your final destination. Yours is where it is. Eastern star shining strong! Guiding me, teaching me! Be Bright and brilliant for you know that I'll be shining right alongside you. We can do the walks again and again. And the learning will not end.

I know that Tim would want me to be smiling and laughing and in time I know we'll do the songs and talks again.

You know how thought of you are! You're my mentor the star. Good old Citizen you haven't changed a bit. Your strength and clever way you told the truth in bits. You're one of a kind and gifted. You mattered! You matter and fever you will matter to me. How right you are about destiny. With love, C.S.E.S.

Contents

Prologue

It was a magical romance...

From the very moment these two souls united, a unique and radiant harmony was captured between them. Each and every enchanted day they shared with one another ended in an array of beautiful memories filled with song, laughter, and playful dreams. This love, so perfect and true, could have only been a gift from above. But with heaven comes hell...

And when the demons of Capri Spettro's past refused to release their wicked grip from her life, it slowly suffocated this angelic love. Those dark shadows would ultimately consume the light in Gentry's eyes, casting Capri's angel away into a mysterious realm of uncertainty. He would escape with her heart in his hands, and leave behind only one hope...That he may one day return...

What would become of Capri in the days that followed is where this twisted journey unfolds, for with this loss also came an unbearable reality. The burden of a painful past now weighed more heavily upon her than ever before. In a world where punishment looms in the dark storm clouds above and tears have a way of flooding the imagination, those who are sinking may instead feel like they are sailing.

During this slow downward spiral into madness, Capri transformed into Eve, and believed wholeheartedly in her life or death pact with the *Big Man* upstairs. Fueled by her childhood dream of marrying "John Lennon", and chasing after what appeared to be an impossible miracle, Capri began walking the tightrope of insanity in pure certainty

Trapped in this bizarre and brokenhearted world of illusion, would the long and winding road to freedom ever reveal itself...or would Capri die trying to find it...

Must have had some nightmare. Lying on my back I stared at the white ceiling and thought... This isn't my room. There was a light above my bed. I couldn't see the sky from the window and what happened to the parking lot? The cars, the van right outside my window? Got up and noticed another bed and someone sleeping in it. I walked around the bed so I could see a face and it was a man. This brought on greater concern knowing that my room in the wacky ward had only one bed.

Well I'll be damned! I'm at Osborne Park! Why would they bring me here? Self thought... Is this placed closed already? There was no one walking around outside.   All I saw through my obstructed vision were trees and a pond.

Quickly I remembered I was allowed a collect call.   I crossed the floor to get to the pay phone and called Nina.   "Nina.   This is Cappy.   You'll never believe where I am!   When I woke up I looked out the window and get this.   I'm at Osborne Park.   It's not even open yet is it?"   I could hear Nina trying to cover her chuckle when she spoke to me.   "Cappy.   You're not at Osborne Park.   We've been waiting for you to call.   You must have really been knocked out when they took you in."   "What the hell are you talking about?   You know they released me from the nut ward on April 8th!"   "I know Cappy, but honey, you are not at Osborne Park."   Nina asked me to hold on and I listened.   She was talking to Pope.   She wanted him to take the phone, but I heard him say you tell her.   Nina was back on the line and said, "Cappy.   You're not where you think you are.   You are in a mental hospital."   "No I'm not.   I *was* in a mental hospital!   Got out remember?   They sent me home."   "Cappy.   Your father and I have waited three days for you to call.   I know it's hard to believe and I'm really sorry, but you are in a mental hospital."

Why wasn't she calling it the South Pavilion like the name it was?   Why all of a sudden is she calling this place a mental hospital?

I knew what I saw out the window.   Knew where I was... or did I?

Psychiatric Examination: 04/12/1989
Name: Capri Spettro
Age: 32 years
Sex: Female
Race: White
Marital Status: Divorced
Date of Admission: April 4th, 1989
Type of Admission: Emergency
Brought From: Firelands

Patient's Chief Complaint

Patient's complaint is that she thought she was carrying a baby, and she went to the E.R. with a sample of her bleeding, but it was just poop in a jar. She is agreeable to hospitalization.

History of Present Illness

Patient is a 32 year old White female who states that she was just recently diagnosed with a Bipolar Disorder.   This being 03-19-1989 at Firelands Hospital.   She is a poor historian.   States that today she felt that she was pregnant, that she went to the E.R. with a sample of her bleeding, which turned out to be just stool in a jar. States that she was willing go to back to the Psych Unit at Firelands, but for some reason was not admitted there. Continues to ramble on and on about being pregnant and that it was just "poop in a jar." She also feels that the radio station in Sandusky, W.C.P.Z. sent her on a wild goose chase to the Radisson and that they made John Lennon look as if he was still alive. She feels that her friends act like they are the Wizard of Oz and she is Dorothy on the Yellow Brick Road. She also feels that she is one special girl. Apparently she went to the Radisson and tried to obtain admission to a private party and was taken away by the police. Patient does admit to some history of depression and wishing that she were dead at times and becomes tearful, but states she would never do it. Patient also feels that Lithium makes her hallucinate and she does complain of blurry vision. Patient states that she has not been sleeping at night, that she has increased her eating and that she has high energy. She also complains of having fast thoughts, but insists that her concentration is good, real good. Patient's speech is obviously pressured. She denies any suicidal ideations at this time.

Past Medical History
Psychiatric - She states her only hospitalization was at Firelands on March 19th of 1989, this year. And that she was in the hospital for about 4 weeks. Medical problems - There is a question of a heart murmur.
Her current medications are Lithium 300 mg.

"Before Chapter One"

" ... What's so important those frenzied dishes?
Want much to tell about them but I need to do my wishes ..."
From: "Because You Are Interesting ... (I Am Curious)"
Words written by Catherine Santi, January 18th, 1985
Oceans of emotions had been beneath the surface long enough. Words were spoken with certainty, I am Eve." A swift reply came with ease, "Then you're Noah's wife." Through phone lines I listened to my older brother, who I shall lovingly refer to as Hermit

After our conversation time told me the sun would make her eastern entrance soon, and through the front window I had it out with God. "I'll rip this rib outta me with my bare hands!" Second plans were made to meet with The Almighty April 27th, 1989. Not one day sooner and never a day late. Timing was non-negotiable and I needed a boat. Where would I find a boat I thought? "Captain! He's got an old canoe out in his back yard. He'd let me use it for a few days." Getting to Montana will be easy. The Going To The Sun Road will lead me right to the palm-treed-paradise that was once mine and Adam's. "Oh I'll be there on the Holy Island and You'll be there Number One! You hear me? You may not wanna hear me, but You do. Pretty fucking hard to forget who did what and when isn't it? One bite off an apple and all this? Hasn't the world had enough?" Silently I watched the puffy-white-spring-clouds for a sign. Something to indicate that I was heard.

Of course God knew I was up to something. He'd get the rib all right, but there would be and exchange for my life... a miracle of a sort... one that He mysteriously granted to me on the evening of March 19th, 1989.

My dad, who I shall call Pope, talked me into admitting myself into a psychiatric ward for a few days. I spent hours preparing for my *"going in."*

All that was left of my gala apparel, proudly worn on St. Patrick's Day, were two bandannas. One white and a sky-blue-colored one. I put them together with all the white clothes I intended on wearing that day.

My white scarf was neatly twisted and tied across my forehead. I wore a man's white tee shirt under a white puffy-sleeved-long-tailed-blouse. Naturally the pants matched both the tops and the under garments too. All was white. I carried my blue bandanna in my pants pocket as a symbol of hope. Pinned on the heart side of my blouse were seven different colored hearts that Noah's two little girls had made for me the previous night Noah steps into the book a bit later. Gold earrings symbolizing Pope's country were on. A finger wore a gold ring and my neck hung a gold necklace. There was one more object I managed to take with me. A small and beautiful brass bell. The tone it rang brought to mind the start of a "John Lennon" song called: "Just Like (Starting Over)."

Pope walked with me through the emergency room doors to meet with the doctors there. They would be full of questions... and I thought... should I answer them?

I felt trapped. Didn't anyone there know that I had a very important engagement to keep? Certainly John would be wondering where I was by now.

After admission "*they*" took me to a psychiatrist's office. That doctor would make a hospital recommendation for me.

A skinny-short man of Asian descent came into the office and took a seat behind his desk. He glanced at my chart. He looked at me with his arm stretched out to one side like he was holding something and said, "Your mind! It's out there!" Well I didn't see anything there and that made me wonder... Who was the real nut in the room, me or him?

How did I end up in that place? A time of make believe? A place where my worth was 500 million dollars, and for something only I was supposed to know. It's been just over ten years since a day presented itself to me. One that was mine and mine alone. Just as then, the memories are as clear and as vivid as that time. That time in 1989.

Never once did I think I had lost mind, though the Doc[1] claimed he knew its location.

I often wondered about writing the bizarre events that took place in my life, but found myself hesitating for fear that I'd hurt important people in my life. The ones that I know and love, and the people I have only dreamed of knowing, yet knowing I loved.

Labeled? Me? Yeah...they did it. The doctors. I'm bipolar. Polar. North. Magnet. B. Two. Two magnetic fields maybe? If that's the case, I thought, then I'm definitely tripolar! Three friends for me! Maybe I lived in three different worlds all at once? My past my present and my soon to be future. Three...my number.

Remember... I was Eve and I was there, third in line, but there.

Naturally God had to be Number One. He favored Adam and made me to multiply. So there it is in simple math. From the moment My Creator made me, He was sure to embed the number three on my soul for life after life and now.

Adam and I lived in the Garden of Eden. It was filled with splendid surroundings. Palm trees, warm breezes in the day of sun and mirrored like seas and skies. Animals that swam, that flew, that trotted along shore fines of crystal sandy shores.

Since there are way too many details about the animals let's get right down to the forbidden fruit.

And it was an apple. The tree I got it from was filled with many shiny green apples. Yes, they were green. After all, I was there, remember?

God would no doubt allow us to eat from the tree someday.

One afternoon white looking curiously at the tree, a slithery, coiled up life on one of the branches spoke to me in a whisper, "Eve. How come you have not tried a bite of the apple yet? God didn't tell you about the knowledge to be gained from it? To be as God? Go on Eve..." I looked at the snake and uttered nothing. I plucked the green fruit from the trees branch, turned away from the tempting voice of the snake and hurried to hide in the evergreens. I stared at this mysterious and forbidden apple. It seemed like the morning had passed. I rubbed the apple with the palms of my hands and looked around for God. He was nowhere to be seen. Then I remembered what the snake had said and took a large bite. The fruit was tart and bitter and I crunched it quickly. My mouth puckered as it was unlike any of the sweet fruits in the Garden. I rushed to Adam to show him that I had taken a bite. I tried to describe the taste to Adam and I told him what the snake had told me. Now don't believe everything you read, for stories have a way of being exaggerated over the centuries. It wasn't the power or knowledge that I was after, but to get away with something.

"Come on Adam, go ahead and try it. God certainly won't miss one little green apple from a tree that contains so many. He'll never even notice." Adam took the apple from me taking a nice big sour bite.

"Eve," saying my name and gasping for a breath. This is not sweet." I looked on. I thought it might make Adam laugh as I did, but Adam began to cough and cough. His fair skinned face grew pink. His breath got shorter and less with each cough struggling for air as he went from pink to blood red. He uttered no words as I watched his skin grow a deep and dark purple. Suddenly Adam fell to the ground. He lay motionless. I knelt beside him, called out his name and Adam said nothing. His once smiling brown eyes now fixed an estranged gaze into mine without a blink. I rested my cheek upon Adam's chest but could no longer hear the pounding from within his body's wall. I called out his name again and then again. I picked up Adams arm from the earth. It was heavy and limp. I stayed with Adam for a long period of time until Adam's body was cold and stone like. I knew, like the night I was born, God would soon be coming when night was upon me. How do I know? I was there, but so soon would be God. How would I answer to

Him? He's going to know, I thought the snake had lied to me. For if what he said was true then certainly I would know what to say to God and how.

There was God. He looked at Adam then at me and said, "Adam is dead." Dead, I thought? What is dead? There was never a mention of this new name. It was Adam and I who named all the living things God had made and we called nothing dead. God went on and said, "I see that he has gone against My request not to eat from the tree of forbidden fruit." "Oh God," I said, "The snake told me that by taking one bite I would know what you know. It was I who gave it to Adam." "Eve look. There lies the bitten piece of apple just beneath the skin in the midst of Adam's throat." I hadn't noticed it before, but there it was just as God pointed out. I most certainly would be punished for this by my Father, but I never imagined that after some ten thousand years, that every woman everywhere would be punished along with me. There had to be a way to make things right! Couldn't that short, skinny Asian man see that?

"Where Chapter One Gets A Title"

In Sandusky Ohio lived a beautiful woman who I shall call Mayor. Mayor's hair was long, wavy and brown. Her eyes green, her complexion, flawless and legs to die for!

Mayor worked at a local business called "The Cameo." She washed dishes there. Little did she know that a young man from across the Atlantic Ocean had made plans to visit the United States.

Pope ended up in Ohio and in Sandusky where some of his San Marino friends had already made America home. One of those friends took Pope to the pizza place when Mayor was at work. Joe introduced them, translated words for them. That's pretty much all it took. Mayor fell for Pope's good looks and accent. What she didn't know is that he would be going back to his small country of San Marino.

Pope once again sailed across the ocean. He explained to his parents that he had fallen in love with a beautiful American woman and could not go through with the prearranged marriage to Maria. Four months later Pope bordered another ship and traveled across the Atlantic to make Sandusky his home and to make Mayor his wife. All went as planned. Pope and Mayor were married in the early fifties on August 9th.

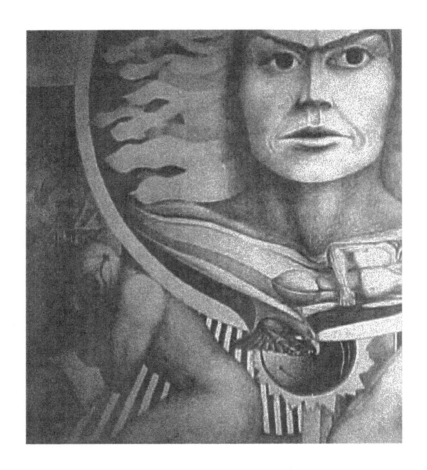

Chapter One: "The Family"

"I try beginnings, but somehow find myself constantly consumed in the middle. Because it seems it's all that's ever left and centering myself is no common riddle..." From: "Because You Are Interesting (I Am Curious)" Written by: Catherine Santi January 18th, 1985

Hermit was the first of my three brothers. Hermit built models. Model cars, monster models and "The Starship Enterprise"

Hermit consumed his knowledge from books. Hermit read comic books, mythology books, "Playboy" books and more and more books in between. But Hermit spent the most part of his time drawing. Hermit drew cars, people, places faces and strange-far-out things. And indeed he was great in all the things he did and does.

Hermit spent much of his time in the back east corner of our house, in his room, growing up and into the permanent and fine artist that he is!

Born second to my parents was a daughter. Pope and Mayor adored the baby girl. They decided to name her after Pope's mother back in San Marino who I shall refer to as Capri.

Capri Ann was warmly welcomed and loved by her new family. I'm sure Mayor couldn't have been happier and she would be daddy's little girl. Then, within three weeks after she was born, Capri was very ill. She was taken to a Cleveland hospital where Pope and Mayor visited her every day. The day after Mayor's birthday, March 22nd, Pope and her went again to visit and be with their baby girl. They went to her room and she was not there. Pope and Mayor rushed to the doctors wanting to know where Capri was! Upon knowing, they walked to the room with heavy hearts and saw their baby laying still and breathless. It sent Mayor beyond reality. Mayor couldn't and didn't believe Capri was dead. She'd be in a mental institution for 6 weeks. I like to think that Capri Ann was whisked by angel wings for a child bearing her 1st name.

Cap dreamed of a tiny girl. A small parcel of smiles, descending from the cloud lit skies, ever so slowly, swaying beneath an umbrella of white fluffy lace. The dream of the child was frequent and always the same. This little girl who'd visit Cap's dreams would be wearing the same white ruffled-bow-waisted baby dress, cute matching baby underpants full of soft cotton and white lacy ruffles. On her tiny feet were a pair of white baby booties that would lace with satin ribbons.

Cap noted the girl's hair was beginning to curl at her ears, as the sun lightened the dark curly locks with splashes of gold... and the dream focused in. Cap was in awe watching Capri Ann float down on the western corner of her front lawn where she stood like an angel from the heavens. Cap never left her front porch to approach tiny magical little fairy. No words were spoken. Yet somehow Cap knew in her heart that this little creature loved her. And ever so small as Cappy was, she also knew that the baby was the sister she would never know in her real world of brothers.

To my parents a third child was born. A daughter. Yes, I am Cap. The third born, living on "C" street, the third letter of the alphabet, being the first initial of my first name. The name I also shared with two other girls on the block. The fun came everyday when the three of us were outside playing and then being called in for supper.

John was next in fine. I believe someone could have snooped in our photo albums and decided then that he would be the original idea behind the "Cabbage Patch Kids." Somewhere between the crawling-almost-walking-stage of John's life, the family couldn't help but notice that his head was larger than most babies. Would it slow him down for a first step? How about balance? Slow John down? Never. For it didn't take us long to see that the pumpkin head was there to conceal the amount of intelligence he was keeping to himself. As for balance?

Now Short Cake was the baby of the family. He had been nicknamed that because his favorite desert was strawberry shortcake. After all, we had a plentiful garden and there were many strawberries.

We were a close clan my brothers and me. We stood up for each other. Stuck together like kids should and it worked well. Our parents were to be respected. If we hurt one another in some way Pope made certain that apologies were in order. But the forgiving we dealt with on our own. Let's say I messed up something that belonged to Hermit. He'd get pissed off and I would say I was sorry and I meant it. Sure he'd forgive me by never ever letting me forget what it was I had done to piss him off in the first place. This of course can last a lifetime and became a family tradition of sorts.

We had lots of kids in the neighborhood and the boys outnumbered the girls. Back then people didn't put fences around their little castles and our night-time-neighborhood kids were free roaming the yards for most of our games. Chase was a favorite. Much like tag, In Chase we had teams of about five, maybe six a team. Naturally the safe spot where you couldn't get tagged and eliminated was a tree that stood all alone in the middle of "George Windaus" yard. Being right near a street lamp it wasn't easily accessible.

Good old Kick the Can. We used "Windaus" property importantly because he was one few people on the block who had a cemented drive. Most of us wore sneakers to play the game, but Hermit would only wear boots and when he kicked the can sparks flew… literally. Hermit was by far my favorite brother.

It was a strange but loving environment. See the Pope and the Mayor were like the difference between a "tsunami" and a back yard pond. Mayor being the pond.

Pope had only gone to school till about the age of 9. He got a job with a cobbler in his village and learned to make shoes. At 14 years old, he carried bricks up the mountain where a third castle was being built. When the Pope became a man, he set his sights on America and found a job building boats at "Lyman Boat Works" People agree that a Lyman boat is by far one of the finer water crafts on the water. And Pope worked and worked and worked.

Mayor did eight years at a private school and went on to her final four years at Sandusky High where she received her diploma and graduated. She took singing and dancing lessons. She studied for years on the piano learning the classical pieces. She knew how to play it well and have a good time.

Pope never had to say much of anything when we would upset him. All he ever had to do was glare at us with those intense Italian blue eyes. Mayor had at sense of humor when it came down to getting us off her back. If it was her nerves we were getting on, she'd say something like, "Why don't you guys go play in the traffic." If we deliberately annoyed her she would tell us to gargle with rusty razor blades. Knowing she was laughing on the inside and out, it still meant to get the hell out of her way, so we could go out and have some fun.

Pope found little humor in it as life was a serious trail he had been blazing for years.

The Mayor spent much of her day with the usual "shit load" of housework as she so named it. She was always busy taking care of us, feeding us, keeping us happy and all the things a mom does in a day. During her free time Mayor would be on the phone with her younger sister Madge talking carnival talk.

When Pope was done at work for the day he was tired and hungry. He wanted his dinner in peace and quiet. But you have to remember that us kids had been in school sitting on our asses for seven hours and again on our bus ride home for about 40 minutes. Peace and quiet would have been the general rule but we had to get away with something.

It wasn't so bad to have to deal with my parents separately, but to have to be with both of them at the same time… that was a challenge. Mayor would hear Pope pull in the drive. She'd cut her conversation on the phone with her sister, and call in the forces to get the dinner table set and ready for Pope.

I set the table. Shorty filled the glasses. John spilled them, and Hermit, Hermit hid.

Mayor would give us a holler, "Okay people, time to eat!"

It was a small kitchen, with blue tile half way up the wall, outlined in black. We sat closely next to each other where the table was neatly cornered in the kitchen.

Pope sat at the head of the table. Mayor, to his right. My left handed brother John, to Mayors right. Backs to the wall were Hermit on Johns right then Shorty and me. I was under the unfortunate and extreme pressure to be seated not only to Pope's left, but directly across from Mayor. Not that I didn't love them, but the Mayor would always instigate some kind of something. She knew it would piss off the Pope and she started with me.

Not that we weren't allowed to have a "normal" conversation at the table, we were, so long as it didn't get out of hand and Pope was able to seriously eat the meal which was now in front of him. All Mayor had to do was take a bite of food, glance up to me with a "Mona Lisa" type grin and kick my foot under the table. I in turn would nudge Hermit with my foot... Hermit would take a chip from the bowl if we happened to have them handy. He'd stick it in his eye, his ear, imitating a potato chip commercial he'd seen on TV. Mayor tried holding in her laughter. Sounded like she was between a cough and a snore. I couldn't help it and I did the same, peeking at Pope. John tried aimlessly not to knock Mayors eating hand with his left elbow. Shorty and Pope continued with supper.

Our ultimate goal however was not yet achieved. The Pope wasn't pissed. He looked up briefly and went on with his meal.

I felt the kick from Mayor again under the table. I kicked Hermit. Johns elbow didn't matter at all, and as for Shorty and Pope, they ate.

The last time around, I started to laugh. Mayor looked at me firmly and said, "Cappy. Your father is trying to eat." (Grinning the whole time). Pope gave me the evil-blue eye. It was hell holding in the laughter. The more effort I put into it, the worse it became and the Lemonade was getting harder to resist. Why? Too afraid that if I took a sip it would explode and enrage Pope, (but that's what we wanted!) Bravely and slowly I took a sip. When I did... Pope was in the direct line of the Lemonade eruption which landed on his face and his food. I removed myself from the table... it would have happened anyway. Pope got a clean towel from Mayor and sopped the mess off his plate of pasta. My back was against the kitchen sink watching Pope. The evil-blue eyes took effect immediately.

The Mayor laughed while she calmed Pope. She admitted she started it all in the first place. Shorty was done eating anyway. John was laughing at something entirely out of context. Where was Hermit? Hiding.

Chapter Two: "Cedar Point-
The Amazement Park"

Sunday nights were "Bonanza" nights and "The Ed Sullivan Show." The "June Taylor Dancers" made the show most worthwhile for me. Uniquely they were filmed from above. The women would form a circle and change movements in their legs and arms. Mayor reminded me to squint my eyes so the girls would look like a kaleidoscope. They did.

Little did Hermit and I know that something better was going to happen one particular night with Ed. He was going to have a band perform on his stage for the first time. This first time band was no ordinary band, this was "The Beatles"!

I can remember being on the living room floor next to Hermit, sitting Indian style with my chin in my hands patiently waiting for the performance. The crowd went crazy as Ed introduced who we had long been waiting to see and hear.

Seemed like most of the girls in the audience called "Paul's" name. Me, I was mesmerized by "John Lennon." Handsome with a voice that caught the world. The man I told myself I would grow up and marry. I figured when the day came, we'd meet, we'd fall in love, we'd be married. I had a long ten years for the growing up to happen and it would have to happen quick! As for Hermit, he bought all The Beatles' 45's and albums as they came out.

Hermit was into numbers long before I knew which one I was and he had just bought a new 45 record. He called me from his room saying, "Cappy, come in here. Listen to this." The song was by The Beatles..". "I'm Down." He had already counted how many times the words "I'm down" were sung and wanted me to come up with the same number. Of course he was as sure as I was. Unless a digitally re-mastered version slipped in a few more I'm down's on us...Hermit was correct with the figure.

We'd battle and argue about certain songs for hours. "Hermit they're not saying lonely." He questioned. "Maybe they're saying lovely?" The competition went until Hermit, as always, remained victorious.

Our house was small, so Hermit and I shared a room with bunk beds. It was later when Pope added more rooms to the place. Being afraid of heights, Hermit took the top bunk.

We used to like talking and singing Beatle songs when we were supposed to be asleep. Pope and Mayor were annoyed, always telling us to knock it off. Leave it to Hermit to find a way to improvise. He'd beat out a Beatle song with the palms of his hands on his stomach and I would have to guess the title. My turn came next to tap one out. Together we'd get 99% of the song titles right. It was a great game and we never thought our parents were wise to it

After super Hermit and I did the dishes. It was a chore we didn't mind doing because it would give us a chance to sing yet more Beatle tunes. Hermit would wash and I would dry. Hermit sang John's part and I did Paul's. We sounded pretty good too. Must have. It never seemed to bother our parents who were just off in the next room watching the six o'clock news.

You might say that me and Hermit were obsessed with The Beatles after a time, like as soon as we found out about them. If friends came over to play, Hermit would ask them if they liked The Beatles, if they said no, he wouldn't let them in the house, nor would he go hang out with them. I went along with my brother. It just seemed like the right thing to do.

At the Catholic School I attended there was a group of us that hung out together, a "click" if you will. There was Paula, Linda, Renee, Diane, and me. We were all in the sixth grade when our parents agreed to let us go to "Cedar Point" by ourselves. We loved the cable cars. Gave us a chance to put on our best British accents for the passer bys. People believed our stories of being exchange students from England. Naturally I was the student from Liverpool where John Lennon began.

One night at "The Point," my friends finally convinced me to ride the roller coaster with them. "The Blue Streak." The thought of it was horrifying but I got in the ride and held with a white-knuckled-grip. The coaster made a slow way to the top of the first hill. For dramatic purposes it stopped, I hoped. Only I was sure it was stuck. The panic set in bad when it took for the bottom of the hill and I screamed. My screams turned to laughter and when the ride was over we had just enough time to get on it again before the park closed. It is the only roller coaster I have the courage to get on... at least I think so.

A few years passed. Hermit and I quit doing dishes together. Well, Hermit did. He was secure in his room with a new toy... an electric guitar. I was okay with it except that John would be replacing my older brother's job. It was a frightening experience. John's balance? What we weren't sure about then... were knew now. Clumsy as clumsy gets. What if something broke or spilled? The family would be on guard.

You have to understand why John's temporary nickname was "the spiller." Mayor would ask him to feed Mud, our dog. John spilled the entire 40 pound bag of dog food. One morning, just before our school bus showed, he splattered one whole gallon of milk on Shorty. Then a Thanksgiving came. Me, Shorty and God help us, John, were told to set the table. Hermit hid out long before that. I laid out the silverware, napkins and plates. Mark filled the nine or ten glasses for us and our soon to arrive company and John spilled them... all of them! You can imagine our terror when we learned that he landed a job as a bus boy. Part of his job was to refill water for the customers. With deep concern Mayor said, "Good God John! I hope nobody asks you for more coffee."

Now Hermit was getting quite good at the guitar. He learned many Beatle songs. We'd end up singing them together. One in particular that we got real good at was one entitled "Happiness is a Warm Gun." Hermit sounded very much like "John Lennon" though he would never admit it.

Hermit was still by far my favorite brother. He was cool. He could draw, play guitar and sing. He was funny and intelligent. I could go to him with questions and ideas that Pope and Mayor would find utterly ridiculous.

Once in high school, for no apparent reason, a click of girls were calling me a whore. They'd laugh and point and it hurt real bad. I got home from school that day and asked my oldest brother, "Hermit, what's a whore?" Hermit gestured with his middle finger, "It's a girl who likes this." "What's that mean?" I asked. "Man Cap, you are stupid." Later that night I was in the bathroom combing my hair when Hermit came to the door and said, "Cap, the only reason the girls at the school are making fun of you is because they're just jealous. You're really cute. In fact if you weren't my sister I might ask you out." "Ha," I said, "If you weren't my brother I might go out with you too."

It was in the spring of '69. I was going on 13 when I heard that John Lennon would marry a second time to "Yoko Ono." He hadn't given me enough time to grow up. I still had 7 years to go. She wouldn't be right for him. After all I was going to be the coolest girl in America someday. I felt a sense of doom. I set my sights on new goals. Number one: To meet all The Beatles someday and number two: John's marriage would never last. Well, maybe it wasn't a goal, but I sure dreamed of it often.

In the summer of '69 I got my first job cleaning rooms at "The Sands Motel." Pope knew the head of housekeeping. Her name was Eda. She, like Pope was born in San Marino, Italy.

It wasn't easy being a teenager making money and saving, so I did what most of my friends did with their pay... I spent it. I bought my own school clothes, supplies and saved a little extra to go to Cedar Point and ride what else? The Blue Streak.

1969 had its good points and bad. "John Lennon" was still married, the Fourth of July flood hit Mayor worst of all. The only place left for her black-lion-footed-legged upright piano... was in the basement. It was drowned and ruined. Mayor was happy because this meant that she'd get Pope to buy her a new one. He did and she was the proud owner of a "Henry F. Miller..". the 100th anniversary edition. The purchase came with six free lessons. Since my brothers three could have cared less, Mayor wanted me, the one who was set on being the coolest girl in America, to take the lessons. Oh don't get me wrong, I wanted the lessons, I just didn't want to be seen carrying the first book down the walk of a busy street to get to the piano store. Book title: "TEACHING LITTLE RNQERS TO PLAY." I kept the book tightly rolled and in a bag keeping a firm grip. Eventually the excitement of being taught was getting to me. I aced the first grade book in classical music in two weeks. It was the numbers below the notes that convinced me I'd remember the numbers and not the notes. Lessons in months... 2 and one half.

Summer was over, school came, "John Lennon" had been married a little over a year and it was official. The Beatles had broken up for good. I was devastated and I thought with intensity... They would have to get together again. But it just wasn't going to happen, and certainly not the way any one would have expected when years later, The "Anthologies" came out.

Hermit never talked about the break up, but he drew. In pencil, he mastered copies of the four photographs that came with The White Album." And many more drawings between and on.

Throughout the course of this book you will see portions of Hermit's art works.
Do you think that this man would have it any other way?
Entireties are invisible...
... Kind of like Hermit.
Thanks to the oldest of my brothers three.   Allowing me to share parts,
if only parts of your work.
You've been an inspiration of intact with impact,
and it is truly an honor to have you as my brother.
Love, Cappy

The Sands Motel would be waiting for me to get to work. That was the summer I began frequenting a restaurant right across Route 250 called "Crook's Den." It became a feel good habit and I started going there every day after cleaning rooms.

One day the man who brought in the milk for the place said, "Hey, you're a working girl now. You should drink coffee." "Coffee?" I questioned. "Ya think?" He sort of shook his head smiling, putting the rest of the delivery away. Maybe a cup of it might be nice, I thought. I ordered it black and hated it. Wondered how anybody could stand it. "Hey Mr. Milkman...This is awful. You want it?" "Oh, I forgot. You're a beginner. Try using some milk and sugar." I took the advice and I was hooked.

In 1971 I decided to save up for my own guitar. I didn't want an electric one like Hermit's, I wanted a twelve-string acoustic. This would definitely drive Pope and Mayor crazy. Luckily for me, Pope was working third shift. Mayor didn't care how late I stayed up. So Hermit took me to a store in Cleveland that was going out of business. I got the twelve string I wanted, made by "Gibson" for 150 bucks.

Hermit taught me some chords, taught me how to tune it. Took time to do it without him. It was months before my finger tips were tough enough to get through an entire song.

Pope didn't care much for music. Even complained to the Mayor about her piano playing. Maybe it was "Johnny Mathis," her favorite singer that really upset Pope. She'd blast "Mathis" on the old "Zenith" till Pope came in the house to bitch about it. He also knew that if Mayor could marry "Johnny Mathis" she'd leave him in an instant. Well, she said she would. We made fun of her favorite singer, never telling her we thought his voice was good. Of course our parents didn't much care for the rock and roll we listened to. Ironically however, Pope and Mayor liked The Beatles.

One evening the movie "A Hard Day's Night" was aired on television. Pope was laying on the floor in front of the set laughing. We asked him what was so funny. It was difficult for all of to get on grip on the fact that it was The Beatles making him laugh.

In my room I'd practice singing and playing for hours. The Beatles influenced me into the direction of rock and roll.

On my days off from work I'd walk downtown to the "Jackson Street Pier" to ferry-boat my way to "Cedar Point." I'd spend all day riding The Blue Streak."

Towards the end of the summer I met a guy waiting in line to ride the roller coaster. He was way ahead of me. Sunday was a good day to be at Cedar Point because the lines were not a wait. It was my turn to ride... l did, and got in the line again. Only this time the guy I saw ahead of me was standing right next to me. He asked to ride the coaster with me. Wow, I thought! This cool rock-and roll-kinda-guy wants to ride this with me! His name was "Gary Perrin" from a suburb in Cleveland. Gary was about 5'8" tall. He had small beady eyes. His hair about medium brown, parted down the middle bushing out in waves to his shoulders. He was about 20 years old.

I couldn't wait to get home and tell Mayor about him, and I needed to get home before six o'clock, because that's when Pope came home from his Sunday card games at the "I.A.B. Club." Mayor wouldn't have had a problem with Gary, except for maybe the difference in our ages. I was a good kid and she knew she wouldn't have to worry. Pope would have forbid me to even go to Cedar Point just for the boys there, let alone a man. It would be the end of the ferry boat rides for me if he knew, so it was a secret saved by me and Mayor.

Naturally we rode the Blue Streak when we got to Cedar Point, but the ferry boat ride in itself was more fun because it gave us lots of time to talk and get to know each other. Gary seemed like a nice guy, so I thought today might be a good one to take him to my house to meet Mayor. We drove in his car. I was nervous about them meeting and Mayor wasn't thrilled about Gary's wild long hair until she came right out and said Hermit looked pretty much the same. She questioned him about his jittery behavior as he sat across from her behind sunglasses. He told her he was always that way. I knew he was high strung like me, but I must admit he was a few floors above me.

Mayor liked Gary and agreed we could drive back to The Point as long as he got me home earlier than normal so we wouldn't bump into Pope.

Gary and I got back to the Park. We hung out sitting in a grassy area next to the bay side entrance. Sometimes we took a break from The Blue Streak and rode the merry-go-round to talk. He didn't come out and say anything to me, but this would be the last time I would see Gary until the summer of 72.

Chapter Three: "The Look Alike"

School was going to start and summer was over, but so was cleaning rooms for another summer. Sandusky would turn into a friendly ghost town again come winter.

Just for something to do, I used to call a local radio station "WLEC" for a song. I'd tell the D.J. my name was Gentry just in case he'd tell his listeners that a song he played was for me. I was 15 and would have been made the joke at the high school for listening to an AM radio station at all. The D.J. was understanding and used the alias name I had chosen.

A lot of the kids I knew in school were experimenting with different drugs. I guess pot was the popular drug. Some took LSD, some took speed and then you had a rare bunch who liked to drop 4 to five hits of the THC. I was in that group. We believed that it was the resin from marijuana.

By now my best friend, permanently, was Winnebago. It was she, me and THC. The funny thing about the drug is you never knew when it was going to take effect. It could take as little as a half hour, or up to three hours. She'd call me up from her house asking, "Hey Spet! Did it hit ya yet?" "No, not yet, I'm still waiting." Later that evening she called again to tell me that it hit her. "Spet! I can see the American Flag on my pillow and it's moving like waves. I can even hear the water. Did it hit you yet?" Just when I was about to tell her it didn't hit, the kitchen table I sat by began to breathe. "Winnebago! My table is taking deep breaths. Can ya hear it? Wait a minute. I'm gonna ask Hermit about this stuff. I'll call ya right back."

Hermit was out in the garage installing a sound system in his new "Fiat" named Betty. I grabbed my long navy coat, ran in knee-deep-snow in nothing but a tee shirt and shorts. Hermit was hooking up some wire when I fixed my eyes on a power light in the stereo. It grew and grew. As it grew larger, I could see a picture in it until it popped like a bubble in my face. I continued to watch it happen again and again with a new picture each time. This made me anxious when I looked at the back of my house and saw through it like cellophane. I wanted to go to "Cook's Den." Running seemed to be the quickest route until Mayor flipped on the side light calling to me. "Cappy! Where do you think you're going? You're not going to The Den tonight. Get in here." She didn't see that I didn't have any socks and shoes on. She probably thought I liked running around like some loon-crazed-idiot. I went in the house and waited for Hermit.

Finally my brother came in. All Betty needed was a test drive to check out the stereo and I was crazy wanting to talk to Hermit, but Mayor was seated at the kitchen table with me and my brother. Mayor would talk to me. When I'd answer, I wondered if I talked soon enough. Seemed like it took me over a half hour to say something back. Something was wrong and I knew she'd find out. All I could do was hope she'd leave the room. Finally my turn came and I told Hermit what I didn't know. "Hermit, get me outta here." "Why?" he asked. "Cause, I'm fucked up that's why." "But you don't look fucked up." "Hermit I'm tellin' you that you gotta get me outta here!" "Why? You don't looked fucked up." "I am fucked up!" "But I told you Cap, you don't look like you're fucked up." "Hermit, Mayor could come back in here any minute and you gotta get me outta here. Something is really wrong!" At last Hermit did something and just in time. Mayor walked into the kitchen to fix herself a fried egg sandwich. Hermit said, "Mayor, I'm taking Cap for a ride in Betty. I want to check out the new stereo in it, see how it sounds." "Okay, but be careful in this weather." That was it and I couldn't wait to leave.

After telling my older brother about the things I had seen, he was sure it was LSD I got and not the elephant tranquilizers I thought I took. He stopped by a friend's house to get me something that would help bring me down, so long as I drank nothing but white milk with them. Hermit asked if I minded going with his friend to "Crook's Den" for milk, 'cause he wanted to take care of a few details with Betty and the stereo. Craig stayed with me for close to four hours. (The time it took for the drug to wear off.) After which I walked home. Home was a two minute run in knee deep snow. This didn't stop me from buying more of the elephant tranqs' or whatever they were.

Summer was coming soon and I was dreading my work at the motel. All that got me through it was the fact that I could pick my own school clothes and go to "Cedar Point."

Sunday I went to "Cedar Point" always wondering when I'd bump into Gary, if he'd show up. Sundays came and went I was at them all, but Gary was not. I got to thinking that he had a girlfriend. One who was more his age and stuff.

The Point was getting boring so I stopped at a department store on the way home to buy an album. There were no new Beatle Albums so I got one called "Bloodshot" by the "J. Geils Band." And I'll be damned if one of the band members on the cover didn't look just like my friend Gary from Cleveland.

The following Sunday came and Gary showed up at my house about 12:30 p.m. Gary greeted me with a hug and said hello to Mayor. She noticed another person in Gary's car and suggested he come in and meet her. Gary hesitated, telling my mother that his friend was really shy about meeting people. Mayor told Gary that the only way she was going to let me go to The Point with him, is if the other man came in to meet her. (So she could check for security).   Gary walked out to his car to talk to his friend and the both of them headed to the front door.   Gary's friend commanded the entrance of Pope's house with his long brown hair and a sunglassed-rock-and-roll-kind of face.   The tall man, perhaps in his late 20's sat across from Mayor who was opposite them.   Sitting in her recliner she studied their faces with her "Mona Lisa" smile and inquiring eyes.   It didn't take her any time to ask questions.   "What is it with you and those sunglasses?   Are you guys on drugs or something?   I mean look at yourself," pointing to Gary who had been shaking his one leg up and down quickly.   "Me?   Oh, I've always been this way ever since I was a kid."   Mayor might have been skeptical except that Gary was quick and clear to answer her.   She accepted what he had said was the truth.

Gary's friend sat back into the couch comfortably.   He wore a T-shirt, jeans and a jean jacket.   Can't say I remember this man ever saying anything.   It's been twenty seven years and I still don't remember.   Guess I'm not supposed to.

I went into the kitchen to get a drink of pop before we left because I wanted to down a hit of THC for the trip to The Point.   Gary followed me and told me to put my pill away.   "I got the real thing Capri.   You've been taking nothing but elephant knock out pills."   He pulled a plastic bag from his jean pocket and showed me the stuff.   It was white-like-crystals of sand.   Gary pinched out a small amount out and told me to snort it.   "Gary I can't snort that.   I've had bad nose bleeds most of my life.   I won't put nothing up my nose but air."   "That's okay Cap, just take this little bit, put it under your tongue and wash it down with some pop.   I'll give you a pin head.   Trust me.   You won't believe how good real THC is."   Looking through an archway leading through to the front room, I made sure Mayor didn't see me put the tiny crystals into my mouth.   I took three or four swallows of pop, figuring somehow the carbonation would make it take affect quicker.

He and I walked back to the living room.   Gary asked Mayor if it would be alright for me to go to The Point with him and his friend.   Mayor asked them both.   "What is it with you guys and those damn sunglasses?   Does the light bother your eyes?"   Gary's friend slid his glasses down to the tip of his nose.   The glasses stopped there and he peered over them looking at Mayor.   Mayor's mouth dropped open.   She was so stunned I thought she was gonna fall off the chair.   Her face was filled with surprise.   After her initial overload, she looked over at me firmly saying, "Okay.   You know what time your father gets home.   And as for you two, make sure she gets back on time and in one piece."

With that the three of us left.   Silent friend sat in the back seat of the car with his guitar.   I sat by Gary who drove us to the Jackson Street Pier where we boarded the ferry boat that would take us to The Point. I having the gift of gab talked their ears off waiting for the THC to hit.

I was still copying "Lennon" then. My hair was long and parted down the middle. I wore round dark sun glasses and I looked pretty damn good. Gary's friend might have passed for "John Lennon" himself. While crossing the bay on the ferry, I turned to this John Lennon look alike and conceitedly said, "Ha I look more like Lennon than you." He said nothing but showed me a shy grin. I was captivated and watched his every move waiting for the T to kick in. The ferry docked. We got off the boat and took seats in the grassy area along the sunset side of "Cedar Point" The mystery man strummed on his guitar for the most part of the day.

Gary's friend took me into the park to ride the merry-go-round with him. We were next to each other on a winged benched seat behind the carousel horses and he played his guitar just for me. The rest is much like rain running on glass. I may never know just who the celebrity look alike was. It could have been the real John Lennon, I thought. The one I wanted to grow up and marry. And I still wonder.

What better place to get lost in! An Amusement park. Close to the big city, but not too far from a place where no one would even think to look. Did the Mania start there? Could Gary Perrin really have been from "The J.Geils Band"? Was he friends with John Lennon? Who knows when it all started and when it would end. All I know is what ever happened in my life happened because it was supposed to. Because in fact it did.

I don't remember the ferry boat ride home or the drive to my house. But I must have gotten home on time. I don't recall Pope giving me the evil-blue-eye or punishment.

Only one thing is true... I never saw Gary and his friend again. And if you were Mr. Lennon, then mine is the pleasure still treasured today.

Chapter Four: "Eye Doodles"

Seemed ever since I was a little girl I liked the boys who played music, sang music.

Andrew was the first boy. We were in the third grade. I watched him in our grade school talent show playing his drums and I was hooked. The crush I had on him lasted through my freshman year at Sandusky High School. I think he knew.

In the eighth grade I like an older guy named Steve. He played rhythm guitar. Later I learned he was a chronic liar. How I watched for a special delivery truck that was to bring "*his and hers*" sweaters from Denmark. Not to mention the roses that never arrived.

He bugged me constantly about my smoking habit, one that he had already so I finally broke up with him. That day Steve came to my house. He was out in the drive talking to Mayor. "Mayor, when Cap broke up with me it hurt so bad I drank a capful of bleach trying to kill myself." "Oh, you poor thing. I'm sorry to hear that. But if you really wanted to kill yourself, why didn't you try drinking the whole bottle." She rolled her green eyes to Steve. Mayor proceeded with her work in the flower garden. It was at this point that Steve realized he couldn't out smart Mayor and made a getaway in his "Comet."

In the evening I would take out my guitar and sing. I longed to be in a rock band performing center stage.

One afternoon a friend of Hermits dropped in. Doug came in the house with one of his buddies named Don. Now Doug worked with Hermit at "The Hotel Breakers" at Cedar Point. However Doug and his friend Don played guitars and were in a band. There it was. That instant attraction for a music man. Don sang and played with his "Les Paul." Then Doug and Don got out their guitars and sang a song by "Neil Young" called "The Old Laughing Lady." Their voices blended well. I knew that somehow I had to make Don my boyfriend.

Being the bold and brassy girl (a name given to me by a former teacher... a nun), I made up my mind to call Don. He remembered who I was but told me that he was already seeing someone. I told him that he should break up with her and start seeing me.

The next day Don was at my door. Damn I was good! Many more days followed as Donald had become my boyfriend and my first love.

Donald was about 5' 10." Medium build with hazel eyes and long light sandy brown hair. He wore a white smile, especially when someone else needed one.

He always, but always brought his guitar with him and if he didn't take it out of the car, he knew there was always my twelve string available. He would sing to me where ever we happened to be.

Mayor would laugh and ask me, "How do you keep from cracking up when Don is staring right in your face singing? I wouldn't be able to keep a straight face." "I love him Mayor," I said. It didn't take long for Donald's parents to adore me just as mine did him.

While sitting in the living-room at Donald's house, his mother walked in with a smile and said, "You know Capri, all my boys marry Catholic girls and you're Catholic." I think she knew that Donald had made his mind up to marry me when I turned 18. I had just turned 16.

Pope and Mayor liked Donald so much that they allowed me to go to the clubs where he and the band performed. There wasn't a problem getting in. Donald and Doug just told the owner that I was with the band and that I'd only be drinking pop. I'd have a great seat where I would be able to view the band playing. They called themselves "Raven."

Donald and I remained together for over a year. Hints from the band members were hints to me that Donald would soon be asking me to marry him. They joked every clean chance they had about Donald being 19 years old and a virgin. I too was a virgin.

One evening the old grade school I had attended was having a dance. I thought it might be fun to go. Donald encouraged me to because his band was playing quite a ways out of town. My folks weren't going to let me go. So I got dressed and went to "Saint Peter and Paul."

The dance was held in the gym and I knew one of the band members. His father owned a music store in town where Donald worked giving guitar lessons. The place that gave me six free lessons.

The dance was over. I saw someone from the band I knew and thought I'd stop and say hello. We talked about five, maybe ten minutes and I reminded him that I had to get the car home, so off I went. The next day, I was walking home from school. I could have rode the bus, but the walk home would take me right by the music store where Donald was teaching. Maybe I'd see him. From across the street I could see Donald sitting at a white baby grand that was in the stores front window. I crossed the street and got closer to the store. Now I could see that Donald was sitting on the bench at the piano with his head hanging down over his guitar. I opened the door and said, "Hey Donald, how'd it go last night? I wish I could have been there. The band last night wasn't as good as yours. I missed you. Donald, what's wrong? Why won't you say anything to me? Why won't you look at me?" He lifted his head up for a moment, looked me directly in the eyes and said, I got nothing more to say to you." "But what's wrong, what did I do? You told me to go to the dance. Is that it?" Then he hung his head down over his guitar, unplugged and played. I think I was in shock. I didn't cry. I don't know what I was feeling. Maybe I wasn't feeling anything at all.

I walked home every day from school for the next ten days and looked for Don's face in the store front window. He wasn't there and I never tried further to find out why he no longer wanted to see me. I missed him. I was going to miss him sing happy birthday for me like he had when I turned 16. A lot of time went by. I was 17 years old and decided to go into the music store to see if Donald might still be there. He wasn't. But a girl who was in Raven for a short time was. She walked over to me and said, "Cap what were you thinking? Why in the world did you ever go to bed with that guy? That's the reason Donald stopped seeing you. Didn't you know that he was saving himself for you? That he was going to marry you?" "Crystal, I never slept with anyone. You mean him?" (Pointing at the owners son) "Did he tell you that? No wonder. That explains it. Crystal, I'm a virgin. I didn't even know what a whore was till I was 14. So Donald doesn't want someone who "he" thinks has already been used. Now he's gone and I can't even explain to him. Thanks Crystal. At least now I know." I cried almost all the way home. But I stopped when I got to "C" street because I didn't want my parents to know why Donald had broken up with me. I kept it inside. I knew someday I would see Donald myself to tell him the truth.

This led me to confine myself more to my room playing guitar. If I wasn't doing that I would be at Crooks Den shooting pool, another favorite pass time of mine. A good friend of mine worked there and taught me everything I knew. His name was Krome.

From about the ages of 15 to 16 , Krome spent much of his free time teaching me all I would need to be a good pool player. He was a great teacher too. I learned well to play eight ball.

After the restaurant closed I'd be back in my room playing and singing. I got a small amplifier and a cheap microphone so I could hear what I sounded like. I sounded good. I had a good range. Clear and crisp, but no style of my own. I'd watch my face in the mirror so I could see what an audience might see someday. Hey you have to look good too. And I did. Mayor didn't mind how loud or how long I played, providing I got up in time for school. Pope, he was working the night shift. Hermit had since moved out and had his own apartment. So it was just me, Shorty and John.

Back in school I took Cosmetology. Winnebago, my best friend would also be in the class.

18

We had the best teacher. Her name was Mrs. Murphy. She was like a second mom to us. And she liked me and Winnebago the best. I know because she pulled the two of us over to the side one day and said, "You girls are my favorite. I'd have you for my own daughters. If you ever need a place to stay, you can always come and live with me and Ken my husband."

She knew Winnebago and I liked smoking cigarettes, so she'd let us smoke in the locker room just off the Lab where the bathroom was. How fortunate we had become. We immediately discovered that not only did the bathroom have and exhaust fan, but a dead bolt lock. Now that we out grew the THC, we could get away smoking pot in there. When we would be in the classroom across the hall from the lab, Winnebago would raise her hand to be excused. She'd go across the hall, into the lab, in the locker room, where she'd enter the rest room. She would take out a pipe, fill it with pot, take a few hits, then leave it in the rest room for me. After she came back to the class, I'd raise my hand to be excused, walk the same path to find the bowl of pot still smoking. I'd take the remaining few hits of pot. Knock the ashes into the toilet, spray some perfume in the room, stuff the pipe back into my purse and buzz back into the class. When I could give Winnebago her pipe back without being caught, I did.

In the meantime, I was dating a boy named Mike. He was from Huron. He played in a band and played a "Fender Jazz Bass" guitar. He reminded me a lot of Donald, my first love. He looked something like him. Mike didn't sing however and we didn't last long.

It was time to think about work. I didn't want to clean rooms again. There was a shoe store close to home and I talked to the manager about a job. Larry, the manager, told me they didn't need any help and after two weeks straight of asking I came out and said, "Larry. You're going to hire me and do you know why? You'll get tired of me bugging you every day, that's why." Larry chuckled. Then one Saturday morning I had to laugh when he called my house to give me the schedule I'd be on for the upcoming week.

I loved my job. It felt good to wear pretty dresses and high heels. Plus I had the advantage of getting all the newest styles in shoes first!

Larry hired someone to be the assistant manager. That man was Gary. Gary, etc, etc, the third. Gary was a goofy guy. Lots of fun to work with. He was tall and built strong. Gary's hair was blonde and receding a bit. He wore thick glasses over his bright blue eyes. Gary was 21 and I was going on 18. It didn't thrill me that I had been working there longer than him and he'd be over me, but I got over it when he and I became boyfriend and girlfriend. Next to Donald, my parents adored Gary. He and I worked together. We ate breakfast together. We did lunch and most dinners as well. We shot pool. We spent most of our time together. Gary wasn't the usual music type person I had dated in the past, but he did like trying. Like the night we were at the pier waiting to ride the ferry boat back and forth across the bay. From out of the blue, Gary jumped from his seat and pranced down the walkway singing the "Cowardly Lions" solo in "The Wizard of Oz." He kept singing the part..."If I were king of the forest...." Not only did he imitate the Lion so well, but people down there stopped to watch this well dressed, highly educated man make a complete idiot out of himself. You never knew what Gary would do next. Shortly after we boarded the ferry, Gary popped from his seat pointing at the bay, saying loudly enough for all to hear, "Look! It's the "Loch Ness Monster"! About everyone stood to see.

One evening Gary took me to a theater downtown to catch a movie. When the movie was over and we left the theater, Gary picked me up to carry me to the car. As we turned the corner there were four girls from my former high school waiting for me. It was over some guy that I was seeing then. His new girlfriend was a 'tough-guy'. She was there to put an ass kicking on me. She set it up real good too. She made sure that there was someone there to hold Gary away from me at knife point, so she could slam my face into the back end of our car. To my surprise, a girl whom I thought was my friend, was the one who located me and Gary, so Tina could beat and hurt me. Months later, Tina and my ex-boyfriend Fro came into the shoe store where I was working. They found me and Gary behind the counter together. She didn't say she was sorry, but Fro apologized. I was amazed. For two years this girl had hounded the life out of me.

Another movie night came and Gary and I went. While we were in line, a short, older, Italian looking man asked Gary how everything was. Gary told him things were fine. I bugged Gary to tell me about the man and after never letting up on him he said, "Capri. Things were getting way out of control with Tina and Fro. The man I talked to was paid to take care of things. They won't hurt you again." "Gary, is he in the mob?" "Don't let it bother you. What matters is all that bull shit is over with." And I it was.

Gary and I probably spent entirely too much time together. After work we'd go out and shoot pool. Gary would put the quarters on the table for me... I would play. It was usually whatever "I" wanted to do.

Every waking moment was time spent with Gary. Gary wasn't less liked by me, I just didn't love him anymore and I wanted out of the relationship. It was going to be hard to tell him. He had been there for me every day together... every day. Plus we still worked at the same place together.

More time went by - weeks - then one night I decided it was now or go crazy. Gary was at my house thinking that we would be going out. We were sitting on the sofa in my parents' house. Night had just fallen and I said, "Gary I can't see you anymore. I'm sorry, but I don't think I love you anymore." "Cappy, I don't want us to stop seeing each other. I'm in love with you. I'd do anything for you." "I know Gary. But maybe we see each other too much. Please don't hate me!" Gary hugged me tightly and cried on my shoulder.

Four months after we broke up, I learned I was pregnant. I asked myself how that could be since I had my periods regular. What am I gonna do? If Pope finds out I'm dead. He'll throw me out of the house for sure. Mayor might have understood but I couldn't take any chances. I was 4 months pregnant when I made plans for an abortion. Gary was totally against it and wanted to marry me. But he gave me the money I needed to have it. It was scheduled for April 22,1975. Graduation was only months away and I wanted to work full time. I wanted all my dreams and no baby was going to keep me from having them come true.

The morning had come. I talked to Mayor about using the car to go to the mall in Elyria. It was a 45 minute drive which would cover the idea that I'd have to leave early. But when I woke her to tell her I was about to go, she stopped me dead in my tracks saying, "Gary called and I know where you are going. You know I have to wake your father. We have to tell him what's going on."He'll kill me if he knows. Please don't wake him up," I cried. "Cap," said Mayor, "he's not going to kill you. And he was up for sure. I heard him stomp into the kitchen. "You're pregnant? I'm going to call Gary." He got him on the phone. Gary told Pope he wanted to marry me, but I didn't want to. Pope was so concerned, saying, "Cappy. What's the matter with you? He loves you. Please don't do this thing." I told Pope I didn't love him anymore. Again he spoke, "But you loved him when you got pregnant. We have enough to feed another little mouth. You don't have to get married." Dad, I already made up my mind. I can't have a baby right now. I have things I want to do." " Pope said with eyes filled, "We'll help you with the baby. You'll still work and have time for fun. Come on. Don't go." I put my head down and asked my mom for the car keys. Pope went back to Gary who was still on the phone and said, "She said she doesn't want to get married. She's made up her mind. Okay Gary. Bye." My father was very choked up. I didn't realize how much I was breaking his heart and Mayors.

It was an hour drive to the clinic and it appeared to be a bank from the outside. Well, it was a bank on the first floor, the clinic where the abortions took place was on the second.

A counselor there talked to about seven girls, including myself. She explained the procedures. One thing I clearly remember her telling us is that we would never forget this day. Since I was further along than any of the other girls, I was scheduled to go to a nearby hospital where I would be sedated for the abortion. I was afraid.

When it was through, I woke in a room with about 15 other girls in hospital beds. Some vomited on the floor because the nurses couldn't get a bed pan to them soon enough. Watching them was making me sick and it wasn't long before I needed a pan myself. The hospital suggested I remain overnight for observation. They informed me that if I signed myself out they would not be responsible for any outcome. After being there a few hours, I asked my friend Mike to take me home. I couldn't bear to be in that place any longer and we left. Got home about 9 p.m. My parents asked me how I was and told me to get to bed and rest.

But at one in the morning I woke to very bad abdominal cramping. I ran to the bathroom and sat on the toilet. I felt the need to push. I figured it was just a blood clot I was passing, but when I looked to see what it was, it "was" a tiny little leg. I screamed for Mayor who was asleep. She came running to the bathroom to see what was wrong. She and I both knew what we were looking at. Mayor tried telling me it wasn't a leg. "Mom, I know what I am looking at. I am seeing a little leg. Look, this is the knee cap and there are five perfectly shaped little toes. Please don't tell me that it isn't, I know what it is." The baby's leg was not coming out. I held the life-less leg in my hand crying, not knowing anything about what I had done. Mayor called Pope at work and told him to come take me to the emergency room. Pope rushed in from work to drive me to the hospital. Confirmed by a doctor there, indeed it was the leg of a 16 month old fetus. My town didn't perform abortions so they wouldn't do anything for me. They gave me a maternity pad to wear until I could get back to Cleveland where the surgery was done. I would have to wait until 7:30 the next morning before I could leave Sandusky to get there.

I didn't sleep for the wait. How could I with a human leg still there. Why didn't they x-ray me afterward, I thought?

The wait at the ER that morn, was nearly two hours. A nurse finally came to the desk and I told her what had happened. She said it was a chance in a million that I might have been carrying twins. This bothered me since twins ran in the family. I was devastated to think that I may have lost the only chance I ever had in having them. The hospital put me under once again to remove the leg. The following day I was released. I left the hospital feeling bad about everything. This would cost me 2,000 dollars more and Gary refused me another dime. It took two years for me to pay for my mistake and it will take a life time to get over.

Gary had become the manager of the Perkins Plaza store and had me transferred to the slowest store of the three. It was the one located in the Sandusky Plaza where a man named Kerry was the manager. Kerry, like me, played the guitar. There was a lot of free time at this store and on those times

Kerry would play his guitar in the back room. Eventually I brought mine in to work and we did duets together.

It wasn't long before the slowest shoe store in the town was going to close and I was transferred to the one in the mall. This would have been ideal except my former boyfriend Gary was at that store. The manager in training position was open there. Myself and another girl were in stiff competition for the job. Gary was constantly sending me home for inappropriate attire. The other girl wore the same things but was never sent home. I was certain that this was Gary's way of getting back at me for breaking up with him and having the abortion. More bad luck… I came down with a serious lung infection that kept me from my job for almost two months. The last week I was sick, I could barely get out of bed to call work and tell them once more that I couldn't come in. Mayor called in for me. The store didn't want anyone but me calling in for the time off. I figured it couldn't be policy, it had to be Gary and I was fired. I would not be unemployed for long. I wasn't a quitter. All I ever had to do was tell myself I was going to work at a certain place and before I knew it, I was there.

While looking for work I shot a lot more pool. The Den was more like a second home to me. It and the coffee. Between games and cups I found myself doodling on the napkins. I figured if Hermit could draw, then maybe I might be good at it too. For some reason I was captivated by eyes. I drew them everywhere. Paper bags, napkins, place mats, just anything. One day while at The Den drawing a group of eyes on a piece of paper, John, a pool buddy of mine and a practicing chiropractor stood behind me and said, "That's pretty good. You know that what you are drawing might be trying to tell you something about yourself. Did you ever finish one?" "Doc this isn't drawing, this is just doodling." I said as I thought about how great Hermit was. Then Doc said, "Well I like it and if you ever finish one I might just be interested in buying it." Doc and I shot a little more pool, had coffee together and day turned into night. Everyone from the Den was goin' to "Gabby's" for more pool. I drove out to meet them only I sat by myself. I just didn't feel much like company, I felt like doodling eyes.

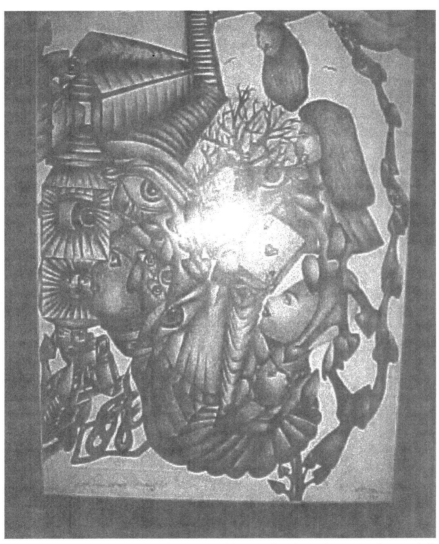

... Little did I know that I would ever finish a drawing, but I did. And sure enough, "John Weatherford", the Chiropractor did indeed buy the drawing you are seeing above. Thanks John! Think you'll ever sell it?

Chapter Five: "My Marriage to Professor III"

Before too long there was a drink in front of me like the one I had bought myself. Just before I finished it there was another one in front of me. Next time the drink came with the man who had been buying them. Professor the III. Professor was a tall, slender built man, about twenty something. His eyes were light hazel and his hair was a natural, tight fro. From a distance his face looked dirty, but close viewed, you could see all the many blended freckles that covered it.

He introduced himself to me and asked if he could call me sometime. After talking with him awhile, I agreed to give him the number to my parent's house. The next day Professor called and asked me out. More and more days followed and soon the days turned into a month. After that month and a date, we were at my parents house on the couch when Professor said in a monotone voice, "Capri...Will you marry me?" I excused myself quickly to use the rest room so he couldn't see or hear me laugh. I composed myself and returned to the living room. I sat next to him and said "Yes." He was not at all liked by my parents.

After getting a phone call from someone else I had a crush on, I told Prof' I wanted to stay single. He didn't like it when he found out the date I had was with Denny. Denny was a guy that I saw when I was 16. He was 25 at the time and wanted more than a pool game. I didn't want to stop seeing him, but I wasn't going to lose my virginity over it. Now that I was 19 and he was more handsome than when I first met him, I was going out with him period. Denny was wonderful. He took me out everywhere and we ended up slow dancing till morning. It was a romantic evening that a lot of women would have envied. However, Mayor made the mistake of telling Prof who I was out with and he wanted to see me as soon as I got in. I went to his motel room so I could explain that I needed more time to think about getting married. But I said nothing when I found him ripping the rail out from the cemented staircase. I was scared and left tor home.

Prof' didn't call and I was off to work at the mall. I met another man named Gary who happened to work at a nearby shoe store. We both liked pool and made plans to meet at "Gabby's" with a group of friends. Prof' came in. He sat up at the bar alone drinking shots. Me and my friends were all shooting pool. The Prof's quarter came up. It would be Prof' and Gary's turn to shoot. I thought for sure Prof' would do or say something to Gary, especially the way he acted when he found out about Denny, but he shook Gary's hand after they shot pool. All seemed to be going fine. Gary had beat

Prof' in the game and racked the balls for the next player. Prof' got a look in his eyes that I had witnessed once before. He got up from his seat at the bar and walked over to our table. Gary was standing by. Prof' hauled off and punched him in the face. Krome was trying to calm Prof' and so was I. I kept trying to tell him that Gary was a friend from the mall. We were all just friends but Professor didn't hear me. He thought I was still his in his mind, I guess. He picked up a bar table, threw it about twenty feet across the room and hit Gary in his rib cage. The police were called but when they arrived Prof' was gone, I told them what happened and gave them Prof's address so that they could arrest him. After which, I followed the ambulance that took my friend Gary to the emergency room. Gary ended up with about five broken ribs and two that were bruised. We agreed there at the hospital that we shouldn't go out anymore and we didn't.

The Prof did not give up. He wanted to keep seeing me. I don't know what happened to my reasoning but I continued to date him.

One night I stayed at Prof's motel room to have a few drinks. I fell asleep. When I woke up I realized Pope would home from work soon. He'd kill me! It was seven thirty and Pope would be off the night shift and at the house at seven thirty five. I didn't have much time. I drove like a maniac, but I didn't get there before him.

I walked in the side door. Pope was standing there waiting to hear my explanation. Pope said, "Kind of late huh?" I answered, "So." This pissed him off royal and he said, "Pack your bags and go live with him then." "Oh fuck you, I will!" He turned to me and said, "Fuck you too." Immediately I thought... How could he say that to me? I packed my things and moved in with Prof'. It wasn't too long and Mayor convinced Pope to let me come back home. But in two weeks after being there I left on my own to stay with Prof'.

I had no idea how my life would change "big time," but it did.

The Prof' had a job as a Chef at a local restaurant and motel. He got me a job there as a desk clerk. I worked my regular 48 hour week and he'd stay late at the bar running the disco lounge. He danced with all the women who came in but I didn't know until I found lipstick on his shirt collar. He denied any wrong doings. Then a friend of mine told me that he was indeed dancing real close with the guests. I tried not to let it get the best of me, but it did. I learned what the word jealous meant. I was constantly accusing him of going out on me since he was never around. He was spending 16 hours a day at a motel complex and it was... complex! In an argument over his hours, our first apartment phone was flying. He threw one at me and missed. I ran up the stairs and threw one at him. He locked himself in the bedroom and it was then that I learned how to kick holes through a door.

No, I didn't leave Prof' I stayed.

One of our mutual friends was having a party for his girl friend and he wanted to take a few of us to Cleveland with them. I didn't care for a particular couple that was going, so I had made up my mind not to talk the entire time.

We got to a nice lounge /restaurant up in the Flats. Prof' drank and drank. He had asked me to dance. I got up and joined him. After only a few seconds he turned and began to dance with the other women on the floor ignoring me completely. I felt so dumb. First I just stood there thinking he was just having a good time and would turn around and face me again but when he didn't, I silently walked back to the table with the birthday girl and her other guests. Prof' joined the group after spending most of his time on the floor dancing the evening away. We were all tired so our host suggested we get rooms at a hotel nearby so we could sober up for our ride back to Sandusky the next morning. It seemed like the right thing to do.

Me and Prof' had a room on the 5th floor. I got myself all tucked in for the evening. There was no way I was going to have sex with a man who was staggering drunk, smelling of booze, so I lay down and close my eyes. Prof' had other ideas. When I refused him, he tore lamps and head boards from the walls that were mounted on. Everything in the room and been ripped from its original roots or tossed about. Then without warning, he jumped on me and wrapped his hands around my throat. I started to choke. I could barely breathe. Just when I thought it was my last breath he pulled me by the hair to the window where he yelled at me. "See that bitch. It's a five story drop. Wonder how you'd look splattered in bloody pieces." I said nothing and gave in to his sexual desires. After, when I knew he was asleep I headed for the bathroom. I locked the door and sat on the floor crying myself into the morning.

By breakfast time with our friends, my eyes were nearly swollen shut from tears. No one came right out to ask what was wrong, though I'm sure they knew something was. Prof' ordered some raw eggs in a glass and drank them down, looking as though business was as usual. We drove home from Cleveland. Everybody but me was in conversation. When we got to Sandusky I got myself ready for work (like it or not) and Prof' was already gone.

I don't know what made me stay with him. I know I didn't want to go home. Who knows what ever made me marry him days later on September 28th, 1977.

When Pope heard the news he was highly disappointed. He said I was marrying the wrong man. I would not be fitted for an original wedding gown. A present my dress designing uncle wanted me to have when the time had come. I knew what kind of dress I wanted too. One like the women wore in the movie, "Gone With The Wind." And I didn't want to be driven away from the church in a fancy car, but a white carriage drawn by two white horses. Something simple. But these and so many of my other dreams would vanish after being married to Professor.

It was time for the wedding rehearsal. The minister of the church had made a grave mistake. When it was time for him to mention the last name of Professor, he mistakenly called him by Denny's last name. He was just married a few days before in that church. Professor looked over to me and said, "That's why you're marrying me." It wasn't the reason. I knew Denny had gotten married and it didn't matter to me in the least.

Soon the day came. We only had one week to get invitations out because we decided one night to get married in one week. Since we both worked at the motel and they had banquet accommodations, we got a room for the reception for free, and the food and liquor were at cost. Entertainment was just a nice stereo and four big speakers.

I decorated the room myself earlier that morning. Bid beautiful yellow and white bells hung all around. The cake was decorated the same.

Mayor got me to the church early to dress. My maid of honor was a girl I worked with from the motel. Her name was Kathy. The best man was Mr. George B. He was a good friend of Prof' and myself.

The music played. My father held his arm out for me and we turned down the long isle way. Just then Pope said, "It's not too late to turn around and go the other way." I nervously smiled. I never would have imagined how many times the words he spoke would sound in my head.

The Prof and I engaged in one dance. He spent the rest of the evening dancing with a girl who worked with him in the kitchen. A black girl who was teaching him the freak. I was furiously getting drunk on the bottle of Champaign that Prof' and I should have been drinking... and I watched them dance my night away while I sat alone.

Just when I thought things couldn't get any worse, they didn't. Because a little girl, about four, came over to me where I had been sitting and said, "Bride. When I go home can I have that big yellow bell up there?" She was pointing to a one that was directly over her table. I smiled at the little girl in her party dress and said, "Honey you don't have to wait till you go home. How about if I go and get it for you right now?" "Oh! Yes thank you!" she said. I climbed up on top the chair, to the table and untied the big bell for her. It was the only bright moment of the evening.

The party was still going strong but I wanted to leave. Prof' drove us to Huron where we were going to live. He was drunk and all over the old Cedar Point Road. Had it been light out it might night have been too bad, but it was dark and rainy. On the left side of the road was a rock break wall that helps protect properties from the lake and a strong northeastern wind. I wanted Prof' to carry me over the thresh hold but he said, "Why? We lived together. That's stupid." Before I had a chance to stop him he tore open envelopes and presents. He stuffed the money in his pockets. I tried to stop him because I wouldn't know who sent or gave us what. I cried after he was through. How will I know what came from who? I wanted to say something personal to our present givers. I did the best I could.

Winter came fast and we couldn't afford the rent on our "honeymoon" home? It was a beautiful home on the lake. Five bedrooms, three bathrooms, a wet bar and a walk out patio from three of the rooms upstairs that faced Lake Erie. Prof' had lost his job and mine wasn't enough to cover the rent. So we moved to a smaller apartment closer to Sandusky, but still in Huron.

Without notifying my parents about the move, they had called the house trying to reach me or Prof'. When no one answered for a few days, Pope thought he better go to the house and see what was going on. When he arrived the doors were left unlocked. The house was not in the meticulous way I had left it. Apparently Prof' had a wild party there without my knowledge. Pope found garbage and cans laying all about the kitchen and living area I think he must have thought that Prof' had hurt me and hurt me bad. When I had a phone hooked up, I called Mayor and told her all that had happened. She told me Pope thought Prof' had killed me. I assured her that I would never leave her and Pope wondering again.

Soon after we moved into our apartment I discovered I was pregnant. Prof' seemed to be in a good mood after work so I told him in the disco lounge about the baby. He looked appalled. I wondered why? He's the one who wanted me to get an attorney to prove that I could have children at all. This news pushed the Prof' further and further away from me.

Trying to get a smile, I dangled a maraschino cherry in front of his large nose and started singing "Rudolph the Red Nosed Reindeer" Before I could get more out than the title, Prof' punched me in the face. His fist slid over my cheek. I grabbed hold of a bar stool so I wouldn't lose my balance. No one flinched or offered me help. I looked at the Prof' and asked, "Why?" He gave me a dirty look and headed to the floor to dance with the other women. I left. I got into my car and drove in tears all the way home. By the time I reached my place, I figured that he didn't mean to hit me. I must have hurt his feelings making fun of his nose. He wouldn't hurt me intentionally. I excused him for the fact that he was drinking. He certainly wouldn't hurt the mother of his child. Especially when it might endanger the baby.

When we could no longer afford the apartment we moved closer to our jobs and lived in a studio apartment. I was six months pregnant.

Prof' found another job cooking. It was about 40 minutes from where we lived in a town called Elyria. The position he held at the country club was kitchen manager and chef.

One evening after he returned to our small living quarters he complained that I made his bath water too hot. He came out of the bathroom and started going through my purse. He threw it on the floor, broke all my makeup and yelled at me. 'You don't need to wear this shit anyway. Who do you need to look good for?" I kept my distance from him and said nothing. Later, when things calmed down and we were in bed I said, "How come you don't make love to me anymore? Come on Prof', let's fool around. Do ya want to?" "Are you kidding," he said, "Do you really think you can turn me on looking like that?" He pushed me off the bed and on to the floor. I picked myself up, grabbed my things, put my coat on and headed for the door. In seconds Prof' stood blocking it. Calmly with a smirk he said, "Where do you think you're going in this weather?" "I'm going to Mayor's house, just let me go Prof'." "Are you crazy? You're not walking in the snow in high heeled boots so just forget that shit. Take your coat off Cappy." I was afraid that he might push me down or hit me so I took off my coat and sat at the desk across from the bed. I sat there until morning. I prayed to God and told him that Prof' wanted a son and wanted his son to have his name. I didn't want any son of mine to have his father's name because it was nothing to be proud of. I prayed for a baby girl. On June 28th, 1978, Christine was born. We moved back to Huron and got a small one bedroom apartment. Prof was still working out of town. Some nights he never came home and I gutted why. No doubt he was sleeping around on me. After the baby was born and I was able to have sex again Prof' would deny me, telling me I had to earn his respect first. He ate away at my soul. "Cappy. You make me sick. You couldn't turn me on enough to have me." Tears were often. I'd leave the room on my own if he didn't throw me out first and cried myself to sleep on the couch.

I didn't know what to do. There was never anyone in my life who treated me so bad, talked to me like Prof' did and I was scared... always. Scared that if I left him he might just hurt me worse. So I stayed.

One evening working at the motel, I met a cute guy named Bobby. He asked if he could call me up once in a white. I explained that I was married, but he charmed me. All he wanted to do was talk. I gave in and told him he could call me but only at the job. We were just phone friends. The phone calls between us lasted hours. It went on for a few weeks and one day Bobby called me where I lived. At first I hesitated to talk but I figured Prof' was out of town anyway and would never know the difference. Besides, it wasn't like me and Bobby were having some crazy passionate love affair. So after talking two hours an operator came on and said there was an emergency call. Bobby cut the conversation short saying, "Okay, talk to ya later babe." Bobby and I had no clue that Prof' heard what was just said and I was terrified.

I called Mayor and told her what happened. I pleaded with her to let me come home for the night. She insisted I was married and had to learn to work things out for myself. But the Mayor never knew what was going on with me and Prof'. No one did. I stayed at my apartment nervously waiting for my husband to come home.

Chrissy was just over 6 months old and needed to be out of mom's room, so I moved her crib in the only place I could which was the corner of the dining area. She was asleep. I was glad because I knew it wouldn't take Prof' the usual time to get home. He would race.

The door flew open. Prof' came in and asked me who I was talking to. I told him that it was just a friend. He was real upset and he lifted the couch's end up trying to make me fall off. I figured I better give him a name so he wouldn't wake up the baby. When I did, he made a call to Bobby's house. Bobby answered and knew by the sound of the voice it was Prof', so he pretended not to be himself. Prof' told the person he was talking to, to leave a message for Bobby. He said, "Tell Bobby that Cap's real sick. She needs him to come over to Huron right away. She doesn't have a car and her phone isn't working." Bobby told Prof' that the message would be delivered. Once off the phone, Prof' went into the bedroom loaded up his shot gun and put me next to the patio doors where we both sat. He put the gun up to my temple. The baby was in direct line of fire. He kept the rifle to my head from midnight until 5:30 am waiting for Bobby. I knew if Bobby would have shown, Prof' would have aimed to kill. Thank God that Bobby out smarted Prof' and Prof' left for work. I went over to Chrissy who was asleep and wondered how to get the both of us out.

There was always something that set off Prof'. Sometimes he'd start a fight because he thought some man was looking at me wrong. Or it would be over a girl who he thought needed his help. He tore up a small bar one evening because another male customer was giving the cocktail waitress a hard time. Tables flipped and drinks were flying. I vacated the premises and walked home alone and humiliated.

When I couldn't get the raise I wanted to keep living in town, close to Mayor and Pope, Prof' moved me and Chrissy to Elyria where he worked.

He stopped wearing his wedding band. Said that working over a hot grill made the ring hot and he'd have to take it off anyway. I fell for it. I knew in my heart that he didn't want anyone to know he was married when he said that all the waitresses at the club were old.

One evening I was alone in the house we rented and there was a giant spider on the curtain. I got a flash light, shined it on the spider so I wouldn't lose track of it. It was big brown and hairy, I sat myself in the middle of the room with my feet up in a chair. Prof' came in and wanted to know what the hell I was doing. I just told him to took. He saw the huge spider on the curtain and said, "How long have you been sitting there?" Until he asked I hadn't realized that it had been over three hours. He smacked it and claimed it was dead. I said, "Prof it's not dead. I saw it web it's way to the floor?" He said, "Cappy. Wolf spiders don't make webs they jump." That kept me up all night thinking the spider would get revenge somehow for its near death. I decided to call an exterminator. After checking out the house, not only was it infested with wolf spiders, but mice and bats. That's all it took. I packed up my clothes and the baby's. I told Prof' I would be at my parents house until he found me a clean place. This was the day I made up my mind to visit the country club. According to Prof', I couldn't enter because I wasn't an employee or a member. The baby went with me when I walked through the front doors. A line of beautiful young waitresses were clocking in. I walked to them and said, "Hi. Has anyone seen my husband Prof'?" About four of the twelve mouths hung open. With no response from any of the girls I said, "Oh I'm sorry. I forgot. This is his day off." Me and the baby left for Sandusky.

Once at my parents house and settled, I needed to get out for a night I bumped into a friend of mine. I told Chico how tired Prof' was all the time. Chico laughed and put his arm around me. "It's not funny Chico. He won't sleep with me." "Shit Cappy. Don't tell me you're gonna stay with him. He's tired all the time because he's fucking anything he can get his hands on!" "Don't lie," I said doubtingly. "I'm not. He's tired alright. Tired from too much fucking. I'm sorry Cap, but why don't you lose him? You're Nice. Too good for him! If I had someone as gorgeous and as sexy as you I wouldn't wanna leave the house. I'd be with you all the time. That's the kind of man you want. Not Prof'. He'll end up giving you some disease or something." I didn't wanna believe what I was hearing, but coming from Chico I knew it was the truth. Sooner or later I would have to face that truth and do something to change my life and my daughters.

Chico was right. Prof' never had a good thing to say about me. He was never around and when he was he'd knock me down in the music department. He'd say, "Christ Cap! Who you trying to kid. You think you are gonna have this big rock band and be an overnight success? It won't ever happen. Not you. You're not rational when you think. That's why I don't want you having a car. You'd probably fuck it up. You're so fucking jealous. You ain't nothing and won't be anything without me. As for you being a singer," he said laughing, "You might make a good prostitute. You'd have to walk the streets and carry your mattress with you because you won't have me taking care of you. Be realistic Cappy. You'll never have what it takes to make it."

So why did I go back to Elyria when he found us a clean place? Maybe it was to hear what I knew all along. For it was there when he finally admitted to having four different affairs. He was putting on a fairly good fake cry when I yelled and said, "Don't ever stick that dirty thing in me again. What did you marry me for? I hate you! You forced me to give you oral sex after you were inside some other woman. I wanted to vomit all over you. I went into the kitchen and got the butcher knife. Stood over you after you passed out on your stomach. I should have killed you then!" "Why didn't you when you had the chance?" he asked, almost as if he wanted me to.

I sort of lost my desire to become the coolest girl in America and I put my music on the back burner for a long time. Friends were ordered out after a while, even though I only hung around with Winnebago. I couldn't have felt worse when Prof' made me call her to tell her she wasn't allowed over anymore. Life would be a lonely one.

Chapter Six: "December 8th, 1980"

Going back home was a smart thing. A break away from Professor now would be a safe one. I didn't want to go back to Elyria and be with him. He talked me into a failed date and it was over. Not legally, but over. After a few months Prof' moved to Arizona... alone.

I took on a job as dental assistant, but the hours weren't enough to take care of Chrissy so a second job was in order. Nights at "The Sands..". again. This time I wasn't cleaning rooms, I was working the front desk. Two clean jobs for a change. Better yet... I didn't have Professor breathing down my neck for the paychecks.

The two opposing shifts started getting to me. Getting home from the desk job by 5:45 am made sleeping worse because I had to start getting ready for the dentist's office at 7:30 am. But one night at the motel, a nice looking blonde guy pulled up on a ten speed bike. He came into the lobby for a cup of cold water. He told me that he had just come from Port Clinton via bicycle. What a pedal. It's at least 25 minutes with a car.

Mike had steel blue eyes and a beach-bum-sun-tan. He kept his beard and mustache neatly trimmed.

Mike and I became well acquainted over the next couple of weeks. He came by the motel on the nights I worked. He brought a card game and got me hooked on "Mille Bornes." Mike usually won.

"Mike, these jobs are making me tired, ya know." "Cap, I got just the thing. Here." He reached in his pocket and pulled out a yellow capsule. "Take it Capri. It's called a yellow jacket. You know, speed. It won't hurt ya." I washed it down with a cup of coffee. About a half hour went by. I ran my hands through my hair, felt the goose bumps and I liked the yellow jacket. "Mike, you got a few more of those? I'd like to buy some for the rest of the week." Mike took a bag from his pocket and asked, "How many?" "I asked, "How much?" He said, "Buck a piece." I bought ten.

The two jobs weren't pulling in enough money so I called a good old buddy of mine from the shoe store. Gene was the district manager and had told me once that if I ever wanted my old job back to just buzz him on the phone. All was set with the call and I would start the following week.

It was good to be back in a business I liked and knew. All of us at the store got along well and would have coffee at my favorite hangout "Crooks Den."

My work schedule was like this: Up at 7:00 am to be at the dentist's office by 8 o'clock. I finished there at 3 pm, walked home because it was a couple blocks away. I'd grab a bite and head for "Nobils..". formerly "Norman's

Shoes." Work was 4 till close. Home time would be about 9:30, giving me just a little time to be with Chrissy, put my feet up and it was back to the motel by 11 p.m. till 5 in the morning and I did it for six months too long. Three jobs was just crazy, and holding on to a saliva tube all day was not my idea of fun, so I quit working for the dentist first.

By this time I was hooked on speed. It started with one or two hits a day. Eight months into jobs and I was taking five just to feel the breeze and I did that five to six times a day. My skin was dry and wrinkled. I was a speed freak, a pot head and an occasional drinker. Sometimes on my nights off I did them all. Speed was easy to get if you knew the right people and I knew the right people. My cousin would get them by the thousands and all kinds. I did the robin's egg, the moles, the black beauties, the yellow jackets, the pink hearts. You name them, I took them. Anything to keep me working.

Anxious and awake I started going out. I'd been turning invitations down because I was still married. This was stupid I thought. Prof' was no doubt screwing every waitress he could get his hands on. I'd go out if the right guy would ask me.

Denny of all people was single and asking me out. The one Prof' was worried about. Oh Denny and I were going out often and things between us were getting close. He dropped in on me at the motel one afternoon. Yes I got afternoons. From nowhere he asked me to marry him. Denny offered to pay an attorney so I could get divorced and all was too good to be true. I accepted. Why shouldn't I? We knew each other for 8 years. Couldn't have been crazier about him. We sort out went out, snuck out when I was 16 years old, just to shoot pool. My insides were shaking thinking about being married to Denny. His father was well established and had one of the finest dry wall businesses in the tri-county area. I knew I would have a secure future for me and my daughter. Except for one thing. The crack that Denny made about taking a hundred thousand dollar life insurance policy out on himself. Just in case Prof' would want to kill him. I took that serious and the marriage idea blew away like dust. Denny and I remain friends.

This was a good thing because I may have never met Nic Angelo. He worked for his father who owned the most beautiful flower and garden shop in town. Nic was one part San Marino like me and his other half, Sicilian. We'd bump into each other on purpose at a place called "The Old Dutch." One of those nights I asked Nic if he'd like to come by the house and try some of the wine that Pope made. Nic liked the idea and about 1:30 am we headed to "C" Street.

After we parked we went inside and I got the wine. We shared a couple of glasses and then Nic said he had to be up for work early. Said he would get a hold of me so we could out sometime soon. I walked out the door with him and said good night.

The following morning while I was getting ready to drag myself back to the shoe store, Pope looked at me and said, "So, I think maybe there was a truck in the drive way last night. A big truck." I was astonished and said, "How do you know that? You were working last night." He laughed and said, "So, who was here?" "Dad, you'll never believe who I am going out with, I'm going out with Nic. You know. Nic Angelo! Can you believe it Pope?" "Nickey? Are you crazy? You're not good enough for somebody like him and besides you're still married." I felt real bad and didn't know what to say to Pope so I thought to myself… Shouldn't he be saying something like that's great? He's a good catch? Why wasn't Pope happy for me and why wasn't I good enough for Nic Angelo? That led me to thinking that I wasn't good enough to go to one of the finest opera schools in the world because I wouldn't quit smoking. Pope liked to put stipulations on me. I was not one of his sons. Was that it? I didn't know and I didn't want to think about what Pope had said anymore, so I concentrated on going out with Nic.

Within a few days Nic called and we arranged to have dinner the Friday to come. He picked me up and we had a wonderful night. We stopped in "The Old Dutch" for a night cap and called it a night.

The next day at the shoe store a man from Angelo's came in looking for me. He said, "You must be Cap. Nic told me to make sure that you got these personally." It was a small tan wicker basket with pink sweet heart roses in it. Nic made it up special for me. I called to thank him.

We had been going put for about two months and one evening out to dinner Nic caught me off guard saying, "Capri. I think you might still love your husband. You guys have a baby together." Maybe you should try to work things out with him." "Nic. Whew! I don't know what to say. I really like going out with you. You are so sweet and nice and he's… well… you would have to know him." "Don't worry Capri, it's not that I don't like your company, I'm just a little uncomfortable going out with someone's wife." I appreciated what Nic said and it was our last date together.

Too soon I began calling Prof' out in Phoenix. It didn't take him long to talk me into getting back with him. He promised me that he had changed. I was down to one job at the shoe store and still taking speed, but I planned to make the big move out west to try and work things out with Prof'.

After leaving the shoe store late one night, I drove down a less busy street to get home. I flipped on the radio and caught the tail end of what had to be a sick ugly joke about "John Lennon." Fortunately The Dutch was nearby. The car screeched to a halt in the lot. I knew the bartender there would never joke about anything as serious as "Lennon" so I hurried in to ask him if he knew what was going on. "It's true Cap. Someone shot and killed John Lennon right out in front of his home tonight. I know how you must feel," he said. "Oh God why?" I cried. "Who would want to kill John Lennon?" "Capri. Let me buy you a drink. Go on and sit down I think you need to." I walked over to the closest table and fell into a chair. I cried out loud. My brain refused to accept the information. It couldn't be true! I finished the drink, waved on to Doug and left.

On my way home flipping channels on the radio, the news was all over. How would I ever fulfill my dream now? No chance of ever meeting all 4 Beatles as planned. I was never going to be Mrs. John Lennon, and I had waited so long. There was nothing more to dream about. I decided that without John, I didn't want to meet the other three. The meaning had none. I don't remember what I did when I got home. More than likely went into my room, locked the door, put on something by John and cried till I slept. Hermit didn't say one way or another how he felt about John's death. Instead he held his own private vigil by putting Lennon's picture from the "Shaved Fish" album on two different tee shirts. One face was white on black and the other was black on white.

John's widow, "Yoko," had asked Johns fans if they wanted to observe his death with a moment of silence. I went down to a record shop in the mall where I knew the two people working there. We talked about her request and thought that maybe we could do something in the mall over the loud speaker system ... manager permitting. Well as it turned out, the manager like The Beatles and agreed to let us give a speech in honor of John, so long as it didn't make any of the customers feel obligated. On December 14th, 1980 our speech was completed by me, "Kristen Whitehouse" and "Chris Dougherty." I was the elected speaker. When the time came for me to read what the three of us had composed I was wreck. With a saddened heart I read to listeners: "MAY I HAVE A MINUTE OF YOUR TIME PLEASE? ON DECEMBER 8TH, 1980, JOHN LENNON, A MAN OF PEACE AND LOVE LEFT US; A GENTLE MAN WHO STRUCK THE UNIVERSAL CHORD. IT HAS BEEN REQUESTED THAT WE ALL OBSERVE A MOMENT OF SILENCE TODAY IN HONOR OF HIM; A PRAYER, PERHAPS A SONG. HERE'S TO YOU MR. LENNON - FOR INSPIRING MY GENERATION TO GREATER HEIGHTS THAN WE WERE TOLD WE COULD REACH."

During the last few words of the speech I broke down and had to take the rest of the day off. I bumped into an old school friend of mine named Richie who suggested we stop and have a candle vigil for John at a nearby restaurant. We spent three hours talking and crying.

In January of 1981, Chrissy and I made plans to fly out to Phoenix with her dad.

Pope got me a used 74 "Lincoln Town Car" I made payments, but told him to sell it for me 'cause it wouldn't be an easy long distance drive with a baby. Mayor was extremely upset that I was going to leave and take with me her first grandchild. So upset, that on the day I was packing, she threw a chair across the kitchen of her home yelling at me. "You can't take Chrissy from me! She's my baby! I watched her first step! I saw her first tooth! I heard her say her first word. Cappy you can't go! Please don't leave!" "Mom, this is my baby. You always told me that my place was with my husband. I am married mom and he lives out west. I'm really sorry, but I have to go. I'll call and I'll write, I promise." Mayor cried and said, "But it won't be the same without little Chrissy here. She's gonna be missed a lot. I love her just like she were my own." "I know mom, I know." I hugged my mom and dad and the hugs for Chrissy were a thousand times more. Before we knew it we were on the plane to Arizona.

The Professor was waiting at the gate of the airport. His hair had grown wild and out of control. Chrissy immediately recognized her father and ran to him. I walked.

I wasn't so sure I had made the right decision.

Phoenix was hot to say the least. It was only January, but the temperature there was in the high eighties. Back home I knew the snow was kicking ass. Speed was also back home. My supplier realized that I was hooked and refused to sell me anymore. I was left dry. What could I do? I didn't know anyone there. And knowing the Prof' the way I did, I wouldn't ever get around to meeting anybody. It was constant on my mind. That and the speed.

He moved us into the small trailer he'd been living in. On the kitchen table were 1 dozen red carnations for me. I could have cared. I got right on the phone and called my parents to tell then I got there okay. Mayor asked if I wanted to keep my "Lincoln" and cut my payments to 50 a month instead of the 100. I told her and Pope to sell it. One week later they did just when I was going to call them to say I had changed my mind.

Prof worked most of the time so me and Chrissy would spend every day outside. It was kind of nice getting up early. You could start working on a sun tan about 7 am. Sun just sort of wakes you up in Phoenix when it shines right in your bedroom window! I'd be out from early morning till early night... about 7:30, while Chrissy played with her toys and her three wheel bike. Prof' saw to it that we had all that we needed at the trailer while he worked. There was always plenty of macaroni and cheese, hot dogs and noodles. Who knows what king Prof' Chef was eating at the country club... and you can bet it was more than steak.

I had been there for about two weeks and still had headaches and stomach aches. I knew it was the withdrawal from lack of speed and I didn't know anyone yet. I didn't have a car to get around, so I was stuck at the trailer all the time. Prof' did all the shopping, if you want to call it shopping.

A month or so passed and we moved into a larger, furnished trailer. Nice things to sit on and a television for those days when there was nothing to do. Chrissy and I still lived on the usual food Prof' stocked us up with. Frankly I was getting sick of it day after day so I drank more and more coffee. More than I ever did. I even began making pictures of ice coffee for long, hot days spent outside. Of course I thought it would get me over the speed I was missing.

Next door to me I saw a woman watering her garden. She seemed close to my age and I thought I'd try to make myself a new friend. Maybe Prof' wouldn't mind. I walked over to her yard with Chrissy and said, "Hi. I'm Cap. We just moved in next door." "Hi Cap. Nice to meet somebody my age for a change. Most of the people in the trailer park here are old. Are you from around here," she asked. "No, I used to live in Ohio. Ever heard of Cedar Point? People from all over America go there in the summer." "Well, I know I don't lead a sheltered life, but I can't say that I have. Oh, I'm sorry, I'm Jackie. What's Cedar Point?" "It's an amusement park. Without it Sandusky would be nothing. That's the town I was born in. By the way, Jackie, I don't mean to be bold, but isn't that pot you are watering?" "Ah so you noticed. Yeah, but don't let any of the old farts in on my secret. I've been growing it all year. Looks good doesn't it?" I laughed and said, "Your secret is safe with me. I used to smoke a lot of it but then I got hooked on speed. The damn dealer wouldn't sell me any to bring out here and I don't know anybody here." "Well Cap! You're at the right place. Got a minute? Why don't you and your little girl come inside." We went into Jackie's apartment. We sat in the living room and Jackie said, "See this bag? Looks like something a bank robber would be hauling money in doesn't it? Well how many do you want?" My mouth watered when I saw the contents. There must have been a couple thousand black beauties in that bag. "Damn Jackie, there are so many. I can't just help myself but I'll buy some." "Here, consider it a welcome to the old folks' home trailer park."

And she handed me about twenty of them. I popped one right away. "Jackie, I have had the worst headaches and stomach aches because I didn't have any of these in so long. I'm gonna watch how I take em. Shoot, I was taking at least five just to get a buzz. You know how ya get immune to the stuff." "I know. I don't do it and neither does my husband, but we have a lot of friends who do. Don't worry about it Cap, if you need some just come on over." "I'll try not to be a pest, but I'm sure I'll be back." "No problem Cap, and hey, it's really race to meet you. What's your little ones name?" "Oh, this is Chrissy." She said hello to my little girl. Chrissy said hello back and we went to our trailer and turned on the cartoons. Prof' would be home and I didn't think he'd make a big deal about the speed, but I wasn't going to take any chances. I hid them in a sanitary napkin box. Things seemed to be going well. Professor wasn't out in the bars. He was coming home. I had a new friend and Chrissy couldn't have been happier. I laughed, remembering the year Prof' and I moved nine times. This would be the last. I liked Phoenix.

Prof' was reading the paper and saw a position up in Montana It was the chefs. "Cappy. We are going to Montana. Up in the National Park. I know I can get this job and I've always wanted to go there. Want to go?" "Why not," I said, "I'm used to moving." There wasn't much choice in the matter. Professor made the call. Landing that job was easy for Prof' and it wouldn't be long before we left Arizona. I didn't want to miss the only friend I made and it was hard going over to say good bye to Jackie. I was going to miss her. Okay, the speed too. She gave me a care package for the trip. I wished her luck on the pot plants. Then Prof' and I packed everything we owned and put in the 1972 "Cadillac." I hated the car. Well, maybe not the car, just the color. Flip-side-dollar-bill-green! Why would anyone want this color on a car like this? Color or not, we were headed to the mountains.

Prof' wanted this to be adventurous so he stopped at a sporting goods store and bought everything we would need to camp out along the way. I don't think it was really the adventure, I believe that there just wasn't any money for motel rooms. Prof' was bad with money.

We went through many states on the way up. Nevada, Utah, Wyoming, Wisconsin. I couldn't wait to get there. The Prof' did nothing but talk about it the whole way.

It took us ten days to get there. We could have been there sooner but Prof' knew someone living in Loveland, Colorado. So the three of us camped out in their back yard for five days.

The Profs' friend was an old one and I enjoyed his company and Colorado. The country there was beautiful, full of grassy mountains and clear skies. If this was any indication of what Montana was like, I was all the more ready to get there.

Chapter Seven: "Palm Tree Paradise"

As noted by Prof', it wouldn't be much longer before we'd cross the state line of Montana.

God's country I thought. It won't be anything like back home. If Sandusky was really home. See I always joked that my town was a subdivision of the Bermuda Triangle. All those people lost at sea? They weren't lost at all. They ended up in Sandtown. Once you're in Sandtown, you never leave. But I managed to escape the triangles deadly hold.

Things seemed to be going well with me, Prof' and Chrissy. Maybe it was the alcohol that made Professor act like he did, treat me the way he did, because all was going well and for the first time in some time I was happy.

There it was. The sign that said: WELCOME TO THE STATE OF MONTANA! This was it. A new life, a new place to begin and maybe new friends.

We approached a booth on the road side where we were asked to stop. Prof' explained that he was on his was to Lake McDonald Lodge to take on his job as chef. The woman at the booth wished the three of us luck and pointed us in the right direction.

It was a fifty mile ride from the Ranger's Station. A long and winding road. This led us to "Lake McDonald Lodge." It was beautiful! What I dreamed it might be. The Lodge itself was built like a huge log cabin. Behind it was Lake McDonald. Very breathtaking. Very deep. 400 feet deep! It was formed by glaciers and you could see the bottom of it at fifty feet. This was nothing like Lake Erie back home.

There was a ferry boat called "The DeSmit" and I couldn't wait for the park to open so I could hop aboard.

We arrived three weeks before the place opened. The care takers who watched the place had been expecting us and showed us where we would live. We walked up the stairs on the side of their house that led us into a very small apartment. You walked into a living room about 14x14. In the living room there was a sink and a set of cupboards below. One window faced the grounds and lodge. Off of that was a small bedroom with a full sized bed. Off that the bathroom, with a sink, toilet and shower. Luxury was not this place. There was no oven or stove top to cook on and we were hungry. We finished everything up the previous night at an Indian camp ground. The "Twamley's" gave Prof' the keys to the lodge and gave us the grand tour. They also told us to help ourselves to anything in the kitchen. Prof' made us breakfast.

The tired three of us went back to the apartment for a good night's sleep.

Within a few days the manager of the place had arrived. There was no one to run the switchboard. He asked if I would until the place opened. That would be two weeks. Prof' stayed in the apartment at night and I was on the graveyard shift. The lobby was huge and decorated with many stuffed animals. Real animals. There were mountain goats, white owls, deer heads, moose heads hanging all around it, the skin of a grizzly bear draped over the railing on the second floor balcony. There were easily twenty to thirty different animals to keep me company in this lonely, lonely place.

After a few evenings on the job a security person had been hired. He showed me how to get a nice fire going in the fireplace. This was no ordinary fireplace. It was about 15 feet across, six feet tall and over five feet in depth. We'd get one hell of a strong, tall fire going. Sometimes it would be at least 7 feet across and 4 feet up. I would curl up on the long couch in front of it watching the flames.

If we got hungry through the night he had a set of kitchen keys and we'd wipe the place out. He was into toast and I was into hot apple pie and ice cream. It became our two o'clock norm' after the first break in. We continued till the place opened. Tough for me. No more kitchen-late-nights kitchen raids and no more job.

Mostly college students came from all over the country to work at the lodges in the National Park. There were at least one hundred working at Lake McDonald. They treated me real nice and adored Chrissy. They went all out for her when she turned three in June. All the employees joined in the decorations, food, and games. Presents? She had more than me and her father could carry.

The kids working there had been instructed not to bring any transportation along because there wouldn't be enough room for all their vehicles. The lodge would provide them with it. I never thought that our car would be the transit system. It became a weekly event. We'd load up about ten people in the car and drive 50 miles into a town called Kalispell. There were a couple of bars that had live country rock music. At first I couldn't stand it. But after a time, when that's all you have you make yourself like it. Television was something to hide in the corner. We only got one station and that didn't come in well. I made due by working lots of jigsaw puzzles during the day while Prof' worked. If Chrissy wanted to play outside I never had to worry about a sitter. The college girls fought over who would take turns watching her. In the evening I got only one radio station. It wouldn't come in during the day at all. But at one in the morning the "Larry King" show did.

43

Surrounded by mountains, Chrissy and I rode the ferry boat every chance we had. We weren't happy if we didn't.

The employees, me and my daughter shared a big room where we ate our free meals. They were good meals too. For a change I saw what Professor was really made of as far as chefs go.

Midsummer came and Mayor phoned with bad news. My brother John's girlfriend had her baby early. The baby weighed only two pounds and was in the Cleveland Clinic. "Mom, John's baby? Why his? It should have been me, mom. John's the good one. I'm the black sheep, he don't deserve this Mayor I do." "Cap," she said, "You shouldn't say that. God must have his reasons. The doctors are amazed at how strong he is for being so tiny. He fits right in the palm of your hand." "Well that does it mom, I'm coming home for while. I want to be there." "Cap, it isn't necessary for you to come, you won't be able to change anything." "Mom, it doesn't matter, I'll talk to Prof', he'll let me come home for a few weeks, besides you'll get to see Chrissy." "Oh, well if you're going to bring my little sweetie pie home, then hurry up and get your ass on the plane now." Mayor laughed, I laughed, and before long I was back home.

I stayed for three weeks. My brother's son was making it. We thought all would be well. At Mayors old house (because Pope had been building a new brick one), I saw Denny's name on the fridge. "Mom," I said, "What are you doing with this number?" "Oh, you know your father. He wants the best dry wall for the house and he said that this guy is the best."

At the old "C" Street house I was feeling a little weak and dizzy, kinda like morning sickness. Naturally I made an appointment with my doctor..."Dr. Buder." He did a pelvic, they ran a urine test and a blood test. All three read negative. The ultrasound would be the positive and I would have my second child in the winter. How would I tell Prof? He'd want a son. He'd have to pick out the name boy or girl. His decision.

The time came for me to go back to the lodge. Saying the goodbyes to my family were tearful ones. In mid July I returned to Montana, and to Prof' who would be having a birthday soon.

Rather than telling him about my pregnancy, I concentrated on baking the ultimate cake for his birthday. Chrissy and I snuck over to the coffee shop everyday to get it just right. We drove to Kalispell to get large gum balls. They were just the right size for the cake we decorated as a pool table.

The students ordered up a couple kegs of beer and the food was endless. People were getting smashed. I watched because I couldn't drink while carrying this baby, the one I still hadn't told Prof' about.

He was doing his share of drinking. By the time Chrissy and I carried the cake to him he was plastered. Prof' didn't see us. I demanded his attention,

"Your daughter has something for you." "Chrissy pie, you made this for me? Check out this cake guys, it's a pool table! How did ya make the balls?" he asked. We told him and lit the candles. Prof' blew out the candles. It took a few blows. Chrissy gave him a big hug and his present. He told her he'd be right back while he took off running from someone who was trying to spray him with whipped cream. The food fight went on for a long time. Me and Chrissy sat outside at a picnic table. I didn't tell her the wait for him would be long. Prof' raced by us and I called to him. "What do you want?" he asked. "The party's been going on for two hours now. Can't you sit with me?" "Sit with you? I don't wanna be with you, I wanna be with my friends. Why don't you go upstairs and do a puzzle if you don't know how to have a good time." A few people sitting with me shook their heads. I turned to Terri and said, "Can you believe that? He's a real prick. If I wasn't pregnant I'd be pretty loaded myself just so I could forget this night. Oh Terri, don't tell Prof' anything about the baby. He doesn't know yet." She promised she wouldn't.

Chrissy and I went headed for our apartment. She was asleep fast. Right after there was a knock on my door. Brenda a cocktail waitress dropped in to see if I wanted somebody to watch Chrissy so I could get out with the other people at the party. It sounded good to me so off I went to the employee cafeteria. It was quieter there and so was Prof' who was in the kitchen ready to take his food filled clothes off and join the two other girls already in the restaurants kitchen sink. Clothes and all, and yes they were bathing. I swung open the doors, "So, you don't wanna be with me, you want to be with your friends? These women? Zip your pants up. You're not taking your clothes off." Prof's face lit up red as he zipped his pants up saying, "Sorry girls, my wife won't let me take a bath with you now." As disgusted as I was, I have to admit that he looked pretty funny with chocolate syrup running down his whipped creamed face. His clothes were drenched with beer.

I went back outdoors to walk around the grounds. About an hour passed and people were headed back to their dorms. I figured I hunt down Prof'. Walking through the employees cafeteria, through the double doors to the kitchen and through it, I took a left, wondering if Prof' was in his office there. He wasn't anywhere else. He'd be there... I was sure, well, close. I found him and one of the waitresses just outside his office. He had his jeans dropped to the floor and ready to pull down his underwear. The waitress whose back was against the wall, saw me coming and nudged Prof'. He looked back at me. I was so mad I wanted to scream, but I calmly and firmly to him, "You just can't seem to keep your pants on tonight can you." Again, Prof pulled his pants back up and zipped them. I said nothing more and headed back to my huddle upstairs.

Maybe Brenda would listen. I had to talk to somebody. This was a good thing and a bad thing. Brenda wanted to talk to me long before I came up with the idea. She told me that one evening on her way back to her dorm, Prof' stopped her and put his arms around her, telling her that he'd be more than happy to walk her there. She told me that she pulled away from him, thanked him and went to her room alone. "Cap. I felt so bad. I wanted to tell you but since nothing happened, I didn't want to see you hurt. You are so lucky to have a family. I respect that and I love children. See, I can't have any kids. When I was about 14, my own father tried to rape me. When he didn't penetrate me, my mother, thank God, believed me and took me to a doctor. I learned then that I didn't have a vagina. By looking, you'd think that I was normal, but there wasn't any opening. I had surgery to correct it. Capri, I'm 29 years old and I never had sex, but when I do, it will be the one I love." Brenda's story stunned me and I believed her because I liked her. She did adore kids and they loved her right back. Chrissy and her hit it off great. Brenda and I spent a lot of time talking about life and things. We got to be good friends and Prof' left her alone.

The next day I made up my mind to tell Prof' I was pregnant because I needed larger jeans. First thing he said is it can't be his baby. Then he reminds me that I was the one out of town not him. I reminded him about his birthday party. He reminds me about the day we practiced for our wedding and he was called by Denny's last name, not his. It took a lot of talking, but when he knew how far along I was, there was no way it could be anyone else's by his. Because I remained faithful. I would travel to Kalispell the next day for a pair of cheap jeans.

The day came and I took a twenty, stuck it in my back pants pocket. (I hated purses) I walked down the stairs and got in the car. I had someone watch Chrissy for me because I just wanted to be alone.

I got to a store there and found a nice pair of jeans for about 16 bucks. I took them to the checkout counter and reached for the twenty. "Oh no, the money isn't here." I started crying. The clerk said, "That's okay, we'll hold them for you right here at the counter, just come back for them." "No you don't understand, I live at Lake McDonald. I had to drive fifty miles to get here. I don't know why I'm crying. It's not the drive. I'm just pregnant. I cry over everything these days. Now I gotta drive 100 miles to bring the money here. It should be funny but it isn't. I'm sorry, I don't mean to go on. I might be back today if the drive don't get me." "You'll be fine hon. I'll keep these up here for you if you decide you want to come back for them today, how's that?" "That's great. I gotta have 'em 'cause nothing fits. I'll be back. Not soon, but back." When I got to my car I was so pissed I kicked the tire and hurt my foot. Drove back to the lodge and found the twenty still folded and laying on the steps to my place. I grabbed it and took off for Kalispell again.

Kalispell was a place I didn't want to go to for a long time after that. Employees from the lodge however, still wanted to go to bars once a week. I couldn't drink and besides, I didn't see them offering me gas money for a hundred mile drunk so I figured they could find their own way.

The summer months brought August. I was tired of the ferry boat all day long so I found someone to watch Chrissy. I needed a good long drive with music. So I took "The Going to the Sun Road." It was a sixty-mile drive one way to Saint Mary's Lake. The view was breathtaking and I fell in love with where I had been living. Tiny and centered between two ten thousand foot mountains was and an island called "Goose Island." Not much bigger than the floor area of my apartment and scattered with a few palm trees and shrubs. I got out of my car and walked down to the edge of the lake. I pictured in my mind that if there ever was a Garden of Eden that this had to be it. How could the palms ever survive the vicious winters Montana was known to have? But they did. I wanted to stand on it. Get a picture of me on it. I believed the road sign I'd seen two hundred feet ago. The Second Most Photographed Area in the World" Per "Kodak." I spent an hour watching it on the mirrored turquoise colored lake. Then I drove off to tour the other lodges and facilities.

On my back to the lodge I stopped at the island again and watched it as sun was setting. I knew then that someday I would have to return if only for a visit.

Before summer was over, I convinced Prof' that Chrissy still needed to be baptized. We would need God Parents. Kate said she'd be God Mother. She worked for Prof' in the Pantry. And Mic, who wanted to become a Catholic priest, said he'd love to be the God Father. Chrissy couldn't have been happier. She had a crush on Mic long before this decision was made. In the cafeteria, when Mic was dishing out lunches to the workers, Chrissy cupped her cheek with her hand and stared at Mic with a big smile. The baptism took place in the employee recreational room and most of the employees attended.

By September's end, when grizzly bears would come down from the mountains to stock up for the winter ahead, we were headed out. Prof' planned that our next place of residency would be the state of Washington. We said many sad goodbyes, took one last ferry boat ride on the lake we had loved so much, and headed back to the apartment to pack our things.

It would be a sad journey to Seattle, because when we were about to leave, Mayor phoned with bad news. My brother John's baby had died. It was difficult for everyone. The baby lived just over a month and the doctors thought for sure he had a fighting chance. He fought for more than a month. I hurt for my brother and his girlfriend, but I did have a new life inside of me that I needed to think about. I put all the negatives behind and left with my daughter and Prof', heading further west.

Chapter Eight: "Seattle. Where Pet Fish Are Popular" ("The Emerald City")

I spent time getting acquainted with Edmonds, Washington a suburb of Seattle. We arrived in late September when the rainy season had already begun.

Naturally Prof' surrounded himself with waitresses again. Of course he was the kitchen manager and chef. This would be serious trouble because they gave him an expense account for business clients. He could entertain them with dinner or serve up the drinks in the lounge. Prof' preferred the lounge area.

With no transportation I stayed at our small apartment. This meant I had to do a lot of walking. Sure, sure, I know. I should have quit my cigarette habit but I didn't. Prof didn't always make sure I had smokes before he went to work. I'd walk to get them. A nice elderly couple was kind enough to watch Chrissy while I walked in the rain to get "Kools." I was up at six every morning because Profs' coffee had to be ready before he got up. After he'd leave I'd get my coat on and slip into the morning fog. Halfway to the store the rain would come without fail. Every day. Really! Every single day. The walk was about three quarters of a mile.

I was soaking wet through my coat and my clothes. I can't emphasize enough that it "did" rain every single day from the very first day we floated into town. At the store an older man looked at me and said, ""Miss? Why didn't you bring your fish along with you?" "What" I asked. He said, "Well everybody takes their pet fish out for walks in rain like this. Believe me... You just don't look quite right without one." I shook my head and thought for sure he had lived in Seattle long enough to be gone. Where, I will never know!

Too many nights were spent without Prof' because he loved his job. I was about six months pregnant and we were not having sex. So one night when I thought he was through at the restaurant I said, "Hey Prof' ... Wanna fool around?" "Can't," he said, "Somebody called in sick. Just play with yourself." And he said that laughing. It wasn't funny. Why did he say it, I thought? What's wrong with me... and him? I'm not fat. I'm just going to have a baby.

I tried everything. I wore sexy nighties to bed. I even pretended to be asleep and said whispering, sexy words thinking it might arouse Prof'. It didn't. He kept to himself in the bedroom and when he wasn't asleep he worked.

December 3rd came and so did another daughter. I wanted to name her Julia after John Lennon's mother, but Prof hated it. He suggested we name her Julie. We did. Julie was born on the same day as Pope. I wanted to surprise him with the news. I called Mayor at 7:35 a.m., her time. Pope would be home from work then. Mayor answered and wondered why in the world I was calling so early. "Mayor, put Pope on. I want to wish him happy birthday." In the background I heard Mayor say, "I don't know why she's calling so early." "Hi Cappy. How are you guys doing," Pope asked. "We're fine. The reason I called was to wish you happy birthday. And would you wanna wish your new grandbaby a happy birthday too?" "Mayor," Pope called, "She had the baby on my birthday." I could hear the happy crackling in his voice. Pope was choked up and wanted to know all the details. Mayor took the phone from Pope and told me how happy they both were for me. Quietly she told me that Pope's eyes were teared up he was so happy. They wanted to see Julie, but Mayor wasn't about to hop on a plane and Pope wouldn't come to Washington without her. It would be up to me and it would take time.

After a rest-filled-four-days at the hospital, there would be no more rest. Prof' was no help at all. The housework was nothing really. Dishes, floors, bathrooms, it was like cleaning rooms. But the laundry would be walking with a loaded basket of clothes out of the apartment, passing four other apartment doors to get to the washers and dryer. The work seemed endless and so was the bleeding. I shouldn't have bled for two months. Losing that kind of iron led me to exhaustion. Prof' spent more and more time at the restaurant. I stand corrected... the lounge.

The kids were good but life generally sucked because I didn't have friends. But I did have Grizzly McDonald. He was born in Montana and I found him at five weeks old. I kept Grizzly for keeps. He proved his worth in Washington. We had to pay our landlords an extra-secret-one-hundred-dollar-security-deposit to keep him. Now Julie wasn't sleeping through the night and I didn't expect it, not yet. She was just two months old. At two-thirty in the morning, the usual time, she woke up crying. By the time I got to her she was quiet and asleep. Grizz' crawled up into her crib and snuggled his belly against the crown of her head. From that night on she slept through the night. Yes, black cats are the best. Grizzly was my third and favorite black cat.

When Julie turned four months old, Prof thought we needed another place. We did and moved into a duplex. It was a nice place. Two stories, two bedrooms and a fireplace in the living room. Did I mention neighbors next door that would soon be our friends? Them too.

Bill and his wife Judy liked to shoot pool just like me and Prof'. One evening I took off by myself to a local bar for a few games of pool. A guy who had been watching me came over to my table and said, "Hey! I've been wanting to shoot somebody good all night. You look like you take the game seriously. Wanna shoot me a game?" Then he wanted to know what kind of car I had. I told him. A 72 "Cadillac." He told me he owned a "Corvette" and wanted to bet. I win... I get his car. Well any fool could see that he was a little on the intoxicated side so I turned the offer down. I didn't believe a thing about the car. We shot and I won. He flirted with me a little. I explained I was married and excused myself from him and the establishment.

Prof' insisted I go to work at a job he already found for me. Working as a cashier in a mini-mart, which of course had a twelve pump gas station. Not to mention that it was only about a mile away from his own job. It wasn't what I would call a job, but we were needing a second vehicle and this would be the way.

He drove me to the gas station to meet the owner. I slouched in the seat of the car when I saw Bruce, realizing that this man was the same one from the bar who wanted to bet cars for pool. He must have really tied one on the night we shot that game because... it was me who told him a week after he hired me, that I was the girl from "Baluga's" bar.

Bruce was a cool guy to work for. He didn't care if we smoked on the job and if we ever worked more than forty hours he would pay us double time. That was ten bucks an hour. Tax free.

I liked the idea of making that kind of money just to stock and run a register. Lots of times I'd call Bruce to see if he needed me to work. Truth was, Prof' ignored me when we were home. Hiding behind boxing games, baseball games and newspapers. The typical call I'd make to my boss was "Hi Bruce, wanna spend the day with your girlfriend, I'll come in." Typical answer, "Sure "B.B," come on in. You know, just take the eighty bucks out of the drawer when your shift is up and mark it down." I'd tell Bruce that I'd be there in an hour and I'd get myself all prettied up and go to work. I sort of had a crush on him. It's hard to explain. He was tall, medium build, light brown wavy hair. His nose was on the large side and he wore glasses. Maybe it was the way he talked. He was cool and laid back. He kinda liked me too. He nick-named me "B.B." Which stood for beautiful butt. Jokingly later it stood for baby boobs. Bruce was just plain fun. I'd show up early lots of times just to be with him till my shift started. Then back to the real world of Seattle.

One afternoon, just before my shift ended, Prof' pulled up to tell me he had a surprise for me, Bruce let me go early and Prof' drove about twenty minutes until we went up a short-hilled street that led to a drive. He parked the car in the driveway of a huge wooden home. "Well, do you like it," he asked. "Hell yes!" I said. "I got the place for five hundred a month with the option to buy it. It looks like just a two story house doesn't it. Well, it has a third level around the back you can't see from here, but that's where the master bedroom and bath are. Oh, plus there's another bedroom on that level. What's real neat is there are only about six other neighbors here and they all keep to themselves. You won't have to worry because this is a real nice area. No trouble here."

It was a big house. There were two living rooms, a kitchen that was at least 25 by 16 feet. Besides the two bedrooms and bath upstairs on the third level, there were three more bedrooms downstairs, a nice workshop and a big room just right for a pool table that was already set up with our other things. Prof' and his buddies spent the day moving everything in place for me. I must admit, I was impressed. I wondered why the sudden change. Maybe it was because I stopped wanting sex with him. I kept refusing knowing that something had to be going on, I just hadn't found out yet. I refused for seven months. He accused me of being a lesbian. Funny, he never accused me of an affair. You think that would have been first.

Things were alright for a time until one morning, after Prof' didn't come home the night before, he called. He claimed he was out of gas and couldn't drive home so he slept in his office all night. I accepted the lie until it happened again only a few days later. Same call, same time in the morning, same shit, only this time I laid into him. "Look, don't give me this shit. You just got paid. You make 700 a week. If you ran out of gas, had a flat tire, even an accident you had the money to pay for it! There is no excuse you can give me that I will believe!" Calmly, he said, "You're right. I want a divorce." I slammed the phone and went into the living room I picked up the recliner that he loved so and threw it across the room. The couch would be next, but there was a knock at the door. It was Profs' younger brother questioning me and trying to settle me down. I yelled. "Are you nuts? You're brother just told me that he wants a divorce and do you want to know why? I know he's sleeping around with someone. Let's get real. Your brother has been screwing anything he could get his hands on since we've been married." Profs' brother had no clue, at least I don't think he did. I was glad to get some of it off my head to somebody. He put the chair back for me, we talked a little, but Jon didn't really want to be involved. Shortly after he arrived, he left. I thought about Prof' and wondered just what waitress made him decide he wanted to divorce me. Rumor had it that he was seeing a skinny little waitress with huge breasts named Sally. He had been taking her to horse races and to ball games. Everywhere! In fact, when it was time for a Christmas party at the restaurant he claimed that it was for employees only. I went to the restaurant and saw Sally leaving the ladies room. I ran up to her and slammed her against the tile wall. "Keep your filthy fucking hands off the Prof', or didn't you know that he was married! To me!" She was shaking so bad and didn't know what to say while she squirmed to get her neck out of my grip. I took my hand off her and made sure everyone heard, "Sally. I could fuck you up so bad right now, but I won't. You can have Prof' you little slut, hell, everyone else has!" The next time I went to the lounge for a drink I was ordered out. Can you believe that? Prof' had told the guys working there to throw me out, permanently.

If things could get worse, they did. Without my knowledge and I'm sure for the money, Prof' told his brother he could live with us. It wasn't that bad if you didn't mind finding your just washed clothes wet and on the floor. Prof's brother was pissing me off. He was the guilty one. Things were always so in order at my house and his lack of respect for that made me damn uptight. I wanted him out. But instead of that happening... Kate popped in. Chrissy's God Mother. Evidently Prof' told her that if she ever needed a job or a place to stay, she'd be welcome. Kate moved in. After Kate, there was another girl who was Kate's best friend and she was moving in too. Why would this be so bad? Because, Prof', Kate and her friend all worked for Prof and worked his shift. Second. The three of them stayed out and partied all the time. I could have accepted it but Prof' would make me late for my job and third was a tough one to handle. Sometimes I was lucky to get five hours sleep a week. Yes, a week. Life was rough.

At my job, Bruce told me I could get a week's paid vacation after six months. When the time came I knew I was headed straight for Sandusky to surprise Pope and Mayor. Bruce didn't think one week was long enough to go all the way to Ohio, so, being the great guy that he was, he gave me three weeks paid vacation and I hopped the next flight home. I arranged to have a girlfriend of mine meet me at the airport so Pope and Mayor wouldn't know. We pulled in the drive about 8 am. The side door was open to the house. I said, "Chrissy. Go in and wake grandma up. Remember where her room is?" Chrissy was quietly going to Mayor's, till she pushed open the door. She stood next to grandma's bed and touched her hand. Mayor's eyes opened, filling them with smiles and elation. "Oh my God, Chrissy! Pope, wake up! Chrissy is here and the baby's here too!" I think Pope must have thought she was dreaming till he came back and saw the three of us in Mayor's bedroom.

Being in Sandusky was great. I spent a lot of time at "Crook's Den." Mayor was happy to have Chrissy back and she didn't mind sitting for me. Think she knew I needed the break. But like time goes, it was gone and our three weeks were up. It was back to the big hairy spiders, Seattle and Prof'. Just didn't seem right leaving my real home behind, but I did with the girls.

First shift was given back to me again when I returned to work. Prof' just partied more now that he had all the room mates for an excuse. All he and I did was fight when he was at the house. Everyone heard the arguments. Since we had moved to the house in the hills, I had no friends again. The people at work were just work. I found myself missing Montana. Wishing to be there away from it all. I missed my guitar and singing. I thought about singing at the Christmas Party back in Montana, held on July 25th held annually back at the lodge. About two hundred fifty some people, guests and employees listened silently to a song done by "The Bee Gee's" titled: "I Started A Joke." The joke was definitely on me. People must have been laughing behind my back. What a fool I had become when I became Profs' wife.

But getting back to Seattle, and to beat everything, the city wanted a nick-name for the tree-y city right when I got there. God! "The Emerald City." Seemed like I had been walking that yellow brick road too long already, and certainly wasn't getting anywhere.

Tired from work, kids I made myself get to bed early one night. Prof' was going to stay out and get shit faced anyway. Kate and her friend were gone out of town. Profs' brother had taken the room all the way in the front of the house on the first level. Profs' room and mine was all the way in the back of the house on the third level. Prof came home and I woke up when he tripped into the bedroom. It was way past three in the morning. All was quiet except for him. He demanded sex. The very idea of just kissing him made me sick. The alcohol smell was all over him and I wanted no part of it. I told him no. Without time to turn away from him he grabbed me by the hair and pulled me halfway off the bed. I yelled for help. But Prof' was quick when he heard me call for his brother. He reached over with one hand and plugged my nose so I was forced to open my mouth for air. When I did he forced his penis in my mouth as hard as he could. I gagged and thought I'd puke. He pulled himself out of me, pushed one of his hands over my mouth and used the other one to restrain me by the throat. Nightmares of the Cleveland hotel trip went off flashing in my head. I made as much noise as I could but it was no use. And because he was drunk it took him a long time. My insides felt like they were being cut and torn. Prof' sheepishly looked at me, and with black, vicious words he slithered out to me, "Bitch! You ain't even a good fuck." I remained on the floor quiet, afraid and waiting for him to pass out on the bed. He used the bathroom, came out and tossed his clothes everywhere. Within seconds he fell flat faced to the bed and was out. Then I got the hell out of the room and ran to check the girls. Thank God they had slept through it all. I went down stairs, washed my face, brushed my teeth and reached for a cigarette and turned on the TV. For why, I don't know because I only stared beyond it and chained smoked till the sun came up.

Afraid to talk, I watched Prof' get his own breakfast and coffee. Like nothing had happened, he left for work. Later Kate came in with her friend. I needed a friend to talk to and I thought Kate would be the one. We were close, but unfortunately not close enough. We both had Prof' in common and Chrissy. But when I confronted her with the night before she said, "Cap I really don't want to get involved." When she said that to me she looked as though she didn't believe a word I said. I called Profs' older sister and she told me that I should call the police and have Prof' charged with rape. I was too afraid to tell the cops. Prof' would just get out of it anyway and hurt me worse. There was no way I was telling the police anything. And that was that.

The summer of '83 was coming to an end and I found out I was pregnant. I didn't want to have anymore of Profs' children. I tried to hurt myself by punching my abdomen over and over, hoping I would have a miscarriage. I even slammed my stomach up against the corner of the kitchen counter. It just wasn't going to happen.

I made up my mind to leave Prof' once and for all. I phoned my parents and told them that I was leaving. Mayor answered. "Hi it's me Cap. I wanna come home. I need 800 dollars to get there. I'll be driving and I don't want Chrissy and Julie sleeping in the car. Can you ask Pope to send me the money? My old boss Gene has my job at the shoe store lined up so I can pay you back right away if you don't mind watching the girls. "Cappy that's an awful lot of money. Don't get me wrong, I want you to come back. Nothing would make me happier, but I do have to ask your father about the eight hundred dollars." She told me she would talk to Pope and get back with me the next morning. The following day came and Mayor phoned me. "Cap, I talked to your father and he said that 800 is too much. It would never take that much money to get here. You're going to have another abortion aren't you? You're pregnant again? Cap? Remember what happened when you had that abortion. Come on home. You don't want to go through that again. Pope said we can help you take care of everything just come home and don't do that." "Mayor, how did you know," I asked. "I put two and two together. Look, we'll send you the money, but we don't want you driving alone with the girls. Can Sue ride with you? Your father said he'll fly her back there. We don't want you traveling over two thousand miles alone and pregnant. And you're pregnant." "Okay Mayor, I'll talk to her. She'd probably love to go."

All the arrangements were made and I would be leaving in a few days. While I was packing I couldn't believe the question that came from Kate. "Cappy. Are you really going to leave Prof'?" Yeah right. She wanted to know my business now, but didn't give a shit about it when I tried talking. I thought she was snooping so I gave her a sarcastic answer. "Yeah." Kate walked over to the living room, sat down on the floor all wide eyed feeling the need to be further involved. 'You know Cap," she said, "It's probably for the best. Prof' acts like he don't love you and I don't think he does." "Funny Kate, I thought you didn't want to get involved. Sounds to me like you can't wait to see me go." I shook my head. Went upstairs to finish packing.

Prof' showed me just how much he cared. He was so thrilled about me going that he rushed out to buy me a real clean "Buick." Even had the transmission totally rebuilt. I met the real Prof' that day and couldn't wait to get to Sandusky for good.

Packed the car, buckled the kids, got Sue and we were off. When driving on Aurora Avenue, a very busy street in Seattle, I could see Prof' wasn't far behind us in the line of traffic blowing his horn to get my attention. I wondered what he wanted. Out of my side view mirror I saw him jump out of the truck. Ran to catch me before the light turned green. He got to the door of the car and said, "Here, you almost forgot the money." Gladly I ripped the four hundred bucks from his hands. He said nothing to his daughters. No kisses, no goodbyes. He left running, fleeing freely like a fly. Felt good to get out of what I never should have walked the isle for.

It took about four days and just over 2500 miles, but we made it back to Sandusky safe. Home never looked so good.

Sue was great company for the trip after I pulled the watch off her wrist and locked it in the glove box. I couldn't take her clocking the time anymore. We would have gotten to Sandtown a hell of a lot faster had I known she was a time freak.

Not much changed on "C" street. The house was still the same and the new home that my father had been working on for his retirement was near completion. In fact, it was right in his back yard. The one that grew all those hundreds of strawberries so many years ago. Mayor kept saying that she didn't want to leave her old house because she'd miss it and the memories. But as time went on, her and I shopped for wallpaper and other household decorations. She was becoming anxious and excited.

I got a hold of Winnebago. Boy was she ever surprised to hear from me. We'd be up to our old tricks of pool and pot in no time. Yep. Home was good!

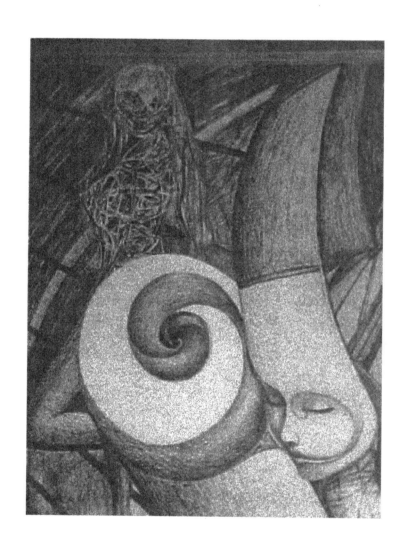

Chapter Nine: "March and April. March On"

Mayor thought right off that I should schedule an appointment with the family doctor to make sure that I was pregnant. Like my first three pregnancies, my tests were all negative. I insisted I was with child but there was nothing that was going to back me up. Figuring I might not be pregnant I decided it might be fun to go to Cedar Point to ride the Blue Streak for a day. It had been years.

Off for a walk through the park, I spied "The Rotor." A spinning wall so fast it holds you against it, and just when you do, the floor drops. When the ride was done, my jeans felt extremely tight. Had to undo the button and zipper. In fact, the zipper was down so far I had to pull my shirt out and cover up my stomach. I knew I had to leave the park and get to Buder's office before it closed. I stopped home to show Pope, who like the doctor, thought, I wasn't pregnant. Found Pope working on the new house and said, "Well, what do you think? Think I'm gonna have a baby now?" He said with eyes wide, "How'd you get so pregnant in one day?" "I'm going over to Buder's office before they close. I want him to order an ultrasound so I know how far along I am." Pope continued to work on the house with a kinda of laugh. Mind you I said "kinda." Pope seldom thought anything was funny. I got to Buder's just in time. His wife told me I could go right back to see him. Standing with my hands on my hips, I looked at Doc' smiling and said, "Well, do you think I'm pregnant?" He was amazed. I told him that I rode the Rotor and the Point'. He figured that my uterus was probably tipped back and the ride helped push it forward. He ordered an ultrasound for the following morning. By the measurements they took, I was 5 and a half months pregnant and due at the end of February 1984 ... Leap Year! The one in which the family learned that Mayor was diagnosed with lung cancer. By the time the doctors realized that she had it, it had already spread through her shoulder, up the back of her neck and into her brain. We were told that mom would have about two years to live. I prayed that she would be cured and my heart tried convincing my brain that she would. She wasn't going to get better.

With heavy hearts we tried to carry on in a normal fashion. Pope continued with the house and his job. Mayor held strong and still planned and bought things for the house in between visits to the hospital.

I was devastated. After I put my two girls to bed I would go into the bathroom, lock the door and cry. I tried not to because Mayor told all of us that tears would not be tolerated. She told me, "Capri, you'll be okay. It will hurt when I'm gone but the hurt will go away honey, you'll see. I saw Jesus and I know that I am going to be just fine. Besides, you'll have a new baby to keep you busy and that baby and those girls are going to need you." It was an enormous lump to swallow but I did. I knew that if I cried she would order my out of her sight. I waited till I left her new house and the tears filled my eyes and face.

More bad was back. A call from Prof' came and I hung up on him. Had nothing to say. Then after a few hours I decided to call back, not to talk to him, but to talk to Kate. I gave her all kinds of shit over the phone. Told her that she was a home wrecker. "Kate you didn't care to hear about the trouble I was having with Prof', but when I was on my way out the door you couldn't shut up! No Kate, you didn't want to get involved. You could care less that Prof' was a married man with kids. You just wanted to party. Well you got him all to yourself, are you happy now?" "Cap I never meant for this to happen, in fact, I'm moving out." "Oh sure now that I'm gone! Like I'll be there to see if it's true. You wanted Prof'. Take him, he's all yours." I slammed the phone down. Kate tried to call me back but I kept hanging up. The Professor called and wanted to talk. He wanted me back. "Cap I'll do anything you say. I won't hurt you anymore, I promise. I was caught up with drinking and a big city and my friends, please, I'll even come back to that sorry ass town you love so much, anything!"

Calls frequented back and forth between me and Prof'. I was consumed with Mayor's cancer and because of that I gave Prof' and me one more try. Had a job all lined up for him at an elegant restaurant about thirty minutes from town. All prearranged. Prof' sold his truck and flew back to Ohio.

Maybe the reason things were going so well between me and Prof' was because he knew Mayor was sick. He let me go hang out with Winnebago whenever I wanted to and it didn't matter when I got home. Sometimes I came through the door at five in the morning. Prof would be sound asleep in the back bedroom...Hermit's old room.

We were sharing the house with Shorty and his girlfriend Chelsea. The house was crowded and emotions were stirring constantly.

It was near Christmas when Pope proudly laid out the new home before Mayor and they moved in.

Pope cherished moments with Mayor not knowing how long they would have to build new memories.

Good news had come from Cleveland. They shrunk the tumor in my mother's brain to nearly nothing. I figured that it wouldn't be long and they would have the rest of her as good as new.

Mayor became an outpatient at the hospital in Sandusky. Her doctor from Cleveland would check in on her. This way she could be home on the week-ends.

It was the 29th of February and I still didn't have my baby. Doc' became concerned that I might be overdue. He suggested that I have the labor induced. It was also the same time that I learned Mayor was a manic depressive. This explained all the months she had stayed in her room, in the dark. Maybe she felt she had no one to talk to. I didn't fully understand it but our doctor told me it was something I could inherit as it's usually passed on to daughters. I was the only daughter and well, maybe Doctor Buder felt he was obligated to tell me... warn me.

All went as scheduled and I was admitted in the hospital on March 2nd, 1984. Mayor was also there on the 3rd floor. She was real excited about me being there at the same time as her and couldn't wait till I had the baby. Turned out I had the son that Prof' so wanted. He did get his father's first name but there was no way he would be a Prof' the fourth. Three was enough. When morning broke, the sun shined down on my little boy's hair. It reminded me of the morning sunrise so I began calling him Sonny right from the start. Mayor was anxious about meeting her new grandson, but since she was in a cancer ward I wasn't allowed to take the baby up there and they didn't allow Mayor in the nursery. We just had to wait four days when we would both be wheel-chaired out.

And the day came. There the three of us were. Mayor, me and Sonny. Had to be the cancer medication 'cause Mayor would never be too loud about anything she said, unless she was bitchin' at Pope. She got the whole waiting room's attention pointing at me and saying, "Look everybody! This is my new grandson and my beautiful Cappy. Aren't the two of them just beautiful." "Mayor please!" I said, "I'm not wearing makeup. Come on... I look like shit." She wouldn't agree and insisted on telling everyone once again how beautiful Sonny and I were.

I stayed with Mayor and Pope for a day. Kept trying to get Mayor to pick up Sonny. She was afraid. "Cap. It's been so long since I held a baby. What if I drop him?" "You're not going to drop him. Julie was only this small three years ago." Mayor was never afraid of anything except for spiders and snakes. I convinced her to hold him. She carefully picked him up and hugged his little face. She kissed his cheek, admiring him like she did all my children. "Cap he is just beautiful, just like Chrissy, Julie. They get it from you, ya know." She handed me Sonny and said, "I don't want to hold him too long, I might drop him." I took Sonny from her.

A few nights shy of April, Friday at 8 p.m. Mayors doctor phone with bad news. "Capri? We placed your mother in intensive care tonight." "Doctor, what do you mean? I want to… I want to ask… but I don't know what to ask or if I should. I mean, I'm twenty-seven years old and I have a right to know how she is, so please just tell me and tell me the truth." He said, "Capri. You mean you want to know how long?" "Yes. I guess that's what I wanna know." Total silence was pounding in my head. Thought he would never give me an answer and I wasn't prepared for it when he did. "Well she might make it through the night, she might even make it through the week end. Capri… I will call you if there are any changes in your mother's condition."

The week-end passed. Monday. April 2nd and one month after Sonny was born, my mother died. Pope called me and my brothers and told us to get to the hospital right away. Her room was silent. Mom wasn't hooked up to the machines and I couldn't hear her breathing. "Mom. No mom, no!" I threw myself over her and clung in endless tears. Pope pulled me up and said, "Come on, stop it, you're a grown woman." Stop it, I thought! This is my mom and she is dead! What will I do without her? How long before the hurt goes away? She told me it would, I didn't believe it and I wasn't ready to let her go.

Professor was still being good to me. He was coming home right after work and doing his share with the kids we had together. Maybe he was being kind because I had just lost my mother.

He let me go see a concert with my best friend Winnebago. Gave me the125 dollars it would cost for a red leather jacket I just had to have for it.

I was so happy to be hanging around Winnebago again. A woman needs another woman to share her feelings with and who better than my best friend of 11 years. We'd hang out at The Well to shoot pool. Serious pool. Winning was everything to her and I. We did not take the game lightly. Neither one of us had changed much since the old Cos' days in high school. Winnebago was still tall, slender and still very blonde. She kept it short and neat. My hair was longer, passed my shoulders and layered around my face. We still had it.

One evening while at the bar and at the table, I proceeded to the green to shoot a straight shot down the corner pocket. Winnebago maintained her position at the bar watching our drinks, purses and the game. I chalked the cue, aimed, leaned to make the shot when a deep, low and sexy voice spoke quiet words in my ear. "How I could make love to you." It was the "how I could" that aroused my curiosity and I was never going to make the shot now, so I turned. Standing there was a tall, strong, handsome man of about 30. His smile was boyish and those bright brown eyes gained my attention. His beard and mustache was short and neat, with splashes of gray and white. His brown hair feathered the sides of his face that lay near his collar. He stood proud, tan, with a bit of sun burn in his cheeks. He told me that his name was Frank Forrest.   Secretly I thought of how cod his name was.   I told him mine.   The rest of the evening is much like an old dream.   I remember only giving him my phone number after I told him I was married.

Prof and I weren't close those days.   We were never close.   Seven years.   Three apart and four together.   We never held hands, never sat together, never danced, never, but never talked.   But there was Frank.   Down to earth.   Honest and dependable.   I took a chance and Frank and I began an affair early in the month of July.   We'd meet at The Well and we'd talk and exchange ideas.   He told me that he painted for a living and that he served in the Marines.   He'd give me the change for the juke box and I'd play the songs.   Winnebago remained my alibi.   She liked him.   She knew how Prof' was to me and told me to go for it with Frank.   I never felt ashamed about the affair because it felt meant to be.   More so when Frank took me to his house to meet his mom and his dog.   His Shepherd's name was Ug.   Short for ugly.   But Ug was by far the prettiest Shepherd I had ever seen.   His mom liked me right away and I liked her.   When we left I thought.   Frank isn't conceited and so handsome.   Hell he could have anybody he wanted.   If a woman liked a soft hairy chest, Frank had that, it was like the colors that ran through his beard and it was soft.   He was easy to look at, and women looked.   Four stood around him one night we were out.   I'm sure he knew they all wanted him but Frank would never admit to that in a million years.   They were always pretty girls too, and I found myself comparing me to them.   What did he see in me?   Funny, up until I met Prof' I never lacked that kind of confidence.   I was always so sure about everything and that part of me disappeared seven years ago.

After my evening with Frank, I'd go home to fiddle with the piano Mayor had left in the old house on "C" Street.   I wasn't too good at reading music.   I was too cool for lessons remember?   So, I'd sit and play some chords that I remembered.   If frustration kicked in, I always had my guitar to fall back on.

Prof' and I ceased all physical contact.   He never wanted anything from me before and now the tables had turned.   I didn't want him.   I was seeing Frank every night I could.

♫ ♪*"Don't You Dare"*♪ ♫
Words and Music by: Catherine Santi in September of 1984
"Don't you dare fall in love with me.
Don't you dare give a damn for me.
I know I'm not the only one to be blamed,

And I'm not feeling wrongly ashamed, oh no!
Hide emotions or throw them away,
Can't learn my lesson on the eve of today.
You came along, now I'm writing a song,
I guess I figured that we must belong-belong.
Are you gonna call me up, are you gonna say hello?
Are you gonna call me up? Don't you think I need to know…
…that you'll be here tomorrow, like the yesterdays before,
Will you love me just the same, or don't you love me anymore?
Time goes by long and too slow,
this feeling inside only grows.
Yet I sit so much, how I cry and I cry,
You just keep me wondering why, oh why?
Could it be that I'm losing my mind,
'cause I let you treat me oh so unkind.
Those feelings inside you're so fine to conceal,
can't help but wonder is your love even real, oh why?
Could it be that I'm losing my mind,
'cause I let you treat me oh so unkind?
Those feeling inside you're so fine to conceal,
can't help but wonder is your love even real, oh why?
Are you gonna give me up, are you gonna say good bye?
Are you gonna give me up, can't we give it one more try?
I can't even play piano, seven years I haven't sang.
Then along one night you came, finally doing it all again.
Don't you dare give a damn for me.
Don't you dare fall in love with me.
I know I'm the one to be blamed,
and all these years of living this pain, oh why?
Hide emotions or throw them away, (I know you love me).
I've learned my lessons, oh I think I can some day
(don't you want me?).
You came along now I'm writing a song,
And I guess I figured it wrong, oh why?"

Chapter Ten: "Christmas Endings and Beginnings"

Things had grown tense in the house on "C" Street. After all, it was Shorty's house now and he and his girlfriend deserved their privacy. Me and three kids were more than enough, let alone Prof'. Shorty and I were still grieving for our mother. She only got to live in her new home a few weeks. Here we were in the house that filled us both with memories of her.

It was September, near fall. I had been seeing Frank over three months. I figured Prof' didn't suspected a thing. But somewhere along the line I let my guard down. One evening after a short night out with Winnebago, I was sitting in Mayor's old recliner watching the television. Prof' came home from work and sat opposite me in the living room, gave me a piercing look and said, "I already know you are seeing somebody so you might as well admit it." I wasn't about to lie because maybe he did in fact know. I had to tell him the truth because I had fallen in love with Frank and I didn't dare jeopardize something that may never happen again. I looked directly at Prof' and said, "Yes, I am seeing someone. " Question, do you love him?" "Yes I do love him and it wouldn't be right to stay married to you anymore." I had to pat my shoulder for that one. Enough strength to speak up at last!

I went in the kitchen for something and a few minutes later Prof followed me in. My face, faced the stove when he said one word..."Hey!" I turned around and he yelled, "Bitch, this is what I get after you dragged me all the way across the country to this miserable scab on the ass of misfortune that you call a town?" Cringing he wouldn't strike, and I forgot how quick Prof' was with a hand and he punched me in the stomach, slapped my face to where I saw black. Struggling to be strong, I held all tears inside. He turned to the back of the house and walked into the bedroom. He came back put with my twelve string, the one I had since I was 14. Walking to the living room he smashed it to pieces against the recliner. Then he took the only two albums he ever let me buy during the years I was his slave, and smashed them too. The red leather jacket? Claimed he sliced it up. When he left he took the only thing we ever owned in 7 years... a television.

The day he moved out was the same day we were married, September 28. I was left with no money, no groceries, no car, no anything! I had no choice but to get something fast... welfare, but while waiting for that, Frank helped me out and taught me to paint houses alongside him. He paid me minimum wage and that was better than the nothing I had. Plus I'd be with him all the time.

After a couple of weeks Prof' came by and dropped off about thirty dollars for food. He claimed that my wanting a divorce depressed him to the point of going on a drinking binge and losing his job. Said he was shooting pool for money and sleeping in his car. I didn't believe a word. When we were first married he was not only living with me but living with an older woman and her three kids. And the big lie then was that he was living in a flop house. I wouldn't never believe a word from Prof' again.

Prof' said that he wanted to see receipts for the food and the food itself. He'd hang around the house till I came back and he'd go through the entire two bags. Of course he got his receipt and the fucking change. And if you don't like the language… !

I was glad to see him leave. The sight of him made me sick. Had for a long time. I was happy with my decision to file for the divorce and couldn't wait for it to be final. I told Frank that Prof' moved out and that my affair with him was no longer secret. The feelings between us were mutual. Frank told me he had seen me one time at a "7 Eleven," thinking he would never see me again. He even remembered just what I was wearing that day. Frank helped me regain my confidence and I felt pretty again.

The day Frank said I love you draws a blank, but he did say it and said it once. I hadn't heard I love you in so long, I wanted, maybe needed to hear it more often. I had to ask him about it because that's how I am. So, one day after work, Frank and I came through the side door of the house on 'C' street. He gave me a hug; he gave me a kiss and told me he'd be back later. Before he opened the door to go, I quietly asked… "Frank, How come you don't tell me you love me anymore?" He put his strong arms around me, hugged my face and with his low, deep voice he said softly in my ear, "Isn't it better if I show you?"

This man wasn't going to repeat those words even if he was singing along with a song that said it. One night he was flipping through a "Beatle" song book and he sang… "Listen, do you want to know a secret, do you promise not to tell, whoa, oh, closer, let me whisper in your ear, say the words you long to hear…" and he stopped. I laughed and asked, "Why don't you finish it?" His answer, "I already told you." After a short time a song came out, that was kinda like "our" song. "Stevie Wonder's" latest song entitled: "I Just Called to Say I Love You." Frank called me on the phone and instead of saying the title of it, he'd recite a verse… "chocolate covered candied hearts…" Sometimes when he I were painting, he'd be on the other side of the house with the radio. He'd call out, "Hey Cappy, ..". chocolate covered candied hearts is on" … I'd put my brush into the bucket of paint and run around to the side where he was. We talked. Sometimes we'd get a kiss in and it was back to the brush.

Working with him was because he was sweet and smiley. He was good with my kids and had no problem changing a diaper. I couldn't believe it. I mean Sonny was not his son!

And when Halloween came up, Frank got each one of my kids a pumpkin. It was after work when Frank had just put them on the front porch at my house. He was about to leave when Prof' pulled up. I didn't dare look out the window. I knew it would be a matter of minutes and there would be a confrontation between the two of them. Prof' would instigate. I waiting in the living room, just out of view waiting to hear a thump, a punch, some kind of body slam but there was nothing. I watched Frank hop into his car and he was off. Prof' came to the door and knocked. "What did you say to Frank," I asked. "Nothing. We didn't talk. When I saw him putting pumpkins down for the kids I just figured he was the better man and let it go."

Prof' gave me the usual thirty bucks for food. This time he didn't wait for the bag inspection and I got to keep the change!

Not all was going well, for there was a constant tension on the home front. I knew that Chelsea, Shorty's girlfriend, wanted to make the 'C' street house hers And we know that two women living under the same roof simply does not work. Why? I don't know. I don't have all the answers. It was hard to accept what changes Chelsea wanted to make and more so because this was Mayor's home where I was raised. That by itself was back burning away in my brain and heart.

Frank would come by often, but never moved in. Maybe he was waiting for my divorce to be final. He lived at home with his mother and his faithful friend Ug.

I had to concentrate more on my own life, my kids and get out of Shorty's and Chelsea's way so they could get on with their lives in private. Good old Pope was working on house that he bought for me and the kids to live in. The rent would be cheap and I couldn't wait to have a place of my own.

Meanwhile Frank and I were frequenting a place called The Well. We mingled and talked to a lot of the people we knew. Frank gave me a few bucks so I could get a drink and I was ready for one. While waiting for the bar maid, I couldn't help but notice a man standing next to me at the bar. His smiling-dark-brown-eyes familiar. His hair was about to his shoulders and lay in dark waves. His walrus mustache hid his upper lip just a bit. His tanned rosy cheeks were either a job out doors or maybe few beers. He didn't look like a beach bum that's for sure. He looked hard-working and was the most handsome man I ever laid eyes on. He stood about 5' 8" tall and was downright gorgeous. I was attracted immediately. He offered to buy me a drink and introduced himself as Gentry and announced to me that it was his birthday. He turned and saw that Frank was talking to a group of women and asked, "What's your name?" "I'm Capri. Capri Spettro." " Ah you're Italian. Pretty eyes too." Gentry smiled, leaned his face closer to mine and said, "When you're through with him give me a call." "Call you? I don't even know your last name!" What was I thinking, I thought? I'm seeing someone. Quickly Gentry said, "Number's in the book. Gentry Mocean III." He seemed certain that I would call. I gave him a curious look, smiled and walked away. He gave me a little pinch to remember him. Another three, I thought? Gary, Prof', Wait! Three thirds make a whole or am I losin' it? This rhyme and riddle filled man, a third? A third of who, of what? As I pondered his idea for me to call him, I walked back to Frank who was still talking to the ladies. At least I think they were ladies.

After our after work drinks, Frank dropped me off at Mayor's house and he left for his. I'd see him later.

Day after day Frank and I painted till the weather would not permit us to do so anymore. By this time I was receiving ADC checks for my kids and food stamps.

It hadn't been an easy year… Losing my mom, crowded in a house where I didn't feel welcome anymore, at least by Chelsea. She thought I wasn't doing enough around the house. Complained that she didn't enjoy picking up after my kids. I remember asking her why I should have to be the one to wash the floor and vacuum. Did she think she floated from one room to another? Arguments were growing heated and one night Chelsea slapped my face. I felt my fist tighten and clench at my side but I didn't dare punch her in the face like I wanted to. Afraid it would ruin my relationship with my brother Shorty, and he loved her.

I walked to Pope's house to look up Gentry's number. He answered. "It's me Capri. Remember," I asked. "Yes, but this isn't a good time." He sounded tired. No harm was really done so I didn't say anything to Frank. For sure a handsome guy like Gentry had someone in his life when I made that call.

Pope didn't even know I had been in the house. He was downstairs, but when he came up I told him about the bitch slap I took. "Pope I want to move into that house tomorrow." "It's not done yet Cappy. It needs carpet, tile in the bathroom, the kitchen and I have to paint it." "Pope I don't care. I can paint and help out doing something, I wanna be in the house tomorrow will you help me," I asked. "Why didn't you punch her in the mouth, you're bigger that her?" "Come on Pope. If I did that Shorty would probably never forgive me. I thought about it, believe me. I had my fist ready. I was mad as hell." "Okay Cappy, I'll help you move in tomorrow." I thanked Pope and started getting things together at the house on "C" street so I'd be ready to leave in the morning. It didn't take long. It was mostly clothes and a few odds and ends.

The morning came. Pope and Frank went with me to Polk Street. Pope liked Frank too. When he met him for the first time he extended his hand across the kitchen table to shake his. Believe me this was a big deal and bigger when Pope said, "Nice to meet you." Something I seldom heard when he met any of my boyfriends. That afternoon when we were all through and I was settled in the house I remembered what day it was. It was 1984, but it was also December 8th. A sad anniversary. "John Lennon's" death date. Would the mania begin here? Why wasn't I paying attention? I wondered about the grandiose ideas starting. Did they begin on that day in 1980?

Fortunately for Pope, he started to see a lady for some months. She was good company for him and he needed that. Her name was Nina. In the beginning I didn't like Nina. I didn't want my dad to see anyone and not someone as young as her. She wasn't even forty! Her voice was sharp and she spoke with much sarcasm. I told my dad how I felt about her and he said, "You don't have to like her, but you can show respect for who I see." So I did. Every Christmas Nina's father portrayed Santa for her kids and she asked me if I wanted him to stop at my house for mine. It was a great idea and Frank looked forward to it too. He said, "I can't wait to see the kids when Santa comes through the door." Not only did he care about me, he must have cared for them. We had two weeks for Santa's drop in date to wait.

In the mean time Prof' called and said he wanted to drop off some gifts for the kids on Christmas Eve. I told him I had made plans for something else. Prof' only wanted ten minutes to drop off gifts for the kids and take off to where ever he said he had to be. Knowing the kids would want to see their dad I knew plans would have to change for me and Frank. But how to explain it to him. I was certain pressure would build and a fight would occur on Christmas Eve. The night would be ruined. My mind worked over time looking for just the right way to put things to Frank and that was all I thought I would have to handle it.

The next day Prof' came by mad. He bitched about working on the house I was in. The one he thought he'd live in. He glared at me. The kids were sitting on the couch near me and their dad. Prof' smirked with poison, carrying on about anything and everything calling me names. "You fucking cunt. After all I did you fucking bitch." He came closer and the kids looked scared. They didn't say a word but they damn sure saw. Prof' gave me a stinging eyed stare. His tunnel vision was me. I cringed wishing someone might come by who'd get me out of Profs' path. With his boots on, he kicked me in the stomach. I dropped to the hard floor, rolled into a fetal position trying to catch my breath. With a sheepish grin and a short laugh he said, "There! That's where you belong. On the ground like a worm." He stormed out of the house and slammed the door behind him. Sonny wasn't old enough to understand, but his eyes told me he felt pain. Julie turned to Chrissy asking, "Why did dad do that to mommy?" Chrissy told Julie not to cry. "Mom! You okay," Chrissy asked. "Do you need help?" "I'm fine. You guys go on and do something, I'll be okay." "But mom can you get up?" "Chrissy, I might not get up right this second, but I will get up. Boy your dad really doesn't like me. Come on. Why don't you guys take Sonny upstairs and play with him a little and I'll get something started for supper."

The girls looked concerned but did what I asked and after about twenty minutes I managed to get up off the floor. I walked to the kitchen to make some coffee and get the kids something to eat. I broke down at the table. How could he do that to me in front of my kids? Why? If he was going to kick me he should have never done it in front of them. He was still scaring me and I knew that I would have to let him come to the house to see his kids on Christmas Eve or he might hurt me worse!

Christmas Eve arrived and I still hadn't said a word to Frank about Prof' coming by to see his kids. I had to just come out and tell him right then! "Frank, I don't know how to put this to you but weeks ago, Prof' came by. He wanted to see his kids tonight. You know the kids are small and they are going to want to see their dad. I thought it might be a good idea if you could just go home and I'll call you when he leaves. He won't stay long. About ten minutes." "What time is he coming?" Frank asked. "He said he'd be here about 8 o'clock." "Isn't that when Nina's dad is coming over to play Santa?" "Yes," and I watched Frank's face look bitterly puzzled. "That's real nice. I've been waiting to see the kids watch him come here for two weeks. But that's okay, I can leave. But I won't be back so don't call me." "What do you mean don't call you? I want to call you. Frank you're the reason I'm getting a divorce in the first place. I love you! Please don't say you're not coming back." But he said nothing. He didn't even bother putting on his coat when he went out into the cold. The lump swelled in my throat bad and the tears were flooding. I needed to sit and I went to the kitchen table breaking down more there Frank was a man of his word. He would not be back.

Santa came and left. The kids had a blast, then their dad came over. Me, I was still crying my head off. Prof' asked, "What's wrong?" "Fuck you! You knew Frank and I were going to be together and that we had plans tonight. Me being the stupid ass that I am sent him home, thinking you were going to upset the holiday for the kids by starting a fight. Now he's gone for good." "Cap, he'll be back. He'll just need some time to get over it. He's probably hurt and like any other man he doesn't want you to see that." "You don't know him. He won't be back. He said so." "I'm sorry. I didn't do this on purpose. I told you once that he was the better man. The day he gave the kids those pumpkins. I had no intentions of starting a fight with him." "Right Prof', you say that now. I know you. There would have been trouble. He's gone and I blame you." "Come on Cap. I hate to see ya like this. Is there anything I can do?" "You got a lot of nerve. Didn't you do enough? Wasn't everything you done enough for Christ's sake?" "Cappy, come on. What's his number? I'll call him." "Are you crazy? I don't want you to do anything; you'll only make it worse. Fuck you Prof' he's gone!" "Cappy let me make it up to you. Let me give you something. It's your birthday tomorrow. Here. Take this and buy yourself a new pair of jeans or something." I took the twenty and said, "There is one thing you can do Prof', I don't have any champagne. You know I always have a bottle for my birthday. Would you mind grabbing me a bottle at the store before you go?" "Sure Cap! Do you want anything else?" "No, just get that for me and then get the hell out of my life once and for all please!"

Professor came back not with one, but two bottle of the bubbly. Told me to try and feel better, assuring me once more that Frank would call.

I popped open a bottle but didn't have Champaign glasses so I used my handy coffee mug of course. It didn't help the crying. Once I started it was hard to stop. I cried easy. My feelings were always easily hurt as far back as I can remember.

Ten o'clock came and I told the kids that if they wanted Santa to come to the house, they needed to go to sleep. The girls hurried up the stairs saying good night from their room. Sonny was already asleep. I went up to check on them and Julie called me in her room. "Mom, we don't have a chimney." Oh, don't worry. I'll leave the door open for Santa." "Okay mom, good night" They were pretty excited about Christmas day.

About a half bottle later, I tried phoning Frank. His mother told me that he wasn't home and I told her about what happened and asked her to give him call me back when he got in, but he didn't call. I tried one more time and his mom said that he didn't want to call me back. He was in bed. I was heartbroken. What would I do? It was nearly 11 p.m. and in another hour I would be celebrating my birthday alone.

The Champaign was going down quick. I had only half a bottle left and this was my second one. I was getting drunk. What the hell, I thought, it's Christmas.

There wasn't going to be the usual Christmas dinner at Pope's house and if there would have, it wouldn't be the same without Mayor. Christmas only reminded me that I was growing into another year older and without my mom.

I phoned Renee at "WCPZ" and asked her to play "Do You Want To Know a Secret," hoping Frank might be listening. Who was I fooling? He certainly wasn't listening to the radio. He was no doubt curled up with Ug for the night wishing he never met me.

I wanted desperately to call him a third time, but I knew I would be wasting my time. He got the message; the rest would be up to him. Only I knew there wouldn't be a rest. The only thing that kept my spirits lifted, besides the alcohol, was the fact that he didn't say I don't love you. He used to tell me that if he ever stopped loving me he would tell me. It only made me cry more. It was just after 11:00 p.m. One hour till my birthday. No cake, no Frank, no nothing. Just the Champaign that was just about gone. Crying stopped when I remembered someone from a September. Someone from The Well, and that someone was Gentry. He told me when I was through with Frank to call him. Except the first and last time I phoned him he said it wasn't a good time. And I was through with Frank, he was through with me.

I decided I had nothing left to lose and looked his number up. I called and said, "Hi. It's me Capri. I happen to have a bottle of Champaign and if you're not busy would you like to come over and have some with me?" "Sure, if you don't mind me coming over in my work clothes. I've been hanging dry wall in my house and I'm kinda dusty." "No, I don't care, it's Christmas!" "Okay. Give me ten minutes. See ya." I turned to the clock to note the time. It was 11:05 p.m. I wanted to see how long it would take him to get to my house. If he was going to come over at all.

I waited and within minutes I heard a knock on the door. I noted the time again. 11:11 p.m. 6 minutes. Damn. Thought it was Frank, but when I walked over to the door and opened it. Standing there leaning up on the rail of my porch was Gentry. He was wearing a cut off sleeved white sweatshirt over a red, long sleeved hooded one with jeans and work boots. Handsome even with work clothes on and I invited him in. "Well, Cap! Where's that Champaign you said you had. I'm kinda thirsty." I pointed to the bottle on the table. Gentry laughed. There isn't enough for a swallow. We need to get more." I looked at the bottle and he was right. I drank nearly two bottles but I didn't feel the effect of it at all when I looked at him. The alcohol buzz just escaped me. What was it about Gentry that made me forget about Frank completely, I thought? Then he tossed a couple hundred dollar bills on the table and said, "We need to get more." "But I can't leave! I got three kids upstairs asleep." "Don't worry, we'll take the "Sharkpooper" and be back in ten minutes. You gotta a key so you can lock up?" he asked. "Yes... but..." "I promise I'll bring you right back." Something about him was trusting so I left a note on the fridge telling Chrissy I would be right back and off we were.

71

We got in the long, old, by reliable, green "Ranchero" and took off for the nearest store still open. Gentry bought two bottles of Champaign. We got back to the house before the ten minutes were up. He opened a bottle and I got another cup. He poured and we drank to the night.

"I'm a little embarrassed Gentry because my house isn't done yet. I had a fight with my brother's girlfriend, so I told my dad I wanted to move in even though the place looks like hell." "It's alright. I'm working on a house and it needs a lot too. Hey Cap, you know I would feel a lot better if I could clean up a little, I'm pretty dusty from the drywall work. Would it be alright if I took a shower?" "You want to take a shower? I mean, I don't care that you want to get cleaned up except that there isn't any tile in the shower yet and the dry wall up there won't take the water." I showed him the bathroom that still had the ply-wooded floor. He laughed at the walls around the tub. "What's this?" he asked. "My dad wrote that there but he's going to use real ceramic tile, not that." "Tell you what you should put up here." Then he took a pencil he had resting at the top of his ear and began writing on the drywall. On one side he wrote mirror and on another he wrote shower caddy or something to that effect, then again he wrote mirror on another wall. I was cracking up. He asked me for a towel and some soap. Gentry started the water up in the tub. With shampoo he filled the tub with bubbles and hot water. I left him alone or tried to. Before he even thought of closing the door to undress, fully clothes and without warning, he grabbed me and picked me up clothes and all and put me in the bath tub with him. He was very amused with this. It was lots of fun. We drank more Champaign. We had a squirt fight with the bar of soap and splashed each other until we had enough water.

I excused myself, ran upstairs to get some dry clothes. Gentry had the privacy he should have had. Like he wanted it. When I came downstairs he was in the living room on the couch smiling and laughing. The Champaign had hit us both. I don't know if he was making a pass at me, but in any case, when I thought he tried to throw his arms around me, I pulled back and we were both on the floor in a fun wrestling match. Gentry kept trying to get a hold of me but I wouldn't let him. I was having the time of my life and was pretty sure he was too.

Gentry started calling himself Pinky. I didn't have a clue why he would want someone to call him that but somehow it fit. There wasn't much I knew about Pinky. I didn't ask his age, where he came from, where he was going and if he'd ever want to take me with him. All I knew is that it was officially Christmas, my birthday, and the best one I had ever had in a long time.

Pinky wanted to see the rest of the house and I told him that the kids were asleep, but he assured me that he'd be quiet so I took him upstairs and showed him the girls' rooms. "That's Julie, I pointed out, she'll be four, Chrissy, that's her, she's 6 and this is Sonny's room. He's just 10 months old." But he wasn't through looking at my house. "Ah, so where is mom's room?" I wasn't so sure I wanted to show him, not knowing what he had up his sleeve, but I took him further down the hall and opened the door to the left. "It's just a bed, king size bed. But then what else do I need?" "Bed!" Pinky exclaimed. "This isn't a bed it's a playground!" He hopped on it and started jumping up and down. "Quiet," I said, "you're gonna wake the kids." "Oh come on mom. It's Christmas. Let's go wake em up and have some fun." Pinky left my room to wake them up. "Hey come on you guys, let's all go to mom's room and jump on the bed!" Startled, they got up and ran to my room. Pinky took Sonny out of his crib, carried him in and sat with him on the bed. They all started jumping. "Come on mom, you gotta get up here and jump with us." I was thinking... What kind of lunatic did I let in? But before ya knew it, I was jumping too.

Funny how the kids took to him immediately. Chrissy the curious one said, "Who are you anyway?" "Ah, you can call me Pinky." The mom in me said, "Okay you guys you gotta get back to sleep." "Oh, but we were just getting started." Pinky said. I gave him a firm smile. He understood and took down the notes. "Okay you guys better get back to bed like mom said." He helped me tuck them all back in and we went back down stairs. We talked a long time.

The next morning, I woke to hear Pinky's announcement, "Come on mom, wake up, it's Christmas. "Blurry eyed, I peeked over to the tree. Pinky was already under it with my kids and they were anxiously waiting to open presents.

I made coffee; Pinky had a little and told me he'd have to leave soon. Was I dreaming? Is this guy gonna ask to see me again or what?

Hey Cap, if you're not busy next week, would you like to go out?" I nearly dropped off my chair. "I'd like that, but I don't know if I can get someone to watch my kids. Things are real tight and I can't really afford a sitter." I felt bad. I didn't want him to know I was getting welfare. He told me that he would take care of it. We made our plans. It was set. He would be at my house at nine the evening we would go on our first date. I thought the day would never arrive. Pinky said good bye to me and my kids wishing us all a merry Christmas.

Reality set in and I thought about Frank. Would he remember my birthday and come around to see me, call me? Like Prof' said, I must have hurt Frank. Prof' was right. Frank didn't show. Certainly he'd drop over and wish me a happy birthday, but the day turned into night and he never called.

Pope called me to wish me a happy birthday, so did Shorty and John. Hermit? I hadn't seen much of Hermit. No doubt he was hiding out somewhere.

I called Nina later that evening and asked if Bink, her oldest daughter, would sit with the kids for me and all was set to go out with Gentry. Her sister Kim was also there to help take care of everything. I went through every stitch of clothing I owned, making sure I would have just the right thing to wear. This man would expect it I'm sure.

I vaguely remembered all we talked about on Christmas Eve, except that "Pink Floyd was Gentry's favorite band, and he knew I loved The Beatles. As far as I was concerned, we had the best taste in bands. That's not to say that I didn't like other bands, but I was a diehard Beatle fan. What could be more important than love? That's basically what most of their songs pertained to. Love was everything and it was something that I had been looking for a long time.

Maybe, just maybe, God put Pinky here for me, I thought. He showed up when I thought my world was just about to pass through hell.

♫ ♪ *"A Matter Of Time"* ♪ ♫

Words and Music by: Catherine Santi on November 17th, 1985
"You never can tell what the words will be,
It's just a matter of time.
You're not so sure about your destiny,
it's just a matter of time.
It's what you live that makes you what you are.
How do you like yourself you've come this far?
Like before , I don't know what this will say,
but if you find a feeling then I guess it's okay.
The longing to believe that what you say is true,
but in a matter of time...
You're telling me over and over that we are through
and in a matter of time...
I'm trapped in a maze of all wrong angels.
Can't get out, they've all been tangled.
If there's away I hope I find it out,
still you have the answers what's this all about?
Thought I don't know where you'll always be,
it's just a matter of time.
I'll run into you or you're gonna run into me,
it's all a matter of time.

Chapter Eleven: "Off-Ten"

My mind was traveling. I still thought of Frank. After all he was the reason I decided to break away from Professor forever. The divorce would be final on the 31st of January, 1985. Frank wouldn't be there, at least there was no indication that he would be. I had to focus on something else.

Christmas Day was winding down. I sat back with the kids. They had a nice Christmas considering our financial situation. I received an ADC check once a month for about 300 dollars and the food stamps came to around 175 dollars. This sucked!

I paid the telephone gas and electric bills. It left little for a good pair of shoes. (I knew about shoes!) I would not stay poor. It "did" matter what people thought! They might think me lazy. It was so embarrassing to hand the grocery clerk food stamps. Especially when the guy next in line is wearing a three piece suit and good shoes! Feeling bad about it wasn't working, so if in a store, in line, and in that same scenario, I'd say to the cashier, "Hell, I put 16 years of my hard earned money into this and I got it coming." The clerk would usually reply the same things, "You're right about that. They barely give you enough and expect to you keep your dignity." "Thanks," I said, "Somebody who understands."

That helped me get through rough times looking for work. My dream was never to be a factory worker, but that's what it would take to take care of everything and get off of welfare for good. It just so happened that a "General Motors" plant was hiring. The plant wasn't the one Pope worked at. It was in Toledo. It didn't matter. If I got the job, I'd move.

Later that evening my phone rang. It was Winnebago. "Spet. Hi. I called to wish you a happy birthday." "Damn this is a surprise! I sure wish you were still living in Sandusky. I don't have anybody to talk to Winnebago and so much is going on." "I know where you're coming from Cap. I don't know anybody in Michigan. We had to move because of Dan's transfer here. It's rough. Things will get better." "Winnebago. He dumped me. Frank broke up with me last night. I can't believe it." Neither could Winnebago after I explained. I said, "Good may come out of it. At least I like to think so. I was buzzed up on two bottles of Champaign and called somebody." "You and your Champaign Spet. Something's never change," she said laughing. "Who did you call Cappy?" "He asked me out. I mean after he came over." "Yes, okay. What's his name?" Winnebago couldn't take the suspense. "Well, his name is Gentry Mocean!" This perked the coffee and Winnebago said, "You mean Gentry Mocean III?" "The third? You know him," I asked. "Spet you're one lucky girl. Let me tell you. He's rich. I don't mean just rich, he's filthy rich! He acts like an average guy. I know I'm married, but I envy you. Shit Spet you dog you. I can't believe it. Gentry? He is real good looking!" "Speaking of rich, not that it matters, but he threw two hundred on the table for more Champaign like nothing." "Told ya Spet. He's rich. That money was nothing to him. He's a catch! Hold on tight!" "You know Winnebago if I think about Gentry, I forget Frank. I'm happy, you know? Like there's something about Gentry. Like he knows me. Hell, I'll be a wreck before Saturday gets here." "Cap! You and him are going to look great together! Hear Dan back there? Spet, I gotta go. We're not done unpacking. Take my number and address down and I'll call you when he's at work."

I took down the address the phone, the city and Zip. Everything a number! My God! How would the world manage without them?

Gentry III, Professor III, Gary III. That ought to do it. That makes three three's. There's that number I thought. The third of my threes! Winnebago made it sound like Mr. Mocean could buy ships though a boat would be nice. She probably messed with my head because she knew I just finished a joint. I went on thinking.

Before I knew it, Saturday had come. I was up early and a frantic wreck all day. It got Chrissy excited. "Mom, Pinky is nice. I like him. He's fun. Maybe he'll marry you mom." "You like him that much huh? Chrissy, I'm not even divorced yet." Yeah, but when you are you could marry him. He likes you mom." "We'll see how much he likes me. He's not here yet. He might not show up." "Mom, he will. He'll be here tonight because he said he would." Looking at Chrissy she seemed so sure. Told my daughter, "He better." But I said it with a smile.

I cleaned the house especially good, constantly on the kids to leave things the way they found them. Everything had to be in perfect order and it remained as such.

Nina's girls arrived about 8:00 p.m. Early, but better. It made for more time to get ready.

I thought about smoking a little pot before Gentry got there, but it didn't seem necessary. Not proper. Proper, I asked myself?

In the bathroom, I fixed my hair, nails, etc... I ran to the living room where my girls were sifted with Bink and Kim. "Chrissy! I got an idea. I'm going to call the radio station; they could play something by Pink Floyd. They'd have to play it at 9, then when Gentry walks in the house, if he's on time, he'll hear it playing. What do ya think?" "Ooh yeah mom. Call them and tell them to play a song for Pinky. Hurry up mom he'll be here real soon!" I took a look at the clock. I had forty minutes.

Stone's the one I'll call at "WCPZ," I thought. He'd put a song on for me at nine if he's got it. The hard part was not knowing which one Gentry liked the best. Nervously excited by the plan there was only one song I could think of. One that was played enough times that if you had the actual bricks you could have built a home. "Another Brick in the Wall" was all I knew by name. Stone answered. Fumbled and put me on speaker. "Hey Stone. I met this real nice guy and tonight we're going on our first date. He's picking me up at nine. Would you get "Another Brick in the Wall" on at nine? See "Pink Floyd" is this guy's favorite group. If he gets here on time, and I think he will, I want him to hear that when he's coming through the door. Only don't say it's a request or say my name. Will ya Stone?" "Sure, I'm looking for it right now. Ah! Here it is, "The Wall." Sure Cap! It may be a minute off, but I'll try like hell to put it on at nine for you." Still speaker talking, I told him I would call him to let him know how it went. Stone wanted to know.

Time was noted. "Shit you guys it's only 8:30 and I'm a wreck! I'll be half crazy by the time he shows up. Do I look alright?" The four girls told me that I looked fine and not to worry. Yeah, don't worry, I thought. Why is Gentry taking me out? What is he looking for? Companionship? Girlfriend? Wife? Get real, I thought. Wife?

I paced the floors listening to "102.7" FM. I set the volume. I went back and forth to the entrance twice for a sound check. I walked into the kitchen making sure I could hear it there. It's where the time was. And above the oven I noted the time again. I went into the living room all jittery and jumpy, "Well, ten more minutes. What if he don't show up?" Bink responded, "He'll be here. Quit your worrying." "Mom, Pinky will be here, I know," said Chrissy. This took me back to the kitchen to check the time. I thought about Chrissy. Somehow in her bright blue eyes she seriously was positive that Gentry would arrive.

I rushed around to the bathroom making sure I looked just right. I hadn't worn a skirt in awhile. But I must admit I looked kinda cute in my blue jean mini skirt, a proper one! I wore a midnight blue sweater and stockings to match. And my shoes were good ones!

Chrissy said, "Mom, you look young in that!" "I am young! Twenty-eight isn't old ya know. You'll see when you get as "old" as me. I gotta check the time. Oh, it's a minute till. Now you guys remember, don't fight, don't be loud and stuff. I want him to hear that song on the radio." "Mom, you did that? You never told us. Now I can't wait till Pinky gets here! He's coming mom. He's on his way," Chrissy said knowingly.

The "'Floyd" song hadn't started at nine. (Me and Stone were sync' in time!) Gentry wasn't there either. I stood in the corner of my kitchen, tapping my foot restlessly on the floor listening to Stone drag on a commercial. What if he can't play it or something? I was going nuts. "Girls, now listen, when Gentry comes to the door, if he does, I'll be in the bathroom. You let him in and tell him I'm not ready yet, because I'm not ready yet! He's so handsome. Wait till you see him!" And on and on I went.

9:01 p.m. The song had been playing about 30 seconds when Gentry was door knocking. I made a mad dash to the bathroom. Chrissy when to the door with Kimmy to let Pinky inside. I listened to his smiling voice when he said hi to the kids and asked, "Where's your mom?" Chrissy, the elected-without-a-vote-speaker said, "She's in the bathroom hiding, Pinky. I told her you would be here and you are. I'll go get her." She rushed to the room to get me out. "Chrissy, they're playing the song. Tell him I'll be right out." "Mom will be out in a minute, Pinky. You want to sit down?" "No thanks. I need a phone book. Where does your mom keep it?" he asked. "I'll get it for you." Chrissy got the book out of one of the drawers in the kitchen and I watched her handing it to him. I made my way in the kitchen with a "Hi. I'll be honest. I'm nervous. I didn't think you'd show up. Chrissy told me you would and here you are." Gentry had his back against the kitchen counter with the phone book. He looked over to me and said, "You look real nice. Pretty." "Thanks, I wasn't sure what to wear." "Do you have a piece of paper?" he asked, "I want the kids to know where we're at if they need to call." "Sure," I said. I grabbed the note pad next to the coffee pot and handed it to him along with a pen.

"That reminds me, I need to make a call before we leave, excuse me a minute." Pinky looked at me with lots of curiosity as I dialed the numbers to the radio station. While waiting for Stone to answer, Gentry's face was behind the yellow pages. (Ring)... "CPZ." "Hi. I just wanted to tell you that it was perfect." Stone had forgotten for a moment who I was and what was going on. This made my call more challenging and I continued... "I called you earlier and you were busy. Timing is the key." "Oh! Pink Floyd! Sorry I got it on one minute late. Did he show up," Stone asked. "Yes! It was at the same time. Hey listen I just called to tell ya thanks and love ya over there. Talk to you later." Stone wished me luck and I hung up. The phone book came down quick revealing Pinky's determined eyes. "Who was that?" he asked. "A friend," I told him calmly with a laugh inside. He looked almost angry when he asked, "Man or woman?" "It's just a friend, okay? Where are we going?" I asked. There were a few seconds of silence as he studied my eyes further with questions. "Courtsmen's." Gentry wrote the name, number on the paper and gave it to the sitter. "Are you ready to go," he asked. "Yes. Let's go!"

We said good bye to the kids and left. Gentry and I got into the Sharkpooper when he asked, "Who was that on the phone?" "It was just a friend of mine." "Was it a man," he asked. "Yes it was a man." While starting the engine he asked, "Who is he?" "Okay. I wasn't gonna tell you about it, but I will. I called a man who is a DJ from 'CPZ. His name is Stone. I only know him from calling there all the time to request songs. I never even met him. Just wanted him to play "Pink Floyd" at nine because that's when you said you'd be here. I didn't know which one you liked the best and it was the only thing I could think of. I've been a wreck all day." "You did that for me," he asked. "Well, you like them so..." "That was nice and you did that just for me? Thank you, but this is how the song really starts." In the push of a button, on his cassette player, the song started from its original beginning. I was amazed. Of all songs! The same one I had played on the radio, he had it set to go. We backed out of the drive and headed to Courtsmen's Lounge."

It was a familiar place. I mean, I knew where it was located. I had played pool in a league there some ten years back.

When we reached it, Gentry said something I wasn't expecting, "Ya know, I'd like to find somebody, someday, who would make me number one in their life. That's all I want." His eyes were fixed personal and he meant it. I agreed, "Yes. It would be nice. I want that too."

We got out of the Shark and headed inside. Gentry opened the door and led me through the people there, finding us seats at the bar. He and the owner were good friends. As crowded as the place was, it was as if the two seats left at the bar were reserved... for us.

Gentry wanted to pick out a drink for me. I loved it. It was a sweeter liquor with a splash of soda and they were easy to drink. We were having a good time just talking. The night seemed to fly like a dream. He introduced me to one of his buddies who was seated to my left. I extended my hand to the suited man who stood up to say hello. I was feeling mighty special. I liked being treated this way.

Gentry and Robert exchanged a few words. I listened smiling. We waited to get the attention of a bartender to bring over another round. Robert spoke to me. "Hope you don't think I'm being forward, but I wouldn't mind being in Gentry's shoes. You are beautiful. You have the prettiest blue eyes. I could look at them for hours." I sensed Gentry was watching me and when I glanced over my shoulder, he was. I turned back to Robert and chatted about five more minutes with him when a hand tapped my shoulder. It was Gentry. He gently reminded me that I was out with him. I gently reminded him, that he was out with me.

The night went on and I think I had about four drinks. I think Gentry thought I had too many because when I asked him for one more, he said, "You don't need anymore."

The time was close to midnight. I was afraid I would turn into something and this prince would vanish out of my life forever. I watched Gentry as he listened to a song someone played on the juke box. It was by "Foreigner," one I never heard before, "... can't stop now, I've traveled so far, to change this lonely life ..." Gentry kind of nudged me and said, "Let's go. I hate this song." I wanted to hear the rest. We were making our way through the door that would lead us out. I heard one more line. " ... I wanna know what love it, I want you to show me. I wanna feel what love is, I know you..." Damn! I wanted to hear the rest. Why did Gentry hate it so much that he wanted to leave? We got into the Shark and he drove me to my house.

Now the alcohol was setting in. He was right. I didn't need any more. We pulled into the drive and Gentry saw me in. I cried and said, "I'm so sorry. I drank too much and you won't want to see me again. Oh this Christmas was so screwed up and I'm drunk. A bad impression right? My mom died six months ago. I can't even afford to have a mass said for her. Is that something? The damn church wants ten dollars for what, to say her name? Pope is upset 'cause we don't go to the grave, me and my brothers that is. I have three. I have lots of three's Gentry. We didn't do the usual kinda Christmas at Pope's house. I can't stop crying, I'm sorry. Really I am. And I didn't drink too much really. I just drank too fast."

His words are brief... to the point. He's saying only what needs to be said and I'm not remembering a word. I have to remember. It's important, I thought! Damn the drinks! He said something to indicate that he was leaving because I watched him leave.

Automatically I locked up. I talked out loud to me ..."Cap, you stupid, stupid ass! Great impression you jerk! He probably thinks you're a drunk. Good! Great!" I got my attention and said to myself, "Self... You just fucked up big time!"

The sitters stayed over. All were sleeping and the house was quiet.

I was in the kitchen wanting something to eat and I wanted fried eggs and toast. "Cap," I reminded myself, "You can't have them now. You'll have nightmares!"

It got me laughing thinking about Kate who worked with Professor, who worked in the park back in Glacier. She told me about it. Told me never to eat them before I go to sleep. I was sure to have nightmares. She was right. I challenged it many times without success. I curled up on the couch and slept and I slept a long time that next morning, but so did everybody else.

In my mind I was still swearing at myself and complaining about how lady like I wasn't. My mind raced... questioned itself. Where are you storing Gentry's words? I can't remember a one. I'm supposed to remember! This is a test. This is only a test. Damn it, I'm gonna pass it too!

It was definitely later. The little church's bell around the corner was ringing. It was 6:00 p.m. I spent the night at the house.

I didn't have a guitar anymore or a piano to play. Time walked on slow that evening.

Wondering if Gentry was wondering about me was what I did always. Chrissy told me to trust Pinky. He'd come back. She knew. And just like magic he knocked on the front door. I saw him through it standing on the porch, leaning one had on the rail to his right, head cocked the same direction and his eyes smiled.

I invited him inside only he stayed for minutes. I brought up the date. Gentry let it go and suggested that we have a Christmas dinner for Pope, Pope's friend Nina and all the kids. It would take place in a week and I would cook the meal. I was embarrassed to tell him that I wouldn't have the money for the food and the food stamps were running dry.

I called Pope and told him about the dinner. He said that Nina would come but her kids had plans with their dad. There would be 7 of us. I was anxious for Pope to meet Gentry. Whether the new man would remain in my life was yet to be seen. The week passed and I spent the day in the kitchen preparing the meal we would have that night. Dinner would be at seven.

Everything would be just right. As a rule, I didn't have any alcohol in the house, except for Christmas, so Pope brought over some homemade wine and whiskey. Gentry brought over two sick packs of "Michelob." I made the introductions nervously. Would Pope like him? Gentry extended his hand to Pope, Pope reached for the shake and the dinner went well.

Gentry talked about all the houses he and his father had built, and there were many. Pope listened. I was paying close attention to Pope. I could tell that he could have cared less about what Gentry had to say and it bothered me. What was going through Pope's head? It wouldn't be long before I would get a hold of Pope to find out just what he did think. When dinner was through Pope stayed for one more shot and he and Nina said good night. Now me and Gentry were alone. The kids were already in bed.

He walked over to the couch and said, "Cap, that was a good dinner. You wouldn't mind if I took a short nap?" My first thought was to tell him to go home after I spent the whole day making Italian homemade soup, pasta and sauce. What nerve! But I politely said, "Yeah, go ahead. I'll clean up the kitchen." I watched him get comfortable as he lay back on the pillow there. Within a couple minutes he was sleeping.

Quietly in the kitchen I washed, dried and put everything away and in order. Sat at the table for a smoke and from there I could watch Gentry sleep. He lay there so quiet without even a snore. I walked into the living room and sat on the floor next to him thinking... A man too good to be true! He'll never want me when he finds out I'm poor. But I wasn't always poor. Will that count for anything I wondered? I went back to the kitchen table and watched him from there. I didn't want to wake him after just an hour. Truth is I was scared if he woke him he'd fly away so I let him sleep another hour.

Tapping him lightly on the shoulder I said, "Gentry. Did you want to get up?" He opened his eyes. He laid there a bit and looked at his watch. "I'm late," he said. "Late," I answered? "Yeah. I'm supposed to be at a party. I should have already been there by now. I'm going to have to go." "I don't suppose I could go with you to this party?" He didn't invite me and I wasn't sure I was ready for his answer and he said, "I can't take you to this party." "Why? I wouldn't like it? I like parties." "Cap it's no place for you." "So I spend all day in the kitchen fixing this great dinner for everybody so you can crash out on my couch and leave. Kind of like, eat and run huh?" "No, it's not like that. I said this party is no place for you. I have to go, I'm already late." "Okay. If you say it's no place for me then it isn't. Well, I'll see you then." "The dinner was real good. Thanks Cap, Goodnight." He left out the front door.

I closed and locked up the house for the night and rolled up a big joint. I smoke it all and cried. Thought I was through with all the crying but I fooled myself. I had no real reason for tears but there they were. Where does this guy come off thinking he can just come over for a meal and a nap? What the hell does this place look like anyway, a supper and sleep? I didn't want to like him, but I did. All my thoughts were how handsome he looked in a dress shirt and leather vest. Then I wondered what he'd look like in a tuxedo. Dream on, I told myself. Had the need for another joint because the first one wasn't enough.

I had a lot on my mind. So me and my brain put our heads together and thought. Much to no surprise we thought a lot alike! "Capri. Be the bright side," Self said. "You had a nice evening!" "But you saw Pope's face didn't you?" "Seen it all your life Capri! If he don't like Gentry that's too bad. You do!" "That's the problem I do. I shouldn't think about getting serious with anybody for a while. That would be best. I'm still legally married. Just had Frank break up with me and three weeks haven't gone by yet! Oh Christ why am I thinking about Gentry? Come on Self. You seem to have all the answers. Why am I still thinking about him? You know me so well. Come on!" We were both fired up. "Oh Capri, now you're gonna start with Capri knows this, knows better, knows everything, supposed to know" "Yes! I am supposed to know!" Self listened. "I don't know how you know when you're meant for somebody, but I know. I know that somebody is Gentry."

The night was closer to dawn. The time about 3 in the morning. I took myself to a room. I called it a room because all it had was a bed a small closet for clothes. I laid down. I thought about different things because different things were happening. I'm getting a divorce because I loved Frank. And if he wouldn't have left, I wouldn't have called Gentry. If I never went to back to The Well I would have never met either of them. If I never left Seattle or Glacier or Arizona. If I never would have left here I'd still be here. Oh to start over again. Maybe I wouldn't be in the situation I am in now. Poor. Really fucking poor! I couldn't get to sleep. Self said, "Don't get yourself going again. Close your eyes and go to sleep. You got all day tomorrow!"

Closing my eyes I pictured Gentry's smile, his dark hair and mustache. But above all... his eyes. Dark brown and beaming, perhaps scheming. Perhaps no meaning. If only I could dream about him. I kept that my thought before drifting off.

I awoke unaware of a dream and wondered about Gentry immediately.

The days went on as normal cold January days do. I had not heard from Pinky.

Got my courage up, asked Pope what he thought of Gentry. He said, "He likes to brag. All those houses." "You don't like him. Maybe him and his dad did build a lot. He didn't sound like he was bragging. Man he was just talking." Pope said, "Well, you think what you want, but I think he's a bum." The Pope was blunt and he meant it. I changed the subject, "Pope, I gotta go, the dryer just went off." "Okay Cap, I'll be over sometime to do more work on the house." "Bye Pope." I hung up the phone and was happy the conversation was not an "in person" one.

This of course led me to think some more, as if I didn't have enough to think about already. The Pope doesn't like Pinky? Why? He was on time, dressed nice, talked nice. Come to think about it, when he talked about all those houses it seemed to bore him.

Numbers. Thinking about how long it had been since I worked last. I counted the time. I wanted to work. That's what was missing. What haven't I done? What would I like to do? I'd still like to have a shot at being a lead vocalist in a great rock band... someday. To have the recognition of being one of the world's finest! If just one record. One album. Calling ourselves "This Is Us." Of course that would be the first song and album title. I wanted to write the song because I could hear it in my head. As I stood in the middle of the living room I said, "Shit! Nothing to play music on and this dark brown paneling is everywhere making life a gloom."

Sitting at the table I watched my view. The red house out the kitchen window facing west. The white house on the east. The garage to the back. The only way to get a view was to look out and up the kitchen window. I watched the sky, the trees and the birds. Watched them often sitting at the kitchen table that sat by the front window. I watched the birds that hung out during the winter. Cardinals, blue jays... others. And I watched the few lingering leaves fall to their death.

Cold colored this winter of blacks and whites and the grays of uncertainty.

Time was toying with me. I wouldn't be a misses anymore at last. I longed for the day to be final and be rid of Prof' for good.

Contacted by my appointed attorney who was Patrick Fitzgerald. He told me that I would need a character witness at the divorce.

Great, who the hell would stand up for me now? It can't be family. I don't know anybody. Winnebago lives in Michigan. Pope. He'd know who I could ask. He suggested Nina. Only Mr. Fitzgerald told me that it should be someone who has known me at least one year. Nina and I were 6 months shy of one year. But I talked to her and we made light of it.

"Nina, this is Cap. Would do me a favor and be my character witness for this divorce?" "Good morning to you Cap, aren't you pleasant," she said. "Please? It's just a little white lie. The judge won't know how long we've known each other. That's all. I talked to Pope about it. They won't check." "Hell, if I do this, I'll have to stand there with my fingers crossed. Better make sure that I keep my hand slightly behind me so the judge can't see. Cappy, maybe I could wear something with a pocket, then, I could put my hand in there. No, that wouldn't look right in a court room." I broke in, "Nina, Prof' said something awful. I'm sorry but I had to laugh. He said I should tell the judge that I found this tramp on the corner selling herself. That's when I supposedly offered you twenty bucks to lie and pretend you know me." "He said that? Well, I could have been at least waiting on a cab." "Really, I'm sorry. Maybe I needed a good laugh. Hey Nina, not to change the subject, but honestly, do you like Gentry?" "Well, he seems nice and he is a nice looking man like you said, why's that?" "Well, Pope thinks he's a bragger and a bum." "Cap. He could be working his ass off, making a good living, or he did, or whatever and no matter what, you know your father is going to find fault somewhere." "You're right. The only guy he ever really liked was this guy Gary I used to go out with. Did I ever tell you he was a third, like Professor?" "No. What's with the Ill's" "Gentry's another third. See I told you about the threes. By the way Nina will you do that for me on the 31st?" "Sure. Cap, let me know what time you want me to commit perjury and I'll be a ready stranger." "Thanks Nina, I appreciate it. I gotta get going, talk to you later." "Damn! It's been such a nice talk too." I knew that voice. Nina wanted to bull shit on the phone a while and I wanted to, but well...

I wasn't thrilled at first about Pope seeing Nina. Wasn't over Mayor yet. Was he? He saw Nina for supper each day and they'd go over to his club.

Nina would go to his house to help out with the laundry. Stuff. Maybe they were helping each other. She became someone I found I could talk to after time and it was often on the phone. Talked about Gentry all the time and at the same time wondered why I hadn't heard from him. I told Nina that I had to ask Gentry for the money to make that dinner.

What would the Christmas dinner be without the soup? I felt bad to ask for money but I was already cut short and it took me seven hours to make the soup. He ate the soup. Worth five an hour. That would be 35 bucks and I began adding. 15 for the meats. 10 for the cheeses. Two shots at 2.50 a shot, that's 5 bucks. The glasses of wine, two? 10 dollars. Hey it was homemade! Let's see, valet parking 4 dollars an hour, rounded off to 4 hours, that's 16 bucks and couch time. Let's see he slept two hours. That's about ten more. Oh and the time it took to go to the store and the gas. Considering I have to let the car warm up first. That takes fifteen minutes each time. Another ten dollars time and travel. I was laughing at the list. This was it. I'll send him a crazy bill and make it look like a real debt. It'll be fun. I'd know where to find him on Neil Street. The Sharkpooper would certainly stand out like a sour apple.

The total bill came to 111 dollars and 50 cents. The fifty cents was for the coffee. The top heading for his bill would read: Capri's Cafe.

The next day, only days away from my divorce, I drove over to Neil Street looking for the Shark. It was on the four hundred block. I looked at the house and jotted down the number quickly in my head. They were fixed permanently. I slid down the frosty road back home before he saw me. At least I don't think he saw me.

When I got back to my house, I made out the envelope and tucked a copy of the bill inside. Yes I made a copy. I put a stamp on it and made sure that the return address was on the inside on the bill. I dropped it off at the nearest letter box.

I called Nina and told her about the phony bill I made. "Cap, I don't know why you don't just tell him you are getting welfare. You didn't have a choice. You needed help for your kids. Why not explain it to him?" "Nina, I already sent him the bill. Besides, I told him it was going to cost about twenty bucks to make the dinner and he said he would take care of it. I haven't heard anything from him and you know how fast food stamps and money go." "I know Cap. Still, I would get in my car, drive over there, or whatever you gotta do and tell him. Say Gentry, we made a deal. I said I would make the meal. You said you'd pay for the groceries. I did my share, where's yours? Capri you know he's got to have twenty bucks on him if he's remodeling a house." I thought about it for a second and said, "Nina, I really want to do that. This month is a killer with the divorce. I'm still short on the attorney fee. I'm paying. Prof' wanted the divorce more than me. He didn't pitch in. Maybe it's only seventy five bucks, but hell, that leaves me with 225 for the month. For bills, cleaning stuff, shampoo and stuff for the bathroom. Doesn't barely leave enough for gas or a can of pop once in a while for the kids. A candy bar is a damn luxury around here." "I know Cap. Once welfare has you, it's like they wanna keep you on it. They give so little and know you need more. You can't work 'cause all the money goes to sitters or day care. Hell, you're better off staying home. I'll bet there are a lot of people out there like you and me who work under the table. Your ex doesn't give any steady money to you for his kids. Now see my ex pays every week, I just get food stamps. Hey I'm not ashamed to use them. I told you I used to work at "Food Town." I made good money there. It gets easier, you'll see Cap. Listen I got to go. What time do we go to court next week?" "Can you be there about 9:45, it's at ten thirty, but just in case my lawyer wants to talk to us before we go in front of the judge." "Yeah right Cap; I'll be the one with my fingers crossed just behind me. Sure, I'll be there." "Thanks Nina. I'll call you later, bye"

I was off to do whatever needed to be done that day. In the days to come, I wondered if and when I would hear from Gentry. Chrissy constantly reminded me he'd show up at the house. Shy was an excuse that she made on Pinky's behalf.

One day, sitting in the living room I heard a knock on the door. Immediately I went thinking it was Gentry, but through the glass stood Frank. I asked him in. We stood around the kitchen just a bit when I told him to come into the living room. Frank didn't sit with me. He stood tall and handsome with some of the painter's sun in his cheeks. His words were of great importance. "I wanna be with you. Could we start over?" I looked up at him from my seated position. He watched my eyes with his. And his were sadly, curiously looking for an answer. "No," I said, "I don't wanna go through that again. You left me on the night before my birthday. I was getting this divorce for you and you left. I was true to you." Frank knelt down in front of me putting his arms around me as he cried with his face pressed to my stomach. I didn't want to let this affect me. I was calm. Frank stood up tall and with pride and said, "You'll take me back. One day I'll walk down your sidewalk, right in front of your house. I'll be in shape and I'll have a brand new guitar for you. When I knock on the door you won't say no." Then he walked quietly out the front door.

I sat in the living room and listened to him drive off. I could still see his face. Had me wondering just how much of that he meant. Would he try to get me back, I thought? Then I told myself to never mind him and concentrate on Gentry and my thoughts of him were off-ten. I killed off a couple days waiting to see if Gentry would show. I was only sending the bill in jest. It was also an obvious way to remind him of our meal-deal without telling him I was poor, but I couldn't wait another day so I called up Bink to see if she would watch the kids long enough for me to see Gentry. There was some beer left at the house from Christmas dinner, so I drank one, just one for strength.

It was just shortly after seven when I pulled up to the house on Neil Street. I got out and went to the front door knocking. "Come on in the doors open," Pinky called from inside. I opened the door slow. There was sawdust, drywall, two by fours and nails and wire. Can't forget the wires, after all Gentry was an electrician. "What's up," he asked. Walking slowly over the boards and dust to get to the what-would-be-dining-room, I answered, "Oh, nothing. I wanted to see what you were up to. Working hard over here huh?" "Yeah, I want to get this place done. Still a lot to do. Who's watching your kids," he asked. "Nina's daughter Bink. I told her I wouldn't be long. Did you by any chance get some crazy bill in the mail?" "The one for 111 dollars and 50 cents," he asked. "Yeah." "Well, I thought you said you would help with the food and stuff and I was trying to ask for it the only way I knew." "Yeah it was twenty bucks." He wasn't reaching for a penny. Feeling like more of an ass I said, "Gentry I really need that money. I hate to ask." Reaching in his pocket, he took a twenty, tossed it to the floor and said, "Here. Here's the twenty dollars already." It was bad enough to have to ask for it, it was worse when I leaned over to pick up the bill. Felt like a beggar on the street. I put the money in my pocket. "Thanks Gentry. Sorry. It was a bad month. Lawyers." "Cap. I have some stuff here I wanna get done before it gets too dark." I knew that meant work when I watched his eyes go back to the saw horses holding his level and pencil. With a lump I said, "Okay. You're busy. I gotta get back to the house anyway, See ya." I saw myself to the front door. Walked down the drive, got in the car and headed to the house.

The hurt was bad and I felt like I had just been used. Was this Gentry's way of finding out if I was poor or not? Did Nina already tell him I was? Why would she, I thought?

More important things were coming. The day I would get divorced from Prof'. I couldn't wait to pick up Nina, get to the court house and get the damn thing done.

My lawyer was there and waiting to meet Nina. She and I would both have to fill out some short forms. Mr. Fitzgerald asked Nina how long she knew me. I thought she'd be kind. "Well, let me see. I met her on a street corner. Her and Prof' paid me twenty dollars to tell you and the judge that I have known her one year. Uhm... What's your name again? Oh! Capri.

That's right, isn't it?" "Yes Nina, that's right. Mr. Fitzgerald..." "Cap. You can call me Patrick." "Okay Patrick. All jokes aside, I've known Nina about six months. Will that work?" "Well let's see. I don't believe the police will investigate the matter. And you Prof', do want this divorce?" "Me? Are you kidding? I'd chew my left arm off to get away from her." My lawyer handed Prof' the papers he would need to sign and we all headed for the court room.

Just as my attorney said, the judge asked Nina to stand. He asked her to tell him how long she knew me. Right before she gave him the answer, she turned back to me a second, then back to the judge and crossed her left fingers together behind her back. Damn I wanted to bust a gut. I knew Nina mentioned that she was going to do it, only I didn't think she would. I turned completely around in my seat and looked at Prof'. He was making stupid faces, scratching the top of his head like a monkey wanting a banana. None of us could keep a straight face. Even my lawyer was having a hard time with it. That was all it took and I busted up out loud. Nina followed, then Prof' and Patrick. Thought the judge was gonna throw all four of us out but he didn't. He said, "Folks. I've been granting divorces for nearly 15 years in Erie County and this is the first time I've come across a couple that was happy to get a divorce. You folks have a great day." At last it was over, or thought it was.

Professor signed a paper, was legally divorced and gone. My papers were not ready to sign and wouldn't be another half hour. This was ridiculous. I wasn't divorced legally, so who was I married too? "Nina, let's go grab something to drink and have a smoke while I'm waiting, unless you want me to drive you home." "No, that's alright. I could go for a "Pepsi" and cigarette myself."

The two of us went down into the lobby to shoot the shit. When the shit was getting way too old we went back upstairs to check my papers. They were ready. I signed and rushed to flee the building. Nina wanted to get home so I dropped her off heading back to my house. I'm not in the door fifteen minutes when Prof' called. "Cappy, I was thinking. I owe you a celebration. I know how much you wanted that divorce. I deserve to lose you. How about you let me take you out to dinner?" "Oh come on Prof'. With you there has to be a catch." "No Cap, I promise. I swear! I'll keep myself to myself and you to yours. Let's go have something to eat to celebrate our divorce." "Okay, why not. I might as well get a free meal off you and it better be a nice restaurant." "Pick you about tonight about seven? We can go out to The Well and fuck with everybody's head, shoot some pool." "You know Prof', it sounds so crazy it might just be fun. Yeah, what the hell, I'll go."

Freedom was off to a strange start, but I knew that there would be no one to have to answer to anymore but myself.

All went as I expected it would at The Well. All our friends thought we were nuts, but they were buying "us" the drinks. Prof' and I shot a lot of pool with other people, left for the place in Huron where we'd have dinner.

Prof' was keyed up on alcohol and on a roll. When the hostess asked us if we wanted to have a drink at the bar before dinner, he said, about me... "Thanks, but we'll take a table now. She doesn't have a lot of time to be out." Curiously the waitress said, "Okay then. Follow me and I'll get the two of you set up." "Set up, are you kidding," I asked. "This is a set up, I know it is." Prof' followed the lead and said, "Now, now. You'll be fine. No one is trying to set you up or anything. You'll have to forgive Capri, her medication isn't working yet." "I told them to double the doses 'cause I'm so damn high strung and they won't listen. They never do. They think I'm nuts." Then I sat, but Prof' wasn't through with our crazy story and he told our waitress Sandy, "You know Sandy, she isn't around people too often. She's been like this a couple weeks now. But you'll be fine, won't ya Cap?" "Sure, I'll be fine if you would get her number already and ask her out." Sandy looked at me oddly. Prof' raised his brows and didn't know what hit him. "Uhm... Sandy, why don't you give Cappy here anything she wants and I'll have scotch on the rocks."

With the waitress gone I said, "Prof, she thinks I'm from a nut house. You started that. And don't worm your way outta the phone number thing when she gets back. I'm not through with you." I knew Prof's type. He definitely liked blondes. Guess because they are... well, they are blonde? Whatever!

"Oh good Sandy, you're back. Look my husband here, I mean my ex-husband here wants to go out with you. He's too shy to ask you for a phone number. You should go out with him, it's a free meal." "Uhm, excuse me... I know I probably shouldn't get personal, but are you two married or what?" Prof' stepped in with compassion. "No. We're not. Cappy hasn't been in public for two weeks. See, she only has the week-ends and I have to get her back to the hospital by 8 o'clock Sunday night. Oh that's tomorrow, Cap." Sandy our waitress said, "Oh, that's too bad. I really thought the two of you were married. You act like it." "Sandy, he's pulling your leg. Well he might like too. This man *was* my husband. We just got divorced this morning and he took me out to celebrate it." "Cappy's telling you the truth. To put it right, we hate each other don't we?" Profs' face was red so I thought just once I'd forget all he did and help him out. "Hate is mild. I can't wait to get back to the hospital tomorrow. I just hope that the next time they let me out you don't do the driving. What's your last name again? I'm going to have you reported." "You'll have to excuse Cappy here; the medications have some ill side effects. They're supposed to go away but..." "Listen Prof', cut the crap, get me another drink and Sandy's number already."

Sandy was laughing but I don't think she had a clear picture of anything going on around her. Maybe she thought we were both half crazy. Maybe I was. I did her an injustice. I walked over to use the ladies room and on my way back I saw Sandy standing at the bar waiting for drinks. Mine. "Sandy? I'm Cappy. I'm not really nuts. Me and that guy at my table were married seven years. Look, here's pictures of our kids. We're just so glad to be divorced, I figured I might as well get a free meal. And he really does want your number. I know he does. Do you like shooting pool," I asked. "Sometimes I do. I'm not that great, but it's kind of fun. Wait. You mean that you want me to go out with your ex-husband that you just got divorced from and you it doesn't bother you?" "No it doesn't one bit. Prof' doesn't know that I'm already crazy about somebody. Could I get your number for him? He won't ask while I'm here." "Well, Cappy, it is kind of a crazy thing, but I'll give you the number. Here, let me jot it down. You guys must have had some marriage." "Yeah, you could say that."

Prof' was anxiously waiting for my return. I took a seat opposite him in the booth just like we started. Sandy came to our table with a bottle of wine that Prof' had ordered. She put it down on the table and said, "Look. Your ex wife told me about the two of you really celebrating your divorce and I thought it was such a cute idea that I want you guys to have this bottle. It's on me." "Thanks Sandy, and don't say anything about that guy I told you about." She smiled and said she wouldn't say a thing. Prof' looked across the table with big eyes and said, "What guy are ya talking about? Did you meet somebody?" That's none of your business Prof'." "Must be pretty serious if you don't want to talk about it." "Look Prof', I had a nice time and all, but life is too serious. Just take me back to the house will ya. Besides, the food sucks here." "It was pretty sorry. I always thought they did better than this. Must be the chef." My thoughts immediately were... The Chef is probably doing too many waitresses to being doing his job! Prof' knew better than to talk to me anymore that night. The drive home was a slower one. We had a lot to drink so I had time to think and I thought about what good came from being married to Prof'. The places I lived. That was it! We moved around so much and I went through the cities in my head. There were 8. We lived in 4 states and went through 26. I saw a lot of America but became especially fond of Glacier National Park.

Prof' got me back to the house. Kept his promise. Kept to himself. The night wasn't over after he left. Alcohol did nothing for me, so while I rolled a joint and thought about the hell that got me through the states. Images came crashing to me about all the shit I took from Prof.

Bad memories came quicker to mind and I thought more about the past seven years of his shit. I didn't want to think about it, but repeating images of it were whirling round and round. Prof' had come in from work one night, late. Chrissy was 10 months old then. Prof' was staggering drunk and wanted sex. There was no way I was doing anything with him, since I was suspicious of him after just three months of the wedding bad blues. "Prof', you've been drinking. How can you come home like that? All shit faced? Don't you even wanna see Chrissy?" "Oh where is my little sweetie pie? Is she sleeping?"

While he stumbled through the hallway, I was sure to tell him to keep things down. He went in her room and patted her on the head, then he came out, grabbed me by the hand and dragged me to the bedroom demanding sex. "Prof', I'm not going to do anything with you. You're drunk." "The least you can do is suck my dick." "I'm not doing anything with you." "Oh come on, just 'cause I was with some beautiful blonde doesn't mean I can't have my own wife. No, I'm just kidding Cappy." Prof' still had a hold of me, but now he held both my wrists tightly. "Just let me go. I wanna work my puzzle." "You and your fucking puzzles. Christ it sounds like you're digging through a litter box. Get down here and do what a wife is supposed to." Prof' pushed my head down. He pressed his penis hard against my mouth and forced himself inside it. I thought I would be sick. He had been with someone and he didn't bother cleaning her off of himself. This brought on ultra strength. I took both hands and pushed as hard as I could at his shoulders breaking away from the head lock he had me in. He laughed and flopped down on his stomach passed out. I ran into the kitchen and grabbed a butcher knife. Slowly I walked into the bedroom. I shook as I held the butcher knife above my head ready to plunge it into his back. For seconds I trembled and the first thought I had then was Chrissy. She just learned to say "Da Da." I couldn't leave her without one. But the days of fear and abuse were over and I thought to myself that no man would hurt me ever again. More joints followed.

So I was a pot head. So were my friends. Never had any bad because of it. Pot somehow managed to untie all the knots with fire. And when the ropes burned away, I turned my thoughts to Gentry Mocean III. This was always after the kids were sound asleep, the radio was going and that was usually around ten. Unwinded often like that, and it became like breathing. Thoughts of Mocean were endless.

Guilt did set in the day I accepted Profs' invitation for pool and dinner. What if Gentry saw me with him? What if he thinks I still care about him? I shouldn't have gone out with my ex, it wasn't right, it just didn't cost anything. Gentry would understand it, I thought. Everything was going great until Self said, "Hey Cappy. Did you forget somebody? What about Frank? He's gone." Self was right. If Frank left because of Prof', it was very possible that Gentry wouldn't come back either. Self pissed me off again and I didn't have the piano or a guitar to take it out on. I blasted the old "Zenith" and sang along when something came on I liked.

Night blinked lights on and off when I woke to bill paying day. I still owed my attorney seven dollars and 45 cents. This would cut me short another month and I'd have to borrow from Pope. After explaining the situation I was in, Mr. Fitzgerald told me I could just buy him a drink sometime and not worry about it. Sure it sounded like a good idea for a second, but only a second. I'd pay him the remaining amount of my bill with him soon... in cash.

Job, I thought. I gotta have a job. There's gotta be a way to get a job at "Genera! Motor's." Hell it's just down the street. I could afford a good sitter, have great benefits. I'm gonna get a job there. Settled! Got out the address book to get Winnebago's number. We talked and I told her that I was wanting a job where her husband Dan was working. I was definitely willing to relocate for the kind of pay this job had. Luck was on my side and "G.M." was hiring. It was the middle of the week and my sitters were in school. I'd wait for the week-end and made plans to go to Toledo for an application early!

For a change Cappy had something positive to look forward to. Self was happy for me, new and free. A land slide couldn't stop me and the ups I was going for.

On a business day, early in the afternoon, I received a call from my attorney. Shit, I thought. He's gonna ask me about the 7 bucks. "Hello Cappy. Or would Capri be better?" "Yes! Capri is better. Then I don't feel like a kid." "Capri. It's a very eloquent name that goes with this kid I represented in court a while back. Very pretty girl too no matter how old or young you are Capri." "Uhm... Getting kind of personal aren't you Mr. Fitzgerald? It's the drinks you called about isn't it. I'll pay." "Nooo. I'll buy the drinks if you'll let me take you out for dinner this Friday. How about I seven, seven-thirty? What time's good for you?" "Sure of yourself yes?" "Pretty sure. I found you attractive and I'm not too sure, but I'm pretty sure that you were attracted to me so I sort of thought you'd have dinner with me." "Patrick. You're sort of right. Seven-thirty's good for me. Tardiness is not acceptable." "Yes Ma'am. Listen Capri, I gotta get going into court and do attorney stuff, so, I'll see you Friday... on time."

There it was again... GUILT! What about Gentry? He hasn't called or come over. He never said he wanted me to be his girlfriend, so I guess there was nothing to feel bad about, but then why did I? Self said, "Maybe you've fallen in love!"

Friday night had come and Patrick was on time. He was the perfect gentleman from the knock at the front door to the restaurant. I was on time. I had just finished four joints just before he got into the drive. The buzz was buzzing and I was ready for lots and lots of food.

During dinner I handed him a questionnaire I had made up after a couple joints. He took the two sheet test, glanced at me oddly and said, "How do you grade a test like this?" "You don't. I just thought it might be fun, something besides lawyer stuff." "Oookay..." and he read each question.

Question one was the beginning where he started of course:

#1. So what are you thinking so far? A) Different! B) read on? C) A and B are correct.

#2. What will people think? A) They don't? B) They'll talk? C) Does that even matter?

#3. You date many women? A) Don't answer that question B) Well... C) Plead the 5th

#4. Answer the following verbally: A) I don't want to answer these. B) I have to finish this.

The correct answer is B

#5 Can we get another drink? A) Sure B) I'd like one myself C) The waitress will be here just about now. And she was. Asking us if we would like anything else. Almost as if it was planned. I'm not quite sure Patrick believed me when I told him that it wasn't. I never saw our waitress before in my life.

#6) Have you ever had a test such as this? A) No I have not. B) I know I have not. C) I am absolutely, positively 100% sure that I haven't. D) All the answer are correct including D. You have never had a test such as this.

We shared a couple more drinks at the table but the food from the bar was starting to give me the munchies. Killed the meal I had only a half hour before. Still hungry, I asked my attorney date if we could have our drinks in the lounge and that I was hungry. The drinks in the bar was a good idea for him too, but he didn't understand why or how I could still be so hungry. I didn't want to tell him.

We sat in a booth across from each other with a light dimly lit over head. "Patrick, I'm going over to the food bar. That Mexican food smells pretty good. Want some?" "No thanks. I had quite enough in the restaurant. How do you do it?" "I manage. I'll be right back." There were so many things to choose from that I took a little bit of just about everything. The plate was over an inch high filled with food. Patrick's eyes popped open. I ate and ate and he talked about what I asked. What it was like being a lawyer.

It wasn't long before I realized I had taken way too much food with me to the table and pushed it aside. Patrick lit my cigarette and I felt like a cup of coffee. He joined me with one and after the bar maid left our booth, Patrick unscrewed the bulb above us and lit the candle on our table. He looked over and said, "Isn't this nicer. Why have the candles here if you're not going to use them. By the way Capri, you look prettier under candle light and red is definitely your color." "Why thank you Mr. Fitzgerald. You're kinda cute yourself. But uhm, don't get any ideas." "I wouldn't think of it on our first date. Well, I think about it, I have... You know something. I think it might be a smart idea to plead the 5th." "Good choice Patrick." "Capri, there's something I have to ask you. Where did you find all the room to eat that food? I mean look at you. You have three kids and don't look like you ever had one! How do you do it?" "Well, if you promise not to have me arrested and send me to jail I'll tell you. Oh what the hell. I smoked some pot before I left the house... Well, not just some pot. I smoked four doobs. Am I in trouble now? Is this were you make a call to the cops?" "No. But why didn't you wait until I got there. We could have smoked it together." "I didn't think lawyers did that. You know what? Why don't you drive me back to my house and I'll roll us up a couple joints to smoke. A night cap if you will. Then I won't feel like I owe ya the seven bucks." "Capri. You don't owe me anything. I'm having a strange, somewhat oddly kind of evening and I like it. Let's go to your house."

Patrick got our coats and put mine on for me, walked next to me on the way to his car where he opened the door for me. What impressed me more than that was the way he insisted that he take my house key, unlock the door, enter it first to make sure there was no one there but the sitter. He paid her, offered to take her home, but Bink wanted to walk and the walk was just around the corner.

I led Patrick into the living room, took out a sugar-bowl off the shadow box because that's where I kept the pot. I rolled up two big joints and we smoked them down to the nothing. He was even cuter with a buzz. I had so much fun talking to him. Patrick was quick witted with a sense of humor who found so many lights guiding in the way of life. He was a power booster and I needed one.

Well, all good things have to come to an end. Patrick told me that he had important paper work to do over the week end and he'd keep in touch. This time I helped him with his coat. We walked over to the front door and Patrick said, "Look. The moon is shining right on your face. I know people must tell you how beautiful your eyes are because I can't seem to stop looking at them. Capri, the date is over and the full moon shines just right on you, almost as if to say kiss her. It would make the night a full and complete one." Well there wasn't time to get the no out and Patrick leaned me over, giving me a movie kiss. It was wonderful and he was right. With the moon and all, it was like we were supposed to. He slip-sided his way out the door thanking me for the great evening, the good pot and the kiss.

Blaming myself for a wrong I felt I did, I thought about the kiss. When I went out with Prof' it was a joke really and he didn't kiss me. I could justify that. But kissing Patrick... I was betraying Gentry and Self gave me a piece of her mind too. "What's wrong with you Cappy? Can't you see what Gentry is doing? Then you go and kiss the lawyer that way on one date! What will you do if you go out with him again?" "Self," I said, "It's none of your business."

I called Renee over at the radio station. Another on-the-air-friend. "Renee, it's me. I need to hear a song by The Beatles. I know it's an old one, but it's been running around in my brain all night. Would you play "She Loves You"?" "Sure Cappy. Hey, while we're on the subject of Beatles, why don't I play the flip side to that. I'm pretty sure it's "I'll Get You." "Yeah Renee, that would be perfect. There is somebody I plan on getting if it takes me till my death day." "Oh, who's that Cap? You haven't said anything about a new flame. Who is he?" "Renee, he is handsome and I think I'm in love. Only I haven't seen him lately. He's gotta know that I listen to this station. That's a long story..." "Oh, you mean the one about the "Pink Floyd" song? Sorry, Stone told me. That was pretty cool. Everything went all as scheduled huh?" "Yes it did. I just hope he's listening now. He'd know these songs are for him if he knows me. But Renee... it's like we both know each other." "Sounds like this could lead to something serious Cappy. I'll get those on for ya." "Okay Renee, I'll call ya tomorrow night sometime when the kids are asleep and keep ya posted." "Sure thing Cap. Bye."

As I listened to the song Renee chose to play, I tuned in to every single word. I would have Gentry Mocean III rich or poor and if for some God un-fairing reason I didn't get him, I would never marry again.

Through the night I listened to the radio station wondering about what Gentry might be doing. Would he be working on the house at this hour, I thought? I checked the time and it was nearly three in the morning. No doubt he was sleeping. No doubt I couldn't. I made more coffee and rolled another joint. Hey, there wasn't anything better to do.

Saturday came, Saturday left taking the same route and leaving me with the same question? Will I see Gentry again?

Sunday morning was up and so was I. Chrissy skipped through the living room smiling big and said, "So mom... I bet Pinky will come over today." "Chrissy, he hasn't been over in a while, so why do you think he'll be here today?" "I just know. He's going to be here mom and I want to see him when he gets here." "Chrissy, if he shows up today I'll give you a dollar!" Chrissy smiled big and said, "Mom can I have the dollar now?" "No you can't. He's not here." Well, the sweet differences of opinion could have went on all day because Chrissy liked to talk about Gentry as much as I did.

Just as an illusionary plan that I was a three dimensional being, Gentry was on the porch talking to Chrissy through the door. She asked him to come in the house, she pulled out a chair for him at the kitchen table and asked him to sit down. This way she could hop in his lap. She burst out saying, "I told mom that you would come here today and she didn't believe me so she owes me one dollar." "Ah! Too bad your mom lost the bet. Come on mom you owe Buff-Bag a dollar." I looked over at the two of them listening to them talk. "Buff-Bag? Were you calling me Buff-Bag Pinky." "Yes I was. And it's Panky. You got a pop the P out like this. Panky!" With good emphasis on the P sound, buff-Bag said, "Okay Panky." The two of them were hitting it off great. It wasn't long before Julie had a question for Gentry." "What should my name be?" "You should be Jules." "You mean jewels, like jewelry jewels?" "Yes, just like that," he said. "Ha ha Buff -Bag, I'm Jewels, like jewelry." "So he nick-named me first and I'm sitting in his lap." This was another thing that could've gone on, so I broke in and asked Gentry if he wanted a cup of coffee. He nodded and said yes.

While all the commotion with Mr. Mocean around, I heard a familiar sound. Coming from Sonny's room, I heard that all too familiar word..."Hungy." Food. It was first and for most thing on his mind the minute he woke up and this way always. I took a mug of coffee over to Gentry, went up to Sonny. Heard the girls asking Pinky what Sonny's name should be. Heard him answer..."His real name should be Sonny. So Sonny is just Sonny." They were pushing Gentry to name me too. There was no way I let the conversation get any further. "No way. He's not giving me a nick-name. I don't want one, don't need one." "What do you think we ought to call your mom," he asked. "You pick it out Panky," suggested Buff. "No thank you Gentry, you don't need to name me please!" I said. "Your mom is real strict isn't she? And very meticulous I see. Maybe we should call her the Old Poop." "Oh, so I'm the old poop huh? I don't think so. You outta be called that for thinking to call me that you Old Poop!" The girls were cracking up. I did too. Sonny? He was eating.

After staying long enough to get me going, Gentry stood and said that he had to get to work. "You know. You should drink "Maxwell House." What was wrong with the stuff I had. It was better than "Maxwell House." Didn't he know that I had been drinking the stuff straight for 15 years?

Pink, (for short), said good bye to Buff, Jules, Sonny and me. But never said when and if he'd be back. I watched him walk down the drive, turn left to walk the walk back to the house on Neil Street. At least I thought he'd walk all the way.

Coffee came to mind. I checked the can I had and it was just about out. I'd have to get more soon, but I'd have to be sure Pinky was long out of the area. Didn't dare want him to know I was going to buy the coffee he suggested. Had to be ready for the next time he'd be back. Buff Bag said he would be.

Baffled. Was I that? Was I dreaming? Who and why is Gentry popping over like he does when he does? He kind of riddle-talked and got a kick out of people who tried to calculate his thinking. It drove me nuts and the thoughts were constant ones of him. Fun ones.

While having a cup of the "Maxwell House" I sat at the table watching the sky. I dreamed of dreams I let go by. The guitar I never played so well, I wished that I had it and I missed it like hell. I'd sing to myself or sing to other people's music the radio had on. It was Mayor's piano I wanted. The answer Pope gave me more than once was no, because he wasn't ready to let it go. The windows' not at a level so I fixed my eyes to the green-less trees. Wishing for warm spring and a cool, cool breeze.

After seeing the way Gentry was with my kids I fell for him all the more. Chrissy, I mean Buff, adored him. Jules had her suspicions about him, like anyone, but found him amusing. Sonny, we weren't too sure what Sonny was actually thinking. He was either "hungy" or climbing.

Frigid February was just that. I hadn't heard from Patrick. Wasn't anybody's girlfriend and I wanted to get out, go somewhere, do something only I didn't want to do it alone. Thought about going to The Well, but I was afraid that I would run into Frank Forrest. It might make me jealous if I was to see him with somebody else. Worse yet, what if he was there at the same time as Pink? Then what? Self helped me make a decision. To stay in the house leaving the cold where it belonged... outside.

It had been a couple of weeks since I had seen or talked to anyone except for Pope and Nina. Nina and I had a few things in common, complicated puzzles, bitchin', the phone, and we did the phone often. Buff would bring up the marriage kick every once in white. She was so sure Pink was the one for me. One evening after school she said, "Mom. You're not married to dad anymore and you know what that means mom. You can marry Panky." "Buff. You know something? Maybe Buff-Bag is a good name for you and I am an old poop, but you have to try and understand something. Pinky didn't..." "It's Panky mom," she interrupted. "Okay, Panky. He hasn't even said that he wanted me to be his girlfriend. He doesn't love me. People should love each other before they get married." "Mom I think you do love Panky and I know he loves you." "Buff, come on now. He never said that unless he's telling you things he doesn't want me to know. You know how he is." "Mom. He didn't say anything to me, I just know he loves you and he wants to marry you." "So now you know he wants to marry me too do you? Are you guys keeping secrets from me?" "Noooo. I just think that's what you and Panky should do." Then she darted up the stairs to tell Jules of news that had no clues.

Without warning... always with no warning, Gentry was at my house one night. It was a little late, but not so that the girls didn't hear him the minute he greeted me. Buff ran down the stairs telling her sister that Panky was here. "Hi Panky." And she was up in his lap. "She really likes you Gentry," I said, "She even tells me when you're gonna be here." "Aah! Telling your mom our secrets?" "Panky, my mom really likes you a lot. She talks about you all the time," Well, Buff got me so I said, "Don't believe her Gentry. I have better things to talk about." Pinky said, "You think your mom is telling a fib Buff-Bag?" "I know she does because I hear her talking to Nina on the phone and she talks about you." Gentry and I both looked at each other with direct beams. There sat my dreams. With him, I knew I hadn't lost them all. Suddenly he sang out some verses that came from "The Wall."

Things could have gone better but I had to have a phone and the damn thing rang. It was Prof'. He wanted to drop off some money for the kids. Didn't want to go to wherever he was supposed to go to make a payment so I'd get it in the mail, so I wouldn't have to look at his face. But he called when he did and I needed the money. There was one problem... Prof'. What would I do about Pink? I'd have to ask Pink to go. If Prof' was to see a man at the house, the money for the kids would stay in his pocket. Prof said he would be at the house at eight. "Gentry, that was my ex on the phone. He wants to drop fifty bucks off for the kids, but if he sees you here, after I just divorced him, he might not give me the money. He won't stay long. He'll hand me the money and go. Would you mind going, coming back about... wait... (I checked the time: 7:55 p.m.) ... Come back in about ten minutes, he'll be gone. Can you?" Gentry didn't say anything, not yet. He gave me a misunderstood glance. What is he thinking, I thought?

"Gentry. I know the kids aren't going to want you to go, but look, it's almost eight and he's going to be here will you say something?" "Ed's. I'm going to Ed's. Got that? I'll be there." "Okay. Ed's. I got it." Gentry took for the front door, stepped off the porch and back walked his way to his car repeating, "Ed's Ed's." "I know Gentry. I know where you'll be." While Gentry was opening the door to the Shark I noted the time... 7:58. Prof' would be here soon. I looked out the door to Gentry and he spread out his arms yelling "Ed's" to me once again.

Needless to say when Prof' got to the house I grabbed the fifty out of his hands. All was done so quietly that the kids never even knew their dad was there. Politely, (yeah right), I asked him if he wanted to see the kids. Fortunately for me he was already late and on his way to Toledo. I raced to the phone when he left and called Nina. I told her I had an emergency and she sent Bink to cover so I could get to Ed's. By ten after eight I was sitting up at the bar next to Gentry. He bought me the same drink he bought me for our one date. It was like heaven to be with him but there was something curiously wrong. "Gentry," I asked. "Are you okay? I mean is everything working alright on the inside? Organs and such?" Gentry looked at me, pulled the hair off the front of his forehead and said, "Look, I'm going bald." "Oh so your hair line is receding a little. You still have lots of it. I love your hair." With a piercing sadness he said, "Okay. I have fucking leukemia! Now you know." Know, I thought? What should I say? Should I say anything I thought?

"Gentry. I can't stay long, but I want you to come back to the house. I got Bink there watching the kids and they all have school tomorrow. Why don't you follow me over there?" "I have a lot to do tomorrow," he said tiredly. "Oh come on Gentry, it's only twenty after eight. You could spend a little time. Buff didn't even get to say good bye." "Why don't you go to your house so your sitter can get home. I'll just finish this beer." Gentry wasn't giving me the straight answer I wanted. I slowly go up from my seat and watched him drink down the bottle of beer almost gone. By the time I was out the front door, he was getting up from the bar stool. I went to my car, he came out the door and got into the Shark. I drove down the road where I'd turn right to get to my house. I expected Gentry to be right behind me but he went straight, no turns. I was sure he'd be over. I had expected too much. I thanked Bink for helping me out in a jam and she walked back to her place. Buff came down the stairs and asked where Pinky was. I told her that he had to leave because he had work to do. She was broken hearted that he hadn't thought of saying good bye or good night to her. I explained the best way I could and it wasn't easy because I had to be sure not to mention the real reason why Gentry left. Her dad.

Naturally I did what I did best. I sat myself at the kitchen table with a cold cup of coffee and a roach. I waited for Buff to go back to her room and then I lit her up. Sighing, I spoke softly to myself. "Why did he tell me he had leukemia and then go? Is he sorry he told me? Why him?" "Why anything," Self answered.

Before I got four good hits of the roach there was a knock at the door. It could have been anybody. I butted out the roach and put it on top the back side of the shadow box. I went to the door and it was Gentry. He changed his mind. Or he drove around a bit to think about coming back. Anyway, he was back and I couldn't have been happier. Same for Buff. Jules was really into her own world and Sonny was where needed to be... in bed... sleeping.

Once the children were asleep and it was me and Gentry he called out to me "Cock-a-roach." "Cock-a-roach?" "Yeah. That's what you were doing before I came in. You don't need that, I'm here. "Cock-a-roach, yeah, well I guess the name does fit me." We walked into the kitchen and Gentry was leaning against the counter by the sink. My spot. He boasted... he said, "Aah! I got the warmest spot." Looking at the ceiling vent and knowing the warm air was blowing right down on him I said, "Yeah, my spot." "Not anymore," he chuckled. Gentry's humor went somewhere else. He walked by the stove and wrote symbols on the not ready dry walled wall. Four of them. From top to bottom they were: Man, Woman, Earth, Infinity. Next to it, off to the right, I wrote the nick-name he had given himself, Pinky. It ever remains under the small, white ceramics tiles keeping it safe.

Wondering what topic to bring up, besides the one heavy one he just laid on me minutes ago, I talked up music. Told him how I wanted Mayors piano, how Pope wouldn't let me have it and how Prof' smashed my twelve string. Pink told me he played drums and guitar. "Do you play 'em much," I asked. "Don't have drums now, but I pick up the guitar now and then." "Damn, if I had my guitar or the piano I wouldn't leave em alone for a second. I miss not having something to take my mind off of things. A reason why you don't play guitar so much?" (curious me) "Yeah. I used to work with a glass company and put my arm through a piece of it. Severed a couple arteries and it's hard to feel where my fingers are on the neck, the strings." "I know what strings are. I had twelve of them once myself. In fact I had that guitar for 14 years then the ass-ex did what he did and life goes on."

"Hey, would ya mind if I went up to take a nap? Just for a little while. I'm tired." "No Gentry. Come on. I'll show you up. Sleep as long as you want." We walked upstairs and Gentry lay on his side closing his eyes. I watched him a minute and took a seat at the foot of the bed. My mind was on what I had said downstairs only minutes ago. Life goes on. After what he told me at Ed's, how could I not think and say the wrong thing? How long would his life go on? The guilt was kicking my ass and my heart. I didn't want anything to ever hurt Pink. This was the man I had been looking for and he's sick. Sick with cancer. Thinking wasn't the right thing for me. I began quietly crying. I couldn't let Gentry see me this way. I had to leave the room, but just before I got off the foot of the bed he asked quietly, "Are you crying?" "No, no. I'm fine. Think I have the hiccups. No maybe they stopped. Well..." "Where you going," he asked. "Just down stairs to make a little coffee. I'm not tired yet. Go on and take a nap, you're tired right?" "Thanks Cock-a-roach."

Downstairs I went, locked myself in the bathroom, cried my insides out and felt so thunderstruck. Leukemia? Jesus! Just when I find somebody I am truly falling in love with and You and Your God give him cancer! I won't stand around and let You get away with it. Not this time. This time You help! I begged You for Mayor and You let her die. I beg for Gentry now. Please don't take his life too?

Drinking a fresh cup of coffee, standing in my spot, I heard Gentry coming through the living room. I turned my back on him and looked out the west window. He would know for sure that I was crying. Then the question came again. "Were you crying up there?" "No Gentry. I told you, I'm fine. Really. And you? What about you," I sighed. "Why you?" "I go to Cleveland every couple of weeks for chemo'." "Mayor had that. Made her real sick." (another mistake on my part) I wasn't even over losing her and now this. Immediately the subject was switched. Gentry asked, "So, do you think your dad will let you have your mom's piano?" "Don't know yet. He's still thinking about it. I'm gonna call him again real soon though. I was the only one that really cared to play it besides her. Now it just sits there. Maybe you could bring your guitar over here. I'd love to play it. I can only play chords but it's something to sing with." "You sing," he asked. "I used to all the time. Especially before I got married. Then Prof' made me feel so bad about wanting to be a professional singer, I stopped." "I like talking to you Cock-a-roach, but I need to get going. Got a lot of work to do on the house tomorrow." "Okay." What else could I say? We said good bye to each other at the front door. I watched him leave in the Shark wondering when I would see him again.

February was about to end and I finally talked Pope into the piano. He reminded me firmly that it was "his" piano and only mine to use. I didn't care. I was just glad it was there. I cracked my knuckles, sat at the bench, wanting for something heavenly sent. Nervous was I at the keys, shaking knees. My first written piano song... a bit long... was after Frank and before I knew Pink. Completed in September which got me to think. What or who was the inspiration for a song I wrote, somehow miracle, I don't get it myself. One was for certain and the certain was Self.

Some things don't ever change. Some things do. My voice had strength, but the piano needed a tune. I called the best, I called "Mr. Moon." He'd been taking care of the pianos at "Oberlin Music Conservatory" in Ohio for some 35 years, plus. He was recommended by the music store in town. Glad

Mr. Moon was around. Not only could he tune the piano without looking at it, he could carry on a conversation at the same time. As he spoke, he taught and quizzed me on the different subjects as far as tuning a piano goes. I'd be right on the ball. Learned it from Pink, I think. Anyway, just when I thought I knew exactly what the teacher had been teaching me and I got the answers right, he was way over my head and I'd fail. I had Mr. Moon sign and date the piano, keeping the Mayor tradition alive. He would be the only one to touch Mayor's piano. Pope's piano. Damn it, I thought..."My Piano"!

Now it was a matter of time. Pink just had to know that I got the instrument in the house, but how? Is he going to show up or do I have to go to him? Guess I would go to Neil Street, because I made up my mind to do it. He had a reasonable amount of time to see the piano by now, I thought. Two days. Yeah, it was definitely time to see him.

The following morning I made some coffee and this was a trick. I had nothing to carry it in but mugs and a stick shift. So that's what I did. I drove with cups filled close to the rim. I drove slow to Pinks' because the coffee was for him. I knocked and he called from inside for me to come in. Carefully I walked along the not done floor, held the cup of coffee out to him. "How did you know I needed a cup, thanks. Oh, Danny. This is Cappy. Cappy, Danny." "I know you Danny. Don't you go with Cassandra?" "Yes I do. Hey, How's your dad been doin'?" "Pretty good. You remember him?" Gentry was trying to think of anything but me and Danny talking, but we were still talking. "Sure I remember your dad. I remember the wine. Does he still make his own?" "Yeah he sure does. He used to make..."

"Danny, turn that up will ya? I like this song. Isn't she something else," Gentry exclaimed. "Drove over here in the snow to bring me coffee." Then Pink came a little closer to me and said quietly, "Tastes good Cock-a-roach." "This really is a good song. After Mayor heard it, liked it, she told me that originally it was a classical piece done by a famous composer, only I can't remember his name. This is "All By Myself" isn't it?" Of course I knew that, but I didn't want Pinky to know I did. "Yes it is. Aah... but you knew that didn't you?" I sort of smirked, smiled at him and said, "Hey, guess what? I got Mayor's piano. Pope finally gave in. Just had it tuned too. You'll should stop over sometime. I know a few things." Gentry watched my eyes and listened to the words of the song as was I. Then he walked over to the front door and flung out the cold swallow of coffee to the snow. Danny was getting ready to go.

Gentry walked over to hand me the mug. "Keep it. Keep mine too." He set down the turquoise and light purple mugs. Then I had to get going. We all said good bye and I rushed to the nearest music store to order the sheet music for "All By Myself." I was going to learn it and learn it fast. I wanted it to be the first thing Gentry would hear me sing. It was much too soon to sing something that I wrote myself if he would end up at my place at all.

The music, the music! Me? Patient? Hell no! I called George at "The Guitar Shop" to see if it came it. I had to know. Luck was with me because the sheet music had been delivered that morning. Called Nina. Got one of her girls at the house so I could race to the shop to pick it up.

The minute I got back to my house I was ready to play it. The chords were easy and in my range. It was easy to learn. I had it down in less than an hour. Now if only Gentry would show, I thought. And I thought some more. This usually spelled trouble for me. And I was very troubled in depth.

I prepared myself to make a call to Cleveland. Talk to someone in the hematology department about cancer. About leukemia. Dealing with this all by myself was getting the best of me just when I was getting back to the best of me.

The registered nurse who worked at the lab was the one who talked with me. We spent a long time on the phone. Filled with distress, she encouraged me to get it all out. So I told her about my Christmas Eve, How Frank left me on the eve of my birthday. "Then Gentry shows up that night and it's my birthday now. Get it? He's like.. .how do I put it? He's kinda like the miracle I needed and I don't want to lose him ever!" By now she could hear my crying and I had kept it so quiet I thought. "Hon, I know it hurts. I know that your hurt is your own and everybody handles things differently. But you know that a person can live a long a life with chemotherapy. Of course a bone marrow transplant could be your second miracle. How long has your friend Gentry known about what he has," she asked. "I don't know. He won't talk about it. He told me he had it and then he leaves me hanging. It's not fair. I want to know all I can! I want him to lean on me, talk to me and I want to be there for him." "Sounds to me like you already are. Tell you what Capri, I can give you other hospitals numbers if you want them. Better yet, why don't I send you the pamphlets we have on it and one that has a list of numbers-different hospitals. If you want, you can call me. Just ask for Vera." "Thanks Vera," here, let me give you my last name and address. Can you send it out today?" "Sure. I'll get it right out today Capri. Remember, call anytime if you have any questions." Thanks Vera. Thanks a lot."

All my finger tips were rolling-tapping at the kitchen table. I needed more coffee, more pot, something! I didn't want to cry but that's all I managed to do. By night fall, late and in the wee morning hours I got stoned and stoned good. I played the piano. Self told me that if I just kept my chin up, play, sing, Pink was bound to feel every vibration and I believed her.

A difficult month was to be dealt with and it was March. March was supposed to be a good time because it would be Sonny's first birthday on the second. There were many birthdays in March. Hermit's birthday was on the fourteenth. Shorty shared Mayor's birthday on the twenty-first of the month. Shorty probably didn't eat a birthday cake, but you can bet that no matter where Mayor was, she'd be blowing out her fifty two candles and Shorty's too.

March was too much. I couldn't take not having Mayor there for Sonny's first birthday. Missed having her around for everything. I was a wreck. I wanted my mom and she'd never be there for me again. It just didn't want to sink in entirely and I thought I was never going to be over it. I had to talk to my doctor. He would have to get me some kind of nerve pills or something before I broke things. Fortunately for me it was time for Sonny's one year check up. It would be a good time to ask "Buder" for something then.

On the third of March me and the kids went to his office. Sonny checked out perfect. Me? I was a crying mess after I told Doc' everything that had been going on since December. Together we agreed that a mild tranquilizer might be the answer. And they were. They were just strong enough to get the shake outta me.

♫ ♪ *"Wasn't It Nice"* ♪ ♫
Words and Music by: Catherine Santi on November 27th, 1985

"I looked up the sky was gray,
four dressed in blue were on their way.
It gets to me the things you say,
wasn't it nice anyway?
On your shelf violet and blue.
Collecting pennies, yeah those too.
It keeps me thinking shame on you.
Wasn't it nice anyway?
We were standing over there,
vaguely laughed and couldn't care,
when you mentioned something about your hair.
Wasn't it nice anyway?
Time and time just passes away.

I know I watch the clock hands turn that way.
That was then and not so long ago,
when you said forget me, just let me go.
I always knew when you'd be here.
Those the days when all was clear.
And all those times I hold so dear.
Wasn't it nice anyway?
The bells are ringing I know the time.
At six o'clock the hours unwind.
At least if nothing else you were kind,
and wasn't it nice anyway."

Chapter Twelve: "Not Another Three!"

Much of March was spent preparing for the cold days I had already been carrying in my head. "General Motors" was not a go. I drove there to Toledo on the Monday following my conversation with Winnebago. Resume was sent out on a Tuesday in the a.m. Called the plant-person-in-charge of applications, to say mine was on the way. Called to make sure they received it. They did. Asked me to turn in another resume. Why? I don't know. Gave them mine when I was in Toledo the first time. Gave in to their reasons and wrote them a letter. My times were a struggle and I wanted life better. The piano helped release frustrations most of the time.

Memories came back and I zoomed in on when I was 16. It was my first audition to sing lead in a band. We did a song by "Neil Young" and I sang it so damn good with them. When that was finished they decided they didn't want a female. Audition #2: was scheduled: Hermit, my big brother went with me. He told the band that no matter how I did, to call me. The rhythm player agreed. Only my audition wasn't with the entire band, just the rhythm player. Wasn't easy singing to his playing. And I thought I couldn't keep a beat! Well I missed his cue because he missed mine. We were off a little. Hermit suggested that I play and sing myself. The rhythm guy insisted he had run out of time. I wrote my name and number on a piece of paper he gave me. Hermit looked directly at the dude and said, "Don't forget. Call her."

They called me. With bad new they called. The rhythm man said, "Capri. I don't know how to say this, but, well, you have a great voice. It's just the not a rock kind of voice. Your voice belongs in front of an orchestra." "No, my voice as far as an audition goes should have been with the entire band. You guys were packing when I got there. You know, I might not be able to play rock, but I can sing it. I sang with a couple bands. People from the audience would want me back up on stage." "Capri, I know you're good, I heard you. We need a raspy voice, you understand. Look, I have to go but you keep singing, you'll find the right band. Lots of luck to you Capri."

Yeah. Right. Sure. The past was gone but the present presented me with a knock. It was Pink. "Gentry. Hi! I'm glad you're here, look," I said pointing to the piano. "Aah Cock-a-roach." He walked over to it and said, "Do you know the song that goes? "... that's just the way it is..." With his fingers ready at the keys he said, "Show me where an A is." I showed him the A and he wanted me to show him the A chord. I showed him a simple one with three notes. He struggled along like a little boy and proudly smiled when he had it. Playing the same three notes over and over he kept trying to sing, "... that's just the way it is ..." I busted laughing. I knew he had been drinking. How much was uncertain. He fumbled a bit here and there. When he talked he was sparkling smart and sharp. Gentry made requests... "Cock-a-roach, play something." I sat back faced on the bench watching him take a seat on the couch. He waited, seemingly captivated. "I don't know too many songs on it yet. I'm might goof. Oh what the hell. After your performance of the almighty A anything would sound good." Happy faced was he.

He laid back into the couch. Crossed and cupped his hands behind his head. He closed his eyes and I said, "If you're going to sleep maybe I should play a lullaby." "Play me a lullaby Cock-a-roach, " he said chuckling. "Well, I suppose it's better than the Old Poop."

The piano notes lightly began a Beatles lullaby, "Golden Slumbers." I introduced the beginning one more time and sang, " ... Once there was a way to get back homeward. Once there was a way to get back home. Sleep pretty darling ..." He wanted more so I surprised him with "All By Myself." "I really love that song," he said. "I ordered the sheet music for it the day you said you liked it. Forgot how much I liked it myself. Took just under an hour to learn it." "Pretty good there Cock-a-roach. I was in a band once. We were called, "Pink Punks Practicing in Public Pissers." I lost it, because I imagined it.

Gentry stayed longer that night. We talked and talked. We rhymed in time. We laughed and laughed more at the piano together. It was a perfect evening until again, I watched him walk to his Shark... to leave.

Went for the roach on the shadow box. Laughed. Lit it up. Got behind the keys. Sang and played till the buzz wore off and I went up stairs. Laying on my bed I thought. Gentry has been coming around more and more. Hasn't even tried to kiss me. Not even a hug or anything. But damn if he ever did kiss me I'd probably have a heart attack. He's making me crazy! I don't want to get hurt again. Twice too much. Mayor is dead. "Fuck all this," I said. Self thought the same so I took an extra tranquilizer to forget.

The next day arrived, somehow it managed to do that without a problem. Oh to be a day!

That morning in with my mail was a letter from a correctional facility. The sender was Henry M. Batturs III. I took it to the table and thought long and hard about the name and then it clicked. I wrote a letter for Frank to him, but why he's writing me I don't know. Don't know him, I thought. I opened it and read it. It simply said that he remembered the letter I sent on behalf of his buddy, that he would be back home in Sandusky soon and wanted to meet me. I didn't write him back. I knew by the date he mentioned, that he would be in town before a letter would get to him. I really didn't think much of it and tossed the letter out.

But a day came and Henry was at my front door. He introduced himself and I politely asked him if he wanted to come in for a cup of coffee. He agreed, took off his jacket, put it on the back of a kitchen chair. He sat up straight in the seat with his hands folded on the table. His hair was brown, just touching his shoulders. His eyes were brown. His mustache was neat. If you didn't pay much attention to a chip in his front tooth he wasn't a bad looking guy.

He told me that he just got out of prison. That newspapers like to trump everything up. He said he had been in prison before for stupid things but only because of an accumulation of things.

Twice I wondered? In prison two times? I never knew anyone who had been in prison, but it didn't matter, I wasn't going to see him again.

Before Henry left, Pope came by the house. He saw Henry sitting at the table. "Pope this is Henry." Pope didn't say a word. He just gave me a look and walked to the back room to work on some closet doors. I excused myself to use the bathroom. Henry reached for a cigarette. When I came out of the bathroom I was face to face with Pope. He said, "Get rid of him. He's a bum." Then just as quickly as Pope showed up to do work, he left. Henry was still sitting straight up at the table.

I explained to Henry that my kids would be up from their naps and that Buff would be on her way home from school. With more reasons I managed to politely get him out of my house.

Was he a sob story? No place to live? No job? Lives with mom? Maybe Pope was right. Maybe Henry was a bum. I saw someone who needed help.

This only led me to think about Gentry. Pope said he was a bum too. Was there anyone that wasn't, I thought?

I got one of Nina's girls to watch my kids one day and took a short drive over to Neil Street to see Gentry. I felt for some reason that it was my turn to make an appearance.

I knocked and knocked again. He was there in the house. The music was blasting away! Familiar music. Beatle music. I took a chance and opened the door slowly. He knew I was in the house. I kind of tip toed my way in, like it made any difference. Gentry glanced at me for shorter than a moment, figuring his pencil-plans for the kitchen. He called, "Sing Cock-a-roach. You know the words." I grinned and said, "I know. I'd like to. But if I start singing you'll shut the music off on me." He knew I was right, smiling big.

Then he picked up a sample of counter top, asking, "You like this color?" It was a nice shade of blue. Sky blue. Robin egg kinda blue. "Yes! It's nice,

I like it." "Come on up here and look at what I've finished." He came around to show me into the kitchen. Gentry stood proud and said, "I made these cabinets myself." "Gentry! They're beautiful! And Pope said you're a bum." Damn. I could have bitch slapped myself. Pink was pissed, "Bum?" "Pope called all the guys I ever liked bums. I know you're not."

Pink changed the subject and said, "You have a "lazy-Susan" in your kitchen. Like to look at it sometime. I wanna build one for that corner." Pointing north. He took me on a tour and showed me where the music was coming from. "See. I got The Beatles on reel to reel. Imports. All of em." "No wonder it sounds so good. I love The Beatles. I sure do miss 'em. Wonder what they'd sound like now if John Lennon was alive." As we stepped out of the kitchen area I noticed the coffee mugs I left for him. High above a cabinet in the kitchen. "I see you still have the mugs." "Yeah," he said, "Keeping pennies in 'em." They were up high and standing east like the sunrise. Hmm, I thought... sitting up there like royalty. One cup king, one cup queen.

When I had to go he showed me out only half way. He stood behind an imaginary line that would be where the living room would end. I looked at him from the entrance and said good bye. Driving to my own unfinished house I thought the usual. When would I see him?

I called and talked to Nina all the time. She was home a lot. She liked to talk on the phone and so did I. We spent a lot of time talking. If we happened to be working on jigsaw puzzles at each other's houses, then our talking would turn to bitching. We liked working on puzzles. I liked the big ones. The three thousand piece kind. You can bitch a lot about one that size. Sit there for hours not finding a single piece. Then one fine day you wake up, then really wake up to a coffee, walk over to a table, and bam! There's that fucking piece. Shit! It's been right in front of you the whole damn time! That's when you slap the piece in! Then the call: "Nina. I hate this puzzle! I'm so damn mad! Last night I spent five hours on it and put a lousy four pieces in. The last two hours I never found a single piece. It pissed me off so bad. I was ready to go through the whole fucking box piece by piece till I found it. Oh get this. The piece of shit was laying right next to where it belonged the whole five hours. Make you sick?" "Christ Cap! I hate that. It's a bitch. The one I'm bitching at is an all white brick building with little pink flowers. The pieces all look alike on purpose. I'm ready to put this puzzle out of its misery. You should come down and look at it. It's making me crazy!" "Go crazy with your own and help me with mine." And then we'd bitch about 'em some more.

Days to nights. Kids asleep. I'd think of the mugs and the pennies they keep. A queen and a kind displayed east and up in a way put together as one single cup. Nights eased in with silent warmth.

I was in the living room when the phone rang. I went to the kitchen to answer it. "You have a collect call from Henry Batturs will you accept the charges?" "Sure," I told the operator. Henry said, "I hope you don't mind. I had to call collect or I couldn't." "Why's that," I asked. "My second night in town and guess where I am. I'm in jail. Once they got your name they never leave you alone. They couldn't wait to put me in here too." "What did you do," I asked. They'll say that I stole something or say I was drunk, it doesn't matter. I wish they would leave me alone. I wasn't doing anything except sitting around on the porch at my ma's house." We talked and then the question, "You and Frank broke up? Thought you mentioned it when I was at your house." "Yes. He broke up with me on the eve of my birthday and my birthday is on Christmas Day." "Yeah, I grew up with him. Cappy, I'll probably get out of here on Monday and it's Friday night. Would you mind if I call you just to have somebody to talk to. It gets really lonely in here. I'll pay for the calls as soon as I get out of here Monday and get a job." "I don't mind. Just make sure ya call after nine at night, this way the kids will all be sleeping and it'll be quieter." "Thanks Cappy. I gotta get off this phone cause somebody else is waiting to use it. I don't mean to sound like I'm coming on to you, but you sure have pretty blue eyes. Well, this dude looks like he's getting kinda mad, so I'll let you go. Thanks for letting me call ya, and I'll call again tomorrow night."

I wondered what this guy is all about. Two days in town and he's in jail? I really didn't want to talk to him, but I felt sorry for him and he was a friend of Franks.

Self and I wanted to call Frank to ask him about Henry. Only I decided it was better to leave him alone. He was probably seeing someone else.

The next night, shortly after nine the phone rang and it was a collect call from the jail. Henry. We talked for a half hour or so until it was 10 p.m. The phones shut down automatically at that time. The next night came, another call from Henry. "Hi Cap. I'm getting out tomorrow. I still don't have a place to live. I can't stay at my mom's because my step dad doesn't want me there. I don't know what I'm going to do. I gotta have a place to stay. I don't suppose I could stay at your place just until I get a job. I know I could have one in a week. I'd sleep on the couch and help you clean and stuff. I'll pay for what I use or eat after I get my first check." Without putting any thought into my answer, I said, "I guess. But just for one week and then you're going to have to go. I'm only doing this cause you're friends with Franks." "Thanks Cappy. It means a lot to me. I really appreciate it. I know you don't know me that well but I won't be a bother. I'll get a job fast and be gone." I checked the clock and it was a minute till ten. "Henry it's that time, my ear is going numb." "Okay, I'll see you tomorrow after court. Thanks again. Bye blue eyes." "Bye, Henry." I was glad to be off the phone. It was time for serious pot smoking. I rolled up three joints and headed for the piano.

I had a good long talk with myself as I smoked the first two joints. Well, I thought... What does it matter if this Henry guy stays here a few days? Gentry never said anything about us being anything more that than what we were. Whatever that is.

I justified the actions that would take place the next day. Most certain as I was, Henry would show. I played the piano to let it all go. What I needed was a new song. Something by me, but it wasn't going to happen... not this night anyway.

Just then there was a knock. It was nearly one in the morning. I knew that knock. Gentry would be at the door and he was. I opened it he came through. He said, "You don't need that." "What? Pot," I asked. "Anything. Pot, pills. You don't need that now because I'm here." I filled up with energy over flowing and round me. I wasn't high on the pot. It just vanished. The high was much higher than any I've known. The name of this narcotic: Gentry Mocean III. Flying free on a high that was better than all. And on this night I knew I had been in love with him more than since the time we first met.

We messed around with the piano and talked like we usually did. (in code) No one would have understood, except for me and Pinky.

Gentry and I took a spot on the living room floor. He laid on his right side facing me. I laid on my left. Both of us elbow bent, holding on to our heads as not to lose them. We talked close in each other's eyes. Warm rays of life poured out of them even if we were hushed. He grabbed a throw pillow nearby and tucked it under his head. I copied. Gentry gave me a pinch and said, "Go to sleep." I laid my head down still facing him. I watched him with his eyes closed. He smiled. I said "Good night." I watched him until he was sleeping, then I closed my eyes. He woke first, very early. Perhaps a dream had told to me wake up just as he did. Gentry was sitting at the table getting his work shoes on. Daylight wasn't yet and I made us coffee. It took some persuading, but I managed to get him to stay for a cup. "Going over to Neil Street," I asked.? "Yeah. Lot to do there. Work, work." As if it bored him already. "It's real nice," I said. "The set up is beautiful." Pink looked seriously at me and said, "I get up in the morning. First thing I think of is work. I wouldn't be thinking of you and you wouldn't be able to handle it." "I think that would be pretty easy to handle Gentry." "You don't understand. You wouldn't be number one. The job would." "I can wait for work and you.

I'll be number one when it counts." Then what he had been thinking came out in words, "It's that time. I have to get to work. Thanks for the coffee. It was good." I started to get up with him to walk over to the door but he said, "No, don't get up. Go back to sleep for a while." I took my seat at the table and watched him seriously head out the door for work. Naturally I got up right after he closed the door behind him. I had to watch his every step. I never knew when he'd be back.

I took the pillow that he slept on and put it on the couch. I wrapped myself in a blanket, put my face to the pillow. I breathed in deep. His aroma still there. I caressed the pillow as I closed my eyes. I focused on him only and I wished him in my dreams.

A nine a.m. phone call woke me and the operator on line said, "You have a collect call from Henry, will you accept?" "Yes." I said hi to Henry. He told me that he would be going to court about ten and would be over around one or two that same day. I said okay and that was it really. Except for the way he slipped in the word Hon' just before he said good bye. Why would he call me that, I thought? I hung up and had hot coffee ready and in my hand.

There were three Maxwell House Coffee cans in the corner of the kitchen. Two empty and one in use. I never thought to throw them out.

My mind was set on Gentry, but it threw me when I thought about Henry. It was two in the afternoon. Henry showed up just like he said he would and I let him in. He brought nothing but himself. We sat at the table and I made more coffee. It wasn't too long after he arrived when he said, "Do you have anything to eat around here? They don't give you much in jail. They don't even give us milk for breakfast. They give ya powdered fruit drink. Even a peanut butter sandwich is better than their sorry food." "I got peanut butter. Do ya want something else," I asked. "A glass milk if you have any. I'll get it, you don't have to get up. Just tell me where the stuff is and I'll make it. Told you that I didn't want to be a bother." "Okay Henry. The dishes and glasses are in that cupboard. The silverware drawer is by the coffee cans over there by the window. Foods to your left from there. And you can see where the fridge is." I watched him go around the kitchen finding what he needed to make the sandwich. He moved slow, but so at ease. I noticed how neat he was. He asked if he could make himself another one and told him to go ahead.

Buff would be out of school soon. I'd have to explain. Sonny and Jules were napping. When the eldest of my three came through the front door she said, "Mom, who's that guy sitting on the couch?" "That's Henry. He's a friend of Franks and I told him he could stay on the couch for a week till he gets a job. He didn't have anywhere to go and I felt sorry for him." "But mom, what about Pinky?" "Buff, Pinky comes over. Mostly when you are all sleeping, but that's all. I know he likes me or he wouldn't come by at all. But he never said he wanted to be my boyfriend." "Mom, then you should tell him that you want to be his girlfriend." She was probably right. She walked passed Henry and said nothing. She raced up stairs to get out of red-plaid-private-school-uniform. We were fortunate enough that the government paid a percentage of the tuition for my kids. I paid the rest. Prof'? He made one court ordered child support check. It would be the first and last check I'd get.

Buff came back downstairs with Jules. The leader was Buff and she said, "Mom, I told Jules about that guy over there on the couch." Jules kept a tight stare on Henry and I said, "Don't worry. He won't be here long." Now she was looking me in the eye... telling me what she thought, "I don't like him."

It was already evening. I had wondered why Henry hadn't gone out for a job. He never even used the phone or newspaper. He sat around and watched television. After supper he did the dishes and polished the faucet. He made it difficult, but I finally said, "Henry, I thought you were going to look for a job? I just wondered why you didn't check the paper or something." He answered, "I know I should have looked for one today, but I just got out of prison not even a week ago. Then I end up in jail for three days. I just wanted to sit down for one night and feel normal. It's real nice and quiet here too. You keep everything neat. You'd never know you got three kids here." "Well they are pretty good kids. They pick up after themselves, 'cept for Sonny. He's a little small. He just turned one on the 2nd of March." Henry said smiling, "I like the name Sonny. He's kinda cute. I like the little guy."

I guess after being locked up, you would want a little freedom to do as you wanted. Freedom meant the world to me when I signed my papers making my divorce official.

After the kids went to sleep Henry stayed up a little while and we talked. He told me how boring prison was. He said, "I wish I would have had someone like you to write to when I was in there. You're so pretty. You don't look like you had any kids." With certainty I said, "I'll never be fat."

The night dragged. I finally announced to Henry that I was going to sleep. I gave him a blanket and headed upstairs. "Night Cappy. Thanks. I appreciate it." "Sure," I checked the kids and closed their doors. I went into my room and locked the door behind me.

I didn't want to play piano and sing. I didn't want to smoke pot that night. Good God, I thought, Henry told me that his full name was Henry Mitchel Batturs III. Another one? Jesus I don't need any more three's thrown in my face! The first third was Gary. He would have adored me forever! (still single) Prof' III took me, made me last, less. Pinky, number

1, yet a third, I've fallen for. Three's and three's and thirds. I'd like to think that the third of the 3's is thinking about me. Sure feels like he is. I'll dream about you tonight. You can't hide from me forever I thought.

It took a long time to go to sleep that night. Interference in the lines... Henry. I shouldn't be such a nice person. What would Gentry think of me if he saw Henry here? I battled myself with questions until I fell asleep.

Morning came. Henry was in the kitchen with coffee ready. "You didn't have to do that Henry." "I can make coffee. It's no big deal," he said, "Look how you treat me. You talked to me on the phone, met me once and I'm here." I felt a sense of un-easy and said, "I don't want to sound upset and thanks for the coffee, but I just like things a certain way. Makes me nervous if my things aren't just right, you know?" All he said was, "Yeah."

I don't remember much of what Henry talked about. He said nothing to peek my interests. He kept himself busy cleaning the house and himself. Fifteen minutes didn't go by without him combing his hair. It looked good enough to go out job hunting. Another day gone and he made no effort. When Henry wasn't looking, I took a couple pills. I didn't want him to know I had any. I wasn't about to share my pot. It was beyond a luxury item and there was only enough for me. I'd have to make it last.

Somehow time escaped. Henry had been at my house one week with no work. He looked at the paper. He looked at the employment page. I said looked! I never said he read! I felt my freedom go away from me. I snuck to take nerve pills and he was on my nerves more than my own children! Henry asked more than a few times about pot. He brought up beer. It was unheard of at my house. Christmas was over and the bubble bottles were empty. I thought it better not to tell him I had a bag marijuana. Sure Henry cleaned the house each day he was there. He vacuumed. He washed the floor and had mentioned that my family didn't have enough vegetables. He was right. I should have given the kids more of them. One day when he was cleaning he said, "You don't have any furniture polish. You can polish chrome up with it nice too?"

I never thought about the polish but the piano came into mind. Didn't matter before. What furniture I had wasn't real wood. I would just damp wipe and dry it all. I said to Henry, "Polish. You're right." I reached for my purse and grabbed 5 bucks. I asked him if he felt like going to the store to get it. With no hesitation he said, "Yeah, I'll go and polish everything when I get back. Wait till you see the faucet." "Okay. I'll smoke a pipe or something while you're gone." "You got some?" Henry asked. "No. I used to smoke it." (used to smoke it till he got here, I thought) "Cap, I've been asking you for cigarettes. I hate asking all the time. See if I had my own pack than I won't have to keep asking for one. A pack will last me a couple days." It was definitely a hint and I said, "Get yourself a pack Henry for going." He came back for a cup of coffee and one of his own cigarettes, mine! This didn't bother me like it should of, but that's because while Henry was at the store I smoked a joint. Blew the pot smoke out the window after I hit it. Henry never noticed. I don't think he did.

"Cap. What's your full name?" "Capri." "I like being called Mitchel, my middle name. Hey can you get some pot? I'll pay you back. I'll pay for these cigarettes as soon as I get a job. You don't have any really?" "No," I said, "Don't like stuff like that around the kids." "That's okay. It was an idea that's all. I sure wish I had something to relax me though. You have anything," he asked? Christ he's been eating and sleeping for free I thought. Smoked my smokes. Finally, after the thinking I answered. "I had some pills but they're gone. I don't know if the doctor is gonna give me anymore because he wants me to come in to see him. See how they worked. I could use more but that'll be up to the Doc'." Ever more persistent, he asked, "When do you see him?" "You know something Mitchel, you're nosy?" "I was just trying to have a conversation like normal people. It was just a question that's all." "Mitchel, I don't have an appointment yet. I don't know when I'm gonna call. Probably tomorrow if you don't quit bugging me with all these questions." "I'm sorry. Are you mad at me? I don't want you to be mad at me," he said. I left the kitchen and walked over to the coffee cans. Henry came up from behind me and put his arm around me saying, "Capri, please don't be mad at me honey. It's not my business. And I like calling you honey. You are a honey Capri." "Just forget about it Henry."

I turned to get out from his arm. I wasn't his girlfriend and I didn't want him calling me honey. Then he kissed my cheek. It pissed me off, but I put a made up grin on and when in to turn on the TV. Henry was right behind me with the polish and rag going over everything. He especially polished the piano. I thought about Mayor. She would not be "present" for her next birthday. I sat on the couch watching Henry and the tears were unstoppable. Henry showed deep concern when he saw me crying. He walked over, sat next to me and asked, "What's wrong Capri? What are you crying about?" "My mom died last year. She has a birthday coming on the 21st and she won't be here." I cried more as I sat with my head in my hands. Henry rubbed my shoulder and tried to hug me but I wouldn't let him. "How old was your mom," he asked. "She was 51." "Hmm," he said, "I'll try to help you get through it. I'm not real good at stuff like this. But did you ever stop to wonder what it would feel like if a little tiny bird just flew up your nose. You know that song about a bird flying up your nose? Well, I just wonder. You know the little feathers would be flapping inside your nostrils and saying how did I ever get in here and how am I getting out?" "Well if I sneezed," I said," I could sneeze it out at you." "See honey, you're not crying anymore."

"Hey. Do you play that piano," Henry asked. "A little. I like to sing. But I'm just learning this piano." I explained. "Oh come on and play one song. I don't care if you mess up. I'd like to hear it." "Sorry, I'm really not in the mood. Maybe later on when the kids are in bed. That's when I practice." He told me then that he couldn't wait to hear. When night came and the kids were in bed he bugged me to play. I didn't want to without smoking some pot. I still didn't tell him I had any and I didn't have a joint rolled. No roaches. There had to be a way to get him out of the living room long enough for me to grab the bag of pot. In was hidden in a gold-trimmed-sugar-bowl on the shadow box.

"Henry, I'll tell you what. I could go for some more coffee. If you make it I'll play something. But I don't know too much remember." Henry said he would make the coffee. He went to the kitchen and I got a bag of pot out and in my jean pocket. I walked out to the kitchen and excused myself to use the bathroom.

While inside, I quickly and expertly rolled a joint. I hid the goodies in my pocket and flushed the toilet. Then I put the joint sideways in the other front pocket so it wouldn't bend. I left the bathroom and headed for the shadow box. Luckily Henry needed to use the bathroom so I put the pot back in the sugar bowl and the joint on top the shadow box, pushed back from view. Henry came into the room and I was seated on the couch. "Well, I think the coffee is done. Are you gonna play something? I really want to hear you sing Capri." "Yeah, I will. I get nervous singing for one person. I sang a song at a "General Motors" open house when I was about 14. There was over a thousand people. That was easy. But one or two people, that's harder for me."

"Well, who do you like? You know, your favorite band." "Beatles." "Yeah," he said, "But they ain't really a group anymore." "You know, I take The Beatles very seriously. You don't want to piss me off when it comes to them. John Lennon might be dead, but The Beatles aren't. And you know why? Because they live right here!" I positioned a fist over my heart. "So, you like The Beatles?" "I still like 'em." "Do you know one by them?" I knew I had to smoke that doob. He was going to know I had some. He'd smell it on me. He'd look for it in the house. I could claim that one joint is all I have. I could let him hit it a few times. I wanted to play.

I got a chair from the kitchen took it by the shadow box wall. Henry asked, "What are you doing?" "Well I'm going to look around and see if I might have hidden a roach somewhere. It's been a while." I stood on the chair looking at him saying, "I already know there isn't a knick-knack on the shelves hiding one 'cause I checked about a month ago. I wanted some then myself. But a lot of times I would hide a roach on myself when I got real high, just to see if I could find it when I ran out." I turned to the back of the shadow box acting very well that I didn't have any. "Tell ya what Henry, I mean Mitchel, there's a lot of dust that's for sure. I'll have to clean it. Ooh wait. Yes! I can't believe this! There's a whole doob stuck between the wall and the box. It must have slid back there a long time ago. It's a little dusty."

While I was talking I had lots of time to rod it through the dust that really was on top of the shadow box. I got down off the chair and took it back into the kitchen. "Hang on Mitchel. I can't wait to light this." Henry said, "Well what do ya know." While taking the chair back to the kitchen, I lit the joint. I took my time pouring coffee and more time taking two long hits before I even thought of handing it to Henry. Stingy? No. Poor. "Here ya go, take a hit." I watched as he took a long couple drags. Wrinkled at my brow I said, "Hey! That's all I have!" Henry passed it back to me and I went to the piano. Taking a longer hit and another to get some sheet music, which gave me more time for another hit while looking for a song to sing. I passed it.

Just then Henry said, "Can I smoke some more? I'm not even getting a buzz." I knew that was a lie. This was the finest pot in the area at the time. Sticky and light green. Like money. "One more?" "And that's it. I'm saving the roach." "Oh man! We ain't gonna finish it? What you gonna save this puny thing for?" "To answer the first question, no. We are not going to finish it, besides you're not getting high and I got a good buzz. As for your second question, I'm saving it for my nick name, cock-a-roach." "Who calls you that?" he asked. The one who gave it to me." "Oh you don't want to tell me?" "Nope, but I am in the mood to play the piano. Excuse me if I drift off when I start. I don't wanna see you upset if I forget I have company. It's the pot." I took the roach that still had another three good hits and stuck it in the cellophane of my cigarette pack.

Henry could have cared less about me playing or singing. He looked bored. He looked like all he wanted was the roach.

"Man that coffee is going right through me for some reason. I'll be right back." I grabbed my cigarette pack lighting one on the way to the bathroom. Once inside I took a couple of nerve pills I had tucked into my pocket earlier. I flushed the toilet and ran the water to wash my hands because I really had to go. I went directly back to the piano bench facing the keys. What to play, I thought? I didn't want to play "Golden Slumbers." That was for someone else. Henry asked, "Do ya know "Hey Jude"? "Yes. I know it if I look at the music or I'll mess up. It's easy, but I don't know it by heart yet. I reached for "Beatles Complete." It was Hermits. He didn't mind loaning it to me because he knew the songs. The radio station wore out "Hey Jude" and it wasn't one I was excited about singing, but I did enjoy singing. Henry asked me if I knew anything else. I told him that I wasn't in the mood to play anymore because I wasn't. "Mitchel. I just want to sit back and take it easy. Maybe there is something good on the radio." Henry found his way to the old "Zenith" console and tuned in a station. Wouldn't ya know. It was "Another Brick in the Wall." Bricks. Is that what you are about Gentry? Bricks? I thought about Pinky as Henry talked about whatever.

It was going on midnight. I wanted to go up to my room and get high, draw or something. I told Henry I was going to crash out and reminded him about looking at the paper the following day for a job.

But that day came and went, and more days as well. I had already gone to Pope for extra money and cigarettes. This Henry guy was breaking me.

Making matters worse, I hadn't seen Gentry. He hadn't been by this whole time and the time was nearing two weeks. I felt bad about the kiss that Henry put on my cheek wishing that it could have been Gentry, wanting it to be him. Did I want too much?

♫ ♪ *"It's All That You Are"* ♪ ♫

Words and Music by: Catherine Santi on November 29th, 1985
"That was you driving by here, I know that it's true.
Think you'd stop in a minute, but that wouldn't be you.
That was you in the morning, at a quarter to four.
Couldn't take if it wasn't, didn't answer the door.
Didn't answer the door.
Didn't answer the door
Didn't answer the door.
I caught you in the mirror, you were looking at me.
Thought that I wouldn't notice, just how quaint can you be.
Tell me how do I leave go, when you're not mine to hold?
But there is a future, that's got to unfold.
It wants to I'm told. Just wants you to hold.
You, you're so cold, that it's bound to explode.
Go. Get out of my way. Go! I don't want you to stay.
Go on and go who needs you anyway.
Go on and go! It's all that you say.
It's all that you say.
It's all that you say.
It's all that you say.
That was you saying to me, you want someone who's true.
I remember it too well and it's still only you.
It was you actor playing, you know it was you.
Please hear what I'm saying, it's all that you do.
It's all that you do.
It's all that you do.
It's all that you do.
That was you who had told me, to go count the days,
of how long it'd been since, since you were away.
It is you who makes magic that takes me this far,
and it goes without saying, it's all that you are.
It's all that you are.
It's all that you are
It's all that you are."

Chapter Thirteen: "History Would Not Repeat Itself!"

On the twenty third day of March I decided to find a job for Henry since he wasn't getting it done. I wanted him out. I was nice long enough, and let him talk me into a six pack. This was it! "Henry, I mean Mitchel, I am going to get you a job and your are going to show up at it. I plan on finding it now. I can't afford to have you stay here anymore. I just can't." Henry said nothing. I grabbed yesterday's newspaper and "read" the want ads. With one glance I saw a janitor job at a cinema in town, one that I had worked at sixteen just before the shoes. I figured this would be the job. I wrote the number down and made Henry get on the phone with the manager. Lucky me! He was hired just like that. He would start on the following morning at 8:00 A.M. He'd be gone once and for all.

Later that night Henry managed to sweet-talk me into buying more beer. I kinda needed one myself so I gave him enough money for a six pack. When he left for the corner store I took a couple take-the-shake-out-of-me-pills and smoked a roach. Pope kept whiskey in a tiny bottle in the house for himself when he came by. I figured I could use a shot. And what did Gentry say? You don't need that anymore, I'm here. But he wasn't here. Hasn't been. I reached for the Italian vinegar bottle that held spirits and I took a big drink. "Whoo! Woah!" I coughed and gagged. I went right into the bathroom to brush the taste out of my mouth. Henry came back with as much beer as he could get for the money. Tall 16 ounce cans of cheap beer. It tasted pretty bad. I wasn't a beer drinker. This night though, I indulged. I told him I was gonna have 4 since I paid. Self didn't want no part of the idea and I gave Henry some of my fourth beer.

My buzz was going. The whiskey warmed me. The pills calmed me and I already smoked the pot I was supposed to. Then the beers made me laugh at the stupid things Henry said. And he said, "We've been talking about this job of mine all day long now. I think we should dwell on it all night. We should really dwell on it a month." "I know Mitchel. Why don't we just dwell on the fact that we are dwelling on the fact that we should dwell on the fact that you have a job. I gotta get some sleep. I don't drink usually and that beer made me tired. Besides, I gotta get up early and it's almost two in the morning. Hell, I won't wake up. I just know I won't be up for Buff if I don't sleep." "I'll make sure you get up. I wake up pretty early. I'm used to it because they wake you up early in jail. They don't have to cause it's so fuckin' cold it keeps ya awake. No heat, not nothin'. It's cold down here too. I wasn't going to say anything but your house gets real cold." Henry sounded as if he was in turmoil. I said, "I'll throw you down another blanket. Congratulations on the job. Good night and stay warm." I walked up the stairs, got in my room and closed the door. I fell into bed with my clothes on.

I forgot about getting a blanket for Henry but he didn't. I heard a light tap on my door and he opened it asking, "Capri. You got another blanket?" Eyes closed I said, "I don't know. I was sleeping." "Say Hon? Could I sleep on a real bed just one night? I won't bother you. Your couch is breaking my back. My neck is killing me and it's so cold ya know. It's a lot warmer up here." "You mean you want to sleep in this bed? You're crazy! I have three kids down the hall. How would it look?" Only I felt sorry for him. "Alright, just this once. Keep your clothes on, stay close to the edge of the bed and let me sleep."

He didn't say anything. He lay down on the other side of the king bed. I watched the closet door while I was on my side facing east. My ears were wide open. Slowly I felt Henry getting closer to me. I remained still and silent. Henry was touching my back, rubbing my shoulders and neck. He kissed my face and said, "Capri. Nobody ever treated me like you. I really appreciate the food, the cigarettes, well, you know, everything. I got a job. I didn't wanna find one right away. I was in prison almost a year. Nobody to call except my mom and who just wants to talk to their mom all the time. Nobody wrote. Then that letter came from Frank and I knew something was up. He never wrote me a letter." That's when I drifted off into sleep. In dreaming, Henry was taking off my pants. He took the sex I didn't want anyone to have. This wasn't a dream but a nightmare! It woke me up to Henry who stole another kiss on my cheek. This was supposed to be Gentry. Why did I drink? This wouldn't have happened.

Gentry was right. I don't need this. Henry heard my sniffles and said, "Hey honey. What cha crying about?" "Never mind, I'm fine. I'm going downstairs to play piano for a while. I just want to be alone don't worry about it." I got up and walked out of the room. Henry said, "You'll be alright." The more I thought about what happened the more pissed I got. The more pissed off I got the straighter it made me. Locking myself in the bathroom, I filled the tub with burning water and bubbles. I scrubbed and scrubbed till my skin was red. I drained the tub and rinsed off and off in a shower. All my efforts failed me. I felt tainted. Why did I let this guy come here? I asked myself. I had three Ill's in my life I didn't need a fourth. This extra number was upsetting the natural flow of the three that had been following me around my entire life.

I started to play and sing anything I could think of. It didn't matter. I went through The Beatles book from start to end looking for ones I knew, only I didn't want to sing them. Then I found some of Mayor's old sheet music. She had the music for "Over the Rainbow." I saw that it was in E flat. Now I could sing to that, I thought. No one who would ever sing it like "Judy Garland" did, this I knew, but there was more to the song. The beginning. The part she didn't sing. It took one time and I turned this lovely lullaby-day-dreaming-notes into a solid rock ballad.

I was extremely proud of it and played a few more times. That put me in the mood to play a few Beatle songs after which I took the couch and fell asleep.

My first thought when I woke up was the night before. I made coffee. I sat at the table and smoked a lot of cigarettes. Three to a cup. I looked at the three empty "Maxwell House Coffee" cans. They were tucked in a corner due-west. Why was I saving them? The night before flashed and the tears came. Doesn't a person ever run out of them? Not me. Mine streamed down my face. I watched as they slapped on the counter just below. Couldn't think about one thing at a time. My head was overloaded. Mayors birthday was three days ago. Gentry is a three. I got three kids. I have three brothers. I was the third one born to my parents. Three jobs at once. Three shoe stores. Same store that changed their name three times. Sailed the Atlantic at three years old to visit my grandparents. Three Beatles. Three Ill's. A fourth third. Three, three and three's and three's! These numbers were for so long a time, that they were beginning to consume me.

Henry came down stairs and said, "Good-Morning. I heard you singing last night. You're not bad. You slept on that couch? Doesn't your neck or back bother you? Mine feels so good now after sleeping in your bed." "The couch was great. I feel fine. I like sleeping on the floor even better. My back feels even better after a night on some carpet. Feels great!" "You must be flippy or something, you'd rather sleep on the floor?" I didn't want to answer him. I looked at him and I was disgusted. But he would be out after today.

Only the day was confused and Henry would be starting his job the following morning. Did I let him stay? Yes, then evening came around, and after the kids were in bed, a couple of guys that Henry knew were knocking on the door. Just like he owned the place, Henry invited them in. They brought beer with them. A couple of twelve packs. It seemed planned. I passed the three of them on my way into the kitchen, when I called out to Henry, "Hey, Mitchel, would you come here a minute." "Yeah, just a second hon." He told his buddies to take a seat and the beer cans were popping open. Henry walked into the kitchen and said, "Capri what's wrong? I saw these dudes at the store and told them about starting a job tomorrow, so I figured it would be alright to party a little. I start at eight o'clock right," he asked? "Yeah! But you should have asked me first. I would have said no. I got little kids here. Did you forget or what? This is my place! I don't keep alcohol here. I don't know your friends. The three of you should go to a bar or something." I was mad! "They won't stay long, I promise. Between all four of us it will go fast. Don't be mad honey. Please?" I tapped my foot to the floor and said, "You mean the "three" of you. I'm drinking coffee."

He took a seat in a black vinyl recliner. I followed in. Out of the two strangers I looked at one saying, "I know you." "I'm Rick. You went to school with my sister," he said. High school flash: "Oh yeah Rick. Your class cooked for us and we did your hair. I did a facial and you had a beard. Remember?" He nodded and we laughed. He was always nice in school. Rick introduced me to his buddy. "Dean this is Capri." "How ya doing Dean?" (like I really cared). Henry passed out the beers. They all insisted I should at least drink one. I stuck with what I knew. Coffee. History would not repeat itself.

Things were quiet. Rick respected the little ones sleeping upstairs. I figured it different. I figured wrong. Things were going fine until Henry boasted. "Hey I got a couple joints here in my pocket let's light 'em up?" I thought I would drop to the floor! Henry pulled out two joints from his pocket, just as if they were his to offer. I had to say something and I did. "Mitchel, since I'm letting you guys drink my share of the beer, then you better pass that to me first." He took another long drag off of it. When I hit it once, I put it out. Mitchel said, "You didn't pass it around." Ooh he was pissing me off. "Mitchel, I'm keeping this. You owe me." "Never mind. I got another one," he said. "She acts flippy sometimes." Flippy??? Dean looked like he really didn't care one way or the other about anything and Rick smiled over at me with wondering questions in his face.

Sitting where I could see all of the guys, I watched Henry. He would go to the fridge' to get everybody a beer, but he was putting an extra one behind his chair each time. He was drinking two to their one.

He kept cranking the old "Zenith" up, getting nothing but distortion, talking way above the music. Rick could tell I was upset. Anyone could have. I yelled at Henry more than once about it! He complained and said I didn't know how to party. This thing needed to stop. I wanted my room.

Henry got louder and louder till I couldn't take no more. "Sorry guys. The beers are done. I'm tired and going upstairs." "Yeah." Rick said. "Come on Dean. We gotta get going anyway." Henry insisted they stay. I told Henry it took me about a half hour to fall asleep and that I wanted to hear the door open, hear his friends foot down the drive at ten. "Rick, I'm counting on you to see to it that the door is locked. Make sure he locks it." I pointed to Henry. Henry gave me a nasty look. Rick said, "No, we're leaving now Cap, don't worry. I understand what you're saying. I'll lock it myself on the way out." Thanks Rick. Oh and tell your sister hi for me when you see her." I said good night to them and went to my room.

I paid close attention to the time on my wrist. Within five minutes I heard the door open, I heard it close and by the sound of it, I knew it was locked. Two car doors opened and two car doors closed. Engine on, car leaving. I lay facing the closet door waiting for Henry to pass out somewhere downstairs. He had to be pretty well in the bag by now, I thought.

I envisioned Gentry. My thoughts said I miss you. Think about you all the time and wish you in my dreams. Through my hopes in transmitting my thoughts, I asked, do you think about me now? You are. I see your smiling eyes. You might be laughing, but I know you hear me. Wanna know what I do to sleep? Have steps I like taking. Step one: I will dream about you tonight and I will remember it in the morning. Step two: I will dream about you tonight and I will remember it in the morning. Step 3: Dream. Resume envisions of steps one, two and three.

Henry came in. He stood on the east side of the room. "Are you sleeping Capri?" I didn't answer. "Honey. I'm sorry. Will you talk to me?" I ignored him. I smelled the beer on him and he reeked. Didn't want him anywhere near me ever again. Henry's voice grew loud and angry, "I don't like being ignored bitch!" He grabbed my hair at the temple and ripped me out of the bed like a rag doll. My head banged against the wall. He dragged me to the foot of the bed pushing my shoulders with fists till I was down. I got up and cornered myself in the east of my room. "You stupid fucking bitch!" Henry yanked me from the corner throwing me against a wall feet away. My body hit it hard. I slid across it off the floor several feet. "Mitchel please don't hurt me anymore. Stop! Please!" I was so shaken it was a struggle to get off the floor. Henry dragged me off the floor by my hair and an arm and said, "You know you're nothing but a fucking whore." I curled on the bed. He stretched his arms to his side, making fists watching down on me. "You're nothing but a fucking dirty whore just like all women!" He threw his body from side to side repeatedly punching the left side of my head. I almost blacked out a couple times. Begged for my safety, "Please don't hit me anymore! I won't ignore you again. I promise!" He stopped for a moment. He turned calmly walking over to the bedroom door shutting it.

My God, the mirror! It must weigh fifty pounds. He's going to kill me with it. I couldn't get up. I tried but tumbled tightly down to the floor. He turned slow and said, "I don't hear anybody crying you stupid dirty bitch!" He kept punching my head more and harder. I was helplessly numb and couldn't move. The beating was sure to kill me if it went on. Suddenly Henry jerked away and stopped. He walked over to the door and I could hear Sonny crying in the next room. Henry opened the door peacefully saying, "The baby's awake. Take care of him." I shook using all the might in my arms to push myself up. I staggered passed Henry in fear.

Little Sonny was standing in his crib, eyes filled with tears looking so afraid. I made my way to him and hugged him. I rubbed his curly blonde hair telling him that everything was okay. I knew I couldn't pick him up and take him down the stairs. My head was spinning off balance as I held on to the crib rails. "Sonny, do you want a bottle of milk? Okay? It's okay Sonny, don't cry, I'll be right back. I'm gonna get you some milk?" He stopped crying. I gave him a big kiss on the cheek and walked out into the hall. I couldn't stand straight. I was at the top of the stairs and as I walked down I had to brace myself against the wall to the left of me so I wouldn't fall. Henry was behind me when I reached the bottom and said, "I'll get him a bottle ready. Thanks Mitchel. Uh, I need to use the bathroom." "Go on honey. Are you alright," he asked. I wanted to say something else but I was afraid to so I went to the bathroom and cried into my hands so Henry wouldn't hear me.

As I wiped my tears outward across my face, I felt a sharp, piercing pain on the left side of my head. I got up slow, braced myself on the sink, and moved the hair away from the side of my face and looked in the mirror. A small bone was sticking out just in front of my ear. Behind, below the temple. I covered it up with my hair. I didn't want anyone to see it. I flushed the toilet and went in the kitchen. Henry was on the landing of the stairs with a bottle. I called out to him, "Let me have that bottle. I'll make Sonny a bottle. Just please give it to me." "Oh, you think I put something in it! I would never hurt a kid. Especially Sonny, I told you I like the little guy." With shaky hands I dumped the bottle of milk into the sink and got a clean bottle out of the cupboard. The bottle was ready and I headed back up to Sonny's room. Henry stood watching and waited for me. "Here you go Sonny boy. Give me a hug and then you go to sleep sweetie, okay?" I hugged him, laid him on his pillow, covered him up and kissed the tip of my finger and touched his mouth with it, whispering. "Good night Sonny, I love you."

Henry was right outside the door. I went by him and into my room to get a cigarette. I sat trembling and painfully inhaling one drag after another. Out of the corner of my low sighted eyes, Henry was coming in my room. Kept my eyes to a wall. "You okay Capri? I'm sorry. I don't know what happened. I didn't want to hurt you. You gotta believe I didn't mean it Hon! You need to lay down and rest. Get some sleep." I had to talk. Didn't want to him to think I was ignoring him and God how I was trying!

"Mitchel, I'm so tired." I realized that the bedroom door was open. I wondered about Grizzly, the cat, and wondered if he might be in, not remembering if I let him in the house or out. Henry got up and came over closer to me and straddled himself over my stomach. He wasn't hurting me but he was scaring me to near death. How would I get away? What's he going to do to me? All was quiet and I smoked the last of my cigarette real slow. I put it out in a thick green glass ashtray next to bed. A small lamp was lit on the night stand. Henry had his pants unzipped, holding onto his penis. He pushed over my chest and said, "Come on Capri. Just open your mouth it's not gonna hurt." "Mitchel no. Please!" I tightened my mouth with a lock on my lips as hard as I could. He pushed his penis against my mouth harder and harder. He said, "Please Cap. It won't hurt. I don't wanna hurt you. I told you I was sorry." Hadn't he done enough I thought? I broke down and cried. "Don't hurt me anymore!" I turned the hurt side of my face away. He pushed at it and made me look at him. He pressed his penis against my mouth again. He forced it in and out of my mouth. I gagged and cried for it to be over. Maybe four minutes went by, which might as well been forever and he said with a grin, "Guess I'm just too tired to cum." He got off me, laid down on the other side of the bed and was snoring in seconds. I had to leave the room.

Took my cigarettes, matches and headed downstairs to make coffee. When I got down to the kitchen, I forgot the reason I came in the room and sat staring at the table smoking. "Coffee." I said softly. "I need some coffee. That's what I need. Okay now. I'll just make some here and then, then, I'll go into the bathroom and puke my guts out." And I did. Brushing my teeth hurt like hell and I did it more than once. I washed my face off. Bumped the bone I forgot about. I pulled my hair up to see it again and I saw my ear bruising and the bruising covered all the flesh. Coffee! I needed coffee. I had coffee.

I stood in Pinky's favorite spot, mine. The warmest next to the kitchen sick. Embracing the hot mug, I silently prayed that he'd show up to rescue me. I noted the time. It was nearing three in the morning. How did this much time go by, I thought? Just then I heard a knock at the door. It had to be Gentry. I set the mug down. I went to the door and flipped the light on. I unlocked and opened the door, but I didn't open it for Gentry. It was a friend of mine named Terry. "Hi Cap. How ya doin'? Can I come in?" "Sure Terry come on in, yes!" I threw my arms around Terry's broad and strong shoulders and bear hugged him as hard as I could. He hugged me back lifting me off my feet.

"Cappy what's all this? What's up Cap," he asked again? "I'm fine. Whatever made you stop over here?" I asked. "I just got off work. Thought I'd stop and say hi. Brought a "Pepsi" with me. Care if I stay here with ya and drink it?" "Yeah. Come over and take a seat. I haven't seen you in awhile.

Let me grab some coffee," and I joined him. "So Cap, what are you doing up? Do you always stay up this late? Hey. You alright," he asked. "You been crying?" "No, no. I smoked some pot earlier. You want some?" "No that only makes me want to drink and I'm trying to quit. I like this job I got. I can use the weight room and that. It's not a lot of hours and the money could be better, but it's a start." We both chuckled.

Then he saw Henry coming downstairs. "What's he doin' here?" Terry asked. "Oh. I let him stay here a couple weeks till he found a job. He starts in the morning and he's gone." Henry came in the kitchen for a glass of water. "Hey Terry, what's up?" "What's up with you?" Terry asked laughing. "Can't you get a place of your own?" "Man ya know I just got outta prison. Nobody wants to hire ya when you come out of there." Henry went into the bathroom and Terry noticed the piano and walked over to it. "Do you play this? Can ya play something?" Slanting to the left, I walked into the room. The light was coming from the kitchen, so the room was dimly lit. I felt the tears stream down my face. Terry put his hands on my shoulders and asked, "Cappy. What happened in this house tonight?" "Nothing Terry, really, nothing! We were just arguing." Terry's voice filled with charge and he stated, "Look Cappy. He's in the bathroom and you are out here with me. You can tell me?" I looked up at Terry for a moment and again said, "Nothing." "Cappy, Henry is a punk. If he hurt you I'll fuck him up right now, but you have to tell me something! Don't say nothing happened Cappy because you were crying at the door." "Terry we just had a fight. Talking I mean. Arguing that's all." "Okay Cap, then I guess you don't need me here." He started to the door. "Terry, your pop. Aren't you going to stay and finish it? Don't leave, not yet. Please stay for a while. I hardly see anybody anymore. Don't go!" Terry looked at me half pissed, half knowing something was really wrong and stayed with me longer.

Henry came out of the bathroom, didn't have anything to say except he was going to bed. Said he didn't want to be late on his first day. Neither me or Terry said a word to him. Terry asked me for my number. Asked if he could call me once in awhile. I gave him my number and he told me where he worked if I ever wanted to get a hold of him. I was relieved to know that I could call someone. And I was too afraid to call the police.

Fear set it once again when Terry told me that he had to leave. I looked at the time. It was after 3:34 A.M. "I wish you didn't have to go Terry. I'll probably be up all night. I get that way when I'm upset." Terry gave me a big, tender bear hug. I wished him good night. He jumped up into the seat of his pickup truck and drove off. I got another cup of coffee, stayed at the table where I ended up falling asleep.

Got up at 6:45 a.m. because Buff was down stairs and dressed waking me up. "Mom, are you okay? Is he still here? Me and Jules woke up last night. We didn't know what to do. Jules was scared and crying so I locked the door and she stayed in my bed." "That was the right thing to do. Don't worry I'm okay. He's leaving this morning. He has a job now, okay?" "Okay mom. Is grandpa coming to pick me up for school?" "You know he always does Buff. He'll be here. You just have a good, fun day in school okay?"

Buff wanted to get her own breakfast. She had a bowl of cereal and some juice. When she was through eating and brushing her teeth she said, "Mom, I'm going to tell grandpa when he gets here." "No, please don't say anything to him. I will, I'll tell him just as soon as Henry leaves for his job. Don't say anything to your grandpa okay? I'll call him up at home." "Okay mom, but I still think you should let me say something. You should call the police on him so they can put him in jail mom." "Buff, there's grandpa in the drive now. Please Buff, promise me you won't say anything to grandpa okay? Promise?" "Okay." Then Buff headed out the door on the sound of her grandpa's third or fourth toot of the horn. I made more coffee.

Forced myself to go into the bathroom. I looked at my hair. A small portion of it was missing just behind the temple area. My ear hurt real bad and was changing colors. It was somewhere between red, purple, well, you know, bruised. Just then Henry came down the stairs. "Good morning Capri. How ya doing," he asked. "It's twenty till eight. You better hurry up or you'll be late for the first day." "Yeah. You know I'll never make it there on time 'cause I'm on foot. Can you give me a ride?" "Mitchel you know I got two little ones still sleeping up stairs. I can't wake them up and take them out into the cold just to get you to work. You knew when you were supposed to be there. You said you could get up on time." I was still shaken from the night, I didn't know what to expect. I certainly didn't think anything I was saying was right and he would beat me more. "Capri, I'll be right back, I left my flannel shirt upstairs." I leaned at the kitchen sink with my mug in my hand.

He came right back down. All dressed. Tee and flannel neatly tucked and buttoned. He brushed his hair. He had a couple swallows of coffee, then he went into the living room for his navy coat and wool hat. He paced the floor a moment and said, "Well, the only way I'll get to work on time is if you let me take the car. I wouldn't be late. It only takes 5 minutes or so to get there. If I'm late, with my prison record, I won't have the job. I gotta have some money so I can pay you back. I told you I would pay you back." "I don't know Mitchel" What do I tell him now? What if I say no? If I say no, he might beat me again. "Come on Cappy I'm gonna be late if I don't get going, just let me use the car for the first day." "Here Mitchel. Take the keys. Bring it back by eleven thirty. By the way, it's not in my name, it's in my ex-husbands name. So be extra careful that you don't fuck it up." "I'm not going to fuck it up. I'll be careful. You know where it's going to be. Thanks honey." Henry dashed out the door. I heard the engine of my "Buick" start. Prof' got it at a good price for the extra-long-road-trip it took to get home to Ohio. The car was backing up slowly out the drive and I stood at the window watching. Henry was careful and cautious. After he drove away, I locked the front door.

Great Cap. You Ass hole! He beat you and you let him take the car? Why did you let him in the house? Why didn't you ask Frank about him? Why don't you call the cops? "If I call the cops, then Henry will only come back and hurt me more or worse. No cops. And I'm not saying anything to Pope." And I carried on with myself. Self said, "Pope told you he was a bum, to get rid of him." The words went over and over in my head like giant church bells. Self was right. She knew, Pope was right. But how did he know? What does he see that I don't? I couldn't tell him. I couldn't tell Nina because she would tell him. I was afraid to say anything to anyone. So I kept quiet.

Suddenly I heard footsteps. I looked at the landing and forgotten about little Henry who stayed that night. Sometime between Dean, Rick, and Henry, Henry's ex brought their son over to be with his dad for a couple hours. I'd completely forgotten. He was about nine years old. He must have dozed off in the girls' room where they were playing. "Henry, hi, I'm Cap, remember? Your dad used my car to go to work. Do you want a bowl of cereal?" "Yeah, what kind do you have?" he asked. "There's two or three boxes here, what kind do you want?" After picking one out I fixed him some. Asked him how to get a hold of his mom. He gave me her number. I phoned after he ate breakfast and was concentrating on cartoons. Tracey said that she could be there about eleven to pick him up. I gave her the address and noted that I had one and one half hour to wait. During that time I tried to get a hold of Prof'. He was living only blocks away from me. Called his place a few times and got no answer. I wanted him to know about the car.

There was nothing left to do but wait. Time went slow till Sonny and Jules woke up and things got going. Jules wondered into the kitchen. I put her in my lap and hugged her, then I got her something to eat. Sonny had to be fed immediately so he was already in his high chair.

Tracey showed up on time. I introduced myself. She seemed jolted that Henry had a job and more so when I told her he had to use my car. I put emphasis on the words "had to" hoping she'd pick up on what happened. I wondered if Henry had ever beat her. "You shouldn't let him drive," she said, "He doesn't have a license." Too many questions flooded my brain, so I asked no more. Tracey stayed till about 12 noon to see if he would show up. No show. Tracey said, "Hope you get your car back in one piece. Just thought you might like to know he messed my car up a couple times." "Thanks Tracey. I'll call ya when he gets back here." I wasn't surprised by her reply. "No, please don't call. I don't even want him to know I came in. I don't see him no more. I gotta go!" She was real uptight, nervously getting little Henry's coat on. She didn't say good bye. Not even why she didn't come back for her son the night before. Tracey more or less fled.

Later came, but my car didn't. I called the manager at the cinema. Confirmed by him, Henry was a no show. Where's my car, I thought? He probably wrecked it. When it got to be 6 p.m. I decided to call Frank. He said Henry did cruise over to his house with the car about four, but that he didn't see him since. I Told Frank that Henry got a job and never showed up for it. Frank said I should have never let Henry take it. He was probably joy riding somewhere and drinking.

Well, there goes the car. I'm royally fucked now, I thought. Then I talked myself out of thinking that, because the car "was" in Profs' name. It would have to arrive somewhere, at some time. But it was the "sometime" that tore at me through supper and early evening.

I had tried Professors' a couple more times with no luck. Buff still insisted I call the police. I asked her again not to worry. She went up to see how Jules was doing and I heard them talking in whispers till they fell asleep. Sonny was out and hour ago. I sat at the table. I looked at the back door from where I sat. In sitting there I realized that I could see every possible entrance to my house. The bathroom window was too small for someone to get in. That, and the noise it would take to break in. I walked upstairs to check in on the kids making sure they were asleep. Made sure that everything was locked up tight. Then I went back downstairs to make more coffee.

The time was nine-thirty in the evening when I heard a car screech to a halt at the end of the driveway by the garage. It was Henry. "Backdoor. Shit! I didn't lock the back door." Yes, I was yelling at myself. I put the coffee mug on the table and that's as far as I got. Henry came in staggering and in a hurry. The headlights were on and the car was still running. I'd been doing typing work at the house for my pool teacher Krome. I didn't wanna make a big deal about the job or the car because he was obviously drunk. "So what are you doing here," he asked. "I'm typing addresses for a friend of mine." "Oh. A friend? How good of a friend is he? Doesn't he know you're seeing somebody? Let's see this." He took my seat behind the typewriter. I stood up and asked him how things were. He ignored me. Just then the phone rang. I looked at Henry and he said, "Well, are you gonna answer that phone or what?" "Yeah, I am."

Watching Henrys every move, I answered. "Hello?" "Hi. How ya doin?" It was Prof'. "What's up? How's the kids?" "Fine. They're asleep. Oh and don't forget, Pope wants to take them to church on Easter Sunday." "Let me see, ah, that's five days from today right? This Sunday?" "Yes it's this Sunday Professor." "Are you alright Cap? What's wrong? You sound bad." "No. Bring it by tomorrow. I can't go shopping tonight the stores are closed." Prof' said quick, "Who's there?" "Yeah. Tomorrow morning is fine. But not before nine. I like sleeping in." "I'll be right over," and he hung up the phone. "Okay Prof', thanks, see ya tomorrow."

Henry smiled a glare back and forth while I talked. But the back and forth stopped when I was through with my call. "What the fuck is this shit?" He pulled the paper from the machine and tore it to shreds. "Don't. I get a dollar for every page. I need that?" "Why, all you have to do is call your old man on the phone. He gives you everything you want, you spoiled bitch." Then Henry tore the pages up that I had completed and scattered them. Pieces where everywhere and he laughed and laughed. He picked up the typewriter and slammed it to the floor. "Henry Mitchell Pick that up and put it back on the table where you got it. It's mine!" I couldn't believe I raised my voice, but I did. To my amazement, Henry picked the typewriter off the floor, gently placed in back on the table sitting up straight with his hands folded smiling. I was standing in the middle of the kitchen under a copper swag light up center watching him.

He stood up abruptly and walked in the kitchen passing me till he was standing in the south corner. I turned to face him. He said, "Give me money bitch." "There's no more." I said. "Bitch! Just give me some fucking money!" Henry slammed his fist up into the lamp, bending and breaking it. I backed away from him as he stood with his fists up to my face. "Listen you whore. I know you must have some money around here somewhere. Find it and find it now!" He shook his fists. Afraid, I said, "There. Over there in that coffee can is some change. Take it. It's all I got. You can take it." Henry reached for the can and poured the coins and counted. "Bitch, there isn't even three bucks here. How am I supposed to party on this you whore." The left side of my head went numb and my balance was off. Scared as hell I waited for Prof'.

"Mitchel, I'm sorry but it's the end of the month and it's all I have. Please just take it. You're going to wake the kids up." Henry made a grunting noise and ran out the back door laughing. I heard a door slam. It wasn't my car. I peeked out the front window, saw that Professor put his truck in the front yard. He must have pulled in engine off, lights off, for me not to hear. I went to the front door to let him in. "Where is he?" Prof' asked. "He's in back. Getting into the car, but don't go back there!" "Cappy what did that son of a bitch do to you?" I pulled back my hair to show him my ear that was now completely black. "I'll kill that mother fucker!" Prof' meant it. "When the car is at the front of the house I will give him the surprise of his life. Just before he's dead, I'll tell him this is for Cap."

The car was backing out of the drive. I grabbed Profs' arm pleading, "No, don't do anything. Just let him go. He'll bring the car back after he's sober, just let him go please!" Professor walked out the door anyway and I followed staying just inside. He stood along the drive way staring at Henry's face. He wanted Henry to know that his face would not be forgotten. Ever. Professor came back in and said, "Well, I'm reporting it stolen to the police. It's in my name!" "I wish you wouldn't do anything right now. Just let him go." Professor asked me what happened and when. I told him everything. He didn't want his kids there in a dangerous situation, so he went up stairs and got them. Said we were all going to stay at his dad's house out on McCartney Road. Jules and Buff were thrilled about going.

While I got Sonny bundled in the baby carrier Professor called the police about his car. Gave the police his dad's number where we could be reached. The 4 of us headed to Prof' Jr's house. The police were going to set up a road block on Division Street. It was a small street. One corner a gas station, one corner a bar, a few houses on each side and a one way. How could they be so sure Henry would even go down that road, I thought? Once at Professor Jr's house I felt safe. Henry didn't know where it was and wouldn't find me. For a night there would be peace. No there wouldn't. 15 minutes after we got there the phone rang and it was the cops. Henry went through the road block they set and drove head on into both cruisers. The officer would come out to talk to the both of us.

Professor hung up and told me that one of the officers had to be rushed to the hospital because he was thrown through the windshield on impact. He was paralyzed from the neck down. "Shit, Professor, I can't believe this! I let him take the car. I just let him take it." "Cappy it's not your fault. You were scared he would beat you again, you had no choice." "Yeah Professor. What kind of a choice do I have now. He'll get me when nobody's around. I know it. He insinuated that I was his girlfriend. I hate him." Professor saw the flashing lights out in the drive way. He was at the door before the cops got out of the car. Prof' asked them in.

One of the policemen asked to use the phone. He told us that he wanted to call the hospital to check on the officer who was paralyzed.

My mind decided to go off alone. The three voices goin' on blended together like a language I couldn't interpret, until the policeman clearly addressed me. "So, Capri, can you tell me what happened tonight?" "What were you talking about with him Professor? You didn't tell him did you?"

Professor looked at me directly. "Cappy! Show him what Henry did to your ear! Cappy just tell him about last night." I looked at Prof', I looked at the cop. "Cappy. I'm Officer Tripstar. From what I heard already you haven't done anything wrong." "Yes I did. I told him he could use the car. It's my fault that that cop is in the hospital. I should have said no, but I couldn't. I wanted him to get the job at the cinema so he would leave." "Cappy, you don't have to be afraid of him now. He's on his way to the jail as we speak. Your ex said he physically harmed you last night? Raped you?"

I looked at Prof' feeling betrayed, pissed. I looked at the guy dressed in the uniform with a gun, the badge and wondered if perhaps he was a hoodwinker underneath his cover. I said to him, "You're my friend? I don't know you sir. You could be another Henry under there. Just because you're dressed like a cop, doesn't mean you are one all the time. I don't know who to trust. I thought I could trust Prof'. He lied because I asked him not to tell you and he did! I thought I could trust Henry because he knew Frank. I only let him stay two weeks. He had no job, he wasn't looking for a job. I got him one then he celebrated with two of his friends, got drunk.

He came into my room and wanted to talk to me. I ignored him. I just ignored him that's all and he kept punching my head. I thought he'd never stop. The blows came one after another. I could barely get up. He hit me like that for more than two hours. So when morning came, he said he was late for work and wanted to drive the car and I told him to take it. I just didn't want him to hurt me anymore, hit me anymore. "Cappy go on and show him your ear," Professor urged. I hung my head down. It shamed me to show anyone. I pulled my hair out of the way. Tripstar shined a flashlight at my ear. "Capri! There is absolutely no flesh color at all on your ear!" Tears escaped and dropped to the floor silent, like me. The officer looked behind my ear and said, "Capri, inside and out, you're entire ear is black. You have a fracture in your face. You should be taken to the emergency room. I can take you." "No" I pleaded. "No! I'm not going there to tell them everything." "Did Henry rape you?" I looked at Professor and said, "I can't tell him. You tell him. I just can't say it. "Sir, what Cap wants me to tell you is that after Henry beat her last night, he forced his dick in her mouth." "Is that was happened Cappy." 'Yes. Yes sir."

The phone rang. There was a pause. The call, for Tripstar. He finished and said to us, "Sergeant Shoor will be fine. That was the hospital. It was just the shock of the accident that caused his body to paralyzed. Just 20 minutes. He's fine." I took a deep breath and exhaled in a gasp. "It was only temporary Prof', did you hear that? He's gonna be okay, thank God! "

♫ ♪ *"In Song #5"* ♪ ♫
Words and Music by: Catherine Santi on December 23rd, 1985

"How can this be, I never see you, never hear
you, never no where are you.
My head plays tricks on me, sees a face,
creates an image, that one of you.
It never fails, I'm always falling calling out
to you and you're not around.
I spend so many days and all these days I've
loved you, but you, you can't be found.
Tell me how do I escape the thought of you when you got that hold on me,
but I love it don't you see? My heart has got control of me.
Once we were laughing, joking, rolling, don't ya think it's funny,
strangers were we.

But now I know that you and I were never
strangers, won't you say that to me?
I can't explain just why it is, but I go on to feel the way that I do.
You eat it up and love it, kinda makes you smile, it's all a game to you.
Tell me how do I deny this love for you? Memories surround me here
only wishing you were near.
You always made my thinking clear.
How many times behind the paper writing
words that come to me 'cause of you?
Were all the things you said to me back then
all lies, or tell me were they all true?
I'm losing my insides, it's empty there, the
soul it stays, I've nowhere to go.
I walk this life alone and that tells you something and you outta know.
Tell me how do I forget your beautiful face?
Something deep beyond your eyes, always makes me realize,
if I think blue, love's still you in song number five.
In dreams, I think of you. In threes will die dreams come true?"

Chapter Fourteen: "Matchbox on the Tracks"

"Yes, that's the good news, "said officer Tripstar, "The bad news is your car was totaled in the wreck." "Great. Now I don't have a car. That's just great. And Henry walks away without a scratch. Nothing broken. Damn him," I shouted. "Well, he was so intoxicated that his reflexes didn't respond like that of a sober person. He obviously consumed too much alcohol to know what was even happening. He'll know after he sleeps it off at the county jail." "But how long will he be there? I mean, he'll be there a while won't he," I asked. "Maybe a couple of weeks till..." the officer tried to explain, until I interrupted... "Wait, a couple of weeks and then he goes free? What's this hold him a couple of weeks mean?" "Capri it means he'll have to wait that long for a court date more than likely. He'll get an attorney, public defender, it doesn't matter and then he'll go again in front of the judge and the arresting officers. He'll enter a plea of guilty or not. He'll go back to jail until he goes back in front of the judge. It could be a few weeks maybe a few months." "Then what," I asked Tripstar? "He could be released on bond. The judge might put a cash bond on him. Someone would have to come up with 10% of that to get him out, but the judge may keep him in. We can charge him for what he did to you, that is for you to decide." "But I let him use the car sir?" "Cap, you got a mirror in your purse," he asked. I got one out, he opened it and made me look at my ear and he said, "Cap, you just tell the judge that he stole the car."

I said no more. I knew that if I had him charged with all this that he'd get out again someday for it and I didn't want him to hurt me anymore. Professor walked the officers to the door. The cops left, the kids were already sleeping. I made myself comfortable on a big couch and curled up with a huge comforter. It felt like I was lying on colossal cotton balls as I sank into a sleep that seemed like days. I woke late the following morning, about 11:00 a.m.

Professor was trying like hell to keep my out there at his dads place. I wanted to go to mine. Which we ended up doing after he fixed the kids a great breakfast.

Walking into my house left me feeling trapped between bad and evil. I didn't want to be there, but how in the hell would I ever get out?

Professor left and told me not to hesitate to call on him for help. I thanked him for letting us stay the night.

The kids had a good dinner and were well ready for bed when nine o'clock came. I got them all cleaned up and ready. Within minutes they were sound asleep. I went back downstairs and got a hot bath ready. I soaked in it sitting

Indian style. I fell asleep. I know because I woke to cold water against my fore head three hours later. It was after midnight. I was exhausted still, and after dressing, I went upstairs to sleep. I turned on the light and walked over to the night stand for a book of matches. Then I saw my hair laying clumped on the floor. I leaned over to pick it up and retraced what had happened exactly. I walked to the wall. I remembered sliding over it. A long four foot scratch was defined in it. My earring, I thought. My pearl earring had made that mark. I laid down on the bed trying to sleep because I was so tired and now I couldn't sleep. The room literally looked as if the walls were coming in around me.

I went out of the room in a hurry and curled up on the couch downstairs. It took some doing, but I finally got the rest I needed.

I woke, sat on the couch, lit a smoke. The first thing that came to mind was the last thing I wanted there. Henry M. Batturs III. I talked to myself. "Well Gentry? Where were you all this time? I'm not the one who you want to make number one in your life? If I am, then I know that wherever you are you must be listening!" Quickly, I sprang from the couch to the kitchen table, realizing that I had not checked the mail since Monday and it was Wednesday! I picked up the two day pile of junk-mail, mostly, except for a brown envelope from Cleveland. I held it like a prayer. I couldn't bring myself to open it, not then. I laid it on the table under the junk mail and made coffee.

Do I go to the hospital like Tripstar said? No, I can't do that. I can't go there. They'll want to know how and why and who and I can't keeping saying it. I can't tell this story all over again. As for pressing charges, having Henry arrested for this, there is no way in the world. He'll get away. He'll get me again. He'll come after me for telling and hurt me worse. I'll be nice to him. That's what I'll do. I'll be nice to him and he won't hit me anymore.

Just then the phone rang. It nearly shook my feet off the floor when an operator said, "You have a collect call from Henry to anyone, will you pay for the call?" "Yes operator." "Please Capri, don't hang up on me. I know you probably want to, but I had to tell you that I am sorry." "Henry, forget it. I'm fine. But I don't think that Professor is too happy about his car. The police told us what happened and it's totaled." "What do you mean, told us," he asked. "Well Professor stopped by the next morning to give me money so the kids could have Easter clothes. The police came by and told us. I guess the cruisers were demolished too?" "How do you think I feel Capri. I get out of prison I go to jail. Here I am again. You gave me a place to stay. You're sweet. I never had a prettier girlfriend before. You even get me a job and I mess that up too and your car, I mean, your ex-husbands car. Leaving you stuck with three kids. Please don't hate me honey!" "I don't hate you." I lied, "I let you stay here because you know Frank. Maybe Frank didn't know Henry's dark side. "Capri hon, don't tell Frank about what I did. I wouldn't want him to know I fucked things up for you, I mean your car and that." The left side of my head could feel the skin crawling sensation on the inside and it made me dizzy. I didn't want to talk. My jaw was real sore. I wanted to hang up on him, but something kept me on the phone for nearly an hour.

I stared blankly out the window for springs signs, some had been showing when a blue jay landed in the front yard. Followed by the one, were three more. I tossed some bread out the door, but before the door opened they vanished out of sight. I waited near the window with a coffee and soon they were back, they picked at the bread like it wasn't what they ordered from the menu and left just as quickly as they arrived. Blue birds. Happy little blue birds. Happy little blue birds fly and fly. Guess those four weren't so happy with the bread.

The mail, I thought. Cleveland Clinic! I took a seat and opened the envelope I was trying to forget about, but couldn't anymore. I read the letter the nurse had personally written to me. She wrote, "Dear Capri, I know there are no real words I can say that will make you feel any less concerned about the man you care so much for and his diagnosis, so I won't write them. Instead, I want to personally write you to tell you how lucky you are. The man you told me about is even luckier because I sensed very well by our conversation today, that you are in love with him. Being loved is special. I wish you and your Mr. Right all the best yet to come, and there will be many bests. Sincerely, Nurse Rogers. P.S. Feel free to call anytime for new information. I'll help you in any way I can. Enclosed is what I told you I would send. Good luck again.

I took out the pamphlets and read them all one by one. I read them out of order and I read them over and more until I quit crying. It took till the next day. I tucked the envelope in a drawer in the kitchen under some phone books and pencils.

On the night of that day I wanted to call Gentry... tell him what happened while Henry was locked up. With absolutely no second thoughts, I got the phone book and looked up the number to The Well where I thought he might be. The owner answered and put Gentry on. "Hi. It's me. Capri. It's important! You have to come here." "Be right over." I heard the phone go blank and when to the front door. Took him four minutes to get to my place. He came in. We sat on the couch next to each other and he said, "I'm here. You can talk to me." "Gentry, I'm sorry! I was trying to help somebody out and he hurt me." He put an arm over my shoulder and my face lay close to him. "Don't worry I'm here now." Damn the tears that were running down my face. I was so afraid and so ashamed. Didn't know what Gentry thought of me having Henry here to just help him out and I didn't want to know. He stayed for a while. We talked. It was warm and nice. He was warm and nice and I loved being around him. When I was already well into tired, he suggested that I get to bed and get some sleep. "I can't sleep up there! This is my bed. The couch. I have to sleep on the couch!" I was shook up worse now than before he arrived. "Gentry would you do something? Like stay? Just until I fall asleep?" "I can do that." "Will you stay next to me?" Gentry turned the lights low and laid next to me on the couch. He told me to close my eyes and I felt his warm hand wiping tears that were left. Gently, I touched the side of his face, his hair. Once again Gentry said, "Relax. Just close your eyes." I did. I slept. I woke. He was gone.

Buff woke up cheerful like always and asked first thing, "So mom, did Pinky come over last night? Maybe I had a dream, but it seemed like I could hear him talking." "Well Buff, as a matter of fact he was. How do you always know about him? He tells ya doesn't he?" She didn't answer me, she questioned me, "Did he kiss you, mom?" "Nooo! We just talked about some stuff and that was that. I was sleeping when he left. Why am I telling you this anyway. This is mom business isn't it?" "Pinky will tell me if I ask him. Next time he comes over I want to ask him. Oh, there's grandpa beepin' the horn." She grabbed for her book bag and coat, gave me a kiss on the cheek and headed out the door. I stayed at the table. Should have walked to the door. I missed watching her climb into the truck to go to school with her grandpa. It was cute, but I didn't want to face Pope after what had happened. Didn't want him to know. As far as I knew Buff never told him anything about Henry.

It wouldn't be long before Jules and Sonny would be getting up, so after Buff took off, I laid back on the couch to sleep for another couple hours. Sometimes the two little ones didn't get up till 10,10:30 in the morning, which was wonderful considering that their mom was a night person. Time for me to be me. Play piano. Sing! Most night-mornings I was up till 3:30 and wishing I had someone to play along with, like Gentry. He had the guitar but never brought it over. Hermit had one and wouldn't come by. Hermit was well, Hermit! Then I remember that Stone from the radio station said he played guitar. He'd come over with his even if he's just learning. I can show him some chords. We could try playing some stuff together on the instruments. Talked to him enough months on the Sunday nights that he worked as a D.J. He knew my dream was to get at least one of my own songs recorded someday. Stone wanted a bigger radio station to work at, like in Cleveland. I talked about Gentry. I think I bored him. It was all I wanted to talk about, next to music. Stone liked talking. And I learned that he liked talking about himself. Stone loved Stone. Maybe I was a little jealous of him, remembering back to a time when I felt like I had the world by the ass.

All the pizzazz I had. World by the ass, I thought. Snap-my-fingers-got-it-kinda-girl. I looked for that girl. I had found her a couple of times and even though I could see her, I couldn't bring her in close, making her me. So I kept her inside, but just to look at.

It was a constant check to know that Henry was still in jail. When he was there I could breathe. I wanted to get out. Needed to get the hell out of the house. The weather was getting nice and I had been cooped up for too long. It was time to go out for a game of pool, pop a few quarters in the juke box. I made arrangement with Nina, her girls would watch my three.

Bravely I drove to The Well and there was Gentry. He came up to me saying quietly, "How ya doin' cock-a-roach? Come on over and meet my friends." I felt afraid. Strange men, but then I told myself that Pink wouldn't let me get hurt. Walking slowly, scared my knees would give in, Pink said, "This is Cappy. Isn't she pretty? She's got the prettiest blue eyes." Gentry wanted to go on but I stopped him, "Quit it already will ya? I might me sexy, beautiful and gorgeous, but I'm not pretty," I smiled. Gentry ready said, "You guys should see her kids! She has three beautiful kids!" I was getting a little pink in the cheeks when one of his friends said, "Well Cappy, you don't look like you had one kid. Gentry was right when he talked about you. You are one very attractive lady." With a hand on my hip I said, "Talking about me behind my back are you now?" He turned a little red, like me and said, "I might have brought your name up once or twice." His buddies were laughing and the second one said, "Gentry man, who are you trying to kid, you talk about this girl all the time." "Yeah," said the first, "He talks about you all the time, no offense Cappy but it was getting real boring. Only now I see why he can't quit talking about ya." Gentry was still trying to deny that he did, but I had a pretty strong feeling that the two back stabbing friends were not just giving him a hard time for a laugh, they told the truth.

He ordered me the drink I liked so much. Just a splash of soda. I spent as much time as I could, until I knew that it was time to for the sitter to be home. I asked Gentry if he would like to come over and he said that he was kind of tired. Entirely disappointed as I was sure he would want to. With a smile-on-the-outside-good-bye, I went home. How did I get home? Pope helped me get a car. It was a well used 1974 "Chrysler Newport." An A ranking tank of an automobile with a radio. Something the "Buick" didn't have. I cranked it up as loud as it would go to drown out any idea that Pink would change his mind.

Sat down in the kitchen immediately to roll a joint. I took a nerve pill and smoked the pot. After I finished the first one, I was rolling up a second one when I heard a knock on the door. I said to myself, "Self, that is not who you think it is." I answered myself, "Yeah he's tired." I walked over to the door and saw my dream come true standing at the front door like always, smiling. I opened the door and said, "Thought you were tired?" Walking passed me he said, "I told you that you don't need that anymore, I'm here." "Yeah, but you were also out drinking so what's the difference?" He sat down and said, "So, gonna play something for me?" And I did. I played "I'm Looking Through You." Beatles. Gentry stayed over that night. We crashed out on the floor like we did the 1st. Only this time I made sure I would be up with him. Like a built in alarm, when he woke, I was up within seconds. We talked over coffee. As always he had to get more work done. I respected that he had to leave.

Nothing yet from him, not even a hug and it was buggin' the hell outta me. Couldn't be because I smoked because he did. Whatever his reasons were I was nerve wrecked.

The next night was a school night, but it was also the day that Mayor died one year before. I needed help with the hurt and pot wasn't doing it at all. I played more pool at The Well and lots of songs on the juke box. Especially one sung by "Phil Collins" called: "Against All Odds." There were many songs ahead. I had a few people waiting to shoot a game as long as I kept winning and I was on a winning streak. An hour probably passed along with a couple drinks and I forgot about the song I wanted to hear until I heard it come on. Mayor came to mind. I knew the odds were 100% against me that she wasn't coming back and I started to cry. Gave my game to the next one in line and sat up at the bar to collect myself. The bartender asked if I wanted another drink and I asked her to make it a double. A man sitting next to me said, "You know, it's not lady like to order a double." I didn't say anything to him. I knew if I did, that as upset as I already was, I would have said something un-lady-like. I drank the drink down fast and just headed straight to the house. A four minute straight drive to the house. Maybe Pink will be there.

He didn't come over that evening but he did show a few days later. He laid back on the living room floor and seemed disgusted about something, so I asked, "How come you don't have a middle name?" He looked at me in an odd, curious expression that went directly to disgusted again and replied, "Because the son of a bitch wanted me to be just like him!" "Your middle name should be Emerson. Gentry Emerson Mocean. Then your initials would be G.E.M." He didn't say anything but it got his mind in a different direction, me, and he seemed to be happy.

It was earlier in the evening and the kids got to see him for a change. Buff eagerly ran into his lap and they talked in code, I think. They looked so cute. He was good with the kids and I loved watching him with them. Professor never spent the time with them in a lifetime that Gentry spent with them in a day. He would make a wonderful father, I thought. And I thought about that often. He took time to look at Buffs home work, praising her for her stars and A's, making me very proud.

The time came for the kids to get to bed and Gentry helped me get them tucked in. It was feeling like a family. It didn't feel that way with Prof'. Came close with Frank. What would make this different I asked myself.

Gentry didn't spend the evening that night, but he stayed late. He wanted to be at the house when he woke up so he could be right there to work on it.

The next day I told myself to drive over and see him. He welcomed me in, showed me what he'd been doing. Just finished some track lighting. It surrounded a platform built up just a step in the east corner of the living room. He had "Pink Floyd" at a deafening height. I went up close to his face saying, "Aaah! You have a brick missing in your wall and I can see you. Trying to hide isn't going to work anymore." "Your eyes been peeking inside my wall, he asked. "It's your eyes. You scare me!" And like a bashful little boy he smiled at me.

Gentry charged to the platform, "See this will be track lights here and here." He pointing to the outline of the floor. Without introducing his act, he went into "Floyd" frenzy singing just like "Roger Waters." Damn, if they ever wanted a fill in, Gentry would be that guy. It was amazing. Then he abruptly stopped and laughed out loud. He was like a little kid. It was what I lacked without him. The coffee mugs maintained their position like royalty in the kitchen. It was good to watch him work and play. Only I couldn't stay. And when I left, I wondered about Pink.

Oh I could have had worse fate, but I already did, Henry was still calling. Scared if I wasn't nice, I accepted the calls. And they were always after nine p.m. when my three were upstairs asleep. I never, but never wanted them to know who was calling. If it sounds crazy that I accepted the calls, it was, but I had to know he was locked up and down. I could open a window for fresh air. I could open the curtains for sunlight. I could sing and play anytime day or night. He was in jail. I could sleep and dream. Of course there was the matter of remembering one.

I talked to Nina on the phone a lot. Pretended that all was fine with me, so that she wouldn't get suspicious and make a mention to Pope. Things maintained a level of light headed bull shitted humor until I made it serious, "Nina, you know that April 22nd is the day I had an abortion. I don't tell everybody, not that I try to keep it secret." "I didn't know. How old were you," she asked. "18. And ya know Pope practically begged me not to. He said we had enough to take care of another mouth. I'm still not over it. I remember the day just like yesterday. They tell ya at the hospital that it will be a day you never forget and they were right. I will never forget it." When she heard the details, she asked me to stop because it had her upset, like sick upset. I felt worse and we both had to get off the phone.

A chance in a million that I was carrying twins. I wondered what the baby might have looked like on his or her tenth birthday. I had a tenth birthday. It was crushing my heart and it hurt so bad that I never gave my baby a chance, a choice. I felt like I hired a hit man to kill it because I didn't have the guts to let it live. This date coming was already tearing me up like it had done for years.

Thank God for Gentry. Seemingly here for rough times, I thought back. The first being the first time we met. The second, my birthday. The third, our first date. He was near when Sonny turned one, just before that or after. He popped in more in March, like a few days before it would have been Mayors birthday. He was there the night before Henry came to stay. He was here in minutes when I phoned him days after I was beaten. Around the day Mayor died he was here. Well come on, I thought, it's that time again Gentry. You gotta come over and see me. I know you can hear me. Self said softly, "You hear me."

I twirled the old chrome "Papermate" pen on the table hoping it would point to the one that I liked the best. And I did that for about an hour while playing with keys for a song. I couldn't write one. I tried Beatles, Mayor's old stuff in the piano bench and my first song. Thoroughly frustrated I asked myself out loud, "Why did you quit taking lessons?" Self knew. "Because... You wanted to be the coolest girl in America!"

One evening after supper, still sitting at the table, reading the paper, Jules said, "Mom, what's that noise?" "Oh, that? Well that's a matchbox. You know, whoo-whoo, chugga chugga, chugga whoo-whoo, a matchbox!" Buff laughed saying, "Matchbox? Jules, it's a train. That's a train hear it? Mom you called it a matchbox," Buff said smiling, asking why. "Hmm, I don't know, beats me." Sonny paid short attention to us as he was finishing his food! But I and myself both paid very close attention.

What made me call the train that, I thought? I can picture in my mind what a train is for crying out loud. I was angry with myself. Had no idea what was going on. I figured it to be sub conscience slip and thought nothing more and I let it alone.

This didn't last because I was having a hard time putting things away. Going back to find them was a maze of sorts. I couldn't find them. I stumbled on them. My purse was in the cupboard with the canned food. I found the newspaper in the freezer more than once and where the hell did I put the dish rag? I would look for it for hours. I finally gave up the search and sat on the couch to think about where I was when I used it last. It was getting the best of me. I already traced my steps pacing and pacing and I was done pacing. "Buff, do you have any idea where I left the kitchen rag? I can't find the damn thing anywhere." Buff came down the stairs and walked over to the kitchen table, picked it up saying, "Mom, it's right here." I watched her dangling it over the table.

Why hadn't I seen it there? I remember now. I was wiping the table with it after Jules spilled her juice then the phone rang. I didn't normally forget where anything was. I kept things in order and was a complete wreck if I didn't know where things were. Now this? I tried to ignore my careless mishaps as much as I could figuring they would subside soon, but they didn't. They went on along with the calls from Henry that were every night. And he made sure he got his free call to me sometime after 9 p.m. Free for him sure, but when I got the bill it was over a hundred bucks! It was never more than twenty five dollars. I had to keep things affordable and it would take one third of the ADC check to pay for the phone. How the hell would I take care of this? I was tired of going to Pope for money at the end of every month, but I had to. There were no full time good paying jobs and I couldn't settle for minimum wage with three kids.

Luckily for me, Prof' was working with the local cable company installing the boxes for the new system. They needed someone to answer the phone there and I accepted. It was an easy job and the money was good. Each of the installers paid me ten dollars to work and it was only 5 days a week and five hours a day. The installers made commission on top their weekly pay. Some of the guys were taking home $800 dollars a week or more, so it was nothing for them to give me ten bucks a day. Providing all the cable guys showed up for work each day, and they usually did, I'd make 250 bucks!

I took advantage of a May that lie ahead. The weather was walking beautiful, so I walked to work. The building couldn't have been in a better place. It sat near the water. Inside from a window facing east you could see downtown Sandusky. North faced the islands on Lake Erie that attract many people across the U.S. To the west was the "The Jackson Street Pier." Ah, but my view from the window to the east was the best. I could see Cedar Point and all of the rest.

There were two ferry boats docked below just outside my window. The boats took me back and reminded me of Gary and his look-a-like, maybe a famous friend and I loved the memories. It was the job that sucked and oh was it boring. The phone seldom rang, so I filed and painted my nails. I called the kids and made calls to Nina to bitch about everything! Like the time wasn't slow enough. I didn't want to watch the clock but I did.

When at last the day was done, a lot of the guys working there offered me rides home, but I usually refused. I liked the walk at closing time. Still light out. Still warm. Best of all I didn't have to be afraid of Henry Mitchel Batturs III!

All the guys at the job like me. The boss was out there and had a split sense of humor. One minute he was all work, the next maybe neurotic and after that it would be a waste of time to figure this guy out. No one fully understood Mr. Jollee. He was warped, yet colorful, distorted and precise, depraved but knowledgeable. Go figure the mind.

His office was in the room just north of mine and he would often call me in if I wasn't busy. He tried his best to get me with him and I loved watching him turn red all over his balding head and face. He'd lay back into his desk chair saying, " You like me. You find me attractive Cool Breeze, I know you do. You're so sexy and those legs are wow! You're great! Damn it Capri! You want to know what it is that you do to me? You do don't ya baby." I slant tightened my lips, shook my finger at him and said, "Cool Breeze? Well Mr. J. Jollee... this Cool Breeze is going to my desk to work. Get a grip J.J. You and I are never gonna happen." Calmly I got up from the seat in front of his desk and went into my shabby little office to answer more calls. Jollee was calling me again, "You know you want me C.B. We'll go out for a drink sometime after work. Sounds good!" "Hey why don't you grow up, grow hair, come back twenty years ago and I'd still tell you to drop dead." He laughed and I heard this crazy idiot talking and mumbling to himself about something. It was usually in musical words from the band "Talking Heads" "… This ain't no party, this ain't no disco, this ain't no foolin' around…" and on and on and on with the same line from the same song. But beyond our strange boss, the job was pretty laid back. Most of the guys smoked pot, and of course so did I if had it. Most morning, before work, I'd catch a little buzz, and sometimes I rolled a doob for the walk to work.

There was a dinner the company was having for the cable installers and I was invited to go by the crew. At the dinner party one of the fellow cable guys named Mike liked me. He had asked me out only days before. I accepted because I was divorced. Of course the Professor heard about it and after we were all through with the food and the wine, we took the party to a serious stage and drank. I drank no more. Professor was drinking whiskey shots. I was watching him close because I knew how he was. He had three or four days to let the jealous rage inside him build and I was afraid he would explode all over me or Mike.

It came like a storm. Professor in a blurred fury punched Mike off his chair and onto the floor. We all stood up. A couple voices in the room were asking Professor why? A couple others were seeing if Mike was okay. Me? I looked up at Professor and turned away with anger when I saw Mike getting up. He held his head high then he took his sport coat and left. In passing he saw me and said, "I'm sorry Cap." "Me too." His face was already pretty red and I know that punch hurt him. It bothered me and embarrassed me for him. Before I left, I got brave enough to speak my mind to Professor. "Mike didn't do anything but ask me out. Why did you want me to work with you guys so you could keep an eye on me? I'm not your wife. I'm single. You had no right to hit him. Remember Prof', we're divorced. Leave him and me and anybody else I choose to see alone."

Professor stood dumb founded for the time. After which I left. It felt good to put him in his place in front of all his buddies. I walked tall to my car to drive home with a roach waiting in the ashtray. I kept it on the tip of a sewing needle to keep it in place. I drove to the pier and smoked it. I watched Cedar Point for a few hits, drove back to the house right away for the phone. It was almost a business taking calls from the jail. I accepted and paid for the high-priced-meaningless-words. It made me feel secure knowing for sure where Henry was at all times, so hell yes I paid for the calls!

May was bursting buds, birds and a closer sun. I had the screens in summer. Barefoot in the grass, barefoot walking, shoeless and I loved it. As long as the weather was warming I opened all the windows to let the fresh spring in. Mornings were great behind the piano. High and singing. Coffee always readily available. And the cans? I had thirteen of the 13 ounce cans of Maxwell House Coffee stationed in the west corner of the kitchen, on the counter.

It was my hopes that Pink might drop in because I had to tell him about the job. And never like clockwork, he showed in the afternoon. I told him about the job, about being the only girl working in that department and about Mike asking me out, on purpose, for a reaction. He reacted, "So, did you go out with him?" "No. It was a bad idea to begin with."

This pleased Pink and we were happy together. Gentry stayed. Had his chit chat session with the kids. This particular day he asked Buff something that I never thought he thought of. "Well Buff, You think I should marry your mom?" Buffs eyes lit up more astounded than mine and said, "Yeah Pinky. When are you going to marry her? Mom, did you hear that?" I remained surprised but composed in the security of the kitchen. I answered her. "Yes," then I listened. "Pinky, I know my mom wants to marry you. You too have to get married you just have to!" "Well Buff, ya know I have to ask my mom first. She'll have to approve." "God Pinky! You don't have to ask your mom. I know my mom wants to marry you, so you should marry her."

I walked to the living-room-couch- conversation that the two of them were handling well without me and said, "Come on Buff, I never said I wanted to marry Pinky." "But mom I know you want to marry him." Pink was having a great time watching Buffs wide bright blue eyes. Happiness was all hers and mine. He was laughing, she was laughing but I said, "Buff, you heard Pinky. He has to ask for his mother's permission. Besides he didn't ask me. I'd probably tell him that he doesn't get my permission." Gentry said, "Then Buff, I'll just wait for you to grow up and marry you, what do you think?" Now I was getting jealous. What if he meant that. It would only be 11 more years for that day to come. He'd be 43. With that in mind I said, "Buff, you won't want some old man for a husband. He'll be in his forties. Unlike your mother who'll still be in her thirties. Younger, better looking, you know." "Your mom is real pretty. She's even prettier when she gets mad, look at her!" Tee heeing away he was.

The night turned time to get the kids in bed and Pink stayed a while. We messed around with the piano and I sang for him. It was fun singing for him because he liked listening to me. From the day he knew the piano was here, he'd come through the door always requesting. "Play something for me." He sat. I played and sang what I recently learned or already knew. More time was laughing and talking, sometimes in riddles, sometime Beatles, sometimes Floyd, nothing was lacking, there was no null and void. The mountains had valleys and we filled them with ease. When talking turned real, it was just as you please.

When we were through playing head games, songs, Gentry stayed with me to sleep on the couch. It was comfortable with him there next to me. My face was close to his as we lay side by side. He smelled so good, I thought, as I lay listening to him breathe. Through closed eyes he said, "Get some sleep."

My God he has his arm around me. I don't believe this. This is heaven. How am I going to fall asleep. Forget sleep. I don't have to sleep. I don't want to sleep. This may never happen again and I don't want to miss a single moment. His eyes were closed sailing in a dream and I watched till I myself was asleep. When I woke up he was there and ready for coffee. With precision, I noticed that Gentry liked the cans he spied in the corner. Kind of like the those coffee mugs I left at his house for the pennies.

Naturally Gentry had to go to Neil Street and work on the house. Working man. Good man with kids. He liked me playing and singing and he liked me. I knew now that he would return again soon and I couldn't wait.

I wanted to sing something that had more power to it. Something to force my voice into war. I grabbed the Beatle book, looked for "Oh! Darling." This in the one, I thought. It'll be easy. The chords were simple. I played the beginning and started right it. I went through it fair, with a mistake here and there. Damn this is hard! It will kill my throat for sure. Loving every minute of it I kept singing. Had to literally yell to sing the words out. Good rock and roll practice. Now whether rumor or not, I had heard that "Paul

McCartney" wasn't able or allowed to talk for a few days after recording this particular song. The point I made to myself was that I would get through this song hurt or not. And I will be able to speak without any quirks.

I started going out more frequently. To The Well. A lot of times I wanted to get there early, so I could get a seat at the bar by the pool table. This way, by getting out about 8 or 8:30, I would be able to avoid the collect calls from the jail. I told my sitter not to accept any collect calls. Explained it to Bink. "If the caller thinks it's that important to talk to me, then they can pay. So, if you get a collect call just tell the operator that you are the sitter. That you cannot accept." She didn't know the caller's name and she didn't know his face or what he had done to me. I wanted to keep it that way.

Ah! The Well. I loved it there and always had fun. I knew the owner Benny, same San Marino blood, as Pope and I liked him. He'd greet me, get me a drink and motion with his light gray blue eyes... Gentry is here!

Occasionally I would bump into a few people I hadn't seen. We'd buy each other drinks and shoot the shit, because after more than a few drinks, shit is what is shot.

Curfew came, so at 11:45 p.m. I would head back to the house. I'd stay up and wait to see if Gentry would come by. Sometimes he did, sometimes not. Most of the time I knew when he would be there, so the sometimes didn't really matter.

♫ ♪ *"True As Blue"* ♪ ♫
Words and Music by: Catherine Santi on December 27th, 1985

"There's only one time, one time in your life
things are gonna come your way.
What kind of answer are you ready to give?
What will be the words you'll say?
Time has no purpose when it's standing, standing still.
You're too busy to come down from the hill.
You won't imagine the dreams and more beyond the door.
The snow keeps falling, outside it's gray and cold
distance and a warmer sun.
Colors are still now, but before had much to say.
Felt like time had moved, time had begun.
There's only one love, one love in my life,
don't want love from no one and loves none.
Somehow I knew him in an abstract sort of way.
Time just stopped, I knew that time was gone.
Time has no purpose when it's standing, standing still.

147

You're too busy to come down from the hill.
You won't imagine the dreams and more beyond the door.
And it your listen and listen well enough,
I'm just being true, as true as blue
It's not been easy, through time I learn and know...
... Time was you in time I'll come to know.
Time was you, was time, I've come to know."

Chapter Fifteen: "Within a Weak Week"

So what did I do with myself in between piano, pot and the bar when I could get there? I had my job at the cable company of course.

Professor came in to apologize for hitting Mike. I told him that he should say his "I'm sorry" for Mike, not me. Naturally he said he would, but you can bet your life if he did, he didn't mean one word.

Jollee the boss, was still trying to get me to go out with him. I had had enough. I told him short details about myself. "I clean houses when I can. I clean this dude's house once a week and I'm there two hours. I make forty bucks. I sit here in a dark nasty office, see Profs' ugly face and you think I'm going out with you? Jollee you are the ultimate pain in the ass." "I bet you have a beautiful ass Cool Breeze!" he said with a big grin. "JJ. turn your ear this way. Please don't say another word or I will quit today. He laughed "at" me, "Cool Breeze, you just love being called Cool Breeze don't cha baby. It's better than some bad ass calling you something you don't like. Some boys like to call a woman a bitch. I see somebody who must have had some tough years. You carry a lot of pain. I know hurt C.B. Take me. A whole lot of people don't like me 'cause they think I'm really crazy! Could explain the reason I'm telling you this. Say. When you want a bottle of wine some night, I'll buy and we'll talk. Just talk. I promise. I like you Cool Breeze, I really do." Certain I wasn't about my boss. He's feeding me a line, I thought. "You know Jollee maybe you're not such a bad guy, but that doesn't mean I'm going to have wine or go out with you." For a minute I thought I hurt him. He proved my theory wrong and said, come on Cool Breeze. Why don't you pull that long skirt up over your knees? It's summer. I wanna see legs baby!" "You don't quit! You're really warped and this is my favorite shirt too. If I stand up and spin around it twirls out. Like a big flat circle. It looks so cool and guess what? You'll never get to see it." With a ha ha ha I walked back into my office.

There were few calls to answer that day. I was lucky to get one call an hour and tired timed hours dragged. It meant more time for thoughts and my thinking thing was bagged. There was Cedar Point across the bay, ferry boats docked the same old way. Wanting it back, to go back twelve years, where problems were a few, when friends were good and the time was cool. Life now a jumble and I was feeling the wreck and some lunatic Jollee was signing my check. Henry would be lurking in safe haven of darkness. Prof' stayed back, yet always in hover. Try and find a four leaf clover, and you might find Gentry. Okay, maybe I was a bit obsessed with him.

There wasn't much going on in May. Gentry still hadn't asked me to go with him so when Mike from cable asked me out. We did. We walked up to "Daly's" after work. It was a couple hill blocks away. Thought he was out of his mind to ask again after what Prof' did. Mike said he wasn't worried about him. Jollee over heard, no, Jollee didn't over hear, Jollee listened in and decided he would join us. Mike thought we'd better drag his ass along with us. We all walked to the lounge and Jollee said he had something important to tell me. "Cool Breeze, I want you to know first that I like you a lot. All the guys working at the cable place like you." "Stop right there Jollee. You're gonna tell me that I don't have a job anymore right? This is why you guys are taking me out. Prof' put you up to it didn't he? He's the one who doesn't want me there. I'm sorry Mike, I'm not mad at you but as for you Jollee, you owe me. Think of this as my getting-fired-drink." "Cool Breeze I didn't fire you." "Good," I said, "And since I don't like you anyway, you can buy me whatever I want. Mike felt bad for me and took my hand. I wouldn't let Jollee hold the other one. He tried, you know he did. "Cool Breeze, I enjoyed having you at cable. So, why don't I come to your house when were through here or I'll take you to mine. "Jollee!" I said, "Are you outta your mind? You're buying me doubles it's over time.

I ordered a draft beer to go along with the shot of tequila Mike bought me. Jollee bought the double and I down-hatched three shots. The buzz wasn't happening fast enough and I wanted a buzz quick. I took a small drink of the beer. Mike took a few minutes to talk to one of his buddies who happened in the place. Jollee was still begging for my attention. I just wanted to get up and walk around. So I did. Floated as it's called, stopping to talk *to* familiar people in my life. Having a ball and the tequila was free. I did two of the four shots in front of me and another sip of beer. Mike excused himself and went to a table where some of the cable guys were sitting. I don't know if he came back to the bar. I felt pretty damn good and it didn't matter. I floated and floated. And I drank and I drank.

Took a break from the walks and the talks, took a seat. Then I saw these people breaking open peanuts by smacking the shells against their foreheads. I walked over to them and said, "Show me that again. Does it hurt?" One of the guys there said, "Here try it. Wait, I'll show ya. Just put it in the palm of your hand and slap it into your forehead you won't feel a thing, watch!" I watched and I was game, "Give one of those peanuts." They were right, it didn't hurt, in fact it was fun, so I went back to the bar to get me some. Broke one, then another, then two and three, did more, did four and did all the more.

Went to the table that showed me the trick and slapped the whole bowl lickity split. Naturally I had to go from table to table to show everybody there how much faster this was and there were a lot of tables with lots of bowls. There was Jollee at the bar, "C.B. I think you had enough to drink. Let me get you home. Don't drink anymore Cool Breeze." "Yeah," I said, "You damn near killed a whole bottle of tequila," said Mike. "Mike," I said, "Watch this. It's the fastest way to eat a bowl of peanuts. More fun getting them! Ready... Watch!" After I did that Jollee said, "That's it C.B., I'm taking you home. You definitely drank way too much." I slapped Jollee across the face saying, "Stand back, I got something to do." And I did...There were still bowls I hadn't hit and I wanted to get all the tables before I was going anywhere.

Things were beginning to blur. Next thing I know Jollee is at my house with me. God only knows how that could have happened. I turned the lamp on and he'd turn it off. Jollee insisted on chasing me all over the downstairs for nearly an hour. It was ridiculous watching him trip and fall through the dark room he made. I was laughing my ass off and he nearly got me. I had to stop and catch my breath. "Cool Breeze, I can't help myself. You just look like sex damn it. Sex just falls off of you and you're making me crazy!" "No Jollee! I didn't make you crazy, but I'm beginning to see you are! Now leave me alone and go home! Just go!" "I'm sorry Cool Breeze. I don't want to make wild hot passionate love now, it would be taking advantage. I'll wait till you're sober. You'll love it too!" boasted Jollee. I pushed him out the door and he stumbled out calling back to me, "You're really great C.B.!" I shook my head, I locked the door.

Then it dawned on me. Laura, who came in to join me at the bar was left there. I told her I would drive her home. She lived with her mom so I called to see if she got home and her mother answered. I slurred the question, "IssssLaurahome? Illlltole Laura lll'dgivweherrrr a ride! Rasbansslay'" She said something and hung up. I passed out.

Next morning, Laura called. "Cap are you alright?" "What happened to you last night Laura? I got pretty loaded I don't remember much." "You don't remember calling my mom last night?" "God I remember now. I bet she didn't understand a thing I said either. I was asking her if you were home." Laura laughed and said, "She told me that she couldn't understand a word you were saying. Hey, by the way, I wanted to ask you something? Why were you walking around with a peanut bowl on your head? Don't you remember? You looked like you were having a good time." "Oh shit Laura. I remember now. I was smashing peanuts on my head. No wonder I got such a head ache this morning. I drank a lot. I never drank like that before. A peanut bowl, damn! Laura is your mom mad?" I asked. "I saw somebody I knew and we ended up driving around a while. My mom never said a anything. She was sleeping when I got in."

"Laura do you have any clue how I got home. My car isn't here?" "You really must have had too much to drink. Four guys carried you outside. One was Mike and that guy Jollee, but I didn't know the other ones." "Shit Laura, I don't remember. Somebody must had really pissed me off or something." "Cap, you looked pretty mad, you told the owners that you didn't want to leave. That's what I heard by the time I got outside to see what was going on. You don't remember me asking you if you were alright?" "Damn Laura! I remember sitting on the sidewalk next to the building, or was I dreaming?" "No, you were sitting there. Then that guy Jollee helped you up and told me he was giving you a ride home. He asked me if I wanted a ride too, but I had someone inside waiting for me." "Laura, I gotta go get my car. Can you come by sometime and watch the kids so I can go downtown to get it?" "Sure. Let me know when you're ready, I'll be home." "Thanks Laura, it won't be for a while, I still feel pretty shitty." "How's one o'clock sound," she asked. "Perfect." We hung up and went to lay down for awhile.

"Shit shit shit!" I swore out loud. "Now, I gotta walk down there to get my car." I sure don't feel like walking to the cable company to get my car and with the way I was feeling it was going to be a very long hot walk.

I went to the kitchen to make coffee, when I noticed a note left by the sitter. You had a collect call from some guy named Mitchel. See ya, Bink. It would be a good day because Henry was still in jail. Then again, he might be out and that's what he called for. He said something about getting out soon. Left with no choice, I had to call the jail to make sure he was there. To my relief they were still holding Henry. I took a deep breath and then a long hot shower.

Coffee was ready and so was I. I felt awake now. I was glad that I got Jollee off of me and out of here last night. Happy that Henry was locked up but I was still having the hang over to deal with. I almost crawled back into the couch with my cat, but I forced myself into the daily routine of house cleaning and kids. After the initial hang over wore off, I was looking forward to the walk to get my car. It was parked in front of the cable building and naturally I would have to go in and give everybody the last word. That which would be mine.

One o'clock came. Laura was right on time. Passing Daly's made me ill, but seeing the cable building just down a couple blocks had made me take a quick change for the better. I walked faster, faster until I got in the building up the stairs to Jollee's office. He wasn't there. No one was up there but another Mike who worked there. A little guy who liked being mischievous. So Mike and I sat up in my old office talking about how wrong it was for cable to get rid of me like they did. Then Jollee made his entrance and agreed. (Like hell he meant that) I didn't want to say anything if front of Mike to Jollee, so I let it go. I had more days ahead to tell Jollee what I really thought of him.

In the meantime, Mike, who had asked me out, dropped in to pick up his messages. He missed me taking them. Boring as it was, it was a job and the money was good. Prof' eventually would have made it difficult for anybody working near and with me. Mike and Mike both agreed they had nothing to do with wanting me out. Thought it would be a fun to leave the cable building, screw any incoming phone calls and have some fun. Fun to little Mike was driving around in his beat up old "Beetle," drinking and smoking pot. I learned long ago that I couldn't mix both. So I took out a joint, Mike did, so did little Mike and off we went. Little Mike is the one who didn't ask me out.

We drove to a small bar out of the way to get started. I drank coffee. Already did the pot. We drove and talked laughing our asses off. We drove about forty-five minutes out of town where I spotted lilac bushes. "Mike," (little one), I said, "Pull into that camp ground I want to get a few of those lilacs to take home. They smell so good." "Sure Cappy, as soon as I figure out where the damn entrance is." I was cracking. Little Mike turned back to me. I said, "It just sounds so funny hearing you swear. You're so little isn't he Mike?" Mike said, "Yeah he is small. Clean cut short brown hair, to go with his size, average." We were doggin' him for fun... he knew and said, "Lay off me, so I'm average!" I tried not to laugh, but it was the pot. Yes, that's what is was, the pot. "Mikey," I said, "You're short, look like a little kid and you're older than me!" "Cappy he sounds like a little girl," Mike said. "Sorry, I don't mess around with little girls."

The three of us were really ripped when little Mike found the entrance to the campground. We ignored a sign about a five dollar parking fee. Silently we all must have figured we didn't have to pay for a handful of flowers.

We came the end of the U-drive where the lilac bush was. I got out of the car and took three small clusters of flowers. By the time I got to the car, the owner was running up to us with a shot gun. He yelled and told us to go nowhere. He already phoned for the Sheriff. Little Mike didn't take the old guy serious. But then he sent someone coming straight towards us was a back hoe. That driver looked happy to have a shot gun too. Now the old man had his face pushed in the window. He demanded that we pay 25.00 bucks for the not paying the five in the first place, plus the flowers. "It was my idea I'll pay for it." I said. I found only fifteen dollars in my wallet. I offered it, but he insisted we pay twenty five dollars. Mike said, "25.00 for flowers? You got to be kidding." The old man reached in and grabbed the car keys right out of the ignition. The three of you ain't leaving until I have twenty five bucks, no, make that fifty bucks since you don't take me serious.

I called the Sheriff." I was nervous in the back watching the guy on the back hoe revving the engine cradling the gun with a smile. Mike said, "I don't have fifty dollars in cash. How about I write you a check for it. It's a good check." "Are you nuts Mike!" said little Mike. "First he said twenty five dollars, Cap tried to give him fifteen. You have no business taking the keys from my car. Second, there is no way in hell those lilacs are worth twenty five dollars. You're nuts if you think we're gonna give you fifty! Don't write him a check Mike, this guy is crazy!" "Oh, so you think I'm crazy huh? Well just to prove you right young man, you can pay me one hundred dollars for trespassing on my property."

The old man meant it as he spit out the words watching for an official vehicle. So was I. Politely I asked the if there was a rest room I could use. He hesitated. He refused me. "Man oh man," said little Mike. 'Where she gonna go? You got the gun and the keys to my car."

The old man agreed to let me go. I got out of the car holding the lilacs and walked over to the bush. I turned back to the old man and said, "I'm really sorry I took the flowers. I'll put them back." And I did. He gave me directions to the ladies room. On the quarter mile walk to get to the ladies room, there I saw the official car on route to the campground. Great, I thought, I'm going to jail for sure! That shit headed old man. This had to be a nightmare. It couldn't be real! But indeed it was. The deputy got out and was about 100 feet from me. Shielding my eyes for the sun, I was sure I knew this person. He looked back at me with his head cocked. He took off his hat, scratched his head and called out..."Cappy? Capri Spettro? Is that you?" "Hi Steve. Yeah, it's me. How ya been? Long time no see." "Same old. Say Cappy, how's your dad and everybody these days," he asked. "We're fine. I never knew you were a cop Steve, can ya help us?" "What happened?" he asked. "Well me and my friends were out driving around, I worked with them at cable, anyway, I saw a that lilac bush and wanted a few flowers. Now he wants us to pay 100 bucks for 'em. One of the Mikes, there's two Mikes, tried to give him a check for 50. Then he made it a hundred because he's nuts Steve! Can he put us in Jail?" Steve shook his head, "Cappy, this old guy is just a mean old man who calls us all the time for little stuff like this. You won't pay him anything and nobody is taking you and your friends to jail. I'll talk to him. Makes the old guy feel better just because we did our job. He does this all the time."

Steve motioned for little Mike to bring the car around for me. The old man gave the keys back to little Mike. Mike and Mike pulled up and I introduced them to Steve. Steve asked how we were all doing. I think he suspected the pot but let it go. Little Mike said, "Do we have to pay that hundred? "No," said Steve, "I told Cappy he calls us all the time. It's fine.

The three of you can go... Oh, and Cappy, say hi to your dad for me when you see him." Little Mike said, "You know that guy?" "Yeah, he's San Marino like me. In fact Pope was engaged to Steve's mom before he married Mayor, my mom. "So did your friend say anything about the fine," Mike asked. "He said that we don't have to worry about paying anything."

The guys drove me back to my car by the ferry boats. I thought about going to up to give Jollee a piece of my mind, but changed my mind. Something eerie told me that I'd see him again. For the next few days I stayed home. Like every day, the collect call would ring from the phone in the hall by the kitchen. Within a weak week I was torn. Repeatedly reminded by Henry to visit him while he was in jail. I was between a rock and a hard place, literally. I stood in a narrow hall, lined with phones and safety glass. In that hall on the left was a wall of brick inside the old building of stone. On the right, was the wrong, where Henry belongs. I sure didn't want to be there. My head was more screwed up mentally than physically. My mind was afraid. It had reason to be. Was I cracked?

On Sunday I would drive to the jail. I would sign in. The cops checked my license They led me to the visiting area. About five or six black phones hung near the windows. I'd walk to any phone available. A jailer would call out Henry's name telling him he had a visitor. Henry came down the steel stairs looking for me through one of the windows. He picked up a phone. I picked up a phone. We talked. He did most of the talking. Talked about how pretty I looked. How nice my hair was. He'd ask about the kids. He complained about the food, the cops and the jail. According to Henry, he shouldn't be there. It made me sick inside to listen to him talk about the freedom he said he missed. I thought about that freedom. My freedom somehow had vanished as well. When I left I realized that Henry wasn't the only one in jail, so was I.

Spring was busting loose and the weather was warmer. June was closer. Instead of letting comfortable breezes blow over me in the night, I locked, latched the windows, the doors and then checking again and over and over. I watched the clock. Listened to the clicking of time and I told myself not to answer the phone. Let him think you're not at home. If all went well, there wouldn't be enough time for Henry to call. Good luck came a couple times a week, that's all. Making those nights my look-outs. Fear stricken.

The ill feeling grew because nobody called collect one particular night. Afraid he was on the prowl, I called the county jail. They knew me when I phoned, for I had done it way too long. I dialed the number, a voice answered, I said, "You got Henry locked up?" "Hi Cap. You can open your windows now." Thanks Wily. That's such a relief." "Cap, you've been accepting those calls from him, you come here to see him. He totaled your car. It just don't seem right, a nice girl like yourself here to see Henry. I remember the first couple times you came down to the jail. I walked you back to the phones. And I remember asking myself... What's wrong with this picture? You looked kinda lost Cap." "Wily, I've been going to that jail for over two months. You're right you know. About lost I mean. I just figure if I'm nice to him he, well, he'll just eventually go away." "Cap, you can still have charges pressed against him." "Oh yeah, press charges. Go to court. He gets out and beats me again. No, no I can't take any chances Wily." "He beat you Cap? You didn't report it?" "No, but one of the Sandusky cops seen what Henry did. What was his name, let me think, uhm, Oh yeah, Tripstar. He was nice, I liked him. He wanted me to press charges. I can't Wily, I know it sounds crazy, but I can't! There's no way in hell!" "Cap, it's not crazy. You're afraid. That's why you call here. You want to feel safe. You can call everyday if you want to. But what kind of a life is that for you? Tell that creep to take a hike." Wily's words hit hard. I had already thought of about telling Henry to stay out of my life. I thought about it every day. And everyday Henry would be lurking in my brain, spinning his webs of fear all around.

Court would be open Monday and Henry might go there... get out. Thank God for Friday. There was a week-end I could feel safe. I opened the windows. Walked in the front yard to feed the birds. The Finches whistled hopped, the robins remained cool while the sparrows hopped through. When the Blue jays squawked, a whole area heard. Pretty but mean and my favorite bird. Particular too. Too good for bread. So one morning I sliced up a "red" apple and tossed it instead. Eventually the four of them soared in scaring the others away. They investigated the food carefully and when they approved, all pieces were taken and I'm sure, eaten. That's what it took and I got them hooked and the four of them came everyday for three square meals.

I always liked doing simple things. Feeding the birds was one, the piano, the singing. Why did life have to get so cruel and complicated?

Sunday came. It was visiting days at the jail. If I didn't go, that wouldn't be nice, I thought. I had been wanting a nice walk, if just to feel more free. That Sunday, I preferred the afternoon.

I went, I listened to Henry and I walked home. On my way I felt the left side of my head go kinda numb. It didn't hurt, it just felt heavy. With a few more blocks to go, I heard someone from behind me calling out, "Capri, is that you? Are you okay?" I turned to see who was asking. It was Pat. A guy I knew from high school. "Hi Pat. Been a long time. How've ya been?" "Good Cappy. Just out for a bike ride." He got off the ten speed and said, "I couldn't help but notice you when I was riding. You were leaning to the left while you were walking. Are you alright? Do you want me to help you get home?" "Left huh! I didn't even notice. That's funny and my head feels numb. Maybe I need glasses. I've been bumping into walls lately too." I laughed a little and concerned Pat smiled saying, "Well, I'm going to walk with you until you get to your house. I want to be sure you get there okay." Me and Pat walked to my house. He got me there just fine. He always was a nice man, a good guy. The same one I knew back in high school hadn't changed. He was more handsome with age and I had to tell him so and I thanked him getting me to my house and off he rode.

Inside the house, constant thoughts of Gentry filled me with awe. There were bells in the air and moons scattered in the night time sky. There was a far off star that I named G.E.M. and I don't have a clue. Am I close to him? Maybe I'm not good enough for him. But why do I feel this way? He's no better than me. In the entire configuration of the universe as we know it, he's a speck of salt like everyone else, but he's special to me. His knowledge is enlightening and Gentry is very precise. What I would call a data information center. He remembers dates and number, where and when. All the things, I do like him. He'd catch me of guard with an eye wink blink. All of him was all I loved.

Thinking… Wishing… now that I could do, and I reminded myself that we were only one date. Though I wanted us so to be life loving mates. Gentry is the third of my three's. Making things whole but complex. He was harder to figure out than a 4000 piece puzzle with every piece being the same color and I've worked on some real bitches. If I had to compare him with one of those, than Mr. Gentry no-middle-name-Mocean the III was in fact…The Puzzle!"

Between looking for pieces and the calls from the jail I felt like a thousand different puzzles thrown in a box. I didn't know what to do until one night Pink came over. I was so surprised! He asked me to sing. I did and we sat together on the couch. We talked a long time, our riddles and rhymes, testing each other's imagination in flight. He handled higher altitudes and was going at the speed of sound. I was lucky if I got going at about 225 miles per hour.

We were having a good evening and the phone rang. It was after 10 p.m. It couldn't be Henry, I thought. The phones shut down at ten. I answered the phone with a calm and friendly "Hello." "Yes, this is the operator, you have a collect call from…" "John, John the piper's son." (It was Henry's voice), "I'm sorry, I think you have the wrong number." The operator said, "I'm sorry." I heard Henry saying in the back ground.."Cappy, Cappy, wait…" I said, "That's okay."

I was hoping Gentry would think nothing of it and he didn't. He only asked, "Who was that?" "I don't know, wrong number." This pleased Gentry and I went back to sit with him. The phone rang again. I didn't want to answer. I knew it was Henry. I knew if I didn't it would ring and ring and ring. I had no choice. I excused myself and said, "That's probably that wrong number again." I picked up the phone to say hello and it was another collect call from the jail. "Operator, I'm sorry, but who ever that is, he's calling the wrong number." I heard her tell Henry that the call was refused. I heard him begging for me not hang up. I hung up. Gentry stood and said with ire, "So. You still talk to him? That was him on the phone wasn't it?" "No Gentry it was a wrong number." Gentry's eyes glared. I had to tell him the truth. "Gentry. You were right. It was him. But I don't want to talk to him. He won't stop calling me." I was digging a deeper hole.

Gentry's eyes were piercing like flames as he raged out the door.

He'll never come back know, I thought. And I can't blame anyone but me. I walked through the living room and back to the kitchen, looking at the things Gentry had written above the stove. They'd be covered soon. Pope said he was ready to put the tile up anytime. I didn't want anything covering up the symbols he put there. It may be the only solid thing left that I have of him. Pencil impressions.

I rolled a doob and smoked it. Then another and another. I was pretty good and stoned, feeling better. I didn't want to think about Henry but I did when the phone rang a third time. This time I let it ring until it stopped. Then I took the phone off the hook once and for all and played piano till the buzz wore off. It was close to three in the morning before I crashed on the couch.

Who the hell would be calling now, I woke up thinking? Tiredly I woke from the couch and noted the time. It was nine in the morning. Next to my coffee mug was a note from my oldest who wrote: "Mom, I got ready by myself. Grandpa gave me a ride and I locked the door. Love, Buff." The phone must have rang 16 times or more, but I had to check the door. It was secure. Then I answered the phone. It was Henry. And like the ass I was I accepted. This call was different, this call was Henry requesting me to give his mom a ride to the court house in a week. He was certain he would be released. He gave me his mother's number and said her name was Merci. I agreed to do that because it would be making me a nice person again. He certainly wouldn't hurt me if he knew that his mother and I were going to meet. Maybe it was the alcohol like he said. Maybe he didn't mean it. Maybe Henry was being sincere. His letters were all anything a girl wanted to here... "I long for the day when I can tell you how truly sorry I am and how much I want to hold you in my arms and kiss you all night. You're so pretty. I love your face. I wish I could touch you right now." He wrote many of them. I foolishly wrote back... to be nice!

I spent the next week going to The Well to drink. If I drank I wasn't afraid. If I wasn't afraid, I could have fun. If I was extra fortunate Pinky would be there.

One night a found a little blue pill on the bar next to my stool. I showed the barmaid working there. "What cha got there Cap?" "I don't know. It has this funny little hole in it." I showed her the pill. "Cap. It's a valium. 10mgs. Take it you'll love it!" "What will it do Migs? I don't want to get all fucked up?" "Oh... in about fifteen, twenty minutes, you won't care. You'll be floating round the pool table. Go on Cap. Take it. I would." I looked at Migs and was hesitant. She looked back at me and said, "Cap, it won't fuck you up. Don't worry. It won't knock you out." "What the hell. I might as well party right?" I took the pill and played pool. By the time I got to the next game, (I had won two), I felt light. I did float over the bar for a sip of my drink and Migs said, "Well, did it kick in Cap?" "You were right Migs. I'm liking this. I get pills from my doctor, but I could sure use these. And you were absolutely right about the floating! I feel like I'm lying out in a boat on the lake and it's just a rocking nice and slow." Migs laughed and said, "See, what I'd tell ya."

Stayed till midnight. Gentry didn't come to The Well and I had to get back to the house. The way things were going, I could very well have turned into something. The kids were all sleeping when I stepped inside. The sitter walked home around the corner to her house. I secured the door and headed to the sugar bowl, that held the pot on the shadow box. Then it was piano time. I loved playing. I still wasn't all that good. I played things pretty much the same. I moved chords up and down the keys and all around. My interest was my singing. Maybe if I get good enough, I could find a job singing with a band a couple nights a week.

School would be over soon. The girls who sit for the kids will be able to stay later on the weekends. They could even stay the night. I'd be getting in about 3:00 am. Now that's what I would call a job, I thought. So I began to get serious about singing and piano. I had to get serious about a lot of things. Henry might be getting out of jail soon. A week. That's serious. He'll want to come over. He'll want to see me. Damn it. I gotta stop thinking about him now. I gotta concentrate on songs, on music, Gentry, my kids and birds. Anything or anyone except Henry Mitchel Batturs the III.

I played and sang till about 3 a.m. I would always stay up that late because the bars in town closed at 2:30 in the morning, giving Gentry time to stop over if he was going to. I'd catch myself at the door or window looking for him or the Shark. After three, three-thirty, I planted myself where I usually did, on the couch to sleep.

The following day I got a call from Henry's mother. He asked me to call her, I said that I would call her knowing I wouldn't. Life went on. Merci (Henry's mom), sounded like a sweet woman. She talked to me about what her second husband did for a living and I didn't hear a word. All I could think about was the possibility of Henry's release. Felt like I just got punched in the head again when Merci asked, "Cappy? Can you take me to court Monday? I don't drive and you could keep me company." How do I turn her down, I asked myself. Self said silently, "You can't. You have to be nice, remember?" "Okay Merci, what time?"

I showed up ten minutes early to meet Merci at 8:50 a.m. She introduced me to her husband Ken. We had a coffee, talked for a few. About my kids, hers and it was time to go. The drive was a short few minutes. I was getting real nervous about going to court. Had pills back at the house for this kind of thing, but the problem was they were at the house.

We pulled in the lot to park and I was shaking. Merci said, "Cappy, you're nervous. There's nothing to be nervous about. We'll just be sitting and that's all." "Merci, I am pretty nervous. I never been in a courtroom before. This is the first time." Merci explained what would take place while we entered the building. Henry was sitting on a bench outside the courtroom. As soon as he saw me walking in with his mom, he stood up smiling, acting like a little kid. Trying to make goofy faces. Merci said, "Look Cappy. Mitchel is always clowning around. I can tell he likes you a lot. He's looks so happy to see you." "Yeah he does Merci." I faintly smiled back at Henry. "Hi mom. Hi Cappy. I missed you. I wish I could hug you now but they got me in these cuffs. Man, I wish they wouldn't make 'em so tight. Mom, isn't she pretty? Can you believe she has three kids? She's so skinny!" Merci chuckled. Then two police officers escorted Henry into the courtroom. Her chuckling stopped. She said, "You smoke right Cappy? If you want to have a cigarette before we go in, I'll wait. You probably want one." "Merci you read my mind. I gotta have a cigarette. Sure you don't care?" (Why was I asking?) "I mean, go on in. I'll join you when I'm through." She insisted on waiting till I was through so we could go into together.

After two smokes, we went in and took a seat in the long wooden pews. Henry was smiling to me from the front of the room. We waited about 45 minutes before the judge called his name. Henry motioned for his mother to approach the bench. She looked at me and said, "Cappy, will you come with me, I'm nervous too. Especially when there's lots of people around." Taking a look about the room, with all the people like she had said, I understood that feeling well and walked up with her. Henry made it a point to stand next to me. Merci made it a point to sign the papers that would release Henry from jail. I made it a point to be nice.

Henry wanted the three to go to his mom's house for coffee and a visit. How could I say no? Merci wasn't going to take no for an answer.

I thought this would be the end of everything. Henry was going to be welcome at his mom's and step dads house but Merci said, "Well, what do the two of you kids got planned for today? You want some money Mitchel? You could buy Cappy flowers or something. Go see a movie?" "Merci, I can't. My dad is coming over to put some tile up in the house. I told him I would help. That's a long job I'm not looking forward to. He wants to finish it today. After he leaves I gotta run errands. My night is shot Merci." "Oh, that's a shame. Especially since he hasn't seen you. Well Mitchel, take the money anyway. Maybe the two of you can do something later." Henry took the money and put it in his pocket and told his mother he would pay her back. Oh yeah, like I believed that!

All I wanted was to be gone. Henry got up to walk me to the door. He hugged me real tight and gave me a big kiss on the cheek. Merci walked over to Ken and said, "Look at the love birds." I needed oxygen. I wanted lots of air. I wanted the radio blasting, the wind in my hair, but the first thing I wanted was to be out of there.

I went home and knew with my guts that Henry would call later. I knew that he would want to come over. Knew that I had to think of another reason for him not to. I had a lot of time to think of one and in time I knew I would.

♫ ♪ *"In The Future"* ♪ ♫
Words and Music by: Catherine Santi in February 1986

"In the future, by the outlook, from the out side
on the walk way near the rain.
See the sunrise, on the east side, thru the skyway
sets the west side just the same.
Do you hear me? I am speaking, from the outside,
here's the rain you will endure.
Are you listening, are you voiceless
from the inside, of the life that you explore.
The places you knew. The faces mat you named.
They haven't changed much if you were looking for a change.
And what's pleasing to the touch, is still pleasing to the eye.
It hasn't changed much in case you're wondering why.
And aren't you wondering why?
Are you wondering why?

You could always turn the world to where it used to be,
but that'll happen on its own eventually.
Things may seem a little off stage
behind the walls of lonely rage.
Moving in time, living in time, constantly it's just a way that we
survive.
Go beyond then, find the future and when you find it
well just remember where it lies.
Look both eyes now, it gets lighter from the years
you've kept yourself from there, within.
Take a chance and, open slowly, hasn't changed much
but it will from time to time..."

Chapter Sixteen: "Pictures in the Clouds"

The day dragged. I paced. I wanted to get out but I couldn't leave the kids alone with a sitter. I drank a lot of coffee that day. I took nerve pills. I paced some more. I cleaned a lot. Anything I could to make the day go and the night come without Henry. Forever without Henry.

After the kids had supper they went to the living room to watch television. I stayed at the kitchen table observing the entrances to my house. This was a good spot I thought, the table. I can see everything. So there I sat. At six o'clock I heard the bells ringing from a little church around the corner. I looked out through the living room window and saw the soon summer night shining down on the neighboring trees. Through them I could see the top of the church. A white painted cross. For a moment I thought of Frank Forrest and wondered what he was up to. Was he painting? Did he have another girlfriend? There was a time when I figured that if Frank and I got married it would have to be in that church. Why? He painted it.

Married. That would be great! To the right man this time. The one who asked my first born..."Well Buff, do you think I should marry your mom?" That's the one. But he may never asked me. Got to get Gentry Mocean out of my mind but how? I'm crazy about him. Self spoke right up. "Get a grip Capri. You blew it. He's not coming back. He knows you've been talking to Henry, or did you forget? Haven't seen him lately have you?" "You're right, I haven't seen him."

"Well, what do we concentrate on Cappy," Self asked. "John Lennon," I replied. He was the number one man I wanted to marry. Gentry is really number two, if he wants me at all. He'll never be the three that follows his name. No one can be the same. I'm the three. That's me! Why couldn't I be number 77, or 165 million. No. I was supposed to be three. Why? How the hell should I know! Too damn much has happened! Overwhelmed and distressed, I learned numbers at my kitchen table whenever humanly possible.

The bluebirds, excuse me, let's call the four, the four who frequented the same. Three times. And I knew about when. Between 8:45 am. and 9:30 a.m. The second time they came to spy was around 11:30, give or take 15 minutes. Last stop was just when the sunlight touched the tips of the trees east out my window and that was around, 5, 5:15 p.m. It wasn't the bells that told me it was six o'clock, it was the colors. It was a big game with Jules and Buff. They'd ask me the time with my back facing the clock. I'd look out that window and say, Two minutes till 6." "Mom, turn around and look!

You knew. How do you do that?" They had to know. It was a hard question to answer, so I gave them the logic. "Well, I sit here all day. After awhile of watching and listening you just know. Just like I know when the blue jays will be here. You can learn a lot just by looking."

I thought about the answer I had given my girls. "By looking," I asked myself? I didn't look at Henry. I did look at Henry. What did I miss? How come Pope saw "bum" and I didn't? Why didn't Pope elaborate on "bum" and give me a run down on the variations? Would I have listened?

The night came and I bolted the doors and locked all the windows up for the night. It was going on ten p.m. and the kids were already in bed for the night. They weren't quite used to the new out-of-school-hours yet. This was good for me because I could play the piano away. But it was bad for me too because I didn't know the where abouts of Henry. He didn't call. Maybe he will stay at his mom's tonight, I thought. Maybe he's with his buddies. Maybe I'll get lucky and he won't call. But then what if he shows up? I walked around the living room, through the back room and checked all the doors and windows again making sure they were locked. Then I called Wily down at the jail to see if by some small miracle Henry was there. Wily told me that he hadn't been picked up for anything since his release that day. Said to lock up everything and not to hesitate to call the police in the event that Henry showed.

Might show up! Yeah, Henry could just show up. Then what? If I tell him he can't come in he might break down the door and hit me again. I won't answer the door, but what if it's Gentry? Self tried to reassure me, "Cappy, you know Gentry's knock." "Yeah, but I don't remember Batturs."

Now I was ready to get high. Rolled a couple of joints and played the guard at the kitchen table for while. A long while. Kept getting up to look out the window. Five minutes later I was at the front door doing the same. I was a wreck. Back and forth to doors and windows went on and on. I knew I couldn't smoke pot while Henry was free. It was freaking me out. It intensified the fear I already had. I couldn't wait to come down. The piano came to mind. I have something to sing with, but hard as I tried to distract myself, I knew that Henry Mitchel Batturs was out there ... somewhere.

Hoping for a quiet knock at the front door, the phone rang. It was 12:30 in the morning. It was Henry. He wanted to come over and see me. He sounded like he had a little too much to drink. He was slurring. He begged, "Please Honey, I want to see you. I only had a few beers with the guys. Hey I just got out of jail, it ain't no big deal to party a little. Will you let me come over and see ya?" "Henry, I'm tired. I was just getting ready to go to sleep. It's been a long day for me. I worked on that tile with my dad all day remember? I'm sorry but ya can't come over." "Sure, I know you probably got some dude over there and you don't want me to find out. I know. A dude gets locked up for a little while and his girlfriend finds somebody else while her old man is in jail. But if you say you're tired and I can't come over to see you. That's Cool. Bye." I heard him hang up the phone hard. He was angry. I was already scared enough. How much longer would it go on? Would he call back? I hoped that he wouldn't.

An hour passed and I was English. Gentry came over. He sprawled out on the couch reminding me that I didn't need the pot. I didn't mention to him that it was a mistake to have smoked it at all. I sang for him upon his request and he talked-sang some "Pink Floyd" for me. We were in sync. I told him about the blue jays and how often they came by. He laughed as though he was the one who directed the birds my way. After the fun and the laughter, me and Gentry curled up on the couch together to sleep.

Morning came early for Mr. Mocean. I woke with him. The coffee was ready and we took our cups out to the front porch. Who shows up at 6:30 a.m.? The blue jays. I never did like getting up early in the morning, but now I did. We watched them play in the yard. One was across the street climbing around the telephone pole. Gentry blurted out. "Aaah! Fric, Frac, Mac and Jack." "Names," I questioned? "Who's the one over there who looks like he's half in the bag?" Pinky smiled. We both knew who was swinging-step-to-step on the telephone pole and Gentry wasn't going to say a word.

When the coffee mug set on the porch, (his), I knew he was going to leave. "Well, I gotta get over to the house." "Okay Jack, you get right over there." He turned to me and chuckled. I clutched a moment in my mind and watched him walk the drive and left east on the walkway. I listened for the Shark to start but I didn't hear an engine. I got up from the porch and walked to the sidewalk looking for Gentry, but by this time he was out of sight. The blue jays were still out so I watched them and thought to myself… you didn't blow it.

Back inside the house a dream came into view. One I had just before I woke up. Symbols. Colored Symbols. Which looked like this: i i i i Blue, yellow, red, green. Well what the hell was this supposed to mean. Four? Four what? The birds? Red, green… Christmas? Yellow… Afraid? A submarine? This dream was saying something and in "color"! Dreams I remembered were always in black in white. What did those dotted lines of light mean? The only thing I could see beyond the fluorescent colored lights was the color black. Four colors. Ordinary common every day colors in a line.

Odd things happened this one morning. Buff and Jules were sitting at the table eating a bowl of cereal. I began telling them about the dream, "And there were these color like lights. They were blue, red, yellow…" "Mom, I know what the next color is," Jules said. Buff took over the situation at hand and said, "Mom, don't say it. Let Jules tell you. Go on Jules, what is the fourth color?" Jules had to finish chewing a spoonful of cereal. You have to understand Jules to know what a wait me and Buff would have. Jules could munch on one bite for minutes. Finally, Buff anxiously said, "Come on Jules, just swallow already and tell mom the color." "Okay, it's green." Seeming not to faze this serious little four year old, Jules went on to eat. Buff couldn't stand it and asked me the grinning question, "Mom, was she right?" "It was green, she's right!" "How did you know that Jules," Buff asked. "I don't know. I just know it was green." Buff was going on wanting to know if there was a trick to this color thing. This was making that dream much more important to me.

Later that morning, well after the mail came, so did a woman who had been going around the neighborhood preaching. I politely told the lady that my religion was a private one and that I chose not to listen. She graciously understood. She reached into a black bag she had and handed me a bible of sorts. Telling me to keep it. She wished me a good day and left. The bible was beautiful and golden in color. Thin lined words inscribed it's title in black. It was very pretty, but I wasn't in the bible mood. I laid it on the kitchen table to look at later. Some things just had to come first!

I got on the phone and called the jail. "Hello, can you tell me if you are holding a Henry Batturs?" "No ma'am, we're not." Great I thought. He's out there somewhere. I'm sure not going to call over to Merci's house. What if he answers? Then he'll think I want to talk to him. I stared out the front window. It was such a beautiful sunny day. I watched the leaves spinning, fluttering, wanting to let the breeze that blew them inside. If only someone would drop in I could have been brave enough to do it.

Terry still stopped over in the evening after work a couple times a week. He'd have a pop and I'd have a coffee. We'd talk for a while and when Terry had to leave, he left as he came. Said good night by lifting me off the ground for a well needed bear hug. I hugged him right back. I knew that his visits were really to see if Henry was coming around. In the three months that Terry dropped in to keep me company and safe, I never told him the truth about that night. I didn't like bringing it up. Occasionally Terry tried.

A day passed. I cleaned and took care of the kids like I did every day. When the day turned to dark and about 9:30 p.m., the phone rang and it was for me. "Hi Capri. It's me Mitchel. What ya doing?" "Hi Mitchel. I'm just listening to the radio. Why," I asked. "I'm sorry," he said, "I know you don't want me around when I'm drinking. But I promise you that I haven't had one beer. I'll be over in a few. Bye honey." Before I had a chance to tell him no on the phone, it clicked off. I heard the dial tone. I got scared. Do

I let him in? I know I shouldn't. I don't want to but what if I tell him no, then what?

I checked all the locks right away. I was secure, except for glass. It's easy enough to break, I thought. My pot! Better hide the pot! Where's Gentry when I need him? I don't even have a number. I can't call him. Can't call no body. Maybe Terry will show up. "Oh forget it Cap," I told myself, "Terry don't come by till after one in the morning!" I can't call the cops because Henry didn't do anything. Why didn't I press charges? Where were my guts? Yellow. That's me.

Pacing about the kitchen floor, smoking one cigarette after another, I reached for the golden book I laid on the table earlier. I took it over to the sink under the light, looking at the vague and different symbols on the cover. I spotted something that sent chills through my head! "iiii" It was on this book! Green came to mind. Then a sudden knock on the door caused a pressure panic and I dropped the bible on the floor. I didn't want to answer the door. I moved by the fridge where Henry wouldn't be able to see me. The knocking got louder and I was sure he would wake the kids. I wanted to call the police but that meant crossing the floor to get to the phone. He'd see me. But if he thinks I'm sleeping he'll leave, I thought. My body tensed waiting for him to stop. I let out a long sigh and seconds later he was knocking on the back door.

Well that was it. I couldn't take it anymore. Didn't want him to wake up the kids. God forbid they know he's here! The girls were afraid of him already. I had to go to the door. I turned on the outside light and saw Henry standing there smiling and winking. "I told you I was coming over. Aren't you gonna let me in Capri," he asked. "I didn't have one beer. You can call my mom if you don't believe me. That's where I called you from." I didn't say anything yet. I looked. He didn't stagger. His eyes weren't red. His speech wasn't impaired. "Okay Mitchel, come in, but just for a little while, that's all. You didn't let me say a word when you called. I have to be up early. Pope's coming over to do more work and I usually help him." "That's okay. I just missed you so much Capri! You have no idea what being locked up is like. You can't even take a shit in private."

Henry agreed to coffee. He'd manage to get whatever he wanted to eat by helping himself. I didn't want him to think I wasn't being nice. Henry didn't like sitting at the kitchen table, unless it was to eat, so he asked if we could sit on the couch for awhile. I agreed. He sat at one end of the couch. I took the other. It didn't take him long before he was sitting next to me. I didn't want him there and I should've been scared, only I wasn't. He seemed sober. He wasn't loud or mean.

167

He tried telling stupid jokes. They were real stupid. So stupid they made me laughed. That's when Henry figured it was okay to start hugging and kissing me. My head battled the fear that crept inside it like a snake. If I don't go along with Henry he'll hurt me. Hit me. The war didn't last long. I gave in and with disgust I let him kiss me. He tucked a throw pillow under my head and said, "Get comfortable Capri. I just want to kiss and hug ya honey." I said nothing. Henry went over to the TV. and put a re-run on of something and turned off the lights. He came over to the couch and made room for himself laying next to me. He said, "You look so good and you kiss so good, I could kiss you all night." Henry kissed my mouth, my face, my neck while his hands were going under my top. He un-hooked my bra. I wanted to find a reason to get off the couch. I wanted Sonny to wake up and need a new diaper, the phone to ring, something, anything, but I had no advantages. Henry pulled my blouse and bra up and out of his way. I covered myself back up and said to him, "Please don't." "Come on Capri. The kids are asleep. Nobody's gonna see."

Henry rolled over and was on top of me. He pulled up on my top above my bra again. He rubbed his face and mouth over my breasts and said, "Don't that feel good. I'm gonna suck your tits." "I don't..." 'You don't what!" He said with fire. "I don't think it's right with the kids just upstairs." Henry didn't say anything. He put his lips on one of my nipples and sucked it hard. It hurt so bad and I wanted him to quit. He continued and with his fingers he squeezed and pulled the other one for a long time. For sure I'd see bruises. He was hurting me and wanting sex. It damn well had gone on long enough! I didn't say no because now I was afraid, afraid he'd beat me. When he was done I got up from the couch and went into the bathroom. I sat on the toilet pushing as much of his semen out that I could while the water was running hot in the sink. I washed fast. I didn't want Henry to get suspicious about anything. I'd take a long hot bath later. When I left the bathroom Henry asked, "Got any pot Capri?" "Wish I did. I'd like it myself," I said. "Tell me! After being locked up so long, I could go for one. Are you sure you don't have any? Even a roach will do, anything!" "Mitchel, I haven't had any pot in about two weeks. I can't afford it. I'm near broke and the month isn't even over." "Oh well, I just thought it would be nice to sit around and get high, listen to some music. I'm so bored."

The boredom went on for me. It was going almost midnight and I wanted Henry out. I pretended to doze off. I'd let my eyes slowly close, open and close until I jerked and opened them wide saying, "Oh sorry. I'm falling asleep Mitchel. And I really do have to get up early tomorrow. I got to get some sleep and I can't let the kids find you here. You're going to have to go okay?" "Sure Cap," he said, "I understand. Can I call you? Of course I can call you. You're my honey right?" I didn't answer that question. I merely said, "Mitchel, would you mind using the back door. I don't want the people living around here thinking that I'm... well, you know." "I'll use the back door all the time honey. He put a kiss on my face before he walked out the door and told me that he would see me the following night.

I locked the doors up. Checked them again. Sat at the kitchen table and guarded all I could see from my position there. I waited about fifteen minutes after Henry left and rolled a nice fat doob. Before lighting it I went around to all the doors and windows again, just in case Henry was thinking about coming back over. Then I waited another ten minutes or so before I got the joint burning. Paranoia set in at first, thinking Henry might come back, but an hour went by and he didn't. The natural thing came naturally...! I smoked another doob, took a couple nerve pills, took a hot bath, changed clothes and went straight to the piano. I thought if I sang something that Gentry would magically appear. I whispered, This one's for you." Then I played "All By Myself" because I was all by myself.

Gentry didn't show up that night. It was just night. I was alone and feeling pretty low about what happened earlier when Henry was over. I wished I would have never let him in. Why in the world would I do that? I must be nuts! He probably thinks that he can just come over anytime he wants now. What was I thinking? I thought. This has to stop and I have to figure out away to make it stop, but how? How do I do that without getting hurt again? If I reject him, tell him to go away, go to hell, go anywhere, he'll find me somewhere off guard and beat me, I know he will.

I was confused and afraid. Knew my thinking wasn't right but I didn't know what to do. I thought about everything Henry had done to me. That made me think of everything that the Professor had done to me. Wasn't that enough? How do I rid myself of Henry? I'm not even married to the son of a bitch and I can't get rid of him? This is crazy. I need help. I don't want to get punched, kicked and raped no more. I didn't know how to make him go away. Why did I let myself get into this? And how do I get out. If I made good money I could move away and not tell anyone where I live, that way Henry couldn't find me. But there was no money because I hadn't found a good job. I would remain where I was. Afraid.

Things took a change for the better, but for the worse. Professor called and said that if I wanted to make some extra money I could clean his dad's house. I liked Professor Jr's house. Prof' said he'd pay the sitter. He agreed to pay twenty an hour. Mark in Huron paid me 40 for two hours. I made sure Prof' knew that I did not want anyone there while I was cleaning. Didn't want to have someone breathing down my neck. I just wanted to clean and leave. He agreed to leave me alone, knowing damn well that I wasn't going to take him back under any conditions. Prof' didn't like "not-having-me" but far worse was he knew he would never have me again.

I couldn't wait to get over to the McCartney Road house. It was so beautiful inside. I went in the house, room to room, pretending that it was mine. I liked to see the mirrors shine and chrome sparkling. Took coffee breaks while I cleaned. Listened to music. There was no one watching my every move. I thought Prof' would try to come see me while I was there, but he stuck to the agreement and stayed out of sight. Outta sight turned into a favor that Prof' would ask, which was to throw in another day a week, only he didn't want to pay another forty dollars. We both agreed that 60 dollars would do.

One afternoon, I was finishing in the kitchen. Unloaded the dish washer and put everything away. I polished up the this and the that's on the counter making sure I placed them right where I found them. Hmm, I thought, I can't do this at my house 'cause I can't find the thing that goes where it should, because I can't remember what it is in the first place. I stood at the kitchen window and looked at the view. Off in the south distance a lonely two lane highway. Much land lay all around the back yard I was looking at. Further off in the east were tall slender trees. The sky was almost Montana. The blue had depth and the clouds were white and puffy drifting west across it. I stood watching out the window and wondering about where I went wrong. How did I go from a wanna-be-rock-and-roll-kinda-person, (center stage), to this? Why me? Why didn't I listen to Pope? Why didn't I turn around and go the other way. Yeah Pope, I should have rolled the ring down the aisle. I should have taken the dress back, I should have just gone back to "C" street and stayed there. But no, not me. You saw the things I wished I could have seen.

I was finishing the last of the coffee left in my mug and noted a white van going south on the road. It was the only vehicle I'd seen in the whole twenty minutes I spent looking outside. Just as I was about to wash the cup I saw a peculiar shaped cloud. I dead stared at what I saw. It was a face. A large white face. I fixed my eyes on this face I knew I had this face seen before. He was with a mustache, beard and longer hair. His eyes gently looking north. So I looked. I began trembling inside. A perimeter of energy shook all around the outside of me taking over.

A cylinder, tall cloud, mighty, was slow, turning like a record. This solid mass used the sky's back ground to clearly place a letter that came one by one. It spelled out the word LISTEN. I looked back over for the face and he was still looking on, so I did the same. Directly next to my silent spinning cloud were two more. They too were letters, G M. Then a number. 2. Again I looked at this face and thought there must be something else I am suppose to see as he still looked north. It was taking all my strength to look at it anymore. I felt tears fill my eyes, not knowing whether or not I should be afraid or thrilled. I looked once again at the clouds. The last was a picture. Clearly it was a man and a woman standing at the bottom of a stair case that went up indefinitely. Her dressed in a gown and the man in a suit. I only saw their back sides as they faced the stairs ahead.

The face was now gone. I wept and held on to my each and every step with my hands to the counter for support. Took a seat at the breakfast nook. I could barely light a cigarette because I was shaking so. Just then Professor came in. He caught me in a situation that I didn't want to explain and I knew he would ask questions and he did. "Cap, what's wrong? What happened, are you okay," he asked. "Yes. Yeah, I'm fine really. I just can't light this fucking cigarette!" "What's wrong Cap? You don't look good, I don't mean you don't look good but something has you real upset." "Professor, I don't know about upset. I don't know. Never mind. You'd never believe me anyway. I'll just go. Where's my money." "Cap, smoke your cigarette and calm down. Might help you feel better if you talk about it." "With you? You'll laugh and make jokes." "I promise Cappy, I won't." "Prof', I could say, but you won't believe me." Professor said, Try me." I described in every detail what I had seen in the sky. The word, the letters, the number, the people, the stairs and the face. It brought more tears to talk about it. Prof said, "Man! Ya must have really smoked some good pot. I don't see anything out there but a few clouds." He was laughing. "Fuck you. I should have known better. Forget it! I know what I saw. I just want to go." Professor knew that he had made a grave mistake in not believing me.

I took the last of the pay I would get for cleaning the house. I wasn't going to go there again. Took off and went directly to Neil Street. I didn't knock. I knew with the music blasting on the inside that Gentry would never hear me so I walked in with a tremble. Gentry was up in the kitchen with pencil and plans in action. I stopped in front of him and said nothing, only looked at him at work. Gentry knew I was there before I came through the door, but when he looked at me he stopped everything. His pencil was neatly tucked between his head and ear. The music was turned down. Happy to see me and he said, "What's up?" I didn't waste time getting to the point. Looked him in the eye and said, "I saw someone today." He asked, "Who?" "He's somebody important." I didn't have a long wait for another question. "Did he talk to you?" "Yes, he said listen." "Listen," he asked. Gentry grew serious and we both knew this man was an important one. He exclaimed, "That's big time!" "Yes. Big," I said. Thought quickly to the time when Gentry said that God put him here for me but that he didn't want to be here for me. Was it God in the sky? The face of Jesus I saw? That's the Face. It could only be Him. I knew that Gentry believed what I said to be true. He was thinking God too.

I would have stayed longer to see and talk to Pink, but I was wordless. This big thing that just happened overwhelmed me with curiosity and caution in search of understanding it. Understanding was the something that I had to figure out myself. And I thought Gentry was puzzling. I left Pink's and headed for the house. People would think me crazy if I told them, so I told no one else.

Things at home were the same. I took care of my kids, I cleaned my house and I sat at the table whenever I could.

I pictured the scene in the sky over and over in my head. What the hell does the number 2 mean? Who is the man? Who is the woman? Listen to them? Listen to who? Listen to G M? Would it be Gentry Mocean? No that's too easy. You know I've had a pretty tough life for some time so why change it now? Great Mystery? Great Magic? Good Man? Okay God. You put a good man in my life. He's wonderful and everything to me, and he claims he's supposed to be here for me. So now what? Speak English do You?

I went on and on into the early night trying to put it all together and have it make sense, but it didn't. I wanted to see Gentry to talk to him. I got to thinking that maybe I was supposed to work this "big-time" thing out with him. The only thing that stopped me was I had no sitter and no number to reach him. Didn't want to call The Well looking for him because Pink was personal. It was going on ten and I heard a knock on the back door. I knew it was Henry. Gentry always came to the front. I went to the door and answered it. I held on to the storm door while it was open and said hi. Henry walked in like he lived there.

Thinking quickly... always thinking, I thought...! I cannot be mean to him! I have to be nice! So, not only did Henry have his foot in the door, he had himself in the kitchen helping himself. First thing after that, a cigarette and the question, "Capri, don't you know anybody who would give ya just one joint? It gets so boring. No money. You can't go out and do anything if you don't have money. Sitting around watching TV gets old." I gave him the answer he got just the night before. "No."

Henry was content watching TV. and munching on something he cooked up earlier for himself. He seemed happy. He acted silly. He'd say something so stupid it was funny and I hated myself for laughing. Then he asked me to play something on the piano. "Ladies and gentleman, tonight, appearing live just for you, is Capri Spettro. She's going to play the piano and sing. There's a little tin cup on set up there if ya want to leave change." Fortunately, I had smoked half a doob before Henry showed up. Was about a half hour into the buzz and I didn't mind playing at all. In fact I wanted to.

Sometime after I shorted out the Zenith trying to get the turn table working... again! I picked up a cheap cassette player, radio, through a company that allowed monthly payments. Anyway, Henry had it and was talking into the microphone hosting his show. I ignored him as much as I could and just played and sang anything that I knew, until the buzz wore off which was about fifteen minutes later. That smoke was a tease. I preferred to double-doob myself, but with Henry there I couldn't. I stashed some pot in one of the "Maxwell House" cans on the counter. He wouldn't find it. There were about fifteen now. Pyramid stacked.

After the recording session was over, Henry said, "Cap we gotta listen to this, I'll rewind it. It sure would be better if I just had a beer. A quart. They sell quart bottles around the corner at the gas station. Wouldn't even cost a dollar." "You know I count every penny Mitchel. But I could go for something myself. Here's some change, go on and get one, but I'm splitting it with you." "Cap, I'll just drink one glass, you can have the rest." Henry thanked me for the money and was back in no time with 40 ounces of cheap beer. I made sure that I drank more than the share I mentioned to him earlier. I'd say I drank 25 ounces to his 15. I liked the beer. Not the taste, but because it kicked in fast. Gulping helped I'm sure. Most important, I wasn't afraid of Henry. It was a good thing until the beer buzz was gone and I was afraid again. I asked Henry to go and he had no objections. As he went out the back door he told me he would be over again. I said good bye. That's all I said. Didn't have the guts to tell him to stay away.

I locked up everything after he left. And like the night before I waited to smoke any pot. I made fresh coffee. Went into the bathroom to look at myself in the mirror. It was like seeing me for the first time and I didn't like her. With disgust, I turned away, turned off the light and sat at the table watching and waiting. It was about a quarter to two. It was safe. Had two cups of coffee and it was "time" for the pot. I rolled it up. As I lit up the first one, I thought more about the pictures in the clouds. The meaning if there was one. Maybe it was a message. I remember when Mayor had cancer she'd stop a conversation with me to say, "Wait, quiet, there's a message coming in, don't say anything." She asked me once if I believed she saw Jesus seven times. I told her that I did. And even more now than then, yes! I believed.

The clouds that formed were better than great. There are no words to describe how they made me feel. The clouds were with meaning. But what it all meant was beyond me and beyond that. Much as I tried, God never complied. I'd ask for a dream, or a sign, something to tell me what was going on. Then I thought about the little lighted dotted lines I'd seen. Could they have anything to do with it? It was getting ridiculous. I had no clue, no clue at all. Damn those clouds on a sky blue wall.

♫ ♪ *"Instrumental Man"* ♪ ♫
Words and Music by Catherine Santi on February 2nd, 1986

"There he is, he will take away what love you give to him today.
It'll break you up inside.
There he is. Never look him in the eye, my friend,
you won't mean a thing to-him and it will break you up inside.
The way he'll make you feel. Up and you're his queen,
Down he'll tear you from the highest thrown.
The things he says in jest are different from the rest,
will wear you down and leave you all alone.
Don't you believe the words he gives to you, oh no!
'Cause he just can't be true
and it'll break you up inside.
There he is, an instrumental man, just sits his time,
better get him off your mind or
it'll break you up inside."

Chapter Seventeen: "Figuring on Nightmares"

You hear about people losing their minds all the time and I wondered why I hadn't lost mine yet. I held a dark secret and his name was Henry Batturs III. It was March when I let that creep in the house. It's almost summer! Three months and he's still around. I'd say it was a pretty sick situation if I was in someone else's shoes, but I was in mine. I had no job and the prospects were looking hopeless. I wanted out and I had no way. Why won't Gentry help me out of it? He said he was working for God. My mind wondered off in endless directions. Blue jays, clouds, numbers, Batturs, battles, Beatles and the life I had. There's a lesson to be learned, but until this ugly thing called Batturs goes away, the lesson continues until the teacher says, "Class dismissed."

The fear was constant. I waited for my God given employee to make it all better. That might be Pink. Then again, the answers may be in the clouds. The clouds! I couldn't get them, Pink or Henry out of my head. What was wrong with me? I should go to the cops. It's not too late. I could get officer Tripstar to speak on my behalf. Prof' would back me up. Buff would. She knew. I sensed both my girls knew what happened the night one week before Easter. Had it affected Sonny? I wondered what Prof' thought. Does he know Henry is still coming around? Does he watch? Did he care? Hell, I must be crazy to think he ever cared! He was no better than Henry. As for Gentry, I knew very little about what he might be thinking or feeling. Maybe it doesn't matter to him. Doesn't he know how I feel? He must know, unless he doesn't want to know.

Times were tough. Prof' only paid support once and that was the first month after the divorce. My kids needed summer clothes. Nina helped me and all my kids got to have lots of nice hand-me-downs. Many months were the same. When the middle of the third week came, I was broke. Pope, thank God, was already helping me too much and he kept on helping. Hey, he was my dad!

Life wasn't just a bitch, it was having a litter! Wanting to be the wife of Mr. Mocean III. Dream on, I'd tell myself. Face it Cap, your luck is Irish. Look at yourself. Do you feel good about anything unless Henry is locked or in your sights? If he don't call or show you call the jail. You wait and hope there will be a next time for you and Pink. "Yeah. That's what I think."

Nina and I became phone freaks. I needed that. I wasn't gonna flip out, I knew. I was tough and I could take it. I went into war when I married the wrong guy. Fell for Frank and he left. Won a dream when the right man was at my door.

It was about 9:30 in the evening when I go a collect call. It was Henry. He told me after he left my house to go to his moms, the cops saw him. Stopped him, smelled alcohol on his breath. He was charged with public intoxication. A feeling of relief was set in my head, because Henry said he'd be in jail for a couple weeks.

Of course collect calls came each night and I accepted, but after them I went straight to The Well to find Pink. Where did I get the money to go out drinking for two weeks? I pawned my wedding band since it never meant anything to me. Got twenty five bucks for it. The alcohol it paid for made me feel better.

One night I no more got one foot in The Well, when a younger girl about 19, was up and in my face totally shit faced. "Looking for Gentry? Oh. You poor thing. Gentry, Gentry pudding pie, kissed the girls and made them cry. You gonna cry over him because you love him soooo much? You're so stupid girl. He's fucked up!" Being ten years her elder and sober, I let her drunken words pass through me like a soul. But I really wanted to slap the hell out of the bitch!

True, I was looking for Pink, but it was only ten. He'd be in later. I needed quicker liquor so I drank beer. When I was ready to order another one, there were shots lined up on the bar in my spot. They went down in a gulp, got me fired up and I was having a blast.

Sitting next to me was Hank. I had met him at The Well months ago. Hank was around 45. A guy who was full of laughs. We talked and laughed until the conversation went hay wire and I told him about Henry. I didn't mention anything to him about being raped and beaten. I told him about Henry wrecking my car and the two cop cruisers. "Hank he calls all the time when he's in jail. He calls collect and he thinks I'm his girlfriend. He won't leave me alone and it's been over three months. He still calls and when he's not in jail he comes over." Hank showed much concern, but before he could get a word out to console me I heard a stern, familiar voice saying, "You're still seeing him. He still calls you?" It was Gentry. God what was I thinking? I should have never said anything to anyone about Henry. "Gentry please. I want to explain to you." Only Pink didn't have anything to say. I stood up tall, face to face to him. Looked through his dark fiery eyes. He looked back at mine. He didn't like who he saw, I knew! Knew that it was time to go back to the house. I apologized to Hank for letting the talk hang in the middle, grabbed my things from the bar and left. It was an easy drive home so long as I kept my head out the window and one eye closed.

When I got through the door I wanted to kick myself in the teeth for what Gentry over heard. Bink was still up. She was welcome to spend the night in my room. Preferably, she went home.

I called Nina to make sure she got home safe. Nina asked, "Cap. You alright. How come you didn't stay out longer? Wasn't Gentry there?" "Yeah Nina he was there, but he overheard me tell Hank that Henry was still coming over." "Henry Batturs," she asked. "Why are you letting him over? Wasn't wrecking your car enough?" "Nina he beat me one night. He raped me. He fucked me up real bad. I never told anybody because I was afraid. I didn't want to press charges either because what if he went free, he'd get pissed off, come back, hurt me again and maybe worse." "Cappy, does your father know?" "Nina, I don't want him to know. The first thing he said, when he saw Henry was, get rid of him. He's a bum." "Cap, you gotta just quit talking to this creep. Don't let him in your house. What about your kids? He might hurt them!" "Nina I know he'd never hurt the kids, I just know. He has a son and I see the way he treats Sonny. He loves Sonny!" Nina, now agitated said, "Capri! That kind of person can't love anyone. You need to have him out of your life for good!" She was right. I knew that, but the fear got the best of me. All of me.

What was I going to do? What's wrong with me? I went to the kitchen table and cried all over it. I thought about Gentry. How he looked at me. What if I had lost him for good? Buff was so sure that a marriage would take place. Sure that Pinky (Panky), would be her dad. This and the alcohol only had me crying more. Had to get this buzz off and took a cool shower around midnight. By 2:30 a.m. I was back to straight and normal. Took a seat at the kitchen table, turned, stared at the coffee cans and said, "Now that? That's Crazy!"

When the clock struck three and Gentry had not made an appearance, I went to the living room to couch-sleep but I couldn't, so I headed back into the kitchen and made myself a couple of fried eggs, toast and a cold cup of coffee. After I ate, I was out.

Figuring on nightmares I woke remembering a dream and Gentry was in it. He pulls into the drive, driving the Shark. He knocks on the door. I let him in. He walks over to the couch, lays on it, looks up at the ceiling. I ask if he reads the letters I sent. He proclaims that he knows all the words by heart. Then I woke up. The day would twist and turn surprise me!

Sometime shortly after the church bells rang there was a knock at the door and Gentry was standing there. Yes I let him! He walked over to the couch and laid down. Looked up at the ceiling. I walked over and sat by him. I wanted to tell him about the dream but he insisted he could tell me the dream word for word. And then he did! "How did you know?" I asked. "It's my job to know," he said with a chuckle. "Your job to know? What's your job?" Gentry's face lit up a big smile, "It's a secret. A big secret! Why don't you sing something for me Big Time." I went from Cock-a-roach to Big Time and I sang!

Unfortunately the good times with Gentry didn't last long and he had to leave. I didn't want him to go, but I didn't tell him so. I watched him walk, getting into the Shark, not long before the sky would fall dark.

Depressed, I went to the piano and tried to make up a song for him. For Pink. But I thought and thought and I just couldn't think. The music was running around in my brain, but the words wouldn't come and it started to rain. Naturally I thought about Gentry again. He came back after he knew Henry was still calling. That was my second chance. I'm on my third now. That fucking three was shoving itself into my face long enough. I had to get this right. I knew what I had to do. I was supposed to be tough. Orion may have left the night time sky, but he was fixed permanently on my right arm, in moles. I came out of some pretty bad times, I thought. I can be The Warrior! I won't accept the calls from Batturs anymore. Searching my heart for strength, I paid for the collect calls that came.

The talks were always the same and about him. The cops had it in for him. The cops like to trump things up. He was bored. He missed me. He wished that he could have his freedom. I was in a very unfamiliar territory and in my own house! I wasn't feeling freedom either. Henry abruptly changed the subject and said, "I hear them talking ya know." What was that," I asked. "Voices," he said. "Voices? What? Do they talk to you," I asked. "They say kill, kill! Ha ha ha. Nah. I'm kidding. Ya get so bored. About an hour ago some dude they brought in last night got some wine. His old lady snuck it in the place. That shit goes on all the time. So I got some from him. Gotta little buzz but I wouldn't mind smokin' some weed. You're probably smokin' a joint now." "No I'm not. I told you I didn't have any." "Cap you don't have to lie to me. I don't care if you're smokin' some. I just wish I could be there with you."

Henry wouldn't stop talking. I wanted another cell mate to need the phone, but the talking went on. "You probably got some other dude over there too. You know. I was seeing this chick, I forget her name. I came home when she wasn't expecting me and I caught her with some other dude and they were fuckin'! So I pulled both of them outta bed by the hair and dragged them downstairs. Once I had both of them on the front porch I bashed their heads in the cement a few times. It still makes me laugh because this dude was bigger than me ya know." I didn't say anything. I got the picture. If he ever found me and Gentry together he'd kill us! I couldn't let anything happen to Pink! I was more than relieved when it was time for the phones to shut down. It was Saturday. The jail gave the cell mates more time, but I didn't know until I checked my clock. 11:00 p.m.

I reached for the nearest roach, lit up, paced the kitchen talking to God out loud. "Hey You! This situation is bad! I prayed for Mayor's cure. You didn't wanna help. That's the way I see things from down here. Where were You when Prof' was pointing a gun to my head? You gotta help me keep Henry away. I can't handle this. It's tearing me up inside. I'm drinking, popping pills, smoking pot! Nothing gets rid of this "thing" in jail! You can hear me. I know You can. Why don't You come down to Earth and talk to me One on one? Do You need me to say it. Okay. I will. I'm scared. I'm scared for myself, my children and Gentry. I love Gentry God. I want him to live and be happy. But You decides who gets leukemia don't cha? We could make an exchange. If You won't help me with Henry, then give me Gentry's leukemia. Give me the cancer. My life's been hell anyway. Please God, if there is a God make Gentry well."

I took my reasons and excuses, my anger, guilt and fear to the piano. I stared at it. I smoked a few cigarettes and played nothing. I went back into the kitchen and got out the information on leukemia I had read and read them over. I re-read the letter the nurse sent. This got me to thinking about the proposal I laid before God. It would be near perfect, I thought. I have rare blood. It would be pretty tough finding a donor for a bone marrow transplant.

Doubts of Gentry ever returning were set. Till there he was on the floor playing with my kids. My three having a ball with Pinky. The feeling I had was good and so warm. Wasn't long before the kids were pooped and wanted to get to bed. I got Sonny ready and the girls took care of themselves. Gentry waited downstairs while I got them tucked in.

The cancer thing was on my brain all the time and after the two of us had been downstairs for a while talking, I brought up the wrong subject. "Gentry. I did cry that time when you asked me if I was. Remember? Well, I wrote a hospital and they sent me these." I handed him the brochures, like a vacation he wasn't on, he exploded with rage throwing all the papers to the floor. His face grew purple with spit in his words. "I don't want this shit in my face!" "But Gentry, I thought maybe I could go to Cleveland with you when you go there." Self and I fought the approaching tears. He yelled again, "I don't want anybody there! My parents don't know, do you think I want you there?" The fury in Gentry raced him out of the house.

Dismayed, I found myself sitting on the living room floor. I looked at the papers laying everywhere. Why can't he accept that I want to be there for him? Why did he blow up on me like that? God, doesn't he know that I love him? Never mind. I think I can answer that question myself.

The next day came and I was wishing it didn't when the phone woke me up at 9 a.m. Henry called collect. I wasn't ready for coffee let alone him.

I'd go to the jail and visit him. Yes it was crazy. But I think I had to see it to believe it. Or I had to let him think that I was being nice so he wouldn't hurt me anymore. And on one of those visits there was someone I had gone to school with. His name was Allen Leed. He was there to see one of his friends. We were in the cold hall way where the phones and safety glass were. I said hi to him and he said hi to me. It wasn't a big deal.

When visiting time was up Allen and I walked out of the building together. We were both parked by the library and stood on the side walk. We talked about the days we went to the Catholic school together and what we were doing now. I was just being Cap and asked Allen if he wanted to stop over for a cup of coffee. What else? Allen said he'd follow me there. We got to my house and we went into the living room. Allen didn't want coffee. He wanted me to go into business with him. And my job would be selling pot. "Shit Allen. I can't sell pot! Don't get me wrong," I said, "I love smoking it and I get it for myself, but I couldn't be a dealer. I got three kids to think about." "Cappy I forgot about the kids. I'm sorry. Here let me give ya some." He opened a black brief case, bag upon bag full of marijuana was in it. Reaching inside, he took out about an ounce. I offered to pay Allen for it. Couldn't take it for nothing, it wouldn't be Italian. He refused money. I insisted I pay. He refused. I gave up. Let him refuse for the last time and took the pot. That was that. Allen had deliveries to make. He saw himself out.

Later in the evening Henry called collect. He said that when they were taking him back up to range 5, and as he passed a window he saw me talking to Allen. "So who was that dude you were talking to. I saw you out the window. He was standing kinda close. I got eyes Capri." Trouble was brewing. "Mitchel, I went to grade school with him. I haven't seen him in close to twenty years. Jesus Christ! It's not a big deal!" "What's his name?" he asked. I told him. Then more questions. "Did he go to your house? Did he fuck ya? He probably did. Yeah. I'm stuck here in jail and..." I stopped him there and said, "Mitchel! Nothing happened when he came over to my house. And yes he was here. He is just a friend." "Yeah right. Just a friend. He'll be back at your house now any time he feels like because you let him come over. He'll be back and he'll be fuckin' ya more because he saw me locked up. Didn't you tell him I was your boyfriend?" I had to think fast. I had to be smart. "Henry, if you don't stop talking like that I'm hanging up." He wouldn't quit. I hung up. Within seconds it rang and rang so much it was driving me nuts. I answered. When the operator went into her speech, I just hung up again. But it rang and rang some more. I didn't pick it up. I let the bitch ring till either the operator had had it, or Henry did. After that

I took the phone off the hook and stuck it in the phone book drawer in the kitchen.

Mentally and physically I was exhausted. Stress was in full attack, so I took a couple nerve pills to help me sleep fast.

Ring, ring, ring, ring! And who knows how many more times the phone rang that morning till it finally woke me up. We all know who it was and yes, I accepted. Henry told me that he was sorry for the accusations he made the previous night about me and Allen. He said that he trusted me. Had better news to tell me. He fired his attorney, claiming the lawyer was an asshole. This would keep him in jail longer. Keep me safe longer. And free.

Evening came and his call was different. Henry's. I didn't hear about the boredom, or the lack of freedom, the missing me, the cops, or anything like that. All I heard, for one month, every night, was the same thing he said he was sorry for. He was sure in his mind that Allen and I were sleeping together. Nothing I said convinced him that I was telling the truth.

But good times were coming this June, like Buffs seventh birthday and a party. It went so well, Buff said it was all her and her friends talked about the next day. There was one thing lacking. She asked me a question that caught me off guard. "Mom, how come Pinky didn't come over for my birthday?" She was heart broken. I didn't know how to answer. Her big bright blue eyes were close to tear territory. "Buff, I'm sure he didn't forget your birthday. You know how smart Pinky is about stuff like this. He's probably working on the house. But remember? You're the one who always knows when he's coming over." Buff smiled but her eyes held doubt. I changed the subject and we looked at the gifts her friends gave her.

It was later in the early evening when dusty, trusty Gentry showed up for Buffs birthday. She ran to the door and said, "Pinky! I thought you forgot it was my birthday." She took his hand and led him to the kitchen table "Mom, Pinky's here. He has to have some of my birthday cake and ice cream too. Come on Pinky!" she said. "Sit down." I said hello to Gentry and he said hello to me. Well one of us had to say something so I did, "Gentry. Let me get you some cake." He looked at Buff and said, "I don't know. What do you think? You know your mom might be trying to poison me." Then he laughed. Buff looked up to him, tugged his sweatshirt and said, "Why would she want to do that Pinky. She loves you!" "Oh she does, does she?" I looked at the both of them and said, "Oh now wait a minute Buff, I never said that and you know it." The little rat told on me. "She talks about you all the time." "Oh she does? What else does she say?" "She says here's a piece of cake. You want some coffee? Or do you think I poisoned that too?" "He turned to Buff again and said, Tell ya what Buff Bag. If I'm going to have a piece of cake then your mom is going to have one, okay mom?" "You eat cake and I'll get the ice cream." I sat at the table at watched him. He really waited for me to take the first bite. But he smiled. Buff was getting the ice cream and everyone was happy. Pinky being there meant everything to her. It meant everything to me.

Gentry stayed till he finished the one cup of coffee he had. And most of the cake. He told Buff that he had to get back to work. She sat back in his lap and gave him a hug saying, "Pinky I'm glad you came over today. I wish you would come over more." " Well I got a lot of work at the house and sometimes there isn't enough time Buff." "That's okay Pinky. I know you won't forget me." The three of us went to the door to see Pink off and memories came. I was wishing I could be a kid all over again. Not seven, but 14. Playing the twelve string singing and dreaming. My dreams had turned into just that, dreams. I still wanted them to come true. I knew "John Lennon" was out of the question. I had my chance when I was working back at the shoe store. Prof' was in Phoenix and I was in Sandusky. I could have driven up to New York City if just for an address. I could have written him. He might have answered. Maybe not. Probably not. No maybe he would have flown in to see me. Maybe that was him on the ferry boat. The look alike. Twenty-one years had passed and the feelings for John were the same. Quietly I whispered, "I love you John."

In the "mean-time" I had been keeping track of the days the Gentry wasn't coming over. July was buzzing by as quickly as the bees flew, as quickly as the kids grew and so grew my concerns. Priorities! What a mess everything had really turned into. How did my life get to be this way? Did I let it happen? Was I stupid? Yeah, that I was. That I am.

On a visit at the jail I met Henry's older brother. He was just leaving and as we passed he said, "Hi, you must be Capri. I'm Henry's brother Tim." I said a shy hello to Tim. "Capri, I'm not my brother. If you knew me you'd like me. By the way Cap, do you have a stick of gum?" "No. Sorry Tim I don't." "Well could I just have the money?" he asked, laughing."You're nuts Tim. Nice meetin' ya."

I was walking to the phones when Tim said, "I'll be outside chain smoking until you're done in there. We can go grab a cup of coffee." What an idiot, I thought as I walked to pick up the phone to talk to Henry, to listen to Henry. After fifteen minutes I just wanted to leave. I knew I didn't belong at a jail going to see the very man who fucked up my head and my life. When I got outside Tim was sitting in his car with his feet hanging out the window smoking a cigarette. "So Capri, wanna go get that cup of coffee?" Tim, I can't. I gotta go, I have three kids there. I'm sorry, but thanks for the offer." "Well Capri, maybe you would like to ask me over for a cup. Do you have any? Coffee that is?" "Tim, are you kidding? That's the one thing I never run out of." "Capri, I just smoked my last cigarette. Do you have one on ya? If you don't I'll just take the money. It's okay." "Here Tim, you can have one of mine. In fact, if you wanna stop over sometime for a cup of coffee, oh well, what the hell. Follow me over to my house, if you don't mind kids and I'll make us some."

Tim and I drove to the house and I made the "Maxwell House." Tim said that he liked my house and the kids. He told me that he worked for "Ford." That he recently divorced with a couple of kids himself.

Tim wasn't the normal kinda of funny, but I liked him. He was nothing like Henry. He asked permission to come by again for coffee. He vowed that he wanted nothing more than friendship and I believed him

One week later on a Sunday afternoon, Tim popped in. We sat at the table. He asked for a stick of gum that I didn't have and politely asked for the money. We drank coffee and he told me about his brother in jail. "Henry needs help Cappy. Can I call you Cappy," he asked. "Sure Tim, why not." "See when we were growing up my dad used to drink and fight with my mom all the time. He'd talk to her and say the worst things, hit her and everything. Henry was only about three or four I think. The rest of us were in school. That's what Henry saw all the time. Did Henry ever mention our brother Ricky? Our youngest brother Ricky was in a car wreck that killed him when he was 18. I think Henry blamed himself, and after Ricky died all Henry did was drink and party." I paid close attention to Tim's words about his brother. Jotted down notes in my head. There was more notes to take as Tim went on to tell me more. "Cappy. Henry will take anything and everything. I don't care if it's speed, downers, alcohol and pot. If it's there he'll take and drink it all. I told him that he needs to see a doctor but he doesn't think anything is wrong with him. He's crazy Cappy! He told me that he totaled your car." "Yeah." I sighed. "It's in the junk yard." "Cappy it's your car. Why didn't you press charges? I would have and he's my brother!"

I went blank. I didn't want to answer that question. I thought that Tim knew what his brother was all about and he was trying to find out why I was down at the jail in the first place. I kept silent. Tim said, "Well will you look at the time. I wasted all this time talking about my brother and now I gotta get to work or I'll be late. Thanks for the coffee Cappy. Oh, by the way, do you want the money?" Tim. No I don't want the money. I would have been drinking it anyway." "Here Cappy. Here's my number. If you ever get bored and want somebody to talk to. Now I'm not a night owl, so whatever you do, don't call me after two, okay? See ya Cappy." I said good bye to Tim and thanked him for the phone number. After he left I noticed that it was an out of town number. It was long distance and my phone bill was high enough. I tossed the number in the trash.

The rest of the night was smooth and quiet. It usually was. The girls liked playing in their room while Sonny tried getting in it. But by 9 p.m. he was ready for sleep. The girls went to sleep when they were ready. I had the whole evening to do whatever I wanted. It was a good night. Henry was locked up and I could open the window. The sounds I had missed I could listen to again. The crickets, the planes the owls and the trains.

Once the girls were sleeping I did what I always did. I smoked pot. I took out the recorder and plugged in the cheap headphone, (ear plug), and listened to the conversation that Henry had taped of himself when he pretended to be a DJ. I listened to it over and over. At least 10 times. What wasn't I hearing? What didn't I see, I thought? It made me sick not knowing the answers, so I put the recorder up in the cupboard hoping that I would forget about it and Henry.

By now the pot buzz was well worn and so was my head. I sat on the couch and rubbed my tired closed eyes. I tried to relax. I had to come up with solutions and figure out problems. I sat, leaned over with my eyes still closed, cupping the back of my head in my hands and thought. In the blackness, I saw a clear, floating purple cloud emerge from the dark. I watched it closely moving my eyes around, trying to see how much purple was hiding in the black. All I could see was purple. I moved my eyes to the right and in the purple cloud that seem to sway slowly I saw a clock. The time was 1:13. Down to the left was what appeared to be a headline from a newspaper. It said: Local 19. I watched it for about ten seconds and the purple cloud was gone. I opened my eyes. They hurt and I felt drained. This happened before. When I was married to Prof' and someone died I had seen a purple cloud, a number and a man. A man who I knew and who died three months after I saw the number nine. Could this mean death too, I asked myself?

Time passed and I was still counting the days wondering when and if Pink would come back. I'd put a check mark on the calendar to keep track. It had been 15 days and the days were like moving my piano from one side of the room to the other. I tried to convince myself that I would never see him again so that my life might get *a* little easier.

One day, being in a brave mood I took a drive over to Neil Street to ask Gentry something. Luckily for me he was standing out in front of the house near the street. I got out of the car and asked, "So. Do you wanna get married?" "Can't," he said," Not now. Lots of family things going on. It wouldn't be the right time." I liked his answer..."Not now." This might mean that I stood a chance after all.

This was incentive. This was exciting. I anticipated that I would be his wife after all. Happily ever after.

On a Friday, Tim stopped over and wanted to know if I'd like to go shoot some pool. "Come on Cappy. You need to get out and have some fun. Have a few laughs. And I'll even pay!" "Tim, it might be fun and it's great that you wanna pay, but what if your brother Henry finds out?" Tim said, "Look Cappy. My brother is in jail and you're not going together. If we want to go out for a few laughs and fun it's none of his business." "You're right Tim. It isn't any of his business. But let's do this pool thing later because your brother calls me every night. It would have to be after 11:00 because that's when they shut the phones down at the jail." "Tell ya what Cap. How about if I call you at ten-thirty, and, if the line's busy, I'll figure you're talking to Henry. If you answer then I can figure that you already talked to him and you can get the heck out of the house for a while. And I'm paying." "Okay Tim. You talked me into it. Hopefully Henry will call early.

After Tim left I thought about who else… Gentry. Thinking of him was endless and always. I thought of how serious his face was when he said "not now." I wondered what family crisis might be going on. Were one of his parents ill? Did they find out Gentry had cancer? What? Who? Where, and the rest of the questions came. Self and I didn't have answers. We remained very concerned and curious.

Later that night I was deciding on what to wear. Didn't want to wear something that would make me stand out, so red was out of the question. Grabbed a tee shirt and threw on a pair of jeans and polished leather sneakers.

In the mean time I waited for the call to come from the jail. The phone rang at ten-thirty p.m. My heart murmured when I answered it. "Hello?" "Hi, did my brother call yet?" "Oh Tim. I thought for sure you were Henry. No he didn't call." "How about I come and pick you up in about fifteen minutes. Just don't answer the phone. Sound good Cappy," he asked. "Yeah Tim. It sounds good to me. I'll see you in about fifteen minutes."

Tim was on time and the phone never did ring. Guess Henry didn't get to use the phone. I was glad that another inmate was tying up the line.

Tim took me to a small hick bar he talked about. Kind of a country western rock kinda bar. There weren't a lot of people there and the juke box was at a level where you could comfortably hear a person talking. Going out with somebody besides myself was just what I needed. I shot a mean game of pool. Tim tried but just couldn't keep up with me. We stayed at the bar for about an hour or so, had a few beers and headed back to my house. Tim pulls out a joint and says, "Hey Cappy. You smoke pot? I brought some with me, but I didn't know if you liked it. Want some? It's free?" I laughed and said, Tim. Pot and coffee are my middle name. Let me roll one for us." Tim said no. "Let smoke mine. It's free remember? Go ahead Cappy, do the honors and light her up!" I did and we smoked that one.

Then I took my pot out of the sugar bowl and rolled us another joint. We smoked about half of that when loud knocking was hitting the front door. It wasn't Gentry that was certain. It had to be Henry. But how? He's in jail, I thought. Tim asked, "Who could that be?" "I don't know Tim. Henry's in jail." Tim was going to answer the door but I stopped him. "Don't. Don't answer it. What if it's your brother?" "Cappy calm down. You just saw Henry at the jail Sunday. Who could it be then?" "There's only one other person who would come over about this time. Frank Forrest's friend, Terry. You know him." "Yeah, I know him," Tim said, "You don't think it's him?" "No Tim. He doesn't knock that loud. Wait. Hold on. Don't make a sound. There's a slab of cement in the drive that's loose. When anybody walks over it I can hear like a ba boom sound. If it's Henry we'll hear it." He's the only one who uses the back door."

Tim was quiet. He put his ear to the wall in the living room that was next to the drive. "I heard it Cappy. That's my brother out there isn't it?" "Yes it's Henry Tim and I'm scared." "That's him pounding on the back door like that? What the hell is his problem," Tim asked. He answered his own questions and said, "He must be drunk or high. Just call the cops on him Cappy. If he finds out that I'm in here with you he'll kill us both." "Tim I'm too scared to go to the phone. He'll see me go to the phone. He told me all about shadows! I can't call the cops. I'm too scared." "Damn. He's at the front Cappy and I'm calling the cops." Tim went to the phone and I followed close behind. I sat in the dark bathroom while Tim called the police. I listened to him and everything else going on. I was shaking. Tim had them on the line and said, "Yeah, this is Tim Batturs. My brother's over here at Cappy Spettro's house. He's pounding on the front and back door. Cappy, your address 709 right?" I whispered, "Polk Street." "Could ya hurry. He's got Cappy pretty scared." There was a long time that Tim stayed on the phone and wasn't talking. I didn't ask. Maybe they put him on hold.

Time moved like a lingering illness and Tim hung up the phone. He came in the bathroom and said, "Capri. The police said they were going to create some kind of diversion. Try to throw my brother off." "How are they gonna do that," I asked. Tim said, "They wouldn't tell me." "Tim, I don't wanna talk anymore. I don't hear Henry knocking. Maybe he's listening at the window. Please don't say anything." Tim nodded. Minutes passed. Life times could have passed. What was taking the police so long?

"Tim, a cop knows that your brother beat and raped me, I told them. "Cappy! Why didn't you tell me," he asked. "I didn't think you'd believe me. He's your brother Tim." "Cappy, I told you that he needs help. I meant that." Just then there were sirens and lights flashing everywhere. Tim went to the kitchen window and pulled the curtain to a side and said, "Come here Cap. There must six cop cars out side. There's cops all over the place." I felt safe so I went to the window to look. Like cats prowling for prey, cops were crawling for a criminal. There had to be 12 or more of them put there with flashlights and night sticks. It looked like a movie. Only it wasn't a movie. It was just another poorly planned out part of my life that only God could have produced.

Within seconds there were as many as eight, nine cops on my porch. Me and Tim opened the door. Some came in, some didn't. "What's going on, I asked. "I'm Sergeant Shoor, Miss Spettro. Still having problems with Henry?" "Yes." There were many nights when the cops would be at my house because Henry was knocking drunk and late. Officer Shoor told us about their plan. "Cappy. We brought a lot of police officers here tonight in hopes that Henry can't keep track of us. All of these officers in your house will get back in the cruisers while they leave me here. After they drive away, we're hoping that Henry will come back. You know sometimes these guys like Henry have a sixth sense when it comes to the police. We'll give this thing a try. I'll just stand back here by this wall next to the door so he won't see me. If he comes back and we think he will, we'll have him arrested." Thanks Mr. Shoor. I wish I could afford to keep one of you guys here around the clock. Henry gives me the creeps."

The plan went into effect and the other cops left the house. I watched them go out the door and locked it up behind me. Tim peered through the window watching too.

Shoor stayed in the house for twenty minutes. Henry didn't come back. Officer Shoor told me and Tim that he'd radio his partner to come pick him up. "Capri," he said, "It doesn't look like he's going to bother you any more tonight. Maybe when he saw all the policemen outside he got scared and ran off. However if he comes back don't hesitate to call. We'll be over right away. In the mean time keep things locked up. I'll keep an eye on the area and if we see Henry we'll pick him up and arrest him. Try not to worry." "That's easy for you to say. All I'll do is worry. Can't you guys call me if you see him? If you arrest him," I asked. " Yes Capri. We can do that for you. Tim, maybe you can stay and keep her company for a little while until she calms down." "Sure. I can do that. I'm embarrassed to say that he's my brother because he needs help ya know." Officer Shoor nodded, and his partner was in the drive waiting for him.

They left. I locked up and was scared all over again when Tim told me that Henry had tried killing him. "Did Henry really try to kill you?" "Cappy he is crazy! One night he came to the apartment and he was running through the place slashing the couch, the lamp shade and then was trying to get me. I don't think I ever ran so fast. I lived closed to the hospital and got the security there to call the cops. He would have killed me Cappy, I know." "So what happened," I asked shaking? "Oh the cops went over to my place but Henry was already gone." "You go back into your apartment Tim?" "Are you kidding? I went back after the cops drove over to the hospital and told me they arrested him for public intoxication on Adams Street." After the terrifying story the front door was getting pounded on again. It was Henry and Tim got on the phone with the cops immediately. They got to my house in less than 4 minutes, but Henry was gone. Again. And again Sergeant Shoor told me that if they found him they would call me.

The night (early morning), had made me a complete wreck. But at last relief came with a phone call. It was Sergeant Shoor. "Capri. We found Henry hiding in some bushes about five blocks from your house. Just wanted you to know that you can sleep tonight. We got Henry locked down at the county jail." "Thank you! You don't know how much better I feel. Thanks for calling. I'll tell his brother. Good night sir."

Tim and I figured we had enough for one night. He thanked me for the good time we did have earlier and I thanked him. I showed Tim to the door. Locked it up good and tight after he left. Then I got out the sugar bowl and it hit me. Remember? I liked numbers? Well, most of them. It was 1:13 in the morning. It was the 19th. That's what the purple cloud was telling me!

♩ ♪ *"Blows The Dream Away"* ♪ ♩
Words and Music by: Catherine Santi in March 1986

"I sit around all day long I think you know what I mean.
I'll say this but it comes out that, and you're so mean it blows the dream
away.
There isn't ever a day I know, when the thought of you don't bring me
down.
Say it's absurd but I'm telling you this,
I know you love me, now how does it sound to...
... you. You know you feel like I do.
And though I wasn't always true
believe me it has always been just you.
Can't you try and understand I don't want your helping hand?
And you know I must be right,
don't you think of us at night, at times you might, I am, so don't go...
... lying anymore. And I'll be waiting by the door
that's been open like before, always for you.

Next time you come, you're gonna stay.
That's what my heart will always say
If this is it, your big game, then I'm insane, because…
… you, make me feel the way I do.
So I'm holding on to you, it's my heart, it's yours, I give it to you.
You know that somewhere down the road,
when you're feeling tired and cold,
there's a place that you can be,
that place is me."

Chapter Eighteen: "Here a Cloud, There a Cloud, Everywhere a Cloud Cloud"

For a moment I went back four years to Glacier National Park. Christmas in July would be here soon. I walked in the kitchen checking the calendar. The 25th was six days away. Six days away. It was the 19th of July. Time goes by ever so slow when you are not having a good time! White clouds, purple clouds, faces and death in the clouds. "Here a cloud, there a cloud, everywhere a cloud cloud. Oh poor Cappy sees the clouds, e-I-e-I-o! Then I took all my frustrations out on the piano after which I slept couch-style.

I woke up to the sound of bells, ringing bells. It was the phone. It was Henry. I accepted. Had to know if he knew about Tim being at my house. I didn't bring it up but Henry did. He wanted to know if Tim had called me or anything. I lied and told him no. I couldn't imagine anything more happening to me and I didn't want to see Tim get hurt too. Henry didn't believe me and accused me of having sex with Tim. He was still sure I had sex with Allen Leed. How could I make him believe me? Would he ever quit? It was time up for Henry Mitchel. He'd go to court to enter a plea. I stayed home where I wanted to be. I knew that he would be calling me later.

Pleasantly taking my mind off of everything were the four blue jays who came on schedule. They squawked away until I realized, oh no, my cat was out there. I took my coffee outside and watched Grizzly running under my car with a blue jay chasing behind. Grizz's black coat was shaking but the bird stood up to Grizzly giving him holy hell.

It went on for two cigarettes. I called Grizzly but he wouldn't budge. The blue jay wasn't affected by my presence and kept at my cat. It was intermission. More coffee and cigarettes. Before I finished the third cigarette, the bird said its piece and flew through a maple tree. Grizzly ran out from under the car and curled in my lap. "Man Grizz, what'd you do, try and eat one of em? Mean things aren't they!" I was laughing and thinking how funny it was to see a cat afraid of a bird. I took Grizzly McDonald into the house and gave him some fresh water and food. I opened up the front window and listened. I heard a whole bunch of blue jays squawking and I literally thought they were having a field day talking about my cat. And that went on for over two hours!

Each day I called the jail making sure Henry was locked up just in case he was calling from a pay phone outside somewhere. Before long Christmas in July came. I took out my shoe box full of pictures. I wanted to look at

Montana again. Wishing I could be there singing again for the party at the lodge. (Without Prof'). I missed it so much. It was a perfect place to have lived, and I wanted to live there for good.

A few days had passed when Tim stopped by to see how things were going. He pleaded with me to keep Henry away. I knew Tim was right and all my rights were wrong. More like gone. I knew that I was terrified of his brother. It would end. It would have to be.

Yes the calls came collect and yes... I accepted and visited Henry. Whenever possible I was at the The Well drinking. Maybe I'd see Gentry and if I didn't I could at least drink myself into a confident brave soul. Some nights I'd get loud but playful. Benny, the owner would yell out, "Hey Cappy. What will it take to make you quiet down? See the parrot over there. That crazy bird! I have to throw a blanket over him to shut his mouth. You want one Cappy?" "Sure Benny! Just make sure Gentry is under it with me. Ah ha ha ha!" Just then, who else but Gentry came sure footed through the door, taking a seat at the end of the bar alone.

He said nothing as he passed me by. I watched his every step. Watched him order a beer. Watched him drink the beer looking ahead beyond the mirror in thought. I was unable to get his attention by staring. I didn't want to look foolish going over to him so I grabbed a couple quarters to play the juke box. I wanted to find just the right song with just the right words so he'd know I played it for him. Maybe then he would acknowledge me in some way. There it was. The perfect song! Believe it or not it wasn't The Beatles, but "The Who." The song was, "I Can't Explain." Picked out a few more songs and went to finish my drink. There were other tunes playing before mine and I figured it would catch Gentry off guard when it came on.

So, I sat and it just came on. I tried not to pay any attention to Gentry, but I had excellent peripheral vision and with that I watched the reflection of his face in the mirror. I could see by a small-smirking-smile that he knew I played it for him. I felt self conscience, especially since I made it pretty clear to Benny that I was crazy about Gentry. I finished my drink and went back to the house.

I smoked pot. Played piano. Hoped Gentry would come over. Gentry was a no show. So I smoked more pot and played more piano. I sang and sang till the usual time. About three-thirty. Giving Pink the benefit of the doubt. It was no use. He wouldn't be coming over tonight. I marked another day off the calendar.

July was not quite over and Henry was released. I let him in the back door like I had been doing as long as he showed up at ten and absolutely not a minute later. I closed all the curtains just in case. I didn't want him to be seen there. Henry assured me that he jumped the fence in the back yard.

Yeah, it was sick, I know that now, but you couldn't have told me that 14 years ago. This of course would go on until Henry would get locked up. On nights that Henry tried coming over after ten I'd call the police. When they arrived they'd ask what the problem was, and again I'd tell them. I explained to them the rules I gave Henry. A cop shook his head at me once and said, "Cappy, if Henry has been drinking and you're afraid of him, then why do you let him in at all?" I couldn't answer him and said nothing.

About a week went by and everything was feeling sane except that Henry showed up at the back door one minute passed ten. I hesitated. I never let him in after ten. He reached down for a plastic bag with something inside and said, "Look, I forgot all about this stuff 'cause I was in jail on Easter. My mom made these up for your kids and wanted me to bring them over, that's why I'm late." He opened the bag to show the Easter baskets Merci had made and I let him in.

He was half way up the stairs calling out to the kids to wake up. "Hey you guys, it's me, the Easter Bunny, I got a surprise for you. I got some Easter baskets here." "Mitchel just let them sleep, they're tired." "Welp, there's Chrissy!" Henry said all smiles. "Come on down Chrissy, you can have it. My mom made it for you," She asked me if it was okay and I told her it was. She took the Easter basket to her room. Jules didn't budge from the door of her room. Henry tried to call her down to get it and when he finally realized that she wasn't coming for it he said, "That's okay Julie, I'll just leave yours and Sonny's on the step."

"Mitchel, Jules is real shy about people. She doesn't really know you at all. She'll pick it up in the morning I'm sure."

I sat on the couch facing the western wall in the living room. On the end. Henry came down the stairs and sat on the other. He seemed distracted about something so I said, "What's bothering you Mitchel, were you drinking?" "Man so what if I had a couple beers. You act like it's a fucking crime to drink. But you can go to the bar and drink and it's not okay for me to have a couple beers?" Henry's voice was a louder than normal but he didn't appear drunk. He slowly, little by little, inched his way next to me on the couch. "I'm sorry honey, I didn't mean to get mad. I try to do something nice, well my mom did, and then it gets fucked up. The kids acted like they didn't want the baskets." "Henry, I told you the kids are shy when they don't know somebody." "I told you I don't like to be called Henry." "Sorry, I don't what made me say that. I won't do it again." "You're just did you stupid bitch. Mother fucking stupid bitch." Henry pulled me off the couch and slammed me into the wall. I fell on the couch pleading, "Mitchel, I said I'm sorry, please don't hurt me!" I was trying to get off the couch when Henry pulled on my head pushing it into the hard arm of the sofa. My chin was pressed against my chest. He sat on top of me and began punching my chest, slapping my face. Then he held me down by my hair

From where I was, I could see the stairs and Sonny's feet coming down them. I said, nothing. Henry didn't see him and I was afraid he would throw Sonny back into his room. My insides felt like a hangover. Henry got louder, "You know something you fucking whore, you would take any dick in your pussy wouldn't you! I bet you even let my brother fuck ya while I was in jail. Allen fucked ya every day. You liked it too didn't you bitch! Bitches are all the same so long as you get a dick in ya. Bet you fuck niggers too don't cha ya whore? Where do you think you're going bitch?" Trying to get up I said, "Please Mitchell Sonny is right here. Please stop! You're scaring him!" Sonny stood between the coffee table and the couch in a diaper and tee shirt. He wasn't even 16 months old. He looked at Henry, then he looked at me. Henry said, "Hi there Sonny. Want to see what happens to whores? Your mother is whore," and he laughed. "Mitchel please! He's just a baby!" Henry had my pants pulled down and he was forcing himself in me. "Sonny..." Henry wouldn't let me finish saying what I wanted to say. I turned my head into the back of the couch when I saw his fist coming at me. It numbed my head. Like a storm over he said, "Sonny you go back to bed. Good night!"

Henry got off of me and I tried pulling my pants up so I could get to the phone. I got as far as my underwear when he saw me and said, "I ain't through with you yet. He punched me in the chest again and tore off my under wear. "You like this don't cha whore. You want me to fuck ya till it hurts don't ya bitch." While Henry raped me again he yelled, "This doesn't hurt you yet does it. I bet you had so many dicks in that cunt of yours you can't even count 'em" I felt sick and nauseous. I kept pleading for him to stop. He got up and demanded to know where the pot was. I told him. When he was getting it I took my under wear and tucked them into the couch. I was going to have him charged with rape once and for all. This would be evidence I told myself. Henry came back with a smile, holding up the bag of pot like he got a reward. He pulled me up by the hair and said, "Well, don't just sit there honey, roll us a joint."

Shaking nervously, I got up to switch a lamp on. Henry jerked me back down and yelled, "Where the fuck ya goin' bitch? I said roll us a joint." "Mitchel I need more light. I was just going to turn on another light so I could see." "I'm sorry hon, let me turn it on for you." Henry reached over me to switch on the light. I pulled out a couple buds peeling away the stems and picking out the seeds. I wasn't fast enough. "God damn bitch! By the time you roll it up I could have smoked it." He slapped me off the couch and finished rolling the joint. I got up slowly and sat back on the couch. I was afraid to move or say anything. Henry smoked the joint by himself. He walked around in the kitchen where the phone was. I thought he was going to cut the wire. I heard some cupboards opening and slamming shut. There was a long pause of silence after he opened one of them. Good God, I'll bet he found Pope's whiskey. I didn't dare look. Didn't want to get up and have him think that I was spying on him.

Henry walked into the bathroom. I could hear him sliding the medicine doors back and forth. My pills, I thought. Shit, I left them right on the sink. I heard the water in the sink running. I kept thinking that not only did he drink the whiskey, he was in there downing the nerve pills. After he shut the water off I heard him urinating. By this time I had to use the bathroom, but I held it in like I did with everything else. When I heard the toilet flush it would be only seconds and Henry would be back in the living room.

"You know something bitch, I got a knife in my boot, Ha ha. You don't believe me do you? Here let me show ya." He leaned and put his fingers in the boot slow. He's going to kill me, I told myself! Fast pictures flashed in my head. My kids, my family, Gentry, Montana, Cedar Point. Henry was pulling something out of his boot. I closed my eyes trying to swallow the lump in my throat. Henry started laughing and said, "You thought it was a knife didn't ya? It's just a comb." And he laughed even harder when he combed his hair in front of the mirror. I figured if I went along with him and laughed he would be nice to me, so I laughed without heart. Henry jerked around and said, "What the fuck you laughing at bitch? Maybe I got a knife. Maybe it's in the other boot. See how fucking stupid you are." He came over to me and pulled me by the feet throwing down to the floor. I heard my back crack when I hit. He said, 'You're not being nice to me Capri!" "Mitchel I'm trying. What do you want me to do? I don't want to fight like this. We're supposed to get along." I put my hands to the floor to push myself up to my feet, but Henry slapped me down to the floor again. I held myself tightly closed using all the muscle I had, but Henry raped me again and again. It felt like the skin inside of my vagina was tearing. It burned so bad. I was trying not to cry from the pain, but the drops ran down the sides of my face hitting cold on my ears. When Henry was finished he said, "Get up honey. Why don't you roll us another joint. I don't think I have a buzz anymore. That pot you got ain't all that great. We get better pot in jail." I was thinking that I would only get beat on some more if I didn't roll it fast enough.

Henry came and sat next to me. I asked, "Can I take a hit off it?" "Well sure honey, it's your pot right?" Henry handed me the joint but I didn't take a hit. I knew I would only be more afraid if I got high so I handed it back to him and said, "You know, on second thought, you go ahead and smoke it. I'm not really in the mood." "How come you just asked for a hit and now you're changing your mind? What are you hiding? Is somebody coming over here? Don't forget, I might have a knife bitch." "No, I didn't forget." "Then you're hidin' somethin' . What the fuck is it whore?" "Mitchel, why would I hide anything? I don't have anything to hide." "You don't?" "No. I swear Mitchel. I really need to use the bathroom, do you mind?" "Sure! If you gotta go ya gotta go." I stood up and Henry pulled me down to the couch. "Mitchel, I have to pee, I can't hold it in much longer. Can I go please?"

Henry was reaching in between the cushions of the couch looking and feeling around. He reached inside my pockets. He found the underwear. "You are one dumb bitch. You were gonna take these to the cops? Well, come on, I'll show you where they're going now." My shirt ripped off when he yanked me off the couch. He threw me to the floor again. He laughed and said, "Oh, I'm sorry, let me help you up." He reached down to me and grabbed my left nipple pulling me across the floor and into the bathroom where he pushed the back of my head into the tub. He put my underwear in the toilet and flushed them. "You think you're smart. I'll show you smart." "Mitchel, I wasn't going to take them to the police, I was going to sew them, you know, fix em." "You are one stupid whore. I've been in jail. I heard so many lies. Bitches like to lie." And he wasn't through yet...

"Come here in the kitchen I wanna show you something. What's the matter, can't you get up on your own?" I got up and followed Henry into the kitchen. He stood in the corner in front of all the coffee cans and said, "Who drinks the whiskey around here? Your other boyfriend?" "The whiskey in the cupboard is my dad's." "Oh come on, you can do better than that. You expect me to think that that's your dads stuff?" "Mitchel, it is! I don't have a boyfriend." "Oh so now I'm nothing. A nobody? Who gave your kids Easter baskets? Who calls you every day? Who comes here every night? I do!"

Henry pushed me. I lost my balance and fell to the kitchen floor. When I got up he was standing in front of me. "Mitchel, I have to use the bathroom!" "Sure go ahead Cap." I took a step in a second he put his leg out and tripped me. "Just remember, I'll be right outside this door. Don't go closing it either." I walked in and sat down on the toilet. When I was going I felt my insides burned even more. I finished and I was hoping that Henry was too. When I walked out of the bathroom Henry pushed me in the living room. He punched me in the chest and shoulders till I hit the floor again. He raped me there three more times. The nicer I was trying to be the meaner he got. I prayed in silence that it would stop. In my mind it would never end. I saw it getting light out. It was then I realized that this had been going on for hours.

I knew the time because I heard Buffs alarm going off. It was Sunday and she and her sister liked getting up early to go to Sunday school at the church around the corner. It was set for six a.m. God please! You gotta help me! The girls are getting up. I don't want them to see Henry here. What should I do? I had to think of something fast. They'd be coming down the stairs in about fifteen minutes. I asked Henry if I could make some coffee. I told him how tired I was. He gave me permission. I made the coffee.

Henry became very polite, lighting my cigarettes and pouring my coffee. I figured I could get up and go see how the girls were doing, since they hadn't come down the stairs yet. I had a plan. I got halfway up the stairs when I heard Henry on the landing behind me, "You don't need to go up there. I hear can hear 'em talkin'. They're fine. Get your ass back down here!" Buff was standing at the top of the stairs and saw Henry pulled me back down the steps. I hoped that she had see me pointing to the balcony upstairs. Praying that she'd know to exit, climb down and go for help. But Henry had me out of view. So much for a plan.

He pushed me in the direction of the kitchen. I went there. He threw a few more punches into the back of my head and demanded! "Get on your knees and suck my dick. Come on honey, it'll make you feel better." "Mitchel I don't want to! I'm not going to! Just leave me alone! Pope will be here any minute to give the kids a ride. Please, just leave me alone!" He grabbed me and slapped me across the face then he forced me to the floor. He unzipped his pants and grabbed the back of my head forcing his penis in my mouth. I tried pushing away but the harder I tried, the harder he pressed my head where "he" wanted it. As fast as it happened he shoved me away with a push from one of his steel toe work boots and said with callous, "Guess I'm not horny anymore." I went over to the kitchen table.

It was a about a quarter after seven. I pretended to be sick, real sick. I thought that if I could have made myself vomit without Henry seeing me, I would have. Anything to make him stop and go. I put my head face first onto the table, holding on to my stomach with one hand. Henry looked over and asked, "What's wrong, are you alright?" "Mitchel I'm sick. Don't think I can get up. Feel so sick I can't even move." "Do you want me to take you over to the emergency room, I'll walk over there with you?" "No, no, my dad will be here at seven thirty. He'll drive me." Capri! I'll take you there." "Thanks, I appreciate it, but I don't think I can get up. I feel dizzy, like I'm going to throw up." "Capri if you want you can call the police, I don't blame you."

Henry reached for the phone and was going to hand it to me. "No Henry, I don't want to. I feel too bad to do anything." I was protecting myself! "You sure you don't want me to take you Cap? Otherwise I might as well get going." A rush of relief went through my entire body. I said, "It's okay, you can go, my dad will help me." I watched him as he headed for the door and he said, "I'll lock it up for you. You wouldn't want just anybody coming in here." I should have been able to believe my ears, but I couldn't.

Buff came down the stairs when she felt the coast was clear. "Mom are you okay? We could hear Henry mom. What did he do to you? Aren't you gonna call the police? I know you wanted me for something when you were coming up to my room. What was it mom? "Buff, it was nothing that would do any good now. Forget it. I'm fine. Why don't you just think about eating something before you go." "Mom I don't want to go today. Jules said she doesn't want to go either. I'll stay here and help you with Sonny." "Thanks Buff but you don't have to. I want you to have fun. You have fun there right?" "Yeah we do, but we just don't feel like it. Jules said she didn't sleep too good. She said she was having nightmares." Nightmares I thought? I wanted to hide away somewhere forever. They deserved better than this. Shit Cap, did it ever occur to you that the kids were scared to go around the corner? "Buff why don't you go back to bed if you're tired. I'm gonna get more sleep while Sonny's sleeping." She did go back upstairs to sleep and I shivered on the couch for a couple of hours.

Me sleep? I couldn't. I hurt everywhere, so I went back into the bathroom. I looked at my back in the mirror. There were rug burns on my spine, bruises on my shoulders. Who knew what my head looked like. Then I looked at my chest. I saw the beginning of bruises there too. I closed the bathroom door to use the toilet. This time when I wiped I noticed drops of blood on the toilet paper. He had torn the skin inside me. Feeling dizzy, I sat on the floor with my head hanging over the toilet and threw up. I remained in the bathroom a long time. I wanted to wash Henry off of me and I knew that a shower wouldn't do it. I'd need a hot bath to clean my insides. It burned like fire. When I was done, I rinsed in a cool shower, wrapped my hair and body in towels and noticed the nerve pill bottle was empty. I checked the cupboard for the whiskey and it was gone too. Henry would take anything and drink everything because he did.

The girls were up in their room. I didn't know if they were really asleep or not. I figured they were quietly talking between themselves. Sonny was still asleep. I knew how tired I was and after the long hot bath I thought I could sleep. There was no way I could relax enough.

I thought about Henry. How could I not? I knew I should have called the police the minute he walked out the door. Even though he was out there somewhere and the doors were locked up tight, I didn't have the courage to call the cops or anyone else. So I drank more coffee and sat at the table wondering how I would ever get myself away from him. It seemed impossible. Unless I call the police, press charges and then what? My only hope was that he would be arrested for something and just be in jail.

The day went by slow like all my days had been going. Time was taking its time and there was too much of it on my hands. I missed having a job. I liked getting a pay check once a week instead of the "nothing" check I got once a month that kept me and the kids living below poverty level.

I was still counting days. Nearly forty days had passed and Pink still hadn't been by. Had to embed it in my head: He Is Never Coming Here Again! My soul felt like it was slipping out and far, while my heart was sinking. This only made me want to get out more and I did, to The Well. Maybe, just maybe I would see Gentry. There were lots of people to talk to and I floated a lot. One night I was sitting in the corner of the bar, to hide? I'm not sure. When who walks over to join me but Winnebago. And you thought it would be Gentry? No way. He was definitely gone. We ordered up shots, beers and sat by the nearest available pool table because we wanted to. Winnebago put our quarters up on the table for a game. She was ready for some serious pod. I had way too many things on my mind and couldn't concentrate on pool at all.

Winnebago knew me well enough to know that something was bothering me and before long the question came, "Cap. You seeing Gentry?" "I haven't seen him in a while. He's been working on a house here in town. He works a lot over there. He said he wants to get it finished." I knew there would be more questions after the answer I gave. "I don't know why he works so much. When was the last time you seen him? You two getting serious?" "Winnebago, I don't know. It's been over a month. As for serious, he never said that he wanted me to be his girlfriend. Winnebago, it's your game." "No. You shoot first Spet" Not really wanting to, I did. Since I wasn't in the mood, I was hoping I'd lose, but to get there I had to win a few first. Losing never felt better. She knew better than anyone, and suggested we get the two corner chairs at the bar before somebody else did. And we got them. Migs came over with a drink that someone bought for me from the other end of the bar. Quickly I turned to see if who it was. It wasn't Gentry, but a friend I knew from way back. I nodded thanks and Phil nodded back.

Times were just like the good old days and things couldn't have been better. As my bad luck would have it, Gentry didn't show up, but someone else did. It was Henry. I faced the liquor behind the bar. Didn't want Henry to see me sitting there. Thought about the mirror ahead of me and hoped he would not see a reflection. I wondered where Henry got any money to go out at all! Then I thought about his mom. She probably gave him a few dollars. If she knew what he was really like, she would turn on him, shouldn't she?

The fun was not going to last, and I wanted to get the hell out of the bar before I was spotted. Just as I turned, sure enough Henry was right there. "Capri, so this is where you are. You told me you came out here so I thought

I would drop in and see you." I had a pretty nice buzz going. He wouldn't hurt me here, I thought, would he? Winnebago not knowing about Henry asked, "Who the hell is that, Cappy? You know him?" I didn't talk, he did. "Hi. I'm Mitchel. What's your name?" "Mitchell, this is Winnebago. We went to high school together. We're best friends." "Yeah we are," Winnebago said, "but she never mentioned you." I shook for Winnebago wondering if Henry would be mad because she didn't call him Mitchel. Henry looked at me upset and acting quite surprised he said, "You mean you never told your best friend about you and me? Capri's my girl, aren't you Capri?" Henry put his arm around my shoulder laughing. I couldn't tell if Henry was drinking or not. With a crowded bar I felt less afraid. I turned to Henry who was standing behind me to the side and said, "Mitchel if you don't mind I don't like people hanging on me in public it doesn't look right." "Hey fuck you bitch. Are you trying to piss me off? You're mine," he said with anger. His eyes grew meaner as his forehead wrinkled between his brows. "Capri! This guy is a real creep. How do you know him? You aren't going with him are you," she asked. I didn't want Henry to hear me say otherwise, so I nodded her a no. She was still in disbelief. Then Henry got nastier, "You know something Capri, if you're a whore then I'll bet your mother is too." I wanted to cry. Winnebago always had more courage than me. She stood straight up and said with pressure, "Her mother is dead! You better quit bothering me and Spet. Get lost!" Fuck you too. If you're hanging out with Cap, then you're a whore too. Don't you bitches all hang out together?

Winnebago looked at me and said, "Don't worry Cap, I'm gonna get the owner over here and tell him what's going on, have this creep thrown out." My head couldn't have hung much lower than it was. I was ashamed and didn't know what to do. I was afraid to walk out and get to my car. Afraid that Henry would only follow me outside and beat me up in the parking lot. Winnebago was having a hard time tracking down the owner and Henry wasn't going away. She turned in her seat looking around the bar.

Winnebago knew the bikers standing around in a pack. They looked like a mean bunch and I needed to drink. When I turned for my beer Henry already downed it. Migs noticed that I was on empty and came over to see if I wanted another one. I told her that I wasn't sure about having anymore and when she saw Henry she said, "What are you doing here Mitchel?" Henry said something to her but I didn't pay attention. Just then a big-bodied-biker came over to me and Winnebago. He looked at Henry and said, "I hope you're not bothering my girls here." He put one of his arms around Winnebago's waist and the other around mine. He lifted us up off the bar stools and our feet ceased to touch the floor. He glared are Henry, "Can't let anything happen to these nice ladies. They're good gals. You better go away and leave 'em alone. By go away, I mean leave the bar. Now!" Henry was scared. He looked at the biker and said, "It's alright man. I wasn't bothering 'em. I was just leaving anyway." Henry gave me a dirty look and left. The biker put us back on our seats. He said hi to Winnebago and she thanked him for his help. "Winnebago, aren't you going to introduce me?" "Sorry, Spet this is Perl. Perl, Capri Spettro. We were in school together." "Nice to meet cha. How do ya know a punk like that? He's bad news. If he ever gives you any trouble out here and you see me, just holler. I'll take care of him for you." "Thanks Perl. I'm glad he's gone. Can I buy you a beer?" "No, but I'll tell you what! Why don't I buy you and Winnebago a drink." Perl called out to Benny. Benny filled the orders. After we got our drinks, Perl made a toast and excused himself to join the bikers he came in with.

Winnebago cheered me up and I learned something. Just because a biker like Perl looks mean and growly, doesn't mean his heart's the same. Last call was called and Winnebago insisted on following me home before I was going to insist that she do just that. She waited till I got inside. I called out the front door, "I'm okay Winnebago. Wish you didn't have to get back to Michigan in the morning. "Me too Spet. Hey, I'll call ya tomorrow when I get back." "Looking forward to it. Tell Dan I said hi." Horns blew and she was gone.

The minute I locked things up I called the jail to see if the cops might have arrested Henry. Wily, the jailer was surprised I was calling. "You're still calling to see if Henry's here, Cappy? Sorry, but as much as I'd like to say he's here, he isn't. Guess you'll have to keep things locked up tonight." I thanked him and hung up the phone. Checked and rechecked all the locks on all the windows and doors upstairs and downstairs. Went to the kitchen, took a butcher knife out of the drawer and held on to it.

Henry left the bar pissed. He'd been drinking and I was too afraid that he'd try to break in. I had to be ready. I sat curled up on the end of the couch with one arm on the arm of it holding the knife tight. Smoked one cigarette after another until I was too tired to smoke. Took the ashtray to the kitchen and placed it in the kitchen sink. Turned off the coffee. Went back to the living room and took the same position on the couch. Each and every sound came in close. Occasionally I'd hear a car, police sirens, a cat, a train, plane and sometimes a cricket. Was taught and learned well how to look for a shadow in the thicket. So full of fear about Henry and I didn't want to be with it. Sleeping wasn't easy and it wasn't until sometime after four in the morning before I did. I woke up late, but was still positioned with the knife tight in my hand. Hoped that the girls didn't see me with it. Guess they didn't, they didn't say anything about it. So when they weren't looking I took the knife and put it way back in the kitchen drawer.

Together the girls already fixed themselves some cereal and took care of Sonny when he woke up.

It was a quiet morning. They usually were. I got the coffee started and called the jail. Henry was not there. So this day was like many others. Always wondering when he'd show up. Would he get drunk and come over while my kids were up? Would he be over tonight? Would he be here at ten? Would he be high? Thought I could tell if a person was drunk. I proved myself wrong when he came over with the Easter baskets. I don't have to let him in, I can always call the cops. They must think I'm nuts down there at the jail calling for him all the time. Anyone who knew what happened and what was still going on had to think that. I hadn't found anyway yet to rid myself of Henry. Thinking about it only made the situation more difficult to live with.

I still let Henry in when he came over. On the nights that he tried knocking on the door after ten p.m. I would call the police. Had the cops at my house at least three or four times a month. They didn't understand and I don't think they cared. They took their time when I called, knowing I was letting him in anyway. I couldn't tell them all that had happened. They would want me to press charges and that would piss Henry off. No, I had to be nice... kept tossing the dice.

A collect call came in one week around nine in the evening. Henry. He was charged with public intoxication, resisting arrest and etc. I paid for the call, glad to know he was in jail. Windows could be open again, but he would call every night. The bill was going up. Of course if I didn't hear from Henry, Wily would hear from me.

One day I received a letter from Winnebago. She wanted to know if I was still having trouble with Henry. She wanted to know details. Told her only about what he did to my car after letting him stay at the house till he found a job. No way in hell was I going to tell her about anything else.

Stranger was that Migs from the bar was curious about Henry. She said she knew him and wondered way too much about the idea that I was letting Henry over to my house. I wondered why.

Things were calmer at the house. Henry was under lock and key. He'd be in jail at least three weeks and I was free once again.

In the mean time Pope was planning his yearly vacation to the old country. He would be gone for two weeks. I never did tell him about Henry. It worried me that Pope would be 5 thousand miles away. What about when Henry gets out of jail? The thought made shudder. He might hit me again or worse, kill me! I needed to focus. Needed to work and since there wasn't a job opening with good pay, I looked around my house to see what I could do to keep busy.

The lawn I thought. It looks terrible and it's the biggest front lawn on the block. It's got to look the best! This will help me get my mind off things, but where do I start?

Nina might know somebody who could help me figure it out. Her former boyfriend was now her boss. His name, Joe. I met Joe on several occasions when I had dropped over to Nina's for coffee and puzzles. Joe was a real nice man who had owned a back hoe, dump truck and other equipment used for his job. I asked Nina if Joe might have a tiller I could use. He did. Nina made the arrangements and Joe brought Nina, his truck and the tiller over to my place after we knew Pope was in San Marino.

I had no idea what I was up against. Joe took a big red machine out and down onto the yard. He showed me the gears and how to operate it. He ran it a minute over the lawn to let me see it in action before I took over. I yelled out, "Joe okay! I think I can handle that, it looks pretty easy." "Okay Cap. Come on. Take it over. Remember... hold on!" Hold on, I thought? I took hold of the handles and then it took hold of me. If it would have moved thirty miles an hour I might have looked like a cartoon character in flight. I yelled over to Joe for help and he ran across the yard taking over. Nina stood against Joe's truck sipping on a cold beer laughing. Well, as you might have imagined, Joe tilled the entire front yard for me. In all, it took him about a half hour. Then he offered to spread out the dirt for me, leveling it with a garden rake. I couldn't let him do anymore. I had the rake I needed and Joe brought over some grass seed and a bale of hay. He gave me all the general guidelines for the rest of the work required, insisting he wanted to help. "Joe, you did the hard part. I couldn't have run that through the dirt and clay in this yard." "Yeah Cap, clay is pretty rough to go through. Are you sure you don't want any more help? How about you Nina?" Joe said, plus, "How 'bout gettin' a rake out to help." "Hey, don't let me spoil all the dirty work. It's okay. You can do it." We all knew (so did Nina), she wouldn't lift a shovel like I wouldn't turn down a cup of coffee. I wanted to do the rest alone because I needed some space and time and I wanted to impress Pope. Yes, the days of pissing Pope of were over.

First things first before the rake, a couple joints, some coffee and the car radio for rock. I was ready to go and dug right in nonstop.

"Damn," I said, "Six hours and I'm still here!" I went into the house for a quick eat, made more coffee and rolled another joint. Buff watched Sonny and Jules. She liked playing mommy to them and would insist they were fine if I grew concerned. Guess I was lucky to have three kids that got along as well as they did. Oh they had their moments, but a few they were.

It was back outside for me. Sat on the one and only porch step to smoke a joint and to take a well deserved coffee break. Then it was back to the dirt and clay.

Oh what a relief. The rest would be so easy compared to the day. I sowed the seeds. I put the right amount of hay over the yard. I pounded wood stakes all around it and tied them together with strips of a sheets. Didn't want some skate-boardin'-bike-ridin' kid happening all over my hard work. I watered everything before and after and then I sat backed against a beam near the step admiring all I had done that day. A little hard work didn't kill me. At least not until the next morning when I woke to a bad back. I was hit and out. I went straight to the emergency room at the hospital around the corner. A couple doctors asked what I had been doing. They were amazed that I worked six hours straight, bent over that way. I told them that I was pretty tough. After a few simple exams they explained that I had slipped a disc in my lower back. They prescribed some medication. It worked. In one hour I was pain free and didn't have to walk like I was stuck in a chair. After a few days I didn't need the muscle relaxers anymore and put them up and away.

Each morning I got up and gave the lawn the watering it needed. Within a week and a half I could see little shoots of green popping out of the dirt. Pope would be back before the grass got good and thick, but it would have a good start. When I knew he was home I didn't want to rush over and tell him, I wanted him to notice.

It was over a week before he drove up to see how things were going. He got out of the truck and said, "What did you do over here?" "Well I worked my ass off that's what I did. What do you think? I even tilled the yard, well, Joe tilled the yard, I did the rest. It took about seven hours." "Yeah but Cappy, there wasn't anything wrong with the yard." "Fine for you maybe, but I wanted it to be more level. Clean out the stones. Nobody else on the block has a front yard this big and I wanted mine to look the best." "Well it looks like it might be." "Pope I ended up in the hospital the next day and they said I slipped a disc in my back because I was bent over the yard for six hours. When I walked it looked like I was stuck in *a* chair." "Well, you always do things the hard way." Pope laughed and went into visit with the his grand kids a few minutes. After which he went to Nina's for supper. Where was the praise, I thought?

Then it hit me. A few months after Mayor died, I worked her front flower garden. I weeded, I planted and trimmed the bushes to near perfect circles. Pope drove by me about the time I was done. Passed the house and headed to his house just around the corner. Now he was pissing me off. I admired the work that took well over two hours and Pope still hadn't come to say a word. Gave him twenty minutes and that was it. The day was hot, my face was red and I was burning with sweat. I went back to his house banging on the door and went in. "Pope, what's wrong? Aren't you even going to come over and see what I did? It took me two hours! I've been working like a dog! How come you never say anything to me when I do something right." Pope was sure and quick with an answer, "If I don't say anything, it's because I can see that you did it right." "But when I do something wrong you yell, you get mad, how come?" "I have to tell you when you do something wrong so you know you shouldn't do it again. But you don't like to listen." "Will you at least walk over and see it?" "Cappy I saw it when I drove by, you did a beautiful job okay?" "K Pope. That's all I wanted to hear." "Okay Cappy then why don't you go home and get cleaned up. You gotta get those kids some supper." "I know Pope. I know. I'm going. I'm pooped. See ya later." For traditional reasons, I honked the horn.

Each morning I watered the lawn. Once in a while a tied off section of the border would be apart from on-coming-night-bike-riding-kids, so I tied them together again to keep my pet project protected. I wouldn't have minded a blue jay in the grass, but they were not visiting. Another couple checks were placed on the calendar waiting for Gentry.

One morning I woke to remember a dream. I dreamed that Gentry had arrived one early evening. I walked outside and stood on the porch as he got of the Shark. He popped out it quickly, hopping over the border of my newly seeded lawn. He jumped around it for a few seconds and said laughingly, "Aah! You think you are going to have grass in before I do?" Laughing on the inside he was pissing me off. I bolted off the porch, ran over to him and politely demand him off the yard. "Do you mind getting off of my grass please? Put my back out over this yard!" (smiling) He smiled back and he removed himself from the new lawn onto the drive. My dream ended.

♫ ♪ *"Morning Coffee Blues"* ♪ ♫
Words and Music by: Catherine Santi - on March 3, 1986

"When I wake up I try die day on.
Find my walls have all gone crayon.
If I just had a bed to think and lay on,
I wouldn't feel all alone.
I think of you, I, I think you listen.
I can love you, I don't think I need your permission.
Have you been testing me? That's what I'm guessing.
Sometimes I feel all alone.
When you coming back to me?
When you coming back to me?

I think it's wise, you should come back to me.
It's hard this being all alone.
Your rituals have all been directed.
Time and time you feel you've been rejected.
You play the fool and now you feel neglected.
How does it feel!
How does it feel!
How does it feel to be alone?"

The Continuation of Chapter Eighteen: "Forward time, backward Time. Never Stepping Foot in the Middle"

One fine-just-darkened-evening a dream came true. A familiar sound approached my drive. I knew it well. This sound was going to bring me nothing but pleasure. I took myself to the front door and out. Gentry got out of the Shark, hopped over the nicely tied barriers that protected my stuff. Jumping up and down on it and laughing he said, "Aah! You think you are going to have grass in it before I do?" He kept that smile. I lovingly told him to get off my grass and he did, stumbling around chuckling. We walked toward each other and my dream come true turned into a nightmare. Gentry grabbed me and pushed the back of my head into the hood of my car and he yelled. "Is this what you want bitch. You want someone to beat on you? You like this?" Gentry backed off and away glaring at me a moment. I stood tall and said, "Gentry come into the house. Come on. Why are you acting like this?" "He's been all over that house (pointing to mine), I'm not going in there!" More nothings were said between us for a minute when Gentry wanted the both us to go in the back yard.

We did that quietly, exchanging thoughts until we stood by the garage. We sat under the pussy willow tree all leafy and green. We talked a lot. Time seemed to stand still for me. I leaned back into him and he was comfortable. Quickly he blurted out, "I want you to be the first one to call, I just got my phone hooked up, the number is 626-3502." Or something like that. I needed to be refreshed. It was totally out of context and he caught me off guard. Then he said, "Don't forget." I ran it through my head for a while as we talked till I didn't want to think about the number anymore. I just wanted to enjoy the time with Gentry. Pink came up with a questionable question. "If you could have only one thing, just one, what would you want Big Time?" A long sigh came from me and I turned to him with a direct answer. "The one thing that I would want more than all the rest, would be to die in the arms of the man I love." Gentry said nothing as he looked at me with depth. "And what about you? What do you want," I asked. He was still looking inside of me. Spoke simple, gentle, kind. " "Everything I said, I said to you in the beginning."

Gentry held me with his arms and I held him back. We were laying under the tree, behind the shadows, when one thing led to the everything and I didn't care if the whole world was watching. I looked up in his eyes and he was looking into mine. The earth was all ours for a time. Strangely, I became short-breathed. I looked at Gentry with fear and goodbyes. I gasped. He didn't understand. I couldn't get air into my lungs and there was no air left to breathe. Gentry's face appeared to vanish. Above me I saw me. That image was looking back down at me under the tree. Gentry stopped and knew something was happening. "Gentry. For a few seconds I didn't see you. Your face was me looking at me. And she was looking down at the me out of breath under the tree. I couldn't breathe. I tried to tell you." Gentry said, "I stopped." And I replied, "So did I!"

I took a detour for numbers. In particular, the phone number that Gentry gave me. I wanted badly to ask him for the number again, but my pride wouldn't let me. There would be a discrete way of relocating the number in my mind, and in time I'd have the seven digits I needed to call. Damn! Location is a must. He wants me to be the first to call. I worked over time.

Before long, the early-early morning was preparing to light the sky. It was about 5:15. Gentry and me were still under the tree talking. Suddenly he stood up, grabbed my underpants and flung them over the neighbors' fence. "Gentry. How the hell am I supposed to get them? The sun is almost up and someone will see me for sure." I was smiling mad at Gentry for his prank. I insisted he cross over the boundaries to get my pants. He assured me he had to be off to work and began to walk away down the drive. I stood up pulling down my tee shirt making sure I was covered properly and followed behind him as he walked to his vehicle. "You think that I am going to go over there and get those you are out of your mind! You can't leave me like this. It isn't funny Gentry." He turned, laughed and said, "Sorry. Gotta go. You can manage." Oh he was loving the reactions from me. After he left I sped around the neighbors' house, behind their garage to get my pants. I put them on and ran back into my house praying that no one saw me in action.

Once inside, I sat at the guard table for a smoke to think about the night. And let's not forget the phone number I forgot. There would be a way to get it and get it right.

Self said, "Forget the number. Get some sleep." But I couldn't sleep. All I wanted to do was think about me and Gentry together just minutes ago. What had happened to me while he was there. Maybe he was really working for God.

This took me back to the clouds in the sky again: LISTEN "Ha!" I said out loud. It was time for, yes, you guessed it. Pot. I had a joint ready and rolled-to-go so I took it and my coffee to the piano. I played around with chords and some songs I knew while thinking about the clouds and what they meant. Until I solved the great mystery it would be just that and constant.

Back to phone number. I called the phone company, pretended to be the newly wedded wife of Mr. Mocean III. Told her I lost the paper I wrote it on in the dry wall and dust. Bingo! It was mine. In a few days, Pink popped in, wanted to know how I remembered the number knowing I forgot. Seemed like he rather enjoyed the way I got the number and the call I made, but in a blink he exclaimed he was building a kitchen cabinets for a gal he called Peaches. "Who's this Peaches?" I demanded. Gentry liked getting me angry but this was early afternoon. He had on a big grin, thanked me for calling and had to work on Peaches kitchen. I wondered... Was I her?

Henry would continue to call collect from the jail every night he was locked in. If he wasn't calling me, I was calling the jail to see if he was there. If he wasn't there I kept things locked and shut in case he showed up. And I knew he would show up.

Yes, after all that had happened I still let Henry in the house. At ten o'clock p.m. and not a minute later. Fortunately for me, Henry wasn't coming over as much. Images lurked in my brain while wondering at the guard table. Just about that time, Tim stopped over to inform me Henry met a girl living right above his own apartment and that he was seeing her. Yes, relief for me! Henry found someone else, but I grew concerned for her. Would Henry treat her the same way? Did he tell her he only needed to stay a week until he got a job? Would he polish the furniture, making himself look like a good guy? Would he beat and rape her? I didn't dare go looking for her to tell her what I knew about this thing she was dealing with, though my heart picked at my brain to do just that. Self told me to let it go, and I did.

Henry was in and out of jail. And when he was locked up he'd call collect and I kept accepting the calls. Money was real tight. I was broke all the time. I didn't want to ask Pope for another dime. I had just asked him for money. I went through my house to see if I could sell something for needed cash. The phone bill was always over a hundred dollars. The only way I managed to keep the service was to pay at least half the bill each month. This never brought the bill down and the thought of being in debt was driving me up the walls. I liked things being paid. I wanted to be responsible for myself and my bills.

After a long look around the house, there was nothing I could find that anyone would pay money for. Nothing of value, except for an pair of 18 karat gold earrings. Pope got them for me on a visit to Italy. He had bought Mayor a pair them when he, Mayor, me and my brother Hermit visited San Marino, Italy. I was 3! I don't remember much of that even though we were there for a few months, however I do remember being 10. The time Pope finally let me get my ears pierced. Mayor gave me her golden earrings and Pope gave me my birthday present early. A pair of real pearl earrings, set in white gold. Back to Mayor's earrings. The symbol in a circle was that of San Marino which consisted of three castles. The newer version had the same design on them except that they were diamond cut and a little bit bigger in circumference. Those were what I pawned for money. The only pawn shop that I knew of gave me $37.50. Yeah, I was shocked. Never knew they paid for the weight only. Pope spent well over 1000 bucks. He'd kill me if he knew what I had done and what I did it for. It was for cigarettes. Henry helped himself to anything in the house. Me being the chicken shit that I was, I let him.

As my rotten luck would have it, Henry was being released from the county jail again. He made it a point to tell me about it when he came over to the house at 10 p.m. He helped himself to cigarettes, the pot I thought I hid well and the food. He told me that he had another girlfriend. Told him I was happy for him. Also told him that if he had a girlfriend it wasn't a good idea for him to be at my house. This didn't sway Henry's thinking. He showed up at my house nearly every night at the same time. On the nights that he didn't show, I called the jail making sure of his whereabouts. This whole thing with Henry was getting way too old and I there had to be a place to lay it to rest... forever.

Gentry wasn't coming around as much and I knew why. It had to be Henry, what else? I thought about Gentry every day. Through the day and all through the night till night was too much.

Many times I wanted to drive over to Neil Street to explain everything going on. With a man on my side I could get through this, I thought. But that's all I did... thought. Never told Gentry about Henry. Never told Gentry how much I loved him. How could I? He'd never believe me so long as he knew Henry was still coming to the house. My house. The one Gentry no longer wanted to enter.

It was around mid summer or later when Huron would hold their annual festival. Never went to one myself and didn't matter if I ever went. Because I never did. Walked out to check the flowers I planted when an old-clunker-of-a-car pulled up in the drive and Henry was the driver. I stayed secured on the porch next to the door waiting to go in and lock up behind me before he had a chance to get to me. Henry yelled out of the window of the car, "Hey Cappy! Ya got a few bucks so me and my new girlfriend here can go grab a few beers somewhere?" I looked at the girl in the passenger seat. She looked very tiny and petite. He hair was long, stringy and blonde. I knew just by a glance that she was much smaller than me. The two of them were laughing and smiling and wanting my money. Even if I would have had any, I spoke up, "I'm broke. Sorry." Henry boasted, This is my new girlfriend so why don't you get fucked bitch." I didn't say anything. Just watched them pull out of the drive and squeal down the road. I went into the house and locked up the doors behind me.

Immediately I thought of Henry calling me a bitch and I knew that that meant trouble for this skinny little blonde. He never used bad language unless he was drunk, high. She was probably already going through what I had been through with him.

More days passed, a few, I fed the birds, watered the lawn, the flowers, when a car sped by honking the horn to get attention. It was Henry. I feared for myself because I thought he would turn right around and come to my house. I fled for the security of my house and locked things up tight.

The next evening I got a call from the jail and yes it was Henry. He didn't say why he was there and I didn't want to know. I was just glad that he was in jail again. It was later when I knew the reasons why he was locked up.

The day he sped by my house honking the horn he was on his way to the festival and he ran into Allen Leed, my friend from grade school? The same friend that Henry accused me of having sex with for over a month. Henry broke a bottle, I think it was a beer bottle, and went after Allen slashing his throat with the broken glass. He cut Allen pretty bad and missed his jugular vein by a quarter of an inch. It could have been fatal. Allen was treated and released from the hospital. Frank Forrest, my ex-boyfriend, encouraged Henry to turn himself in because Allen wasn't about to press charges. Allen would rather get even. So Henry turned himself in and was locked up for a long time in the county jail. This led to more collect calls. Calls that I would accept only to find out what was going on and why Henry did what he did to Allen. Rumor had it, that Henry tried to steal something from Allen's house. But I didn't believe that for a minute. Henry M. Batturs III did it because of what he thought when he thought of me and Allen. For me, the guilt built. I prayed for a day when I could confront Allen. Let him know that I was the reason for Henry's actions. Time passed and eventually I did bump into Allen at the store. Told him my concerns and I apologized for what had happened. Allen hugged me and told me not to think that for a minute. He said I had nothing to do with it. He claimed Henry was a sick dude who would get pay back in time.

Getting braver, I ended up telling Frank about Henry and what he did. One evening, afraid of not knowing the whereabouts of Henry, I phoned Frank and asked him if I could have his shepherd at my house for protection. Frank laughed and suggested he come over himself. I made a place for him to sleep on the couch. I slept on the floor next to the couch. It felt good having him there. Didn't bother either one of us that he had a girlfriend. Well, it did me just a little because he found her so fast. Only months after our break up and just weeks after Henry beat me. Frank had stopped over to introduce the girlfriend. She didn't look like she wanted to be at "my" house. She wanted to leave as soon as she got there. She never smiled and it made me wonder what Frank ever could have seen in her. She was so plain and kinda lifeless. She was shorter than me with brown eyes and brown hair passed her shoulders. Petite. He name was Sherry. Oh, I almost forgot the most important part of them coming over when they did. Henry was there sitting right smack next to me, making it look as though the two of us were going together.

Fall was upon me and the cold winds took no time pushing their way into town. I kept myself busy raking leaves, watching for and feeding my four feathered friends. Buff was back in school so now it was just me, Sonny and Jules for the most part of the day. Things were quiet and I continued playing piano in the evenings after the collect calls from the jail came and went.

I hadn't seen Gentry in some time and it was killing me inside. Why wasn't he coming over anymore? Did he mean it when he said he was never going to come into my house again? He must have meant it. I missed him and I kept missing him wondering if I should make a move to see him or what.

I wrote him letters telling him things that were going on over here at my place in hopes that he might get curious and want to come over, but he didn't

Before I knew it the falls life was short lived and the snow was falling. Around the same time I had to think about getting my teeth fixed. Again I made a final plea to the Pope for the money I needed for root canal work and crowns but he wouldn't budge. He told me how brave Mayor was when she had all her teeth pulled to wear dentures. But I was only 28. I couldn't get dentures, I only needed four teeth fixed. Why didn't Pope just loan me the two grand it would have costed?

I had long talks with Nina about dentures. Nina had both upper and lowers. Told me something that was very important. She said, "Cap, you have to remember that when you have your top teeth pulled, your face isn't going to be the same. It's going to change. Your mouth will never be the same again." On the cheery side of things she said, "Think of this Cap! You'll never have to worry about another bad tooth ache."

In November I saw a dentist who referred me to a specialist. This was best for me. I would be put under to have the back top teeth pulled first, leaving me something to eat with. Going to the dentist was almost as bad as having a baby.

The very day after my teeth were pulled Henry was released from jail. He came to my house at ten like nothing ever happened and insisted he was sober. He wanted to explain to me about this new girlfriend, (like I cared).

Foolishly I let him in. Especially after what he did to Allen. What if Henry ever found out about Gentry? What in God's name would he do to him?

Henry and I were sitting on the couch and I told him I was getting my mouth ready for an upper denture. My mouth was hurting bad. I turned my back on him for a minute and he punched me in the back of the head. I started to shake. I got up to sit further away from him and asked, "Why did you hit me? What the hell is a matter with you? I never did anything for you to lay a hand on me!" He answered, "I'm sorry honey, I don't know what makes me do the things I do." Then he came over to sit by me and he put his arm around me telling me he was sorry. I moved off the couch and sat on the floor ignoring him to watch the television, wishing he would just leave. He grabbed me by the hair and turned me around to face him. He had his pants unzipped and his penis in his hand. He pushed my head next to it and said, "Come on honey. It won't hurt you. Just suck on it a little. You'll feel better. Come on." "Mitchel are you crazy! I'm not doing anything for you or with you. Even if I gave a shit about you I wouldn't. Christ Mitchel, I just have eight teeth pulled yesterday, please leave me alone. Don't hurt me!" Henry didn't listen to a word I said and forced me to give him oral sex. Then he jerked off the couch and said, "You don't even know how to give a guy a blow job bitch. I'm going over to my new girlfriend's house. She's even skinnier than you." Henry got his coat, hat and left out the back door. I locked it up tight and headed for the bathroom. I wanted to wash my mouth out with soap. This would be the end of Henry. I ran the water in the bathroom sink until it was as hot as I could stand it and put some in a glass. I sipped the water and moved it slowly around my mouth so I wouldn't lose any blood clots. Last thing I needed was a dry socket. And if anyone knows about dry sockets...!

The next day came and I called the jail to see if by any chance Henry was locked up, but he wasn't. This meant that I would have to be safe and at the guard table. Nights like these passed slow because I didn't want to do anything that gave me pleasure. Didn't want to play piano and sing for fear I might not hear Henry coming if he had any intentions of coming over. I had to be ready.

How much more did I have to go through before this would all come to an end? How do I make it end? I questioned myself all the time and failed to come up with the solution to my problem. I could kill Henry, I thought. But how would I ever get away with something like that? It seemed the only way to end it. I prayed that he would die. I wanted him dead so that I could go on living in peace again. But it would take more than a bullet to do it and I wasn't about to buy a gun. All I could do was hope that somehow, by some freak accident, Henry would die.

I talked to Wily at the jail about Henry and how I wanted him dead. Wily said, "Well Cap, you could be driving one night and Henry could fall into the street drunk and, well, you couldn't stop in time and you run him over. Believe me, you would be doing yourself a favor and the police department. We have all had it with Henry Batturs. Then of course you could back up the car and run him over again. Just tell the cops you were so upset at what happened that you didn't know what you were doing. Hey, you were confused, you were scared about what happened. It could easily be an accident." I was shocked the words had come from a cop and pissed that I didn't think of it myself.

No, I never did go out driving around looking for Henry to stumble into the street. I blew the idea of running Henry over hoping that his time would come on its own and it would come soon.

Though cold as November came it warmed up just a little when Nina and I thought of a way to make a little extra cash. We'd make the Italian soup I made for the Gentry Christmas and sell it to the "I.A.B." club. Hermit was in charge of the kitchen. We agreed to make two thousand of the ravioli-shaped and filled pasta. Nina and I had no idea what we were going up against.

The day came to start making them. Nina came over to my place for a change, (I usually went to hers). She brought her own beer. I kept the coffee brewing and the pot smoking. We cooked the meats. We blended the meats with the different cheeses and etc. We made little balls just slightly smaller than marbles out of the ingredients and placed them in plastic containers till we were ready to stuff them in the little square suits. A late morning and an afternoon passed when we broke for supper. After which Nina would come back over and we continued with our work. The first day we put in about twelve hours.

Let me give you an idea about what a bitch it is to make caplitz. I would rather scrape, prime and paint a two story house. Glaze the windows and every detail to painting a house, then to make the soup. Took nine hours for me to make 500 alone. My calculations were way off when I thought Nina and I could make two thousand in eighteen hours.

Nina showed up the next day after supper, about six-thirty and we worked and worked. She was content making the balls of meat and tossing them in a large wide bowl in front of her. We laughed and joked for the most part. Like I said, for the most part. About midnight, neither one of us could stand the job. Nina was literally getting sick to her stomach just looking at the bowl of meat. "Cap, I can't take this anymore. It's making me sick. I don't want to make these freaking meatballs ever again as long as I live!" I turned around to look at Nina. She was grinning. She wasn't even looking at the bowl while she rolled and tossed a meat ball in the bowl. She was beat. I understood, but it didn't keep me from laughing my ass off. We were nearly delirious after the hours of the same old shit. We knew we weren't getting paid union scale and she wanted to go home. I told Nina to go and that I would finish the rest myself. What was I thinking? Nina apologized for not being able to help out anymore, but I didn't blame her, I knew her pain.

So ahead of me was yet another three hundred and fifty caplitz. "Good Lord! Hurry," Self said, "Tell Nina to get her ass back here now!"

I rolled up a joint and had some vodka there that Nina had brought over for me. It went well with grapefruit juice on the rocks and it helped to get through the mess I had left.

I called the radio station and luck had struck. Stone was on the air. We chatted a long time. I told him that I was making this crazy Italian soup and it was making me want to break something. Stone never heard of them and wanted to know all about them. I told him all about the little bastards I had been making for nearly two days. Stone cracked. He couldn't believe that making this soup was so difficult. I wanted to challenge him and asked him to stop by to help me finish if he thought it was so easy, but he suggested it first. I took him up on the idea. Gave him my address and directions to my house. He told me that he would be there after his shift which would be about 1:00 a.m. and we talked till his shift was over.

After talking for nearly a year over the phone with Stone, I was looking forward to meeting him. Felt like I knew him. Self said to get going on the bitch of a job I had ahead. Coffee was in order and of course it was brewing. Thirty "Maxwell House" coffee cans had control on the west kitchen counter top. That control I could live with.

One thirty in the morning and a knock was at the door. I knew Stone was on the way, but I wanted it badly to be Pink. I walked over to the front door, looked out the window and saw the face behind the radio. I opened the door and said, "Stone?" "Yep, that would be me. We finally meet at last." he said. "Come on in. Did you bring anything over to drink, because I don't keep alcohol around." Stone pulled out a bottle of wine he picked up at a convenient store and laughed, "I'm not much of a drinker myself. I would rattier have a doob to smoke. Love pot. You?" "You came to the right place. I just happen to have some "handy." "Ah!" said Stone. "So do I!" Stone pulled out a small pipe and the clear plastic bag of the stuff. I have to admit it looked better than what I had. He insisted that we smoke his and I had no objections. Stone filled the pipe jammed. Cool I thought. This guy knows how to smoke pot. I watched him light it. He inhaled large amounts of the smoke into his lungs. His face was real red before he finally exhaled the smoke. "Ah! That worked. Here Capri you take a good one." "Damn Stone! Ya got some lungs there! I never saw anything like it before." Stone gagged out a chuckle and handed me the pipe and asked, "So are these caplitz?" He picked up one of the pasta filled squares studying it. "Yeah, that's one of the little bastards. You can't know how long it takes to make them bitches. I gotta finish this tonight. I can't take it anymore. In fact, Nina, the lady who was helping me took off earlier." Stone said, "Looks like fun. I'll help you with the bastards." Stone was ready to dig in. He washed his hands off in the kitchen sink. I handed him the stuff and showed him how to make them.

He rolled out a little dough and made a few caplitz all by himself. It cracked me up because I could tell by his facial expressions that he was not having the fun he thought he would have. Once was all it took for Stone. He suggested he'd make the meat balls. Like Nina, he had the easy job.

Stone was cute too. He stood about 5'10." His hair was light brown with gold highlights passed his shoulders. His eyes were hazel sitting behind of pair of dark brown framed lenses. He had a mustache that neatly lay over his top lip.

After he finished his wine, smoked more pot an hour had passed. We talked a lot about ourselves during that time. I learned that Stone played a little guitar and liked singing. "Stone, I love the guitar! Don't have one close do you? Like the car," I asked. "I thought you would never ask. I wasn't sure it would be alright to bring it in this late with your kids sleeping." "Are you kidding Stone! They could sleep on the engine of a freight train with the whistle blowing. Go on and bring it in." Stone ran out to his car, got the guitar, came in and shook a little snow off. We took a break from the soup and sat at the kitchen table while Stone tuned the six string acoustic. I couldn't wait to get my hands on it and it would take five minutes to get the dough off of them.

Stone jumped right in singing something by "Neil Young." I like Neil. Loved his voice. Stone was a good singer too. His voice was crisp. He pronounced the words clearly. Maybe it had something to do with being a broadcaster. He handed me the guitar and said, "Okay Cap. Your turn." I played a few chords and that was about it. My finger tips hurt bad. It had been some time and the calluses were gone. I told Stone I couldn't play it anymore. A couple minutes was enough for me. I gave the guitar back and told him some of the songs I used to sing when I did play it. He asked for the chords. I told him. He played. We both sang. We weren't half bad! Then I looked over at the mess I had ahead of me. Those damn caplitz. I had to finish them and that was that. I stood up and told Stone I really had to finish. He offered to make more of the meat balls. And we worked another hour.

By now our minds took off. Holding a meatball in my hand I looked over at Stone and said, 'Ya know what? I have had it with these fucking things! I can't take it anymore!" I grabbed a meatball and slammed the bitch to the ceiling and it stuck. Stone's eyes opened wide and said, "That's what I call food that really sticks to ya!" I looked up at the caplitz still stuck to the ceiling. I reached for another one and said, "Stone, grab a meatball and put the damn thing to rest!" I threw the next one up to ceiling and Stone followed my lead. By the time we got over this laughing frenzy we were in, there were at least fifty meatballs stuck to the ceiling. "I don't care if those stupid little soupy bastards stay up there forever." Stone looked up and said, "I don't think they're going anywhere Cappy. But I gotta move. It's almost three in the morning and I have to be at the station by 9 today. I don't want you to think I don't want to stay for the clean-up but I didn't know it was this late." "Stone I would have had to do it myself anyway. Say, what else do you do besides being a-fill-in-one-night-D.J.?" "I work on the commercials and that. But I'd like to end up full time in a big station out of Cleveland." "That sounds like fun, except I could never sit and talk to a mike all night. I'd crack up. Ya know when I get the laughs I can't stop. Especially when I know I'm not supposed to be laughing" "You should stop down there sometime and I'll show you what I do. You know where it is don't you," he asked." "Sure. I lived here nearly all my life." "That's right, I forgot."

Stone was from a bordering state and was fairly new to the area. I told him that I'd stop down at the radio station. He said he'd show me how things were done. He put on his coat and locked the guitar into the case. I thanked him for the his help and told him to stop over again. "We won't be making caplitz will we," he asked. "No way Stone! I'm not that crazy. Next time I'll supply the pot. You just make sure to bring over the guitar." "Not a problem Cappy. Well, I'll see ya soon." I watched him slip slide to his car then I locked up. Talking out loud to myself I said, "You still have this flour mess to clean up yet Cap. You won't sleep if you don't. Well? What are you standing around for? Get to it." And I jumped right in.

By five fifteen in the morning the kitchen was back to normal. Not a trace of meat on the ceiling. No flour in sight. Caplitz counted and bagged. 2,000. The floor was swept, the dishes were done and everything shined. I was exhausted. Within seconds I was asleep.

Didn't sleep long enough when the phone rang at nine-thirty. It was Nina wanting to know if I got everything done alright. That woke me right up. We both bitched about the job for an hour and felt better. Then the kids were up and I needed off the phone to get them breakfast. Especially Sonny.

The day was bright and snow filled. Though it pained my eyes to look at the white covered ground, the day was cold with fresh!

It's April 22nd, in the present, the day I had an abortion. I remember because I can't forget. Like so many other things I could never forget and I didn't want to remember.

Before I sat down this evening to write, I looked out at the spring night skies. It looked like snow would fall, or it wanted to. My mind is going in all directions. Forward and back. Never stepping foot in the middle.

It's 1999. The infamous three's again. I had figured on finishing this some months ago but I didn't figure that it would upset me so much. I thought I was losing it again! Last year in March I admitted myself to the mental ward after a night of drinking. It seemed that no matter what I did to get down off this energy burst nothing worked. I blamed it all on the book. This one! After talking to a social worker, a doctor and a nurse, I let them admit me to the ward. I paced about it remembering the good times I had there. Then the reality set in when I found out that you only got to smoke cigarettes about every four hours. This meant I had to go home. I could no way in hell live like that and I missed the kids. Since I turned myself in, the only way I'd get out, was to stay the night and wait to see the doctor in the morning. I slept. Woke to the doctor. Went home.

Not wanting this to happen again makes me put the book down off-ten and not write for weeks. Buff tells me that it would be so cool if I would just lose it once more time. She tells me I'd have a best seller for sure. She plants the seeds. Magazines, talk shows? That only happens to other people not me, not number three. It's 1999. March was when this therapy should have been copy written to say the least. The number is Law! But that's another story entirely!

I am 42 years old. But I lived the 42 years. That's puts me well into my forty third year. These three's of mine keep getting in the way. If they would just leave me alone for a while maybe I'd finish this book once and forever. It's starting to feel like caplitz!

I went to the radio station and met Stone for a tour of the place. I liked "WCPZ." Stone showed me albums that had different sound effects on it and how he placed them into commercials. Showed me his small office and the broadcasting studio. I met one of the regular D.J.'s there. He explained and showed me how they put songs on the air. It was quite the learning experience and fun. Afterwards I invited Stone over to play more guitar. I told him just to call whenever he felt like dropping by.

A couple nights passed by and he did call me from the radio station to tell me he was coming over and bringing his guitar. I couldn't wait.

When he arrived we got right into the guitar. Well, not right into the guitar. First we smoked some of "my" pot. Now that I have that straight... We played lots of things. I started to remember more of the stuff I played when I first got my twelve string. Later we were having a blast changing the words to a "Jim Croce" song entitled "Photographs and Memories." If you will beg our pardon, "Jim," these are the words:

Pornographic memories. Dirty books you sent to me. All that I have are these, to remember you.

Pictures taken long ago. Put into a porno show. I took all my friends to see, they were proud of me.

But we sure had a good time when we snuck in the back door. You were nothin' but a rotten

sleaze bag of a whore.

Pornographic memories. All the smut you gave to me. But whatever you think you might be,

you're not worth the fee.

But we sure had a good time when we snuck out the back door, you were nothing but a sleaze bag of a whore.

We re-worded a few songs. It was always fun to hang out with Stone, providing I knew that Henry was locked up tight. I never mentioned anything to Stone about him. Henry was still jail and I accepted the calls. Are you as tired of hearing that as I am writing it?

Winter was soon to be official as December kicked in cold and furious. Stone came by about once a week to play some guitar. I would show him the little I knew on it and played the piano. We were having fun the two of us singing and goofing off. Stone liked his D.J. voice and more so when he heard it through an amplifier and mike. Hermit gave me that amp when I was 14. Stone loved himself all the more and wanted to buy it. Well, I needed the money so it I sold it to Stone.

On another night that Stone came by we were doing what we usually did and spent many the hour at it. About 12:30 in the morning there was a knock on the back door. The knocking went on for a few minutes then stopped. Stone wondered why I didn't answer and the truth came out. "Cap, I don't understand why you didn't have him charged with anything. That guy outside needs to be in jail. In prison!" Stone looked more scared than me! "Stone! I couldn't do anything. I was too scared. See, he stopped knocking. He probably went to this other girl's house." Just then, Henry was knocking on the front door and much louder. I knew he was drunk or high or both. Stone wanted me to call the cops. I was scared to go to the phone. I couldn't let Stone see me that afraid! I secretly talked myself into going over to the phone. "Stone. Walk to the phone with me, will ya?" "Sure Cap." The call to the police was made by me. Henry was knocking on the back door again. Scared he was able to see movement in the hall, me and Stone took ourselves in the dark bathroom. He peeked out the door every few seconds, wishing for a cop. I asked them to stay on the line with me until an officer arrived. One look would have told you that Stone wished he had never come over. He kept asking me the same question... "Will he break in your house Cappy?" This

218

made matters worse by making me more afraid. The cops told me the only way Henry would get into a house was if something was left un-locked. Stone found no relief when I tried to calm him. Police said they'd be right over, but right over to them meant fifteen minutes. They were tired of coming over for the same thing. I was too embarrassed to tell Stone just how many times they were here. Naturally when the police arrived, Henry had vanished. One of the officers said, "Cappy. This thing with Batturs doesn't make sense. He's really got you. He knows all he has to do is knock on your, and your terrified. He's probably over in the bushes somewhere laughing." "Well it isn't funny!" I said. Stone stepped in, "You guys are going to look for him aren't you?" "We will, but he's probably out of the area. If he comes back call us." "Sure will, and thanks," replied Stone, "I will call if he comes back."

After the cops left I asked Stone to stay a while just in case. Stone was hesitant, but he stayed. We weren't tired, but when day light hit, Stone left for home.

Daylight came through the eastern window. I checked all the locks again and took for the couch. Like other mornings, Buff got herself ready for school. Fortunately for me, my seven year old knew to "always" lock the door behind her. Unfortunately I thought, I shouldn't feel fortunate.

The first thing I did after getting up was call to see if Henry might be in jail. He wasn't. He was out there, somewhere.

It was hard to stay home, but I knew that I had to. No going to The Well hoping to find Gentry so long as Henry roamed. I couldn't stand being cooped up and I wanted to fly, but the creep in my life wasn't a cloud in the sky.

I invited Stone over a few times after Henry showed up that night. Stone had reasons not to come over. And I knew it was Batturs keeping him away. Knew it would be difficult for him to admit, but I never gave up. Stone eventually stopped over, but did it during the day time hours and it just wasn't the same.

Before long, Henry was charged with public intoxication and placed in jail again. Ten months had gone by since that day I let this stranger into my house. I can't count how many times he was in and out of jail in just that amount of time. I was only glad that he was where he belonged.

I could travel now. It was almost Christmas. Almost my birthday and only one birthday wish. That Gentry would be here like he was in 1984.

Christmas shopping was over. I was glad. It was the one thing I despised the most about the holiday.

When the eve of the day came I had some extra money so I went and got a couple bottles of cheap champagne. They'd be for after midnight this night. They would be for me and a certain someone I was hoping for.

Midnight came and I couldn't get myself in the mood to take one sip. I didn't want to celebrate my birthday with nobody.

The kids were well into dreaming and I wanted to do something. I rolled up a couple joints and smoked them both. Then I went into the closet and grabbed a gallon of paint Pope left when he was working on the house. I decided to paint the bathroom upstairs. Took everything I needed for the job and went straight up. Music! I had to have some music so I went back down the stairs for the boom box and one bottle of champagne.

Got comfortable and ready. I drank a couple glasses of the bubbly and called 'CPZ to talk to Renee. It was later, about 1:30 in the morning, Renee would let us both choose what songs we wanted to hear in the next set. We were literally running the show. I was literally getting buzzed. Told her that I was painting the bathroom. I looked about the room and saw it very sloppy. Very sloppy! Knew this must have had something to do with the fact that I wasn't using a glass for the champagne anymore. I just drank it like country.

After a couple of short messy hours, the bathroom was painted. So was the floor, sink, tub and toilet. What a wonderful birthday it wasn't. Cleaned up the mess I had made, took all the stuff downstairs, called Renee to tell her I was gonna pass out and we wished each other a Merry Christmas. I woke up to a bad hang over. It was too early. About seven. My head hurt like no other hurt. I thought maybe if I cracked open the other bottle it might help, but I waited and made a pot of coffee. The first sip only made the matter in my head worse. Seemed unreal that I had to force myself to drink coffee and I did that for hours. Time came to clean the house and think. In a number I was 29, but in life I've lived them years out. Thirty's where I'm actually at. The first day of 30 anyway and it made perfect sense to me. Plus it had my number... three.

♫ ♪ *"Places. Questions. Words."* ♪ ♫
Words and Music by: Catherine Santi in January 1986

"What's he doin' on your floor?
Take my keys, no, take yours.
You don't need him anymore.
It's what you once had said to me.
Tell me is he on your mind?
You often knew the right lines.
And don't you see him time from time?
It's what you once had said to me.

Throw the ashes in the fire.
You are my one desire.
Just sit pretty and be quiet
It's what you once had said to me."

Chapter Nineteen: "Wishes... They Come Later. Much Later."

It was a joint, a glass of warm champagne that gave me the courage to go to Gentry's. I walked in unannounced saying, "Gentry. It's Christmas. Brought some champagne over." Sternly, without lifting his head, his voice said, "I'm busy." I knew the look. Understood that I had just made a complete drunken fool out of myself. He wasn't happy to see me. See me drunk? See me at all? I don't know which, but it was something. I went out the door, into the cold, into my car and back to my house without him.

The day went even slower. Buff wanted to know where Pinky was and if he'd be coming over for Christmas. I didn't have all the answers, so I gave her the only one I knew was certain, "He's busy."

I didn't like being in my 30th year so far. The day started wrong and stayed that way.

It was the first time in a long time that I couldn't wait for the day to be over just so I could get some sleep. I had no desire to stay up and play piano and sing. Sing about what? Sing about who and why? There wasn't a touch of spirit in me at all. To make it simple, I didn't feel like doing anything. And the days passed...

Stone got brave one evening and walked to my house after work with his guitar. It was about ten-thirty in the evening. I was caught off guard. Stone always called before stopping by.

Naturally I let my radio friend in who was ready for something hot to drink. I made him the tea he requested and I did the coffee. Had 41 coffee cans standing pyramid style, neatly taking the west corner counter in the kitchen. Yes! I was keeping count! Stone curiously asked about them. I never gave it much thought until then. "Is there some reason why you have all those cans on the counter? I mean, are they full or what?" "Stone, remember Gentry? You know I go on about him all the time." "Yes you do talk about him all the time, but what's he got to do with the cans?" "The first time he had a cup of coffee here, he said I should drink "Maxwell House" and ever since then I've been buying it. I don't know, I just save the cans. For some reason I just can part with them. Besides, they look pretty cool sitting there don't ya think?" Stone agreed they did look pretty neat.

Well as you might have guessed, once Stone was warmed by tea, we were ready for some marijuana. He took his guitar out of the case and went into the living room. Stone brought beer over and insisted I have one. Didn't want to hurt his feeling, telling him that I hated beer, so I had one. Of course none of this matters, but what happens later does.

Time went by pretty quick considering. Time always went slow for me when I had a pot buzz going. Before I knew it, it was almost 3:30 in the morning. Stone was real tired and pretty buzzed from the pot and beer. I knew he would have to go out in the cold to walk home. The walk was 4 miles from my house. I didn't want to see him get arrested for public intoxication, even though I think he was more tired than anything. He asked me if he could crash out on the floor. He was already laying on his back staring at the ceiling. I didn't want to say yes, but I didn't want to say no, so I said yes. By the time he knew he could he was already curled up on the floor with his coat for a blanket. Stone said good night and I sat at the guard table wide awake.

About a half hour or so when by and there was a knock at the door. A familiar one that was warm and light. I went to the door. Lo and behold it was Gentry! I couldn't wait to let him in. I couldn't believe he came. Never thought he'd come into my house again, but there he was just inside the door and the door was closed. He walked by the kitchen table and said, "Who's that?" "That's Stone from 'CPZ. He walked over here to play guitar. It got late so I told him he could crash out here tonight. Gentry didn't like it and said, "Wake him up! Tell him to go home. Here take my keys, no take yours. Just wake him up. He can walk home." I didn't say a word to Gentry. I turned to Stone and nudged his shoed foot with mine. "Come on Stone, wake up. I'm sorry but you'll have to leave." "Oh okay." Stone looked up at Gentry like he knew him. He was polite about everything and thanked me. In no time Stone was gone on his way home and in no time Gentry was at the kitchen table and we were sitting across from each other. He looked into my eyes and said, "You don't need him. Why don't you and I make music together." I didn't understand what he was saying. I'd heard it in old movies. Was he proposing to me? Was he asking me to be his wife? Finally, I asked, "For how long?" "For as long as you want." There must have been something wrong with my head. This wasn't clicking in my brain. It wasn't complicated, it just wasn't sinking in. Here is the man of my every dream, right in front of me, saying all the words I longed to hear and I failed to listen.

He didn't stay long. He had to be off to work early, maybe. Maybe he didn't want to tell me that he wanted to go home and sleep. He didn't mean what he said to me I thought, he's mad. Angry because there was another man in my house. What was wrong with me? Was I cracking up? I let him leave just like that? Why, but why didn't I answer him, talk? Damn it! Why didn't I tell him that I wanted to do just what he suggested? It put me and winter where it belonged, in black and white.

Oh this was an uneasy feeling. A new feeling I hadn't dealt with before. How was I going to handle it? If I could handle it at all.

Wasn't handling anything right. I couldn't get rid of Henry and never filed one charge against him. He'd call collect, I paid. When he wasn't in jail and at my back door by ten, he was in. What was it that Gentry felt for me? Sharp knives for fun, or did he feel the same way about me? If he was shooting cupids arrows I wanted to catch everyone of them, but Batturs was in the way.

January was about over. Tim Batturs stopped by and wanted to pay for a cup of coffee and a stick of gum. I welcomed him in. Tim filled me in on details. Vital information about his brother. Tim asked, "So are you still letting Henry in the house Cappy?" "Why," I asked. "He's out of jail. He's hasn't been over here, really?" "No Tim I haven't seen him. When did he get out?" "Well let's see now, he's been seeing the girl who lives upstairs in his apartment building. My brother really hasn't been over here Capri?" Tim had a large question mark in the middle of his brows. Relieved but scared I said, "I'm so happy he hasn't been here. I'm glad he found somebody else, maybe he'll leave me alone!" Tim knew I was really afraid, he tried his humor on me, "Cappy. Would you happen to have a stick of gum?" "No, sorry Tim, I don't." "Well, then can I just have the money?" Digging into my jean pocket for a coin, I slapped a dime on the table and said, "Here. Please take the money. I want you to have it." Tim was shaking his head a smiling a no. "Tim, really! I really want you to take the dime. Please! Maybe you'll quit with the stick of gum question finally already! I can't take it anymore." "Okay, I'll take the dime, but you have to let me pay for it. I'll give you ten cents for it okay? Fair?" "Tim, if I take the dime back then you will ask me that stupid question for the rest of my life! I insist that you keep the dime... for free!" "Hmm, I can keep this dime? No charge? You don't want the money? So can I just go ahead and take the money?"

Time to get serious. Henry was free again and my life was locked.

Grocery store was going there during day hours only with Henry on the loose. It was right around the corner. One minute tops. I went right after Tim left the house. Decided to splurge on myself and get something to drink. I mean drink! I didn't want to be afraid. I wasn't a wine drinker and there wasn't any champagne at the store. I grabbed two six packs of beer, took it home and tucked it in the back of the fridge. It was an odd thing for me to have beer in the house. I only drank on my birthday. Used to. Drinking was getting regular since I let Henry Mitchel Batturs III in my life. He destroyed the natural pattern of the threes that had been following me for years.

Every morning and every evening I would call the jail to see if Henry was there. Unfortunately for me he wasn't. This kept me on a constant watch for him. Especially at dark. I checked my porch lights and spot lots every night to make sure they worked. I locked and literally bolted the door with a steel kick bar that hooked under the door knob. Prof' got it for me and told me that if the creep got in anyway, I could use always use the kick bar to bash his fucking head in!

I didn't smoke any pot. The fear was intense enough. I played little piano or music. I wanted to hear everything. I wanted to see everything. I watched for shadows that might move in the dark. I looked behind hedges and trees with my heart. If movement be seen I watched still ever so. I just couldn't move off my guard that you know. Lift the curtain open just a corner crack wide and I stared at the night things and I wondered inside. This thing has to stop, you can't live it no more! I turned from the window eyes set to the floor. I remembered I bought a few beers to be strong, so I reached for a can after can I was strong. I told myself this: You're feeling tough like a fight! If Henry creeps over tell him he's outta your life. This time my luck was lucky when Batturs didn't come. Had a butcher knife to sleep with because I'm so scared of guns. I woke to find the knife still clenched in my hand. I put it away and I knew the kids wouldn't understand. Then I did what naturally came next. I made coffee and called the jail. Henry wasn't there. It was February of 1986, and the month wasn't short enough for me. I tried very hard to think of the best way to handle the situation at hand. I could still press charges. I let him wreck the car and get away with it. What was wrong with my head? I wasn't just losing things in the house anymore. Did he damage my thinking? My logic? My brain would not cooperate.

My brain. Ha! Now that's an interesting subject. I thought about what my brain must be going through after all it had gone through with me. Somewhere locked in this brain of mine are all the things I've seen, done, been, thought, dreamed and everything from the start. Where did I start from? I thought about that and remembered trying to explain something to Mayor when she was alive. I said, "Mayor. If God created us to be like Him and God always was, always is and always will be, then so are we." Mayor looked at me with that Mona Lisa grin, rolling her olive green eyes. "It's like this Mayor. There was a time when we never were. So we were not. Always. Now we are because here we are. When we die we will always be. Like God! Back to the beginning where we always were." Mayor questioned it over and over and thought the idea impossible. I explained it to Hermit and he understood exactly what I meant.

It's been 15 years since Mayor died, but now she always is! Back to where she was in the beginning. Just like she always was and will be. How do I know this? Mayor pops in on me. Tilts the shadow box a little so I'll get it straight. It was mine when she decided she wanted nothing old in her new house. Just cleaned it the other day. I put back all the little things I had been saving. There's 3 coffee mugs, a tea pot, a sugar bowl, lighters I collect, pictures and 5 little wishbones. Wishes. Now they come later... much later.

It would take more than a wish to get rid of Henry and I took no action what so ever. Before long he was back at the back door. Henry was sober and only stayed for a few minutes. He wanted to know if I had a few bucks so he could go get some cigarettes. Said he was playing cards with his buddies. Well he and I both knew it was the beginning of the month and the welfare check had leftovers then. I decided to take the bite and give him three dollars so he would leave. Huh! What do ya know. He took the money and left. More importantly he didn't return. I was shook up after that. Took me a good couple hours at the guard table to get my shit together. I was a knee-shakin'-mess, so I stayed straight and drank coffee. Lots and lots of coffee.

Then I remembered the beer. If I have some, I thought, I won't be afraid. So I took a beer to the living room, sat on the couch and listened to the radio. I called 'CPZ to request a few songs. Before long I was catching a pot buzz at the piano and singing. It felt good not to be afraid. Time must have been right. Henry was hooked on this other girl and happy days returned.

The first week of February was at an end. That night, about midnight, Henry called and wanted to come over. "Mitchel it's after ten. You can't come here." "Oh come on Capri let me over, I only had two beers. It ain't nothin'. Man you think two beers get me drunk? Come on let me come over Cap." "Forget it Mitchel I'm not letting you over. I can tell you're drunk. You're slurring your words. Don't come here." I was scared out of my mind. I couldn't believe I was saying these things. Now what did I trigger? Henry got extremely agitated, "Bitch! I'm coming over anyway. Fuck you. I'll be there in 15 minutes." He slammed the phone and I called the cops.

"Hi. This is Cappy Spettro on Polk Street. You know where I live. Batturs just called and said he was coming over. I told him on the phone not to but he wouldn't take no for an answer and I'm scared. The cops tried to calm me down. I interrupted them, "I'll tell you where he lives. I think I know what streets he uses to get here because he jumps the fence in my backyard. Will you look for him please? He's drunk. He was slurring and swearing and I'm afraid, I have three little kids upstairs." The dispatcher said they would send a car over to look for him in. After about 15 to 20 minutes, a cruiser pulled in the drive and an officer came to my door. Was I happy! He told me they found Henry and told him he was not welcome at my house. They took him back to his apartment under the conditions that he stay there. Otherwise they could have thrown him in jail for public intoxication. The officer told me that Henry was more than willing to accept the offer and went back to his place without a struggle. I was assured again. The feeling safe part would take some time! When the police left, I drank a couple more beers, took some nerve pills because I just wanted to sleep, and I did.

The next morning I received a phone call. I thought for sure it was Henry, but it was a cop from the police station who was concerned about me because of Henry. "Hello. Is this Capri Spettro?" "Yes... Who's this?" "I'm officer Cradal. We arrested Henry early this morning. He's in jail. I'd like you to come down to the station and look at what would have been you had you let him in last night." I sat at the table and said, "What are you talking about? Why should I come down to the station? You did say Henry was in jail right?" "Yes I did. I want you to come down here to see the girl Henry beat last night. You need to see her cuts and bruises. Why do you girls keep letting him in? He is going to end up killing someone one of these days. Capri, please! Maybe you'd think twice about letting him in your house if you would just look at her. She has bruises from the top of her head to the middle of her chest and back." I felt myself cringe all over. My skin was crawling. "No. I don't wanna come down there. I can't. I don't want to see her. She lives over in the same apartment as Henry right?" "Yes and he did this to her in front of her baby!" I instantly saw Sonny's face the night he helplessly watched Henry punch and rape me. Again I told the officer there was no way I would be at the station and I hung up.

Later that day after supper, I sat down to read the paper. There it was in black and white. I felt worse inside than earlier that morning when Cradal told me the story. He beat and kicked her with work boots for over an hour and a half. The story went on to say that the girl blacked out more than twice. Each time she tried to get up, Henry would only kick her again knocking her out of consciousness. I read the story over and over that day. I ended up cutting it out and putting in my wallet where I was sure to see it every day. Kept telling myself if I keep reading the story I'd find the strength to be through with Batturs. Period.

That night the phone rang and it was a collect call. Yes. Who else? I accepted. Why, I don't know. I just know that it was beyond necessary.

Henry told me lies. Wishing I would have let him in. Because If I would have, he wouldn't be sitting in jail right now. So now this was my fault? I couldn't take it. He was nuts! I made an excuse to get off the phone and when he wouldn't take no for an answer. I hung up. Of course the phone rang and rang and rang. And after four attempts and many, many many rings, it stopped.

I knew he wouldn't try to call anymore that evening because the phones at the jail were off by ten.

I went upstairs to check on the kids. As usual, they were all sound asleep. This was great for me because I could get the pot out of the sugar bowl and play the piano.

Steel toed work boots! That poor girl, I thought!

Morning arrived like it always did. Things were back to a settled norm'. Henry was in jail and with his bond set at over 24,000 dollars, he'd be in for a long, long time. I was free again. I could open the windows again! I could walk to the corner grocery store even in the dark! Freedom's well worth a wait. If only you-know-who would show up! Pink had not been to my house since Stone was found crashed out on my living room floor.

Henry would call collect. I'd accept. I'd pay. Still. I could hear officer Cradal's voice going off in my head. I couldn't imagine what the other girl must have looked like when Henry beat her with his boots. I heard Cradal's voice asking me to come to the station to see what I would have looked like had I let him in that night. I reached for the article that I had saved from the newspaper about Henry Mitchel Batturs III. I read it and I read it again. My skin crawled. I felt off balance. My heart went out to that girl. That girl that I should have gone to see at the police station. I wondered if she was getting calls from Henry. Did she go and visit him at the jail? No, I thought. She wouldn't. Then it began. I talked out loud to me. Self got me going that way. "Cap look at what he did to you and you were first in line to see that asshole. What can you say about that?" I answered myself and Self said, "Yeah, I was there. You still accept the calls. You are the ass here Cappy!" Self went on, "You could do something about it and you don't. What the hell is it going to take? Don't you love Gentry? Now's the time to get this creep out of your life once and for all Capri Elizabeth!" Self had to get in the last word and I let her because I knew she was right.

Lose Gentry forever? This has to stop! Why do I keep accepting the fucking calls? Why do I let him in? Must be out of my mind! Like God will help me now. Oh, I get it. I have to learn the hard way, the way I've always learned. And Pope reminded me of it off-ten! Yes. My life wasn't one fucking party, it's one big and bad clam bake. Some life. Just when someone wonderful is in my life and in my story, someone else was thrown into it, tearing up the pages and ruining the cover.

It was mid February. Henry was still calling me. One evening he asked me why I wasn't coming to see him. I lied and told him that my car wasn't working. I was very surprised when my lie didn't upset him. Then I got hit with a brick and figured that the other girl he beat and raped was going to see him at the jail. Of course. That had to be the reason. I soon learned from Henry's brother that indeed she was seeing Henry at the jail. Tim filled me in on many details. It turned out that this tiny woman, he had been seeing, beating, was married.   Not only was she married, but her husband was in prison. Oh this was some soap going on here and it was all too much.

One Sunday night I decided to go to the jail and ask Officer Wily about Henry and this other girl.   Wily saw me and more questions.   "Cappy, I don't get it. What keeps you gals coming down here to see this guy? Did you see her after Henry beat her?" "No. Cradal asked me to come to the station Wily, but I couldn't.   I just get sick all over when I think about it." "Well Cappy, you must not be too sick, you're here aren't you? You did come to see Henry didn't you?" "Wily, you don't understand. It's like being in jail myself.   I know that you say he is here all locked up. I call you every time I don't hear from him. You don't get it.   I have to be sure that he is here." Wily sighed. He handed me the visitor's papers to be signed. I went in and saw Henry. He didn't bring up the other girl and neither did I. I stayed only for a few minutes. Planned on getting there just as visitation was about over. Left the building, got in my car and headed to the house. Henry did not phone me that night.

I amused myself in the kitchen polishing my cans. There were 46 coffee cans now. They meant a lot to me. They looked so great in the west corner of the kitchen. I had so many that I had to spread them out from the corner. They now lined up against the white tiles to the sink and under the window just left of the original pyramid beneath the cabinets. There were blue cans with white lettering, blue cans with yellow lettering. Some of them carried printed words, some of them were in script. The arrangement had to be perfect.

Didn't have my own teeth on top anymore. It was very devastating and I hated the dentures. My face wasn't the same. Nina was

right.   The dentures would be my secret.

With Henry being locked and secured in the county jail, my life was less a prison. I got out a little more and stopped at The Well.   Sure I shot pool, played the juke box, but I was there for Gentry.   As my lucked took a turn for the better, he came in. As the bad luck would get me, Pink didn't talk to me. Sat some four, five bar stools away, but not close enough for me. He saw me shooting pool.   Been playing over an hour.   Was tired of playing against poor competition so I gave my cue to the next player. Told him he could have my game.

Sitting back at the bar I used my excellent peripheral vision and watched Gentry. He was still watching the pool players in progress. I wanted him to talk and for him to talk to me. Look at me.   See me and hear me. Immediately I thought that it had to be the teeth. Mine. Maybe he knew I had an upper denture. Maybe he doesn't want me anymore? He probably would want a girl with her own teeth. He'd never kiss me and now I didn't want him to. Began to feel real bad about the dentures and bout Pink who wasn't giving me a second thought. Or was he?

When the players were through and the cue sticks were planted in the wall, Gentry stood up at the foot of the pool table and said, "I only do this a couple times a year. Who wants to challenge me?" He looked so tired and worn out. Is he wanting my attention or is this his way of wanting some for himself? I watched him put the quarter and rack the balls like a pro. Wondered just how much he did know about game. Gentry glanced around the room for an opponent. His eyes deliberately passed mine. He looked extremely serious. Was his mind focused on the game or something much more? Was the much-more me? Self said not to accept the challenge and I didn't. I watched to see who would play him "the" game of pool. Pink played and won with ease. He put the cue down on the table and sat back at the bar to finish his drink. I wanted to congratulate him but I remained quiet and to myself.

A while passed when a friend of mine came in and joined me. His name was Tony. His last name was French. Well, it wasn't literally "French" Okay, the name originated in France. I don't go for many men with blonde hair and blue eyes, but Tony could have been bald and still sexy. His hair was just below his ears. He was about 5' 10" maybe, slender build yet strongly built. His eyes were set back with a rich hazel color. He kept a neat mustache. Tony had it made. He was kind of like a rough and tough kind of looking man, especially if he skipped a shave for a few days. Yep, he loved the ladies and had no problem attracting them because he was "fine"!

Girls were always flocking around Tony. But tonight he wanted to sit and talk to me. Tony started, (this was every time we talked). "So Cappy. You're gonna make a record and I wanna buy it." "Tony, your last name is pool, come on think about it.... "Tony Mojea" ... I'll be watching for your tournaments on the tube." We laughed, but we meant every word and proceeded to the table for great games of eight ball. Ultimately, Self and I wanted Gentry to be fucking jealous! But he was getting ready to go after last call. Pinky was out the door, and I excused myself as best as I could from the game. Like every winter before I was stricken with tonsillitis. Smoking and drinking wasn't helping and Tony and I were yelling over the music. I looked over at Benny the owner and said, "Don't lock me outside now. It's cold out there." Benny smiled and asked me to make it quick.

I got out the door after Gentry. He was standing on the porch just outside. I didn't have a chance to say anything to him when he quickly came over to me and grabbed my throat with his arm. All I could get out was his first name. I pushed as hard as I could to get away. Couldn't understand why he was doing this to me. I felt my gold necklace snap off my neck and hit the cement. Now I was mad! I kicked and pushed trying to get to the door. No one could hear me. Tried like hell to yell when I broke free, for a second, only my voice came out in whispered squeals and no one could hear. I broke the grip Gentry had on me, turned the door knob of the door but it was locked. Gentry walked back to me. I pushed him away and pounded on the door. Pink was just about to grab me again when the door flung open and Tony stood there with a cue stick aimed right at Gentry's face. Tony only had to look at Gentry and Gentry was gone. "Capri, do you want me to take care of him for you?" "You mean beat him up? No, I don't want anyone to lay a hand on him. Tony I know why he acted like that. It's a long story. He probably hates me and I think he has valid reasons. Call me crazy Tony, but I love that guy!" I gotta get to the house. I'm really tired. I appreciate what you did. I mean I'm glad you opened the door. It was getting cold out there." "Cold out there Cappy, that dude was hurting you and you're talking weather." "Yeah, well you know me Tony, I'm nuts! Hey, remember now, I wanna turn on the TV. one day soon and see you shooting professional pool" Okay Cap, but you have to give me a copy of your first record." "You bet cha. Later Tony."

Back at the house I thought about what Gentry had done. Funny… even though it wasn't funny, I realized I felt no pain when he did what he did. You'd think that it would hurt, but it didn't. The only thing that hurt me was my necklace. It made me so angry knowing I couldn't afford to get it fixed. I received it as a wedding gift from my relatives in Italy. It was an small medallion of the Virgin Mary hold the baby Jesus in 18 karat gold. I got home and put the necklace up on the shadow box. Made the mistake of having fried eggs before I crashed out on the couch. When I woke I went straight for the shadow box to look at my necklace. It woke me up in a hurry pissing me off! Damn, I thought, how the hell am I going to get this fixed? Self said "Gentry should pay for it. It's his fault. He broke your necklace. You never take that necklace off. Think! You have been wearing it every day for nine years! That's a long time. Make Pinky pay Capri Elizabeth!" Self meant business! "You're right. I know you are. He should pay. But he won't because I'm not going to ask him." Self lowered her head and we both cried.

Teary-eyed I sat at the guard table drinking a cup of cold coffee. Looked up and out the window wishing it was spring. My life was a blending gray. Wasn't it enough that winter already left my world so colorless? I must be losing my mind! Batturs! It's all his doing. He has destroyed my life. I can't take this. I gotta do something!

I washed my face and pulled myself together, made more coffee. Made the usual call to the jail making sure Henry was there.

231

That morning when I checked the mail I found an odd envelope that had come from some attorney's in Cleveland. I opened it. I took one look at the first page and it made me sit right down at the table immediately! They're going to sue me? The cops are going to sue me for the damage on the two cruisers? One hundred and fifty-thousand dollars? Yeah, like I have that. I don't own a thing! The thoughts raced on. It wasn't my fault. I was afraid to tell Henry he couldn't use the car. I didn't want to get beat again. I could still press charges. Self silently reminded me that I might lose. Henry might try to get back at me for taking him to court. I talked myself right out of pressing any charges.

Then something hit me. Never went to see what my car looked like after Henry joy-ride-wrecked-it. Made up my mind to do that after I called Pope about the law suit. Pope was to the point. He told me not to worry about it. I had nothing they could take anyway. He was right of course. It's his house I live in. Pope bought the furniture, washer, dryer and all of it. I laughed and said, "Hell. I don't own shit!" A bell went off in my head and I heard it clearly. Tripstar the cop, told me to say that Henry stole the car. The police would believe me. Of course they would believe it. I took in a deep breath and sighed, "Yes, the police will believe me."

I prepared myself mentally. Read the newspaper clipping about Henry like I did every day since the day he kicked and beat Laurie. I imagined just how brutal it must have been. Self talked me into going to the junkyard to see the car. On my way there I thought of the officer who went through the windshield of his cruiser, wishing it would have been Henry. Bob, the owner of the car graveyard was there. "Hey," he said, "I wanted to buy that from you. Why did you do that," he asked. "Bob, I didn't do it. Some jerk I know took it and hit two cop cars. I'm being sued for 150 thousand dollars." "No kidding? It was *a* beautiful car too. I wanted to buy it from you." Bob took me to the car and slapped the hood, "It's a shame isn't it? That was such *a* clean car too." "Yep." "Well Cappy, look all you want." Bob headed for the office. I was afraid to get inside. From the driver side, through the window I saw that the steering wheel was pushed toward the seats. The entire dashboard of the car was pushed forward almost a foot. I opened the door that was bent up pretty bad and made myself get in it. When I did I pretending to be at the wheel. Leg room gone. Damn Batturs! He should have gotten a couple of broken legs not just some easy-ass-bruises! I opened the glove compartment and found a now tarnished tin I had used for spare joints. Shook my head and said out loud, "He smoked that too!" Put the empty tin in my pocket. I saw enough and waved good bye to Bob. With speed I had to go somewhere. To the Sandusky Police Station on the other side of town, conveniently on the east side of town. Not too many blocks from Neil Street where Pink was still working on the house. Of course I drove by to see if the Shark was parked in the drive. There or not, I didn't stop. He would have to come to me now. He broke my necklace damn it!

When I arrived at the station I walked in and luck was standing right in the lobby. It was Officer Cradal. "Hi Cap. You should have been here that day to see the girl that Henry kicked and kicked." "Cradal I know. I didn't have the guts. I didn't want to see what would have been me. It makes my skin crawl thinking about it." "It should. That was almost you. Steel toed work boots Cappy. Head, face, chest, back and more bruises. She could hardly open her eyes. You're a nice girl. One of these days Henry is going to end up killing somebody. He's sick Cap. I've dealt with guys like him for years. I go to clinics and I see psychopaths all the time. Everybody loves a psychopath and do you know why? Because they are the world's best liars. You keep talking to him. Laurie visits him at the jail." There were patient eyes watching me and I paused long enough.

"Cradal, look." I opened my wallet and pulled out the newspaper article. "See, I cut this out and saved it. I read it and read it and read it. I have read it every day since it happened." "Are you still talking to him Cappy," Cradal asked. "Yeah, if he calls I accept. I'm scared. Scared if I don't accept the calls that when he gets out he'll hurt me again. Tripstar was the only cop who saw what Henry did to me. My ear was black inside and out. I had a bone sticking out in front of my ear." "Cappy, why didn't you press charges? He would have gone to prison where he belongs." "Again, like I told you Cradal, fear! What if he was found not guilty? He'd want to hurt me worse for pressing charges. I didn't go to the hospital, doctor or nothing. Didn't want any reports made."

"Cap, I'm going to get something that I'm not suppose to show anybody outside the police. Have a seat and I'll be right back. Don't leave on me now." I sat down on the brown wooden bench and lit up a cigarette, waiting. Cradal was back with 3x5 index cards. There were five in all. "Cap, these are all the charges that we have on Henry Batturs. Look at them and look real good! One charge you won't see anywhere on these cards is domestic violence! Look! Why don't you girls report this stuff?" Five cards, I thought, numbers and lines so I counted.

Distractions, additions and multiplications. Ten lines a side. There was a line down the middle of the card. The lines were numbered. 1 through 10 on the left side. 11 through 20 on the right. Then I flipped the card over. Same, different numbers. Right side 21 through 30. Left 31 to 40. And Cradal was right. There were no domestic violence charges what so ever. He tucked the cards under his jacket and slipped them in a pocket there. "Cradal I don't want to keep talking to him. I hate him. I just don't know how to get out of it." "Cappy, you just get out of it. One day, he'll probably be on death row. What if you let him in one night because you think he isn't drunk or high and he kills you and your children? Your children Cap! You can't take risks like that, you have to protect those kids and yourself! I'd hate to get a call and find out that the call was your street, your numbers and find you dead! Please think about what I'm telling you." "I will. I have imagined the worse. Thought the possibility that he'd kill me and the kids. I read this article every day. It seems to make me stronger. I just now came from the junkyard to see my car. It wasn't easy. Believe me Cradal I do think! Sometimes I think so much, I feel like I'm losin' my mind and thank God he's in jail!" "Yes he is locked up... but it won't be forever. Laurie didn't press charges either." " Yeah, well, uhm, I'm really sorry but I gotta get back to the house. Don't worry Cradal, I won't say nothing about those charges you showed me. I needed to see them. It'll help me. Thanks, thanks a lot." "Sure Cappy, and remember, don't let Henry in your house!" "I do want this to stop, but really Cradal I gotta go. I'll see ya."

It was back to my house. I drove west on Neil Street and the Shark wasn't in the drive. Naturally once I got through the door of my house I had coffee ready. Cold, but ready. Of course there was a fresh pot brewing. And the pot was acting funny. This percolator Frank gave me. It was playing tricks. Sometimes it would rumble till the coffee was good hot and black. Then other times it would go through all the motions making no coffee at all. Just hot water. Like with everything else, it had a third trick it would slip in on me every now and then. It would bubble and brew the coffee, take a break and not do anything at all. Once the break was over, which sometimes could be up to two minutes, it would start brewing again. This left the coffee looking like tea, making me angry enough to wanna shine the stupid pot just to get it off my mind! And I did just that. I took out the some soapy steel wool pads and shined her good inside and out and the little bitch had the audacity to do whatever it wanted and when. "Capri, you're losin' it." "That I might be." That was Self.

I spent a lot of the time thinking about what Cradal said. Henry might be mentally ill. Maybe he really does hear voices! He told me he did. He'd laugh, but maybe that was a way to cover the fact that he really was. I wondered how many other girls had been through what I'd been through with him. Wondered how many more there might be. I knew I would get away from Henry somehow, but it was the somehow I had a hard time finding. Where was that time, only God knew. Or did He?

It was near the end of February. One evening I got a call from Migs, the girl who tended bar at The Well. She called to see if Henry was at my house. This surprised me because Migs never called me ever! I told her that he was in jail and I told her why. Migs broke down and told me that he crawled into an open window at her house one night and punched her head a few times. It set my wheels rolling! Does she keep the same dark secret I do? Did she continue to see him after? I didn't ask and I didn't wanna know. The phone call hence forth was cut short. I told her I'd see her out at the bar soon. That was that.

Shit! Migs said her dad was sleeping right upstairs when that creep broke in. This guy is sick Cap! He doesn't care who is around. Babies, dads! Maybe he will end up killing somebody someday!

I received a couple more calls from Migs. She asked the same question she did the first time. Again I told her that Henry was still in the county jail.

I knew then that Migs had to be as afraid of Henry as I was. Otherwise why would she be calling me to see where he was? Why didn't she just call the jail herself?

As short February persisted on taking its time leaving, Henry was calling me collect. The same boring things were his topics. Complained about the blacks tying up the phones. Complained about the food and he complained about being locked up. I wanted the conversations to end sooner than later. My lips moved and said things that never meant a thing. It was a front. An act. It was fear. I couldn't think clear. Hiding things on myself, to search and search. Slurred my speech waiting for the blue jays to perch. The days still a chill, the nights ever cold. I can't forgive. I can't forget all that I had underwent. I talked to God I knew He was there. The clouds in the sky had made me aware. I told this to Pink and he knew it was so, because he's working for God, because he told me so.

Then a call came one night from The Well and it was Gentry on the line. "How ya doin' Big Time? Got something important to tell you." Felt like my soul took off in flight to surround his. A lump grew in my throat. "I'm getting married!" "You can't Pink, you can't!" Stunned, the phone was being hung up at his end, while I stood in a trance. This must be a dream and I'll laugh and I'll laugh. Time went quick and then a knock on the door and it was Gentry don't you know it? He just had to tell me more. I opened the door distressed, till I saw the gleam that shined in his eyes. Pink knew I was mad. He liked getting me that way. "So, you think it's okay for you to be here? I mean, after all you're getting married. What would the little woman say if she knew you were here?" Gentry laughed and walked in. Stood at the kitchen sink waiting for me to claim the spot he took because he knew it was mine. "Hey, you can't stand there, that's my spot!" I walked over and pushed him shoulder to shoulder wanting him away from my spot! He laughed even more and said, "I like this spot. It's the warmest spot. I'm not moving," he said chuckling. "Like hell! You get over on the other side of the kitchen.

You're getting married remember? Go on move!" I pushed him again. Pink laughed more making his way to the other side of the kitchen, (and that was only about five feet). He backed into the counter and leaned. "Okay. I'm on neutral over here, but you have to stay in yours." "No, I don't think so. Who's this girl you say you're going to marry? You can't marry her!" Gentry beamed into my eyes smiling, "Why? Why can't I marry her Big Time?" "Because. You don't love her that's why!" With a grin he asked, "How do you know that?" "Because I know. I don't know how I know, I just do." "Tell me Big Time," he said, "Tell me how you know?" He was still smiling, trying to act like this marriage thing was so serious. He and I both knew we could read each other's minds and the game rolled on.

"She won't make you happy Gentry. Then again, I don't know her. Maybe she will. Anyway, she better. Make you happy I mean." He face grew curious-serious and he asked, "Oh, so I shouldn't marry her?" My face grew the same, I thought it was a game. There went my heart again. I knew the only way to show him I loved him was to let him go. Wishing I would have said yes when he wanted to make music with him ... together... forever. Calmly and bravely I said, "Gentry, I don't think you love her, but if you do and she loves you too, guess you should marry her. I just wanna know you're happy. She better take care of you damn it!" The lump in my throat grew more and it was harder holding back the salted tears. I started back to my neutral side of the kitchen when he held my arm and said, "I can't marry her. I don't love her. Who should I marry Big Time?" "Oh, you think you're so funny don't you Gentry Mocean. I should tell you to leave." He jumped right in saying, "You want me to go, I'll go. It's late anyway..." I jumped in immediately if not sooner and said, "Oh no! You're not going anywhere yet!

Tell me what's going on. Still working for God? He's making you do all this right? You're driving me crazy! Why do you do this to me?" "Think I should marry you," he asked? "Me? Yeah. You should marry me, but see we're perfect together. And since there is nothing perfect on earth, we can't be married. God wouldn't like that now would He?" Pink was precise, "Oh so you think we're perfect together? Hmm. So we shouldn't get married. Yeah you're right, we can't. Okay. Why don't you play something for me Big Time?" "You know Gentry you have a lot of nerve asking me to play something for you. Should throw you out you know that?" "Oh! If you want me to leave that's nooo problem!" He was still tee-heeing. "Oh no! You're not going anywhere! You're staying with me." Gentry laughed his way into the living room. "So you think you can make me stay now?" "No Gentry, I don't think I can make you stay, but we both know you want to." Pink laughed more, went over to the couch and laid back into it waiting for me to play and sing. I did. Then we talked, we laughed and night went on. Nothing happened not a hug or a kiss. I waited so long for a moment like this. It wasn't in my dreams, it wasn't happening in life, and I knew more than ever I should be this man's wife. We lay face to face on the couch to talk on. I slipped into sleep, morning came, he was gone. I love him, I thought! Did he feel the same way? And I wanted him to be the first one to say. Would the time ever come? Was a time planned to be? Would time be the never, as it seemed much to me? Would I go life time to life time finding him each time each time. Would it be just like this time, would he ever be all mine?

Pondered the questions, it was daily that's that. Kept saving the coffee cans, got high, petted the cat. The next day was like any other. Drank plenty of coffee, played more piano and finished off the pot I had left from the night before. It was a normal day as days go, but a call came that had changed all that.

Batturs called. He was messed up on something. The call was from the county jail... collect. He told me that one of the trustee's managed to sneak some wine and pot into the jail. He was passing it around to a bunch of the guys locked inside. Henry told me it went on a lot of nights. He spoke boldly to the black men he really feared. "Hey, man I'm on the phone. Like, could you keep it down a little?" Yeah, that was about as bold as Batturs could get. "So, Capri, what are you doing? Drinking? Pot? You know you are." "Yes Mitchel. Is a matter of fact I'm high right now! Good pot too!" "How much do you have," he asked. "We've been getting high in here all night. I got a pretty good buzz goin' on. Hey, there was this dude in here when you came to visit me that one time. Last time. He said he knew you." "Yeah, who was that? I didn't see anyone in there I knew. Got a name?" Henry got angry and loud, "Man, I can't remember the dude's name. Some guy. He was leaving when you came in." Ha, I thought, he isn't telling the truth. I always looked at the names on the visitor's list to see who was there. Seldom was anyone there to see him, accept for Laurie. "Well?" I asked again, "What's the name?" "Man I told you I can't remember. But he knows a friend of your mother. He said your mother is a whore." "That's it Mitchel. Shut up. I'm hanging up. Don't call..." "Wait. Don't hang up. I didn't say it, this other dude did. Don't hang up. Come on. I just want to talk to somebody. I've been in here a long time. It's so cold in this fuckin' place."

The interruption worked but I needed more information. "Okay, but you find out this guy's name Mitchel. I mean it!" "I can try. I don't even know if he'll come back over here. He was here to see somebody else and that dude is getting out tomorrow. He just said that your dad used to take your ma over to this dudes house to get fucked and then your dad would go back to pick up the whore and take her home." I hung up the phone and immediately called the jail. I asked for Officer Wily but he was off that night. It didn't matter who after that. "Sir, My name is Capri Spettro. I just received a call from Henry Batturs. He said dirty things about my mom and she's dead." I fell to tears. Officer Ganes, who was on the phone with me said, "Miss, you can press charges. Phone harassment. If he calls you again, he'll be charged. He could get anywhere from 1 to 5 years." "You're serious? Will it work? Do you think he'll try to call me. I'm afraid of him. He hurt me. He wrecked my car. I'm scared." "Knowing Henry, I don't think you'll have to worry about him calling you again. I can go and tell him right now that this is what we will do if he tries calling you anymore." Without hesitation I said, "You'll tell him now? Can I wait on the line until you do that? I have to know what he says." "Tell you what. I'll call you as just as soon as I pass on the information to Henry. How's that?" "Great, but will it be long?" "No, it's not that busy. I can probably get back with you in about five minutes or so. Oh, and miss, if he calls you before I get there to tell him, just hang up." "Okay, I will. Thank you."

We hung up our phones. Mine rang. It was Henry calling collect. I hung up. He called a second time, I did the same. Then there was silence. I figured that Officer Ganes was talking to him at that moment. I watched the clock. Four minutes passed. Five then six. " Damn! When is Ganes gonna call me back?" And I paced the floor. Seven! The phone rang and it was Ganes with the good news. He told Henry. Henry said that he wouldn't call anymore. And he didn't. At last. It was over.

♬ ♪ "I Used To Love You" ♪ ♫
Words and Music by: Catherine Santi on March 14th, 1985

"*I used to love you, back then I guess I was obsessed.*
I used to love you, don't get me wrong you're still the best.
Don't you know what I'm trying to say?
When you feel what is real and I still feel that way.
And...
I used to need you, like no one else I knew before.
I used to need you, until I just could need no more.
Don't you know what it is that you do?
Tell you this, it's too much for just one to go through.
I used to want you, that is no secret to conceal.
I used to want you, so least for now I should be real.
You oughta know what I'm trying to say.
When you feel what is real, well I still feel that way."

Chapter Twenty: "Part One: The Game. No Playing Pieces."

March of '86 had glided in, landing swiftly on time. Spring would be near, if only a number. The no more collect calls gone, gave me a few extra dollars, but just a few. Good jobs were gone, if ya call factory work good. But without that kind of income, sitter expenses would be stupid. Yeah, March was wonderful. A real fucking hell. Memories of March ran round in my head. Mayor gone and it's March. Met Prof' in March. Beat and raped in March. Yeah, so much for spring.

Desperate for work, I called Nina for ideas. She told me that I could get a grant from the government to get some college education. I thought about the idea of going to school again. But going to college didn't feel like me. Didn't want to be anything but a singer. Self ran the show. "Some singer I'd be now. These teeth ruined what we looked like. Looked good!" Damn it! If only Pope would have loaned me the money for dental work. He should have let me go to the Italian opera school. So I smoked! Why wouldn't he let me get a job at Cedar Point like all my other friends? Why didn't I take that brand new ladies shoe store out in Wisconsin when I had the chance? Why did I marry Prof"? Why did I do anything I did? Jesus! I was driving myself nuts thinking about it. How hard it has been. Poking round in my brain was Pope, "You always had to learn things the hard way." So why couldn't he have made things a little easier while I was growing up? "Aaah, kinda late for that now Capri." So Self reminded me.

I let the ideas of going to school float around in my head thinking of what I would go to school for. That would take a lot of thinking!

In the meantime I had to concentrate on what I had to work with already and it wasn't much. While me and Nina were having our usual morning bitch puzzle talk, she surprised me. Said that housing development was accepting applications for renters and that her landlord agreed to be a part of the program. Nina talked to Pope about doing the same for me. Pope liked the idea of getting a steady rent check so he signed himself up. I knew he would.

The day came for the applications. Nina and I arrived thinking we arrived fairly early. We knew there would be others wanting a chance. We took our numbers. Nina was 56 and I was 57. Our wait would be a lengthy one and we worried we weren't there soon enough. But the wait paid off. Nina and I were the last two applications they were going to take for that year. We fit the bill for "poor" and got the benefits of having most of our rent paid. Since Pope was more to me than just a "land lord," the 40 bucks I was supposed to pay, he'd let me borrow. He knew I would end up needing it.

Now if I could get a job under the table I could have it made. But there were no jobs. Could have easily found a job cleaning rooms again. Knew people who would pay me under the table to do the dirty work, but I was through with that. I waited. Looked for something better, if something better was out there somewhere.

March was well into the second week and spring would officially be. Made calls to the jail, making sure of where Henry was. Took long enough to get *"that"* creep outta my story.

Gentry hadn't been over in so long and I wanted so much to tell him everything ... the truth. But I didn't have the courage to call him and I certainly wouldn't drive to Neil Street. A letter. Yes, I'll write him a letter. Letter number one was sent, but I heard nothing. Thought about another plan, plan number two.

In the mean time I was working on another song. It would be my eleventh. Gentry had no idea that I was writing them all for him. But hadn't he been able to read my mind well enough to know another was in the making? Or had it had me tuned out?

The rent was paid, I finished a song, I wanted to celebrate and Henry was gone. I would go out this night for fun! I threw on my jeans, a red sweater and my gray wool scarf. It was quite the scarf. Hanging in front of my clothes, it dropped down to my knees. It looked good. I looked good. Even my teeth weren't going to get in my way! Tonight I'll go somewhere new, by the bay. Me and my car headed north to the downtown area I parked in front of a corner lounge named "Daly's." Felt real nervous going into a new place, for the first time, and the place was big. I decided to take a friendly seat at the bar if I could find one. The night was early and Daly's was hopping.

It wasn't normal for a bar in Sandusky to be have this many people out and drinking green beer none the less. Then I spotted a two or three green hats. There were shamrocks planted everywhere. Coasters, tee-shirts, napkins, shirts. Saint Patrick's Day! That's why the place was so busy. That's why the green beer. After finding a place to sit, I figured I'd order a glass of the green stuff, just to get into the spirit of things. After a couple of them, I floated around talking to people I hadn't seen in a while. Felt good to be out and about with people, good people. Everyone was having blast. Going to The Well would bring me down if Pink wasn't there, so I stayed at Daly's because the Irish in me wanted to.

Later in the evening I saw someone I had a crush on when I was 14 years old. People called him Winky. I went over to him to see if he remembered me. "Excuse me. Aren't you Winky?" "Yes I am. How ya doing Cappy. It's been a long time." He remembers me, I thought? Wink said that I hadn't changed a bit. He called over to the bartender and bought me a drink. I thanked him and we talked for a while. He called the bartender over again, telling the man that in wanted to buy every green carnation behind the bar. "Cap, I wanna get one for you and all the lovely ladies tonight. Want one?" "I'd love one. It'd look good on my scarf don't cha think?" Wink agreed. The bartender told Wink it would be nice to leave some for the other people who might want one. Wink put up a friendly argument with the young man for about five minutes, gave up and bought one for me. It was a beautiful shade of mint green with a long stem. Wink pinned it on my scarf, gave me a little kiss on the cheek and said, "Happy Saint Patrick's Day Cap." "Thanks Wink. Thanks for the flower. Smells so nice and I seldom get flowers." "Are you kidding Cap? A pretty girl like you should get flowers every day." "I appreciated that Wink. But everyday would be a little much don't ya think?" "Cap, I'll tell ya what I think. You and me ought to take off and go out dancing somewhere. You like to slow dance? I do. Want to go?" I could tell that Wink had a good alcohol buzz. Even though the invitation was an innocent one, I felt like I was betraying Gentry. "Wink, it sounds like a lot of fun, but I got three kids home and I didn't plan on staying out much longer." "Oh come on Cap. Let's just go for an hour, a half hour. Just a little while. What do you say?" "Wink I'm sorry. Wish I could but I can't." "Oh I see. I bet there is somebody out there already isn't there?" he asked. "Sort of. I think. I'm not sure yet. I mean I am sure, but I'm not sure if he is sure. Get it?" "Cap, I may be a little drunk, but it's not hard to see that you are in love with someone. He's a lucky man!" I thanked Wink for the compliment and said I had to get going.

On my way out I saw Max Sparks. A cop who worked for the Sandusky Police. He called out, "Capri. How are you? Why don't you join me and my friends for a drink?" Thanks Max, but I need to get to the house. Can't make the sitter late." "Are you sure you can't stay for one?" I wasn't about sit with a bunch of cops, and as hard as it was to resist his shining white smile and good looks, but hey … he was a cop and was going to the house to get high!

Glad to away from the crowd and loud music. The quiet was just what I needed. I made fresh coffee, took the carnation off, got it in a vase and placed it on the piano. Then I headed straight for the bag of pot I just bought. Now that the phone bill was lower and the rent was paid, I bought an ounce and it was pot heaven for me. Never bought that much at a time! Took it over to a desk and rolled a joint, smoked it and then I repeated that. Wasn't quite ready to get behind the piano, so, instead of smoking another one, I thought it would fun to clean the seeds and stems out of the pot. Dumped the bag of it on top the desk. "Oh what the hell." I rolled and smoked another joint. Just then there was a knock at the door. It was not a familiar knock, but could it have been that familiar person? I answered and it was not Gentry, but Max Sparks the cop! I didn't open the door all the way. Kept the chain lock on. "Hi Max. What the hell are you doing over here?" "Hello Capri. I'm know it's late, I'm sorry. But when you left the bar I got to thinking about how you were doing?" "Me," I asked. "I'm fine, but what are you doing here? You're a cop." "What's me being a cop have anything to do with it?" he asked. "Cause I can't ask you in. You're a cop!" "Why not Capri? Oh! You have company?" "No Max. I just think you might arrest me if I let you in." I held the joint to my right so he couldn't see it. "Capri I wouldn't arrest you for anything. Now will you ask me in?" "Max it's illegal." "What is?" "This is." I showed him the joint. " Capri I'm not going to arrest you for one joint." "Okay Max, I let you stand out in the cold long enough. Guess you can come in. But you have to promise me that you won't arrest me after I do." I took the chain off and opened the door letting Max into the house.

Within three steps he could see the desk and all the pot I had laying on it. Right away I said, "Well? Wanna arrest me now?" "No Capri. I told you I would never arrest you for anything." It was a load off my shoulders. Max and I relaxed and talked. Naturally being a cop he asked me if I was through with Batturs. I told him about the phone call that put a stop to everything. Max was glad to hear it. I had some beers in the fridge and we drank them. I smoked more joints. Max knew I was gonna smoke the stuff on the desk. Who cared? Not me. After the green beers and the beers and the pot at the house, I didn't care about anything, not coffee, not nothing, not Pink. But I should have because time made it's passes and so did Max. Yes, there was sex and when it was over, Max didn't run out the door like that's all he came for. He stayed, we talked. When he gave me his reasons why he had better be going, I didn't mind. I wanted to be alone, need to be because I knew that I had done something terribly wrong.

Felt so ashamed of myself. I should have gone out to dance. At least this would have never happened. Winky didn't know where I lived and I wouldn't have told him. Max did know where I lived and I let him in. What a fool I was, so much alcohol. I wanted to sober up, clean up, but all I accomplished was putting the pot back in the bag. I passed out on the couch. Morning came. It took some doing but I dragged myself into the shower first thing. I thought I could wash the night away. I felt miserable for what I had done. Couldn't believe that I let it happen. I tried to make myself think it was a dream, but Self and I both knew how very real the night before was.

A few days passed. My money situation was short. I called Prof' and told him that I had to have some money. He owed me. He owed the court.

He owed it to his kids. He should have thought himself lucky. The child support he was supposed to be paying for three kids was just 120 dollars a month. After talking to Prof', I got the usual response, "I'll see what I can do."

A couple more days went by and one early evening Prof' stopped over. He claimed he had 100 dollars to give me that came with a condition. The condition was that I have sex with him. "Are you out of your mind Prof'! There is no way! How could you ask me something like that? You make me sick." "Geez Cap. You act like we never did it! We were married seven years. That ought to be good for one more time. You're the one that will make out." I still couldn't believe what I was hearing. "Prof' I'm not your wife anymore. I won't and will not have sex with you ever! Pay someone else." "Cap, why give it away when you can make a little money off of it? Didn't you just have Max Sparks over here the other night?" I was curiously pissed and asked, "What? Are you watching my house or something? How did you know he was here?" "I just know. He used you Cap. He's married. Did you know that?" "Married? Max? How do you know so much Prof'? "Maybe you're wrong. He can't be married. Or he..." "Or he wouldn't have what Cap? Had sex with you?" "Prof', it's really none of your business, but I'll tell you. Yes I did have sex with Max. But I would have never done anything with him if I knew he was married. You know me better than that." "I know Cap." "You're no better Prof'. You want me to give it up just to have what my kids got coming."

Professor didn't say anything. He just watched me a minute. I thought about the kids. They needed things. We all needed things. I didn't want to call Pope for help. I didn't want to have sex with Professor. I was in a bind. Felt bad enough about getting drunk and stupid. I felt worse that I let things get out of control with Max. What would Pink say if he knew? What to do? Hurry Cap and think of a way to get the money. "Prof' just give me the cash will ya? It's not for me it's for the kids. You're suppose to pay." "Cap, come on. You know I'm not gonna give the money to you for nothing. You're dad is taking care of you and the kids. You know if you need something all you have to do is call him. He always helps you out." I knew Prof' well. I knew that no matter what I said he wasn't going to give me a dime unless I had sex with him. "Professor... you make me sick. I need that money so just give it to me. You want the sex, I want the money first. I live here you don't. I make the rules. You don't. I can't stand you and hate you! Don't put your hands on me, don't hug me, kiss me or nothin'! I'd only puke all over you."

Professor took out the money and hesitated giving it to me. I took the money out of his hands and his pants were un-zipped. I didn't want to look at him. Hated him so much for all he had put me through. I wanted it over and I wanted it over before it began. I grabbed a blanket that was folded next to the couch and threw it over my face and said, "I don't want you looking at me either." "That's okay Cap. If you don't want us to look at each other, it's okay by me. I don't care."

From head to hips I stayed covered with the blanket. I put my head on one side and concentrated on looking at the blanket that surrounded my vision. Except for one problem. I kept wondering how long it would take Prof'. Unfortunately I let him do this to me. Fortunately it didn't take long. I reached for my jeans that were at the knees and pulled them up. Kept the blanket over me and said, "Prof' leave! Just go. I want to hear the car start up outside before I even get up off the floor." "Come on Cap. Was it that bad?" "Yeah. That's the last time I will ever let you con me into your sick game. I won't sell myself to no one again." "I'm sorry you feel that way Cap. Things might have been better if we never married, just dated." "Prof'. I got my money. You got what you wanted. Just leave already!" I heard him buckling his belt. Next sound. His car keys. He walked away and to the door saying, "Well, see ya later. Bye!" I heard the door close. Heard the car start up in the drive. When his car drove away, I pulled the blanket off of me and headed into the kitchen. I put the money away in my purse. Went to the bathroom and filled the tub and tried to wash this and the other evening away. Oh I was doing great. I tried to cover one bad night with another. How could I be so stupid? Prof' just wants me to think that Max is married because Max is much better looking than him. "Listen to yourself Cap. Do your hear what you are saying." Self was always butting in when she wasn't wanted. Then I answered her, "I know, I know. What I did was wrong with Max and it was wrong with Prof'. Hell, I don't know what I'm doing anymore, and worse, I don't know why." I heard Self saying to herself, "I thought you knew?"

This was a night marked for drinking. Made plans to get out that night to go to The Well. Migs was tending bar and had my drink ready before I even sat down. I slammed some quarters in the juke box and planted one on the pool table. Night was headed for serious thoughts. I didn't let anything distract me. I played a lot of pool, a lot of music, and I was there a long time. Hours passed quickly that evening. It was near closing time when Gentry floated in for last call. He didn't see me or he didn't want to see me. There was a good half hour before Benny would tell everybody it was time to go. Normally if Gentry came into the bar you couldn't un-glue me from the place. This night I wanted to leave the minute I saw him and I did just that. Grabbed my things off the bar, got my keys out of my pocket and headed for the door. I bid the owner and Migs a good night. Walked passed Gentry and said nothing to him. Gave him a quick look and left the building. I drove to the house carefully. The last thing I needed was a D.U.I.

It was just after two in the morning and I locked the house for the night. Left the porch light on just in case Gentry would stop. He didn't. I stayed up till about five in the morning singing and playing the piano. Finally I could stay awake no longer. The liquor wore off and I was tired. I turned off the porch light and curled up on the couch to fall asleep.

When morning came I realized that I thought about nothing at all. I only went out drinking. Drinking just let me forget the reason I left the house in the first place. I left to think. I ran into Pink. I said nothing to him, he said nothing to me, not a wink! Man oh man! What am I doing? I thought. I finally got Henry Batturs to leave me alone. Sparks had me, Prof' had me and I was drinking. I wondered if I was turning into an alcoholic. Thought about how many drinks I would have in a night. It started with a couple and became about seven or eight. I talked myself into the fact that my body was just getting immune to the alcohol. That didn't mean I was becoming an alcoholic. Facts remained. All the wrongs I had made. I spent the day cleaning the house and doing laundry. I tried "not" to think about anything. Of course there was one exception. Gentry remained constant.

Buff began growing curious about where Pinky had been lately. It was hard explaining to her that he just came around when he felt like it. Positively Buff stated, "Mom, I know that he will come back. Maybe he just wants to surprise you. You know he always comes back right? I wish he would come over when I'm awake. I miss him. Will you tell him the next time you see him that I miss him and I want him to come over and see me?" "Sure I will Buff, if I see him." "Mom you could always go to that place. Could you go tonight and see if he's there, Please?" "Buff, I don't know. I was just there last night and he didn't even say hi to me. I don't know. I can't spend all your dads money at the bar, this money is for you guys!" "Well mom, you could go and not spend any right?" "Yeah, you're right. Okay, if I can get someone to watch you guys tonight for a little while, I'll see what I can do." "Don't forget to say Buff Bag misses him. Jules said she wants him to come over too. I don't think Sonny really cares." "Oh, you know your little brother. All he ever has on his mind is food."

When it got to be about eight p.m., I really didn't feel much like going out. Didn't get much sleep the night before. I was hoping Buff would forget what she wanted but she didn't. She asked me if I was going to go out. I looked at her looking up at me with those big bright blue eyes and I couldn't turn her down. I made arrangements with one of Nina's girls to watch the kids for me. Went out about 9:30.

Drove over on Neil Street and I didn't see the Shark so I headed to The Well. Made up my mind before I left the house that I wasn't going to drink. Buff was right. I didn't have to spend money to go out. Not on alcohol anyway. I had coffee.

I didn't see Gentry and asked Benny if he had. Benny pointed to a group of guys standing half way through the place and said, "He's standing right there Cap. Had a little too much last night? I almost had to throw a blanket over you?" "Come on Benny don't kid me. I wasn't loud was I?" "No, you were pretty quiet last night." "Don't mess with my head like that Benny? You should throw me outta here ya know." Benny shook his head and we both smiled. I drank half the coffee and decided it was time to talk to Pink.

I was real nervous about walking over to him, especially with a couple of his buddies standing there. Had to keep in mind that this was for Buff. I made my way to him. He stopped and turned. I said hello first. He said, "What's up?" "Well, I came out here because of Buff." "How are the kids?" he asked. "Oh the kids are just fine. It's Buff. She misses you. She came up to me earlier today wanting to know why you don't come and see her anymore." "She did huh? Must be pretty pathetic when you have to use your kids to get a man." He sneered as he turned his eyes away. I was mad and made sure he knew it when I raised my voice and got firm, "Is that what you think? What I told you was true! It was for Buff! I wouldn't use my kids to get a man and especially one that thinks so. Good night Mr. Mocean." Walking away, I felt the lump in my throat and my heart breaking. I didn't want him or anyone see me cry. Gentry gently took my arm to hold me from leaving, "I didn't mean it." I tugged my arm away with my back to him and said, "Forget it. I'm leaving." And I left. I didn't drive straight home. I lit up a joint I had and drove around to smoke it. I back tracked my way to the house and when I drove down on Neil Street I let all the tears out. I knew I would have to hurry and get myself together. Buff would never believe that I didn't see Gentry if she saw I was crying. She'd be up if she had to make herself do so. I drove till I knew I'd be composed enough, until the joint was gone.

Wasn't going to be no easy matter. I didn't want to lie to her about not seeing him. I walked in and Buff came running up to me asking, "Did you see Pinky?" I choked back the tears when I didn't tell her the truth. She held back enormous disappointment and went up to her room. I felt helpless. Then a knocker was knocking at the door. Buff ran to the door and when she got to it she said, "Mom, it's Pinky, he's here, he's here!" She opened the door and yelled out smiling big, "Pinky you finally came over. What took you so long?" "I've been doing a lot of thinking," he said. I watched her looking at him, smiling big with joy and thinking how wonderful this was. He had her little hand in his and he walked over into the kitchen taking my spot and

I let him. When I told him at the bar that Buff missed him he knew it was the truth. I saw this now as I saw it then. He made me so angry and would he do it again. I wondered without aim. Is this a big game?

Then I sang and I sang and he stayed yeah he stayed. Buff was happy and so was Jules. Sonny was sleeping just waiting for breakfast. I was happiest of all. So happy that I had forgot about all the music I had left scattered all over the piano. Some of the stuff was other people's songs, but mine were buried in the books and pages there. I hurried into the living room to get at the mess. Stuffed all of it in a folder nearby. Not neat and entirely out of order. Buff tried to stay awake, but she'd been fighting to keep her eyes open. Jules got off the couch first and said good night to me and Gentry. Headed to her room. Weary Buff hugged Pinky a big hug good night and mom was after. Told her that I would be up in a minute to tuck her and Jules in. I offered Gentry a cup of coffee, but he didn't want any. I checked on the girls and Buff was already asleep. Jules was still awake and asked if me and Gentry were going to get married. "Jules, I don't know. He never really asked me." "I heard that Jules," Buff said. "Buff, I thought you were asleep?" "I almost was till *"Jewelry"* opened her mouth and woke me up." "Buff, just leave me alone I was asking mom." "You guys, stop it now. Don't start! Just get some sleep. Forget about this marriage thing okay. He didn't ask me." Buff said, "Mom, he'll ask you. Are you going to say yes when he does?" "He didn't ask me. I don't know. Just go to sleep, come on! He's gonna hear us talking up here." The girls both decided that it was time to get some sleep. Thank goodness!

When I came back downstairs Gentry said, "Who was that guy with you the other night at Daly's?" I had to stop and think. Like I didn't do that enough. "Oh, you mean Winky? He just bought me a flower for Saint Patrick's Day. Wait, how do you know anyway? I didn't see you there." "I know." "Oh, you know huh. Well, Winky asked me to go out dancing with him too." "Where did you go?" he asked. "Nowhere." "So did you go home then?" "Yes. I came straight here." Gentry got up off the couch and made a mad-dash for the folder of music on the piano. He clutched it laughing and said, "I think I'll take these home with me." "Oh, no you're not. You're not taking my music any where!" He started flipping through the pages and then he looked at me with a big grin and said, "Which ones did you write for me Big Time?" "I'm not telling. Now give them back." I stood there with my arms folded, tapping one foot on the floor waiting for him to hand them over. He kept holding on. He rolled up the folder and held it even tighter. "So you're not gonna tell me which ones are mine? You don't have to tell me. After I read 'em I'll know." I thought to myself... if you only knew they were all for you what would you say? Would it matter? Would it mean something? Would you tell me?

I watched his smiling eyes and I could see his mind growing curiously solemn. I wondered who should speak next. I waited. It was his turn and he came back with a the big one, "Why don't you and I get married?" My knees grew weak, my stomach fluttered, my heart murmured fast and I sat down on the arm of the couch trying to look cool and collected. I watched his eyes. Knew them well from somewhere. Perhaps another place or back in time. Oh this man is mine, but this man has been drinking. I answered him with the correct answer. The one I had to give him, "Ask me when you're sober." He was caught off guard with my answer and said, "Well, then I guess I'll just take these home with me tonight and look them over." The phone rang. Buff and Jules came running down the stairs. This was going in all directions. I answered the phone and it was a friend of mine from across the street. "Hi Cap, how's it going?" "JoJo, I can't talk to you right now, Gentry's here. You remember me talking about him?" "Oh that's too cool Caps. Say can you do me a big, big favor? Could you give me a ride. It's only a few minutes from your house, my house, what's the difference right?" "Jo, I can't right now. He just asked me to marry him. I don't want to leave now he might go home." Just then Gentry called out to me, "Who is it?" "It's Joanne from across the street." "What does she want?" Joanne over heard and said, "Put him on Cap, maybe he'll give me a ride." "Jo, are you out of your mind! There is no way! Don't you understand? You know under different circumstances that I would, but please don't do this to me tonight, please?" "What does she want Big Time?" "She wants me to give her a ride." "That's no problem, I can give her a ride." I handed the phone to Pink.

There went my heart again. I knew if he left he wouldn't come back. When he was through talking to Jo, he gave me the phone and I thanked her. She knew my thank you was pissed off. Jo was 17 was a very persuasive person. Gentry would be ready to go in a minute. Now the girls came forward and wanted to why I turned Pinky down. I overheard the three of them talking about it when I was on the phone. Buff was excited! Jules was real happy about it too. I didn't want to tell them what I had said to Gentry. I didn't know how to explain it. Gentry seemed elated that I had to come up with the answer. Ooh he knew just how to get me going every time! Then Jo had to call. "Gentry, are you coming back after you drop Jo off?" "Nah, I'll probably go home." "But Gentry you just got here." "You need to get your girls back into bed and I need to get going. "Aaaah," Buff sighed with raised brows." "Yeah, I gotta get going Buff and you need to get back into bed." "I know Pinky. I will."

Buff was stronger than me. Her and Jules said good night to Pinky as the they went up the stairs. I could hear the two of them giggling and I knew they were talking weddings. Mine. Gentry was up and had his jacket on. Jo was at the door a knocking. I let her in and introduced her to Gentry. She told him where she needed to go. I looked at them both and said in a beg. "I wish I could ride along." "Don't worry Caps. Good old Gentry will be back to see ya." But I knew better. After they left I wanted to rip the phone out of the wall and break it. I wanted to break something, anything, but I didn't have anything I could afford to replace. I grabbed my bag of pot and rolled a few joints instead. Went immediately over to piano. Played all I knew and the songs I wrote about Gentry, hoping that where ever he was, he was listening.

Just as the night became comfortable again and I had my mind tuned properly, the phone rang. Wondered who it was. It was after eleven and no one called me then. I picked up the phone. It was a reminder of the earlier great evening I had. I said, "Hi Jo." "Hey Cap. I just wanted to tell you that I got here okay. Is he back yet?" "No Jo. I told you he wouldn't. That's why I didn't want him to leave when you called. I knew he wouldn't. Damn. I'm sorry Joanne, it's not your fault that you called at the wrong time." "I'm sorry Cap. I didn't mean to mess up your night. Don't worry, he'll be back over. You're too pretty." "Thanks Jo, but pretty isn't everything. Hey Jo, isn't he the best looking man you ever saw?" "He's nice looking, but he isn't my type. You two would look good together though Caps. Are you gonna marry this guy or what?" "I told him to ask me when he was sober." "Good answer Cappy girl." "He'll ask sober if he loves me." "He better Caps. Hey, well I'm gonna get off this phone. This is a blast over here. Tell your honey next time you see him thanks again from me. Don't forget now." "I won't Jo. Have fun. Talk to ya tomorrow."

I hung the phone up and went for a cup of coffee. I sat at the guard table looking out over the dark sky. Oh how I had wished the night was different. I wanted it to change and go back. I wanted to go back and go back and back as far as I could. To the beginning. To the time that I first stood next to him and our eyes met. That time. Start from there. What a wonderful thought. If only I could go to the beginning and start all over. I wouldn't mess it up that's for sure. It would be perfect. Then I talked out loud because I wanted Gentry to hear me. "Did it ever occur to you that maybe we are suppose to be perfect because we were perfect in the beginning? Like Adam and Eve? You're Adam and I am Eve. We're back! We got another chance at being perfect, all we have to do is be together. Can't you see that?" Of course he can see that! He's working for God, I thought. God told Gentry that he was supposed to be here for me. Only he doesn't want to be. Now What?

Are you gonna help me or do I look like Dorothy from "The Wizard of Oz"?" "Oh Brother! This is getting ridiculous," Self cut in.

"Look at all the coffee cans you have Cap! How many now? Counted lately? Don't lose sight of the numbers! Count this, count that. Check the time. Double check the locks. Three three three. This is me, God, are You hearing this? If Gentry is Adam then he's number two. And if the Bible is telling the whole truth then I am number three. Because I was third, am third and always will be third. Yeah Cap. Like you're really Eve," Self went on. "Anything is possible," I replied.

In truth, I liked believing that anything was possible. Maybe I am Eve. Maybe Gentry is Adam. Maybe that is why Gentry drew those symbols on my kitchen wall. Man, Woman, Earth, Infinity. Could be why his eyes seem so familiar. Maybe that's why we are so perfect when we're together, because we are suppose to be. It made sense to me. Nuts! That's what people would call me. They'd think I was losin' it. I lit up another joint, grabbed a sheet of paper, a pen and sat down at the table to write. Not anything in particular, just a good doodle.

My all chrome "Paper Mate" was my mate and it turned it, spurned it. Twirled the pen on its side on the table quietly watching the middle that looked like a steel ball bearing. Like other nights, I pretended it was a compass. East naturally was the direction where I wanted it to stop. Pink's location. Figured that if I concentrated on the pen stopping east, Pink would come over. This is when Self had to tell me what to say to make it work. "Come back over, come and see me. You know me well, I'm number three, for we are all a number plain to see. Here I go talking in rhyme, but I can't help what happens all the time. My words are simple ones, but words I say are true. The one perfect pair on Earth and that's me and you. I want to hear you knocking, I want to see your face, I wish that you'd get back here at my place. The night isn't late and I'm up with your songs, I'll sing you to sleep this is where you belong!

I quit with the rhymes and I put the pen away. Nothing I wanted to draw and my thoughts ran out of things to say. Took a seat at the piano, sang songs and thought about my wishes. Then of course, I smoked pot. Smoked and played and smoked and played trying to get my mind off of Gentry, but I couldn't. Self was still wishing when outside the house, was a knock on the door. One that I knew. Took me courage to go to the door, afraid it wouldn't be him. Peeked out and saw Pink standing just outside on the porch like he had the first time (11:11 p.m.) "Gentry, I thought you weren't coming back!" "Came back to hear one of the songs you wrote for me. Play one for me Big Time." "I don't know, they're kinda personal." He laid back into the couch like he always did. Cupped his hands behind his head and asked for a tune. "I have to warm up first. Then I "might" play one. And I said, might!" "You'll sing one for me Big Time." We both knew that I would and I did. Gentry loved it as much as I did myself, but a question would linger. When would he hear all of them?

Gentry fell asleep. Pink slept ever so handsome, so quietly. I watched until I fell asleep myself, but when I woke up he was gone.

Coffee and pot were definitely in order. And not in that order. "Three!" I caught myself saying outright! "Number three is still following me. First Max and Prof'. And now Pink! Jesus Christ girl think! Why oh why did you even let the cop in the house? You let Prof' have you for 100 bucks. Then Mr. Right comes back and you let him take you to the "couch." Guess I didn't want to say that Pink and I had sex, because that's all it was without a kiss. That makes three fuck ups. Three in only a few days!" Brother was I right. Man was I wrong. I was bringing myself down to a place where I'd never been before. I was always true. Okay, so I went out on Professor when I had seen Nic. But I was separated from Prof' for a year. God only knows how many women he had taken to bed! Here I am making mistakes. Three in a row. One person... one very familiar and comfortable person is in my life. Wants one thing...To be number one in someone's life! You're the coolest girl in America alright, I thought. The coolest at fucking up!

Things didn't get any better, in fact, things only got worse. A day or two passed and Prof' was at the door wickedly angry. "You gave me gonorrhea. You might want to go talk to your good buddy at the police station. That's why he messed with you. He didn't want to give it to his wife." "Professor, the way you are you probably gave it to me. That's why the hundred bucks. It was a cover. One to cover your ass!" "Okay! I will admit I was wrong about the other day. You're right. I owe the money. But I didn't come here to argue with you Cap. You need to go to the health department and get treated. They'll ask you who you've had sex with and they'll want names." Shocked I said a name I didn't mean to say. "Gentry!" "Would he be the guy you didn't want to tell me about? The one who drives the green "Ford"?" "So what if it is. It's not your business." "Well, don't you think it's his business? Look, I wanted to tell you. The nurse told me at the clinic that a lot of women won't have any symptoms and things can get real bad if its left untreated. I gotta get going. Thought you should know. Oh and uh, I hope it isn't so hard for you to tell uhm... what's his name, Gentry? Bye" It was easy to despise that man! The sarcasm in his voice. Gonorrhea? Capri Elizabeth! Prof' might be telling you the truth. Get to the health department, thought I and Self.

How do I to tell Gentry? Do I call him? Do I go see him face to face? No, I can't. First I have to go to the health department and get checked out.

It's possible that Professor is just lying through his teeth. A sick lie just to find out who drove the Shark.

Like I said earlier things got worse. I went to the health department. Got checked. Had gonorrhea. Got mad. Real mad! But feelings changed in an instant when the nurse gave me a clipboard and form. A place for names of anyone I had sexual contact with. The forms were filled and I left. Being in such a hurry to get the medicine I needed, I never thought to ask what they did with the names.

What the hell do I do about telling Gentry? He has to know. I should be the one to say. How? A letter? "No time to joke around, he didn't answer the first one, remember?" "Yeah, I remember." The battles went on with me and Myself, (of course only when the kids couldn't see or hear). I thought and I talked. Played and sang and talked some more till it got to be about 4 a.m. Planted myself where I had for some time. The couch. I lay facing the ceiling in thought about what I would do the next day and I did that till I drifted off in hopes of a dream.

The dilemma only grew dimmer, remembering the day before. Slowly I strolled to the kitchen to make more coffee. Then, I thought, I thought. I think too much, I thought. So, I stood at the window watching for spring. There was splatters of snow on the oncoming green. I'd wait for the warm colors that were soon to be seen.

Reality hit. I sat. I thought... naturally! I have to find a way to tell Pink. And the question for the day was "How"?

Why did I do what I did? Why didn't Max tell me he was married? Why didn't I ask him? Why and why and why? I ruined it Pink? You won't want me anymore after this. There are no more chances. You've given me three. That's my number and you know it! In thinking I grew out of control in anger. Three is after two. You're two. So you are what? Smarter or better than me? Remember Adam, you had a day before me. Just one. What would you have done without me? Good God I'm thinking like a crazy person! Normal people don't think like this do they? Why didn't You make us both on the same day?! And I thought the question would be how!

Good Lord, I'm back to this again. How do I tell Pink? Maybe the health department will notify him. They won't tell him it was me that gave his name out. It would be the easiest. Damn! I should call a nurse over there and ask her what they will do with the information they got from me. No! I can't! I feel bad enough. This is just another thing I'll have to work out myself. After all, I got myself into it.

The day passed. Night made its appearance and it dragged. Wasn't much in the mood for anything, except maybe some truth. That truth would come from location. From one person. A place where I could find Max Sparks and

I was in a turbulent, venomous kinda of mood. It would not be pleasant. I checked the clock. It was 9:30 p.m. Shit, I thought, it's a school night! I don't want to call Nina up and ask if one of her girls can come by. But I'd call. I'd ask. She'd remind me about nights I said I'd be in on time and I wasn't. Well I tried the call anyway. It turned out just the way I expected it would, but it didn't matter. Luck was knocking at the door. It was Jo from across the street. I grabbed her arm and practically dragged her in.

"Jo, I need your help real bad. I have to find this cop. If I don't, I'm gonna go off!" "Cap's what's up? What cop?" she asked. "Jo if I tell you this do you promise not to say anything to anyone?" "Sure thing Caps. What happened? Something's wrong." "Yep. Every fucking thing is wrong Jo! I got gonorrhea. I got it from a cop." "What about this Gentry dude you're so crazy in love with? Why would you want to have sex with another guy Cap? What's up?" "Well Jo, I'll start from the beginning..." After explaining the whole nasty mess, I asked if she wouldn't mind keepin' an ear open for the kids who were already sleeping. Jo agreed. It was a marijuana moment indeed! I went to the shadow box and took the sugar bowl down. Rolled up a quick doob for the road. I thanked Jo and headed out the door. Ready!

Drove down to the pier side of town, north, smokin' the joint. Parked and put the car on idol. I listened to the radio. I thought I would have to do a lot of thinking, but then it hit me! The police station! That's where I can find Sparks. High as I am, I'm going! I rolled down the windows and turned the heat off. I put the roach in the ashtray, put the car in drive and I drove. Parked. Turned the car off and went in the building. Asked where Sparks was. They didn't know so I asked where I might find him. The offered to radio his whereabouts. Politely, because I was buzzed, I told them not to. It would be more fun driving around to find him myself. Cops didn't know I was high? Feeling bold, I drove directly to the county jail. In the back of the building was a small parking lot. I didn't notice any city cop cars, just the county vehicles. I decided while I was there I would see if Wily was on duty, shoot the shit with him for awhile. Wily was telling me that Laurie was still coming to see Henry on visitation days. I figured as much. I did it myself. I asked him if Henry was still locked up. Naturally he was. For how much longer was not yet certain.

While talking to Wily I noticed a couple of cruisers pull in the drive. "Wily, it was nice talking to you, but I might have business to attend to." "Business?" Wily asked. "Yeah, it may have pulled up outside. I gotta check it out. See ya later!" Flash...! I was standing on the cast iron landing. The few cops, some eight steps down, knew I was around because Max Sparks was there and he saw that my eyes held a poisonous glare. Calmly he addressed me, "Hello Capri. What brings you here? Thought you were finished with

Batturs? I don't get it. Is this guy great in bed or what?" He turned to his fellow officers with smiling shiny whites. "I didn't come here to see Batturs. I was looking for you." I walked half way down the stairs maintaining my position above him. "You never told me you were married." "Yes Capri. Thought you knew that." Self spoke opposite strong. "Didn't want the little woman to get gonorrhea so you gave it to me! You ask about Batturs? Is he good in bed. You think being raped and beat is bed?" I had to be level with the boys on concrete. "Capri, it's no big deal..." "No big deal? I have a life but what gets me most is I thought you were my friend." "I am Capri." "Yeah Max. Some friend. Couldn't say you were married. Didn't want the wife to know you picked up the disease. I feel sorry for her because I was married to a guy like you." "All you have to do is go the health department Capri. Five days and it's gone." Sparks pissed me off because he kept smiling like he placed best at show. "Max. Thought I should tell your wife, but I won't be the one to hurt her." I moved through the clustered cops to get to my car. Max called out good night, like it meant anything. Self thought, fuck him! I listened and went straight to the house. Jo ran home and reminded me to have coffee ready in the morning. Like I wouldn't?

Turned off the porch light and locked up things for the night. I went upstairs to check on the three little ones all sound asleep. Headed back down the stairs and made coffee. While it was perking, or maybe not, I went for the pot. I sat at the kitchen table and rolled enough joints for then and the next day. Smoked two waiting for the coffee to brew, or not. Turned to look at all the coffee cans I had on the kitchen counter corner. Sixty would be soon. "Shit! The porch light! Gentry might pop in!" I raced to flip it back on. Peeked out the window with a whisper, "Come over Pink. We need to talk I think." Asked God about relaying the message and bid Mr. Mocean a good night, where ever he was.

It was time for the piano. I took me, coffee, pot, pen and paper and we took our proper places and positions. Everything had to be laid out just right. Made me a nervous wreck if it wasn't. Played and sang some of my own songs. A couple of good blast-out-your-voice-singing songs because Max had me so fucking mad! Oooh! This was feeling good! Feeling good enough to throw a piano at him. Then I thought about Gentry. He must know by now that I gave him a disease. Prof' said, he'd know. Wish Gentry would just come over so I could get it out in the open. Honesty should count for something, shouldn't it? Pink was a no show. He did not come over when I woke to a day. I stayed home and waited for night, to sleep.

Morning came to before I did. I slept in late. Fortunately for me so did the kids. Buff was in school. Jules was like she wasn't even there. Quietly she played life seriously. Sonny had to be followed like a shadow, climbing here and climbing there. Climbing everywhere I swear!

Day 3 ... and later that day... about a half hour before the sun would descend and disappear westward, Gentry calculated the proper time of arrival. The girls were at Sunday school around the corner in the little white church. Gentry took his spot on the pale blue sofa and laid back.   He's not asking me to play anything for him. This was bad for sure. I sat next by him to talk to him about what I did.   What I got from what I did and what I gave him because of what I did.   "So how ya doing Gentry?" "Same. Tired, working. What cha been up to? Where's the kids?" "Jules and Buff go to that church around the corner for Sunday school. They make things, paint and sing. They go twice a week." He asked about Sonny. No, Sonny wasn't eating he was napping. The conversation was off to a great start and I didn't know where to begin. "So, aren't ya gonna play something for me?" "Hmm. Yeah I want to, but I gotta talk to you about something." "What?" he asked. "Health department call you or anything?" Gentry masked his face with a smile and said, "No, should they?" "Gentry I had something. Thought I gave it to you. I didn't know anything was wrong with me." I wasn't able to read his face. Wasn't he mad? Does it matter? Is it over? Then again, he was at my house smiling his brown beaming eyes and again he mentioned music. "I thought you were gonna play something Big Time." I got up from the couch and walked over to the piano.   Feeling courageous, I decided on singing something else I had written for him entitled: "In The Future."

Gentry knew it was for him and said, "I like that.   Did you write it?" "In February.   It's Jules favorite song.   Whenever she hears me singing and playing, the first thing she wants to me to play is that one.   She's not even 5 and her favorite Beatle song is "I Am the Walrus" and it's a struggle because I'm just learning it." Pink wanted to hear a couple more. He did. Then shortly after that he stated that he had to go. The good-byes always sliced my heart right down the middle and I couldn't stand not knowing when and if I would see him again.

When the girls came home I figured it was best not to tell them Pinky had been here. It would hurt Buff bad! Jules would be sad, but sad for seeing her sister that way. Sonny didn't care one way or the other. On traveled life.

Two bad Marches in a row. Count 'em. Counted the reminders I know. Mayor's birthday coming and she'll be fifty three. Batturs slid into the story. Raped and beat me and beat me.   April was up and coming, the coming of number two. Mayor died on that number and I wished it wasn't true. Pink was marked that number and it was messing with my head. "God I work hard for living and a raise would help," Self said.

This wasn't getting me anywhere fast, so I waited for April to come and to pass.

April one I felt just fine! April two was un-ending time. I wanted Mayor to hold Sonny more than the one time she did. "Can you see him mom? Aren't the kids cute? It's a shame that Jules and Sonny didn't have you around longer so they could have remembered you." I talked to the Mayor on the evening of the second while the kids were sleeping. She heard me. She must have. A gust of "Emaurade" her favorite perfume, slid through and up the living room.

Up until about the middle of the month things were moving by pretty quick. April 22 would be coming. The baby would be 11 this year. Why did I have the abortion? Why didn't I listen to the Pope? Counselors told me and the other girls that it would be a day we'd never forget. Don't know about the other girls, but I didn't forget. April 22nd and I relived that day. That day I went to Cleveland and paid someone to kill my baby. That's what I did! The reality of abortion! It hit me hard! My heart hurt so much and I couldn't stop crying. Had to get my head into something else, so I smoked a lot of pot. When that didn't work, I took two nerve pills until I was tired. Numbers filled my head and I counted and added. Two! Sonny born on a 2. Mayor died on a 2. 22 had two two's. Gentry is a man with two names. Gentry might be Adam. Adam was definitely two! "Jesus Christ! And I thought all I had to deal with was the threes!"

I pictured paradise in my mind. What it must have looked like. What it would have been like to have but one other human being to share that life with. What a place it was! Sand and palm trees. Warm windy breezes all through the days and the nights. Swimming in the clearest of waters or riding gracefully on the back of the forgotten Unicorn. Look very hard and you might just see one.

April left and May arrived. I thought about plan B. Remember? I wrote a letter to Mocean and got no reply. Plan B was simple. I hid behind a pen and paper and wrote another letter. With so many words, I couldn't find the right ones. Plan B failed. He didn't respond, (a 2nd time). That did it! I wasn't going to write a third. I went to Neil Street to question him. Of course the real reason I went there was because I missed him. He hadn't been over in some time. When I got there he was outside. He was working around the front porch. I parked the car, got out and said, "Workin' hard?" "Yeah. What's on your mind?" he asked. "You." Then he saw a man across the street and headed that way to talk to him. I followed him and said, "I came over to talk to you about something Gentry." "I know," he said. Pink greeted his friend who was just getting ready to go inside for the night. They talked for a couple minutes when the man said that he'd talk to Gentry another time, he went into his house. I was standing next to Gentry not knowing how to bring up the letters.

Without giving it any advance thought I just starting talking, "I've written you two letters and you don't call or come over or anything." He was brief, "I didn't open 'em. I have so much mail laying around. I don't have time. Been busy." "Yeah but these aren't bills or junk mail or whatever, these were letters I wrote you. Why didn't you open them and read them Gentry?" "I didn't think it was important." My mouth dropped. I said, "Not important? Maybe if you would have read them you would have seen that they were! But if you think that way, then why don't you go ahead and burn them." Calmly he replied, "I did. They were good for gettin' a flame rolling ha!" "I don't care what you did with 'em! You didn't wanna read 'em fine!" Things got worse and he made sure that they did. Aren't cha gonna write me another one?" "No I don't wanna be part of your fire. Start it alone." Pink laughed as he crossed the street to get to the house. I was so pissed I didn't know what to think. I got into my car, pulled outta the drive and thought about the look on his face.

He seemed happy to see me go, I thought. What nerve! If he thinks I'm gonna waste my ink and paper on him again he's out of his mind! This made me feel sane and I was in a song writing mood. Went straight to Mayor's piano and nothing. Nothing at all was coming to mind or coming out right. After a couple hours of pure frustration, I quit and went back to numbers. It was nearly forty days since Gentry had been to my house. I've been counting since I asked him about the health department. He's the third of the Ill's in my life. And he's number one in my life. Why were things going for me, the way they were going? Because I guess they were supposed to. My life had fixed nine tough years on me and I blamed the abortion I was still paying for. "How long God," I asked. As with Gentry, there was no response. Maybe this is hell? God didn't wait, I'm in it right now! Some joke number One, and You see me crying.

Days went by slow. I even thought about writing another letter. It would be my signature letter to Mr. No Middle Name Mocean. My third! My last. Throughout this particular day I found myself reaching for the paper, reaching for the pen. Sometimes I'd catch myself holding one of the items. I put the pen, paper or both back to its proper place.

Buff was home from school. Jules was happy to see her and Sonny, well Sonny was climbing on something. We talked the school talk. Jules and Buff went up to their room and Sonny climbed step by step after them.

The night was a quiet one. The kids were asleep by nine. I had a lot of time to stay up and mess with the piano. But that's all I did. I still wanted to write something new. The other songs were getting boring and I needed a change. Stayed up getting high till three and came up with nothing.

Again I reached for the pen and paper and began writing Gentry. The letter was short. I wrote that I wanted him to burn this with the others. Two wouldn't get it. It was sarcastic, but then I'd go to almost telling him that I loved him. Then I'd blow up in his face for not coming to see me. I wanted to know if God relieved him of duties. When the letter was completed I read it over a few times. Went for an envelope, but was stopped when my hands decided to tear up the letter and throw it away.

What was the point? He knows it was me that gave him gonorrhea. He must hate me knowing for certain that I slept with somebody else. He'd never want me anymore because I ruined it all. I've loved him the instant he stood at my front door on Christmas Eve. And I was sure it was love I saw coming from his eyes, through the storm door glass. And that winter was warm!

Before I went to sleep I called Renee at "WCPZ." When she answered I asked her if she would put on a "Beatle" song for me. Well, not for me but for Gentry. I could only hope that he might be listening. She played "She Loves You," and suggested another to go along with it. After the first she played, "I'll Get You." I called her back up. "Renee, it's me Caps. Thanks for not saying who the songs were from, for not saying his name either." "Cap. Why didn't ya want him to know? You love him right?" "In answer to your first question, if he was listening he'd know! But why let him be know he's sure, even though he would be. Never mind, if he listened, he knows it could only be me. In answer to question two, those fucking two's. You know about them right?" "Yeah Cap and don't forget the three's!" "Yes Renee. No, but really...what can I say? I love him and never felt like this. He keeps me on my toes and I love it. But lately I've been messing things up. He hasn't been to my house in 43 days today. I can't stand it. I'm losing him and if I lose him I may never find him again." "Cap he wouldn't be making the right move if he doesn't get you before someone else does. You're a once in a life time kind of person. He'll be back. Give him a little time," she said. "Well you know pretty much what's been going on, I call ya enough!" "Cap, ya know. It'd be a shame for him to lose a girl who has a number one hit on her hands. Let him wonder when your song breaks the records. You'll have millions and smoke lots of marijuana!" That put me in the right mood, "You're right Renee! Well, I'm gonna hit the couch. Don't look like Mr. Right is coming over anymore tonight, this morning." "Okay Cap. Hey. Keep me posted. Give me a call. You know when. When I have the time and we can talk."

After talking, I checked the locks and the kids. Couldn't wait to get downstairs and sleep. I turned out the lights, left the radio on and curled up on the couch. Laying there, I thought... If I can't have you here Gentry, I

259

have a pillow. One you've managed to stay on for 43 days. In a sense, you never left. This put a smile on my face. I pushed my nose right into the pillow breathing in deep. Yep, he's here alright. Just then I heard Renee say, "Hey Cap, if you're still awake, I'm puttin' a song on for you, so pay close attention." So I did and wondered what the third song would be. Number three, like me, was "I'll Be Back." I thought of numbers falling asleep. Three Beatle songs. Each song had three words. Forty-three days. Gentry Mocean, no middle name the third. Three brothers, three kids and all the other 3's that had taken over my life. I didn't want to think about them anymore, but it was hopeless. They refused to leave me alone.

I put my thoughts on Gentry and only him. Concentrated on each and every moment that I had with him. They were so clear, so "right-now" and so right. Perfect! Like we are supposed to be. Hoped to dream about him that night like I did every night. And I hoped for it until I was absorbed in a deep sleep.

When morning came I tried to remember if I had dreamed of me and Pink. Which only means that if I did I forgot. It was pissing me off. I talked to God about it, "One little dream is all I asked for. He hasn't been in one. Did he tell You that he doesn't want to be in my dreams?" Then I got to thinking that maybe they were both in it together. For real!

I didn't want to start thinking crazy things first thing in the morning. Not before coffee! So I sat at the kitchen table reading yesterdays paper. Stumbled on it when I went in the fridge for orange juice. It still wasn't easy reading. I found that I was reading different letters backwards. Sometimes I'd have to read one sentence two or three times before it would make sense to me. Oh and the numbers, we can't forget the numbers! Numbers is my thing! I knew them well. But not when it came to reading them. Especially phone numbers. I dialed the numbers in the wrong order. I wrote most of the numbers, phone numbers backwards. And I was always playing like hell to make a simple call!

This only brought Henry to my attention and I quickly went for the phone to call the jail. He was still there thank God! Thank God for something!!!

The little ones were still asleep so I figured on a couple of doobs and of course, coffee. I called Nina and kept her up with current events. Told her how I made an ass out of myself by going over to see Gentry. "Cap, you worry too much. You're taking this too seriously. You need to lighten up, let him come to you. Does he call you? Does he take you out? Why do you keep doing that to yourself? You'll make yourself crazy! Why not take care of you?. You're single and free to do what you want. Just have fun." "Nina, I do try to have fun. Some fun going out alone. And you're right. He don't ask me out. He called once! Ha Nina, just one time." "Then don't sit around there all the time. Come over here and work on this puzzle with me. You can bring Jules and Sonny with you. Oh, I forgot, you have to be there at the house so you won't miss Gentry. No you wouldn't want to come here and work this great new puzzle. 2000 pieces! You want to sit there at your house all day long and wait and wait." "Nina, I can't help it. He doesn't come over as much as he used to and I love him. I don't want to miss him any more than I already do!" "Maybe you just think you love him. You've only been single a little over a year. You had a rotten marriage and you want to be in love, think you are in love with who? The first nice looking man you see?" "Come on Nina, you might be a few years older than me and you may know life better than me but I do know what I feel. And it isn't that I think I love him I know I love him. Always will and I know that.

Back when I was first seeing Prof', I asked Mayor how I'd know real love. She told me that when it happened I would know." "Okay Cap, so you let's say that you do love this guy, are you still going to hang around the house waiting? What I'm trying to tell you is this. Don't make yourself so available. Go out for an afternoon. Wouldn't it be nice if he showed up and you weren't there? Then that would make him wonder a little. Hmm, where's Cap? She's always here. Get it? If you do that then maybe your friend Gentry might get curious enough to want to be at you house every day. Isn't that what you want?" Of course I knew she was right. But I was me after all.

When the kids were up it was full steam ahead. And with nicer weather they were not wanting to go out. Yes I said that right. Not wanting to. Why, I have no clue. They were happy to be inside playing and watching cartoons.

It was time for a can count. I figured as long as it was time to shine them up I might as well. Filling the western corner of my kitchen were 62 "Maxwell Coffee" cans and they looked just grand. It was a shrine. A private sanctuary I had assembled for one man. Gentry Mocean III. This led me to ask the air around me a question, "Wonder how many pennies are in the mugs?"

Again I was concerned with numbers. To get my mind off the numbers I rearranged the cans. Of course this only led me right back to numbers. 62 cans. Six and two makes eight. Half of eight is four and half of four is two. It's had been 44 days that Pink hadn't been to my house. If you add those fours together you get the same answer as the last one. Two! Now I was really thinking and wondering. Hmmm, if I add 44 and 62 together will I end up with a third number 2? Quickly I ran the math in my head. 106. Half of that is 53 and when you add the five and the three together you get eight and that breaks down to a two every time. "Damn it Gentry, that's you and you need to be here." After my outburst I took a break and stood at the window looking for more spring. The four blue jays should be here, I thought. I checked time. It was eleven-thirty a.m. They would be here shortly so I broke out the peanuts and tossed some out the front door watching and waiting. One by one they flew into the grass for lunch. I watched until the four of them were flying due east. I knew where they were going. They were going to over to Neil Street. At least that's what I told myself and Self believed it.

While I was scouring the kitchen sink I heard a vehicle pull up in the drive. I continued shining the sink listening to the idle of the engine. It was not the Shark. I turned to look out the front window and saw only the tail end of a small black truck. Curiously I went to the front door and peeked out. It was Gentry. Since he didn't get out of the truck I walked out on the porch. He began first. "Well what do you think? I just got it. It's new." "You look good in black," I said. He smiled. I asked, "Wanna come in for a cup of coffee?" He answered me with a question totally out of context, but I was ready, "Do you know how long it's been since I was here last?" "44 days," I said accurately. This put an even bigger smile on him, that and he was proud of his new "Ford." Gentry stayed only to show me his new toy and told me he had things to do. I was desperately disappointed that he didn't want to stay with me longer. I watched him back his way out of my drive and my life again, wondering, always wondering when and if he would return.

With great weight on my heart, I played hell getting Mr. Mocean off my mind, but it wasn't going to happen. Why didn't I listen to Nina? I should have told Pink that I was real busy and had to get back inside before he made his excuses to leave. Damn I was good at pissing myself off! But it sure beat crying.

I reminded myself that my four, blue-feathered-spies would be here just before sunset to scan the area. This put me in a better mood! Enough that I wanted to play and sing, so I did. What could be better than that? I'll tell ya, a little pot to go with it. But there was something better than that. After that. A song. Although it was bitter sweet, it was new and it was about Gentry. I titled it: "Time to Say Good Bye." Took only minutes to write but it left me much more to think about. Why would I say good bye in a song? Gentry was still coming over? "Get real," I answered myself. "He only came over to show you his truck!" Maybe that is the only reason, but I convinced myself that it wasn't. He came to see me. Yes, he must have wanted to see me and he used the truck as an excuse. That's what he did!

I mastered the evenings and loved the nights that were mine. I didn't have to be mom. When the kids were asleep I punched the clock and kept myself on-call. I could blast music, I could yell rock and roll. I made up love stories about me and him. I'd do the talking for both of us. And by now we know who the "him" is don't we?   And each time that I did these actor, actress roles, I was the one with a broken heart in the end, and they always ended just the same, with Gentry telling me it was over forever.

I kept my theatrical disasters to myself.   Always thinking... If anyone ever found me out, they'd think I was crazy.   Lock me up in some insane asylum. Hell I knew I wasn't crazy, unless talking out my scenes were!   I was betting with myself. Betting that if a shrink heard me, he'd call it something. And Poof! I'd be gone.

Some days passed still wanting so badly to see Gentry.   While talking to Nina one day, she told me that her younger daughter stayed home from school to help her with some things around their apartment.   From a mom's point of view, you might call that a "legal-skip."   I couldn't wait to ask Nina if Kimmy might be able to come over an hour when she was through.   Luck was with me.   Nina told me that Kimmy was already done and could come over any time. I asked, "Half hour?" Nina answered, "Sure."   I sped in and out of the shower. Clothes were ready ahead of time.   Got my hair dry in ten minutes, makeup in five. I had a few minutes to wait before Kimmy would show.   Sat at the table drinking a cup of coffee and smoking a cigarette.   When Kimmy knocked, I jumped.   Couldn't wait to get out the door.   I quickly explained that Sonny was already down for a nap.   She knew Jules was easy to watch. I checked the time and told her I'd be back about two, two-thirty.

As I drove out and down my street, I thought that Pink might be at The Well for lunch or a beer so I drove there first.   I went inside and sat at the bar. Benny was working that afternoon. He knew what I would ask before I would ask every time. "Cap, you know what you ought to do?   You should pick up a six pack and take it over to Gentry.   He'd like that after working all day and then you two could see each other." "Benny, do you really think he's there?" "Where else would he be?   Why don't the two of you just get married and get it over with! Maybe both of you are crazy!" he laughed, "If you want to see him just go over there Cappy, it's easy." "Benny, could I get a cup of coffee? I need to think about this." "Sure Cap," he said shaking his head.

I wanted to go over to Neil Street, but I didn't know how I could get away again at supper time.   I hung out at Benny's bar for a little while and went back to my house to think.

I called Nina, told her about what Benny suggested to do and I told her that I wanted to.   She didn't think it would be a good idea, me going after him again! I knew it she was right, but I had to go.   I told her that Gentry would be expecting me. Kinda figured Benny would call Gentry to tell him I was coming over.   I thought Gentry probably put Benny up to it anyway. Nina still thought I was making a mistake and gave me one hour.   Her older daughter showed up about 6:30 that evening.   I was well ready to go when

Bink got there. I kissed the kids and went straight to a drive through for a good six pack for Pink. Then it was Neil Street. Pronto!

I was in luck. The "Ford" was in the drive. I walked up onto the porch that was finished and knocked on the door. From inside I heard Gentry say, "Whoever you are, go away, I'm busy." I smiled at the closed door and said, "Gentry. It's me. Would you open the door?" "I said I was busy, just go away." I stood there not knowing what to do next, so I talked at the door a second time, "Oh come on, I brought something over for you. You won't even open the door? You can't be that busy!" Just then the door opened. I said nothing when I saw him standing next another woman. Older! I'd seen her somewhere and Pink said, "Told you I was busy." I looked at him, he looked at me. I looked at her and she was looking at me the whole time. I turned away from all the eyes and slowly stepped off the porch. As I walked to my car I heard the front door close behind me. I got in and held my head high when I really wanted to cry. All I could see was his face and I knew this woman was just a big lie. He was getting even, getting back, but something wasn't right. I drove away shaking and cried half the night.

Who was this woman and where did I see her before? Why would Gentry want to be with someone ten or more years older than him? And she looked like such a bitch! He was only 33 and I was twenty-nine. Was this the reason he was wasn't coming around as much? He found someone else he wants to be with? No! This can't be happening! She can't have him! I'm supposed to. I know that and so does he. What's this, I thought, more games?

The nerve! Seeing him with someone who could never be me. "Get real Cap. Pink told Benny what the scheme was. And the scheme was to have you drive to him and find him with her!" Maybe it was true. I couldn't blame him for wanting to hurt me. I knew I had hurt him. Didn't he know that it was unintentional? God? He knows I never planned all of this. Doesn't he? In my thoughts, in anger I asked God more questions. This got something to do with the apple? I gave it to Adam? I tempted him? Didn't you tempt us? Oh, and by the way, who got the fuckin' snake goin'? Never mind. You never answer me. I have to figure out what Your precious clouds were trying to tell me. They were saying something right? Well tell me who and what I'm supposed to listen to and when for that matter? Did Pink see the same clouds? He believed me didn't he? He had to believe me. Wasn't he supposed to?

That was enough. I couldn't take what I was doing to myself anymore. I called Migs up at The Well. Asked her if Gentry was there and she told me that he was not. "Migs, where else would he go, do you know?" "I don't know Cap. Try the "Cameo." He mentioned the place one night." "Thanks

Migs. I'm there." Migs chuckled. I hung up and made plans to go out later that night. It was a Saturday so Nina wouldn't mind if one of her girls came down for a while to watch the kids.

About nine p.m., I drove to "The Cameo." It was only blocks away from where I lived. On my short trip there a verbal memory came to mind..."This is the place where Mayor worked before she met and married Pope!" I was nervous, anxious and I was there. I parked on a side street and looked around for Pink's truck. It wasn't in sight but that didn't stop me from going into the place to take a brief look about. All around the bar, the seats were taken. I looked at the faces behind the drinks and not a one was familiar. Aah, but there was a face I knew. The face of the woman standing inside the door at the house on Neil Street. She tended the bar. She glanced over and saw me. I dead bolted a look back and walked into the ladies room. I locked the door behind me and noticed a chalk board on the wall with different names and numbers on it. Looked at myself in the mirror and thought about the woman behind the bar. A guy at the bar said, Hey Norma, can you set us up with another round over here? I laughed out loud. "Norma? What the hell kind of name is Norma?" Norma Mocean? Doesn't even sound good. Now Capri Elizabeth Mocean sounds great!" I did the next natural thing and erased the black board and wrote my new name on it. Then I wrote Norma's name on the board with a big X over it. I flushed the toilet like I had used it. Ran the water I would have needed, brushed my hair and applied more lipstick. Knowing I looked just fine and younger, I walked out of the ladies room. Now in her sight again, Norma asked, "Anything I can get you?" Quickly, with a shit eating grin on my face, I replied, "No, I already have it."

As I walked out I thought... Ooh that was great Big Time! She will be sure to say something to Gentry about this.

I drove out to The Well and told Migs what I had discovered. Maybe she would mention it to someone and that someone might tell someone else. The plan was to let Gentry know! Then again, he probably already did.

I didn't stay at Benny's place till close or too long. It was midnight and Gentry hadn't come in yet. I wanted to get back to the house to get high because I left un-prepared. Usually took a couple joints with me for the road and I needed some badly.

I flew down a main road that got me back to the house in under four minutes. Pulled in the drive and ran into the house. I had a good reason for running. Spring spiders were hanging all over the front porch.

The kids were all asleep and I sent Nina's daughter home. Plan C would take its place. First a cup of cold Maxwell House, then the pot, then the plan. The plan was very original because it was mine. It would consist of words. It would require ink and paper. Lots and lots of paper because if one "I" wasn't dotted just right, I'd only scrunch it up and throw it away. Three. Three again and again. The 3rd plan is to write a third letter with the three things I have here in front of me at the kitchen table. Three plans, three letters, three things. Maybe it's the stamp that's been throwing me off. I won't use a stamp. I'll take it to his mailbox myself.

I wrote and I wrote until I couldn't see straight anymore. It had to be perfect because that's what Gentry and I were when we were together. Was he afraid of perfection? Is that why he keeps himself hidden behind a brick wall? I wondered just how many bricks he had laid. How tall was the structure that kept Pink inside so often and more still. Speaking out loud like I had so many times, I exclaimed, "We are perfect and you know it! We were first and you know that too. You are Adam. I am Eve." And I meant it as I stood facing due east sending out energy thoughts that were sure to reach him. Then I asked God about the apple. "They weren't red yet, right?"

I stayed up the night with the letter and got nowhere real fast. I needed to do something to get my mind off of Gentry. As for Norma, she will never have him. No one really can, I thought. Because he was mine to begin with. When there were only two in the beginning, excluding God.

When the clock struck eight I went for the lawn mower in the garage. Brought it out and left in the driveway. Strolled around the front and back yard to see what I was up against. The front yard was easy to mow. It lay level and smooth. It better! I didn't slip a disc for nothing. It was the back yard that concerned me because a section in the middle was higher, giving me hills to climb. And I thought I had mountains. I didn't want to do it. I knew I'd be put off wind when I was done, but then I saw a brick. One brick. One red brick and it was laying right smack in the middle of the yard. I stood by it then looked around for a truck. A little black truck. Hmm! I was thinking... Pink! I told him that he was missing a brick from his wall and that I could see him. "I saw you! And maybe this is the brick!" Pink had to be the one to put it here. Who else? I picked it up, held it like a trophy and looked over the parking lot again for Pink. He and I both knew who put the brick there. I smiled, took myself and the brick back to the garage so I could put it neatly away. After I cut the lawn, I took me and my coffee to the front porch. Took the one step for a seat and lit up a cigarette.

It was a beautiful spring day. The birds were chirping. The crows were cawing. The squirrels were dancing and playing around the trunk of a big old maple tree. I was thinking about the brick when just then a blue jay swooped and jet landed in my maple tree. It was planted left of center in the grass. It flew off just as quick. The other three arrived right after and number one came back. Was hard to tell them apart. Fric, Frac, Mac and Jack. I ran in inside to get some peanuts. Took 'em out and tossed them under the tree. Why I started thinking about an apple I'll never know. But since I had one in the house, I went back inside, chopped the apple into little pieces and threw my birds a treat. They didn't waste any time getting their beaks into them either. When the apple was gone, so were they.

"Cap don't start it, not out here on the porch where all the neighbors can hear you." Shit, I thought, I better go in the house and talk there.

The kids were asleep and my thoughts continued as I talked and paced the kitchen floor. "Four. Four Blue Jays. Four Beatles. The albums? They had red apples on them and then they went green. Wonder what that means?" I started singing part of a Beatle song… " … Well it's past my bed I know. And I'd really like to go. Soon will be the break of day, sitting here in Blue Jay Way…" Self said, You gotta stop this crazy stuff before we end up in a straight jacket!" When I was through having it out with her, the girls were awake and Sonny was hungry.

I stayed home that Sunday with the kids, it was a good day until I got the kids all tucked in for the night and started thinking more about the brick which led me to thinking about everything I was already thinking about earlier and it was driving me nuts!

I had to call Renee at the radio station and tell her about it. Had to keep her updated with any valuable information. She needed to hear about the brick and I needed to tell someone. Nina would already be in bed and she wouldn't be as interested. Had to make myself wait to talk to Renee after one in the morning because until then, she'd be busy. But I did call to request a song and held nothing back. "Renee, it's Cap. Would you play "I'm Looking Though You" for the guy who is driving around in the little black truck." "Hi Cap! Sure will. This is for your Mr. Right, right?" "Right." I said. "Right. I'll get it right on for you. Alright?" "Alright with me." We both knew that we could have gone on indefinitely with the rights so we *left* them alone. "Good morning. This is "WCPZ." I'm Renee. Good to have you rock and roll listeners with me tonight. Got a request from a friend of mine. This songs goes to the man drivin' the little black truck. You know who you are. Here's "The Beatles" with, "I'm Looking Through You." "Gentry Mocean no middle name the third! Fuck you!" I couldn't take it anymore and called Renee. Had to tell her about the brick!

♫ ♪ *"Time To Say Good Bye"* ♪ ♫
Words and Music by: Catherine Santi in May 1986

"It's too late for us, time to say good bye.
It's too late to even stop and wonder why.
It's too late for us and time to say good bye.
It's too late for me, too long to take you back.
Well in a song I find a way to say, well, that's just that.
It's too late for me and time to say good bye.
And there's a place I'll never out grow.
And I've come too far to know.
Then you released me from a vacant dream.
And the dream was just, the dream was just a dream.
It's too late for you to come and say hello.
It's too late for that, I truly have to leave you go.
It's too late for us and time to say good bye."

Chapter Twenty: "Part Two: The Game. No Rules."

"What's up Caps?" Renee asked, "Strange things tonight. There is this guy on the other line and I think you should talk to him." "How do I do that? You got his name and why do you think I should talk to him?" "See Cap, I can put the two of you on a line together so you can talk. I think you need to hear what he has to say. I think it's your Mr. Right. He seems to know an awful lot about you. As for his name, he won't tell me. Do you wanna talk to him," she asked. "Who else could it be? It's gotta be Pink. Sure Renee, put us through, I'll talk to him." I don't how they do that at the station, but they did and she had the two of us the phone.

The man talked first. "Hi, how are you?" "I'm fine and you," I asked. "Good. Did you request that Beatle song a minute ago? I just had a feeling that it was you." "Yes, I did. Who are you?" I asked. "Well that has to stay a mystery. I don't want to give you my name. Might spoil everything." "Spoil what?" I asked." "Oh nothing. What's your name?" he asked. "Well, since you won't tell me yours, I think it's a good idea that we both remain anonymous." "That's fair. So you like the Beatles huh? My brother likes 'em, but he likes "Pink Floyd" best. He goes around telling everyone he has all the their albums, but it's really me who has them all." "Really? Cause I know a guy who says he has all the albums." "It might be my brother. He thinks he's "Roger Waters." "This is getting very interesting," I said, "Does your brother play guitar too?" "Is a matter of fact he plays the guitar and the drums. He used to be in a band and get this, the name of the band was "Pink Punks Practicing in Public Pissers." "Don't go away," I said, "I have to get something. Be right back."

The strange voice I was hooked up with said he would wait. I went for a piece of paper, pen, got back to the phone and started to jot down everything he said that was "in common" with Gentry. Gentry said he had all those albums. That was number one on the list. Playing the guitar was two, playing the drums was three. Then the band. The list grew as the two of us talked. By the time the conversations was over between me and the voice, I had made a list that went from one to forty. I couldn't believe that the man was telling me all the things Pink had said, and he wanted me to call him and talk some more. "But who do I ask for when I call, if I do call you?" I asked. "How about if I call you about the same time tomorrow night, this way my brother won't be around bothering me. Can I call you tomorrow about one-thirty?" I didn't hesitate with an answer, "Yes. Call. I wanna hear more because I've been jotting down some things you've said since we were talking on the phone. You won't believe this!" "Are you going to tell me?" he asked. "Maybe I'll tell you about it tomorrow if you call." "Oh, you don't have to worry about that, I'll call and I will be on time. Talk to you tomorrow. Wait what's your number?" Now I hesitated. "I don't know. Maybe this is wrong. I don't even know your name." "Yeah, but I don't know yours either. What if I give you my number? Will that work for ya?" I thought for a moment and said, "Okay. Give me the number. Wait. Who do I ask for?" "Don't worry, I'll answer. It's my place, but sometimes my brother thinks it's his. Tells everybody it is." "That's interesting too. I'll call you tomorrow... same time." "Yes," he said, "same time."

Me and the mystery man had been on the phone for over two hours. The very minute I hung up I called Renee to tell her about the guy on the wire. I asked her this one question. "Renee, what in the world did he say to you that made you think I would want to talk to him?" She said, "Cap I don't know. I think it had something to do with that Beatle song you requested." This led to another question, "What about the Beatle song?" She simply said, "He liked it and wanted to hear another song so I played it. That's when you called and he was still on the line with me. When I told him that the Beatle fan was on the other line he seemed so nervous and excited I thought for sure he was your Mr. Right." "Well it wasn't him, but he was indeed very eerie! I was getting goose bumps. It almost took my buzz away. Know the feeling?" "Yeah I do Cap. I know. That's the best high." "You're right. And speaking of high, mine is almost wiped off the board. I gotta go roll one up."

"Capri. You gonna call him tomorrow?" "You're damn straight I am! I wouldn't miss it! It's crazy. Real crazy Renee!" "Roll with it Cap. Call me up tomorrow and we'll work on a set of songs to play." "You know I will. Thanks. Talk to ya tomorrow morning. Probably around 3. Depends on what mystery man has to say and I think he'll say plenty." "Yeah Cap, let me know what's up with that. That is very very eerie!" "Okay, I will. Bye!" "I'll put something on for you Cap. Talk to ya tomorrow."

I turned up the radio and smoked a doob. Sat back into the couch re-reading my list. I counted them and this time I numbered them just to make sure that I had counted right to begin with. There were forty. I was shaking the whole time I went over it. The albums, the name of the band, the guitar and I knew Gentry had a brother. The drums, "The Beatles," "Roger Waters" and Christ Pink sounded just like him! Reels to reels. Gentry had them too. The truck was on the list to name a few. I was having a blast and it was driving me mad, I laughed when I cried when I was never sad. It had to be Pink who devised this new game, to talk to this stranger, the stranger with no name. "No name!" Self shouted. Like Gentry no middle name Mocean, who was the cause of the commotion. But why this voice, this voice unknown I hear on the radio air? Pink you were with this guy, weren't cha? Weren't cha right there?

There was no way he could have known all that he did. He knew about a girl who got beat up. He knew that I lived by the hospital. He knew what kind of tree I had in the back yard. He knew exactly which house down I was from the east corner of the block. I should have been afraid I suppose, but I couldn't be even if I wanted to. This was to amusing and I wanted to get as much information as I could. I wanted the brother's name.

It was hard falling asleep. Slept only four hours that night. I had to be up for Buff at 7:15 to make sure she was off to school. This morning she had something to say about my getting up with her. "Mom you can go back to sleep. I can get ready all by myself." "Buff, you're only seven ya know. I have to make sure you eat something and brush your teeth." "But mom see. I already ate a bowl of cereal and look, I brushed my teeth seeee! You can go back to sleep." I un-knowingly raised her independent. "Buff, I do need some more sleep. I'm pretty tired. Just make sure that the door stays locked until you see grandpa's truck in the drive way and make sure that it is locked when you go out." "Okay mom I will." Buff gave me a kiss good morning and waited for her grandpa. I went over on the couch and curled up. Buff didn't know it took me some time for me to sleep, especially after a cup of coffee. And the cold cup I started to drink was close to kicking in. I pretended to be asleep. Didn't want her to think she wasn't a big girl. I heard the truck pull up. Pope tooted the horn a couple of times. Buff went out and closed the door behind her. After I heard the truck going down the road I got up just to make sure the door was locked. It was. I should have known.

Like I said, it took me a while to fall asleep. It was that way for a lot of years. It used to piss me off bad when Prof' could explode at me, then sleep in seconds. It took me almost an hour.

Lucky for me Sonny and Jules slept till about 10 that morning so I got all the sleep I required. But the day dragged waiting to get on the phone with the mystery man.

When the time came I was fully high and I dialed the numbers that would get me in touch with him again. Only there was no answer. I let it ring at least six times. I even hung up and dialed it again just in case I miss-dialed in the first place. The phone rang again with no answer. Called Renee at the radio station and she was flipping out. "Cap. It's you. Great! Your mystery man is on the line and he wanted to know if I could get a hold of you." "You're kidding me. I just tried to call his place twice with no answer." "Hang on Cap, I'll tell him." "Cap, he said he heard the phone but couldn't get to it. He wants you to call him again." "Oh man Renee. I can't believe this. Is this a trip or what?" "I'll say. It freaked me out when I heard you on the other line. It was like seconds apart when the two of you called. Do you want me to tell him that you'll call?" "Yeah, go ahead and tell him. Play some Beatles for me will ya. No, don't do that. Maybe mystery man would prefer some "Pink Floyd." "Sounds good to me Cap. Keep me posted."

I called Mr. X up and we talked a long couple of hours. He seemed to be on the down side of something and wouldn't give me a hint as to what it was that pulled him there. I tried to figure out why the excitement had vanished from his voice but it was hopeless. We didn't talk much about his brother and we didn't talk much about my mystery man, Pink. I wasn't about to disclose Pink's name to someone I didn't know, even though I figured that Pink put this guy up to everything. Maybe this is a new part to his game. And the game was working. I was into it with my whole heart and soul. When the conversation between me and him ended, he asked if he could have my number to call me the next time we talked, and that would be the next night. 1:00 a.m. I told him that I'd give him the number only if he promised to be in a happier mood. He agreed.

The next morning at one, he called. I heard fumbling in the background and I knew there was something or someone else in the house with him. I asked him what the bumping noises were. He explained that he had some boxes stacked that came down. Told me that the place was almost empty really, and any little noise echoed. Well, right away I added to the list. Pink's house was empty because he hadn't finished it yet. I was only getting more curious about anything and everything the man had to say. He kept his promise too. He was in a good mood and we laughed about a lot of things we were saying to each other, because so much of what we said was familiar to the both of us. Our talk was winding us up and we both wanted off the phone at the same time. Before we hung up, we made plans to talk again.

Called Renee and told her that I still couldn't get his name because he wouldn't tell me. It was a constant question that I had asked him throughout our long talks of mysterious eerie things. He'd ask for my name, but I'd never tell. Figured he knew. He had to. Why? Because he was suppose to and the list made it obvious.

Calls continued on and off for about two weeks. I thought I was doing a pretty good job at playing a game that came with no rules or instructions and thought for sure I was winning when Mr. X called in the afternoon. Catching me off guard was not in his favor. He said, "Hi, I'm sorry I called during the day. But, hang on a minute..." I heard him pull the phone away from his mouth and he was talking to someone else in the house. I listened with my ears peeled. "Come on man, stay off that, it isn't finished yet." Then

I heard a man laughing and a stumble, I think, and Mr. X was back on the phone. "Sorry. That's the reason I called you. Man this guy is a pain!" "Who are you talking about?" I asked. "Oh, it doesn't matter." His voice raised away from me to whoever. "Man I told you to leave my stuff alone it ain't yours!" The background man said, "All mine, ah ha ha!"

When Mr. X was back I said, "Don't you have anything in your house? It's got one hell of an echo." He asked the background man, "Hey, what do we have here? A cooler and a, what else? We got something to cook on don't we?" "Aah but we are missing something," said the background man. And the man sounded like Gentry. When Mr. X was on the line with me I said, "Who is that your brother? The one you told me about?" "Yeah, it's my smart ass brother who thinks this house is his. Man quit messing everything up will ya already." "Is this the one who thinks he has all the Pink Floyd albums but they are really yours? Your brother?" He changed the subject and said, "So, what have ya been up to? Talk to your friend at the radio station lately?" "Yeah, I call her a lot. She plays lots of songs for me. Why don't you let me talk to your brother, maybe I know him?" I could hear the background man mumbling about something when Mr. X said, "Yeah. So! I'm looking through it too. Get your own man! Hey! I'm sorry for all this. He can be such a pain in the ass. Wait. Wait, I'll be back. Hang on..." I could have sworn he said Gentry. "Man I told you to leave that shit alone! I know where everything is!" "It's all mine, ah ha ha ha!" said the background man. The phone was back in hand and Mr. X said, "Yeah. It's my brother. I know where everything is in here. He says it's a mess. This place isn't done yet. I got so much to do, ya know. He comes over and wants to drink and party. So what are you doing? Playing your piano? Written anything? Didn't you say you wrote songs." "Yeah, but not in a couple of weeks. Hey, didn't I hear you call your brother by his name? His name is Gentry?" "Oh my brother. Uhm. No, Don't think I have a brother named Gentry. He was talking too. It was probably hard to understand. I'd tell you what his name ought to be, but you seem like a pretty nice girl so I won't say it." Just then the background man burst out laughing, trying to put his mouth in restraints. It sounded like Gentry.

It had to be Gentry. Who else? Why all these calls back and forth? Me and Mr. X talking I mean. "Oh come on mystery man, why don't you let me talk to your brother?" "I don't think that would be such a good idea. Hey wait man what are you doing?" The dial tone came quick. Hmm, I thought, who hung up the phone. I tried to call back but the line was busy. Tried a second and a third, always a third, and it was still busy. I gave up. No I didn't, I waited for a call from him at the kitchen table. The phone rang and it was Mr. X. "Hi. Sorry about that, but my brother didn't want to wait to use the phone so he walked over and pushed the buttons and you were gone. I did mean to get right back with you but I figured I'd just let him make his call to get him outta the way." "Is he still there?" "No. He left. About time too. He was gettin' on my nerves. He likes doin' that, especially when he knows I'm talking to a girl." "Are you sure his name isn't Gentry? He sounds just like this guy I'm crazy about. Oops. I told. Damn!" Told what?" asked Mr. X. "Oh, never mind, it's not important. Besides, I can't stay on the phone too long." "Are you going to be around later," he asked. "Sure." I told him. "Call me later on. Like say one, one thirty, if you're up." I'll be up mystery lady. I'll talk to ya then."

Damn! That had to be Gentry over there with him. I've been to Pink's house and it was empty except for building materials, tools and stuff. This Mr. X was becoming more and more a huge mystery to me.

He called at one thirty that morning like he said he would, but the conversation was slow paced and to put it frankly. Boring. I listened for sounds or words that might be in the background but I heard nothing and no one. I tried to get Mr. X's name, but again he declined to say. After talking with him for about a half hour, the talk was over till the next one.

For the rest of the night I had 'CPZ tuned in. It was my background for piano. While the songs played on, so did I, unless one came on the radio that I liked and I had to crank it up. "Yes! Ten decibels Mr. Mocean, if this radio would go that loud!" Self couldn't control herself, wishing the room would have answered. Quickly I turned to see if the shadow box was tilted, thinking that Mayor might at least be curious. The shadow box was straight and so was I. I reached for the sugar bowl and headed to the piano where I was supposed to be.

When I woke up I wanted to call Mr. X. I thought that it would be a good idea to catch him off guard. Truth was, I was hoping his brother might be the one to answer. Thinking of the brother made me hesitate. I didn't call Mr. X that morning. I was as patient as I could be and waited for the afternoon. I prepared myself well and when he answered I said, "Oh, I'm sorry, I thought this was Greg." Mr. X goofed and said, "No, I'm Steve." "Sorry," I said and hung up. I had his name and I wanted to call him again, but when, I thought? Can't call now, that would be too obvious. Wait, I thought. Prof' told me that if I wanted to get away with something to "be" obvious. People are less apt to notice. I took the advice and called Mr. X right back. He answered again. I said hello again. He knew who he was talking to now. Then again, maybe he knew who it was just seconds ago. "Some girl called here looking for some guy named Greg and I swore it was you. "It was," I said. "Then you know my name is Steve. Do I sound like one?" "Guess if your name is Steve, you sound like a Steve." "Do you wanna tell me yours," he asked. "Why not. I'm Capri and I feel a lot better knowing your name. Do I get to know where you live, or are you suppose to keep that secret too? Wait, before you answer, do you know anything about a brick?" I waited while he sighed a short pause and said, "No, I don't. And if I tell you where I live, no, I better not tell you where I live Capri." "Why not?" I asked. "I don't wanna say, you might get mad or something." Tension grew. I knew it sounded demanding when I said, "Look Steve, we've been on this phone kick for over two weeks. If you don't wanna tell me where you live, I think it's time we meet face to face. You can come here. Today. Now."

Self was sure he'd say no, but Steve said, "Yeah. It would be nice to see the person I'm talking to. I could come over, but it will have to be about 7 if that's okay with you." "Yeah. Seven is a great time. But how do I know you will show up?" I asked. "You'll know. But you have to give me the address first don't you think?" I laughed. "I guess the address would help." I snuck another question in before we said good bye, "Did your brother stop by to mess up your stuff lately?" "Yeah he did. Last night when we got off the phone, he brought a twelve pack over and wanted me to stay up and party with him." "Did you let him in?" I asked. "No I didn't let him in 'cause if I would have let him stay here drinking, then he would have ended up crashing out on the floor like he always does." "What's wrong with that," I asked. "Cap, I like my brother, don't get me wrong, but he's such a pain! If I let him stay, and it has to be on the floor, he'd be moving this here and moving that there. He doesn't know how to leave things alone. I told you that remember?" "Yeah, you did. I'm like that too. I like everything where it belongs. I'm a neat freak. Well, listen, I'm gonna get off the phone. You are definitely coming over at seven right Steve?" He assured me that he would be close to on time, give or take a couple minutes.

The rest of the day went slow. Very slow. The house was already clean. The girls were up in their room playing. Sonny was taking a nap.

I passed time in the kitchen wiping this and shining that. For the first time I wondered what Steve might look like. Would he be tall or short? Brown eyes or blue? Maybe they're hazel, maybe they're green. Is he super nice or really mean! What if he's just like Henry Mitchel Batturs, oh no! Why did I let my address go?

My worries subsided when I got to thinking that Gentry was behind it all. I had to get real. "Cap." I said to myself, "Come on. What's with you? Gentry has to know this guy Steve. Steve told you a name of a band that his brother was in, remember?" "Yeah. Can't forget a name like "Pink Punks Practicing in Public Pissers!"

To kill time, I counted the cans. There were 71 and brewing. It would be a matter of space. Cans will definitely have to start pyramiding in the south corner of the kitchen.

Just as I was finishing there was a quiet knock on the door. I looked up at the clock and it was a couple of minutes before seven. Hmm, I thought, it's gotta be Mr. X. I went to answer and the man outside the door said, "Hi. I'm Steve. You're Capri?" "It's me. Come on in. Nice to finally meet you." I didn't say it with enthusiasm. Steve didn't look anything like Pink. There was no way they could be brothers. Steve was about 5'10." He was average in build and was very fair skinned. His hair was light-light blonde and curly. His eyes were blue. Steve was not ugly, he just wasn't my type. I would never have given him a second look had we bumped within a crowd. However, I remained polite and asked him to have a seat at the table. I offered him a cup of coffee. Steve declined. After a few minutes of small talk, I plunged right into the main business and the game was the business!" "Do you know someone named Gentry," I asked. "No, why?" "Well, you wouldn't tell me if you did, he wouldn't want you to..." and I rattled on. "Wouldn't want me to what?" Steve asked nervously. "It doesn't matter. It's just that all the things you said about you, are just the same as this guy I know. I wrote it down. I'll show it to you." I went to the piano and got the paper with the list. 41 in all on it. He looked at it and said, There's someone like me out there?" "Yeah. Hey Steve. Where do you live? Are you going to tell me? After all you're here. It's fair."

Steve looked down at the floor a moment and when he raised his head up he pointed north and said, "Over there by the hospital." "Where abouts by the hospital?" "In that green house over there. It faces this way." I knew the one. Knew that from his house he could see mine. Well, he could see the second level and the back of the garage and that was enough for me. I was convinced that Mocean put him up to spying on me. Why would someone who called the radio station want to talk to me? Why did Renee think it vital? Did Gentry put her up to it too? The game was a master! And I surrendered. "Steve. You're nice, but this is kinda creepy. I thought someone I knew put you up to talking to me. I was wrong. I think it'd be a good idea for us not to call each other anymore. No offense. Okay?" Exit Mr. X. Game over, or was it?

No one showed me how to play. What was I supposed to do or not? Well I never saw or heard from Mr. X again. I was tempted to drive pass the house he said he lived in, but what if he saw me? "Capri," Self said, "He's been watching you!" "Shh. The kids are gonna hear you Cappy." Quietly I listened and sat at the table for coffee and to think!

"Spet. He's not just rich, he is filthy rich..." Man how I wanted to call Winnebago and tell her about this thing with Mr. X and all, but her number was unlisted. I knew her sister was married, but not to who. Knew her mom had re-married and moved to where I don't know. It was too much to write in a letter so I put it in a book.

I wondered what kind of things could be bought if a person was "filthy rich." I suppose you could buy and sell people all day if you wanted to. What if Mr. Mocean III was very wealthy? What made him come into all of that? Is it a business? It couldn't be Moceans Sugar Company? I buy it. It's across America. It's everywhere! It's been around for years and years! I was betting that I hit it just right. Maybe Gentry didn't care about the money thing. Maybe he didn't like being a sugar man like his father. To hear Gentry talk, you'd think that his dad was made of salt.

Pink liked being an electrician. I saw his works in the Neil Street house and he was genius when it came to sounds, wires and light. You name it, Pink did it better than right. Thought about the last time I'd seen Gentry. Wondered when and if he would pop in again. Tried telling myself that too much time had gone by. I'd never see him again unless I went to Benny's place.

By now, most of the people there knew I was crazy about Pinky, that I loved him or they should have. So if I stopped in to shoot pool or something and Gentry wasn't there the word would be certain to reach him. Nina again told me that it would look like I was chasing him. She would thought me crazy if I explained that looking and waiting for Gentry was beyond my control. Believe me! Looking for him was like working on a huge puzzle. The piece is there you know it is. You've gone through the box a hundred times like paws in the litter. You know it's only a matter of time before you find it. (unless it's lost), Immediately I thought about the game. What if this is just a game? What if Gentry set out to have a girl fall in love with him, just to see if it could be done? Maybe that explains why he loves getting me mad. No I said to myself in silence. He wouldn't have made jokes about it to Buff! Would he go that far? Would he play this part to the end? Doesn't he know that he would break her heart too? He can't be heartless. I've seen the little boy in him and he knows it. I've watched him play and sing here. Self and I both watched those dark brown eyes too many times and they read serious.

On nights when I could I went to The Well. Sometimes Gentry would be there and on those nights he kept a distance between us. Giving me a reflected smile from the mirror he was sitting by near the bar. On other nights, I'd get up my courage to walk over and say hi. No direct eye contact while he'd nod a hello. Though no words were exchanged, I knew what was going on in his head. He was trying to keep things from getting personal when he knew they already were.

On the nights I didn't go to Benny's, I stayed home... waiting. The porch light was lit. The piano was in tune. Thanks to "Mr. Moon." I wanted to hear Pinky say, "Play something for me Big Time." I didn't care if he was filthy rich or if he only had one bag of sugar to his name, I loved him and that was all that mattered. The days that followed dragged on slow but August came as it did you know. School would be just weeks away and Buff couldn't wait to be there the first day.

I was happy I had a little girl that liked going to school and of course Jules couldn't wait for it too. Sonny? It doesn't matter now. He'd get there.

I watched the leaves changing colors. Couldn't wait to watch them fall and blow around. Looked ahead to the next Christmas. Will I get what I want a third time around? It had been a rough three years in this house and I thought about all that happened. And I mean all! I went back in time and dreamed about starting over again. What my life would have been like had I not married Prof' the III. Why did I do that? I just wanted to be a rock and roll singer first. Marriage and kids would come later, maybe. If the marriage happened I intended on having four boys and naming them in order, John, Paul, George and Richard. Wanted to be in my room on "C" St., playing my first 12 string and singing with my real teeth! I wanted to be 15 going on sixteen. Wanted to grow up and marry John Lennon like I always dreamed I would, only John was gone and dead. He was killed. Killed on December 8th. I moved here on that same numbered day, four years after that tragic fact. Why didn't I see it in one of my purple cloud purple visions? I could have run up to New York to save you John! If running was in order, believe me, I would have run like hell!

I stopped myself from continuing a dream that was never gonna happen and focused on the present. What a fascinating combination we would be! Pink and me.

The fall days were growing emotionless. Nearly all the leaves had died and dropped. I'd rake them every day because I had to, because I was suppose to and because I liked it. It kept me busy in the morning and it went real good with coffee and pot. I'd get myself so into it, that unless it was attached to earth itself it wasn't on my new grass and the yard looked beautiful.

Too much time was going by without Pink stopping over and time couldn't move slower. I did however find the time to get out. When I did, I was going on a personal treasure hunt at The Well. There were times when Gentry was physically there and nothing more. His mind was focused on something but for him to see and no one else. I wondered what he thought of and this threw a cut in my heart. For there was a time when I could tell what he was thinking and it was becoming a part of my past. Was he thinking about himself? Was he thinking about me? Was he thinking about Norma or leukemia, his house or job? I was lost and I wanted a compass, but the game came with no playing pieces and I wasn't sure who's turn it was anymore. I only knew that if this was a game I wanted someone to finish it. I wanted to know how to win and who would.

Ooh the things I was thinking since Mr. Mocean no middle name the third came into view! Why is he doing this to me? Doesn't he know I love him? Can't he tell by looking at my eyes? I feel so much when I am around him. Doesn't he feel that I'm aiming right at him? It wouldn't be right for me to tell him first. If he loves me than he should tell me. He's wasting time. Unless... unless he is making sure he loves me before he tells me. Yeah. That must be it. He probably thinks about it all the time. He's testing himself. When he's not coming over it's just to see how long he can stay away until he misses me and has to see me again. It's the only thing that makes sense. He isn't coming over for sex so what else could it be? To play with your head," Self reminded me. "You think so?" I answered with a question and Self left it unanswered.

December was getting the best of me. I didn't want to see winter blanket my world with snow and ice, but it would. It always did!

It was time for a puzzle. A big puzzle! Something with lots of pieces to help me get my mind off the game. Bought one with 3,000 pieces. I couldn't wait to get the box open and check it for difficulty. "This will be hard for sure. Lots of branches and sky." Self had her say and I called Nina. Had to let her know what I was up against. She had a bitch of a puzzle of her own. I know... I saw it. Nina put over two months into it and had a ways to go. Took some doing, but I convinced her to walk around the corner to see mine. Nina took one look and said, "What! Are you out of your mind? No thank you Capri. Ha. You'll be doing this one all winter." "That was the general idea. Come on Nina. Now I got legitimate reason to bitch. This one outta piss me off for good."

I did the puzzle every chance I had. Hours were spent just to get the frame together. If I wasn't at the back table, I'd be at the kitchen table with coffee. Always coffee and always thinking. Thinking about what to do next. Was there anything to do next? When will Gentry come back? Is he coming over again? He has to, I thought. I'm through with Batturs doesn't he know that? Who does he have spying on me now? Who put the brick in the yard? "Shit! I'm back on the brick?" I continued questioning myself in length. I couldn't stand it no more. It was time for pot and piano.

Too many days went just like the one above. I had to go to The Well. Had to drive down Neil Street and I did it whenever I had a chance. Couldn't stop at the house when I knew Pinky was there. Who else might be there? Didn't want him to want me to go away again. I was feeling bad enough, not feeling good enough for him. Was that it? I'm not good enough for Gentry? Maybe I'm not. Maybe he wants a woman with her own money and job. I don't have my own money or a job. Maybe he doesn't want to take on a family. I had to be realistic where it counted. Gentry was never married and I was.

Going to The Well too many times and not seeing Pink there was hurting like hell. I needed new faces, new places, when someone from Benny's told me that I might like a place called The Barrel.

Off I went. The bar crowd there was my age and older. People were quieter, more mellow. It was a place where you could float around with ease. The big plus was that most of the time you could hear who was talking to you. After going there more than a few times I learned who the owners were. Their names were Lloyd and Mary Fazio. Pope knew 'em. But I didn't know he knew, until he knew that I was going to The Barrel. More Italians, but Mary and Lloyd couldn't have been nicer.

November was getting closer. I could hardly believe another birthday was so near. Didn't want to be thirty because the number itself sounded old. Then I quickly reminded myself that I wasn't turning 30, but that I was just starting my 31st year and that sounded young! Now that I had myself in the right frame of mind, I made a silent wish. Please God! Let me have another birthday with Gentry. Will You let him know that? I'm not so sure he's hearing me these days. Then I sprung from my seat and went to my spot in the kitchen. I figured I better say what I gotta say out loud just to make sure I was heard. "I need Your help God. Are You listening to me? Number 3? Remember? Cap? I love him God. Won't You send Gentry my way on Christmas? One more time?" Positive energy had been draining outta me for years, leaving me feeling nothing but doubt.

November had come and gone and December was upon me. More three's I thought. Pope and his granddaughter Jules, both shared their birthdays on the same day, December 3rd. Naturally if you add the 1,2, and the twelfth month, you get three. Then when you add the month and day together you get six and that can be broken equally in half one time making it three. Me! I ran through the three's in my life that night after Jules turned 5.

December continued like any other. The days and nights were cold and snow was making its presence known. I'd get out as much as I could and go to The Well. Of course I went for one reason. If the reason for going there, wasn't there, I headed to The Barrel for a peek.

It was around that time when I met one of the tenders there who shall be referred to as Ladie. Ladie was 5'7" tall. In my opinion she would have been more pleasing to the eye, if she weighed about 30 pounds less, for Ladie was a pretty woman. Her mane as she called it, was long, full, feathered and brown. Her eyes were big, brown and clever. Somehow we hit it off right from the start. I think it had something to do with the "in-common's" we had. Coffee and pot.

A lot of nights after going to The Well looking for Gentry, I'd pop in The Barrel to say hi to Lade and anyone else I knew. December went much like that and it was closer to Christmas.

It was about two weeks before the day when me and my kids realized that Grizzly had not been home since the night before. And it was night again. The kids were upset. Jules and Buff were crying asking me if they would ever see him again. I reassured them and said, "Grizzly probably got scared by a blue jay. He's probably afraid to leave his hiding spot. He'll be back. Don't cry." "Yeah, mom's right Jules," Buff said, "He'll be back. Come on. Let's go play "Barbies." Jules looked at me and I wiped her tears with my hand. "Jules, Grizzly will be back. You go up and play with your sister. "He'll probably come to the door meowing at three in the morning." "What if you don't hear him mom?" she asked. "I'll hear him Jules. How can I not? You know how loud he can be." Jules shook her head to agree with me and tried to smile. She went up to her room to be with her sister Buff.

Now I was becoming concerned about my cat. Had him since he was about 6 weeks old. He always came when I called him. I thought about the night before. Called him once and he came to the door but he didn't want in. I asked him in but he just stood there a minute and looked at me. Then he darted off the porch and took off. I was up late and called for him a second time and when he didn't show up I figured he was busy goofing off somewhere. I let it go then, but I couldn't let it go now. He wasn't at the door this morning when I got up either. This isn't like Grizzly, I thought. I waited till the girls and Sonny were all sound asleep before I called for the cat. Didn't want to see them hurt again if Grizzly didn't show up. It was after 11 p.m. when I called for him. I watched and waited. Called his name again and whistled, (he knew my whistle), but Grizzly was nowhere in sight. I walked out to the side walk. Looked in every direction and saw no fresh paw prints in the snow. I walked back to the house and called him one more time. Again I waited and watched, but my cat was not hearing me or not listening. I wasn't sure which and I didn't want to know. I closed and locked up the front door leaving the porch light on.

When morning came the girls first words were about Grizzly. Jules, the seriously depressed little one said, "Mom, I don't think Grizz' is coming back." "Mom, what if Jules is right? What if he got hurt and he can't get home?" Buff asked. "You forgot. Grizzly came from bear country remember? He's tough." No more was said. I could tell by their faces that they didn't buy one word I had said and I couldn't blame them. I knew something was wrong. I too did not believe we would ever see Grizzly McDonald again and we didn't.

Christmas was close. I had to get things fixed fast. This was something I knew I could do. Kittens will help them forget about Grizzly. I went right to the newspaper without hesitating. Read the pets adds and found lots of free kittens. I called and asked about all of them. When I knew I had the right litter I was at somebody's house picking out a couple. They were all cute, long haired kittens. One was colored light caramel. The other was a white and light tanned tabby. I asked the woman who placed the add if I could come by Christmas Eve to get them. I explained to her that I needed the kids to be sleeping before I took them home because they were presents. The woman told me that she would be more than happy to hold on to them until the night would come.

In the meantime I wondered about my own Christmas. My birthday. Would I have a cake so I could make the wish official and blow out 30 candles? Nah. I wouldn't get that unless I made it myself. Prof' was a chef from the get go. He never made me a cake. Now I had myself down in the face again missing Mayor. She always made my birthday special. There was always a little something extra for me at Christmas, making the day feel more like my own and not everybody's. But Mayor wouldn't be here for another Christmas and going to Pope's just wasn't the same without her. Had to get my mind off Mayor and focus on the kids. I didn't want them to see me down, so I thought more about the kittens. They put a smile on my face and I knew they would do the same to the girls. Christmas would be a happy time for all three of my kids, for kids it should be.

On the Eve of Christmas I bought myself two bottles of champagne and hoped for the best. The kids were real excited about the next morning so it wasn't as easy getting them to sleep. I told them that if they went to sleep fast, then morning would get here quicker. It worked. I called Nina. "Nina, it's me Cap. Could you do me a small favor and I promise I'm not going out drinking." Nina answered, "What now Cap." No she wasn't mad, but I usually called for something and the something was always a sitter. "No Nina, I don't need anybody to watch the kids. I wondered if you wouldn't mind baby-sitting a couple of kittens for me till the kids are sleeping. They might run up the stairs and wake the kids up. I don't want to spoil the surprise." "Well alright. I'll watch the kittens. When are you going to get them?" Nina asked. "I don't want to go over to this woman's house too late. What if I call her and ask if I can get them at ten. Would that work for you?" "Sure. I'll just keep them in the basement and when the kids are sleeping you can come over and get them," Nina said. "Great. I'll call her now and let her know what's going on." Then Nina asked, "Cap, who is going to watch the kids when you go? Is Joanne stopping over?" "Gee Nina, she knows I got champagne here. She already asked if she could come over and try it. You know she's not 18 yet, but we made a deal. She said she'd watch the kids for me if I let her have some. I told her that I would after I got the kittens home. So I'm set." "Well alright then Cap. I'll look for you around ten." We hung up and I couldn't wait to get the kittens to the house. My house.

Looking into the living room at the tree I felt down hearted again. It was the eve of my birthday and all I could think about was Gentry. Immediately I recalled December 24th 1984. The time was 11:11 p.m. when Gentry knocked and entered my house for the very first time. I noted the time and the time was just 9:20 p.m. "Cap don't worry," I said to myself, There's still time. Don't give up hope. You might hear that knock again tonight." "Yeah. Who am I kidding. He wasn't here last year and it was all I wanted. What would make this birthday any different?"

I phoned the woman about the kittens. All was set. Called Nina and told her that I was going to keep the kittens in the downstairs bathroom till morning. Besides, after I picked them up, I just had to play with them. Jo asked if I was going to open a bottle of champagne. I turned to look at the clock. It was just about 11:00 p.m. I didn't explain in detail why she would have to wait until 11:11, I only told her that I had something else to celebrate besides my birthday. And besides, it wasn't my birthday. Not yet.

When the hands pointed to the numbers on the clock that indicated the precise time, I walked to the front door, looked at the porch unattended and cold. I turned off the porch light. I put my outsides on the inside and popped open bottle number one. "Hey Jo, in the cupboard over there you'll find some glasses. I'm gonna smoke some pot." Jo's curiosity peeked, "Cap, you'll let me try some? I never smoked it before, what's it like?" "Jo your mom would kill me if she knew I let you smoke pot are you crazy!" I reached for the sugar bowl on the shadow box and brought it over to the kitchen table. Took out enough to roll a joint when Jo asked, "You keep your marijuana in a tea set?" "Sure, why not? It's trimmed in gold isn't it pretty?" "You're nuts Cappy!" she said laughing. Thank you very much," I said, "This is tea time." Jo watched me roll the doob and said, "Caps. You gotta let me try a little. I won't tell my mom or my dad. They'll never know." To her parents she was 17, but when that birthday numbered her, she was into her 18th year, so I lit it up and handed to Jo. "What the hell, it's Christmas right?" She took a hit off the joint. She coughed and coughed some more. Her eyes watered fast. "How do you smoke this Caps? You cough like this?" she asked. "It's gotta be a big hit for me," I said, "But the cough gets me higher quicker." "Let me try it again. I don't feel anything yet," Jo said. "Go on. Inhale it slow. Hold it in for as long as you can. Go easy Jo because this is real good! It creeps up on you. You'll see what I mean." Jo took a hit and held it in. Then she took another one and held it in. "Cap I don't feel a thing. I feel like I did before I took the first puff, hit, whatever ya call it." "You know something Jo. The first couple of times I smoked pot it didn't do anything to me either. Guess that's why I took pills. Pills are easy. Water and down they go. No cough. Unless you choke on the pill." "Cap you crack me up. Let's have some champagne. Maybe I'll get a buzz off that." "Yeah. Go on and pour. I'm gonna roll up another joint." Jo couldn't wait to have something that would give her a buzz. Probably because she never drank anything till this particular night. If it would've been poured into a champagne glass full, then it only took Jo half of that to get all pumped up on the stuff. She was stumbling, laughing and having a great time.

It was after midnight. With JoJo being drunk, I told her to stay at my house until she sobered up. She told me that she'd be able to pull it off and wanted to go home. I couldn't change her mind. She swore she'd be in deep shit if she didn't get to her house... So... Off she tumble-walked across the street calling back to me, "Tea Time!" Once she got into her house I locked up but not for the night. I stood and watched the outside for a cigarette and I went to check on the kittens.

I couldn't resist playing with them till things nearly got out of control. The little tabby was checking out the view from the bottom of the stairs. I picked her up and said, "If you go up those stairs you won't be a surprise tomorrow morning." She crawled on my shoulder and cuddled the back of my neck purring. She and her brother were back in the bathroom. Both of them pulled up with their paws to get into the litter box. They needed a boost. I got a pillow from the living room and wrapped an old towel around it and laid in next to the box. They used it with ease. After business in the box was done, the two of them got comfortable and slept on each other. They looked so cute I hated to move them in the cabinet where I had set up a bed, but I did. Like earlier, I left the light on for them...

... then it occurred to me. I shut the porch light out! What was I thinking? I was thinking that I was born sometime before lunch. My official birthday would be at that time. Whenever that was. So I went back to the front door to turn on the light. I watched for Gentry. There was nothing out there that indicated he was going to show. I headed back to the sugar bowl on the table. Drank more champagne but it didn't feel right. I decided to call 'CPZ and ask them to play something. I had to think real hard about what I wanted to hear. There were so many Beatle songs to choose from and the words had to be just right. I went through the different songs in album-order the best I could. Then it came to me. Gentry asked me to sing him a lullaby. "Golden Slumbers" was the one I played and sang for him first. I dialed up the radio station and Stone answered. "Stone hi, it's me, Cap. Did I tell ever tell you when my birthday was?" "No, I don't think so. When is it?" he asked. "Now, and it's a rip off cause I'm not getting what I wished for yet." "Let me see Cap. Does this have something to do with the man?" "You know it does Stone. Will you play "Golden Slumbers"?" "Well hell yes Cap. It's your day. Tell ya what. Since it's your birthday, I'll play the whole album side for ya." "That would be great! Thanks a lot. I'll go turn the radio on. Talk to you later." I could hear Stone fumbling around the studio as we said good-bye and Merry Christmas.

My spirit wasn't into the holiday. I cleaned up the glasses, put the bubbles in the fridge, wiped off the table and kept only what needed to be on it. My pen, some paper and coffee. Wrote thoughts, words, names and of course numbers. I thought about the year 1984. I had met Frank Forrest in early July. Prof' was still legally my husband and living with me and the kids. I meet Gentry on the 22nd of September. Six days later on the 28th, Prof' moved out. Hmm. It hit me like it should have back then. There were three men. In a period of three months. I tried to find this three amusing, but it wasn't gonna happen. What happened? More pot of course.

Just when I was good and buzzed I could hear Stone loud and clear through the speakers: "This is Stone here tonight coming to you live from 'CPZ. Got a request going out to a friend of mine. It's her birthday. Happy Birthday Capri! Hope you get what you wished for." I stopped everything and got over to the piano. I played and sang along pretending that Gentry was back-laying on my couch listening. When the Beatle songs finished I turned down the radio and stayed at the piano for awhile. Played and sang hoping that Gentry would feel the energy and charge over. I stayed high and played till nearly four in the morning. He did not come and I was too sad to be tired. I sat at the kitchen table to think with the pen. I am thirty going on thirty-one. Life was wow! Look what life has done. I was three, I am three and I will always be three. The numbers don't change if you can't let them be. What's going on? Is it nothing, will I fall? Did I want it so much I just imagined it all? Oh it couldn't be truth these things in my head, I was Eve you were Adam choked on an apple and dead. Do you hear me? Am I crazy? Can't I just have the dream? I wonder if the numbers are part of a scheme. I played poem games keeping sharp and alert. Before I knew it the morning light was coming through the window. It wouldn't be long and the kids would be up, because I was going to wake them up.

Eight o'clock was all I could stand. The kittens were put into Christmas wrapped boxes with hidden air holes. I went up the stairs. "Come on everybody. Let's go see what Santa brought you. There's all kinds of presents under the tree." The kids half asleep, raced down the stairs and headed straight for the tree. I joined them and gave Sonny and Jules what belonged to them. Buff found her own without a problem. Then Buff found a box with all three names on it and said, "Mom what is this?" "Well just open it and find out," I said. Buff turned the box on its side trying to open it. With the top facing a wall ahead, a kitten ran out of the box and around the living room floor. "Jules it's a kitten!" Buff exclaimed. Jules face lit up and she said, "Oh mom it's so cute. I love it!" "She is cute isn't she," I said. Jules was holding the kitten to her face. Just then the other one was tumbling under the tree and Buff spotted it. "Oh my God there's another one! Look Jules. There's two! Mom got us two!" Buff's eyes were happy teary. Sonny? He opened his presents then immediately wanted food.

They were having a wonderful day. My day? It couldn't have gone any slower. I watched the clock over and over. I knew better. I should have removed all time telling items from the house long ago. God knows that my "own" numbers were consuming me enough. That is... if He's been paying attention.

The clouds, I thought. The clouds said Listen. They said 2. They said GM. They showed stairs. There was a man. There was a woman. There was a Face. It was real. It was there. It was there for me. It was there for a reason. The one I still wasn't sure of. Out came the pot and the pen. I was up to numbers again.

Just then the phone rang and Buff raced to answer. It was Ladie from The Barrel. She wanted to stop over and leave me a couple doobs for my birthday. I agreed quick because I was running low.

Ladie was at my house by the time a half hour went by. The coffee was brewing in an automatic maker. The temperamental percolator that proudly made me nothing but hot water was out. For good. I poured the coffee and Ladie rolled a joint. "Cap, is it going to be okay to smoke this with the kids here?" she asked. "Ladie I got cool kids. They don't say anything to anybody. Buff knows I smoke pot and so does Jules. Sonny doesn't know what it is so light it up." Ladie passed me the joint and said, "No. You light it up. This is your birthday." "Thanks!" I said, striking a match. After the one Ladie rolled, I brought out mine.

The day went pretty good despite all I wished for. Ladie excused herself telling me she needed to get something from the store before they closed. She was back in a flash and was in the kitchen fumbling around by the microwave. (Back to me) She turned slowly with a chocolate cupcake. It held one lit candle. Ladie said, "They were outta cake!" Then she sang the happy birthday day song for me. I was stoned and it was so funny I cried. "Ladie this is the nicest present I got for my birthday. Thanks." "You said that nobody made you a birthday cake in so long, well, never mind the rest. You're suppose to make a wish and blow out the candle." I didn't say anything. I was too choked up and teary eyed. I wished my wish again to God. Surely He would listen to me on the day that He gave me life! I blew out the candle and composed myself. "Ladie. I think we need more coffee. I'll make us some more." "Cap, I've been meaning to ask you about that. Why do you have so many coffee cans? Are you collecting them?" I answered her question the best I could, "Looks like it, but I'm not really. One day this guy Gentry told me I should drink "Maxwell House" coffee, and now I have all of these!" "Do you know how many you have Cap?" she asked. "Of course I know. I shine 'em up all the time. There's 72 empty cans. There's this one I haven't opened yet and the one we're using. So there's 74."

Ladie admired the cans and told me how good they looked sitting on the counter. I admired them too.

As the night crept in Ladie told me that she had made plans for the evening and would have to be going. I told her I was going to Pope's for dinner. Ladie handed me enough pot for a couple joints before she left and said, "Hope you get what you wished for Cap. You deserve it." Maybe I didn't, at least that's what I was beginning to think.

In the next hour that followed I spent time getting the kids ready to go to their grandpa's house for supper. They were excited to go. (hoping for more presents). My brothers would be there. Hermit with his wife and kids. John and his wife, Shorty and Chelsea, Nina and her kids would be there with Pope. I show up with the kids, no husband or boyfriend. This made me want the dinner eaten and over with. I wanted to go back to the house. Afraid I would miss Gentry and I was sure he didn't know where Pope lived. When the feast was over I got up to help Nina with the dishes. That's when the jokes started. Hermit called out from the living room, "Cap aren't you 31 now?" Pope jumped in and said, "You were born in '55 right?" I walked over to the living room. Hermit was grinning. I looked at him, the Pope and said, "I was born in 1956! I turned 30 today you guys. "Are you sure?" asked Pope. "I thought you were born in '55." "That's it. I've had it. You two have been doing this to me for years. I was born in '55 Pope okay? And yes Hermit I am 31. Technically I already did the 30 years." Of course Hermit understood that. Pope didn't care less. Neither did I. I wanted to be at my house. Went back to helping Nina with the dishes when she insisted that I didn't. Being brought up half Italian, I didn't insist that I stay and help like I should have. I couldn't wait to get where I wanted to be all along.

The kids gave their grandpa a big hug and kiss wishing everyone a Merry Christmas. I said good night.

We drove back the same way we went and passed Neil Street. Gentry's little black truck was not in the drive and the kids were none the wiser.

When we got through the door of the house Buff and Jules wanted to know if they could play with the kittens upstairs. I didn't have a problem with that, but I took precaution. I took the litter box upstairs to the other bathroom. I closed all the other doors and showed the kittens where it was. They climbed in and looked around the box and the room. Then they both hopped out and ran down the hall where Jules and Buff waited. They each picked up a kitten and went in their bedroom. Sonny was out like a light on the chair downstairs. The little guy had a big day. Had a lot of good food at grandpa's. I carried him upstairs and got him tucked in for the night.

Buff wanted to know if I had any yarn laying around. She wanted to have a ball of it for the kittens to play with. So did Jules. Good old mom made two balls for each of the kittens to play with. I added a piece of yarn about three feet long to each one of them so they could get the kitties to go where ever the yarn went. They made for great lures. I told the girls to guide them down the hall every so often so they would remember where their litter box was. They learned fast.

I could time out mom and be Cap for a while. So I went downstairs to get all the things I would require for thirst, for notes, for fun. But I wasn't having any fun. It was ten dark-out and glacial. Didn't look as though I was going to get what I wished for, who I wanted. I didn't call Gentry at the Neil Street house and I wasn't about to call his parents. I could only hope he would be over before my birthday ended.

Boom! January was and it was February. I'd see Gentry as often as he was at The Well. Pink sat by himself. I was the one who would walk over to him. If it felt comfortable I'd half-sit at the bar with him. We'd talk. It was to the point and meant nothing. I'd go back to my seat and wonder if it was the leukemia that made him moody, because other nights he'd talk in code to me from across the bar laughing. I'd be sure-worded, quick and smiling. As long as this was going on, I had made mind to call him at the Neil Street house the next day. When the next day came, I called.

The phone rang and I got an answering machine. I could faintly hear music in the background while I heard Gentry's recorded-voice saying: "Hi. This is Gentry. I can't come to the phone now. Leave a message after you hear the tone." The background music was still going and the words being sung were: " ... to let you go, and if you lost your love for me, well you never let it show, there was no way to compromise..." (tone). I didn't leave a message. I called the number again and again just to hear Gentry's voice. The first time I heard it there was something wrong. It was the way he said it that sought my aura. He was leaving me in some way. Only I didn't know in what way. Is he going to die? Is he going away? No. He wants me to say something and I don't know what to say.

I went to The Well, to The Barrel and I drove over to Neil Street. I couldn't find Gentry anywhere. I missed him. His laughing, his playing, he riddles and rhymes. The church bells are ringing and I know the time.

Me and Ladie were hanging around together just about every day. She would come over for coffee and pot, or I'd go to The Barrel for coffee, already potted-up. Ladie and I talked and talked. She talked about the man or men in her life and all I did was talk about Gentry. Whoever I talked to, I talked about Gentry because he was all I wanted to talk about!

I was glad to have someone drop by the house and Ladie was always there. Many hours were spent at the kitchen table. Many more coffee cans would pyramid up. More pot would be smoked and more going out was an order. I went out nearly every night. It didn't take much money because most of the men I had met at The Barrel bought drinks for me. Ladie would always slide me free ones when she was tending bar. I'd go home with most of the money I had left with which was about two dollars. Whenever Ladie and I would go out for drinks we seldom paid for any, but the first. Each night after night, drink upon drink, Ladie and I hung out and smoked pot. When the times were over and I was back at the house, I'd sit at the table and gazed at thoughts in the air. I was wishing that Pink was there. Each day that went by I was loving him more and more. How I hated myself for ever letting Batturs through the door.

But one night fortune had struck I was certain. It was early evening, after six or so. Benny, the owner of The Well walked up to me and said that Gentry wanted to talk to me about something. Of course I asked Benny why, but he wouldn't say, just that I should be at The Well at ten o'clock. I finished the coffee I ordered and went straight to my house. There would be hours to kill and I wanted them to go by quickly.

First things first. Fed the kids, cleaned the kitchen. All was set. Sitter lined up and standing by. I'd have to look just right. Did my hair and face with all the Cos' I had in me. Questions came stampeding. Why The Well? Will Pink even show up? What will he say? Self said softly, "Maybe he's gonna ask to marry you... sober." Sober? Marry him? This meant only one thing because Self saw me reaching for the sugar bowl. "Don't do it Capri. You don't wanna be high if he's going to ask you "the" question!" I put the sugar bowl back and took something for my nerves instead. With an hour left I played the piano. I lied. I tried to play the piano. My fingers just refused to hit the right keys. I couldn't even play the songs I had written myself so I took another pill with a cup of coffee and paced the floor until I couldn't take it no more. It was 9:45 p.m. I called Nina and told her I was ready to leave.

First thing I did when Benny told me the news was make the arrangements priority! Kimmy would get to my house in under two minutes. It only took four minutes to get to The Well and I arrived early. About 9:51. I walked in taking a seat at the bar, a few barstools away from the door, ordered a drink and Benny brought it over. I asked him if Gentry was still going to come. "Cap, it's not ten yet. Give him time, he'll be here."

I sipped on my drink a few sips and asked Benny to break a dollar. I put the quarters in the juke box and played some songs while I waited. .

It was almost ten. My patience were gnawing me. I grabbed my purse off the bar and headed for the ladies room. Checked my hair and my face, pinched my face for blush and headed back into the bar for a seat. Gentry was nowhere in sight. It was ten o'clock when I called the owner over. "Benny, Gentry isn't here. He isn't coming is he?" "No Cap, he's here. He just came out of the men's room see?" I turned to see if Benny's words were true and I did not see Gentry. "I don't see him." Benny just nodded his head and aimed his eyes to the west side of the bar where Gentry was standing. "Benny?" I asked, "Should I go over there?" "Yeah Cap. He's probably waiting for you, go on." I left my things at the bar and walked slowly across the room.

Gentry was behind the bar looking for a particular brand of whiskey. I sat down at the end of the L-shaped bar and greeted him. His hello was a brief hi. Gentry found what it was he was looking for and grabbed a shot glass from the bar. I watched him pour a shot and drink it down. He was well into thought and calculations. "Gentry," I said. "Whatever it is you're having, I think I could use one." "Sure," he said. He took another shot glass out and put it on the bar in front of me. He filled it and I swallowed it down. "Gentry, Benny said that you wanted to talk to me." I looked at his eyes and waited for a reply. He came a little closer, but not close enough and said, "Cap. I don't love you. I never loved you and I will never love you." My heart pounded hard inside my chest and I could hear every beat. Then he said, "Find somebody. Find a nice man, I'm not the one for you." My eyes filled with tears. It felt like my heart was pushing like hell to get through my skin. My voice quivered and I looked up at him and said, "But I don't want to find somebody else Gentry." "Cap, I didn't want to make you cry. You want another shot?" "Yeah! Please!" I tried hard to keep my tears under control and I drank the whiskey down fast. I put the empty shot glass on the bar. Gentry said, "Cap. Find someone else because it's not going to be me. Sorry." "You're sorry? Not as sorry as I am." Bravely I stood up and took one more look at Gentry. It felt like it took forever to get to where Benny was and it was Benny I was after. He saw my anger and hurt. "Benny. How could you do that to me? You know how I feel about him. You told me to come here at ten o'clock to get my heart tore out? Just like the time you told me to take Gentry a six pack. To find him with Norma! You planned this! I know you did. I thought San Marino people were like family. Well you're not family no more. I will never patronize you establishment again. Hope the two of you have a good laugh." Benny tried to get an "I'm sorry" in and an "I didn't know." But it wasn't gonna work. I would never believed him and I would not go back to The Well.

I cried and cried all the way home and all through the night. Didn't sleep. I couldn't. I smoked all the pot I had left and four joints wasn't doing a thing. I never felt so devastated in my entire life. The one person I've loved every single life time doesn't love me? All this time it was a game? A joke? "Cap. It was nothing. Nothing to him." Self said. "But that can't be true!" I replied, "He loves me. I know he does. He didn't mean what he said." "Then why did he say it?" Self always tried getting the last word in and she did this time.

I pretended to be happy on the outside the best I could. I spent a lot of time cleaning the house and working on the damn puzzle. The one on the table until reality set in again.

Ladie dropped in and hours were spent talking over coffee and pot. She got to know the kids real well and they liked her too. There were times when Ladie knew I was down and out over Gentry. If the kids were loud and out of hand, and it wasn't often, Ladie would firmly remind them," Buff, Jules and you too Sonny, your mom needs a break. She does a lot for you. Don't you think that you could be quieter for her? She has friends too you know." The kids didn't say anything, but they did listen. When Ladie would leave it was about the time she had to start getting ready for work.

It would be back to waiting and wondering more about Pink. And it was the waiting that was getting to me. March had crept in. I went against every three I stood for. I sent a fourth letter to Gentry.

A few days later I was busy doing something. Buff called to me from the door saying, "Mom, Pinky's here." She handed me something he had handed her from the driver side window of the little black truck. I walked out to the porch happy to see him, when he spit on my shirt. With angry eyes he said, "Don't send me anymore letters and quit calling me!" I started to ask him what it was I did, but he backed out fast and sped away.

I went back into the house and looked at the envelope that Gentry gave Buff to give me. It was the last letter I sent. Un-opened. Just below, where I had addressed it were the words Gentry had written with rage: "Don't bother me for the rest of your fucking life." I had to sit. This is it, I thought. He made it real. I damned him for giving it to Buff. What if she had seen and read those words. No, he didn't want me to call again, but I did. I gave him enough time to get back to the house and dialed up the numbers. He answered and when I spoke one word he hung up. I called again. It rang. I got: "Hi. This is Gentry. I can't come to the phone now. Leave a message after the tone." And I did. "I know you hear me. You don't want letters anymore, okay. But you should never have given Buff the one you wrote on. She doesn't need to see things like that. What's wrong with you? She's only eight years old!" I hung up this time.

He spit on me. "He spit on my shirt!" I looked down at the faded picture on the tee-shirt and realized it was the same one I was wearing the night he and I spent time under the tree by the garage. I dragged myself up the stairs to get a clean one. The one with the picture of lemons, the one I should have thrown away, I put in the dirty laundry basket. Washed it, dried it, folded it and kept it never to wear again. Talked myself into believing that it had a memory worth saving.

Good Lord what did I do to make him hate me so much? Why would he do this to me? He doesn't think Henry is still coming around does he? He's got to know that he isn't! What did I ever do but fall in love. Why did I have to fall in love with him? Why! Why? Because I was supposed to. Because I did.

It wasn't over, not by a atom bomb. There would be explanations for everything in the end. And I convinced myself that an end would never be. Oh the third month had brought me down like it had before. I should have never let any man come through my door! Then I did, and I did, and I did it three times. I asked myself often "Am I losing my mind?" A love so absurd? A game? No. A cloud. God's letters were quiet but planetary loud. I read in my head the words letters and 2. The face in the sky, Christ was that You?

Poetry, song were the things that I did and I wrote another song that Gentry wouldn't hear. In all there were 15. Each one would get better and better. Or maybe the old ones just got boring. Pot was easier to obtain now that Pope was getting his rent on time. If pot was hard to find, I'd find Frank Forrest, via his mother Barb. I'd call and ask for him. He was never there. Barb assured me that her son would get my message. Sure enough Frank would be at my house within the hour. Frank always managed to get me a bag when the people I dealt with on a regular basis couldn't. Frank always asked for a joint from the bag and I gave him a hard time every time. But in the end, he'd get one and leave, but he never left for good. Since he left me on the eve of my birthday we maintained a solid friendship. It didn't matter if he was seeing someone or living with someone. Frank might pull in my drive and we talked for a cigarette. It was habit and we did that for a long time. He was comfortable and I could never dislike him.

I wondered. I was always wondering about something. Something that happened. Something that might or might not happen. And now I wondered if Gentry thought about what he did. Was he going to make up for it somehow? Would he at least tell Buff he was sorry? He better, I thought. I ought to go find him and tell him face to face what I think!

I went to The Barrel and confided in Ladie. She was on my side. And my side changed. I decided not to go looking for him. It was his turn. The game couldn't be over.

One day, about mid-March, just shortly after the church bells rang and the blue jays headed to where ever it was they headed, Gentry pulled up unknown to me. He lightly knocked on the door and walked in. I was standing at my spot in the kitchen thinking. Fear turned me quickly in the direction of the door. I lost control of my legs, my arms and my balance. I held on to the sink where I was standing. Strongly I stated, "You should have given the letter to me. Why didn't you burn them like you did the rest?" Gentry was still smiling as he walked into the living room to take the couch. He laid back into it like he always did. I walked over to him and sat at his hip. "I know all of them by heart Big Time. And you're right mom. I was wrong," he said. "Oh you make me so mad Gentry Mocean! What are you trying to do? Drive me crazy? I should throw you out you know that?" And I told him that trying not to smile. "Aah! But I want to stay. I want you to play something for me. Will ya Big Time?" And I played. And we talked in the language he and I understood. Then he was gone. When Buff and Jules returned from Sunday school I didn't tell them that their favorite person dropped by, because I didn't know if and when he would return.

This March held a treasured memory and I wanted more. To be happy "all the time" like years and years before. Gentry makes all of that happen with a single snap. Course maybe he has his doubts about you Cap. He could be playing with my head but God knows he has my heart. It's happened many moons away as it happened from the start.

Maybe Pope was right. Maybe I was stupid. Hell, he only drilled it in my head forever. I didn't wait on Gentry's arrival. I called the house on Neil Street. Listened over and over to his recorded voice. I left message upon message. He never replied. He never called back. He wasn't coming over. I didn't know what to think. I almost called the nurse in Cleveland. I wanted to ask her if Gentry's behavior was due to leukemia. One minute he hated me and the next he had to love me! Changed my mind and went back to The Well... angry.

I took a seat close to the pool table and the bartenders. I ordered a sweet liquor with a splash of soda. The first drink Gentry bought me on our first and only date. I got change for the juke box and headed to it. On my way I saw Gentry sitting at the end of L shaped bar. Never saw him sit there before. I noticed the coat he had on right away. It was softly colored in white. My first thought was cashmere. My second! The anger. I went back to the bar and slammed down the drink. Then I ordered a double. I played one game of pool and lost. I returned to the bar. Sat down to finish my double. There were four drink chips sitting in front of me. I had a pretty good buzz going after about three more doubles. All I could think of was Gentry sitting in his neat white coat and how he spit on me. The more I thought, the more angry I was getting. I watched him drinking his beer, sip by sip from the bottle as he stared into nothing ahead. I called the owner over and said, "Benny, you might want to throw me out. You probably should have thrown me out a long time ago." "Do you want me to throw you out?" Benny asked. "No. But after I do what I gotta do you might." "You planning on breaking up the place Cap?" "No. I'll just get a little loud. And don't throw me out till I'm done." Benny shook his head asking, "You want another drink?" "Okay Benny. But just one ice cube. Enough to chill it because it's freezing in here."

While Benny was getting my drink I needed to use the bathroom. I watched Pink till I didn't want to be obvious and walked to the ladies room. I went, washed my hands, fixed my hair and lipstick. I went back and took my seat. I turned and watched Gentry on purpose, and I didn't care who noticed. I continued to stare and stood up. Took the cube out of the my drink and walked across the floor of the bar till I was next to Gentry. He did not turn to greet me. He kept his distant stare and sipped he beer. This enraged me even more. I made vocal the thoughts that were in a blaze and said, "Don't sit there and act like you don't know me!" He wasn't concerned. Calmly he pretended I wasn't there and took another drink from the bottle.

The game had turned into a battle. I threw my drink in his face and said loud and clear, "That's for spitting on me!" I stood and glared. Gentry picked up his bottle of beer and took another drink setting it back on the bar. He said nothing. He did nothing. The anger I was feeling made me straight and on track. I walked over to the juke box. It was blasting and I needed quiet. "Benny," I called, "Can you turn that down a minute?" He nodded and said he would when the song playing was finished. A couple of people asked why I would want to do such a nasty thing to Gentry. One girl in particular, who just started working there said, "Why did you do that to him? That's cold. He's a nice man. What do you have against him Cap?" I answered her in the way it was required, "You know something Patsy, you don't even know me well enough to ask and it's really none of your business." She got snotty and said, "Well, I'm going to make it my business. What you did to Gentry was wrong. You should tell him you're sorry." "Pasty, stay out of it. You don't know the half of it. For that matter you don't know any of it." Just then I heard the music get softer. I could hear all the people talking amongst themselves.

It was time to say what I had come to say and I called out to Pink, "Gentry Mocean III, I know you can hear me!" I silenced the room and I carried on, "God wasted his time when he made you! He broke the mold because He wasn't going to make the same mistake." I watched Gentry's every movement. His motions were slow or time was taking it's time. He put the bottle on the bar and held it. His eyes kept fixed ahead. His head lowered with dishonor. I made a direct about-face-left and left.

To my house was I. Got out of my cold coat and shoes and made some hot coffee. I took a long look at all the coffee cans I had saved and for what? Took a seat at the table and thought about what I had just said to the man I loved so much. What was he thinking? He had to be thinking, I thought. Why did he ignore me? He was just here for Christ's sake! He told me he knew all the letters I wrote him by heart. Or was it a lie? If it was then why? He asked nothing in return. Not a hug, not a kiss. So what was with all of this?

With adrenaline still pumping on the inside, I knew it was tea-time. I took a seat behind the piano and got high. Good and high! It made me think more about the things that were fun and the things or people who made me laugh. That naturally led me to thinking about Pink. I had to force my brain into another direction. What have I learned? I thought about the men who did me wrong. Professor totaled them all. But I learned something from him. If you want to get away with something be obvious. Frank taught me that showing someone you love them means more than saying the words. Henry Batturs re-taught me to eat my vegetables, polish the furniture and always lock up everything good and tight for the night. Oh but Mr. Mocean. He was the teacher of them all! He showed me the ease of fun and laughter. It was what was missing all along. He brought the kid inside me back to life. I loved playing word games, our song lines, then my mind abruptly went into reality. I talked to myself. "After what you said to Gentry, do you think for one minute that you will ever see him again?" Good Lord!

"Whatever possessed me to say that? What in the fucking world was I thinking? Well, are You going to help me?" Self answered. "Like He's gonna tell you what to do." Yes. This was all my doing. And I knew that this was something I would have to fix myself. It's trust, I thought to myself. Gentry doesn't believe in me and I don't blame him. I played and sang like I did every night. And time went slowing waiting for April. More bad days. I tossed the two and the twenty-two numbers around in my head. I didn't care much for April and March wasn't going like I thought it would. Nothing was. Badly as I wanted to, I didn't call Gentry. I would have only gotten the recording and the recording would make me miss him more.

On a Wednesday Sunday-School day, while the kids were away I was at the piano when I heard a tap on the door. I stopped singing. Gentry walked in, sat down in the red velvet queen chair and said, "Go on Big Time. Don't stop. Play something for me." I looked at him and said, "Oh like I should just play something for just anybody who comes walking in my door right?" I was smiling. He was smiling. A face I couldn't resist. For I had seen the boy in him that all the others had missed. And he knew it! "Okay Gentry, I'll play something."

He relaxed back into the chair saying, "Sing it to me Big Time!" And I did. I sang "The Long and Winding Road." Gentry wanted to hear me sing a song I wrote for him. I thought about the words to them all in a flash and there was no way I could. Then I asked, "Do you write songs for me?" He got up from the chair and laid down on his side on the floor. "Come here and sit with me." he said. I sat Indian style next to him saying, "You got a guitar. Ever write a song for me?" "Why do you think I have that song on the answering machine?" he said. "I don't know. Why?" I asked. "I put it on there just for you." And his eyes and words were solemn. I wanted so much to believe that he was telling the truth. But then why didn't he ever call or come over when I was brave enough to leave a message? I check-marked my brain this time: (Gentry doesn't trust me). It explains all that's happened or all that hasn't happened between us. If indeed there was an "us." He never made mention of it, and I stayed clear of that direction. I wanted him to say it first. To say that he wanted him and I to be together. To stay together. We were together that evening for an hour or more. Pink got up and said, "I gotta get going." "Why?" I asked. "Because you scare me that's why!" "I scare you? What do you mean I scare you?" "Look at them eyes!" "What about my eyes? I like 'em," I said. "So do I. That's why you scare me." He walked out of the living room, passed by the kitchen table and was about on the outside. I walked to the front door with him. I wanted him to hold my hand or something before he left, but it wasn't going to happen. I noticed his truck wasn't in sight. Wondered if he walked over as I watched his steps down the drive turning left, heading east on the sidewalk.

Damn him! I thought. What is he coming over for? Does he want me or not? I wish to God he would tell me already. He's driving me nuts and he knows it. I bet you can hear what I'm thinking right now and you're laughing your ass off at me aren't you Gentry? Well, are you?

Most of my days were spent thinking just like that. I never wanted to stop thinking about Pink. And my thoughts were constantly on him. Sure I did the mom things. I cleaned the house, I cleaned the clothes. I cooked the food. The kids got fed. Did the dishes and when night was mine, I wished my wishes...The answering machine song was put there just for me? Like the spit on my tee-shirt it was! I called the number up to listen to it again. With Gentry being "afraid" of me, it wasn't likely he would answer the phone and I didn't want him to. I listened to the words of the song called "Separate Lives." It's such a beautiful song, I thought. But why did he pick that one? Maybe, just maybe because there's a line in it that talks about a wall. Of course! A wall. What else? He tried hiding behind the brick one he had mastered in his mind, till I came along, noticed one of the bricks was missing and it turned up in my back yard! If indeed the song was put there for me, then what is he trying to say? If I knew that, maybe it would explain one thing. Why I suddenly scare him! My thoughts became vocal and I took a seat at the piano. "Mr. Gentry no-middle-name Mocean the fucking third... If you can hear me and I know you can! Ha, smiling aren't cha? This game you're playing is getting ridiculous!

You started it. You know the rules and regulations. Hell! Try looking for a space to land on when you can even find the board! Why don't you just come out and say whatever it is you want to say to me. Be done with it. Or start it." I was getting myself all frustrated thinking about Gentry, so for the rest of the night I sang all the songs I had written for him. Then I'd sing songs by other people. The ones I knew. The ones he liked. It was hopeless. No matter what I did. No matter where I was or who I was around, I couldn't get my mind off of Pink because I didn't want to! 2 years and 5 months of certainly not knowing what was what! But whatever it was, May set in motion, and Mocean was once again knocking on my door. I couldn't believe it! He just told me to find someone else! Told me he would never love me! It didn't matter. I loved him and I let him in like I had done each time he made an appearance.

We walked into the living room. He took his place on the couch and we talked our talks until he asked me what he always did, "Play something for me Big Time." I sang and played. The early morning hours sped fast.

Pink was alert, sharp and suddenly wanted to go up on the front balcony of the house. I followed him up the stairs and unlocked the door. We walked out. It was a beautiful morning. I watched the eastern sky with Gentry. We lay on our backs watching planetary alignments. Venus was center-beneath a crescent moon. We looked until we couldn't see the planet anymore. With big eyes, Pink said, "Hey did you see that?" "You mean in the tree?" I said. He stood up and answered, "It was big! What do you think it is?" Before I had a chance to answer, (and I didn't want to move), I saw this huge something rushing over a big maple branch. So did Pink. "There it is again. You see it?" he asked. "See it? Did you hear it?" I asked. I was scared out of my mind. It really looked like the neck of a brontosaurus. Pink suggested, "It could have been a real big snake." I got a little braver and was sitting on the balcony floor, still looking into the old tree when Pink asked, "Do you think this is little?" He was talking about his penis and he was laughing. He had unzipped his pants. To put it nicely, he was ready for sex. I laughed and said, "Would you put that away." Laughing more, Gentry said, "Ah ha ha, so you do think it's little." I shook my head and didn't say anything. I turned away. And I forgot about the tree.

The moon was about to fade from view, when Gentry laid me back down on the balcony. "Are you crazy. What if somebody sees us?" I asked. "Who can see behind this wall," he said. I looked around. The height of our fortress was about 3 and half feet tall. No one would see us. I couldn't say no. I didn't want to. I was in heaven when heaven closed the gates. Gentry stood up laughing at me. He said, "It doesn't matter what time I come by you let me in. He opened the door to the house and went down and out the front door. I got my clothes back together just before he was about to leave my house. "Gentry!" I called, "Where you going? Why you leaving?" I asked quick. "You make it too easy bitch! Don't ya know how to make somebody want you?" He shook his head and I could hear him chuckle as he walked away.

I went into the house, passed the room I used to sleep in. I looked at the bed that Pink had called my playground. I tried to smile and couldn't. I went downstairs for coffee, took it out on the porch and sat on the step smoking a cigarette. Bitch, I thought. He called me a bitch! What if the neighbors heard it? What would they think of me now? They'd seen the cops here enough when Henry was around. Did they need to think that I was some kind of whore? I grabbed my coffee and went back into the house. I couldn't have felt worse.

I'd been up and down on a merry go round and I wanted it to stop. Why does he pretend he doesn't care about me? Why would he treat me just like a piece of meat? I justified it all by reminding myself that he was scared of me.\

♫ ♪ *"Feeling Natural With You"* ♪ ♫
Words and Music by: Catherine Santi in July, 1987

"Ya keep me wonderin' and that's alright.
Even though it's hard to sleep tonight.
But by the morning things will look alright,
I'll be right here thinkin' of you.
I guess I left myself wide open.
I certainly wasn't lookin' for love.
So we jumped the rope and now I'm fallin',

I'm fallin' for you, fallin' for you.
It wasn't so hard to do.
You came so natural to me.
Can't get over feelin' this way, feelin' natural with you.
You can hang around as long as you like.
Because I'll like you twice as long.
What a feelin' that's come over me,
I believe we can't be wrong, somehow I know we belong."

♫ ♪ *"Take The Hand"* ♪ ♫
Words and Music by: *Catherine Santi in June, 1987*

"Love can come and go so easily, anytime, anytime at all.
There are some chances to be taken, if you're willing and ready for it
all.
Love should never hold no secrets, loves just, loves just a dream away.
Don't give up because you're wearing a down.
Be tight, hold strong and take the hand.
There must always be an answer, if the questions your command.
But you'll never find the answers to these if you fail to take the hand.
We all have a lost a love we'd swore be the one.
And when it's gone, well what you gonna do?
We tell ourselves that it's the end of the game,
and over again, it keeps coming back to you.
The sun can break the cloudiest day.
So don't lead your heart astray.
For what you hide someone will find it again.
As the sun keeps rising every day."

Chapter Twenty - "Third Part: The Game.   Regulations"

T'was about mid-May and all through the house. The memories clashed and I wanted a spouse. I needed a place to go to where I could hide out. Where no one would know me. That afternoon, on a Sunday, I chose a place where I used to shoot pool, Make Limber.

When I got to Make Limber I ordered my drink. A double I think. Just then across the bar was someone I knew from high school. He was drinking with a woman almost twice his age. I didn't say anything to him because he didn't realize I was there until he turned his head and looked directly across the bar back at me. "Cappy! Is that you? he asked. "Hi Bobby. Sure has been a long time. I almost forgot your name," I said. "Hang on Cappy. I'll get my drink and join you." I watched him as he talked to his lady friend a few seconds. He came over and stood next to me and said, "You look beautiful! I mean real beautiful!" Thanks Bobby. How've ya been?" I asked. "Ya know something Cappy? I always had my eye on you back in high school. You were pretty then, but now! Damn woman! You're gorgeous! It's your eyes. It was always your eyes! I bet you hear it all the time don't cha?" he asked. "You mean they don't scare you Bobby?" "Why should they?" he said taking a seat. "Never mind. It's not important. Hey, won't your girlfriend get upset if you're over here talking to me?" I asked. "Cappy, she isn't my girlfriend, just a friend. If I was going to have a girlfriend, because I don't have one ya see, then I would want her to look just like you. Are you seeing somebody?" he asked. I didn't know the correct answer so I told him what I knew, "I guess I was."

He looked puzzled and said, "Well the man couldn't have been in his right mind to let you go. You were always so pretty in high school and I looked like a high-hippie 'cause you know I was. I didn't think you would ever go out with me so I never asked." "You should have asked," I told him. "Damn woman! You mean I waited how many years for a yes? That was a yes you would have answered, yes?" he asked. I had to laugh. He was so cute. He had curly brown hair and brown eyes. I just loved the brown eyes. "It's been twelve years. And yes. It was a yes I was telling you about." "So, if I ask you for your number, because I'm going to ask you for your number, will you let me call you sometime? Like later on?" Bobby handed me the matches waiting for my response. "Sure, why not. Let me get a pen." I reached in my purse and grabbed the first one. I jotted the number inside the match cover. Bobby held it tight before he put it in his wallet. "Why are you putting the book of matches in your wallet? Why not in your pocket?" I asked curiously. Bobby replied, "Because I'm damn sure I'm not gonna lose this number!" I stayed for a while longer and Bobby and I got reacquainted. He was fun to be around and I needed someone to help me get my mind off of Gentry. Then I got to thinking about what Gentry said. He told me to find somebody else. I wondered if Bobby would call and I wondered where that call might lead if it was made.

The phone rang later that evening at my house and sure enough it was Bobby. He wanted to take me out. I sort of figured that was why he wanted my number to begin with. He didn't know my real number was three. And he didn't know that I was in love with number two. And he wasn't going to. This is what Gentry wanted and this is what he was going to get. I told Bobby that I would go out with him that upcoming Friday. But before that week went by, Bobby popped over one afternoon to say hi. He met the kids that day. Told them that he was going to take me out to have some fun. The kids seemed to like Bobby well enough and I liked him too. Bobby called me every night up until the Friday we both waited for.

I didn't know where Bobby was going to take me until he got to my house. I let him decide. He thought The Barrel might be nice for starters. I drove. Been to the Barrel enough times to know the regulars by names. The added plus was that I knew Bobby from school. He was one of the good guys. I wasn't the least bit uptight and couldn't wait to go out the door.

We began the evening early and left the house about 6 p.m. Bobby was dressed like he was living on a Hawaiian Island. Comfortable khaki-colored shorts and the shirt was, well, like I told ya, Hawaiian. He was slim and tan and walked a very laxed walk. I wore a jean mini skirt and a soft navy tank top. I had nearly every color imaginable in stockings. I wore sheer navy of course and a pair of good shoes. High heels.

While driving to The Barrel it occurred to me that if I am out with another man, like I am, it wouldn't be long before Pink would be aware. Now I really couldn't wait to get there and be seen with Bobby. Bobby was good looking. Taller than Gentry, and Gentry stood about 5'8."

We pulled up in the stone parking lot and got out of the car. Bobby led the way, opened the door for me to enter first. Like a queen I entered. Directly in front of me, a few feet away, sat Gentry at the bar. He didn't see me right away. But I was sure he did when Bobby and I passed by him to find a table. "Bobby, there's a couple of seats right up at the bar, let's take 'em." I said anxiously. "Cap' I'd do that for you if my back wasn't like it is. Here's a table right next to it. Wanna sit here?" he asked. "This is fine Bobby." Bobby stood up until I took a seat. I made sure it was the chair that was

302

facing south where Gentry was. The view couldn't have been better. Bobby said, "Cap. Stay right there. You won't leave will ya?" he asked. And he looked so serious. Then he said, "I'll go up and get us a couple drinks so we don't have to wait. What do you drink?" "Something sweet with a splash of soda, just a splash." This gave me time to make eye contact with Gentry. My peripheral vision was just as good as his. I caught him looking at me a couple of times while using it. That lasted only seconds and time was running out. I just kept looking at his face until Bobby came back with the drinks and it didn't bother me one bit when Bobby apologized for it taking so long. My mind was on one thing and one thing only. Gentry.

We were sitting at the table catching up when suddenly, Gentry let Pink speak up and with the emphasis on the P, he said, "Peaches!" He was talking to me and I knew it. I looked over. He had that big walrus mustached face just smiling and chuckling away. I knew this was prime so Big Time recited a line from a song I had written about him. Across the room and fast with a comeback I said, " ... You off-ten knew the right lines..." Pink and I both knew we had each other's attention, so did Bobby. I'd completely forgotten that I was with him. I didn't even hear what Bobby was saying to me. I just got up and told him I'd be right back. I walked over to Gentry.

"Hi Pinky! What's with the peaches? You and I both know it was an apple." Pink looked at me with a chuckle and he kept up a smile and asked, "Is that your new boyfriend?" "New boyfriend? No. I knew him in high school." "Aah! This is a date?" he asked with a grin. Big Time didn't want to keep things secret so I revealed another line from my song and I said, "... Your rituals have all been directed. Time and time you feel you've been neglected. You play the fool and now you feel rejected...?" "Maybe your friend is missing you over there. You should get back over to him," Gentry said. I wasn't bold or brilliant or Big Time. I stood closer to Gentry and whisper-talked a verse from another song I'd written for him, " ... Throw the ashes in the fire. You are my one desire. Just sit pretty and be quiet. It's what you once had said to me." I told Gentry that I had better get back to the table. He agreed with his eyes and those eyes grew far and away on purpose. I felt it when I walked back over to sit with Bobby.

My heart ached. I wanted to cry. I was shaking all over and needed a chair bad. Bobby said, "I thought I lost you there for a minute. Who was that man you was talking to Cap?" "Oh Gentry? Just somebody I met when I used to hang out at The Well." The subject was closed and Bobby already had another couple of drinks at the table. I drank down my watered down drink so I could get to one that had more oomph! I needed something to stop the trembling. It was so obvious that Bobby asked, "Cap? You cold or something? We can move to another table." "No, I'm fine. The drink will do it. They usually do." I covered myself good, I thought, until Gentry walked over to the table. He stood and extended his hand to my friend and said, "Hi. I'm Gentry." I cut in and made introductions. "Gentry. Hello again! This is Bobby. Bobby this is Gentry." Bobby politely said, "It's nice meeting you. So you know Cap here huh?" "Yes. And she is one special lady." "Gentry why don't you join us, sit down?" Bobby looked like he didn't care much about the my idea, but I didn't care because Pink was already sitting next to me. Not close. Just next to me. "Let me buy you two a drink. What are you drinking Bobby, I'm buying," Gentry said. "No that's alright," said Bobby. Gentry didn't take no for an answer. He knew I wanted him there when he called for a tender to bring over the drinks.

I was feeling warm and nervous the whole time Gentry me and Bobby were sitting at the table together. Gentry was going on and on about me. "You're a lucky man. Wait till you hear her sing and play piano. She writes her own music and she's got real good kids. Beautiful. Just like their mom." Bobby watched Gentry carefully as he laid back into his seat. His arms crossed and he said to Pink, "Yes. I'm proud to be with her tonight." On purpose, I crossed my legs so that I could brush one of them against Pink's. I was thanking God that the bar was loud and filled with people because after I did that Pink looked at my face and then my legs. He said to me softly, "You sure do have sexy legs Big Time." "Think so?" I asked.

He loved me, I knew he did. Why was he letting me go? It didn't make sense. I was feeling dizzy and I wanted room. I needed air. I couldn't take the situation inside, so I excused myself from the table telling Bobby that I was going outside for a minute. He didn't ask why. I got up and felt my knees going out. I was trembling inside and all around. I couldn't stand without holding onto something. And I held on to each and every chair and table as I made my way outside the building. I leaned up against it and let the tears gush out. I couldn't take being in love and not having who it was I loved. And that man was sitting with me and my friend! How do I go back in there, I thought? Maybe I outta just go home and not say a word to anyone. I had to collect myself. I had to wipe the tears away clean. It would be only a matter of time and Bobby would be looking for me to come back in. Just then he walked out to find me.

"Cap. The man in there isn't just somebody you met is he?" he asked. "No Bobby. I told you, I met him at a bar," I said with a sniffle. "Caps. You're in love with him aren't cha?" Bobby asked. Again I lied and said, "How can that be Bobby? I hardly know him." Then he said something that took me off the guard I had kept so long. He leaned one arm up against the building and said with certainty, "Well, he's in love with you Cap." "Bobby that's crazy. I told you we're just friends." I thought I would drop to the ground when Bobby continued, "Look Cap. While you were out here and I was in there, the man came right out and told me he was in love with you." I didn't say anything.

We went back inside and I sat next to Gentry on a cloud. Bobby said, "Look, we can't stay much longer, we got plans. Let's finish up these drinks and get going Cap." Gentry said, "Don't go. Let me buy you another drink." Bobby tried to get a word in but I was quicker and said, "Sure, let's stay for one more Bobby. I'll take one Gentry." Bobby declined and excused himself. He went to the men's room. Gentry and I watched each other. His eyes looked like they were melting away. He said, "You really are one special lady." I was still trembling and it took all I had in me not to cry. Just then Bobby came back to the table. Gentry said to him, "You got one special lady here. She's smart, she's pretty. And if she ever says that she loves ya, you can believe it. Because when she loves, she loves for real." Gentry's eyes weren't melting. They were tearing up. Not a one slipped down his cheek. I couldn't bare looking at him that way. It was killing me on the inside not to be with him. I'd have to leave with Bobby. After what Pink had just said, Bobby announced that we had to get going. "Bobby." I said, "We didn't make any plans. We can stay here. Besides, I like The Barrel." "Yeah, come on and stay for one more," Gentry asked. I was all for it and Bobby insisted we had to leave.

After telling Bobby that I wasn't in love with Gentry, how could stay? I was already too obvious. Bobby stood up. I stood up. Gentry remained seated and said, "I wish you didn't have to leave." Bobby said nothing. But I did. I leaned over and put my mouth right next to Gentry's ear, touching his face and said, "Me too. Take care of yourself." I stood up straight and I looked at Gentry before I left. I think we both wanted to break down. I forced myself to leave The Barrel and him. I couldn't drive so I asked Bobby if he would. "Cap? What's wrong? You are in love with him aren't cha? he said. I broke into a thousand tears and answered Bobby the best I could, "I don't know what he and I were, if we ever were. I just know that we're not." "I'm sorry Cap. I know where you're coming from." "Bobby, just drive me home will ya? I'm sorry. I blew the night. I'm just not much in the mood for anything now except to be alone." I cried even more after saying that. And I cried all the way home. My face was dripping with mascara. I looked like hell and felt worse than that. Bobby was very understanding about the whole thing. When we got to my house he said, "Cap. Have some space. Why don't you call me when ya wanna do something. I'm not going anywhere." "Bobby you're so sweet. Thanks. I need a little time to think. I'll call you, you can call me. It's okay. Doesn't matter." Bobby stepped off the porch. We said our so longs and he walked home.

I went in an immediately got high. I played and sang. Then I stopped singing and playing. Talking out loud I said, "He's in love with you Capri!" This took me over to the couch. I remembered the way Gentry looked when I was about to leave with Bobby. I thought about his tear-filled eyes. This made me cry. Why didn't he just come out and tell me that himself? Why did he tell me that he never loved me, he didn't love me and he would never love me? Now he loves me? In love with me? God! He has to be in love with me. That was no actor playing in Gentry's face today. That sorrow was as real as the love I have for him. Why is he doing this to me God? Why? Didn't the G M in the sky mean Gentry Mocean? It had to mean him. And maybe the number two means that I will have another chance to have him in my life forever. A second chance. Maybe the man and the woman at the bottom of the stairs was me and Gentry. Was that what You were trying to tell me? Oh tell me now because I don't know what to think anymore. First he wants me. Talks about wanting to marry me. Asks me to marry him. Then he doesn't love me and now he's in love with me. Well, which is it? There was no purpose in asking. God never answered me, at least not in a way that I could hear.

The night went along slow and high. After a couple days Bobby called to see how I was doing. I was passed the tears and told him I was fine. The day was early and I asked him if he wanted to come by for a cup of coffee. "I want to, but I can't do that ya see. Because then it wouldn't be a surprise," he said. "Hmm. So you like catching people off guard. Okay. I like surprises. Surprise me! Bobby, I don't mean to be rude or anything, but the kids are at Sunday school. I figured I better take a nap while I have the chance ya know?" "Sure Cap! Have a nice nap and I'll talk at ya later." A couple hours later passed and I woke to find Bobby sitting on a chair next to the couch. "Hi Cap. Sleep good?" "Who let you in?" I asked with a yawn. "Buff did. I told her that I wanted to surprise you." "Well, I'm surprised that's for sure! Shit! I must look like hell!" I sat up and fussed with my hair. Bobby said, "Don't worry about your hair. You could be covered in flour and still look beautiful." "I bet you say that to all the girls don't cha Bob!" "Cap, you have to know you look good. I see the way the other guys look at cha. And no, I don't say that to all the girls. Why don't cha lay back down and rest. I wasn't gonna stay long. I got a couple things to do back home. I only came by to see you and to give you these." Bobby handed me a card. The flower was already in a vase on the end table next to me. I thanked him and laid back down. Bobby winked and said, "See ya next time Cap. Don't forget about me too soon." "I don't see how I can with this pretty flower and a card. Thanks again for coming by. You really surprised me." As Bobby headed out he said, "There's more where that came from. Bye Cap." I re-read the card and placed it next to the vase and fell back asleep for awhile.

In a couple of days I decided to go over to The Barrel myself. It was a habit. Just liked being out talking to people. Felt good. This particular evening, Bobby happened in. I joined him for a while and we made plans to go out somewhere. Bobby told me that a friend of his just bought a bar he and was throwing a party. Well, it sounded alright to me and the following night we went to The Pine. The place was jammin' with people. It was a small place and the music was blasting. Bobby hand-walked me through the crowd of people and took me up to the bar where one of his buddies let me have his seat. I thanked the brawly-biker-kinda guy and was surprised he let me have it. Guess I figured that most guys who looked like "rough and tough" weren't about to give their seat up to no "woman"! Was I wrong. Most of the guys in there looked like bad-boy-bikers, but after Bobby introduced me, I was greeted kindly by all of them. I liked them and they seemed to like me.

Bobby wanted me to meet his friend Gary. Gary had long straight, light sandy brown hair and a long beard to go with it. His voice came out sounding like an old worn out drill sergeant. He looked at me and said, "Wheels!" "What?" I asked him. "Wheels! You know. What gets you around." Wondering what Gary was saying, I said, "You wanna know what kind of car I drive?" Gary busted out laughing and whistled. He said, "No, I mean your legs. What gets you around! And if you don't mind me tellin' ya, ya got a pretty set of wheels, Wheels!" He whistled again. I blushed. I had to wear the mini skirt with nude stockings and the good high heels. Bobby walked up and put his arm around me. He looked at Gary and said, "You kept an eye on Cap for me?" "I sure did. Kept my eye on them wheels! Hmm, hmm, hmm!" Gary turned to me and said, "That's a good name for ya Wheels!" "I like it," I said. "So Wheels, ready for another drink?" Bobby asked. "Sure Bob-bet! Sorry Bobby. It just came out like that, but that's what I'm callin' you, I'm callin' you Bobbet! Bobby laughed and said, "Okay Wheels."

There were helium balloons all over the ceiling with long ribbons attached. Bobbet asked, "Want one Wheels?" "Yes, the red one. It will look good with my top." He went for it and brought it over ready to tie it around my wrist. When Gary saw this he stopped Bobby and said, "Wait, wait! This is The Wheels! Give me that balloon. I'll show ya where it belongs. If you don't mind Wheels?" "I don't know Gary. Oh what the hell. It's a party right?" "Don't mind do ya Bobby?" he asked. Bobby said, "No." We were all standing so Gary asked me to put a foot on the seat of the chair. I did. He tied the end of the ribbon around my ankle, christening me "The Wheels." And it stuck! Before I knew it everyone was calling me Wheels. Even people

307

who didn't know me. This name was as cool as Big Time, as cool as Cool Breeze and I liked it.

Bobby and I were spending a lot of time together. And before I knew it July was here. He wanted to take me to a Sunday service. He told me most of the people I met from The Pine would be there, but the main reason was he wanted me to go was to meet one of his best friends. One like a brother to him. I wasn't one to go to church and asked him what to wear. It was whatever I wanted. He explained that the services were always held outside unless it rained. And sometimes the rain didn't matter. I had my doubts about this shin-dig, by my curiosity was peeked and I wanted to go.

The day came. I wore jeans, a tank top and some good polished, white leather sneakers. We drove to a house, not a church. It wasn't about God. It was about beer-drinkin', whiskey-drinkin' and cookin' on the grill. Each Sunday they gathered at the owner's house for fun and laughs. Bobby introduced me to The Captain who was cooking up the chicken. Captain was about 6' tall. He had very dark brown wavy hair. Not short, not long. Just right. His eyes were brown with tan through them. He was a good looking man. "Hi!" he said, "Say Wheels, would ya mind takin' over the chicken a minute? I promised the kids I'd play something with 'em." Before I had a chance to say a word, he handed me a long fork. I turned to Bob and said, "Bob-bet! I don't know nothing about cooking chicken outside!" "Wheels it doesn't matter. Most of the guys here will be too buzzed to notice. Shoot Wheels! Some of these guys start coming over at six in the morning!" "And they do this every Sunday?" I asked. "If they didn't have jobs they'd be doing this every day!"

I walked around with Bobby and he introduced me to some of the women there. They were either married to the guys or girlfriends. They were standoffish and I felt out of place.

I stuck to Bobby and we bumped into Gary, (he was a 6 am.er!) Then I noticed Captain. He was jump roping through a "hula hoop" and then a jump rope. The Captain was good too and seldom missed a skip. I told Bobby that I wanted to give this jump rope thing a try. Bobby said, "Have fun!" I ran over to Captain who was jumping alone and said, "Can I jump in?" He asked, "Can you?" "Of course I can." I waited for just the right moment. It had to be cool. Did it just right. We continued jumping. Captain said, "You're good Wheels! Let's see how long we can go before one of us misses." "Okay," I said. We jumped and we jumped and we stared into each other's eyes.

The Captain liked me and I knew because he said, "Wheels I find you very attractive." But I was seeing Bobby. That was the first thing I thought when Captain said what he said, and right after he missed a skip. He took a rest and went to check on the chicken. The chicken that I was supposed to watch and let burn. "Captain I'm sorry about the chicken." "Wheels. Look around. This crew will never know the difference. Trust me." I went over to Bobby and Gary. Bobby leaned over to kiss me and said, "What cha thinkin' Wheels? I told you these were a good bunch of people. Are you having a good time?" "Yes I am is a matter of fact. Captain sure can jump the rope Bob-bet!"

Out of the corner of my eye I saw Captain sitting on a lawn chair alone in his back yard. I told Bobby I needed to used the rest room because I really needed to use it, and he told me how to find it in the house. I left the picnic table we were sitting at and watched The Captain on my way to the door of his house. He was staring off thinking of something serious. It looked that way to me. I went into the house and found the rest room okay. Took care of me and went back outside. I stopped on the porch and saw Bobby talking with a bunch of his buddies. I didn't think I'd be missed so I walked over to Captain. He kept his eyes ahead. I at his side said, "Okay, back here all by yourself?" "Yeah," he chuckled, "I'm fine. And I'm not by myself." "What do you mean? I asked puzzled. "Can't tell ya," he said. "Can't tell me. Why?" I asked. "'Cause you're seeing Bobby that's why." "What's he got to do with it?" I asked. "Bobby's seeing you and I can't tell you no more. It's a secret." "I can keep a secret Captain. You can tell me. After all, that jump ropin' ought to be good for something." "Okay, I'll talk, I'll talk! Wheels you're driving me crazy because you look so good and there's something else... Your eyes are real. I can't say no more. I told you too much. You see Bobby. Sorry! Subject closed." "Okay Captain. Same to you." Captain asked, "You mean that? Never mind don't answer that. I don't wanna know. Besides I have to keep telling myself that you see Bobby. You better go see him. Go on Wheels." "Yes sir!" I saluted The Captain and made my way back over to Bobby, Gary, Mike and Gino and Gene and on and on and on.

The time was getting late and had to get going. I didn't want to leave. I wanted to stay and keep an eye on The Captain. I know I shouldn't have wanted to because I was seeing Bob-bet! We left for my place and Bobby headed for his. All I could think of was his best friend.

Oh it was hell that night! I put myself right in the middle of a triangle and I wanted a way out. I was in love with Gentry and I never told him. I was seeing Bobby because Gentry told me to find someone else. I liked Bobby a lot but I knew I could never feel for him what he was feeling for me and he was falling in love. To put my life in the order it had always been, The Captain completed the three-sided-figure I managed to get inside of and I thought... Now what do I do?

I was tired of the situation I was in. Each time Bobby took me somewhere I'd look for Gentry. If Gentry wasn't where we were, there was a good chance Captain would be. And when he'd see me he yell out in his deep voice. "Wheels!" Bobby didn't have a clue that me and the Captain had an attraction for each other and we kept it that way. For a little while. A few times, when Bobby came over he brought two of his friends. Gary and Nate. Nate was like a "Charles Branson" kinda-of-guy with lighter hair. His arms were strong and I was always asking him to flex one for me. Nate wasn't into showing off, but after buggin' him enough he would. He had great arms. I loved feeling one when he tightened the muscles up in it. This didn't bother Bobby. Bobby trusted his friends with me. I did whatever I wanted. Said what I wanted and so did he. He knew that his friends would never try breaking in the middle of what we had. Until...

... Captain had all these fish that he wanted to fry up. Well, between Bobby and him, they talked me into letting them have a fish fry at my house. Poker and all the beer and booze you could drink.

The table in the back room was open. By that I mean I didn't have a puzzle on it. So we set the chairs up just right. We got the cards out on the table and the beer. I showed Captain where everything was in the kitchen. He showed me how he cooked things up. We had most of the fish already to fry. Captain suggested that we take turns cooking while the five of us played cards.

I was sitting across from the Captain and he made sure of it. Bobby was sitting to my left. Gary and Nate were to my right. Captain was watching me over his cards ail night. I was looking back. Bobby was looking on. As for Gary and Nate, they were busy puttin' on a good buzz and never noticed. But I did. I knew Bobby could see that something was there between me and his best friend. The situation was getting increasingly tense. Exciting!

Captain and I took our turns in the kitchen watching the fish. It was a few hours into the card game and my turn to for kitchen duty. Not more than a minute went by when I turned to see Captain standing there beside me. He looked me dead in the eye and said two words. "Kiss me." "Bobby's right in the other room!" I nervously answered. Captain just took me in his arms and gave me a long and sensuous kiss. It made my heart pound like thunder and my knees went weak. Captain looked at me and said, "I have been wanting to do that for the longest time." "Me too," I answered. Then Captain gave me a book of matches and said, "Write your number down for me Wheels." "What if Bobby sees me?" I asked. Captain had a plan and said, "I'll get back to the cards. You write it down. I'll ask you for a light when you get back there." I nodded yes.

Captain left the room and Bobby came in. "What's takin' you so long Wheels? The cards are getting cold." "Guess I wasn't putting enough salt on the fish. Captain was showing me how much to use. I'll be right there."

Bobby gave me a kiss on the cheek and headed back to the card game. I grabbed the first thing that could write with, and put my number in the book of matches. I slid them in my side jean pocket and pulled the fish out of the pan, salted them just right, and carried the big plate back to the table. After the five of us snacked on the fish, Captain, in his deep, deep voice asked, "Hey anybody got a light?" Gary had a good buzz goin' on and was quick to get his lighter out for The Captain. And at the same time I said, "I do." I tossed the matches. Captain caught 'em, took the light Gary offered and said," "Don't care if I keep 'em do ya Wheels?" "No. Go ahead. I got a whole box of them in the kitchen."

Well another hour or so went by. Nate was through with poker and passed out on the recliner in the living room. Gary asked if he could crash out on the floor there. Bobby said that I would be in good hands and told me he had to be up early for work. I walked to the door with him and he gave me a little kiss and hug good night telling me he would see me the next day.

This left me and The Captain in the situation we wanted from the start... To be alone. Captain walked into the back room and shut off the lights. He cut through the living room and back into the kitchen to me and said, "Those guys are out cold." "Yeah they are. You gonna make sure they leave before my kids wake up?" I asked. He was turning all the lights out in the kitchen and said, "Yes. But I'm gonna kiss you first. Like I wanted to the first time!" I thought about the first one and if this was going to be better, I knew I would be hard to resist almost anything! Then he kissed me. I was kissing him back and loving every minute of it. He was sending chills all over my body and I didn't want it to stop. But it did. I sat up quickly and said, "The door! I didn't lock the front door!" "Want me to lock it Wheels?" Captain asked. "Yeah," I whispered. He locked the door and came back saying, "Where were we." He wrapped his arms around me and gently lay me down again when there was a knock at the door. Pink! I thought. Oh no! Captain said, "It's Bobby. Don't let him in." Before Captain said not to let him in, I already wasn't going to. I went to the door and quietly opened it. Just enough for head room. Bobby said, "You got three grown men in there Wheels! You're safe. You don't need to lock the door." I could tell by his searching eyes that he suspected something was going on. I pretended to be tired and said, "I lock the doors no matter what. Habit 'cause I got three kids remember?" Bobby said, "Yeah Wheels. You're right. Sure. When I was walking home I got to thinking about you and that made me wanna see ya again. So that's what I did Wheels. I wasn't gonna ask myself in. I just wanted to say good night again." I didn't know what to say but good night. Bobby didn't try to kiss or hug me. He wanted to but he didn't want to. He walked tall and away and said, "Good night Wheels. Oh yeah and lock the door." He put his hands in his pockets and left for home.

Captain was still in the kitchen. I walked over to him and said, "He knows something is going on, I can tell. I feel so guilty. He knows! I know he does!" Captain put his arms around me and kissed me. He held my face in his hands, looked into my eyes and said, "Who do you want to be with?" "You," I answered. "Then don't feel guilty. I want you Wheels. I wanted you since the first time I saw you at the house." The talking was over. Captain kissed me over and over. There was nothing that was going to keep us from making love so we did and we did.

I don't know if it was love in an instant, but I felt very strongly for Captain and he did with me. We went dressed into the living room and found a place on the floor. Captain lay on his side and I laid with my back against him. With his arms wrapped around me he said, "See how good we fit together laying like this." "Yes. I know what you mean. It's real comfortable. I like the way we fit." I told him. "Me too. How did we do that so fast Wheels?" he said laughing. "I don't know. Guess it was supposed to happen, "Wheels. Gonna tell Bobby?" he asked. "It will break his heart Captain, but yes I'll tell him. I'll have to. Captain said, "I'm not tired. How about you Wheels? Feel like talking?" "Are you kidding! I don't want to sleep. This is nice. I like being with you." I turned to face Captain who said with a smile, "I like being with you too. Say Wheels, what's your real name?" "Capri. But people call me Cappy or Cap'. You can call me anyone of them, but I like Wheels the best. Hey, remember that song "Lennon" wrote?" " ... I'm just sitting here watching the wheels go round and round..."? That's why I like Wheels so much, and our names sound good together, the Captain and The Wheels. Wait! Don't say anything. What's your name?" "It's Corbin," he said. "Corbin. I like that name. It fits you."

The night passed by fast and Corbin and I talked straight through it. He wanted his buddies to get going before the sun came up. He didn't want the neighbors to think I wasn't a lady. Nate was easy to get up. You couldn't shake or talk Gary awake. I tried, when Corbin showed me how it was done. He walked over to the refrigerator and got a cold beer. He went back to Gary, put the beer next to his ear and popped the top. Gary woke up drilling the words, "We'll see by the dawns early light!" I couldn't believe it. I was rolling and laughing my ass off. It was a sight. Gary grabbed the beer, sat up, took a big swig, stood up, lit a smoke and while heading he out he said, "Thanks Wheels. See ya Captain."

It was shortly after that Corbin would be saying good bye. He reached into his pocket to make sure he still had the matches with my phone number in it. "Don't wanna lose this. I'll call you Wheels, after I kiss you good night,

I mean good morning." Corbin kissed me good night, I mean good morning and was off west in his truck. A "Chevy."

Then it hit me. It was the first night I didn't think about Gentry. Corbin was the reason and I didn't feel guilty. Wait, I thought. I'm thinking too far ahead. I still have to break this off with Bobby if I'm going to see Captain. I'll have to tell him the truth. I wouldn't expect him to accept anything but the truth. I had a lot to think about.

Just then the phone rang. I answered, "Hello." "Wheels! Good morning again. Told you I'd call ya later. Is this later enough?" "Captain, you crack me up. Yes this is later enough. What are you doing?" I asked. "Laying here in bed. I'm smoking a cigarette trying to figure out why I can't stop thinking about you. Miss me?" he asked. "Yeah I do and I'm still wide awake?" "When are you gonna tell Bobby? Do you want me to talk to him?" he asked. "No. I think that since I am, was, his sort of girlfriend, I should tell him. I will. I want to say everything just right ya know?" I waited for a reply. Then Corbin said, "I don't think he's gonna like me after he finds out about us. We're good friends me and him." "I know, " I sighed.

Captain acting like a Captain said, "Hold on tight Wheels. Might be a stormy ride." "A roller coaster ride," I said laughing. "Better get your sleep Wheels. I'm gonna give it a shot. I got your number in my head. I'll call you when I wake up." "I hope so. You better call me Captain and that's an order!" "Yes Ma'am! I will. I can't wait to go to sleep. I'll be able to call you back quicker. Okay let's hang up and go to sleep." "Wait! I said, "Who's gonna say good bye first?" Captain had a perfect plan and said, "Let's both count to three out loud and then say good bye at the same time. Okay? Ready? Start counting." We both counted. "1,2,3 and said good bye. Then I said, "Are you going to hang up?" "How come you didn't?" he asked. "Oh no. Are we going to have to go through this again?" I asked. "Yes! Let's try it again. Only this time we both have to promise that we'll hang up. Go on Wheels, promise." "Okay! I promise. I promise that when I say good bye I will hang up. Okay. It's your turn." Captain said, "I promise the same thing you just promised. Ready? This time we hang up the phone Wheels. Get ready to count. Ready? One, two, three, good-bye." I said it along with him and hung up. I picked up the phone again to see if he hung up. And guess what? We both did that and we were back on the phone.

After breaking our promise, we promised that we wouldn't break our promise and we counted again to the good bye. I didn't pick up the phone again to see if he was still there. So I don't know if he picked up his to see where I was.

I strolled to my piano where I wrote a song. I thought I could tell Bobby about me and Captain. That early evening I went to The Barrel. I needed a friend to talk too and Ladie had become my closest confidant. I told her about what happened between me and Captain. Between the two of us we could find no answer to the problem. And the problem remained. I still had to tell Bobby. Then Bobby came strolling in The Barrel. He walked up to me, kissed me on the cheek and said, "Hi ya Wheels. You and your girlfriend Ladie been doin' the gossip?" "Why not? It's fun and it's free," Bobby smiled. I looked over at Ladie as if to say, now-what-do-I-do? Her look back was, I-don't-know! Then she said to Bobby, "We don't gossip. We're are adult women who tell the truth." "Do you always tell the truth Wheels?" Bobby asked me. "I don't lie," I told him. "Say Wheels. You wanna go to The Pine?" "Sure Bob-bet! But let's have a drink before we go. I haven't talked to Ladie since yesterday. Do you mind?" Bobby said, "Ladie get Wheels whatever she wants." Bobby and I sat and talked for the drink. Small talk. As small as I could make it without saying anything about Captain. I reminded myself that it would be far worse to tell him the truth in a public place. This matter would be set-private.

After our drinks we headed to The Pine. It was only a minute away via car. We parked right out in front of the building, got out and went in. The place was packed. There was only one table left and it was next to the shuffle board. Bobby and I went up to the owner and ordered a couple drinks. "Bobby, since I got that job under the table I come in here almost every day after work for a drink or two. But you knew that. I just can't get over how nice everybody is!" "Yes. They are some good people Wheels."

There were a lot of people that I knew in The Pine that day and they all said, "Hey Wheels!" But there was one guy I had never seen before. He looked like bad news. He acted like bad news and drunk bad news. And for sure he sounded like bad news when he yelled across the room to me.

"So Wheels. That's you right?" "Yeah, that's what they call me. How ya doin." I asked just to keep things polite. I turned for Bobby, but I forgot that he went outside to talk to the cops about something. Then the loud mouth said, "I'm Jake! So Wheels? How 'bout showin' me some titties?" I needed help with this guy. I looked at Mike by the bar window. He held his beer up, nodded a hello and went on talking with a group of guys. He probably didn't hear what Jake said. It was so loud in there that afternoon. I had to stand up for myself.

I fixed my angry eyes on Jake and said, "In the first place where do you get off calling me Wheels? Just leave me alone." "Come on Wheels. Lift up that shirt and show me your tits!" Nervously I grabbed my drink. There was nothing in it but a couple ice cubes. I slammed it back down on the table. A cube landed on the shuffle board. I needed a towel and quick. I had to go right passed Jake to the owner. I yelled for him to get me a towel and fast. He didn't hear me.

"Hey if you don't want that shuffle board ruined you better get me a towel." The owner glanced over for a second and ignored me. Then Jake blasted out, "Wheels threw ice on your shuffle board." Kenji, the owner, finally came over to me but yelling, "Why do you wanna fuck up my table Wheels?" "Just hurry up and give me a towel already!" I demanded. He tossed one to me and said, "You better hope you didn't ruin it!"

Jake was laughing and said, "Have fun Wheels!" I ignored him. I got the ice off the table that had melted some by then. I didn't just wipe the table, I polished the table until the dust cloth glided over the wood with a push. Knowing there was no damage done, I took the towel back over to the Kenji and said, "Why were you yelling at me? It was an accident ! I know about wood. I wouldn't do something like that on purpose. I yelled for you twice right after it happened. I wanted to clean it up right away but you didn't hear me. You heard him instead." "Who?" asked the owner. "Who? The one who's given me a hard time since I got here. Will you tell him to leave me alone? See if he would have left me alone, then I wouldn't have gotten mad and slammed my glass on the table. Then the ice wouldn't have landed on your precious shuffle board." I was ready to blow! "Oh so you broke one of my glasses too! You can pay for it Wheels! Better still, you can leave!" he ordered! But I wasn't done. "Oh. So after coming here every day for almost two month you're telling me to leave? You should be telling him to leave! I never seen him here the whole time I've been coming around." "You must be drunk Wheels, I said leave and don't come back!"

Finally Bobby was back and now wondering what the hell had happened. "Bobby he's throwing me out for good because he thinks I'm drunk and threw ice on his fucking table." I had hoped that Bobby would have said something to Kenji, but he didn't. Guess he didn't because he didn't see or hear anything that happened. Maybe in his heart he knew something was up with me and Captain. All he said was, "Let's go Wheels. We don't have to stay here. Too crowded even for me." Bobby started walking through the people and to the door without me. He turned and said, "Let's go Wheels, come on." "I gotta grab my cigarettes, hang on." Then I turned to Kenji and said, "You know maybe I didn't come in here and spend fifty bucks a day to get drunk, but I did come here because I liked it and the people. And I'm sober. It takes more than your watered down drinks!" "Outta here Wheels! Now!" he demanded.

I got my smokes off the table and reached into my pocket for a quarter. I walked up to Jake held the quarter in my fingers and put it right up to his face. My face was there too. I felt strong and said, "You see this quarter

Jake? See that phone over there? Do you know that all it would take is one call and your friends will start to wonder where you are! Don't fuck with me! You don't know who you're dealing with!" His beady eyes got tighter. He grinned a pissed off grin and said nothing. I tossed the quarter in the air, caught it without looking, dropped it in my pocket and made my cool way out the door.

Bobby wanted to know what exactly when on and I told him. That's when I learned the owner was moody. Moody? I thought. He's more than that. He's a coward because he couldn't tell some wanna-be-biker to leave me alone. He's probably crazy!

After that, I just wanted to go home, get high and play piano. I told Bobby that I would talk to him later. Captain called wanting to know if I had talked to Bobby yet. I explained what happened and told him the time wasn't right. Captain seemed anxious to have me all to himself and I was waiting too. We both agreed that we would stay apart until Bobby and I were.

One week passed and I still hadn't said anything about Captain. It was too hard because Bobby was going out of his way to show me a good time. I went everywhere with him and on those every wheres, almost all the time, The Captain would be there and then he was on my mind. I'd watch him close from far away and he watched me right back. In time I knew Bobby would read our faces. Within the next week, I'd un-tie the laces.

Bobby called and told me that he was gonna have a cook out. He wanted me to bring the kids. His daughter, (Buffs age), would be spending her weekend with him. I told Bobby that I would make it over but the kids would stay home. The reason I was going over there alone would be explained when I got there.

I had the day to think, but the night was soon to come. I got a sitter and left my house about six p.m. I drove over to The Barrel for a few shots of courage. And I drank them with a splash of soda.

Ladie was not working that day. There was just a handful of regulars there. I said hi, they said hi. I went about my own business.

Four drinks and small-talks later, I drove to Bobby's. There were a lot of people still there. I met Bobby's daughter Caroline. While she went off to play, I prepared. Bobby took my hand and led me through the back yard. I let him do the talking. I wasn't ready yet. Our steps were slow, mine were heavy. After about a half hour of taking my nods and short replies, Bobby led me into the house.

"Wheels. You're not talking much and I think that you have a lot you want to say." I looked down a moment, just a moment, then at Bobby and said, "Yes. I want to talk to you. I've been wanting to." "Come on in here and sit down Wheels." Bobby led me to his room. I took a seat at the foot of the bed. Bobby sat beside me and said, "Talk to me Wheels. I don't wanna have to hear it from somebody else." I sighed a long sigh. I felt the lump in my throat. It was cutting like a knife. I had to let it out. "Bobby, remember when you asked me about being in love with Gentry? You knew I wasn't telling the truth." "Hey Wheels, I know what you're going through. Like I know what Gentry is going through because I'm in love with you too! But I won't ask you to stay with me. I wouldn't make you happy. Not all the way like it should be and you deserve that." "Maybe I don't deserve it. I wasn't true to you! The Captain, me and him? Well, I mean that night…" Bobby stopped me there and said, "Wheels I'm not blind. I saw the way you two looked at each other. I know what you did. You don't have to tell me. I probably won't talk to Captain anymore. Friends don't do friends like that. He could've waited till after this talk we're having." "Bobby I don't know what to say. When I was with you all I did was think of how much I really wanted to be with Gentry, and then when I met Captain he helped me to forget about him."

"Wheels! I think you are looking for someone who is exactly like Gentry and Wheels, you can't replace people." Bobby stood up and I was crying. He held out his hand and said, "Come here Wheels. You need a shoulder." I reached for his hands and he pulled me up. He hugged my face and I hugged his back. Bobby assured me and said, "You'll be alright Wheels. I'll be alright. We always be buddies you and me. This doesn't mean we can't be friends and I wanna stay friends with ya" I pulled back to look at him and said, "That's what I want. I want us to stay friends. I was so afraid you would hate me or something." "I could never hate you Wheels. I told ya, I'm in love with ya!" "Bobby, I wanna go. I gotta drive. Listen to music or something." "Wheels," he said, "Play the piano and sing Wheels. Sing some songs. Sing one for me." "I will Bobby. I will." I didn't want to say good bye so I turned to leave. Bobby called out, "Be good to yourself. I turned and with teary eyes I said, "Yeah."

I was out of the house and crossed the yard to get to my car parked on the street curb. I didn't want to go home. I wanted to talk to Pink but I wasn't sure he wanted to talk to me. I ended up going to my house.

I called The Captain and told him about going over to Bobby's. I was still pretty lump-throated, and wasn't ready to see him. Captain understood and we didn't stay on the phone much longer than that. He would call me the following day or see me on familiar territory. The Barrel. Sometimes we'd go to a place closer to Captain's house called The Black Out. Maybe named that because it was the only building at the end of a dead end street surrounded by trees and the train tracks. Lots of the same people who went to The Pine could be found there. The Black Out was the kind of bar where you could sit and pass a doob from one end to the other. Not that it was legal to smoke pot, just that we all got away with it and the owners didn't care.

I got together with Captain a couple days after our call. I felt very uncomfortable being seen with him at first. I was sure his family of friends knew that I was the reason Bobby wasn't talking to him anymore. The women in that group never did warm up to me. Far worse than any of that was going to a place with Captain and finding Gentry there. Most of the time he wouldn't even look at me or he tried not to. When he did, I wasn't sure what his eyes were saying and they were always saying something!

Captain and his gang of buddies liked to drink. I wanted to fit in. So I began drinking more and more trying to keep up with the rest. It helped me to keep my mind off the one person who wanted me to forget him in the first place.

Most nights were spent drinking with Captain and there would be wild times ahead for me.

I was lining up baby-sitters all the time. If Captain took a day off work, I'd have a sitter. Most nights would be nights away from my house. Sometimes I wouldn't get home till three, three-thirty in the morning. On other nights I wouldn't get home at all.

I don't know how I let things get the way they did. If I wanted to sit on Captains lap at the bar I did. This was a side of me I never knew existed. The more I would drink, the more I didn't care how I acted. I changed my Cos' perfected cut off jean shorts. On the outer leg side of the jean shorts, I tore a two inch slit in them. After a couple of washing and frays, they looked great. I'd forever wear tank tops but I added a new look to it all my own. I took an old soft sweat shirt and cut the body part of it shorter so it came to my waist. I cut the sleeves short, but not "cap." Then I the used the scissors one more time and made the opening for my head larger. Much larger so that when I wore it inside out over my tank top, it would fall off of one shoulder. To complete it all, my leather sneakers would always be polished and shined. My hair was passed my shoulders and feathered all around. It was summer and the sun highlighted it for nothing.

One evening dressed this way, sweat shirt cut and red, I went to The Barrel to see what Ladie was up to. The minute inside, a familiar face was sitting there. It was Perl. The big and bad "Outlaw" who saved me and Winnebago from Batturs once. He took one look at me and said in a growly loud voice, "What do you call that, the rape look?" The bikers were laughing and roaring. Were they going to give me a hard time or was the question in fun? Not knowing gave me the courage to laugh along and I said, "I like that. The rape look. And I look good in it too." There were whistles and oohs.

It became my signature dress. I liked it. It turned the Captain on. He turned me on and you can take it from there.

Now I was never much of a gambler except for some good knock poker games. But the Captain loved playing the bar tickets and soon so did I. One evening at The Barrel, Captain encouraged me to sign for the weekly drawing. A buck. Funny, I thought. All this time I've been coming here and I didn't know. I signed my name next to a number. My number was 10.

That following night we were at The Barrel again. Not just to drink, but to win the drawing. It was up to about 235 bucks. I looked around. Captain looked around and we both came to a mutual agreement. I needed the money more than anyone else there. We drank and drank till it was close to winner-time! Captain looked over at me and said, They're gonna call the number pretty soon. We gotta cross our fingers." I agreed and crossed two fingers on each hand. Captain followed and added another set of crossed, fingers on both hands. I copied. Then he said, "Wheels, we need to cross our arms together. I did. He did. We entwined our crossed arms together. We both looked down. I knew what Captain would want next and I was right when he said, "Okay, let's cross our legs. I put out an ankle, he laid his on mine. I put my other ankle on his and he used what was left. We were set. There couldn't possibly be any thing more we can cross, I thought. Till Captain said, "Okay Wheels, now just when they are about to put a hand in the bowl for the number let's cross our eyes." "You're goin' too far! There is now way I'm going to sit here all crossed-eyed and stupid looking." "I'll look pretty stupid then because I'm doing it. Come on. You wanna win? Keep thinking about your number. Number 10. Then cross your eyes." Captain was going to do it and I knew it. I was laughing and refusing all the way until I watched for the hand reaching in the bowl. I concentrated on the number. I thought, fuck it and I crossed my eyes. The winner was in the hand of the bartender. She called out, "Number 10." Captain said, "Wheels! That's you. Did you cross your eyes?" "Yes and I won! I can't believe it!" Captain yelled over to the bartender and said, "Wheels over here is number ten!" They checked things out and handed me all the money. Captain told me not to buy everybody a drink, (cause they were asking). He wanted me to have all the money I won and a twenty dollar loan till payday. I loaned him the twenty and tucked aside the money like I didn't have it at all. I had something in mind that I wanted and this wasn't quite enough. I'd need a little more.

July was near over. Captain and I started a late afternoon from his house on bikes. Bicycles that is. I really had not worked out since Sonny was born and I wasn't sure I was up to drinking and biking. I wanted to drive my car. It wasn't much to look at and it gave me plenty of trouble, but it sure beat peddling. It was either hop on a bike or be left behind. This was an excursion that Captain and one of his buddies had planned and I didn't want to go back to the house. I wanted some fun. I locked up the car and hopped on a bike. Captain and his friend were way ahead of me on the street. Captain would yell back at me to catch up if I could. Well, it took some doing, but I caught up, or he let me.

We stopped at The Black Out for a couple of drinks. We hit a few smaller bars on the way having one in each. The final destination was in downtown Sandusky where a live rock band was playing outside. There was pop and food and beer. Lots of beer.

We parked the bikes in the back of someone's truck. Captain knew the truck owner. We headed to the ticket stand. Captain bought some tickets and got our first round with them. We walked and talked to everybody we knew. Captain always introduced me to anyone I hadn't met as The Wheels. The girls, well, the new and the others were still distant and cold.

Round two and I was ready for another beer but Captain wasn't. He handed me a ticket and told me to help myself. I went to the stand and got a beer. On my way back a face in the crowd put me back at the guard table. It was Henry. I said nothing, but had to pass him to get to the Captain. I was about three feet away from him and he said, "Aren't ya gonna say hi to me Capri?" I changed my mind about not talking and did, "Woman beater!" He tossed his beer in my face and called me a whore. I went by him quick to tell Captain what happened. I wanted to leave, but Corbin wasn't in sight and the reason he wasn't was because he was behind me, about ten feet away. He had Batturs back side to the concrete. Gary was near and yelling, "Come on Corb' hit him! Punch that fuckin' punk!" I walked only a couple feet closer to watch.

Captain was sitting on Henry holding him down with one arm. He'd look at Gary and back down at Henry. He held up a fist. Then he looked down at Henry again and looked back up at Gary laughing and said, "I can't, I can't hit him." Captain jumped off of Henry and Henry took off running. The police were nearby and got Henry in the back of the cruiser right away. Captain explained what happened and they took Henry to the county jail like they always did.

Captain came back over to me and said, "I'm sorry. I know I should have kicked the shit out of him for what he did to you. I wanted to but I just couldn't do it. I'm sorry Wheels." He didn't have to say he was sorry, I was the sorry one. Because when I saw Henry I thought about losing Gentry who was out of my life more than likely because of him. Pink told me to find someone else. I talked to Gentry in my head while we took our bikes to The Barrel for a few more beers.

Gentry was there. The same spot he was in the last time we exchanged words when I walked in with Bobby. The place was packed. I walked behind Captain and we made our way to about the middle of the bar. I excused myself and went to ladies room. I cooled my legs face and arms from the bicycling. I shook my hair into place and went back out.

♪ ♪ *"Touching Venus"* ♪ ♪
Words and Music by: Catherine Santi in July, 1987

"Across the mirrors, across the styles,
the lit up faces, some sober smiles.
When you looked my way, I crossed the sky way,
and touching Venus, oh love was our way again.
I'm through with losing, with you I'm winning.
Take my heart we're, we're just beginning.
My inspiration. I don't need the wall.
You are the one who completes it all.
In you forever, take my heart and all.
You are the one who understands it"

Walking between the tightly packed crowd, I focused on Captain where he was standing with a group of friends and Captain had many of them. I went directly to him and stood by. I wanted to be sitting with Gentry who was sitting alone. I could feel Pink's eyes on me. His energy surrounded me. My mind and heart were set on thinking only of him.

At The Barrel I joked and laughed and talked. But it was no use. In the back of my mind, in the front of my mind, right in front of me in the flesh was Gentry Mocean III. How could I not think of him? Off went my mind in search of answers why Gentry ever entered my life at all.

So he built this wall. He knows that a brick is missing. I saw through it and he knows I did. Maybe that's why he's soooo scared of me, I thought. Then again maybe he's the brick. He just don't know where the wall is. Reality gave me a bump and a tight squeeze around the waist. Captain and the no-motor in the bikes were ready to leave. Normally, with Pink being near, I would try and delay whoever I was with. I didn't do that to Captain, I just made sure that on my way out I'd take a good look at Gentry.

The space between Gentry and I was about 15 feet. I began the walk out. I looked at him. He looked back at me. It was obvious that he did not like seeing me with someone else. Couldn't he tell that my eyes were saying that I wanted to be with him? Why didn't he reach for my hand and ask me to stay? I would have.

I left feeling sad. I wanted to get the bike back to Captain's house to get my car and get back to my house. Play piano, smoke pot. What I did best. I knew that I wasn't going to get Gentry off my mind that night.

I sat at the kitchen table to roll a joint. Bobby came to mind. I remembered that he said, "Cap, you can't replace people." With one night I forgot all about Gentry. Just one night. When the mornings came after a night of drinking, I thought about Gentry. There wasn't a day I didn't and I had to tell him.

The next day Jo from across the street came over for coffee. I needed another point of view. Nina had only been telling me that I thought I was in love with Gentry or I just wanted to be. It would bring me down. So I told Jo about how he wanted me to see other people. I told her about the way he looked at me the night before. Jo, who had just turned 18 gave me her out spoken advice. "Caps! You have to tell him that you love him. Why see anybody? Just 'cause he told you to find somebody else doesn't mean he wants you to. Did you ever stop to think that maybe this is his way of testing you?" "Jo I never thought of that. But you're forgetting something. He told me he would never love me." "Caps, I might be only 18, but he's afraid of you. He probably loves you as much as you do him. If I were you, I would go over and tell him what's up! I'll watch the kids." I didn't say anything. I watched Jo's face. She had the look of certainty. One that I lost, found, lost, found and lost. Just never had the guts to hang on to it.

But she was right and I said, "Jo. I'll go over there. I want to. I don't care if he thinks I'm chasing him or not. All he can do is tell me to leave. Oh Jo! What if he does tell me to go?" "Cap! He's not going to tell you to leave. How can he resist you?" "Jo I hope you're right. Well, I guess I'll get ready. Hope he's there." I had the shakes, but managed to get ready. I thanked Jo for watching the kids and I drove to Neil Street. It was about mid-afternoon and when I got there the little black truck was sitting in the drive. My gut told me that he was inside. I parked the car and slowly walked to the porch. For a split moment I thought about turning around and leaving. The door was all I could see and I knocked gently. In a lax voice I heard Gentry say, "Come on in." I opened the door and walked in looking for Pink. He was sitting on what you could call a bench. One that ran the width of the front-north window of the house. Tucked under the space between it and the floor was a guitar. I walked over and took a seat at the far end asking, "Is that your guitar?" "Yes," he answered. "Care if I take a look at it. I used to have one." "Sure, go ahead." Gentry said. I slid the case out and opened it. It was a beautiful guitar. Better than the one I had. I took it out of the case and asked Gentry if I could mess with it a minute. He didn't care. In fact, the look in his eyes the minute I walked in should have already told me that his thoughts were somewhere else.

I fumbled with the guitar. Trying to remember something simple. Although Gentry's guitar was easy playing, I couldn't play a thing. I put the guitar back in the case and slid it back under the bench. "Gentry. You know I came over to talk to you. It's about this guy I'm seeing. He's nice and has a good job at General Motors but I can't get my..." "Then you should keep seeing him. He seems nice enough," he replied. "You know Gentry," I said, "When I was seeing that guy Bobby, you know who I mean, you met him. I never for one day..." Gentry stopped me from finishing my sentence again, "Look Capri, you're a nice girl. You are. This guy Captain, seems to care about you." I sighed and said, "I think so. Well, I don't know why I came over here. Guess I just wanted to say hello, see how you're doing. I'll just get going. Hey, you know? Maybe sometime you'll let me borrow this guitar. I'd take good care of it." I felt like such a fool because Pink said nothing more. I left feeling worse than ever.

My knees shook as I made my way out to the door and headed for the house. I went inside devastated. "Well Cappy? Was he there? Did you talk to him?" Jo asked. "Yeah. I shouldn't have gone. He wasn't happy to see me. I'm sorry Jo, but I don't want to talk about it. Would it be rude if I said I just wanted to be alone?" "No Caps, I understand. Just pick me up a bag of chips when you go to the store. Cap, he'll be back. Cheer up! Doesn't he always come back to you?" Sonny was napping. Jules and Buff were upstairs playing with their dolls. Me, I did the usual. I got high, went right over to the piano and wrote "Touching Venus."

Thought I could will Pink over with this new song. Thought for sure that he was still sitting at the window thinking. Deep thinking something, someone, or some place. Was it me? I wanted it bad for it to be me. I tried hard to read his thoughts that once was so natural for me. Nothing was coming to mind. So as time went on to August, I kept running with The Captain.

All we did was go out and drink. I was getting used to it and to keep up with the rest of them I started drinking shots of tequila. I felt stupid never remembering which came first, the Lennon or the salt, so I just downed the shot without them.

About mid-August I was at home waiting for Captain and Gary to stop over. Minutes before they arrived I received a phone call from Henry and it wasn't collect. "So whore, what cha doin'?" I hung up fast I went to lock the front door. Just then Captain and Gary were getting ready to make an entrance. "Captain! Henry just called and said. Well he's got me scared. What if he calls back?" "Wheels don't worry. If the phone rings again, I'll get it," he said. And the phone did rang again. I took a deep breath. Captain answered the phone with his deep voice and said. "Hello, (silence), who's this? (silence), Oh yeah where are you? (silence). The phone went down. Captain said, "Gary stay with Wheels. He's at the corner bar." "Captain, what did he say?" I asked. "What you said. I'll be back."

I heard Corbin's wheels squeal all the way around the corner. It screeched to a stop. Within about two minutes Captain returned with a laughing smile and said, "I don't know what he looks like. I was ready to beat the shit out of this guy till the one next to him said that Batturs wasn't even there." Gary said, "What cha gonna do Corbin?" "Go back. As soon as Wheels tells me what he looks like." I gave his description to Captain and he flew out the door, racing them wheels around to the corner bar again. This time the time was going slower. I turned to Gary and said, "What do you think is gonna happen? Henry carries a knife sometime and I'm scared." Gary said, "Henry's a pussy! Excuse me Wheels. But he's a punk. Captain can handle him. Ain't nothing gonna happen but an ambulance to take Batturs to the hospital. Corb' will fuck him up." "Gary I don't want Captain to get into any trouble over me." "Wheels Corb' ain't gonna get in trouble. He's a big boy. He'll handle it. Trust me."

I trusted what Gary said. I waited for Captain to return. About ten minutes later he did. He told us what happened. "I go back into the bar, I look around for the punk and I don't see him. So I ask the owner Ed, if he seen him. He says Henry? Hell, he probably made that call to you guys from across the street. I don't let him in here. So I go across the street. I knocked on a house and asked the girl who answered if she knew him. She said there was somebody who just moved out but she didn't know who. Ed said he's probably hiding inside somebody's house laughing his ass off." Shivers ran up and down when I remembered the cops telling me that he was doing that to me. Good God was this starting again, I asked myself?

Gary was amused at what happened, turned to The Captain and said, "Hey we need more beer and I still gotta take care of a couple things." Captain answered him and said, "Yeah, I almost forgot. Sorry Wheels. I told Gary I'd help him out. It won't take long. We'll pick up a twelve pack and come back as soon as we're done." "How long Captain? I'm scared of this guy. What if he's hiding on my block somewhere?" Captain came over to me and gave me a big hug and kiss. "Wheels when me and Gary go through your door, you lock it up. Keep it locked till we get back." We kissed again and they were gone. I locked the door. I waited and waited. I wondered how long it would be before the both of them would return.

Time might as well stopped. I quit looking at the clock after a half hour passed. I didn't think they were coming back. Then about fifteen minutes later I heard Captains "Chevy" pull into the drive. The two of them walked out smiling and laughing. I unlocked the door. Gary came in first and said to Captain, "I never saw anybody shake so bad." Captain said to Gary, "Yeah! Did you see the look on his face when I told him to wake up?" "Hold on!" I said, "What are you guys talking about? Who's face?" Gary wanted to tell the story and began by saying, "Well see Wheels, it isn't very nice to call Corb's girl a whore so we had to find out where he lived. We went back across the street from Ed's, and another neighbor was nice enough to oblige us. So we went there."

Captain jumped in and said, "I parked the truck around the corner of his apartment building. Some guy was outside and I asked him where Henry lived. He pointed to the door. Me and Gary walked in." "Yeah we did Wheels," Gary jumped in, "Henry was sleeping on the couch but not for long," Captain continued, "I walk over to him, kick his leg and say, "Hey, wake up!" I watched as the two of them kept the story going, Gary took a turn and said, "Wheels you should have seen his face when he rolled over and saw Corb' standing over him. He was shakin' so bad wasn't he Corb? Wheels, the punk gets up 'cause Corb told him to. Wants to know if he can have a cigarette. That fucking punk's hand was shaking so much he couldn't even get the fucker lit. Oh Corb's a nice guy, he lit it for him and then he grabbed him up by the shoulders and dragged him out on the cement. You know how that corner is over there on Monroe Street. Fucking Corb' had him laid out on the cement. Henry is begging for Corb' to get off him. I kept saying, Kick him Corb'. Come on, punch him." "So what happened?" I asked. Corbin said, "I got the dude out there. Gary was yelling for me to kick the shit out of him. He was just about ready to come over and knock Henrys head with one of his crutches when I picked him up by the shoulders again and almost threw him on the front step." Gary finished, "Wheels, you should have been there. This punk was so scared. Now we got the neighbors outside because they wanna know what's going on. Corb looked at him. Fuckin' Batturs was still wantin' to hit a cigarette so bad. It was killing me! So Corb goes up to him and says "You don't call Capri Spettro. You don't drive down her street! You don't even say her name!" According to Captain, Henry had agreed to the three demands.

I felt like I must have meant a lot more to the Captain than he cared to admit. He never did say how he felt about me. Not in the three words one might expect. And Batturs stayed out of my life.

Captain and I saw each other a lot. More time was spent drinking and partying out and about than anything. During that time I was missing Gentry and wondering if he was seeing someone too. I kept it to myself. What I couldn't hold in, I confided in Ladie. She was with no doubt my best friend. Whenever I wasn't at The Barrel, and I was there off-ten, Ladie would be at my house. There was nothing we didn't talk about, except for what we didn't say.

Things were going as wrong as they could go. The drinking continued with Corb' like the coffee I drank. One day we took ourselves, my kids and a few of his friends to a private beach on Lake Erie.

The kids were having fun playing in the sand. They stayed to themselves and away from the water. Me, Corb' and the other adults were getting wasted. The day was very sultry and it didn't take long for a drunk. I got pissed about something Corbin said and slapped him down on the sand with one hand. Corb' got right up and did the same thing to me. I saw black and hit the sand. All I remember was waking up in my living room on the couch. Gary and Corb' were passed out in some chairs. A note on the television was left saying: The kids are with me and Chelsea. Call me when you see this, Shorty. I pulled the note from the TV., woke the guys up and said, "Well, my brother has the kids. You guys ready for a beer?" Gary and Captain got up and we raced off in Captain's truck. We went to The Black Out and got drunk all over again, though I don't think the first one had completely wore off.

When the bar closed I was driven home. I got in and passed out somewhere. The next day, Shorty called me wanting to know if I was okay. Then he told me what happened. "Caps. I have the kids here and they are fine. Buff told me that you came out of the bathroom and fell to the kitchen floor. She saw blood everywhere and couldn't get you up!" "Blood?" I asked. "Yes Cappy. Your little girl thought you were dead. She called a lady down the street from you, I guess you know her. She's a nurse. She went over to your house and cleaned you up, changed your clothes and got you up on the couch. I'm gonna give you a little time to get over the hangover you probably got." "Okay Shorty, thanks. I do have one hell of a hangover. I feel terrible. It was so hot on the beach. Didn't take long to get loaded in the sun. I don't even remember driving home. I did drive didn't I?" "Yeah. You drove. Don't you remember taking them to a drive through to get some hamburgers and fries?" Just then I noticed a cup from where we had gone. "Shorty! I had a black out. I don't remember any of it. And if I don't remember it, I wonder how I was driving? I must have been all over the road." "Caps. Relax. You made a mistake. It was a big one but you didn't mean for it to happen. It happened. Drink a cup of coffee. Take a shower or something and I'll bring the kids over this afternoon about one, one-thirty." We hung up and I headed back to the couch to get more sleep and I slept till noon.

The first thing I saw was the cup from the fast food place. I picked it up. It was warm and watered down. I stared at it a good long time. It made me take a seat fast. "How could you drive drunk with all those kids in the car?"

I asked myself. "Gotta keep up with the Captain." I answered. This led to a question. Why was keeping up with him so damned important? Would I lose him if I didn't drink along with him? I didn't want to lose a man who could make me laugh, make me safe, had a job and home. Was Gentry right? Was Captain good for me?

Shorty returned my kids to me on time. He lectured me about the drinking. I didn't care to hear it because he didn't go through anything like what I had. What could he know, I thought?

The kids were glad to see that I was alright. I could tell by looking at the girls that I had them very worried. I felt ashamed. It came back to me after the kids were home. The Captain and I were in the bathroom. We had sex. The blood the kids saw was from my period. I passed out on the floor with my pants down. It must have looked horrifying to them. Shorty wasn't making it up. They really must have thought I died. I knew the drinking would have to slow down but it was the slowing down part I couldn't get right.

I still drank, but never at my house with the kids. I stayed out late. Jo from across the street watched the kids as long as there was pop, chips and some place to crash. Each time out with Corbin was the same. There was always laughter and fun. He kept his arm around me keeping me close to his side. When I was with him, the conceit echoed in my head, "Ha! Look at you. You're with the Captain!" I envied not a single woman!

One afternoon I went to The Barrel with Corbin. There was a new barmaid. A beautiful young woman with dark feathered full hair. Her body wasn't petite like mine. Her figure was fuller. Her eyes were brown clear and sharp. Something inside of me went off and my immediate thought was that Corbin would fall for her. That same day, Captain introduced me to a good friend of his, The Mad Russian. Mad Russian and Captain had been tight for years. He was easy to like and I liked him right away. His sense of humor was quick, witty and wild. Always laughing and joking. Always. He could take a person with no mouth and having them grinning from ear to ear. But there were things going on behind the scenes. Things I was not aware of. A meeting took place. And a place would be taken.

Things went on with Captain and me but in a different way. We saw each other like we always did. We'd drink and laugh and talk and run around hoppin' the bars. But when we'd get to my house the conversations we had weren't quite the same. Corbin was upset with me about something. We were standing in the kitchen. He raised his voice to me. His deep throated voice grew louder with anger. He raised his hand to strike me and dropped it just as fast and headed out the front door. I stood in the kitchen terrified! I didn't know what to do. A thought ran through my head fast... What if he's just another Henry Batturs with a job? Just then Corbin came back inside. He looked at me still angry. I looked at him afraid. He slammed his hands down onto the kitchen table and nearly knocked it over. I froze and he said, "You know what really makes me mad? I can't get mad at you Wheels! Look at you! You have so much! I don't think you know just how much you have! Look around Cappy! Do you know what I mean?" He sat down. I took a seat at the table not afraid anymore and said, "What do you mean I have so much? What do I have? Oh I have welfare. That's what I have. I don't have a job. Besides my kids, what do I have Corbin?" "Look at all you do. You can make music Wheels. I can't even write a poem! You draw! You're so much all rolled into one. You got real good kids too! You get to watch them and the whole neighborhood grow up." I was at a loss for real words. Corbin never said things like this to me before. I suggested we go out on the porch.

We sat on a wooden-back-benched seat Pope had made. The night air was warm and breezy. We enjoyed it together on the porch and smiled with the nature of the night.

My next door neighbor came over and asked if Captain could help her get her ill husband out of his wheel chair and into bed. She felt bad about asking and explained that the nurse who usually helped couldn't make it. Captain was real sweet and told Mrs. John that he would be happy to help out. While he was in her house, my neighbor to my east had just pulled up and was getting out of her car. Her name was Cappy, like me. I walked over and talked to her while waiting for Corbin to return. I asked her if she ever saw him at my house and she told me that she did. I said, "Cappy, isn't he handsome? You know sexy?" She agreed and said, "Yes. I didn't want to say anything but he's real sexy Cappy. That deep voice! Doesn't it drive you crazy?" "Yes. I love listening to him talk. His voice makes him even sexier! Oh! Here he comes Cap," I said. Talk to you later." "Okay," she said. I took a seat on the bench.

Corbin was standing by the front door facing the house east of me. He said, "Hi Cappy" (to my neighbor), and I quietly heard her say hello. She was no doubt blushing. Still facing her house he said to me, "I love you Cappy." The words threw me off the guard table, but my reply was like his and I said, "I love you too." After we exchanged these very important words things took a drastic change. Corbin wasn't seeing me as much. I found myself looking around for him in the evening. I'd go to The Black Out, The Barrel. I would drive passed The Pine slowly and look through the window. His truck had turned invisible and I couldn't find it either. He was busy if I called for him where he worked. He'd answer the phone when I called him at home but the conversations were always cut short with excuses he made and I believed them.

I had to quit calling and driving all over the place for no one. It wasn't finding him. I needed to talk to Ladie, so I went to The Barrel for me. There was one small problem. Ladie was not working that night. The new girl that had been hired most recently was. Her name was Tammy. There was a couple of guys sitting at a table in the back. They were friends of Captain who called out to me, "Hey Wheels!" I nodded and promised myself that I wouldn't say anything about Corbin to anyone except Ladie.

Tammy came over and asked what I was having. I asked for a coffee... black and I paid.

After drinking half a cup and ready for a warm up, Captain walked in. He was surprised to see me. I was happy to see him. He walked over to me but not close. He didn't put his arm around me like he always did before. "Corbin, aren't ya gonna give me a little kiss or something?" I asked. Just then one of his buddies yelled from the back table, "Look out Captain. You got double-trouble." Captain looked back at Gene, nodding and grinning. "What does Gene mean Corbin?" I asked. "Hell he's drunk. Look at him! How ya been Wheels?" he asked. "Okay. Is a matter of fact I'm more than okay. Tonight I came in here for me!" He looked at me sitting on the bar stool with woeful eyes. Was he sick? Did he lose a family member? Captain said, "Well that's good! You need to get out for yourself sometimes. It's good for you."

Captain and I had little to say that night. He made small talk very small. I looked around for Tammy who was busy cleaning tables towards the back of the bar. I wanted to get more coffee but it didn't seem important enough to interrupt what few tables she had left. I waited.

Corbin was off somewhere else. Don't get me wrong, he was still in the bar standing close, but not any closer. When I saw that Tammy was through cleaning up I had changed my mind about a refill. Something told me to leave. Told Corbin I was going. I expected him to say not to leave or something, but he wished me a good night and told me to take care of myself. I stood up and gathered my things and faced him. I didn't ask for another kiss, but that's why I was standing in front of him. He didn't even give me a pat on the shoulder. I yelled out good night to the guys at the back table. They laughed and I felt certain that they were laughing at me.

On my two and one half minute drive I was wishing that things didn't happen like they did at The Barrel. It was a place I like going to so much till what happened, happened. I pulled in the drive. The kids were up and surprised to see me in early. Buff asked me if I had seen Corbin. She said some of the other kids in the neighborhood wanted to play another game of kickball with him. I told her that I did and I kept the conversation as short as possible. I guess it never mattered much to Buff. Corbin that is.

Occasionally she would say, "Mom, I sure wish Pinky would come over!" All I ever answered to that was, "Yeah! Oh well." I didn't want her to know how much I missed him too. And I still missed him more now than anything.

Corbin tells me one night that he loves me and tonight, this cold shoulder. I needed someone to talk to and Ladie was either not home or sleeping. I got out the pot and smoked joints.

A few days shortly after my meeting with Corbin, he got a DUI and had to serve a ten day jail sentence. He was fortunate to get put on work release. He called me collect once from the jail to tell me what was going on. He didn't call me from the job on his break. I was getting nervous. Something was wrong. Very wrong. It wasn't making sense. I thought about other guys I had seen before. Bobby said he was in love with me and he loved me enough to let me go. Bobby told me that Gentry said he was in love with me. But if that's true, then why does he want me to find somebody else? Corbin said I love you Capri and then makes like a chameleon and on and on and back I go. I don't know, I just don't know. I try to find some reason but it comes out so-so. I take the hands in my mind to turn them the other way and I know I can't go back and play.

It would only be a couple of more days and his time would be fully served. I was sure he would call and come over then. Maybe he was going through some rough times when I saw him at The Barrel last. Maybe that's why he ended up with a DUI. Maybe this jail time has given him time to think and he will tell me what's going on.

My instinct was off. Way off! He didn't call me when he was out. He didn't call me from home or work. I hadn't seen him in over two weeks. August was over and September was just beginning.

Like any other early evening I drove over to The Barrel to catch Ladie working. To my surprise Captain was at the bar with two of his friends. There was a seat, two seats away from Captain and I took that one. I said hello first for a change. They were quiet with their greeting, like strangers. So was Corbin. "So Captain!" I asked, "What cha been up to?" Captain grinned a shy smile, looked to Gary, to Mike and then to me. He held up his left hand and said, This." My eyes grew large when I saw the band on his finger that announced commitment! Laughing, I said, "Come on Captain this isn't funny. You didn't get married." "Yeah he did Wheels. I was there at his house when he married Tammy," Mike said. "I was his best man Wheels. He's telling you the truth." Gary said. "Captain, you and... So that's what that guy meant when he said double-trouble. You didn't have time to go and get married. Did you really marry Tammy? I can't believe I'm asking you this Corbin?" "During work release on my lunch break." Bravely I held my head tall and cool. I held up my drink to the Captain and said,

"Congratulations Captain." The four of us clicked our drinks together and Corbin said, "Thank you Wheels."

Captain knew that this wasn't easy for me to take. I could see that he felt bad about hurting me. Once more I got my courage up and said, "You know. The very minute I saw Tammy behind the bar I figured that she would be the one you would fall for. Funny how that happened." I teared up and sat my drink down on the bar. "Well, see you guys." I didn't want to hear anything more. They said their goodbyes but it was as if they were out of an old forgotten dream and I couldn't remember any words. I left The Barrel. Once out and in my car, the need for crying had stopped before it happened. I knew that Tammy and Captain were in love and I was happy for them both. After the day I was glad that it happened. It took me back to reality.

I knew that all Corb' and I did was drink. It wasn't what "in love" should be. I loved Captain but I was in love with Pink. Still. And I wondered then if Gentry knew about Captain getting married. I wanted to tell him but I chickened out and left it alone. Maybe, just maybe he'll be out taking a walk and he'll end up at my door again. I wanted to believe it with all my heart that he wasn't through coming over. There would have to be another time. After all it's his turn, I thought. Unless the game is over.

Meanwhile, Jo from across the street had turned 18 over the spring and wanted to know about moving in my house. I hadn't used my room since March of '85. So I said she could.

The kids liked her. Sonny couldn't say her name correctly and Jo Yan became the nick name.

I didn't know how much to make a friend pay as far as rent goes so I charged her 30 bucks a week. She'd watch the kids if I felt the need to go out and I did that a lot.

Jo had wanted to go out drinking for a week straight since the day she turned the legal drinking age and asked if we could. I agreed. Together we scraped up the money it would take to drive to the "Wild Waves" in Vermilion, Ohio. It was twenty minutes or so east of Sandusky. So, on we went. In all the time I thought I was heavy drinking with Corbin, I never saw anyone put so much alcohol away and walk cold stone sober like Jo did. She insisted on trying each and every drink that came in a shot glass. She must have had thirty five to forty shots. I was absolutely amazed at how cool she was when she left the building. After our drunken week there, and we got pretty loaded, it was back to The Barrel for me. I could go there with ease. Tammy didn't work anymore after she married Captain. Ladie was there more often and it was her I was looking to talk with anyway. Who better than my best friend.

331

After a rough day at my house I went to The Barrel to see Ladie, only she wasn't working. She was sitting at the bar next to Gentry. I took the seat next to Ladie. I wanted to sit by Gentry but I couldn't. He wouldn't have wanted me to. Would he?

Ladie and I chatted for a few minutes. I talked more about Captain getting married like he did. Not breaking it off first... not even verbally. I wanted a reaction from Gentry. It was getting his attention. I saw him lean inward to peek over at me while I was telling Ladie the details. I remember telling her, "Ya know Ladie. It would have hurt less if he just would have said something to me instead of going behind my back. I knew he wanted to be with her. It makes sense now. Why he didn't call, come over or anything." Ladie said nothing, but Gentry did. He tapped Ladie and said to her, "You mean you never told Cappy about us?" Ladies head and eyes looked down. They did that a lot anyway. But this was way down. I looked at Gentry. He seemed happy to piss me off. And he did piss me off. Worse than that was her! I looked at her with disgust. I wanted to slap her. I hated her. How could she sleep with the man I was in love with? Did it matter that he wasn't seeing me? Did it matter that I was seeing other people? No. It didn't. Because I knew who it was that I really loved and so did she. I didn't know what to say. I kept looking at the both of them until I couldn't stand looking at them anymore. I left my unfinished coffee at the bar, grabbed my cigarettes, matches and headed for somewhere. I ended up at the pier. I parked there and blasted the first good song I found on the radio. I stared off at Cedar Point. I tried to get the image of Ladie having sex with Gentry out of my head but it was no use. The more I pictured it the more angry it made me. I wanted to believe that this was Gentry's way of hurting me. It must have hurt him to see me with someone else. But if I'm right, then why isn't he seeing me?

After the pier I went to my house. Took my time going there because I had to drive by The Barrel to see if Pink's truck was still there. It was gone. Ladie was there and for a moment I wanted to go inside and tell her what I really thought of her. But I did nothing. I figured it was she who owed me an explanation. I wanted to hear it from her and I wasn't going to ask. I didn't call her. By the next day she was at my house. It was morning. The first thing she said was, "Capri will you let me in? I want you to understand what happened and why. Can I come in?" I had to know if this was a sick prank Gentry was playing on me so I agreed to let her in.

We sat down at the kitchen table after we poured our own cups of coffee. Ladies eyes were all over the place. The piano, the windows and the coffee cans. She knew who they stood for and the topic came up at last. "Cappy, I don't know exactly what to say about what Gentry told you." "So it's true?

I asked with a sigh. "Yes it is Cappy. It wouldn't have happened except that I was scared Cap! One night someone broke the window out of my door. I couldn't find the landlord to fix it. Anyone could have gotten in." I asked with anger, "So, what the hell does that have to do with you and Gentry having sex?" "Please understand that I was afraid Cap! The next night I was out getting drunk. I was with Red. After he went home I was scared. So I drank even more, plus Red gave me some pot. I smoked a couple joints and Gentry showed up. He was drunk too!" Ladie explained but it wasn't working, not for me! "Ladie! Drunk, straight... what's the difference? You should've said no! You know that I'm in love with him for Christ's sake! How could you do that to me? Why?" Ladies big brown eyes grew wider with worry that our friendship was over. She pleaded and said, "Capri. I know I should have said no. I figured you were seeing Captain. I thought you were over Gentry. Capri I was drunk and wasn't thinking. I was scared and let him in for that reason. The rest just happened. I didn't want it to happen but it did. I'm so sorry. Wish I could go back and change it but I can't." For the time it took to pour myself a cup of coffee, get the sugar bowl, roll a joint, I said nothing. I thought...

... She slept with him, the bitch! He did this to hurt me. Well it worked Mocean! Can you hear my thoughts now you prick! You had to do it with my best friend? You knew it would get to me. You fucking told me! Just how cruel can you be? (Ladie got more coffee). I watched her as she poured. I really watched. Why would Gentry even want to sleep with her, she's fat! At 5' 7" she has to weigh at least 170 pounds. I have three kids and still weigh 123! Why her? I finished rolling the joint. Ladie said, "Cap, if you don't want us to be friends anymore I can leave but I will miss you." I bit on my bottom lip and tilted my head over to one side and said, "Well, this is all his fault Ladie. He wanted me to go out and find someone else. He told Bobby he was in love with me. So he knew that sleeping with you would nearly kill me or worse drive me nuts! It worked and it hurts, but I would miss you too. Let's just light this joint and make like it didn't happen." "I'm ready for one Cap. Are you sure you're not mad at me?" she asked. "No." I told her. And I lied. After a couple hours of the bull shit, Ladie had to get ready for work. She left and I was glad.

I thought the first week of the month wouldn't never end but it did. Gentry would turn 35 this year. Born during my favorite season and on the day it started. September 22nd. There's a set of two's for ya! Two 2's are a four. Half of that is two. Well Gentry is two. And September is the ninth month. That's three 3's and that's me. Definitely me!

333

I told the truth and I let Bobby be so I could be with Captain who wasn't in love with me. Things were all wrong and I didn't want to be free. I went to The Barrel every night.

I bumped into a guy named Shay.   Me and his mom drank together a lot there.   He was just about to go out and smoke a joint.   I didn't wait for an invitation and said, "Well, let's get out there then."   Shay and two other guys who were with him walked out as I led the way.   When we were in the parking lot and heading for Shay's car, I noticed that one of his friends was nice looking.   With the alcohol in my system, the shy in me was gone.   I walked around this man and said, "Hmm, you're kinda cute!" He smiled and said, "Yeah?   You think so?"   He got into the passenger side of the door, took a seat leaving the car door open.   He lit the joint and passed it to Shay.   Shay passed it to me and I passed it to... I don't know who.   Never was introduced. After the man in the seat took another hit he said to me, "Do you wanna sit down?"   "Nah," I said, "There's no room... bucket seats."   He said, "There's plenty of room.   I'll move over."   "Okay you seem nice enough," I said.   I sat. "So what's your name?" he asked.   "It's Capri, but you can call me Wheels, lots of people do, at least the people I like and I like you.   That and you're cute. Wait.   You didn't tell me your name," I said.   "You didn't ask me?" he said. "I didn't give you a chance."   He told me his name, but I shall refer to him as Priest.   Priest said, "You're pretty cute yourself.   Why don't you write down your number for me and I'll call you.   We can do something."   "Oh no!" I said, "I don't give my number out to someone I meet just like that.   But I'll tell you what.   You can give me your number and maybe I'll call you."   "Okay. I can understand that."   I watched him take a small piece of paper from the glove box.   He jotted the number down and handed it to me.   I looked at it and tucked it in my jean pocket.   "Thanks Priest."   He asked me if I hung out at The Barrel a lot.   Of course I told him I did, hoping that he would pop in again sometime.   Priest told his friends that he was heading for home and said, "It was nice meeting you Capri.   Maybe you'll call me sometime." "Maybe I will." I said.

After Priest took off I went back inside for a few more drinks.   I kept a picture of him in my head.   I compared him to Gentry knowing very well that I shouldn't.   Priest was not as handsome as Gentry, no one was, but he was good looking.   His hair was wavy brown.   He kept it cut very short and all of it was neatly combed off and away from his face.   He was clean shaven.   His eyes were brown.   He stood about 5'9."   His weight was good on him and I was growing curious.   I finished up at the bar and hoped Jo would be up so I could tell her about Priest.   She was sitting in the living room watching TV. and eating chips.   I called her into the kitchen and said, "Jo.   What am I gonna do?   I met this guy tonight and he gave me his phone number.   He wants to go out. I don't know him. He could be anybody, but boy is he cute." "I say you should call him up. Does he have your number?" she asked. "Are you kidding! Look Jo. First Bobby and I let him go for Captain, then Captain got married. That's two. You think I should go for three strikes you're out?" "Hey Caps. Third time's a charm. I still say you should call him. Talk to him. If he didn't insist on your number and gave you his, then I'll bet he's a real sweetie." "I don't know Jo. I just don't have much luck in the "seeing someone" thing ya know? Besides, I still care about Gentry. What's the point?" "Cappy, you're missing the point. The point is that it was Gentry who told you to find someone else. So go for it girl. Don't sit around and wait for him. Have some fun. Call Priest. Who knows!" "You know Jo? You're right! Gentry told me to find someone else. And if it takes the rest of my life I will!" That's what I told her, but that's not what I really wanted. I didn't want to see anybody else. I certainly didn't want to get seriously involved. I waited and thought more about calling Priest.

Jo had been buggin' me about Priest for a few days. I gave in to her and called him. I was nervous and hoping he wouldn't answer, but he did. I asked him if he remembered me and he did. He said that he was sitting out on a dock on the bay where he lived. He asked me if I wanted to join him. I told him to hang on. I held the phone away from my mouth and asked Jo what she thought about it. She told me to get my ass in gear and go! I got back on the phone with Priest. "Where do you live?" I asked. "I live just over the swamp passed McCartney Road. You know where that is?" Priest asked. "Oh! So you're the swamp monster huh? Maybe I better stay home. I don't like crossing water. Scares me. Especially when I don't know what's on the other side of the swamp. You could be a serial killer or something." (Jo elbow-nudged-me) "Well, I'm not a serial killer or a swamp monster I promise. We don't even have to go in the house. I'm sitting outside having a beer. It's nice out. Come on over and have one with me." I heard him and I liked his voice. He seemed so mellow and laid back. He could no way in hell be a Batturs. I looked at Jo giving her a shove and she was nodding yes. "Okay Priest. Where's the house. I'll stop over. It'll take me a little while to get there. Oh and I'll try not to talk so much because I know I talk a lot." Priest said, "I'm a good listener." Then I'll see ya in about an hour. The extra time is in case I get lost." "Okay. See ya in a bit." he said. I was a mess. A total wreck. I got ready. Told JoJo to keep his number near the phone. She insisted I stay out as long as I wanted. I didn't want to stay long. Didn't know this guy. I was real jittery so I headed to The Barrel for a drink. Had to try and loosen up a little before I went to Bay Bridge. Monsters and swamps and Priest, oh my!

There wasn't a whole lot of regulars there and Captain's crowd had faded from the place after his marriage. I had about two tall whiskeys and soda. I was still pretty nervous but I made my way across the west side of town, passed McCartney Road, over the swamp that led to the house. I pulled in where Priest said I should. He met me at the car. We said hello to each other. He suggested we sit out on the dock and excused himself to go into the house for a couple beers. He was out just that quick and we walked over to the bay. The view was beautiful and still. Further to the west was a big bridge that lit up against the darkened sky. To the east where rail road tracks that also crossed the bay. Priest was lucky having each and every sunset for a view. I talked and talked. Told him I did that when I was nervous. I took him up on the beer he had previously offered, to slow me down. Then Priest reached into his pocket and pulled out a bag of pot. Think you can roll a doob?" he asked. "I roll pretty good." "No seeds or stems," he said. "I wouldn't have it any other way," I stated. I rolled the near perfect joint. Gave it to Priest. He passed it back to me. "You light it." I had no problem with that. And after that we smoked another one.

I didn't waste time and got to a point. "Priest. You seeing anybody? I mean do you have a girlfriend?" Priest didn't beat around the bush. He told me that he was dating three different girls. No, really! Three! Their names were Shelly, Debbie and Debbie. It wasn't sitting right with me. Oh three was definitely my number, but I wasn't going to upset it by being number four. I skipped over the thoughts running through my head, saving them. "Priest. What kind of work do you do?" "Right now I'm working for a glass company." I asked him if it was the one in town. He told me it wasn't. It was a big company that paid good. Told me that most of the jobs were out of town. There were lots of times he would stay at a motels and go home only on week-ends.

A lot of time went by. It was almost 11:30 and I wanted to get back to the house to play the piano while I still had a buzz. Priest had to be up for work early. When I suggested that it was time for me to leave, he wanted me to stay longer. And I asked, "Don't you gotta get some sleep?" "Yeah but I don't have to go in. In fact I think I'll take some time off. We could go out for dinner tomorrow night." "I don't know Priest. What about Shelly, Debbie and Debbie?" "What about 'em?' he asked. "Priest I wouldn't mind going out to have dinner but I can't. I can't go out with somebody who is seeing somebody and you're seeing three other people." I was thinking... Damn! At the same time he said, "I don't have to see them anymore." "You mean you would tell these girls good bye just to take me out to dinner?" "Yes. But I was kind of hoping we'd go out more than just once. There's a lot of nice restaurants across the bridge." I thought about it a moment and agreed to have dinner with him the following night and gave him my phone number. "Priest, I have a roommate and she told me to stay as late as I wanted, but I gotta get to the house and play piano before the buzz is gone. Ya mind?" "No. Why should I mind? Then Priest tossed me the bag of pot and said, "Here, roll one up for yourself." "Are you sure?" I asked. "I got enough. While you're at it, roll two. I could go for another one." I thanked him and cleaned enough pot for a couple doobs. I handed one to Priest and tucked the one he gave me in my cigarette pack. He helped me up off the wooden dock and walked me back to my car. "I'm glad you decided to come over Cappy." "Me too Priest. Sorry if I talked too much." "I told you I'm a good listener. I'll call you tomorrow and we'll make a plan." "Okay. I'll talk to Jo about watching the kids. Well, thanks again for the pot Priest." "You're welcome."

I got in the car. He said good night and closed the door of my car. I drove off. I saw him in my rear view mirror. He was watching me drive away until I couldn't see him in the mirror anymore. Told myself not to look left out my window to see if he was still standing there, but I did and he was. I tooted the horn, headed east across the swamp and to the house.

Naturally Jo was up and filled with questions. I told her about the three girls and his job. Told her that he was going to take some time off from work to take me out. And I told her that I was going out with him the next night. Jo was more excited than I was. She was already figuring on what I should wear and how to do my hair. Me, I just wanted to light that other doob and play. So I did.

Jo was an early sleeper and a deep one. The piano didn't bother her one bit and neither did my singing. Like all nights, me, myself and I stayed up in hopes that Pink would change his mind about me, but he didn't.

Morning came early and Jo was already to her house and back to mine without fits for me to borrow. Priest called. It was early afternoon. He suggested picking me up about six that evening. Everything was set.

Me and Jo spent the entire day trying to figure out what I should wear. She had some of the cutest clothes. Clothes girls her age were wearing. I knew I could get away with it. I still looked twenty three, (us Capricorn's are lucky that way) I ended up wearing something of hers. I looked like I should have been sailing on a yacht, wearing white baggy pants and a long sleeved sweater. The navy stripe was four inches in width across the front with a silver anchored emblem. Jo suggested I wear her sandals. They weren't really sandals, but woven white leather shoes. Great with suntan on your feet. And I always had a good tan in the summer.

Time was ticking fast. Jo was at the door and window watching for my date. I was still in the bathroom touching up my face and hair when Jo came rushing to the bathroom. "Caps. Somebody just pulled in your drive!" We both went back to the door.   As the man got out of the car Jo asked, "Cap. Is that him? He's kinda cute, but he looks like a priest!" (this is where his nickname really began), I looked at his clothes.   He was wearing a black shirt.   The collar was an inch up on his neck and had three white buttons there.   Hmm, I thought, a Catholic Priest!   "Jo you're right.   He does look like a priest.   I can't do it.   I can't go.   I'll crack up every time I think about it!"   Just then Priest was at the door.   He saw that me and Jo were laughing and was curious as to why.   Jo bluntly stated, "Sorry I'm laughing.   I'm Cap's roommate JoJo.   I can't help it.   You look like a priest!"   "Damn it Jo," I said. I turned to him.   "She's right Priest, you do look like one."   Priest smiled and asked if it would be alright to roll a couple doobs before we left.   No problem here, I thought.   Mine was almost gone and Priest sat at the kitchen table rolling while I drank a few more swallows of cold coffee.

We spent a few minutes at the house and I introduced him to the kids. He seemed to like the kids okay and the kids took to him.   They didn't warm up to just anyone.   Maybe Priest was a good guy after all.

He told Jo that we'd call when we got to where ever it was we were going. He wasn't sure yet and I didn't know the town he was taking me to at all.   I kissed the kids good night and told Jo that I'd call her in a little while.

Priest and I drove to Port Clinton.   It's west of Sandusky and over the beautiful bridge you can see from his back yard.

We stopped at a few of the nicer lounges for drinks before we found a restaurant Priest picked out.   Everything was great and Priest was nice company.   He told me that he was recently divorced.   Like two months before we met.   I asked him when his birthday was and he told me July 25th. Christmas in July.   He was 10 years older than me and I thought I might be too young for him.   Priest was the oldest man I dated and I felt somewhat intimidated by it.   He was 41.   I figured that he'd know so much more than me and anything I'd say would sound immature or stupid.   But I was wrong. Priest enjoyed listening to me talk.   Priest was right.   He was a damn good listener.

The place we ate dinner had a nice lounge.   We went inside to have a night cap.   It was warm and cozy.   There was a round fire place in the middle of the room.   The black baby grand piano sat on a platform next to a window that viewed the paddle wheel.   When the night was over Priest drove me safely back to my house.   We pulled in the drive.   Priest checked his money.   He curiously asked, "Did we spend 50 bucks?"   "I don't know.   Why?" I asked. "If we didn't spend 50 bucks then we didn't have a good time.   Did you have a good time?"   "Yes I did.   It was a lot of fun.   Sorry you didn't get to say too much.   I talk a lot don't I?"   "I enjoyed it.   You made me laugh and I had a good time."   Priest hardly said anything and it was nothing like the talks that

I had with Gentry. There I was comparing again. I thought about Bobby. I thought about Captain. I thought about Pink and what was happening.

I asked Priest if he wanted to come in for something to drink and he asked for a cold glass of water. He and the glass were planted at the kitchen table. Priest took out the bag of pot and said, "Go ahead. Roll up a couple for yourself." I didn't ask any questions this time. Shoot, he rode around with a half ounce on him and it was a pot mine. I seldom had enough cash for that much. I rolled a couple and said, "Priest? Care if I roll up one more? I'm just about out. I'll get it back to you. "Don't worry about it. Hey, while you're at it roll one for me. I need one for the way home." "Thanks Priest!" He watched me clean and roll the joints. Priest curiously asked, "How many coffee cans do you have in here? Do you know?" Did I know. Little did he know that I always knew that number. I answered quick, "90." "90 ? How long have you been collecting them?" "I never thought of it like a collection. Somebody told me that I should drink that coffee and then all this. They've been adding up since February 1985." (and it was 1987) "Is it crazy or what!" Priest said, "No. It's different. They look good there." This made me feel less intimidated by his age. It was easier to be myself once the cans were accounted for. They were a quick-eye-catcher!

Priest was through with his water and I was done rolling the doobs. He thanked me for going out with him and wanted to know if I wanted to go out again the following night. I told him that I would.

Priest and I were going out every night. There wasn't a place in Port Clinton that we didn't go to. But my favorite place was a country-kinda-rock-kinda-place. And it was only a minute from where Priest lived. Pinball! It had the coolest pin ball machine! This was something that the two of us indeed had in common. Each night ended up at the "Rockin' Country Tavern." Priest would make sure we had plenty of quarters. He wasted no time and bought a roll of them. If we went there in the afternoon and kids were playing, Priest would buy them off the machine like he owned it. While he did that I went to the bar to buy the quarters with the bill Priest gave me. He was good. He beat me a lot. I didn't care because when I did win, I'd repeatedly dwelled on my victory on purpose to get him siked for the next game. No matter what I said to interfere or to make him laugh while he played, he'd keep his eye on that shiny silver ball never losing sight. On went the nights out with Priest.

It was around the 10th of the month or so when I happened to be listening to the rock station in Sandusky, 'WCPZ." Was I glad I tuned in. They were giving away tickets to see "Pink Floyd." I had to win those tickets. This would be the best birthday present for Gentry. If I can win those tickets, I thought, maybe he would want to go see them with me. When the time was right, and the DJ announced for a tenth caller, or a 16th caller, or whatever number the caller, the phone was in my hand. I pressed and pressed the number with lightening speed. I'd either get a busy signal or a "Sorry, try later..." The concert was only days away. 6 days. I called and called. I stayed up later than normal. I called and I kept calling. There was no way in hell I was not going to win. I would win and that's all there was to it!

After five days of calling the station I was losing faith in myself. It was about 7 p.m. and Priest stopped at my house before he would head to his. I had the radio going. We smoked a doob together when the DJ announced for a caller. Buff called from the living room, "Mom. Let me try. Maybe I'll win the tickets. Me and you could go see them mom!" I handed her the phone and told her the number. I told her to keep calling if she got a busy signal or until they announced a winner on the radio. Buff pushed the buttons on the phone almost as fast as me. She called once. Busy. She called again. Busy. "Keep calling." I said. "I am mom, I am!" She pushed the numbers fast on the phone. I saw her eyes grow wide and her mouth drop open. She was almost in tears and yelled, "Mom! I won, I won! I won the tickets! I'm the tenth caller! I can't believe it!" "Buff, I can't believe it! I've been trying for days!" "Wait, hold on mom he's saying something. " Priest asked, "What did Buff win tickets for?" "Pink Floyd" is going to be in Cleveland! I love them! Whenever I hear them, I make cassettes because I don't own anything by them. Wish I had all their music. Here I go again. Talking too much. Buff just won two tickets to the concert and I'm siked!" Priest was happy for me. Then Buff handed me the phone with much despair and disappointment saying, "Mom, I can't go 'cause I'm not old enough. If I'm with you can I?" she asked. "I'll talk to 'em and find out what's up." I took the phone and the DJ explained to me that I would have to drive to Toledo to catch a bus that was taking the winners to the concert, and you had to be 18 to be on that bus. There was no way she could go because of the rules and they were basically, take the bus or you don't go.

She was devastated. I felt so bad for her. "Buff. I'm sorry. I wish you could go. But look at it this way. If you and me go to one when you're older you'll remember it forever." She shot up the stairs to tell her sister the good news, the bad news. First thought I had was how to tell Pink about the tickets. That I wanted him to go with me. Priest said, "I haven't been to concert in years. We'll have to take plenty of pot and beer for this. It'll take us an hour to get to Toledo then we'll have a two hour ride to Cleveland." He invited himself! I couldn't be rude and undo it. Damn! I had to be nice, much as I wanted to tell him different, I said, "Are you sure you can go? Won't you lose your job? You took a lot of time off work?" "They don't care. I can take a day off any time. They're not gonna fire me. " Well there was no way around it. The concert was on the 16th of September and that night was the next. I was just going to have to go to see "Pink Floyd" with the wrong person!

Before Priest left he told me what time he would come by and pick me up, and I let him. Told him I'd be ready. "I'm ready for take off," Priest said, while he headed to the door, doob lit and all. What was funny was that take off would be a mosey because Priest was more like turtle speed. After he left I went back to the kitchen table to think.

Buff came down the stairs and asked if I was taking Pinky. "Buff, he'd be perfect that's for sure. But Priest kinda invited himself and I couldn't say no. And the concerts tomorrow night." I tried my best to explain things and she said, "Mom, I could call Pinky and tell him to take you. You should go with him. He would take you mom. Let me call him." "Buff don't! I don't want you to call him. He won't go. If he goes it's probably because he already bought a ticket." "Okay mom, but I still think you should tell Pinky before it's too late!" I shook my head with a smile to Buff. She knew I'd end up going to the concert with Priest. He didn't know a single song from another. He didn't know any of the words, where as Gentry knew them all. Guess what mattered was that I would be there. And maybe, just maybe, so would Pink.

The next day came and by early evening we were off. Let's make this quick. We drank so much beer and smoked so much pot on the bus to Cleveland, that I remember very little about "A Momentary Lapse of Reason" ... The Tour! I kept telling myself to myself, "Open your eyes. Get your head up. This is yow favorite band in the whole world and you're falling asleep!" It didn't work too well. By the time I straightened up everyone was getting up to leave. I walked with Priest through the crowd. The band stopped for an emotional amount of time when suddenly they performed one more song called, "Shine On You Crazy Diamond." This song filled me with streaming tears, wishing it was Gentry with me, loving it too.

Priest and I left for the bus after the concert was over. I slept all the way to Toledo and woke long enough to get off the bus and into Priests car. Slept until I got back to my house. I woke up and we went inside. "Priest. Look. Remember the lady bug I put in my pocket before we left?" "Yeah, I do." "It's still in there crawling slowly over that big marijuana stem. See?" "He probably likes you." "Priest, I think he's stoned." We both agreed it had been a long night, so Priest was off for his home across the swampy road, and I needed more sleep.

Of course that wouldn't last too long, as Buff would be up early wanting to know all about the concert. Eager to hear everything, Buff woke me up asking how the show was. I told her how I was falling asleep, but had remembered seeing a man sitting about 20 rows ahead of me. "From behind, he looked just like Gentry, I swear it looked just like him. I wanted to walk up and see if it was him but they got security guards there that won't let you. "Mom, I bet that was Pinky. He's just like "Pink Floyd," it's his favorite band!" It could have been him Buff, he turned his head once, and from the side it looked just like him. Priest didn't know Floyd from "Led Zeppelin." I should have been with Pink. You were right." "See mom. It would have been more fun with Pinky. He would've been acting like Pink Floyd. Singing! I just like Pinky so much mom! I bet he likes you too." I long-sighed and said, "I don't know Buff. He hasn't been here for a while." "Yeah but you know Pinky mom. He might surprise you and come over just to see if you went to the concert. And maybe he saw you too." I laughed, made coffee, but on the inside, my daughter had got me to thinking. If that was Gentry at the concert then maybe he did see me. But he didn't need to see me there with Priest. Oh yes! Buff and I knew who it was that I should have gone to the concert with because it's something I thought we were supposed to do. Just like we are supposed to be together. Like we were in the beginning. Where it all started.

Priest ended up going back to work. It would mean lots of nights of him being out of town. On those weeks before he'd go, Priest told me to take how much pot I would need for the days he was gone.

A couple days passed. I was still trying to remember the concert, but more about the man who looked just like Pink. And was he thinking of me?

That morning something came over me. I went in the bathroom and took a good long look at myself. My hair was great. My eyes looked even better. I saw a very attractive woman in the mirror. It was making me sick. I stared and thought about how many times boys and men told me about how beautiful my eyes were. How sexy I was. My hair was gorgeous. I couldn't take no more. The compliments were often and had gone on for some twenty years. Enough was enough. I went for my purse where I kept my hair cutting scissors. Then I headed back to the bathroom where I washed and cut my hair. I wanted it short. No more waves laying over and passed my shoulders. This was going to be at the neck short. The cut was just below my ears. I feathered it all the way around from front to back and kept the style full. It was just beautiful. I was amazed at it myself, but I had to put it to the test.

I walked to the corner grocery store to see who'd notice first. The first person who said anything about my hair was a woman standing behind me in line. She said, "Excuse me. But I love your hair. Where do you have it done?" "I don't. I cut it myself. I've been cutting my own hair for about 13 years! I got my Cosmetology license in 75" "That explains it then. You did a very professional job. It looks very good on you!" I thanked the stranger, paid for my things and went back to the house.

Later that day, after supper and after all the dishes were put away, I made a pot of coffee. There was someone knocking at the door and I knew it couldn't be Priest. He was out of town. Buff went to answer and from the bathroom I heard her say, "Pinky! Guess what? I won tickets off the radio station for a Pink Floyd concert only I couldn't go." I heard him ask, "Oh! Who did?" She answered, "My mom." I came out of the bathroom and Gentry was sitting laid back on a chair at the table. His head was cupped by his hands. "Who did you go with Big Time?" I answered quietly, but I answered, "Just a friend, a man." "So what! I saw "Pink Floyd" when "Roger Waters" was there and you didn't." I was lost for words because he knew more about the band than I ever would. I leaned to the kitchen counter with my back against it. Stood with my arms crossed as I watched his eyes. Pink said, "You hair looks good short." "You like it?" I asked. "Yeah," he said, "It's high time you got some class about yourself." I raised a brow to him and said, "Since when does hair have anything to do with class?" He changed the subject, "I see you put on a few pounds." He was pissing me off. "Oh! So now I'm fat?" "You're not fat, but it's about time you put some weight on those bones." He chuckled like only he could. I went to him and sat on his lap. Yes I did. I said, "Bones huh? Look at you!" I said the wrong thing and got up. Took a seat next to him. Of course he could be losing weight if he wasn't in remission, I thought. But Gentry didn't let what I said bother him and he didn't stay long. He got a good look at the cans, he had to! Everybody did! He didn't say good bye when he left. He looked upset when he learned that I was at the concert with someone else. I wondered when I would see him again and I was damn tired of wondering.

I dated Priest for the remainder of 1987 and on into 1988. The relationship we had wasn't like any other I had since my divorce. Priest worked a lot. And when he didn't work we'd go out for dinner. He drank a lot. Oh Priest was a cool one with alcohol. He didn't get all mean and stupid, just mellow and laid back. I liked this! If he was working close to home and not staying at a motel, sometimes he'd spend the nights with me. He'd come over about 8:30 in the evening. By nine his head would be resting on my lap as he lay snoring lightly on the couch. I'd tell him to go on up stairs and sleep. Then I told him I was gonna roll a couple of joints and meet Ladie at The Barrel. Told him that I'd be back by the time the bar closed. He'd say no problem and was off to sleep. I'd roll the doobs and it was off to The Barrel.

But this was about all our relationship was. We didn't hold hands. He seldom put an arm around me. He kissed me one time, I think. We had sex once. He was pretty drunk so it didn't mean anything to him so it meant nothing to me. Was there something wrong with me? Other men found me irresistible. Maybe it was the hair cut. Oh well. On things went just the same and it was getting real boring. I wanted more attention and I wasn't getting it. No, I didn't go looking for someone else. There was always that somebody else to begin with.

Priest would want to spend most of his week-ends with his one and only son. I couldn't blame him, except that he seemed to want nothing to do with me while that was happening. It really bugged the shit out of me. What really pissed me off was when Sandusky was going to be opening a Radisson Hotel. It wasn't the place itself that got me mad, but what Priest did. He rented the biggest suite they had and took his son and his son's best friend to spend the night there. Doin' dinner and the whole fucking nine yards! I told Ladie, Nina and Pope. I told anybody who would listen. Why in the world wouldn't he want it to be a night for me and him? I let Priest know how much it bothered me. He didn't say anything about it. We kept seeing each other. If nothing else, the pot was plenty and free.

It was March when I had made up my mind that he was going to sleep with me or I was out. I had feelings for Priest and he wasn't giving me any affection. I called him one evening and said, "Priest! I'm coming over to your house tomorrow morning at 5:00 and we are going to have sex." I hung up the phone. I went to couch early that night. Had to be sure I'd get up on time. I went to Priest's house, to his room and we had sex. Downstairs I explained to him that him and I had to end our...? We both understood, we both cried and are still close friends today.

♫ ♪ *"Voice In The Wind"* ♪ ♫
Words and Music by: Catherine Santi in September, 1987

"I could hear the laughter inside. I can hear your voice in the wind.
I can hear you breathing the air even when you're not in the room,
up the stairs, down the hall, down the hall at the end on the left.
Alright the right when you left.
I had sought the solemn and strong. I've been where I don't belong.
But to me there's always a trace... the emptiness that's wearing your
face.
For me it's been ideal, but I can't conceive if you can't be real to me...
... Do you know what I mean? I'm sure you know what I mean.
I wanna thank you for what you have done.
You let me go and now I know you are die only one.
I outta thank you, you're one hell of a guy.
Oh I think you are but have no real reasons why.
So let me tell you for the time, just one time,
I thank you so truly from the heart of my mind.
If one day when you're not too blind,
and you come by to change your mind.
If there's words I just cannot say.
Would it be worth it anyway?

Made a choice. What a choice,
it's smearing your vision that constant incision you feed.
Or don't you know what you need?
I'm sure you know what I mean."

♫ ♪ *"Won't Say Good Bye"* ♪ ♫
Words and Music by: Catherine Santi in November, 1988

"I wish you would give up, still what have I done wrong?
We'll be friends and good ones at that, only how long, how long?
Please go away, I am busy, only I just wanna say hi.
Before I ever have the chance to say it's always first good bye.
So I won't say good bye anymore,
for it's said we'll meet once again.
No I won't say good bye anymore,
I'll see ya round my friend.

No I won't say good bye anymore,
I believe the old cliché.
I won't say good bye anymore,
it's just easier this way.
Yes it's been a long, long time, you replied to my delight,
So I won't say good bye anymore, I'll only say good night"

♫ ♪ *"Only Love"* ♪ ♫
Words and Music by: by Catherine Santi in December, 1988

"Here I go again, soon colors will disappear,
I'll just have to mark time alone.
I keep you to myself and you won't give me a day.
You are all the love I'll ever need.
And if you come by, you won't see me cry.
I'll remember you and just how you feel.
You're the only love that's in my heart.
There I go again and what I couldn't learn till now,
I've got to let you go on and be free.
And with my heart I'll see the warmest times were.
I've got the very sweetest memories.
And when you must go, you won't catch me crying.
You're the only love there is for me.
You're the only love I'll ever need.
You're the only love I'll ever need."

Chapter Twenty: "Part Four?: The Game. A Beginning To An End. And Three's Upset!"

Priest wasn't right for me, not Bobby or Captain. Three was enough. Told myself I would share my life with no one. Not then, not ever. No one that is, but Pinky... the exception. How could there be anyone else for me? I talked to myself out loud in the car, "Do you hear me Gentry? It's me. Big Time. Ya know the one who was three from the beginning? I am speaking, are you voice-less?" Self took over..."Capri! Until it is over, it isn't over." So on Marched March.

Sonny turned four. After that day I felt like I had finally made it through the bruised memories that always came with March. The month would soon be over.

I still hung out at The Barrel. Made a lot of bar friends there. They were a good bunch of people and I enjoyed them all. There was Harris who owned his own electric and plumbing business. He upgraded me to "18 Wheeler" and many people still called me Wheels. There was David. David laid carpet for the store his father owned. No matter what he talked about he was always smiling and laughing. He was notorious for saying, "I'll just have one more" and he said that for hours. There was a lady named Sherry who was a regular there. She was probably ten years older than me or more. Sherry looked great. She could still get away with wearing a mini skirt and high heels. Her hair was short and very blonde. She caught the attention of a lot of men and was always good for a laugh, unless it was good advice you were after. Sherry was real and to the point. I like that in a person. Her kids were old enough to bar hop and they became regulars too. Harris's daughter Trace was cool for young and she'd party with me and Ladie. The three of us agreed that "Clairol" should put our faces on their hair color boxes. My hair a golden brown, Trace the blonde and Ladie a burgundy wine, we were on time. The list of regulars could go on and on. Aah! But yonder came a new regular. A fresh-out-of-high-school-regular. Couldn't have been twenty, if that. And the twit came with a name... Wanda.

I didn't like her from the get go! She wasn't very bright. Not in life! Though she acted like she had lived. She had very short and light brown hair. It was much shorter than mine. Mine was growing out and just touching my shoulders again. Who was she kidding? Compared to me?

Wanda would bring her clan of class mates along and the bunch of them made me nuts! They played music on the juke box that nobody liked. They were proper in manner, proper in dress, but there big-nothing-all-talking just made me want out. I ignored the bunch the best I could and most of the regulars, well they understood.

Towards the end of April in 1988, who does Wanda end up seeing but Gentry. I could not believe what my eyes were seeing. She was with him all the time and they were coming on my territory, the place being more mine than theirs. Gentry hung out elsewhere most any other time. Now they were habitants of where I went for peace and a good time. How could I have a good time looking at the two of them together? Jesus! He's old enough to be her dad! What does he see in her? What's he thinking? I thought. Did he feel the need to feel young? Hell he was four years from 40! Was he feeling unattractive? In my eyes, no. He was very, very handsome. Yes, I was playing favorites. I had every reason to. I was still in love with him. What could this teenager know about real love? He'd be sure to see this, wouldn't he?

My guesses were way off track. It wasn't long after they were seeing each other that Mr. Mocean himself had decided to introduce the two of us. Standing in the crowd at The Barrel one night was Gentry. I watched him for about five minutes. Apparently he was waiting for Wanda to come back with the drinks. Well, when she was coming back with "the drinks," I was just about to make my way passed the both of them to freshen up. I held my head high and tall when Pink stopped me and said, "Hi Big Time. Wanda this is Cappy." Ding-dong Wanda busted out and said, "Hi. Gentry and I are getting married, aren't we hon?" Oh! I could not contain myself for a second. I gruntingly cracked and said, "You really think you're gonna marry Gentry? Honey, he's not going to marry you." The dingy didn't know what to say, but Gentry did. He took one small step, was eyes to eyes with me and said, "You really are one special lady!" I went beyond deep-looking into his eyes and he further said, "You scare me ... Big Time!" "Boo!" He laughed and I smiled. Wanda, she tried.

I found this all very amusing. She really thought she had what it took! Did she not hear what that man said? He wasn't boasting about her! I was the queen sitting highest by the king at the top of the eastern wall where the mugs had collected pennies. Not her damn it! This meant war.

But the war already started before I thought of it. Gentry and Wanda exchanged some loud words and he was out the door. I knew that he had way too much to drink. Didn't want to see him walk anywhere in that condition and Wanda pissed me off letting him go that way. I walked over to her and said, "I thought you loved Gentry." "Oh, I do," she said, "But I'm not his taxi driver. He can walk home and get hit by a truck for all I care." I shook my head and told her just what was on my mind..."And you love him? If you knew anything about real love, you would over look the anger and see to it that his life is safe." "Oh, you don't know Gentry. He's probably ready to go somewhere alone for the week-end. He likes to do that. After he has that time , he'll miss me and be right back."

Like she knew. Time was wasting and I wanted to leave, but there was something she needed to hear first and it would come from me. I stood tall next to her and said, "Listen Wanda. I love Gentry and don't you forget it. If something happens to him I will personally blame you. You see these week-ends you say he loves so much aren't at all what you think. He has chemotherapy because he has cancer. That's where he goes for a good time Wanda! You piss me off. I'll make sure he gets home alright! That's love!" I left the bar and got into my car and drove the route I thought for sure Pink would have taken on foot and got to Neil Street. I knocked but no one answered. I checked the door to see if it was unlocked. It was. I walked in and saw Gentry standing over by the north window and he was on the phone with someone. Someone named Janie.

He was quietly talking and the words sounded pleading. I couldn't make out what he was saying and said nothing. I turned to look out the window to my left to ignore what I couldn't hear anyway. After a short time I turned back and Gentry was getting ready to hang up the phone. When he did I said, "I just wanted to make sure you got here okay!" He raced towards me with fire and rage. He grabbed me by the shoulders and shoved me down into the couch. He was pulling at my clothes. For a second I was afraid, then I got just as mad and pushed him off with one good heave. I almost tripped when I got up to leave and yelled at him, "Stay off of me!" He tried again to grab my arm but my reflexes were sharper. I backed away and said, "You know? I must be nuts to want you so much!" With bitter feelings I walked to my car and kept walking while he in ire said, "Leave for good this time!"

I couldn't wait to pull out of the drive and go for one. I drove to the pier. Didn't turn the radio on but got out to listen to the sunset. I wondered who Janie was. She obviously made Gentry angry enough about something that he took it out on me. Why me? I asked myself. Self had no answer. The next day I would learn more about Janie.

It took several days before I found out who upset Pink so much. It happened to be the daughter of a dentist. My dentist. One who I worked for eight years ago while holding "two" other jobs! Gentry and her had seen each other at one time. She was living somewhere in Florida the day they were on the phone. That information was from the dentist who I had an appointment with.

Janie did what I do not know, but whatever happened between her and Gentry must have upset his life. Maybe this was his true love, his soul mate. Maybe she is the reason he told me to find somebody else. I was full of questions. How could she not want him, I thought?. If she didn't and I found out she didn't from a private source, then why doesn't he give up? I answered myself. For the same reason I don't give up on him. Because I am in love. Falling in love just happens. It catches you off guard and keeps you there forever if it's real.

The status... tense. I was drinking and smoking more. I had to get my attention on something else. How to make some money. This will give me less time to think about this make believe wedding and Janie.

Over the winter I drew a picture. It took about one month to finish. Guess you could say I copied Hermit's work by using a pen. It was a collage of profiled faces whose necks connected to the next face. Each neck was the forehead of the face to follow that formed a circle. Other odds and ends were in the drawing. It was finally complete. I figured ten dollars an hour for the drawing and the price was at 175 dollars. Firm! I lost this original because an old friend of mine came up from Florida to see me. A friend since I was 14. Since I hadn't seen him in years, I showed off my last piece of art. The lost one. I gave it to him because of what you haven't read yet. I wanted it out of the house. Then I started this book. I called J. Luis and asked him if he'd run a copy of the original so that I could show my readers. Joe said he'd do it. Said he'd send two in a tube. Well, the tube never arrived. I gave it fair time. I waited three weeks. I phoned Joe and he was certain that he sent it. I didn't believe him. My reasons were justified. When I gave him the original he said that the people down in Florida would buy that up in heart beat. He said, "I can get prints made of this and sell 'em for 25 bucks a piece." I told him that I didn't care what he wanted to do. Gave it to him because I wasn't going to be drawing for a long, long time, if ever.

He acted special because he had my original. I drew one for my pool teacher Krome when he got married. Captain got one for his birthday. But someone told me that his new wife Tammy found it and threw it out. Doesn't matter. The only one that mattered was the one Joe failed to send a copy of. And if it did get lost in the mail, he didn't put a tracer on it. He could have made another copy. It would only cost a buck and I would have paid. No. Joe must have sold the original. It made the only sense. Poor Joe! He was so happy that he was going to be mentioned in the book as a good friend. Well, it started that way. But it sure as hell didn't end that way. And that way it shall remain!

Back to April, 1988, before I ever gave the drawing to Joe, I took the drawing to The Barrel. I asked Lloyd if I could display it in the bar in hopes that I might make a sale. I offered him 15% of what I wanted for it if it sold.

But Lloyd didn't want anything. He hung it left of the cash register. This was the perfect spot for it.

It stayed there many many nights. It got odd stares. Heads turned this way and that way to view it but no one seemed interested in the price or the artist? Artist? I can't call myself an artist. That name fits only one person in the family and that's Hermit!

It was not taking my mind off of Gentry and Wanda like I thought it would. I spent a lot of days drinking coffee, smoking pot. Most of my nights spent, were at The Barrel drinking.

Jo had long since moved out and back home. We didn't get along as roommates but stayed good friends. I told her about Wanda. It turned out she knew who I was talking about. Well, JoJo knew where things stood when it came to Gentry. She insisted to get me all dolled up for a night trip to The Barrel. "Capri! When I'm through with you, there's no way that Gentry will be able to keep his eyes off you. You'll look gorgeous!" Jo flew home and back with a dress for me. It was blue-sky-blue. The sleeves were short but not quite capped. The neckline scooped. Very simple. Nothing sexy. Just neat and nice. Jo had the accessories to go with it. White-flat-woven-leather-shoes and matching belt. She suggested I wore the belt loosely around my waist so I could gather an inch of dress up through it and let it drape slightly over the belt, giving it a lax look.

I was the only one who dealt with my hair, but Jo wouldn't have it any other way. I gave in to her, like most people did. She styled my hair with a curling iron. I liked it feathered all around just the way it dried, but I must admit that when she was done with my hair and I my make-up, I could have easily passed for twenty! I was afraid to go out looking so pretty. Wasn't used to wearing anything like this. I was strictly jeans and cut offs, depending on the weather. The outside was in my favor. Jo's favor. We both started our sun-tan-competition and the sky-blue-blue-dress was the right color for the day. I would not go out alone. I was a nervous wreck. Jo was going with me. We set out for the experimental-excursion at 7:30 p.m.

I wanted to sit at the bar. Jo insisted it would look more lady-like to be seated at a table... that and she didn't like sitting at the bar. I agreed so long as I could sit at the very table where Gentry once insisted that I stay. In that spot I would be able to see everyone coming and going. We got something to drink and talked a lot.

Jo never told me till then that she was joining the Air Force. This called for a song. "Jo, I wanna hear something on the juke box. I'm gonna get some quarters." "Wait Caps. I wanna check it out. See if there's something that might go with this bash were having." Jo walked over to the juke box. I knew the songs all in all. The ones I liked. I had no idea what might be appropriate in her eyes. She played lots of them. When she came back I asked her what she played. She wouldn't tell me. "Okay Jo. Get us a couple more drinks." It was my turn to pick out a song for her. Like she did to me, I would do to her. I wasn't going to tell her, she'd know!

I came back to the table and Jo said, "That man sitting at the bar is staring at you." "What man?" I asked. She used her eyes and nodded her head for indication. It was Pink. His eyes were fixed on mine in a glance. I turned fast. "Jo, don't you remember who that is? That's Gentry. The one I'm crazy about! I can't look at him." I turned my chair hoping he was watching and wondering why I was doing it. I tried to ignore him. Now Jo had him in her sight dead ahead. "Cappy! I'm telling you that he has been straight-staring at you since you went over to the juke box. He loves you Cap! Look if you don't believe me. You know why he can't take his eyes off you?" she asked, "Because Caps, you are just gorgeous! Nice sun tan. That dress looks better on you than on me. Keep it Caps, I want you to have it. Hell I'm going to the service anyway, I won't need it." I thanked Jo for the compliments and dress, but now she had me going. Was he still staring? I had to know so I nudged Jo with my elbow and said, "Is he..." She stopped me and said, "Ah! Wait. I know what you're going to ask me and the answer is yes.

He hasn't stopped looking at you! He is still straight, and I mean straight-looking at you! Just you! What's with him? I know he wants you. Hell he is in a flood of love with you!" "If that's true," I said, then why doesn't he join us? Why doesn't he say hello?" Jo said, "Maybe if you would turn around and look at him like he is looking at you he might want to come over. Did it ever cross your mind?" I told Jo I had to quit talking about him. My heart was only breaking more. Jo was trying to cheer me up and the timing couldn't be better. "New York, New York" played. And "Frank Sinatra" was the singer. "Long loved! Long live!" Jo stood and said, "This is the song I played for ya because that's where you belong. You belong in the big city singing and playing all your music. I can see your name in lights girl." I was laughing and agreeing that I'd make it. Someday. We had a few drinks in us by then. I had a couple joints before I left the house. We were a little loose and both got up, made like we were a couple of "Rockets" dancing and singing along. I was having a blast and remembered that Gentry was there. Out of the corner of my eye I caught a brief smile directed to the performance he'd just witnessed. I wasn't embarrassed by that, just felt un-cool when I had to pass him to use the ladies room. I went back to the table and noticed that Pink wasn't at the bar and sat down wide mouthed. Before I had a chance to say or ask, Jo said, "Cappy. He didn't leave. He's in the men's room. Do you think he's going to leave? He knows he has to stay and make sure no one else gets you. He's been watchin' you all night. Get real Cap!" "I have to stop talking about him Jo. I should cut my hair short again." "Cap I'd have to hurt you if you touch that hair. It's beautiful. Wish I could do mine like that. Wait till it gets longer! Come on you know you look good! What's wrong with that? Flaunt it baby, flaunt it!" she conceitedly said. "You're right Jo. I do look pretty damn good if I must say so myself. So I will say so myself. I look damn good!" "That's the spirit!" cheered Jo.

I was waiting for a song that I played on the juke box. I needed to hear it just about then. Sure I looked great for a night. I laughed, had fun. I sang. But I still wanted Pink to be sitting with me. Always with me! What was going through his mind as he watched me? It bothered me. But what bothered me now is I can't remember the song I played for Jo. Wanting to leave was what I wanted to do until I thought about what Jo said earlier. That maybe he is sticking around to make sure someone else doesn't get me. I had to go before he did. "Jo drink up. It's getting late. Let's go." "Takes a lot of guts Cap!" she said, "I know how much you wanna stay, but get this. He's going to see us leave and he knows we're going home. Where else is there? Once he can't see you in front of him he'll wonder about you. Hell, Cap! He'll be thinking about you right up until he falls asleep tonight." I shook my head and we both got up from the table. I looked at Gentry for *a* moment. Tried to hide my curiosity, but I was sure my eyes would give me away. I felt a blush coming and I knew it was time to go directly to the piano.

Jo went her way. I went inside to roll another doob and I sat at the piano to do it. I was in a hurry. I was hoping Pink might stop at the house. I wanted to play everything I had ever written about him, for him. I needed him to hear. But as my lousy luck would have it no other way, he didn't come to my house that night.

I became a regular at The Barrel. Occasionally if Gentry popped in that's all he would do. A drink and gone, unless of course he was there before me. A night like that came and he was already there and drinking, full of smiles, talking to everyone but me. I noticed Wanda wasn't around and wondered about that. She hung on him like dry wall.

The Barrel got a new trivia game. It was a machine of full questions that me and Ladie were hooked on. After playing an hour, we took a break and sat at a table close to the questions. I watched Gentry. He was standing behind the bar like he worked there, and only three feet away from my drawing. Then he turned and saw it. I watched even closer and turned up my ear volume. He reached for my picture to look it over. He seemed to take an interest in the collage of eyes and faces I had inked. My how quickly people change when they realize that they are now the ones being watched. He saw me watching him. I wrinkled my forehead. What gives him the right to remove it from the wall? I thought. The price tag was clearly marked on the frame.

Just as I stood up he said, "Whoever drew this must really be scrambled!" I was already walking to him. "Scrambled huh! Give it to me. Unless you're buying it, it belongs on the wall." I was taking a gentle hold on the frame to get it from him. He said, "Hey if somebody is gonna buy it then they should be able to take a good look at it!" "Oh who are you kidding Gentry!" I said, "You're not going to buy it." The picture did not go back on display. It had been there for a couple months. No one knew was coming in and I figured it to be a "no-sale." Gentry was showing my scrambled picture to a few sitters at the bar. I was getting very upset. "Gentry! If you wanted to buy it I wouldn't sell it to you!" With smiling sarcasm he asked, "Why not Big Time?" I answered just the same, "Because it's not for sale anymore!" I took my picture back to the table and finished my drink. I invited Ladie over to the house with me. I needed someone to talk to and I needed pot. I left the bar wishing things didn't go like they did, but they did. I guessed that they were supposed to.

Ladie followed me over in her car. We were both the not proud owners of our "Chevy Citations" Maybe it was the colors. Maybe they sucked really. Maybe we got the ones that were built on a Friday. Whatever. We had problems with them. Pope helped me out with the piece of junk. He stuck over 2,000 bucks in it. It didn't deserve it, it needed a bullet. Now that was an idea! It was another thing Ladie and I had in common. We could bitch about the cars. We got to my house and did the coffee and pot. Ladie left after a time to go looking for love.

I sat at the piano. Did that night after night hoping Gentry would return. He did not. I continued to go to The Barrel on those nights after nights. He wasn't coming in anymore. I wondered if had run off and married that dingy little girl.

May passed and it was June. The blue jays still visited in a full set of four. And one fine day there was a knock at my door. I went to it and leaned back into a wall to brace myself for it was Gentry. He stood tall and neatly dressed. I was so used to seeing his head cocked slightly to the left, with him using his right hand to lean up on the rail of the porch.

Then it hit me. He was sober. He was totally straight and sober. I only seen him this way a handful of times and I was a wreck. He asked through the screen door, "Can I come in?" "Sure. Come on. What are you doing over here? Aren't you supposed to be getting married?" I asked. Gentry came through the door and walked right over to my spot in the kitchen. I had to take a seat at the table.

He spoke as I stared off out the window. "That's why I'm here. I came over to thank-you. She's gone." "Hmm. You're welcome." I turned to him and asked, "Want to sit down?" He walked up to me and took my hand, led

me into the living room and said, "Play one more song for me Big Time."
I sat at the piano and thought... One more song? I played and sang one I
wrote for him in '86 called, "Places. Questions. Words." When the song was
about through he stood behind me. I could feel him wrap his arms around
waist. He put his cheek next to mine and said, "I just wanted to hug you one
more time." I closed my eyes and held tight to the moment. When I felt the
warmth of him away from me I turned. Once again he led the way, taking
my hand till we were at the kitchen table. I sat down.

He sat across from me. I reached my hand across the wooden table till
my finger tips touched his. We'd been looking into each other's eyes saying
everything unspoken. I was surging with energy all around. I had to tell
Gentry what I was thinking. "We lived before. You and I. On a ship. On
great waters you and me." Gentry looked deeper into my words and eyes.
I waited for him to talk. He didn't just come over to thank me. He sat
tall in the seat across from me and folded his hands on the table in front of
him. I slid my hand off the table and on my lap with the other one. Then
he said what he really came over to say. "We can't be together. I can't tell
you why. Just remember that I'll always love you." I said nothing. Did
nothing. Didn't cry? My heart hurt so bad that it felt like Gentry had a
hold of it and was trying to take it out of me. He stood up and went over
to the door. Looked back at me while I sat in shock. Completely lost! He
walked out the door and I jumped up off my chair, raced to the door, but I
didn't call to him. I watched him walk down the drive and he didn't look
back. He knew I was watching and I knew that this was no game. This was
real. This was life. My life. Whatever it was that Gentry and I were, only
he knows and God The Almighty knew for certain. And it was on that day
I knew, he would never return.

Later that night it hit me like a thunderstorm. I blasted Beatle songs I
had recorded. Pink Floyd songs for Pink and my eyes were buried in an ocean
of tears. It went on for months. And it went on for years.

My life had been ripped to shreds. How was I supposed to go on without
him? How could he tell me he would always love me and then leave me?
Why couldn't we be together? Why can't he tell me? There has to answers
if there are questions, I thought. I would find them if it took a life time.

I needed to do something. Had to work. Get out of the house and I had
to quit bothering my head with all the questions. Things took a turn for
the better. Nina who was doing the book work for Joe, (the one who tilled
my yard), well, Nina said that he needed someone to drive one of his dump
trucks. I knew I could do it and I didn't turn it down. The pay was under
the table at seven bucks an hour. I would begin the next day. I was to be at
Joe's house in Huron by 5:30 a.m.

My day started at four-thirty in the morning. I woke. I showered. I dressed in cut-offs and a tee shirt. I gulped down a few cups of coffee and by passed the pot. I would need to be straight for sure.

When I got to Joe's he led me to the truck and asked if I could drive a stick. Of course I could. They didn't call me Wheels for nothing. The truck was easy. We'd fill the two trucks that Joe had and headed to our first job. It was on the old road to Cedar Point. We would be building a break wall for the private residents there. It was trying work and the weather was rainy. But I passed. I got the job. Working 6 days a week if I could. And I did. Sometimes a day could go on till it turned to close dark.

Driving was bore, a drag, but the jobs when done made it all worthwhile. I was proud to tell my bar friends that I helped build a break wall for the folks who lived on the lake. Great to say I helped make a parking lot for a car dealership, a street in Port Clinton etc... We did a lot of asphalt work. There were many trips to the diesel fuel tank. You have to line the bed of your truck with it or the asphalt sticks. Diesel fuel smells bad, but when I got to see a nice lookin' fellow-truckin'-kinda-guy, it got my mind the fumes and off of Pink... for a time.

Last stop was Joe's. I parked my single-axle red truck off the drive next to the back hoe. I wanted to run that baby. That looked like a lot fun. Eventually I got a stab at the big yellow machine. Joe let me fill my truck with a load of top soil. I got the hang of it after a bit... Okay, I nearly back bent the machine over. It was gonna topple, but Joe caught me in time and jumped in to get to the gears. Thank goodness. I decided I wasn't ready for the back hoe yet. And I wasn't ready to quit the job. But soon school would start and there would be no sitters. No sitter... no job.

I was getting bored. More time to think. More time for pot and illusions of Pink. There wasn't a day and I would ever forget the time that he left, the time that we met. The numbers were coming and coming in twins. September 22nd. Fall. Where Pink's birthday begins. Good God I'm doin' it again. I have to say this, rhyme all my words. This thing about Pink was getting absurd.

I found myself dwelling on the numbered, numbers in my life. The damn three's for one! The two's for second of course. The rest didn't seem important. Except for number 19. Every now and then I can hear Captains deep voice in my head shouting it out. He never did tell me what that number meant. I started to think that it had something to do with me. Why not? And there was something that Gentry couldn't tell me? Maybe Captain played a part in Mocean' game. But that wasn't a game. And if I am wrong then it was a cruel game of fucking with my head. Capri. Cool Breeze, Big Time and oh let's not forget The Wheels! You listening Gentry. Watch me big time! I don't need you, I thought in anger. I have me, my kids, the piano and that's all I need!

I wrote two more songs. Of course they'd make great presents if only I could play them for Pink the birthday boy. I knew it wasn't going to happen. So who and what the songs were about were for me to know.

Restless and kinda missing the old red truck, I looked around the house for a project. It had been in the house all along. A desk. It was an expensive desk. It came with a wooden-framed-mirror to hang above it. That alone weighed 40 pounds. One of Pope's friends were buying new furniture again, and again they gave me things they didn't want. The desk and mirror were for Buffs room. But we all shared it and kept it in the living room. It looked good there.

The paint had to come off the desk mirrors frame. I wanted the job to be easy. I called different hardware stores. They told me what I could use but I wasn't about to spend the money. There would be a shortage that month, so the suggested products were out. I looked around the house for something to take the paint off with. There was a brush for painting but nothing that would make the job easy. I could get all the sand paper I wanted for free from Pope. I tried the paper but it was running over the desk like plastic on steel. There was some kind of a hard shell finish that I couldn't get through. I looked around for something, anything. All I had was a flat screw driver, oh, and a hammer. A lot good a hammer would do. I took the screw driver and used it like a scraper. I worked on an area behind one of the back legs to see how it would work. It worked. After I was through with that I continued. I smoked many many joints working on the fucking desk. And you'll know soon know well enough why I called it that. The name has never changed!

Day after day and in the hotter than normal weather, I chipped away at the desk. I'd start about ten in the morning and finish about 5 or 6 o'clock. Sometimes longer. The coffee mug was in arms reach and of course the music was blasting.

After working on the desk for 8 days, it was finished. Mirror frame and all. It felt almost as good as glass. I wanted to get to a hard ware store right away. I had to spend something to protect the back breaking work!

When I got to the store, just inside, I had seen a familiar face hidden under sunglasses. I heard the deep voice say, "You don't remember me do you? But I remember you. You're Cappy. Cappy Spettro!" I knew who he was right away, but his short friend with curly red hair butted in ahead of me and said, "This is Jimmy." "I knew who you were the minute you smiled," ignoring his friend. Jimmy said, "Yeah, but I bet you don't remember my last name." I just started to get my mouth opened to say it when his friend, pissing me off again said it first. Next thing I know the three of us are in the isle looking for some wood protectant. I ended up getting nothing but confused.

Jimmy said that him and his friend needed a ride to the drug store. They wanted me to go in and buy them cough medicine. It required six dollars and a driver's license. You could only buy it once every 24 hours. I thought for a minute. Figured what the hell. I smoke pot. I drink. To each his own. I drove them there. They gave me the six bucks and I did like Jimmy instructed me to do. I was real nervous about getting this stuff. I wondered about having to show my license. Do they turn these names into the cops? I asked the pharmacist for a bottle of it. The only thing he wanted was a driver's license and a signature. He wrapped the bottle in a bag for me. I took it to Jimmy and his buddy. Next stop? Some place for a tall lemonade-to-go. I drove up to a drive-thru at a fast food place, where they both bought large lemonades.

I paid attention to how Jimmy was dressed and how he looked. It had been 15 years since the two of us saw each other. I had the biggest crush on him when I was 14. He was the main reason I started going to Crooks Den. Jimmy worked in the kitchen then. Now here he was at my house 15 years later. He stood about 5 feet 10 inches tall. He loved being tough looking, thinking it made him look cool, and he was good at it. He wasn't muscular but I liked that. What color would you guess his hair and eyes to be? If you said brown, you're right. I fell for the men with dark hair and eyes. His hair was passed touching his shoulders. He wore a "Harley Davidson" scarf around his head for a band and a "Harley Davidson" shirt and "Levi's" What else? I liked his mustache. I liked his voice. He was kinda sexy and old memories re-surfaced. Jimmy introduced his friend. His name was Roger. Roger was a short guy. You know his hair color if you were paying attention. His eyes were light bright blue. He had strong arms and he was a roofer. I asked Roger, "So do you like your job? Don't you get real hot up there?" "Yeah it gets hot. It's an alright job if you're crazy enough to do it!" he said smiling. Jimmy explained that they were both working for a guy named Mic', doing the roof for the high-rise downtown. "I'll bet there's a view. The bay, the islands and Cedar Point!" Jimmy said, "Yeah Cappy, you should come up there sometime and see what we do."

James and I both turned and looked at Roger. Roger had been sitting with his chin cupped in one of his hands the whole time and he was staring at me. He looked like a little kid about 15 who was having a "first crush." "Rog," Jimmy said, "What is it man?" Jimmy looked back at me and again at Roger who was still staring and said, "She's pretty isn't she Roger?" "Huh? Yeah Jimbo." He was still looking at me when he answered. "I know you probably hear it all the time, but you have the prettiest blue eyes. I can't stop lookin' at 'em." Standing up acting very theatrical was James. He said, "Well you can quit looking at her bro' 'cause it's like this. I saw her first!" Roger defended his rights and said, "No way man, I saw her first at the store." "Hey fuck you man! I've known this girl for 15 years!" I played the ref…"Okay you guys! We came over here to look at the desk. You said you'd help me figure out what to do with it."

Jimmy walked over to it. He walked around it and stuck a thumb in the pocket of his jeans. He rubbed his fingers down across his mustache and said, "So you did this desk? How long did it take ya Cappy? It looks alright!" "Are you kidding me? It took me eight days to get this desk like this. I had to use this!" I showed him the screw driver. He took it and busted out laughing. "You mean to tell me that you scraped all the paint off of "that" desk with this? Cappy, they sell stuff to take paint off." I explained to him why I didn't go that route and then I asked him, "So now that I nearly killed myself working on "the" desk, what do you suggest I put on it to protect it?" Jimmy grabbed a drawer and walked over to Roger. Between them they talked. Jimmy came back and named some things that the hardware store did not. I wanted to go off and get something for the desk and Roger said, "Cappy, we don't know nothin' about wood. He just wanted a reason to see you. Ain't that right Jimbo." Jimmy walked over to his friend and said, "You got a big mouth Rog! Who was trying to kiss her on the way to the drug store man." Roger put his head down, then lifted it up looking at me and said, "Cappy, I'm sorry." "Sorry Roger!" exclaimed Jimmy. "You only had your head right in between hers and mine dude. She don't want your goofy ass."

Roger kept on smiling and laughing. Jimmy was performing but I think he really hurt Roger's feelings. Roger did have a crush on me. It was damn obvious! Jimmy asked me if I was seeing anyone and I told him that I wasn't. He told me that his wife Cindy wanted a divorce. I couldn't imagine why. He was cute, sexy and he was working. What more could she want? We spent the rest of the evening going over old times. Well, we took Roger back to his house first, back to Huron. I drove. Roger still wanted to give me a kiss on the cheek. I wanted to let him because I felt sorry for him and because I felt that way, I wouldn't let him.

Me and Jimmy stayed up half the night talking and it was getting real late or should I say early. By now he had had a couple of 40 ounce bottles of beer and the half bottle of cough syrup. I let him pass out in the chair.

The next day came and Jimmy was up early. He got me up. (I was on the couch) He asked me if I had any coffee. Good God! It took him that long to see that I had coffee? "Jimmy, do I have coffee? Are you crazy?" His eyes got big and he said, "Cappy. Did you drink all that by yourself?" He was laughing. Of course "the" question would come, it always did. "Cappy, how many cans ya got there, huh?" I knew that number. Quickly I gave him the answer, "92." Question 2 was "when" did I start holdin' on to 'em. I told him. Lo and behold there was a third question which was "why"? I didn't know the answer to that myself. I just kept letting them collect and grow wider around the kitchen counter

I made the coffee. Jimmy had a quick cup. Before he left he wanted my phone number and I gave it to him without questions. He told me that he'd try and help me out with the desk after work, if I didn't mind him coming over. I didn't. I had such a good time the night before that I was looking forward to another one.

Later on in the day and too late to see my doctor at his office, my back went out. Now this had gone on for years. Got the bad back from Mayor. Then there was the added problem associated with the new fucking grass I had to have. I couldn't stand up so I walked like I was sitting in a chair. I called my doctor at his house to tell him. He ordered me some muscle relaxers and something else. I got to the drug store okay. The car was easy. I could sit. But when I got into the store, I knew the pharmacist was going to let me have the jokes I didn't need. He seen me come in for this before, but I was always able to stand straight. Let's say I was stuck that way. I was in no laughing mood because laughing wasn't easy. I walked to the back of the store and talked first. "Listen pill man," I said, "Don't give me a hard time please. And whatever you do don't make fun. I can't stand up." He said, "Cappy, how many hours did you sit in the chair marathon?" Yeah, it looks like it," I said, "Pill man don't do it! Don't make me laugh, I can't take it. This time it's a mess! Look at me!" "I'm trying to look at you Cappy but you keep looking at the floor. What's wrong with you?" he asked, and how did you do that?" "Can you believe it was a desk that got me like this?" "What happened? Did one fall on you?" I took my prescription out of the store. Put the two pills in my mouth and swallowed them down on my own saliva. Hey! I hurt!

If the drug store trip wasn't bad enough when I got back to my house Jimmy was already there sitting on the front porch waiting for me. More questions. More jokes. I was hot, tired and pissed. I answered the questions and I took the jokes. Jimmy and I walked in the house. He stood in the living room, he put his thumb in his jean pocket, took a hand to his mustache rubbing it down. Then he stopped and pointed at the desk laughing his ass off. "Aye Cap. This is "the-fucking-desk" that did all that huh? You got hit." He was crackin' up. "Hit? Yeah I guess I did that." I had to sit. It took James a while, but when he was through busting up over me and the fucking desk, he understood it was no joke!

Me and Jimmy spent the night talking and talking and mostly about the-fucking-desk! That was 1988 and 11 years later it is still called that name with pride and great pain!

The night was done and Jimmy and I couldn't even look at each other anymore without busting a gut. It got so bad, Jimmy had to leave the living room. It was the only way we could keep from laughing ourselves to death. He got about four feet away and he dropped to the floor. I looked over to see where he went. Looked over the couch and he was down on his knees with his head into the floor nearly out of breath and laughing. This got me going again and I tried to tell him to get up. Holding on to his guts he said, "Cap. Please. I can't take no more. Go in the kitchen. Go somewhere. I can't even get up off the fucking floor!" I went into the kitchen and thought my face would burst. Ten minutes passed. Jimmy managed to get off the floor. He walked in the kitchen and out of the corner's of our eyes we saw ourselves. It was hopeless. We were at it again. He made a direct left into the living room where he wouldn't see me. Where I wouldn't see him. I went in after a while and Jimmy was asleep on the couch. I was laying on the floor watching an old movie on the tube and dozed off. I forgot to take the back medicine. When I got up the next day I felt okay. I could stand up no problem. Problem was sitting down. I took the pills that would take at least one hour to kick in. Can you imagine what it was like to use the toilet?

I made coffee. Me and Jimmy tried to remember what was so funny the night before. I think we were glad it slipped out of minds. It was time for Jim to get down to the high rise. As for the fucking desk it stayed the way I left it. Finished without a finish.

Jimmy was around all the time when he wasn't working. It didn't take long for our teenage crushes to be upon us. In about two weeks not only were we an item, Jimmy moved in.

Can't begin to count the hours we talked and talked. He remembered how crazy I was about the Beatles and told me a secret. "You know somethin' Cap? When me and "the" ex bought "John Lennon's" "Imagine" album, every time I listened to it I thought about you. Cindy always thought I was thinking about her. You always loved John Lennon. I bet you still do don't cha?" This got my attention big time and I said, "You were thinking about me? That makes feel kinda special James. Most people who go back as far as you and me remember how much I loved The Beatles. They sang about the most important thing in the world. They sang about love." "Yeah they did. When he was killed you came into my head right now. I said to myself, I'll bet Cappy is taking this hard." I was choked up but I stayed tough and said, "Jimmy, I don't think I'll ever get over it. How can I? Do you know when I moved in this house? December 8th. Great fucking day ha? This year he'd be 48. I miss him. I miss him too much!" "A lot of people do Cappy, you're not alone." "Jimmy it messes with me all the time. If I didn't have three kids and that creep "Chapman" wasn't in prison, I'd take fucking pleasure in blowing his brains out. Sure, I'd go to prison, but I'd go there knowing a lot of people would've wanted to do the same thing. They'd be thanking me. Shit! I'd be thanking me!"

We learned more about each other. Jimmy had three daughters, a house in Huron and a wife. I also learned that he loved to drink and he drank a lot. He could get very loud and mean when he was drunk. But I dealt with it. From the time I learned he liked his case of beer, he promised he would never hit me.

Around the beginning of October I received a call from Jimmy's wife Cindy. Cindy and I both were crazy about him when we were kids. She and I talked for a long time. She explained that she only threatened to divorce Jimmy because she hoped it would open his eyes and close his mouth to the alcohol that was ruining their marriage. She asked me if Jimmy ever hit me. That question took me to a stand at the guard table. I looked out the window and asked myself, how do I answer her? Jimmy probably beats on her when he's drunk. Like Batturs did me. My heart answered with truth and I said, "No. He promised not to. Cindy, I'm sorry. I wish it was me instead of you." "No you don't Cap! I've put up with this drinking for 20 some years. I got my babies to think about. He needs to think about! But his beer is first, last and always." She talked with anger and despair. "Cindy he loves you so much. All he talks about is you and the girls. He wants to be with you. I can tell him to leave 'cause truth is I've been in love with somebody since 1984. He's handsome, hardworking and intelligent. I can't say I don't love Jimmy, 'cause I do, but like a brother." "Caps. Whoever that guy is, you better hold on to him. There aren't many of them left." We talked over an hour. We learned a lot about our lives that day. "Cindy I feel bad about you and Jimmy. He always liked you more than me when we were kids." "Caps. Don't tell Jimmy I made up the divorce, but I had to." "Don't worry. I won't. You're a strong woman to put up with it all these years." We both had lots to think about.

John Lennon is dead. Been that way nineteen fuckin' years! Can't implant it in my head. Reality should have kicked in by now. I thought it could. Thought it would. But it's 1999. Three nines. Another three. Just what I need! Like I said, they never end, they never do, they never do, because they're not supposed too. Add the three nines and ya get 27. Two and seven is 9, divisible by three and that's me. Good Jesus! I'm writing the book! What more do Ya want? Did I misspell? Did I accidentally use a wrong date, a year? Would "Sir Paul McCartney" even care? I'd like his opinion or if he thinks it's okay, 'cause it's therapy Paul, tryin' to be sane these days. The book has become a job with no pay and I struggle and hope they won't lock me away.

These are the kind of things that happen when I'm trying to write this book. I figured it would be done by now. I'm Big Time. I'm Cool Breeze! Fuck! I am The Wheels! But I am no writer. I don't know what the hell I am doing. Something inside keeps telling me that I'm supposed to do this... so I do this. I put myself at risk each night. If I continue telling the story I may lose my mind again! If I send it off to publishers and they reject me I might lose it, find it, fucking kick it down the road! The brick one of course. God really help me if it sells! I'll end up calling the state mental hospital myself to make sure they have room. And I want to smoke!

Might be and may be. Could be or should be. What if this, what if that? It's the next day and I can't get laid back. Things and thoughts are rolling in my brain, then it fucks with me more so hey, I complain!

Getting on with the past as it was. Jimmy and I were still seeing each other under my roof. Cindy was right about the drinking. Jimmy knew he had a problem but did nothing about it. He'd get to talking about the same thing for hours and hours. The more he'd go on, the louder he'd get. How did Cindy handle it I thought? Two months was almost over and so would this thing with James for sure. He was scaring me and sure it scared the kids. I was certain in my head that eventually he'd break his promise and hit me. No man was ever going to hit me again!

One night Jimmy and I took Old Red for a ride and ended up going to The Barrel. We stayed long enough for one drink. Jimmy loved showing me off. He couldn't get over that he was seeing me. That I was seeing him. He loved the way I walked and let's not forget the eyes. Well it just so happened that a bunch of nasty lookin' bikers were in the bar that night. I didn't know them and they weren't with "The Outlaws" that's for sure. Jimmy couldn't wait to tell the boys my name and that I was his old lady.

We were standing and about to leave. One of the nasties said, "Jimbo, Where ya headed?" The Jimmy I didn't know said, "I'm gonna take Cappy home, spread her legs open and lick her clit." I looked at Jim. I didn't say anything. I opened my right arm out and with everything I had I bitched slapped him across the face nearly knocking him down. He wasn't laughing anymore. He was pissed off real bad. His face wrinkled. I did that in front of the boys? I knew I fucked up. I rushed out the door and then I ran like hell. Jimmy got out and hopped in Old Red. He chased me down and told me to get in the truck. He swore he wouldn't hit me. I was still scared to death and refused. Stopped running because I couldn't run anymore. I just wanted to get to the house and fast. So I walked that way. Jimmy was on me the entire time. Once again he said, "Cap. I don't lie. I'm one mad mother fucker! You don't know how bad I wanted to fucking hit you. But I made you a promise. I'm not gonna break it. I won't hit you. Just get in the fucking truck Cappy. You ain't walkin' home alone. It's dark out." "You'll hit me." "Capri Spettro. Get in the fucking truck before you really piss me off. I said I wouldn't hit you and I won't. Not now, not ever!"

Well I got in the truck. I sat close to the door and said nothing. Jimmy yelled about it for the two and one half minutes it took to get to my house. And it didn't stop there. It went on for hours. He yelled and dogged me all night about bitch slappin' him like I did. Since he wouldn't budge or shut up, I stood up and said, "I'm gonna take a walk till you cool off." I went straight for security at the hospital around the corner. I walked in the hospital and called out to the first cop in sight. I told him what happened and that I wanted somebody to come and get Jimmy out of the house. The big dark cop said, "Now let me get this right. You say that you hit him and now you want us to come and get him out of the house. He should be the one calling the police not you!" The cop laughed but I didn't. I finally got him to call the station so they'd send a cruiser over to the house. I met the cops in the drive and they came into the house with me. Jimmy said, "Oh great Cap. You hit me, you leave and bring the cops back with ya? Thanks a lot!" It took some talking but the cops took my side and told Jimmy that it he would have to take himself and his truck out and away for the night.

Jimmy left and I locked up. I took a seat at the guard table and rolled a few joints. I had some cold coffee in my cup there. Drank it and smoked the joints one after another. I thought to myself, Man, I hit him hard! The only other person I did that to was Captain. Captain hit me back but Jimmy kept his promise and didn't strike. It was the yelling and swearing that scared me enough and I wanted the cops there in the worst way. I knew what getting hit, kicked and punched felt like and I promised myself that I'd never get hit again. Jimmy will understand, I had hoped he would anyway. They didn't send him to jail. Shit, he's probably sleeping somewhere in that truck of his if he is calm! Guess this will be a wait and see what tomorrow brings.

The next day came and when the work day was over for James, I heard Old Red pulling into the drive. I went to the door and walked outside. Jimmy was grinning. "You done being mad at me James?" "Oh, I'm not real happy about gettin' hit! That pisses me off a lot!" "I had a good reason to get mad at you. How could you say that? You made me sound like some cheap slut. I'm not and you know it!" He replied, "No you're not. I don't know why I said it. The boys were all there and I was proud as a mother fucker to have you with me. Their old ladies look like shit. Believe that! You beat 'em all!"

"I appreciate that James. But friends don't talk like that about their friends and we go way back! You hurt my feelings bad. That's my hang out man."

Jimmy walked up to me and gave me a big hug. Holding me he said, "Cap. You been through some shit. I didn't show you any respect last night. You were always a nice girl. Still are. Man I love you! You're Cappy!" He loved me?... "Jimmy you said you love me?" "Yeah I do. You're a sweetie-pie... you're smarter than most chicks I know and you're pretty. Ain't much on cookin' though are ya huh? I love ya Cap!" "I think I feel the same way about you James!" "What's with the James, Capri?" Jimmy asked with a chuckle. I looked at him in a rugged rough-n-tough stand, thought about how shy he was at 14 and said, "Well, we're not little kids anymore Jimmy." "Okay Cappy. "Aye! Ya know you're gonna have to ride on the back of my "Harley." Cindy never would ride with me. You and me will be ridin' tough too. I'll have the prettiest girl in town on that bike!" "I don't know James." "Don't know what Capri?" "You might be drunk and kill us both. Uh... no thanks Jimmy." "Cappy! I promised I never would hit you and I didn't. I will be sober and you will ride on my "Harley.""

The next morning, two in the morning, I heard an engine. It was Jimmy and his bike and the bike looked beautiful. It was the long chrome fork that added to it and I wanted a ride. James was prepared and sober. He wore his black leather jacket, jeans and boots. I was the good guy in the white leather jacket and the white leather sneakers. And we looked good sitting on the jet black bike. Jimmy told me to hold on to him tight. We drove down a route 250. Good-traffic-kinda-street. But it was after two in the morning so the cars and trucks were light.

We stopped at an all night restaurant for a burger and a pop. We stayed long enough to eat and we left. Then the rains came. Jimmy went back into the restaurant to get some paper towels for the seat of the bike. He came back out with a bunch stuffed inside his jacket. He wanted to get it started and he prided himself on being able to kick start the bike the first time. As his luck would have it a few people were getting out of a car just when James was wanting to be cool. The bike didn't start right now. He looked at it and said, "Bitch!" He tried a second time and said to me, "Cap. This is not fuckin' cool", as he laughed he went on … "The bitch don't wanna start and when I do get her goin', and I will, we'll get stung by the fuckin' rain, huh!" he laughed. I started to lose it too. We were both cracking up. It was so funny to watch him kick start the bike. By about his sixth attempt, he got her runnin'. He dried the seats off and told me to climb on first. He was definitely right about the stinging ride home. The rain hit like tiny needles over my face and hands.

Jimmy and I took our relationship lightly through October and November was cutting in. Cindy was right about her husband. He most definitely had a drinking problem. He could go a couple a weeks without. I'd treasure those days. I got to know the real man. He was sweet, enjoyed the outdoors and he could cook! He liked working on things. And when it came to "Chevy's," there wasn't much he didn't know.

This side of Jimmy everybody liked. It couldn't be helped. He was cute, he was handsome, he was smart, he was quick with wit. He's lines, original. You wouldn't be crazy to him but he'd tell ya, "You ain't on the fucking porch!" When he'd have to leave my house, he'd say "I'm breakin' camp." When you come in the house, the bar, "You cleared the door." And there are far too many more. I don't really think it's a good idea to write, I kinda feel like I'm falling off the porch tonight.

James was still coming around even though I told him that I couldn't deal with him. Most of the time he was sober and when he was drunk I have to end up calling the police. He never hit me, he kept that promise solid. He'd get so mean looking and loud and all I could picture was a scene that took place in my old bedroom when Batturs beat me and beat me. James didn't run when the cops came. He calmed down and cooperated with them. He'd get in the back of the cruiser, look at me from the window saying, "Thanks a lot Cappy."

By Thanksgiving things were out of control. A big box a food came from the Catholic school so I could prepare the traditional meal. And James knew it. I spent the entire day cooking, cleaning and taking care of the kids. I was whipped by six but dinner was on the table. James was late. I made the kids wait a little while longer, giving him time to start the dinner with us. About a half hour later, we gave up on his on-time arrival. We were just about to sit when drunk and mad as hell Jimbo came flying through the door. He took one look at the table of food and flipped the table to its side. Food was everywhere. It got real quiet fast. I shook and the kids were hiding around a wall by the kitchen. Jimmy looked at me and said, "Sorry Cap. I fucked up your Thanksgiving. I'm breakin' camp before you call the cops. At least one thing was clean. His getaway.

Me and ail the kids pitched in and salvaged what we could. We tried to forget about what had just taken place. James was enraged! I was through with him. I would tell him the next time he came around. And he would.

November was just about over. James pulled in the drive. It was after the kids were in bed. To my surprise he was sober. He couldn't have been more sorry about how he ruined things on Thanksgiving for me and more so for my kids. I accepted his apology and we sat at the guard table.

Jimmy drank coffee. It was a good thing and I had plenty of it. "How many ya got there now Cap?" he asked. "Oh "the" cans! Grow fast don't they? There's 118." "You should slow down on it Cap. So, what up? Huh?" he asked, "You're still sleepin' on the couch I see." I sighed and said, "That's my bed. Gotta be ready for anything." "Still can't sleep in your room Cappy?" "No. I don't wanna talk about it. I wanna talk about us. Jimmy I love ya and I always will. I also know that I don't wanna deal with it anymore. Can't. You need to get help, get things right. Cindy still loves you Jimmy and you're crazy about her. There's time to make things straight before it's too late ya know that don't cha?" "I know. She told me that she was trying to get me to quit drinking with the divorce shit. I got a house. It ain't much but its mine. I do own that and Old Red. Doesn't make a good night's sleep, but aye!"

My heart was going out to him and his out to mine and he said, "Cappy. I hate seeing you sleep on that fucking couch. You got a bed. A big bed to sleep in! There ain't nothin' up there that can hurt you. "Jimmy, I can't sleep there. The walls will come in all around me and get black. I'd just freak out!" I shook thinking about what happened three years ago and Jimmy took me by the hand saying, "Come on. Get up Cap! I'm going up there with you. I can't leave here knowing you're afraid." I knew he was right. I knew the only way to get over my fear was to face it. I took his hand and we went up to "the room."

Jimmy turned the light on, walked in, sat on the bed and said, "See. Just a room. Four walls, a closet, nice little end table here. Come on Cap, sit down and let's talk. You look like you need somebody to talk to. You can always talk to me Cappy." I was at the north wall. I ran my hand along it. Teary eyed I looked at it and said, "It's still here. You can see it, see?" Jimmy got up and said, "What Cappy?" "See this line in the wall? This long fucking tear, scratch, whatever the fuck you wanna call it?" Jimmy put his arm around my shoulder. Tears dropped to the floor. Mine. From his heavy heart he asked, "What happened in this room!?" "My ear. My earring. These!" I told him, touching one of the pearls I was wearing. "How the fuck?" his face puzzled up. "That mother fucker! Tell me Cappy. I'll fuck him up. Tell me what happened!" I pulled away feeling cold and numb. My thoughts were slurred and the answers came out that way. "Seee, a, he uhm... he grabbed me. He uhm, he threw me. He, I mean... the side, this... this ri-right side, side. Uhm. Hit first." I was shaking my head back and forth nervous and anxious to just get the fuck out of the room.

Jimmy stood back, took a glaring stare at the wall. He turned to me and hugged me warm. "That is never gonna happen again Cap. It's over. I promise." He backed up and his face was right in front of mine and he reminded me again, "I promise you that. Bet. I keep a promise Cappy.

Nobody is gonna ever hurt you again!" I broke. Broke out crying. Laid down on my stomach and buried my head in the pillow. I didn't want Jimmy to see me out of control and not in tack. He sat next to me, rubbed my back and said, "Cappy, you've been through some tough years huh? You can talk to ole Jimbo. "Jimmy. Damn! There was so much shit in my life. Christ I'm 31 and I bet if you took a thousand 80 year old women there wouldn't be a one that's been through what I've been though. Prof' fucked more with my head than my head, ya know. I get divorced to be with Frank. He leaves. Oh, did I tell you I had an abortion? I hate myself for that. Was before Prof'. A third. Prof's a third. Then I meet the third of my dreams. Then Batturs a third, comes along and fucked up what I might have had with Gentry. He's the 3rd third. I told ya about him. And the day "he" tells me he'll always love me, he leaves. I hurt Bobby to be with Captain. Guess he just wanted a pretty drinkin' buddy till he found the girl he loved and married behind my back. Priest and me are still friends. That's one good thing huh?" James held me and said, "Two good things Cap! I'm not gonna just forget you. You and me are special tight. We don't see the other one for sixteen years and then Bam! It's like we've been hangin' out together all that time." "You're right Jimmy," I said composing myself. Jimmy took his worn, soft flannel off and said, "Here. Wipe your eyes. They're too pretty to be crying. You got the prettiest blue eyes too." I took the soft red shirt, dabbed my eyes dry and handed back thanking him, but Jimmy said, "Nah. You keep it. Looks better on you. Never wore it much when I lived here, huh!" "Jimmy. I can keep it? I love this shirt. And you're right. I do look better in it then you." I rubbed the soft flannel over my face.

Side on side with our chins in our hands James tried to make me understand, "Cap. There's a reason for all this. You've suffered with bad stuff and shit for a long time. But ya know, it's the people who go through years of it that get the reward. You'll see. Might not happen tomorrow, but it will happen. You got it coming." Curiously I asked, "Ya know how many times Pope said that to me? Ya been talkin' to him or what?" "Look at what you have Cap! My old man didn't do nothin' for me. Your dad got you a house. That car. The old boy don't know much about cars does he, huh." Yeah," I said, "To think I could have dropped an engine in a '68 "Camaro" Could have had a ten-thousand-dollar car easy. Three thousand bucks Jimmy. Everything mint, just needed an engine. V-8. 350, you know. Shit, between what he paid for that car and the money he stuck into it, he might as well have seen it my way." "Red ride Cap?" he asked. "Yes. Fucking red red! Damn it! I look good in red." My head was cocked up all smart ass and he said, "Yeah. You looked real good drivin' Old Red. You're the only one who could drive her as good as me. Nobody could keep her runnin', but you did. You didn't grind the gears, you shifted her real smooth. Fuck yeah, you could drive Old Red tough!"

I was glad Jimmy came by. He knew how to bring me out of a down. I was in a good mood. He suggested I listened to some Beatles. That took us back downstairs. James took care of popping a cassette of songs I taped from different radio stations. I made more coffee. Smoked pot. James stayed straight. We didn't make the night late. We listened to the Beatles till the songs were up. Jimmy thought time was late and that's when he got up. He said, "Cappy. You and me will always be good friends. I love you." I knew that kind of love and that was easy. "Jimmy, you know I could never hate you. Too many years! I love ya too. Thanks for being here. I didn't think I had anything to say and then I...." "Cap. That's what friends are for." Jimmy and I gave each other a big hug. We parted ... smiling ... friends!

By now we should know where his departure led me. It led me straight for the pot for one, the piano for two and finally the couch.

I thought about the straight talks Jimmy and I had. I had a nice house to live in. Maybe none of the furniture inside matched, but we all had a bed of our own. There was plenty of food. I had a car. Not the car of my dreams, but it took-me-there-brought-me-back! Guess I had all I needed but I wanted more.

I thought about the three's that were creeping in the core. December, December, a one and a two. Of course a three. Of course that's me. Jules has a birthday on the third day and Pope, well it's the same way. More three's and three's. God don't give me a break it's a old reminder of dead number eight!

I thought out loud and talked to myself and I was all ears. "So, how ya handlin' the 8's Cap?" I said. "What do ya think? Look at the year will you! It's 1988. It's been eight years since Lennon was shot. I moved into this house on the eight of this fucking month. And you ask me a stupid question like that!" That made me shut up fast.

The birthdays went well. Jules turned seven. I told her that Mayor could see her from heaven. Then the maddening of eight came to me like before, there were four eights too many, I didn't want anymore. I thought about the number four and brought it down to two. Well we all know by now who's who. The month carried much depression so I wrote some songs for total remission.

♬ ♪ *"And You Are Forever"* ♪ ♫
Words and Music by: Catherine Santi on July 1st, 1988

"I remember a time when nothing seemed real and nothing too new,
only you.
Though the memories are quaint. Do you think it's too late if I put it to
you?
It's down to you.
If when I look up, won't you give me a smile?
How many steps I gotta take before you lesson me miles?
Surrender the storm, well it keeps us apart.
And if I never really mattered then how'd you break my
heart at all?
And oh! You'll come and go for a while.
For me you're all I have on my mind.
You see the years are quick from our sight
These dreams are ever still in the night
and you are forever, you are forever.
The days can't be taken away and these days, these days are mine alone.
Alone? Oh you left me this way but you know you always can come
home."

Song Finally completed on September 14th, 1991 by: Catherine Santi

♬ ♪ *"Music (Soul For Song)"* ♪ ♫
Words and Music by: Catherine Santi in October, 1988

"Far beneath what feels like a dream
I'm finding out that on the nail you hit the head most every time
and it's opening my eyes.
But I do want to wake up, to what I memorized before?

Afraid to think that I am not, who I always thought I should have been.
No one can walk a road as such be it real or fantasy,
no one can but me.
Now just as then. The dreams as it stood long before I knew
the reasons why it lost its way and beckons for me every day,
but still that something in the way,
I can't see what it is for sure.
A fair hello to younger me, a soul for song eternally,

perhaps a lonesome side of me and you can make us one.
One and one equals one."

I spent most of the month day dreaming about Gentry. Wondering how he was doing? Was he seeing anyone? Did he think of me? Might he pop in on my birthday? Would I get a cake? Ha, who was I kidding it was further than late. I turned 32 on that Christmas Day. I shared it with my kids. We did the traditional thing. Me and my brothers would take our families to Pope's house for the evening dinner. Nina and Pope made a great dinner. The grand kids played together and had lots of fun at grandpa's house. When it was time to go, and I was ready hours ago, I packed up the kids and we were off.

The kids played with all the things they received for Christmas. By ten p.m. they were exhausted. I tucked the three of them to bed and headed straight for the sugar bowl. After a number of joints I was ready. Ready to go nowhere because my hang out was closed for my birthday. Most places were. My birthday sucks, I thought! "What do I do now?" I asked myself. Self said, "Why not count the cans?"

"Okay." I went to the kitchen and counted them. Christ there's 126 cans! Yeah, that's right. I picked up one yesterday because I knew the store would be closed. So I bought eight? Jesus! There it is again. Maybe Jimmy was right. I should cut back on the stuff. I thought about that and asked myself, "Why?" "Yes. Why?" Self replied. She was always buttin' into my business.

While I wasn't having a shin-dig I got a call from Prof'. He had long since moved out to California. I told him that the kids were in bed, that I could get them up. He said, "Don't wake up the kids. I got some things I really need to tell you." "Yeah, like what bull shit now Prof'?" You have to remember how much I loathed this man. He was a cheat, a liar and a manipulating son of a bitch. Bored, I let him talk. "Cappy. This isn't easy for me. Took me a long time to grow up. I want to tell you how sorry I am for the way I treated you when we were married. I treated you like shit. I was a real piss poor excuse of man. A stupid young fuck up." "Yeah you were," I said. I stayed standing by the wall where the phone hung. Prof' continued, "I know you hate my fucking guts and I don't blame you one bit. I was a real mother fucker. I lied to you, I hit you and I cheated on you. When you met Frank and wanted a divorce, my eyes opened. Too late, but they opened." "Oh well," I said. "Cap. You have been through more shit than anyone I know. Me. Then Batturs. And everything else. I know you got this thing for that Gentry guy. I hope it all works out. You suffered a long time and it's people that go through years of suffering that are most rewarded." "Oh brother! Have you been talking to Pope and Jimmy too?" I asked. "What?"

371

he said. "Never mind." "That's alright. I didn't expect you to hear me out. Telling you I'm sorry makes me feel better inside. I hope someday you will believe that. Well, take care Cappy." I could just see him rubbing his eye with a finger or raising his brows. That's how he looked when he'd told all the lies. I let my phone say good bye – "Click."

I felt like someone just threw the guard table at me. I went to it and sat down. Prof', Pope and Jimmy all talked about the reward. The reward one gets in life for suffering. Why the hell does a person have to suffer to be rewarded and who's handing them out? I want mine now!!!

The treacherous threes were there in the lines. Three people. Telling me the same thing word-for-nearly-word. I wanted out of this triangle of a life I'd been in. Make me anything but a three. It was hopeless. I turned 32 this last birthday. I knew I did those years already. I was in my 33rd year. Or maybe that's more like 33,000 years. Maybe I really am Eve, I thought!

There seem to be no escape. By mid January I accepted it. By month's end I was enjoying it. How many people can say this, I thought. I've had three of everything. A lot of it good, some of it bad, some I wish I had never had. I loved my kids and hated Batturs a third. I loved a man, he was the third of my thirds, but three sentences to me from him were final words. I had three guitars. Prof' broke the first. I got a "Gibson Les Paul" and exchanged it for "Gibson" acoustic six string. Couldn't quite tune a 12 like I used to. Where did I get the money? Not from the win I made at The Barrel, that went for the kids. I got the money when Ladie and I went on a lucky to excursion to private club. We had three dollars between the two of us. We bought three illegal tickets. We won. We bought more. We won more. And we kept on winning till we walked out with close to four hundred dollars. Ladie said, "What are you gonna do with your half Cap?" "I'm gonna get a guitar." That following day I went to a shop downtown. One of the guys there named George, sold me my second. He let me exchange it for the acoustic, my third. That was so out of context! I don't even own a guitar now. But that's a long story that doesn't belong in this one.

By end of January of '89 I had one hundred and thirty two cans on the counter. They were a bright sight to behold! Ladie and I talked about the cans. I told her that Maxwell House ought to come up with wall paper and curtains and stuff with pictures of the cans on them. Maxwell House canister sets, dishes and mugs. I liked the idea of the mugs. I wanted a set of them bad after I saw a commercial about the coffee and a mug that looked like the can. I took a picture of the cans on the counter and sent it along with a letter to Maxwell House. Asked them where I could get a set of the mugs. They answered me and told me that I might be able to find them in one of the finer department stores. Great I thought. I'm on welfare. I don't do finer department stores. I tossed the letter out and the idea and when the first of February came with my check, I went to a cheap store looking for mugs. I was very restless because I hadn't slept in a couple of days.

But that didn't keep me from the store. When I got there, I found some cups. My attention was caught immediately by some sitting on the bottom shelf. Why? Eyes. Each one had a single outlined-blue-eye on it with words. Now I had been drawing eyes for about 17 years and I was slap happy enough. I knelt down and reached for one of the cups and read what was printed on it: Clinic for diseases of the Eye! Well, that's all it took. For no apparent reason I busted out laughing just like Jimmy did the night he couldn't get his face off the floor. I was crackin' up and completely out of control. I looked at a lady who thought I was gone for sure! While losing it in the isle I said to her, I'm sorry if you don't find this funny 'cause it's fuckin' killin' me!" She looked at me with pity, I looked at the statement on the mug still laughing my ass off. I watched the lady walk away, wishing I could have. I sat on the floor of the store trying like hell to get up and that took me about five minutes. Maintaining myself wasn't easy. I ended up buying four cups. Why didn't I buy three? I don't know. Never thought about it till now.

I showed them to Ladie. I handled it better that next day. At least it was in the privacy of my house when I cracked again. This time I had the counter in the kitchen to prop myself. Ladie couldn't see the humor either. But it was there just as plain as the glasses over my eyes. 'Cept I didn't wear any then. My vision was excellent. Was excellent!

We used the new mugs. I was a little afraid at first. Afraid I might the blow the first sip of coffee straight out my mouth laughing. Instead, it went down the wrong way. I gasped and coughed. Ladie got up and was hitting me on my back to help me get the coughing over with. Thought I was gonna die. I was brave and gave it a second try. I had to remember what just happened before and I took a small taste, then three and then four. Cup after cup and pot's after pot's and joint after joint and I was ready for take off. Where I was going is yet to be reached.

February, I thought. What special events are in this month? Well, it is no one's birthday I know of. Valentine's Day will be cute. The girls will make me something in school, I think. I don't have a boyfriend and it's okay because I don't want one. With that in mind, I went out to a bar a little out of my way. One I hadn't been too since drivin' the dump truck.

I went in and stood up close to the bar to order quench. My drink went from what Gentry bought me to something I could afford. Whiskey and a Lemon-lime. While waiting for the bar tender to tend to me, there was a group of younger guys standing near. One said, "What are you drinking." I answered, "Why?" "I'll buy ya one, that's why." I overheard one of the guys saying, "She's a bitch." Ignoring him, I turned to the guy who asked me anything to begin with and said, "I don't need you to buy me a drink, I got my own money." "I'm sure you do," he said, "I just thought I'd buy it. Damn! You "are" real bitch, you know that! You got something against men?" Little did he know! I fired at him! "Yeah I do. So get the fuck out of my face you're pissin' me off!" "What a bitch!" he said. His friends weren't looking too happy anymore. They were takin' his side but I got the last words in. "Damn right I'm a bitch. Put a lot of years into it. You know? So why don't you and your little friends run out and find someone your own age to play with. I don't do games."

I got my drink and drank it. Ordered one more and had it down quick. The place was full of a younger crowd and I wasn't into its mood. I took off for The Barrel. Drank a lot of alcohol there and kept count of the drinks. I took the long thin straw that came with it, shaped it into a triangle and hooked it to an earring by making one end of the straw small enough to fit it together. That night I had linked 14 straws together that lay in front and passed my shoulder. People wondered. They asked. I told them. "Just counting. Gotta count." The ones who didn't know me shook their heads. Did it matter to me? Not much did. I was into my own world of numbers.

February had a week to go and things were changing fast-lickety-split. I stopped sleeping. Not that I didn't want to, I wanted to. I just couldn't do it. I tried drinking. I mixed in a few valiums, I smoked as much pot as I humanly could. Still no sleep. Figured I didn't need any and I liked that. Gave me more time for numbers and things. Like day dreaming pictures of persons not seen. Where are the people hiding? They give me no traces, and Mocean I guess, found some new hiding places. Where ever I went he was out view. All the dreams in my life times just took off and flew. So I stayed with the numbers it was the right thing to do. It would help keep my mind off of dear number two. Oh I figured out I was number three a very long time ago. I thought, I am Eve from the Garden. I was there. I know.

So three isn't so bad just 'cause Mocean is two. Together we were first to begin multiplication. See? More numbers. Numbers that would go on and on and on. You are born a number. You live a number. You die a number, but the number doesn't stop.

They didn't for me and March arrived. I had been working with some chords at the piano and the words were running late. Sonny's birthday was very on time. He turned 5 on the second day. That evening after the festivities and the kids were in bed, I was restless. I was still not requiring any sleep. I was strictly pot and coffee but I had to get out and do something.

I woke Buff and told her that I was going out for a little bit. Sleepily she said, "Okay." I raced down the stairs. Drank some cold coffee and rolled a couple joints. I got my favorite red sweater, jeans, leather sneakers and the scarf. I just came back from the closet. I wanted to measure the length. I never did. It's seven feet long and over a foot wide.

Back to back then. I drove to a place called McJams. They had a pinball machine there I loved turning over. I arrived about 10 p.m. The place was packed with standing room only. I got a drink and change enough for pinball. No was standing there so I had it all to myself. While playing, drinking and already potted up, I kept thinking of words for my song. They came to me. I knew exactly what to say. I had to get back to the piano. I clocked the time. It was 12:03 a.m. Officially the third day of the third month. I bumped into someone cute on my way out. I almost knocked him over or was it the other way. No. It was his fault and then he introduced himself to me. His name was Steve. I told him that it was three minutes after midnight and I had some where to be. He said, "Will you turn into someone?" Hurriedly I said, "No, I gotta get home and finish this song I've been working on for too long." Interested, he told me that he had musical experience and wanted to help me out if it was okay with me. "Shit, yeah! I got a guitar at the house. You can play along." I didn't even listen for his reply. I told him to follow me to my house.

Grabbed my smokes and headed out. He followed. We got to my house. I walked him in. He looked into the living room and said, "I thought you said you played piano." "I answered, "Yeah I do but I got it in this hall next to the kitchen. This way I can play when the kids want to watch TV. Check this little blue light I got hanging over it. I love working in low light. It's only a 15 watt."

We walked by the piano and I turned on the clear blue bulb. It was pretty. Steve said, "So what's this song you're working on? No wait! I don't even know you're name. You never told me." "You're right I didn't. It's Cap. But I don't like it much. I'm getting it changed to Autumn. Autumn Sky. What do ya think? I love fall and I love the sky. You should have seen the letters there once. And the... never mind. You wouldn't understand. It was huge. It was for me. So I changed my name. Call me Autumn." "Okay Autumn," Steve said, "I like that. Autumn Sky. So let's hear this song." My voice was raspy from all the singing but I liked it. I sat at the piano. I played the short introduction to "Always For You." I got the words out in a song, right where they should belong. Though short and sweet the song sang strong. This is the song:

♫ ♪ *"Always For You"* ♪ ♫
Words and Music by: Catherine Santi on March 3rd, 1989

"It was always for you.
It was always for you.
And when there's nothing here to do,
it's still only you.
Now I've come to know.
That I have lots to show.
Those wasted days are gone and I want you to know.
That it was always for you.
And there's so much more to do.
I'll go on and get what it is I love the most
And it beams for me and those qualities,
they'll come alive, they'll come alive in me."

I could tell by looking at Steve that he could have cared less about the song. His acting was no good to me. He made suggestions. I wrote them down. I didn't have the heart to tell him that his ideas sucked. I tried it with his words and played it off that I liked his better. He acted again, but I knew that he didn't know a damn thing about music. He wasn't kidding me! I was Eve. I'd seen it all. "Steve. When I left McJams, I checked the time. It was like magic. It was three minutes after twelve. Three. See everything happens to me in threes. I sped up the list of all the 3's in my life up until I reached Batturs.

I went from nice to "don't fuck with me." Enraged I looked over at Steve who was casually leaning back against the end of the hall wall. My shorted out vocal chords spoke in fire, "Damn him! He was the one who ruined it all for me. He just kept punching me and punching me over and over. I could barely walk. He threw me against the wall. I don't use my room. Haven't slept up there for almost 4 years this month. A three. He was a three! They might as well all have been three's, like me. I've been three all my life. Got a particular number that's been following you around? Trust me, when you know your number it never will let you forget it. Not fucking ever. I don't even sleep on that fucking couch anymore. I don't sleep at all. Don't want any more nightmares. Do you have nightmares? I just want to hit Batturs over and over again till I'm worn out. I want to fucking beat him like he beat me and he fucked my jaw up. I may never get to be a singer now because of him so I'm gonna sing till I can't sing no more. That fucking bastard! Go … damn him!"

I punched the refrigerator as hard as I could. Steve calmly said, "Autumn, here, if you wanna hit something, hit me." "Hit you? You didn't do anything to me," I said. "Come on Autumn. I'm this guy Batturs and I'm standing right here. Hit me. Hit me as hard as you want to. I won't hit you back. I can take it. Come on, hit me what are you waiting for. Come on, I broke your jaw, I ruined you. Here's your chance." I let loose. I went up to him fast. My fists already clutched and solid. I plowed into him like a prize fighter. I punched him over and over again in the stomach and chest with all I had. He didn't flinch. I don't know how many times I hit him but it had to be over twenty for sure! I stopped as suddenly as I began. He looked at me and said, "Feel better now?" "Yeah I do. Did I hurt you?" I asked. "You pack a hard punch for a tiny woman, but no, you didn't hurt me. Autumn, I don't mean to be rude, but it's almost 3:30 in the morning. I gotta get some sleep. Aren't you tired?" He said, he asked, what difference does it make? I shouldn't have to follow the laws of proper writing because I'm about out there.

Told Steve that I didn't sleep. My mission in time was too important for that. Was going to record that song one way or another. I had to. Had to tell Gentry that I loved him, somehow. This song would be the way.

I explained all of that to Steve. He looked at me and said, "Autumn. I like to stay, I'd even like to see you, but I think you have a lot of problems that you need to work out. Too many problems for me. Don't get me wrong, you're a nice lady with good qualities. Then I know me. And I know that I couldn't deal with all this right now." "Problems? I've had some but they don't bother me now. Wanna know why? One. My song is done. Two. You let me hit you. Three. I'm Eve. And Eve was number three." "Okay Autumn. Like I said, I gotta get some sleep and you gotta do what you gotta do. I'll see myself out."

I didn't want him to go but it didn't matter when he did. I locked him and the rest of the world out for the night. I was either playing piano, or working with numbers at the guard table. 12:03 penned on one of the many sheets that laid strewn on the table there. I wrote it. I added it. No matter what I did to change it into a more positive number, the more negative three was becoming. I wrote the number in various ways. Child-like. Angry. Roman numerals and they were the worst, so I gave God some hell for being the first. "You sent me pictures in the sky. I ask Ya each day for what and why! You said not to eat the fucking apple because You were curious as to what we would do. You installed that curiosity in me and everyone else You game with." I could have gone on talking to The Almighty, but He didn't reply. Not ever, until maybe those clouds in the sky!

I went back to the song I finally had words for. I played it until dawn. I almost called it "Blue Light Special." Then I thought about who I had written it for. Gentry Mocean III was more than something that made my kitchen look like outer space. He was space. Gave me space. But why I thought? Why did he say we couldn't be together? Why can't he tell me the reason or reasons why? Why in all the skies around me did he say just remember I'll always love you? "What's the point?" I asked out right to anyone who would listen. Of course I was at the piano alone at the time and I answered the question with another, "What is the fucking point?" It was hopeless. Me and myself had been at it for years. We still didn't know the answers so all that remained were questions.

Ladie came over early one evening and she happened along with a joint for the both us. Or should I say three of us? Do you wanna take over the writing? I honestly don't think I can get to where I have to go, needed to go. That's what "they" would say. The wrong "they" would lock me up now if they knew what I knew. Knew what I was thinking that is. What I am thinking is what I am wondering. Am I going mad? That's what some of the "theys" call it. I still see purple clouds and their disasters. I know that fatalities will hit. They always have. I can't stop them because I don't know dates and times. With the numbers all around me you think I'd figure them out. You may not be able to reach with a hand to touch what I see but no one can see what was meant for just me.

Back to "the" book. The fucking book that sits in floppy colored disks and pages. Notes and pages and pencils and pens. Lots and lots of cigarettes. It's nearly one in the morning. September 1st, 1999 and I'm trying to avoid the book again.

Ladie directed a serious question to me, "Cappy. You're getting so skinny! Aren't you eating? Do you want me to make you something?" Like I needed more questions. "Ladie, I'm not hungry. I don't think much about food. I've been busy working on numbers. I think if I work real hard and use as much of my brain as I can, I might even come up with the lottery numbers." Ladie looked concerned. I showed her how not to be. I handed her a deck of cards and told her to shuffle them good. She did. I told her to place the deck face down on the table when she was through. "Ladie. I'm going to put my hand on the top card for a minute. It takes me a minute to feel them. If it's a high vibration the card will be red. If it's a deep, low and slow vibration it will be black. I may even know the numbers or suits. For some reason I get the sevens and tens right. Go figure. I'm three. You'd think I'd know the three's by now." Ladie looked at me with uncertainty. I put the palm of my hand on the top card. It felt warm like summer. "It's red. Hearts, I think. The queen." Ladie flipped to the card to reveal it and sure as I'm sitting here the card was the queen of hearts. I went on to the next and the next, till I completed the entire deck. Out of the 52 cards I knew the right colors and shapes of 50. I managed to get the sevens and the tens. I got a hold of a one eyed jack and I immediately thought about the blue jays. Ladie was astounded at and wanted to know how I did it. I couldn't describe it to her. It was like not being able to touch a purple cloud.

She wanted to bring this weight thing up with me again and it was pissing me off. I didn't care if I was thin or fat or whatever. I was who I was. And it was high time I liked me. There were lots of things to like, I thought. "Get off the weight Ladie. So maybe I lost a little." God how I wanted to tell her how awful her fat legs looked in a tight mini skirt. She was jealous I thought. "A little Cappy! You lost a lot!" she said. "Ladie fuck my weight already. What's the fucking difference? I'm strong. I'm smart. I'm three that's why. I'm somebody who has been around a long time. I've been through enough, seen enough and had enough. I like me just the way I am and if that doesn't suit anyone else, then they can run, drive, fly their naked bodies elsewhere." "Cappy are you okay?" Ladie asked, "You haven't been acting the same. Are you sleeping?" Christ I thought. More questions. I said, "No and why?" "Cappy, when was the last time you slept?" Ladie asked. I answered honestly, "I don't know." Naturally I being "her" best friend, she suggested I get some sleep. I suggested we go out and drink. We did the drinking. She probably thought that a few drinks would make me tired or something. It's not important. We went to The Barrel and drank till the bar closed. I had 17 straws hanging from my earring and I didn't even catch a buzz. Ladie thought something was definitely wrong. Suggested diets, relaxation techniques and doctors. She should have never said the "they" word around me. Why in the world would I need a doctor, I thought? I never felt better. I can do anything I want, say what I want and I did. "Ladie I don't need a doctor. Quit with the fucking questions and the suggestions and the what's wrong with me. Do you think I ever forgave you for what you did with Gentry? I hate that part of you as much as I do Batturs. You had to fuck Gentry." Ladie tried to explain. She couldn't make it right. I left for the house and straight to the guard table.

After getting there I made some coffee. While it brew I rolled some joints. What else? Had lots of pot for being on welfare. It's a matter of money management and I was quite qualified at the numbers, so long as some four didn't come along and fuck with my threes. Maybe those blue jays weren't so great after all, I thought. I was always thinking. And if I wasn't always thinking, well, then I was always thinking. I used the piano, I used the pen, I had fine-fine pot and lots of coffee drinking.

One night on the seventh day of March, three, yes three men came to my door. I knew 2 of them and the one for years. Their names were Mike and Harry. I asked them to come in but they were in a hurry to make a sale.

I looked at the short blonde, who was a rough-but-cute-kinda-guy and said, "Who's this?" "I'm Jeff," replied the stranger. Mike said what they came over for without hesitation, "Caps. Got a bag of black beauties here. The real ones. There's 30 here if you want 'em. I'll sell 'em to you for 25 bucks." "How about 20?" I asked. Mike agreed and I asked them in while I got the money. They remained just outside the door. I came back with the cash, said good bye, thank you and blah, blah blah. I wanted to get to the point. I hadn't seen these capsules in years and couldn't wait to pop one.

I took them over to the guard table and poured them out of the plastic bag. I began counting them. When I got to the 30 count, someone was knocking on my door. Quickly I put the pills back into the bag and tucked them into the pocket of my jeans. I didn't want to answer the door. What if they were setting me up? I didn't know this little guy Jeff. Maybe it was the police at my door. I just bought drugs. Not to mention the smell of pot everywhere.

The knock continued so I chanced it. I flipped the porch light on and it was Jeff. The wild-blue-eyed-guy I met a minute ago or so. I opened the door and said, "What happened to your friends? For a minute I thought I was getting busted by the cops." "Busted? No," he said, "But something didn't feel right. I wanted to come back to see if you were okay. I told the guys they shouldn't have sold them to ya so I brought back your twenty." "Jeff come in. You're right. I don't need these pills. I don't need anything to stay awake. That's easy." I handed him the bag of pills and he gave me back the money. I offered him some coffee. He looked at all the cans and said, "Are you sure you have enough, ah ha ha." "Yeah I suppose it does look funny when you see it for the first time. Aren't they something else? I got 138 cans now!" "Then it's pretty safe to say you like coffee," Jeff laughed. "Very safe," I said.

I liked talking to Jeff. He was sincere. He looked rough, tough and probably didn't have a shave for a few days. He looked good like that. His hair was light sandy blonde that just touched his shoulders. He combed it neat and I liked his blue eyes. He was about five foot seven with a small strong build. We talked that evening at the guard table loaded with paper and numbers. Jeff never asked about the notes and numbers. He was interested in me. We were both divorced. We both had kids. He broke out pictures of his and I led him up the stairs to show him mine who were asleep.

We headed back to the first level and I made more coffee. I offered Jeff some pot and we smoked a couple joints. We spent hours talking at the guard table. Jeff was getting tired. It was past 4 in the morning and I knew he needed sleep because he said he did. I told him that he could sleep on the couch as long as he didn't mind me playing the piano. He said, "I was kind of hoping you would say that. I think you and the little ones need someone to take care of you." I liked what I heard. It wasn't threatening. It would be nice to have a man around the house. Jeff crashed out on the couch. Piano would've been too much to break out on him so I stayed at the guard table and messed with numbers. 3 for March. 7 for the night I met Jeff, the 30 for the pills and the 2 in the sky.

Jeff woke about 9 am. He wondered and asked, "Did you stay up all this time?" "Yep," I said wide-eyed. "Had some figures to work on." "Are you a book keeper or something?" he asked. "No. I just got a thing about numbers. They're very important to me. They mark things, people, places and on and on." Jeff's tired reply was, "Hmm." I'd been on a coffee frenzy and needed more. All I had left was what the pot brewing. It made me a wreck. That and I had one pack of cigarettes. Jeff didn't look like he was going any where real soon so I asked him if he would keep an eye on Sonny for me. I could add to the family of cans. Jeff stayed and watched Sonny. I grabbed my scarf and headed to the grocery store around the corner. Come to think about it, everything I needed was around the corner. The grocery, the gas, the hospital. The school was even around the corner. The corner was just a little bigger. For that matter, everything is really right around a corner.

While waiting in line to pay for the coffee, I noticed some pins for sale. Buttons if you will. A black round button that read in white letters: I LIKE BOYS. Right under it was one the same in coloring, but it read: I LIKE GIRLS. I grabbed one of each. On the bottom shelf there was a basket with odd pins. I found one that almost passed for brass old and worn. It said: When God throws you lemons. Make lemonade. I knew I had been hit with the sour yellow footballs many suns and moons so I got the small rectangular pin too. I attached it to my scarf right after I paid for it. It looked good there so that's where it stayed.

I couldn't wait to show Jeff the pins. He wasn't as excited as me. He didn't know and understand me yet. It was a wee bit too soon to tell him everything. He told me he was going home to get cleaned up and asked if I needed anything. I told him no. He said that he would be back over in about an hour. It didn't matter to me. He wasn't going to come back. Why should he, I thought? And what's with this "he" thinks that me and the kids need someone to take care of us? I'm doing just fine. I looked around the house. It's neat. It's clean and it was the eighth of March. I grabbed for the pen already at the table, got a sheet of paper and began writing them. 3,8, 7, and 30 for the pills. It would be Mayors birthday this month. It would be Shorty's birthday on that same day, the 21st. It would be Hermits birthday before them both on the 14th. Is there something I'm missing? I asked myself. Self stated, "Yeah. Your cans." "Thank you." I said. "You're welcome," said Self. 140 cans, I thought. Gotta open one and get a fresh pot going. After

I opened the 139th can and made more coffee, I wrote 139 down with the 3,8,7 and the thirty for the pills, I rolled some more pot into joints.

I smoked the pot and drank the coffee. Checked the paper and the horoscopes. I had to see what they said. I had to read all the signs that pertained to me. And they did. I read Gentry's. A Virgo. I read mine. Capricorn. I read Pope's a Sagittarius. I even read Mayor's, the Aries. Ladie was a Leo. She made it obvious talking about her hair like she was a lion. I kept up on Prof's. Cancer. Know your enemies I told myself.

Just for fun I read the pet adds. I found an ad for free puppies. I had always been a cat lover but I was thinking about Sonny. He was five and old enough to be responsible in taking care of one. Always thought that a little boy and a puppy were so cute together.

As luck came my way and it didn't much before, Jeff came back and on time. I was happy to see him. He came in and sat at the table. He looked so cute, I thought. We had coffee and talked. Told me that he lived off of Monroe Street on a corner house with his mom. It was only minutes away on foot and that's the route that he took. Jeff wasn't driving because his license was under suspension. It made me feel good to know he wanted to come and see me. I waited for the right time to tell him who I really was.

Rather than jumping right into Eve, I told him that I was going to get a puppy. I explained that I already called the people who were running the add. Told him that I was hoping he'd come back so I could hurry and get the pick of the litter. Once again he had no problem with me driving a little ways out of the way for the pup. He watched Sonny for me and I was off. The driving was about a half hour from my house out in the boonies somewhere. The lady gave me great directions and I found the big farm house and pulled in the long drive. Parked, got out, walked up to the door and rang the bell. I heard a dog barking beyond the door. The man of the house answered and said, "Are you the gal from Sandusky who wants a puppy?" "Yes. I'm Cappy. How many do you have?" "Oh! I'm sorry. Come in Cappy. It's cold out there," he said. "She had, the mother had... What I mean is the mom had 9 this time. It's her second litter." In the kitchen, I saw the man's wife who looked at her husband and said, "It was ten. She had ten this time!"

She walked into the dining room and said, "Hi Cappy. I keep the mother and the puppies down in the basement. Come on I'll show you." I followed her through the kitchen and down the wooden steps that led to the puppies. They were all so adorable but one stood out above the rest. I pointed to it and said, "Is that one a male?" "Yeah he sure is. He's a cutie isn't he? Do you want to pick him up?" she asked. "Yes." His little ears were floppy and his eyes were darker brown. His coat was jet black and white-white. His front paws were touched with white and little black spots. His black tail was curled and soft. I looked at the Mrs. and said, "Yeah. I want him. What two dogs made this little guy?" "Well his father is a Smore and the mother is a Cocker Spaniel. Only I think he favors his mother. That's mamma over there," she pointed. The mother was a pretty dog. She wasn't a small dog, she wasn't a big dog. She was just right. The one I was holding would be a little bigger than his mom being a male and I couldn't wait to see him grow up. I thanked the lady and the man for the cute puppy they let me have. Told them that I'd take good care of him and so would my kids.

I put the little guy in the car and we were off and going north back to my house. I turned the radio on looking for Beatles or Floyd. Somehow one of the bands would always be on one of the stations I listened to every time I got into the car. Is was getting to where I could tell one of the kids to tune in the local FM station because I knew The Beatles were playing. Buff was astounded. Jules was impressed. Sonny didn't care one way or the other. He just wanted to get to where ever we were going, so he could get back to the house and eat.

Well on the way home with the puppy sitting in my lap, I thought about what to call him. It had to be something special. I looked at his bright colored coat of black and white. "Thomas Edison" came to mind. Before there was light, everything was dark. At least that's what "they" say. "Edison" invented the light bulb. Flip of a switch and you have light. Edison would be one of his names without question. How nice! No question! Petting him I said, "Who else would you like to be?" No he didn't answer but you know who did and she said, "Why not Maxwell." "Hmm," I said, "Maxwell like the coffee or "Maxwell Edison" in The Beatle song "Maxwell's Silver Hammer"? "Perfect!" I exclaimed. "Naturally," said Self. "It's still missing something I thought. It needs more. What? What? "A middle name." A voice was spoken. I heard it before. Talking to myself was one of my favorite things. At least I listened. "Okay. What would be a good middle name? And don't tell me. It'll come to me. Ah yes! His entire name will be Maxwell LP. Edison? LP. for albums." I looked briefly at the little pup and said, "You like that? You're Maxwell LP. Edison. You stand for a lot!" I couldn't wait to get him to the house. The girls were in school but Sonny was home. He fell for Maxwell right away. It was the picture that was always so cute in my head. A boy and his puppy, then the puppy was fed.

Max was 11 weeks old when he came to live with me and my three plus one. See how sneaky the fours can be? Jeff reminded me to get the little guy his shots when he turned 12 weeks old. Then he said that he had worms. This worried me. My Maxwell LP. Edison with worms? No way. "Jeff he can't have them. We gotta get rid of them. What can we get him? Capsules or pills? Do we give him drops? I don't like seeing the little guy dragging his tummy like that. It has to bother him. Are you going to say something or aren't you going to help me?" "Geez Caps. If you would slow down a little I could say something. I got some stuff at my mom's house. I'll run over there and get it. He'll feel better in a few days, but it will take a little longer before all the worms are gone." "Thanks Jeff. When can you get it? Are you sure you have the right stuff? Is your mom and dad going to mind you using it or is it yours? Do you have a dog Jeff?" I liked being the one to throw questions, but Jeff interrupted me and said, "Caps, I'll go right now. Be back in about fifteen minutes." I gave Jeff a big thank you hug and he went to his parent's house.

I went to the phone book and looked up the number of the best veterinarian in town. I made the appointment for Maxwell and marked it on the calendar. Then I noticed another marked day. A dentist and patient meeting. I would be that patient. I hated going to the dentist. What more could they do? I barely had anything left that was mine. I made a mental image of the number day I had to go. Number 13. A one then a three. Like God and me. This was carefully planned so I armed myself with my pen and my hand.

The girls were now coming in from a day at school. Both of them talking at the same time, trying to tell me what they did in school that day was going through one ear and out the other. They didn't have a clue. Jules and Buff were too excited once the puppy came over to their feet. "Oh mom!" Jules said, "You got a puppy? How come you didn't tell us you were getting one?" she asked. I couldn't get an answer in because Buff started in with questions. "Mom! Where did you find him? Did you buy him? What are we going to name him?" This was too much for me but to handle. But I was supposed to. "Girls. One at a time. First, I didn't know I was going to get him till I read yesterday's paper. I didn't buy him I got him for free. A couple out in the country had ten to choose from. Maxwell was the cutest." "Mom, that's a perfect name for him. You drink that coffee. And the cans!" Buff said laughing. I had to tell the girls what his name was in full. I said, "Wait now. You don't think I would give this little puppy one name do you? His whole name is Maxwell L.P. Edison!" Buff and Jules loved his name. Jules said, "What's LP. stand for?" "It's what a record is called," I said. "Yeah but mom," Buff cut in, "LP. could stand for lucky puppy." "Hmm," I said, "There's no reason why it can't stand for both."

The rest of the night was centered around Maxwell Edison. He was adorable. Me and Jeff told the kids to take it easy with him until he felt better. He told them about the worms. The kids understood that Maxwell was no toy. They gently pet him till he was ready to play and tumble. Jeff was right. By March 11th he wasn't running his stomach along the floor. He stumbled and fumbled and looked so cute doing it. On the evening of the eleventh

I stayed up with Maxwell until I could teach him to speak. Then to speak pretty. He already had the sitting part down pat. The kids taught him that in the early evening. It was after 11 p.m. before I got to thinking about how to do it. I didn't have any treats. I only had his food. Guess that's what I'm supposed to use, I thought. Jeff was already asleep on the couch.

I turned on the boom box. I had taped the song "Maxwell's Silver Hammer" off a radio station on a cassette. I popped in the tape. I forwarded it to the song and sang along, singing it to Maxwell. His curly tail was wobbling around in excitement. He was softly and playfully growling. I looked at him and said, "Are you talkin' to me Max?" He liked the new sound he just learned he could make. I had to turn the music off to listen to him. He was laying about ten feet from where I was standing. I bent over and sang. " … Maxwell Edison, majoring in medicine calls her on the phone..." Maxwell sat up. He growled lightly. He knew his name. "Maxwell! Tonight I'm teaching you to speak." I went into the kitchen and he slip-slided behind, right behind me. I grabbed a few pieces of his food, squatted down on the kitchen floor and showed him a bite. He sniffed it and I pulled it away. I said, "Maxwell. Speak!" I made his growling sound. He cocked his head and stared at me with his tail just a wiggling. "Come on Maxwell. Speak boy!" I made like him and growled. He growled. I repeated the words and he growled again. I gave him the bite of food. I could see he was looking for more to eat. I wanted to see if he would remember what I had taught him. I made the little guy wait till I drank a cup of coffee.

Without giving him fair warning I said, "Maxwell. Speak!" Ah ha! He did. I gave him another bite, picked him up like a little baby and said, "You're one smart puppy Maxwell LP. Edison. Now you're gonna learn to speak pretty. I'll have to get down on the floor with you again, but I don't mind. I know you'll learn this fast. Come on Max." He growled a little growl and wig-waggled his tail about waiting. I asked him to sit. He sat. I said, "Maxwell. Speak pretty! Come on. Speak pretty!" I barked like a dog. I repeated this a second time. I showed him the bite of food. He growled. "No Maxwell. Speak pretty, like this..." I barked and barked. Jeff came into the kitchen and thought it was the pup. I told him that I was doing the arf-arf sounds trying to teach Maxwell to speak pretty. Jeff said, "Could you two hold the racket down. Arf a little quieter will ya? You should try to get some sleep Cap; it's almost three in the morning. Do you ever sleep?" 'Why should I?" I asked.

Jeff said nothing and returned to the couch. I continued with school. "Okay Max. Maybe we were getting a little loud. Okay, I lied. It was me, but it was supposed to be you. I don't want to be up barking all night. So let's just learn one more thing tonight, I know you can do it boy." I didn't bother showing him the treat. I said, "Maxwell, speak." he growled. I said, "Maxwell, speak pretty!" I did an arf-arf. Max copied. I said it again. He barked again. I pet him and hugged him and told him how smart he was. I had another cup of coffee and a joint. I was going to put Maxwell to "the test"! I cleaned his bowl and gave him some fresh water. He drank it right up. I finished the joint and still had coffee. "Maxwell!" I called for him. "Sit!" He sat. "Maxwell, speak!" He growled. "Okay Maxwell. Speak pretty!" He barked a few barks. I was so happy I clapped and applauded him. This woke Jeff. This didn't upset Jeff. He tiredly walked into the kitchen and said, "You two are still at it." "Stay up with us will ya Jeff. Come on." "Are you kidding! Somebody has to get the girls ready for school. Will you just try to keep it down so I can get some sleep and take care of things in the morning?" "Maxwell can speak and speak pretty. He's so smart! I'm sorry if things got a little loud. He knows it now so I won't need to bark anymore. Go on back to sleep. We'll be quiet. I'll just make some coffee and write, draw something maybe." Jeff thanked me for the peace and quiet he was now going to get. He curled up on the couch and within minutes he was sound asleep.

The coffee was being made and so were joints. I sat at the guard table.

The day turned 10 am. It was time to get Maxwell Edison to the vet. He had a bath hours ago. He was going to be a beautiful dog when he grew up I thought. Jeff was on deck and had already taken over the ship. He got the girls up for school. Made them breakfast, combed their hair and took care of Sonny. Me? I did what I wanted.

I left the house with sweet smelling Max and we were off. The vets was only minutes away. Like The Barrel. All the other dog and or puppy owners were fascinated with Max. Me and Max sat on the floor. He was sitting for me. He spoke and he spoke pretty. When a couple people asked how old he was and how long it took me to teach him they didn't believe me. Really, they didn't!

It was time for Maxwell's first check up. The Doc' came in and said, "That's a fine looking Cocker Spaniel, what's his name?" Looking briefly at his chart he said, "So you're Maxwell LP. Edison." He pet Max and playfully made him feel at home. "Doc," I said, "You called Maxwell a Cocker Spaniel. Why's that? I wonder because his father is a Smore and his mother is what you said. Isn't he just a mutt?" "No. He's all Cocker Spaniel. It can happen that way. You're lucky to have him. Did you buy him?" he asked. "No. He was free." "That makes you even luckier. People sell Spaniel pups for about 200 a piece these days." "Really? Hmm. I'll have to tell my oldest daughter about this. She said the L.P. could stand for lucky puppy." The doctor gave Maxwell his shots. Told me that I was doing a fine job in caring for him. Hell, I knew that. I was sent back to the receptionist for my bill. Luck didn't usually come my way, not good luck but today it had. I didn't have to pay in full. They broke the payments down to three. No! I am not making this up. I remember everything. I know the numbers and they go on in spaces. I know details, the places and especially people's faces.

Back at the house, Jeff had just finished getting Sonny fed, cleaned and dressed. He was doing the dishes. I told him about Maxwell's visit to the vets. Enough about the blessed dog. I had the next day to think about. The dentist! The nice little men who can only pull or fill a tooth because you got welfare insurance. I would have paid back for the crowns Pope! This is a problem, I thought. They certainly aren't going to give me tooth-by-tooth-implants!

I needed to get my mind off of the dentist and told Jeff I was going shopping. I wanted to get some scarves, bandannas. Ones that looked kinda like a man's hanky. You know, those reds and blues. Throw some white in them. I wasn't one to shop at the mall because I hated the mall. I worked at the mall. I stood on soft carpet in heels at the mall. I sold the shoes to the people who walked on the soft carpet making their shoes more comfortable and they would buy them from the mall. I ran my feet off at that mall and that's all. "Hold on Capri," I said to myself, "You made an important speech at that mall!" "Yes. I did." I replied. I didn't want to remember it. It flashed through me like a cold soul.

"Jeff I'm going to the mall. Back soon. Bye bye Sonny." I was out the door before Jeff had a chance at choice.

I drove out to "The Sandusky Mall" and parked out in front. Went into a small shop. It had small items for women. Costume jewelry necklaces, belts, hats, gloves and this and that. In the back of the store I found the bandannas I was looking for. The colors were too many to mention. I had to buy the right colors. They had to mean something to me. A reason for buying them in the first place. I forgot the reason and bought thirteen. What caught my eye most was the label. Each had this printed in and on a corner. "Freedom. Made in America With Pride."

Leaving with a well framed mind, I went to the location where I made the speech. I spoke to John in a whisper, "Remember? It was right up there John." I saw that a few people over heard me having this conversation with no one. I thought they would never understand how my dreams turned into false hopes and enraged out of controls.

Days later, when it hit me that Lennon was shot I wasn't sure whether to believe it or not. I grew teary eyed. I sat at a fountain and hung my head weeping. I missed hearing a new release by John. I missed news of him. I miss wondering if The Beatles would ever get together. Millions shared this common question. We got the answer on December 8th. The day I moved into the house. I had to compose myself quick and get the hell out of the mall. I ran down the long hall that led to all the glass doors. I located my piece of shit car and headed for a plaza. There was a real dirt cheap store there. I wanted one more thing. A new top. A blouse, a shirt, something. From my car I already saw the long blouse hanging just inside the store. It was bright yellow. It had small swirls and odd shapes in bright rich colors of red, blue, purple, green, white and black. Best of all it had a long tail on the front and back. I slipped it on over my tee shirt. The tails reached to just above my knees. The buttons started at the collar and went all down the front. Black buttons. It was four bucks and I had to have it. I took up to the cashier. In an isle close by was a brass bell. It stood about 5 inches tall. It only cost one teeny tiny dollar. I had the bandannas, the shirt and a bell. Drove back to the house to show Jeff.

He could have cared less about what I got at the store. It was a woman thing. I took the new things back to the dining room table where a puzzle was usually in the making. I laid the bandannas out next to my jeans and shirt. This was one wild outfit and I couldn't wait to see how I was going to where everything. Just then something in my brain took me to The Barrel. The way I hung straws off an earring to count the drinks. I could do that with some of the scarves. I could tie one at each ankle. I had to make sure that when I tied the bow at my ankle that the built in label would be perfect in view. I folded the scarf in the shape of a triangle. Jimmy taught me this. Where the two corners meet you begin folding in towards the longest area of the scarf. Inch by inch I had it folded just so. I tied it around my ankle and made the bow as best as I could. You could clearly read the nickel-sized label. I did the same to my other ankle. Since I already had the jeans on I tied a corner of a scarf on the right belt loop. I took the bottom end of that scarf and attached another one. I added two more to those and repeated the process on the other side of my jeans. That took care of ten but there were three more to go. I tied one around my forehead. It passed above my ears, through my hair, where it ended up tied at the back of my neck. This was a good look. I made sure that the label would be center on my forehead. It was obvious to me where the last two would be folded and tied. I put one on my thigh just above my knee and did the same thing with the last, except it was on the other leg. I put the shirt on. I pinned on the buttons at the collar. One on each corner. I put the lemonade pin on one of the large pockets that hung lower that my jean pockets. This was convenient-apparel. I could put my cigarettes in the pocket, my matches, my keys, my ID, my comb, my lipstick and compact. I had to go out and try it out. Told Jeff that I would be back later and went to The Barrel. I walked in and got all kinds of expressions and stares from the people at The Barrel and it was cracking me up. You couldn't help but notice or wonder!

I had a few drinks there. Had a few laughs with the regulars. Had to get to the house. I rushed through the door like the boogie man was after me. I was totally out of breath and short-winded. I knew I needed a cigarette and quick. The illegal kind. I got the pot from the sugar bowl and smoked a bunch of roaches that accumulated over time. The resin buzz was best. I grabbed a couple of nerve pills and had a cold cup of Maxwell House. The cans number didn't grow any further since the last count. There were 140 of them. Did I need any more?

That evening at the house I sat at the table writing numbers and numbers and more numbers. Dates and times. Birthdays. The falls, summers, winters and spring thing numbers. Pope's age, my age, Jeff's age, my kids ages, my brothers three and Mayor who would be 56. The year I was born. Well, one of them anyway.

Jeff was upstairs tucking the kids into bed for the night. I called up to him. "Jeff. I need you to come down here a minute and hurry!" I had been bugging him the entire night with numbers and things and he was well worn with my questions and ideas. I was going to win the lottery, remember? He answered me with exhaustion, "What is it now Cappy? I don't know why you don't sleep. You need to get some rest. Listen to yourself." "I am listening to myself and Self wants to know if you know anything about boats." Jeff looked at me troubled and asked, "Why?" "Didn't you say you were a carpenter or you are a carpenter? Because if you can build a house, it can't be that much harder to build a boat. Could you build a boat Jeff?" I asked. He was brief and said, "If I had all the right tools. Why?" On I went, "Damn Jeff. If you could build a boat, and not just any boat, say one about 50 feet, customize it, make it special, how much do you think it would sell for?" "I never thought about. I guess a person could sell it for about 250 thousand. I don't know. Maybe more" "No kidding Jeff? How long would it take to build one if you had everything you needed?" I asked in excitement. "If I worked on nothing but a boat it might take about six months or so." And he said it so laid back, I couldn't hold back. "Jeff you and I could have a lot of money."

We could live in Montana at one of the national parks. Be the care-takers. The parks are closed all winter. You could build one boat every winter. Each boat could be unique. Have its' own personality. Everyone of them should be designed a little different. Hell we could go all out on the interiors. People could special order one. In that case they would have to pay at least 300 thousand dollars! They wouldn't mind a wait. People like buying something hand-made and original. Shit Jeff you could retire after making about four or five boats. That would be an easy million. Handle it right and it could take care of you and me and all of us the rest of our lives." "A million could do that Caps but you have to have the money to get started. You'd have to have thousands of dollars to get the materials for a boat that size."

Then I explained that that was the very reason I had to work with the numbers. "Jeff. If I keep working at the numbers I'll hit the lottery and give you the money for the first boat. Shit! You wouldn't need to build the boat. We'd already have the millions." I laughed and laughed. Jeff chuckled and shook his head. Then the conversations took a turn to serious and he asked this question, "Capri, why don't you let me fix you something to eat. I've been here a week? I don't ever see you eating. You can't live on coffee." "Jeff I wasn't going to say anything but I wear an upper denture. If I eat, the plate puts pressure on that little muscle between your lip and gum. It hurts like hell because the fucking little muscle in my mouth is swollen now. I cut into twice chewing and it's not going to happen a third time. You think I'm going to hurt myself on purpose? I'm fine. I don't need to eat! Okay!" My voice was enraged.

Jeff remained calm and said, "Alright Caps. You don't need to yell. Christ, you're gonna wake those kids up there. The only reason I wanted you to eat is because you're nothin' but skin and bones." "Oh!" I said, "So you think I'm a bag of bones huh? Who do you think moves that fucking piano from wall to wall when I change the living room around every six months? I do because I can. I bitch slapped this one guy down to the ground and he was six feet tall. Not a punk. Not skin and bones. Shit I arm wrestled a guy standing up, both of us. I put him to his knees and you think I need to eat?" I was extremely agitated. I stood at my spot in the kitchen wanting bad to hit or break something.

Who can write on a night like tonight? It's September. The ninth month. It's the year 1999. It's 1999! The time is 11:55 p.m. Good! Today at the store I wrote out the checks date just like this: 9-9-1999. Being in a mood I had to say something to the clerk about numbers. "Will you look at all those nines!" She laughed and agreed about the nines saying, "There are way too many nines in this!" Earlier in the evening I was thinking about "the" 9's. I knew right then I had to add those nines and they came to 54. I added the 5 and the 4 and came up with a nine. I divided it by three and got a three. And the time was 11:55 when I wrote it above. I thought that this was a good number. Then I had to add it up it comes to a 12. That's another three. "Enough, I can't do this anymore." "Remember Caps. Therapy." Yeah me and myself still talk to each other... when no one else can hear.

Today, in the present, I wanted to break something I couldn't afford to replace. Since money is tight, I went to the grocery store because I was supposed to. I grabbed the few things I needed. Most of the people waiting to get checked out did. I was behind them about fifth in line. I spoke so all could hear me, but the words were directed to the cashier who sees me about every other day. With perfect pronunciation I commanded, "Let's get another line open over here." The clerk looked over and said, "I thought that was you. What are doing? Did the harvest come in or something?" "No. I own this place. I own a lot of stuff. To be frank, I own just about everything in Erie County." A young black girl was in front of me with her little baby and said, "Then tell me how I'm supposed to get 12 dollars of food with the 11 I got." I said politely, "Simple. Just walk out the door without paying!" She made like she was going to do that when I heard the old lady behind me laughing. I was on a roll. So was the cashier. With my hand cupped to the side of my mouth I announced, "Attention! Attention all shoplifters..." Cashier continued saying..."Yes. Shoplifters. The specials are in isle five." "Really! What's the point paying the cops if don't got somebody committing a crime? Hell if my hands weren't so full I'd be down that isle rackin' up the free-bees."

Cashier, me, the old lady behind me, the old man behind her and the young black mother with the baby all must have been thinking I was out of my mind. They tried hard not to let me see them laugh. I turned to the people behind me and said, "And the great government pays me to be like this! Now who's crazier, me or them? Go out of your mind and get a check a month for life." By this time I was checking my items and the clerk said, "You found the harvest alright! Having a little fun today huh?" "Hell yes I am! But no. No harvest. I am having the worst life this life today. I thought perhaps I'd pop into the mental hospital for a short vacation. I might even wanna live there. They have a room with my name on the door. Why wait? Miss out on all the good times going on in there? The place is a fricking scream! Hell! I loved it there!" I'm not so sure that the old woman and man in line fully understood what they were hearing. They looked at me with puzzles and worry. I didn't want them thinking I might be some insane-criminal-type or something. Whatever they were thinking I had to clear the matter before I broke camp. "Hey! What can I say? It's true. My own kids think I'm nuts. You can laugh. I do, but I gotta go to the place that makes me this way. Spend a couple hours there and see what you turn into!" Well the old lady broke up at last. This made for a good exit so I calmly and dramatically said to the cashier, "Well I think I'll drive over to the drug store and "really" act up."

I left the store in my car and headed to the house. I did the normal things I do in the evening. As little as possible. Then I came up to my room and I sat at "the fucking desk" trying to tell you the story and I can't. I want to draw. I want to listen to music real loud. Sing, something, anything! I gotta know that I can get through this without losing my mind. But I started it and I have to finish it. I gotta get through it once and for all. I know my life and I know it well. Writing the first draft was lived-again-hell. The start that was simple but I need the number that will mark the last page. So I wrote the book over again. That is three times too many and I'm short in the calm. Where I end up is where I belong.

All of this just to keep my mind off the dentist the next day. I stayed up. I drank my coffee; I smoked my pot and played with the numbers. Singing was becoming a struggle so I sang in whispers.

The next day came. I knew it would. I headed over to see the family dentist. They took an x-ray. You sit down in chair and rest your chin on a tray. A machine that takes the pictures of your teeth and bones goes all around your head. It quick its easy. But it led to a problem after the dentist looked over the black and white pictures. He called me back into his office and said, "Capri. I think I want to send you and these x-rays to the specialist in town. I'm not real sure what's wrong. It's your left jaw bone. It's very thin." "Thin? Doc, what do you mean?" "I can only guess as to what the problem is since I don't have another x-ray to compare. It's possible you were born with it. It could be that your jaw is deteriorating and lastly it could be cancer." While he looked at the charts I said, "Doc. Cancer? There is no way it can be cancer. I gotta sing! You don't know how long I dreamed of being a singer! Can it be fixed? What needs to be done? Who are you sending me to, the specialist I mean? Can I go see him now?" The Doc heard my questions in panic and said he would call the specialist on the phone right away. After the call was made, me and my x-ray left, and we headed straight to a small medical building right around the corner from house. I told you that's where everything was.

Fortunately for me I didn't have to wait. This new doctor was interested in viewing my jaw the minute I walked in the door. On the lighted screen he pointed out what was wrong. He said, "Capri. The bones in your face on the right are normal. Now look at this side, your left, where the joint is. It's almost as thin as a dime! It looks like the bone is deteriorating. I'd like to send you to Akron. There's a TMJ center and doctors who specialize in things such as this." I was freakin' out in the chair and had to stand up and get things straight with this man. "Doc. You don't understand. I have to sing. I gotta make a record." He answered with concern, "You also have to eat Cappy. But be careful about what you eat. Take smaller bites. Maybe try softer food." He still didn't get it! "Doc. I don't eat. I don't have time. I have to get one song recorded. Just one!" "Cappy, you have to eat to stay alive. I want to get an appointment for you over in Akron as soon as possible. You're bone is so thin that if I were you I'd be careful when you need to yawn. It could break." "Okay. Okay. I understand. But what can they do to make it right? I'm in a hurry." I said. "I can't say for sure what they will do for you. They may want to reconstruct your jaw. They may take out the jaw bone that's thin and replace it with one of your ribs. This isn't something that heals in a day Capri. Your mouth would be wired up a good six to eight weeks. That's why I'm encouraging you to concentrate more on eating. If the doctors decide to do this procedure you'll need to gain some more weight because you will definitely lose weight."

That was all I wanted to hear. "Bye Doc. Thanks for seeing me on such short notice, but I gotta sing while I can. I don't have two months." I didn't listen to anything else he said I was already out of his office. I walked out of the building and back to my house leaving my car in the parking lot.

On the way home, (2 minutes tops), all I could think about was what I had just heard. My jaw could break if I yawn? I gotta sing! What happens if I yawn too big and it does break? "Then you're fucked," Self said. "Yeah," I answered, "I would be fucked for good wouldn't I?"

To the house I got and through the door. I went straight to the piano. Conveniently I put the shadow box right above it where I could reach the pot with ease. I reached for a pre-rolled doob and lit up. I sang and sang and sang. Jeff was trying to get my attention. I ignored him until minutes went into hours. I played and sang from 4 that after noon until about 9 that night. Then I went to the guard table.

Anybody that I talked to I yelled at. It was the only way for me to get my voice out and I did for days. Jeff couldn't take it anymore and said, "Capri, give it a rest. You haven't stopped singing or talking since you got here!" He angered me. In a demon-like-voice, I filled with rage and yelled, "Get the fuck out of my face and leave me alone. Go to fucking hell on your way out!"

An abrupt silence crashed around me and the house. Jeff walked away into the darkened living room. My eyes followed his steps. He was going through what few books and magazines I had by the light of the television. While he did what he was doing, I did what I had always done. I thought. And the only thing I could think of at the moment was what and how I talked to Jeff only moments ago. Where did that voice come from, I asked myself? I didn't have the answer.

Jeff walked over to the kitchen table where I was sitting. I knew I had to tell him I was wrong but when I started talking he said, "Cappy honey, you don't have to say you're sorry, just stop yelling. Somebody's gotta watch out for those kids or you're going to lose them! Why don't you just be quiet tonight? Let everybody else get some rest. Do something quiet. Why don't you read something!" And Bam! Of all the books he could have put on the table in front of me, he chose a Beatle book. Jeff walked into the living room, sat on the couch, propped his feet on the coffee table and fixed a stare to the television saying nothing.

I took the book from the table. The title: "The Love You Make." I opened the cover remembering that I never read it. It was a gift from Prof's sister for the both of us on Christmas of 1983. I quickly closed the book and held it tightly in my hands. This is the last thing I need now, I thought.

I didn't want to read! I didn't even want to look at the cover. But I held on to it. I stood it on the table pages closed. Someone had written across them: Love You. Who I thought? When? I asked myself. Furthermore... Why? A question I could answer at last. I'm supposed to read this book. That's why. So "Y" was where I chose a place to start, making sure I found the exact page where the ink finished the letter. I opened it. It was page number 396. The first line that caught my eyes were these: " ... John was the only one missing..."

I reached for the pen on the table and wrote the dates. Third line up from the last line I had read in the paragraph. "April 27, 1981" The day that "Ringo Starr" married actress "Barbara Bach."

I wrote down 4, slash, 27, dash, 1981. I toyed with the numbers. "4, hmm," I mumbled. "Four Beatles. Four blue jays, four coffee pots, four radios, four telephones and four thirds. And I thought everything happened to me in threes!"

Like a genie inside the book, wanting to be magic lamp, I found it hard to resist and rubbed my hands over the words in it. I kept page 396 marked and began to read from where I had caught that one line about John.

The words began to make more and more sense as I read them. And the numbers were endless. Every month, or numbered day, or money and taxes I wrote them that way. Pages upon pages were strewn on the guard tables with numbers I had found in the book. You'd think I was a messy kinda book keeper if you gave it a quick look.

Book in one hand, and writing the numbers here and there. The story had grown importantly rare. When I reached the part about an island somewhere off the coast of Spain, I was certain that this was a hoax. Nobody is really writing about some fuckin' island off the coast of Spain somewhere out there. That's "Goose Island" they are writing about. "My God in Heaven," I thought out loud, "This book is about me!" I kept quietly thinking. My jaw. The rib. Goose Island. God we both know that's all that's left of the Garden of Eden. Than I am number three. I am Eve. I spoke to Number One and said in whispers, "I'll be there on that island on the 27th of April. I have something I want to give You. It doesn't belong to me. Maybe Doc' was right. I might have an extra rib! The Rib!"

Chapter Twenty One: "The Book. The Bell. John Lennon Is Well"

There had to be a reason for this Beatle book. What was wrong with my thinking? Oh sure, I know... I have to read it three times. After that, thinking was effortless.

Simple, I thought! This book contains vital information that has to do with now. It most definitely goes in Lennon's direction. The direction that made millions upon millions of people believe John was shot dead. Why not? The hoax about Paul's death went overboard. People looked for messages here and there. Hunted through the albums for a picture, a clue. The fools. We the fools. And fooled we were. But I knew different. The Beatles would never do something like that again. Or would they? Of course they could. Why not invent the notion that John Lennon was shot and killed on December 8th, 1980? Sad news that would travel around the world with certainty and tears. The dream of the Beatles ever being again would be erased from all of us who loved them dearly. Without John Lennon the dream was over. But what if it wasn't over? What if John Lennon, the man who was shot and killed at the "Dakota" wasn't John Lennon at all? What if that man was just a look-alike? And maybe that look-alike was hired to do a job while John Lennon was getting settled in the states.

What was this man's job? He would be the one walking the walk. The walk that led him to the archway of Lennon's home where he would be shot five times, "Hollywood" style. Where was the real John Lennon when this mystery man was being whisked off to be saved? He was going for a ride with Paul, George and Ringo that would take the four of them to a place where they would not be discovered until they were damn good and ready. They knew that this would be the greatest hoax. The world would be filled with the magic of the Beatles again. And The Beatles would take their proper place on earth. Not only as the most popular band but the greatest rock and roll band that God ever wanted... again.

This was more than a stunt for publicity. The four of them knew that their names were already living on. But the world would be amazed and half crazed when they learn that sometimes more than a name lives on. Like John Lennon! He isn't dead! Christ it's all in this blessed book!

I damned myself for not reading it sooner. The big picture was very "right in front of me" all along. And I was going to be part of it all. The slow twirling cloud spelled LISTEN. To what? To who? Maybe music! Maybe merry go round music? Like the kind you can find at Cedar Point about 15 going on 16 ! years ago when I was 15 years old goin' on 16 and I rode that merry go round with nobody else but John Lennon himself. I spoke to John hoping he could hear me and said, "Ya had to get off the merry go round 'cause I was too young back then. You would have to wait for me to grow up. Fucked up when I married Professor! You had to act fast and three years later you pretended to pass. It's been 9 years! You like the number nine. It brings you back to me 'cause I'm three all the time! My name's hidden in your musical schemes. I know all the words and I know what they mean. The nine years in the making and the day is coming fast. You were never in the line of fire you're the present not the past.

Page 396 and I added the numbers. I wasn't surprised by the sum. It was number nine when I was done. It was number me when I was done.

"Maxwell" I called, "Here boy, we gotta learn something new today." Had to teach my smart little pup how to speak without the sound of my voice.

I reached for the brass bell that took a place on the shadow box. I told Max to sit. He sat. "Maxwell I know you probably don't know what I am going to tell you but you'll figure it out won't cha." Max growled a happy growl. I asked him to speak. He did. I asked him to speak pretty. He did. Then I said, "Max! That was great! Now all you have to do is learn how to do it with this bell." I explained. His curly tail waggled as he walked up to the bell to check it out. He gave it a Spaniel sniff then looked at me like an A student wanting more knowledge.

"Maxwell LP. Edison! They may have to wire me shut for a couple months. Doctors might need to take a rib outta me to make my jaw right. That's why this bell is so important. Now watch me. I'll hold the little dinger here and tap it against the bell. Listen." I tapped the bell three or four times and said, "Maxwell speak." Of course he did. He knew the word. I tapped the bell softly again and said, "Speak Maxwell!" He spoke. It took no more training than that. I tapped the bell and said nothing. Maxwell spoke. "What a smart boy you are," I said petting and rubbing his belly. I took the bell again and tapped it using my finger. He spoke. I knew that he had this down. Just had to teach him to speak pretty! He was more than ready. I took the bell by the handle and shook it. I said, "Maxwell! Speak pretty." Yes, he barked. Again, the words. I did just what I had done before as far as lessons go. By the time I shook the bell the third time and said nothing, Maxwell barked and barked. A test would be next. The finals took place. Bell ringing. He spoke and spoke pretty by listening to just the bell. One job done well if I had to pat myself on the back for its completion. And I did.

That night, much later in the night I called my brother Hermit. He answered, "Hello." Emotions flooded with explosions and I stated, "I am Eve."

Hermit quickly said, "Then you are Noah's wife." The conversation escalated as I told Hermit about the book I had been reading. Hermit asked, "Ever hear of the book called "Catcher in the Rye"?" Sick rushings went through me and I said nervously, "Yes! It's in The Beatle book." "Cap," Hermit said, "Are you standing or sitting?" "Standing. Why?" I asked. "It's the kind of book that might give you the creeps." "Hermit, when I read the title the words kinda sound like it's saying catch her in the eye. Hermit, how creepy are you talking about? Is it going to scare me mindless?" "No," he said, "You just might want to sit down." I did. I took a step to my chair at the guard table. Hermit told me about the children playing a game on a hill of rye. Chills ran through me as he went into more detail. I looked at The Beatle book closed on the table in front of me. Listening to Hermit describe further on goings in "J.D. Salinger's" book, I opened mine and I opened it to the very page that read "Catcher in the Rye." "Hold on Hermit! I just opened this Beatle book right to the page where the title is. Damn! Don't think I want to hear any more about the story. Don't tell me. Better if it sounds like catch her in the eye. Me… my eyes. Me and somebody's eyes meeting. Maybe me and John Lennon's eyes." "Caps! You're forgetting something. John Lennon is dead." "Hermit, just because they say that John was shot and killed doesn't mean he really was. He could have had it staged. Maybe things weren't all that great at home for him. Maybe he wanted out. Maybe he wanted to be John Lennon The Beatles. Maybe he always wanted to Hermit. There are these pictures of him in this book and you can tell that some of them are not the real John Lennon. See there were two John Lennons. The one that got away and the one that was supposedly shot to death. Jesus I'm tellin' ya Hermit John Lennon is not dead! This is "The Magical Mystery Tour" and he's alive!" "Caps. It's all very possible but not likely." We spent the next two hours talking and talking. I talked Beatles. We both did.

I checked the date and it was the 15th of the month. A number to add. To make a six. That's divided by two, that's three. Me! Fifteen would be a positive number for me. I looked for the negative immediately. It was like questions. If one can question, than one can answer. Eight. The negatives 8's in my life. A tragic day in 1980. Four years and four blue jays later, I move in on that very eight. Of course the positive of that was nine. Being that John Lennon's birthday contained a nine on an October day. Making number nine more than positive. It's a few months longer than the nine years that passed when the greatest stunt unknown to the world would be known at last.

I had to talk to Jeff. He was asleep on the couch. I walked over to him and shook his shoulder "Jeff! Wake up! I have to tell you something very important. It's about you." Tiredly he sat up, rubbed his eyes, face and said,

"What is so important Capri? Couldn't it wait till morning?" "No it can't." I said. "I was talking to my older brother Hermit awhile ago and he said that if I am Eve than I am Noah's wife. Well that got me to thinking. You said you could build a boat if you had all the right materials and tools. You're Noah. See? You built the Ark. That's why you came here when you did. You came here because you thought you had to save me and the kids again. But you don't have to Noah. Because I thought I was supposed to marry Gentry Mocean III. After talking to Hermit I figured it might be you I was supposed to marry 'cause we were once. Can't have you or Gentry because I figured that John Lennon isn't dead at all. It's all in the book you told me to read. He's alive and I'm going to marry him because I'm supposed to. He's waited a long time for me. Almost 16 years Noah! He's been watchin' the Wheels alright. Watching me! This book is all about the time we met at Cedar Point. He played guitar all afternoon. We sat next to each other on the merry go round there. It was real Noah. You'll see how real this is like everyone else will. I can figure out when too because it's in the book. I'll know. The radio will help. They've been playin' lots of Beatles lately. Something is going on Noah I'm tellin' ya." "Jesus Christ Capri! You woke me up to tell me that I'm Noah and that you are going to marry John Lennon! Capri! He's dead." "He isn't!" I insisted." But Noah insisted that I go about my business and let him sleep.

So I did the business. Mine! How great it will be to see John after all these years!

I kept "WCPZ" radio station tuned in at all times. Certainly something would be said sooner or later. Why else would they be playing Beatles so much? Because they are being paid to, I thought. But by who? I watched out the window waiting for my blue jays. It was warmer than most days. I walked outside and the first thing I noticed was a silver car. It passed my house slowly. The men inside were all in sunglasses. Suit-and-tie-kinda-guys. No sooner did the silver car pass when another one was coming from the east. Same kinda guys in the car, sunglasses and all. They're watching me. They must be. Silver! The Beatles were once called "The Silver Beatles." That's why the silver cars, I thought. Just as I turned to go back inside for more coffee a third silver car passed by house. The men? The same.

I got more coffee but I stayed in the house. I locked the door. I had to be sure these were the good guys. Each time I looked out the window for a blue jay or just to look for a view, there was a silver car was going by the house. Never, but never did the men take off their sunglasses and I wanted to know who they were.

I phoned the radio station and a D.J. answered, "WCPZ." "Did you happen to notice all the silver cars in town? I asked, "Never mind. I might give it away. Play a Beatle song for me will ya? People need to know that I'm paying attention." "Okay!" he said, "Which one do you wanna hear?" "I am a die hard Beatle fan. I'll let you pick it out." "Okay. I get it. You don't want the wore-out-played-over-and-over-kinda-song. Got just the one for ya. Hell, I'll do a block. Where ya callin' from?" I answered, "My phone!" "Sandusky?" he asked. "I have to be." "Wanna share a first name without listeners?" (more questions...) "Sure, why not. I'm The Wheels." "Cool name ya got there, Wheels. Be glad to get some Beatles on for ya real soon. I'm kinda partial to them myself." "Thanks, I'm tapin' 'em Mr. D.J.!" "Thanks for listenin' Wheels. Call in a request anytime. By the way, you can call me Rick." "OK, Rick. Thanks again. I'm gonna get my cassette ready. Will you do me one more favor?" "Name it Wheels! I really love that name! Wheels!" "Me too Rick. Could ya not say anything until the songs start and end so I get a good recording. Can't quite afford cassettes if you know what I mean." "No problem. You got it Wheels. Enjoy!"

I went over to the boom box and set up the cassette. Fast forwarded it to a few seconds from the last song recorded. Hit the pause button, record button. Listened. Waited. "Ah ha ha." I cracked when the first song started. "You Know My Name. Look Up the Number." So I did. I peeked in the book for the number. It had to be in the book everything else was. Ah, and it was. 1975! I was eighteen, legal and you're were still alive. Something bad about number five. Like what it might feel like to be buried alive.

Song two was beginning to play, so I turned the volume up. "Watching the Wheels." Now I was rolling on the floor laughing. That dude really likes that name." "I do too!" Self exclaimed. No wonder Gentry starting calling me Big Time. He said that he couldn't be with me and he couldn't tell me why. This is why Big Time! He always introduced me as "one special lady." Was he paid to set me free? Or could he fore see? For sure he saw. He knew I wanted to marry John Lennon when I was seven years old and I continued wanting until 1980. I'm 32 now and half is sixteen and that makes a seven! Do the cloud stairs mean I'll finally reach heaven? Maybe I should listen to merry go round music.

Song number three was ready-set go and I loved it don't ya know. Rick chose the song "Revolution 1." My favorite "Revolution" song. He knew what to play and I was wondering what his fourth choice would be. It was perfect like he knew what I had been thinking. The last corner of the songs was "You Never Give Me Your Money" " ...What a sweet dream, came true, today..." Was the D.J. in on this too? There was something about my story that carried solidity. And it stayed that way.

I had errands to run and found the silver cars were more than just three! In fact silver cars were all around me. Everywhere I drove, down small streets and mains, the silver cars and sun-glassed men had always remained. Then out of the blue, white cars were passing up with the silver's and I didn't like the white cars. Naturally they were the bad guys. I watched for them and there were many. Behind the wheel I convinced myself that they were the bad guys. What was I into? There were so much around me that I headed back to the house and locked up tight the doors behind me.

I tried explaining to Noah that somebody was out to get me. That I must have said something to the wrong person. The bad guys wanted to get me and hold me for ransom. 500 million dollars. This was Big Time! Noah caringly explained that a lot of people drove silver and white cars, and wore sunglasses because of the sun. I didn't buy it. "Noah. I'll bet the "FBI" and the "CIA" are in on this. This is big money I'm talking! Lots and lots! Somebody could end up getting hurt or even killed. This plan was long in the making. I'm sure The Beatles saw to every detail. They won't let anything happen to me. Especially John. Jesus! It's been nearly 16 years! We have every right to start over without fail. We've earned it. Deserve it. Don't you think Noah?" Noah shook his head saying, "Capri what the hell are you talkin' about? And what makes you so sure that John Lennon is alive?

Why don't you eat something and get some sleep already!" It was the back to the not eating and sleeping thing I thought. "Noah. I only have so much time to get things done. I gotta call "Atlantic Records." I'm sure if I explain things, they will put me through to "Phil Collins." He must know by now that I'm supposed to call him to do one of my songs. I don't want no money Noah. I just want him to sing it. Make it great!" "Cappy nobody from Atlantic Records is going to put you through to somebody like "Phil Collins." He's probably home and if he isn't, they're not gonna give out personal information about his where abouts and phone number." "Noah, forget it. I'm calling." I was pissed off bad. "They know me Noah. They are paid to know me. Lots of people are. Watch all the silver cars Noah 'cause they're watchin' me. Don't ya know who I am? I am The Wheels. Big Time." Noah shook his head again. Was almost laughing. He seemed disturbed and said, "Caps. Go on and call. I can't tell you what to do. You won't listen to me." "You're right. I won't. If I listen to you I wouldn't get anything done on time. Time Noah! Numbers! I know the numbers. You watch me get through." I called information and got the number for the record company. A woman answered with a friendly good afternoon and a how may I direct your call? I said, "I know this may seem a little peculiar but I am supposed to talk to "Phil Collins" today at this time about a song of mine he's going to record." "What is your name Ma'am?" she asked. "I can't tell you my name. Just tell him that Wheels is on the phone he'll get right to it. He's expecting my call now and if you don't put me through this could cost me a half million dollars!" "Ma'am I'm sorry, but I can't give you any information on Mr. Collins. I can tell you that he isn't here. I'm also sorry to say that we are very busy here and don't have time for calls like this. Have a nice day!" She hung up. "She hung up on me Noah! Can you believe it?" "I told you Capri, but you won't listen. Come on why don't you eat something. I'll fix you whatever you want. I'll run and get ya a steak." "Ya gotta keep bringing up the food thing! Every fucking day you bring up the food, the sleep. I'm sick of it. Eat? You want me to eat? Okay Noah. I will. I'll eat something but it's gotta be fast and I'll make it." He stood at the kitchen table and watched me race for the cupboard that had the cereal boxes. I took the puffed rice. I filled a cereal bowl, dumped a couple teaspoons of sugar on it and got the milk out. Poured the milk, reached for a spoon and did it all in less than three minutes. Do you think it pleased Noah? Hell no. He told me that he was going to get some things from the store. I looked out and it was pouring down rain... didn't want to drive in it. Noah did and picked the kids up from school too.

I was really let down by the record company. Phil was expecting me. Now what am I supposed to do? I checked the Beatle book and there was nothing that indicated that I should have called Mr. Collins at all. I let it go and put it out of my mind quick. Called Ladie at The Barrel to see who was there. She said things were pretty slow and wanted me to drop in.

I told Noah that I wanted to get out. I needed to drive. He gave me a look that said I shouldn't because I wasn't sleeping. "Noah! Can't you understand that sometimes there are things that are more important than sleep." Buff came running down the stairs calling for me, "Mom! Can I go to a play at the high school. It doesn't cost anything and it's only for a two hours?" "Sure Buff. I think I can afford something free! I was just going over to see Ladie for a little while. I can pick you up when it's over. When's it start?" I asked. "4 o'clock." Buff said eagerly watching the clock. I was always checking it myself. "Well, it's ten to four now Buff. Are ya ready?" "Yeah! Let's go! Mom, could I have a dollar for a pop or something if they have it?" I reached in my jean pocket and gave her two. I turned to Noah and said, "I'll give Buff a ride and see ya shortly after the church bells ring." To my surprise Noah had been paying some attention and said, "Oh, okay. Sometime after six. Well just be careful driving. I'll keep an eye on Jules and Sonny here. Fix 'em something to eat. You might want some when ya get back." I turned to Noah and gave him that look. That look he was getting was me saying: Don't start on me with the fucking food eating thing now! I was in no mood to be verbal. Got Buff to the play. Behind me, I noticed a silver car closely behind mine in the drive of the school.

One man alone. No sunglasses I thought as I watched him in the rear view mirror.   Why doesn't he pull up closer so I can make out his face? Thought by now he would pull around or something.   Guess this guy is waiting for me to make the first move. I drove away slow and he waited a few car lengths before he did the same. He kept a distance behind me, I drove straight back to the house.   Fortunately for me I had to stop for a red light. He remained behind the "yield to pedestrians" lines where he wouldn't be too close. The light turned green and we both were on route.   He turned left at the light I had already been under and through to get back to the house. Then on ward ahead I got stuck at another red light. I stopped. I glanced all around. The car behind me was white.   Four neat and darkly dressed men wearing sunglasses. I got scared. They were going to get me I knew it. Under my breath I said, "Where's the fuckin' silver cars when you need "em?" Sure enough two were in sight. One stopped at the light ahead of me. The other pulled behind the guys in the white car.   I would get to the house just fine. There will be a silver car down my street somewhere when I get in the drive. I know. Only I didn't go straight to the house. Feeling safely guarded by my men in steel, I drove down to the pier to check out the view.   I parked my car facing north. I watched Cedar Point. The peninsula that it sat on. The rides, "The Blue Streak," my favorite but better.   I was 15 goin' on 16 and you said, "I'm gonna get her!" Who was the man behind me ?   I stayed at the pier until I noticed a couple of white cars loaded with sun-glassed men. Since there wasn't a silver one to comfort me, it was to the house and back to the book. I waited for the bells to remind me that I needed to pick up Buff.

Noah didn't think I needed to drive. He said "Capri! You look pretty worked up maybe you shouldn't be driving. I'll go and pick up your daughter. Why don't you set the table!" Why, I thought? I don't eat. I stepped in and said, "How quaint. You want me to set the table. Ha. I'll set the table and you deal with the white cars. I've just about had it with them. Oh shit, the book! Here, I'll show you what I'm talking about because I know you are going to say something along the order of...Capri, what the hell are you talking about? Here. Here *he* is, right there in that picture. That's "Mal Evans." He's was behind me when I dropped Buff off at the school. He's one of the good guys though. He saw that I could see who he was and he turned off and there wasn't a silver car in sight to help me. I went to the pier and it wasn't long before two white cars were there so here I am. Make sense now?" Noah looked up at the clock and said, "I better get Buff. It's six o'clock now." "Okay Noah. I'm sure there's a silver car close to the school just in case." Noah only nodded as he took the keys off the kitchen table.

When Noah returned he told me that he had made fish and potatoes and whatever doesn't matter. What mattered was the fish. Noah was a Pisces.

Noah was allergic to fish, and I was rolling about it so much I had to sit at this dinner. Noah didn't take a bite of the fish. He fixed something else for himself. Don't remember what it was. It doesn't matter, what mattered was the fish because I wasn't eating anything either. This was a thing that was always upsetting to Noah and sure enough he said, "Cap. Try a bite. Something! Some vegetables, some..." "Okay, okay Noah. I'll take a bite of fish for you but only because you can't. Then will you please get off of me about eating?" I took one bite of fish. I chewed enough. I swallowed it. Rinsed it down with some coffee, lit up a cigarette and said, "There. I ate. I'm 32 years old. When I'm through finishing everything that I'm supposed to do I'll eat!" I left the table and went into the kitchen for more coffee. Sat at the guard table and opened my Beatle book to the pictures. I studied the faces. It was sure I would remember all the ones that I would need to know for later because I wasn't through doing what it was I was supposed to be doing.

I looked at the face of "George Martin." The Beatles Producer. There was a man named "Sir Joseph Lockwood." He looked important. I made sure his face would be ever firm in my mind. I studied the faces of the men who wrote the book I was in involved with. That I am involved with! "Peter Brown" and "Steven Gaines." How clever the two of them and the thoughts continued. The book had a copy right in 1983. Three years after John was dead. Missed. Numbers were added up quick as I did. It wasn't 4, 1 or dear number 2. It was three. It is me! 1 and 9 is 10 plus 8 is 18 plus 3 is 21. See the three?

Pope and Mayor named Capri Ann after Pope's mother back in San Marino. So she was number two. I'm three. At least my parents were nice enough to give me my own middle name. Sue. How do you do? Who was it for? Was it a replacement? A replacement was I? That's all I am is a number? But why number three why? I was growing very curious and serious. Thought back to age number nine. Easter was the best friend of mine. We short-cut-walked to a corner store off my street. Through a back walk-way we took. Old or not used head stones stood cold next to a wall face. I must have turned white on my friend by the place. I stopped dead in my feet and said with a stiff and pointed arm, "Easter! That's my name on that stone. See? Capri Spettro!" Eyes wide and open Easter said, "I see Capri!" I told her about the baby my parents had before me that died. It hauntingly amused me and gave me the chills. I called out to Noah told him the details. Enraged in a storm I called Pope for the truth in the tale. He answered politely, "Hello!" "Pope this is Cappy. I want to know why you named me after a dead baby!" "What are you talking about Cappy?" he asked, "Me and your mother named you after my mother." I thrusted into the conversation with bolts and thunder, "You named me after a dead baby! "She" was named after your mom!

All those times that Mayor sang that song to me on the front porch she was thinking of the first daughter she had not me! You went across the Atlantic five times because you had to go there and find a baby girl to adopt for Mayor so she wouldn't miss Ann. You don't care about me! Who's with you? I can hear someone talking in the back ground?" Pope's voice was in a tremble and said, "It's Nina Capri. What is wrong with you? Why are you asking me all this stuff? You weren't adopted. You are my daughter and you were Mayors too!" I dug at the Pope. "You didn't have to give me the same name. You could have called me Holly. I was born on Christmas. I deserved to be known for who I am. I am a constant reminder of a baby that died. I hate you for naming me after her!" "Cappy! She loved you your mother. You were her daughter and you are still my daughter. You don't sound good. What's wrong? Are you okay?" he asked with a shaking accent. "I'm fine!" I yelled at my father. "I'm just fine. I don't like the idea of that snake being over at your house. She's just using you Pope. She's a snake. I hear her hissing in the back ground! Tell her to mind her own business and keep her slithering tongue inside her mouth before I come over and yank it out!" "Cappy! Enough! Tell me what's wrong so I can help you, you don't sound good at all."

I listened to him talk but his words were becoming less important. I was back on track and said, "Pope. The only thing that is wrong with me is I didn't get my own name. I didn't get to go to opera school. I just wanted some truth that you can't or don't want to tell me and that's fine. Wanna know why?" "I did tell you the truth Cappy. I don't know why you don't believe me," he said.

"Wait!" I said, "You didn't ask about the why. Is that snake still there? I don't want her listening in on my business. Pope, I am in love with John Lennon. You remember who he is. He was with The Beatles!" "Capri, Capri! How can you love somebody who is dead? You can't be in love with a dead man!" "Mayor is dead right? And you still love her?" "Yes I do. I always will! But you can't love John Lennon, he died. You can't love somebody you don't know honey! What's a matter with you Cappy?" he asked crying. "Pope. You should be happy for me! John Lennon isn't dead. He's alive. And we did meet a long time ago when you were out playing cards. I went to Cedar Point on those Sundays. Mayor told me that she wouldn't tell you. Guess she didn't huh?" I laughed but stopped when Pope said, "Maybe I should come over to your house and see if you need anything! You want me to come over?" "No no! I don't need anyone to come over. I'm fine, really! Maybe you are right Pope. Maybe John isn't alive. But he was one of The Beatles and I loved

The Beatles. You even said you liked "em." "Yeah. I liked them guys in those movies. Now, are you sure you're okay?" "Sure I'm fine. Noah's been taking care of me and the kids. Oh you never met Noah! He's real nice Pope, you'd like him. He knows how to build boats. That's why I call him Noah. His real name is Jeff but I like calling him that and he don't care." "Well that's good. You take care over there. If you need anything you call your old dad okay?" "Okay Pope." I hung up first without a goodbye.

I wasn't satisfied with what Pope had said. There was more to this and he was in on it. He had to be. Hmm, I thought, maybe I'm not supposed to know what I already know. Maybe I shouldn't say anything to anybody. If the silver cars are taking care of me like I'm sure they are, then they are listening. So could the white car guys! They probably heard my phone conversation with Pope. The two sides undoubtedly know that this will change the course of action that would be next. Certainly The Beatles would have a backup plan. "Shit!" I said. "They concocted this crazy thing!" "And had years to do it," Self responded. "Yes! Years and years! You're right! Ah ha ha ha." Just then Noah butted in from the living room, "Who the hell you talking to Capri?" "Me and me," I said, "I'm so used to not having anybody here, that I just let what I was thinking out without thinking." "Oookay," he said smiling. "I'll be quieter next time. We'll both be." Noah didn't say anything. By the way he looked, I don't think he knew what would be appropriate.

It is the present. But it was the night of June 6th, 1998 when I felt the need to take a break from the book and get out with some friends. I was only away from the house for a couple of hours and in that time I had smoked a little pot, and drank about 4 beers, at least I think I did.

While out with my friends I started to hear voices. I wasn't sure if it was Timothy Smiths voice that I was hearing, but it sure sounded like him and I thought for sure that he or someone was trying to tell me something. The one girl who I knew better than the other people was worried about me. I had told her that I needed to go to the local hospital because of the voices. She begged me not to go, but I knew there was no other way. The problem with some mentally ill patients is that they "turn" themselves in. I was one of them.

I drove over to the hospital and was examined by the doctor on call. He in turn called a social worker named "Ralph Hancock." Now I have met him before and he was just a great guy. I told him what I had been doing with the book and all. He suggested that I stay one night in the nut ward, and leave the book alone for a couple months, so as not to lose it again... my mind that is. He also encouraged me to finish the book as it may benefit others who were just like me. So I took his advice.

The following day I met with the shrink who knew what med's I had been taking, and knew of the book I was trying to write. He released me that morning and I was back home.

I was afraid to pick up where I left off as far as the book was concerned, and I did manage to stay away from it for quite a few months. But in time, I was right back on it. I had to look back and realize how I ended up in the nut ward while trying to write the story. I had to make believe I was insane in order to remember everything that had happened. Each night about the same time, I would talk myself back into 1989. And for a few hours, I admit I was not quite right. But I maintained, and managed to finish without another trip back to the hospital.

So, back to 1989 ...

♬ ♪ *"You And I (All That I Wanna Be)"* ♪ ♬
Words and Music by: Catherine Santi in June, 1986

"I could write of you forever, not hard at all for me to do.
Imaginations run away with me and that's all I have of you.
I have written you some letters, and you claim you haven't read.
I say go ahead and burn them. Wish I said this instead...
... You and I, I was building a fantasy.
You and I, I know we are meant to be.
You and I is all that I want to be.
We could make a sound all our own, ideas are yours and mine alone.
Do you word a song for me? With this for you this I have done.
There's no one who can sway me, I will do what I will do.
But it's feeling kind of empty. Bring the strings. Let's see what we can do.
Make a mistake and knock on my door. Tell me, tell me any lie.
Say to me you never saw me before, as I look through your eyes.
I can find no ending. When I turn and look it's always you.
Oh I could put it all behind me, but this instead I do...
... You and I, I was building a fantasy.
You and I, I know we are meant to be.
You and I, it's all that I want to be."

Chapter Twenty Two: "Code Name Adam"

Much is on my mind as much as it was in 1989.

The 16th of March was getting closer to the next day in clock-time. The kids were already in bed and I was feeling just fine. Noah so close to falling asleep as time was in drive. Me? I'm elated because John Lennon's alive!

I tuned in WCPZ for hints if you will. They were there. They got paid. This is all too strange. Commercials. I thought. Good God they are using commercials to get to me. I listened and listened well. The old familiar voices were those from a cartoon called, "Rocky and Bullwinkle." The two of them were engaging in a conversations and not in sync'! I don't think. Bullwinkle was certain that he was the best electrician ever, explaining to Rocky about this wire and that wire, red and a black. I knew what that meant of course. The positive and the negatives were all in the scene. Rocky was off elsewhere. Out there! How long have they been watching me, I thought, as Rocky talked furniture. Furniture? He rambled about the kinds of styles for sale. "Early American," "French Provincial," "Modem" and the good old "Country." The hi-fidelity system Bullwinkle said he could fix like a pro, well, he touched the wrong wires together and you know how that goes!

I took notes at the guard table. The furniture he talked about is mine. I had all that in here! My old boss from the "Sands Motel" had given beautiful and expensive pieces of furniture over the years I've been here. Thinking of those years made me think of those years before. I was 13 when I worked at the motel. I was 23 when I worked at the motel. Twice was enough. I certainly wasn't going to let that be a third! So I destroyed the thought of ending up there at the age of 33.

I kept the radio on all through the night. I called and requested "Beatles" with might. They played when I called and station was new but they were being paid and I knew by who. But they didn't. There had to have been a code. Something as simple as a young boy walking down the street with a large brown envelope. He was generously paid to deliver this mysterious package to the radio station I talk of.. .WCPZ. He takes it up to the main man. It is handed over to the one who's supposed to receive it. The young boy excitedly hurries off. The main man opens the envelope. Enclosed: a check and instructions. The check would have to be authentic. It would have to be a certified check. It would have to be a lot of money to take over the station for I don't know how long! A million at least. Hell if I owned the station and the instructions were harmless I'd take the money and proceed. Naturally I stayed tuned in.

I gathered up all the clothes I wanted to wear when the day was lit. I washes my jeans, my yellow-long-tailed shirt, the thirteen scarves and a blue tank top. Laid out the buttons and the pin and put them near my Maxwell House Coffee cans. After the clothes were washed and dried, I folded the jeans and the tank top but the shirt and the scarves had to be perfect so I ironed them. I laid them down carefully on the back room table. All was set. By six a.m. I knew that things were going to start happening fast. I didn't need The Beatle book for references but I kept it close for coming events. I played with Maxwell L.P. Edison. I used the bell. The morning guys would be on at seven. Do they have instructions to follow, I asked myself? Self answered saying, "Come on Capri! They've been watching a long time." "Yes they have," I replied.

I allowed Noah to put a stop to me driving the car. The kids told him that I was all over the road. Ladie made mention of it to me directly one night. I stopped dead in the middle of an intersection and said, "Look. See? There they are. Four men sitting in the silver car that just passed us Ladie!" Ladie was recovering from me slammin' the brakes and said, "Capri. That was four little old ladies in that car! What are you doing?" she asked. I was in the middle of making a U turn to follow the car. Ladie said, "Capri! You shouldn't drive hon." "I have to drive Ladie. I gotta catch up with them. You don't understand. Those four people in that car work for the CIA or the FBI, I'm not sure which ones they were but they are watching out for me. They want me to follow them." I rushed down Columbus Avenue. The street that divides the east and west of Sandusky. The middle. For once I was in the middle. Center front stage. Ladie said again, "Capri. Those were little old ladies! Why don't you drive me over to your house so I can get my car. You shouldn't be driving." Was she being paid too? I thought. No. There was no way they were going to pay her a thing. She fucked up big time with Big Time when she fucked Gentry Mocean for the sake of fucking. She liked it. She needed it. She had to have it or she would literally break down and cry. I drove the bitch to her car. By the time I got there I was pissed off and didn't feel like doing anything but concentrating on numbers and John.

So the story of the not driving my car began but not for long. Noah would take the kids to school. He told me that he would be back about noon. He needed to buy groceries for the kids. My kids. He wanted to pick some things up from his parents' house. I was glad to have some time alone. I wanted it. I needed it. I had to have it.

At seven when the DJ's came on the air they began a program with a mystery guest. It was up to the listeners to call and guess who the person was. This was for me too, I thought. The man they talked to over the air waves sounded like a very old man. The old man claimed to be around for a very long time and was tired. I listened to other people call in their guesses. They were wrong. I knew I would get it. Was supposed to! I called. DJ answers: "Got a name for us caller?" Me: "Yes, but I'd like to ask a few questions first. "Mystery man…" "This nice young lady wants to ask questions. Excuse me miss, we ask the questions. Other people are trying to call in an answer." I heard a click. "Just who in the hell do they think they are hanging up on me?" I asked. I answered quick. "They know who I am. They are just going by the book. They will want me to call again." I did. Ring, ring: "WCPZ, have you figured out who our mystery guest is?" Me: "Yes. You said that you've been around for a long time and that you're tired." The mystery man said, "Yes, very tired." DJ: Hold on. Who's running the show?" Other DJ: "Ma'am the man is very tired and we need a name not a question. Thanks for listening." Click. They hung up again. Well, I'll show them. I called back a third time. I got right through on the first ring: " WCPZ, got a name for us?" Me…"Yes, Adam!" Click. I was getting closer. They didn't want me to say it over the air in case the bad guys were listening. I over stepped to quick. Each time after that when I called and the DJ heard my voice they wouldn't say anything. They just kept hanging up.

Damn! Why did I have to say that on the air? The bad guys in their white cars probably had no clue about the large brown envelope and the young boy who delivered it. The code name. I must have said the code name. ADAM. "Of course, that's it!" I said slapping a hand down on the guard table. "Yes!" It was in the instructions. The main man read them. The perfect name. The perfect code because I was Eve. "I am Eve! And 'CPZ is on my side!" I shouldn't say a thing. The commercial! The electrician. Mocean. An electrician perfectionist! That was his job. To bug my house. To know all there was to know about me! He's been in it from the start. He received a certified check and instructions.

But how would The Beatles know about Gentry? I asked myself. I was nearly nudged by Self when she said, "Pope must have told them!" I cut the conversations short with myself and concentrated on Eve. Me. The apple was becoming more and more important than ever! It was a green apple I picked from the tree bearing many. The Beatles record company was called "Apple." "Apples, apples red and green, red and green. Red and green?" I asked. Then I pictured the albums themselves. They went from red apples to green apples. Opposites in taste. Sweet and sour. Positives and negatives. I was an energy tower. I'm the one the wind blew across the ocean and they want me back. He wants me back! I jumped with excitement and said, "Capri Lennon! Now there's a name for ya Jack!" I thought of the blue jays who were named by Gentry. Is he listening to me, I wondered? I looked at the clock waiting for the guessing game name thing to be over with on "the" radio! I wanted to hear some music. And I wanted to hear Beatles. I played with the numbers going on in my head to figure on when. Three and four and that is seven. Can't break it in two without having a half. Seven, seven, it doesn't belong. I got the fucking numbers a jumble. I'm three! All this time I thought Pink was two? So who is who? "Come on Cap, so what if you were wrong?" Self knew and said, "It was Lennon all along." I added the numbers. Never had before. Simple math. A five. "It doesn't have anything to do with this morning!" said I. "Time," Self said and reminded me, "catch her in the eye!"

Sitting at the table with the boom box near I said, "Fuck that now Wheels. You gotta about a half hour to know precisely when they are going to do that block of Beatles. "Ah ha! There might be an explanation for number five after all!" Nine! The day John was born. They'll do Beatles alright. At 9:05." I watched the clock and watched it steady. The boom box was set, paused and ready. And The Beatles came at exactly 9:05 a.m. Only they didn't play a real block of Beatles. One of the four songs was something John did after he had left them. One I had never heard before. Then three came back to mind. They played three Beatle songs and it pissed me off. If they were going to do a block, then why did they play a song that wasn't really Beatles? The five was making sense. The songs that John sang, yes I did say "the songs," were two. Three Beatles and two that John re-made (and well) made five! Three were for me so he had to be number two!

Morning passed and Noah returned. "Noah it's the 17th right? That makes 8 and eight is four and four is two. What would you do?" I asked. "Cap! You really do need to take a rest and sleep. It's the fifteenth," he said. Tapping my foot and folding my arms I said with a grin, "And the next thing you'll tell me is it isn't March." "No. I wouldn't say that Capri. It's March. I'm sure of it," he said. "Then I'm off a little. Off by two days. Two! Maybe I'm supposed to be off by two." Noah shook his head smiling, "Yep! You're off!" "Off to the see the wizard," I said. Conversations ended. I got serious. I wanted my car. I had to get out and do something. Roam streets, look for cars. Silver ones, white ones. I had to be aware because there were so many of them out there. Only Noah denied me that and I let him.

I stayed in and wondered about how I could have moved ahead two days. It upset me. I went to the piano, I rolled up some joints and got high. Stared at the keys. I couldn't put my fingers on them. I couldn't play because for some outrageous reason I couldn't remember anything I ever played. And the day turned into the evening.

What do I do? I called Prof' of all people. I was almost outta pot and hadn't seen Priest to buy any. Noah was no way on this earth going to give me anything but care. I was down to a quarter once and I knew that would be gone in a couple two three days. I wanted to be ready. Prof could mail it to me and have it here in a few days. I dialed up the number. Prof answered, "Hello." "Prof' it's me, Capri. Look, I got some big things going on now that I can't talk about. I've been watching these silver cars and white cars and the radio station won't take my calls and Noah doesn't want me to drive and I want to drive. Pope won't admit that he's not my real dad, Ladie is a fucking slut and I could play the piano if I could remember anything but I can't remember so I don't but I want to. They watch me, they hear me now. Both of them. All of them and there are many many people. A lot of people. You should see this town. It's very silver is the only way to put it and I got about a quarter once of pot left and I wondered if you could mail me a quarter once because what I have won't last but a few days and I have to be ready cause they'll catch me off guard or they'll try to. Except that I was off two days so you see that's why I want some pot. Will you send me some please Professor ? I'll pay for it. I'll have more money then I'll know what to do with. Can you get me a little?" At last I paused. Prof' said, "Capri! Wait. What? Slow down. What's wrong with your voice ? You sound bad Caps." "Get me the pot or not Prof'? Just answer the question yes or no. I can take it. I'm not afraid of you anymore. Fuck you!" I was about ready to hang up after telling him that when he broke in and said, "Capri. I'll send you a fucking elbow!" I questioned this, "I don't want body parts I want pot." "Capri. That's what a quarter pound is called out here. I'll send you the elbow first thing tomorrow and you'll get it the day after that. I promise." "Thanks Prof'." I hung up.

"Damn Noah. I'm getting a quarter pound of pot in two days. I don't have to pay for it! See I am very important! Prof' is in on it too. There are a lot of people in this Noah! It's all in the book. This changes all the numbers. I gotta get the numbers right. Maybe I'm reading them backward. But you can't do that with numbers. Or can you?" Noah made his way through and said to my surprise, "Why not relax! Do what you like to do best. Play the piano and sing all you want. It's your house. I'm just some guy who thought you needed somebody. I want to be here for you Capri. So if it makes you happy do it. I can curl up in Sonny's room." "Noah. You know there's a room up there with a bed, use it!" I said. Noah cocked his head and said, "But that's your room." "I don't have a room up there. This is my room. All this." I said pointing with both hands to the guard table and the piano. Noah was happy for a bed was he. I clocked the time, tickity-tickity-three. It was the earliest start of the next day. The "16th" of March.

I went over to the piano and starting to play and sing with ease. I liked the raspy-in-the-voice-kinda-sound I attained, so I played and sang underneath the one light lit downstairs. The blue light just left overtop the piano, enough light. Soft but cool light. I was singing the most recent song

411

I had written. I set a smoke in the ashtray when out of the bottom of my eyes I noticed my thigh was bleeding. I called out to Noah. "Noah! Noah! Hurry, hurry please! My leg is bleeding! I don't know why it is bleeding there is not cut! No glass!" I heard Noah rushing down the stairs to be at my aid. "What's wrong with your leg?" he asked looking at it calmly. Noah was always calm, always. "It's bleeding Noah! It just started bleeding and I didn't cut myself or anything, I'm scared Noah! Something is wrong with me! Why am I bleeding? Help me! Make it stop!" He was looking about the piano, the ashtray, anything that I might have hurt me and found nothing. He said, "Let me get something to clean your leg. Let's find out what's going on. It's not a lot." "Yes Noah but I have rare blood and I don't want to lose a drop! This isn't logical." I was terrified.

Didn't like something if I couldn't make sense out of it. This was new to me and I was scared. Noah walked back over to the piano bench and washed the blood of with a nice fresh and warm wash cloth. There was no cut. No pin prick of a cut. Just then the blood was there again, a drop at most. I got scared. "See Noah. See what I mean!" "Capri. Look. Look at your arm. You cut your arm and probably from this piece here that's holding up the piano. You're lucky the kids didn't get cut. Didn't you know it?" he asked. "No." I saw the back side of my lower arm and sure enough there was a good inch cut there. "Noah. Whenever I did it, I sure as hell didn't feel it. It doesn't even hurt." Noah insisted on getting it nice and clean. He played nurse and placed the bandage on very carefully and comfortably in place. "You alright now Capri? Need anything?" "No. I'm fine. I was freaking out when I thought I was bleeding for no reason. I wanted to know the reason and you found it. That's it. I'm sorry I woke you up. I'm gonna quit playing for a while and listen to the radio. See ya in the morning Noah." Noah kissed the top of my head and said, "If you need me, just come and get me. It's okay. Good night or good morning." "Good-morning Noah!"

He left the kitchen and I heard him go up the stairs. I listened to the steps down the hall till I heard the door close. Then I stopped listening. I tuned WCPZ in case I was missing important data. And the ribbon on the wheels recorded it all for back up.

The early morning hours of the 16th passed as they always did. I figured that if I was off by two days, I'd just repeat what I had done two more times to make it three. It'll be all fine. Straightened out! Days wise. The 16th would be the second time or day two. Then the sun light peeked in through the curtains and it was.

"Noah. Wake up! I have to talk to you! About the book!" Oh and I was yelling for joy from the infamous guard table where I was spending most of my time. Noah came down the stairs in a flash. "What Cappy? What about the book?" Guess he was getting used to the out bursts. He was so calm and I was so opposite. "Noah. It's all here. You put the book in front of me and told me to read something. I wasn't born here. I came from someplace else. I was named after a dead baby. I was replaced. I didn't go on a trip to Italy with my parents. I was brought back from somewhere when I was three. See, there's the three. Don't you get it Noah? It's so simple. Pope sailed that fucking Atlantic Ocean five times. Now there's a number for ya" "Caps. What are you talking about? That book is about The Beatles." "Noah! The book is about me! You just have to be me to know that. Nobody else could have realized it. It wasn't about them. You know, when I was a little girl, about three going on four, Mayor used to sing this song. The song was titled my name. Only it was apostrophe O. An Irish Cappy. Who was she really singing it to? Me? Or the baby that was really hers?"

Just then, Buff slipped and fell down a couple of steps. I got up from the queen seat to see if she was okay. "Mom. How did grandma's picture get here?" she asked me. "Mayor? You mean her picture was on the stairs? I had it on the shadow box Buff." "Well that's what I slipped on mom. How did it get here?" "I don't know. I don't know. See Noah, just when I start to talk about Mayor, Buff slips on her picture. I told you how she comes around and tilts the shadow box. She's trying to tell me something Noah." "Maybe she is Cappy. She's probably trying to tell you the same thing that I've been. Eat and get some sleep. You need that Cap. Look at yourself, you're losing weight. You gotta eat hon." "Noah. You don't get it! Time is running out. I am Eve! Don't you remember? I gotta face the music and make things right! Why is that so fucking hard to understand! You don't believe me do you? So if you don't than fuck you Noah! Leave me and myself the fuck alone and get the hell out of my face." I left the kitchen.

Noah followed and asked, "Where are you going Cappy?" "Jesus Christ Noah. I'm gonna take a fucking bath. Where are you going Noah? You gonna watch me and make sure I do that right? Get away from me!" I shoved him out of my way and closed the bathroom door behind me. I turned the water on and made it as hot as I could stand it. I sat on the edge of the tub knowing that hell was hotter. I got out of my clothes and into the water. The room started to steam up as I began to wash, face first. While running the wash cloth over my arms, I looked at them real good. Skinny, I thought? This is fucking muscle! What does Noah know? Why is this bath going in slow motion? I stopped. I reminded myself that I had something to do. I had to be clean if it took the night, then I would deal with God!

I sat like an Indian and faced the wall. The tiled wall that covered what Pink said should be here and what should be there. I didn't want to think about him. I wanted to get out of the bath and be ready, but when I started to wash my back I stopped dead cold. "Noah! Please help me. I can't do this. I can't. Noah? Aren't you coming to help me?" Noah came through the bathroom door out of breath. "Cappy what happened? Are you okay? Won't you answer me so I can help ya hon?" I had fixed a stare in the water looking for a reflection of me. I couldn't see her there. I didn't know how to answer Noah and God only knew how much I wanted to. "Cappy, please. If there's something I can do. Did you wanna ask me something? Whatever it is I'm here for ya." I brought my knees up to my chest, wrapped my arms around them tight. Shaking. I broke down and cried. "Noah. I can't wash my back because it isn't mine. If it was mine I would be able to feel it but I don't. It isn't mine Noah! It's somebody else's and I can't do it. It's sickening to wash something you don't know. It's lumpy and rocky. Will you do it for me Noah? Please?" Noah knelt next to me on the floor, took the wash cloth from me and washed my back. "Cappy, it's your back honey. You won't eat. You gotta eat Cap! I can see your bones that's how much you need to eat. You don't wanna be stuck in the hospital for weeks or longer with tubes in your arms? I can't let you get sick!" While Noah talked I listened. He could see my bones, I thought? What if Noah is right? What was he trying to tell me? It was the same thing the Doc' told me. If I wanted to sing then I have to eat. I knew then that I had even less time to get done what I had started in the "third" place. "Noah. Thanks. I'll be okay. You can go now. I'm gonna shower off and get dressed. I'm fine, really." "Okay Cap. I'll be right in the other room. If you need me give me a holler." "Thanks Noah." While drying off and getting into some clothes I knew there was no time for food, even if God Himself handed me an apple.

Needed to get my mind off of Him and the clothes I put on. What's wrong with me, I thought? I should be wearing the stuff I just bought! I folded the 13 scarves exactly the way Jimmy taught me. I ironed them with steam. The colors came to life with rich meaning. The white one stood for peace. The powder blue for hope. The red one, like a rose, for love. I had to have an orange one. Why? Because I hated the color and that's what it stood for. Green for the earth, yellow for God, black for life, does it sound so absurd? Navy blue for the Universe, pale pink stood for Pink, the deep turquoise of course for Saint Mary's Lake and the lavender Goose Island, I thought, I think. Thirteen stole base all on its own. Teal stood for home.

I got into my "Levi's," put a red tank top and tucked neatly in the jeans. The very-yellow-and-very-long-tailed-to-the-knees-shirt was next. I buttoned the black buttons to the waist and the rest lay like wings. A top button undone because it was needed for things. I wore the collar of my shirt up. It was side-back-around-my-neck-to-the-other-side. The scarves were tied on last and all very neat. For it were those I wore that took the highest seat.

Enough rhyming words to get on with the book. This is where I tied them and how it did look. The white one around my forehead. The powder blue went twice around my left upper arm and bowed. The red one wrapped above my left knee. The orange one I hated so much didn't get the respect of its bow being seen in the front. I tied it above my left knee, like the right, kept the bow in back and outta sight. I wore the green one around my right arm. The others hung like gowns. On the right belt loop of my jeans, I tied corner to corner four scarves that nearly touched the floor. Yellow, then black, purple and navy blue. Opposite the left, the same. Pale pink, deep turquoise, lavender and teal. For real!

I went to the kitchen, took a seat at the guard table filled with numbers and papers and cassettes and notes. I had a cup of cold coffee handy, oh, and let's not forget the blessed Beatle book!

I smoked many cigarettes and joints at the table going over the book for accuracy. I had all the positives and negatives worked out because that's what's life was all about. Something was still missing. It was back to page 396. It was John.

How I wonder where you are. Up above the clouds so high, you picked me and I know why. Long ago when we were three, the merry-go-ride was featherly free. You played guitar and I know now about then. It wasn't a look-a-like it was you Mr. Lennon.

This ADAM thing was well organized. Everyone has been in it for a long time. But why would they make me wait as long as I did, I asked myself? "Because you married Prof' Caps!" Self shouted. I demanded the right answer. But Self was right. She usually was.

I picked up the paper to check the horoscopes. After reading all the ones necessary, I cut that section out of the newspaper and hung it with the others on the wall to my right, just before the front door. They didn't seem important anymore.

Suddenly and without warning, I could hear Winnebago's voice in my head saying, "Caps. He's not just rich, he's filthy rich." I tuned her out but not the words. What if Gentry is filthy rich? Is John Lennon the reason why? Pink's been in on this? "Cappy, Cappy, Cappy! Don't you remember what he told you?" Self asked. "Yes. That he'll always love me, that we can't be together and he can't tell me why. He can't tell me why? He "can't" tell me why because John Lennon is the WHY! It was all in the sky. Listen… Merry-go-round. A 2. Another chance. The two people at the bottom of the stairs ready to go to the top. My heart. Flip flopped!

A house! Now that was important. I wanted out of the one I was in. I had to took in the paper again. "There must be something in there for me," I said. "Why not look for a new home to move into?" Self suggested.

I opened the paper again. I knew just what I wanted. Something near the water where I could see the sunrise and the sunset. I wanted a yacht 100 feet long. I couldn't be happy with a boat anymore. This life was going into luxury and I wanted it all and I wanted more.

Noah came downstairs while I glanced through the ads and said, "Caps. Your kids are asleep for the night. I gotta get home and get some rest." "But Noah! You can't leave me here alone. It's your job to take care of me remember? What if the bad guys see you leave?" "Cappy. No one is going to hurt you. I don't live far. I can be here in less than a minute." "Noah, how can you do that without a car? Do you want mine?" "Caps. I can run can't I? I left my number here for ya. All you have to do is call and I'll be here quick. See?" "You really are leaving me Noah? You won't be back?" I was afraid.

Noah pinned up his number on the wall next to the horoscopes and in large letters he wrote: IN CASE OF AN EMERGENCY CALL NOAH AT ###-####! "Cappy. I'll be back. Your kids might be used to you singing and playing and yelling, but I'm not. I need a few hours of good sleep and I'll be back over to take care of things. Tell you what. When I go out the door, lock it up, wait about 45 seconds and call that number. I'll answer. I promise!" "You're sure Noah?" "Yes Cappy. I'm sure. And remember, lock the door." I grabbed Noah and hugged him with all my might fearing that this would be the end of me. He went out the front door and diagonally crossed the yard and was outta sight. I locked up just like he said and watched the second hand of the clock tick away. I called the number he left hanging on the wall in 45 seconds like he told me to. He answered. "Caps?" "Noah! Thank God. You were telling the truth. What would I do without you?" "Well, you can let me sleep a few hours and you won't be without me. I told you that if you have any emergency that I will be there in less than a minute. I live right on the corner of Monroe and Central." "Why didn't you tell me Noah?" "You never stop talking long enough to let me tell you anything. Now will you let me sleep?" "Yes Noah. I will." "Good night Cappy." "Good night Noah."

I went right for the ads in the paper. I had to get my mind off of not feeling protected. I didn't want Noah to know that I didn't feel safe without him. I couldn't help the fact that he needed sleep and I didn't. I needed a house. A home!

There it was! The perfect house. The add read: Mother of three needs home. Plenty of water and utilities paid. Call ###-####. I called the numbers frantically. A man answered. "Hello?" "Yes. I was calling about your add in the paper. The house? Do you by any chance know Gary Perrin? He's coming from Cleveland to tell me where I can find Adam." "Miss. I don't believe I know anyone named Gary Perrin. I think you have the wrong number." "Sure, I forgot. You wouldn't tell me even if I was right. You're not supposed to tell me." Sir, I'll let you go. I made a mistake." "Wait!" said the man, "Don't hang up. You say your friend is coming from Cleveland. Is he flying?" "Probably," I said. The stranger on the line said, "Then he'll be flying outta the airport there. If you know Huron, there isn't a place to land here, so he must be using a smaller plane. He would land at the airport in Sandusky wouldn't he?" I got excited. "You're right! I never thought about it. Thanks. That means that he could be driving to my house now as we speak. I have to get off the phone in case he is trying to reach me." "Please, don't hang up. I don't know who you are, but I like talking to you. I don't have a lot of friends and I find you very interesting. Won't you at least tell me your name? This way if I run into your friend Gary, I can tell him that you're waiting for him." "No, I can't tell you anymore. The world will know soon enough. I gotta hang up sir, really, thank you." And I hung up. The man's voice seemed hauntingly familiar. I wondered if he was Gary. I had to get my mind off the phone call. Staring me right in the face was the blessed Beatle book. I didn't want to pick it up but Self wanted to... the bitch! She flipped the pages back and forth and let it open where it did. And it opened to the page where her and I could clearly read the words that stood out like they did before. "Catcher in the Rye." I got scared and remembered that Prof' lived in Texas. The Lennon's" went there once. They must have given Prof' a copy of the book then. Good God! I have to call Prof'!

I dialed his number and anxiously waited for him to answer. "Hello." "Prof', This is Cappy. You need to take the book and get rid of it." "What book?" he asked. "You know, "Catcher in the Rye," that one. Get rid of it. Bury it, burn it, blow it up if you have to but make sure you don't keep it on you anymore. You'll be killed. They know all about everything. They know because I haven't been able to keep my mouth shut. Trust me, just get it away from you!" "Caps. I don't have that book," "Prof', look around. It's there in your house. It's probably well hidden. I know it's there. I know too much. Please Prof'! Think of your kids!" "Okay Cappy. I'll find it and when I do I'll throw it in the Pacific Ocean." "Great Prof'. Now they know the ocean. You tie a brick to it, wipe off any prints and drive. I mean drive down the coast where you live at least a few hundred miles and throw the bitch as far as you can." "Cappy, consider it done. Bye." Prof' hung up. I could only hope that he was going to get to it!

I closed the book. Wanted to call Noah but I knew that I couldn't. This was nothing that concerned him, or did it?

I jetted up the stairs and told Buff that I was going to The Barrel. I didn't wait for an answer. I knew things would be okay. She had Noah's phone number if there was an emergency. I flew down the stairs, so did all the scarves I had hanging on me. I grabbed The Beatle book off the guard table. I had to show Jerry and Ladie what was going on. Ladie would be at work and Jerry would be there. He was always there waiting for me.

I went out the front door, Beatle book in hand and locked everything up behind me. I drove to The Barrel. Sure enough Jerry was sitting at the bar and Ladie was at work. I pulled up a stool next to Jerry and said, "Jerry, look! It's in this book. You won't believe it!" "Geeze Cappy. You're getting real skinny. Are you okay?" he asked. "Yes Jerry. I'm fine. Check out this book. Fuck! What is taking Ladie so long to bring me a cup of coffee. Look at the tramp talking her way out of her panties when she needs to serve me!" "Cappy, what are you talking about?" Jerry asked. I opened The Beatle book and showed Jerry trying to explain to him that I was what the story was about. He didn't believe me and it was easy to see. So I opened my mouth again! "Jerry, the CIA, the FBI and so many other people are in on this. I know that's it's hard to believe, but it's the truth. Nobody's really supposed to know what's going on except me." "Soooo Caps. How did you figure that all this was about you?" he asked. Just then Ladie came over and said, "Caps, I'm sorry but I was so busy down at the other end of the bar I didn't even see you come in. You did want coffee right?" "Of course I do Ladie." "And you better put another pot on. That's all ya got there." Jerry told her. She did and I answered Jerry's question before Ladie came by too late with the coffee. When I told him that I was going to come into 500 million dollars, Jerry asked with a smile, "Ya gonna buy me beer then?" "I thought you would believe me Jerry. I'm telling you that John Lennon isn't dead. He is alive and it's all in the book! The Beatles didn't want anyone to know until I figured it out. Now I know and soon so will everybody else." I didn't realize that Ladie over heard the conversations I had with Jerry and pretty soon the Mrs., owner of The Barrel came out and called me back into the kitchen.

"Cappy. What's wrong?" "Nothing," I said. "Cappy, you're sick. You need help," she said gently holding my hand. I pulled away in anger and said, "I don't need any help!" "But Cappy, you're all skin and bones, look at yourself! Go home Cappy. Get some rest and eat something. We don't want to see you in the hospital honey. You need help." I heard the owner all I wanted to. "I don't care what you think I need. I'll leave here only not for rest and food but because I have things to do that cannot wait anymore. Don't worry about me. I know what I'm doing." I walked out of the kitchen and said nothing to Ladie and Jerry on my way out. All I could think about at the time was how I opened my mouth in a public place. What if they have The Barrel bugged too, I thought? And here I am with all this information on me. I gotta get it to the house where it will be safe. The numbers. The fucking numbers. They're evil. Numbers are evil in the wrong hands and I'm the only one who can know them, say them. Can't tell anyone about them.

The book, the numbers and the notes were secure at the guard table where they belonged. Feeling restless I didn't I want to sit at the house. Noah wasn't there to stop me from leaving. There had to be a place where I could go and not be heard. A place where there were no bugs. My destination... The Pine. I felt safe and parked right in front of the bar. There were no silver cars. Maybe it was all the kick-standing "Harley's" gaiting the lot.

Felt right at home and floated around talking to all the people I hadn't seen since Captain. A good forty minutes or so zoomed by and it was time for a seat. Kenji and his wife were working. I knew he saw me, but Kenji took his time at getting to me. I wondered if he was still pissed about the time he threw me out. Then why didn't he throw you out yet, Self thought.

Kenji walked over and said, "What ya havin'?" "I think I'll have a White Russian." "Okay." Kenji turned to make the drink, turned and said, "We're outta cream Wheels." "That's okay Kenji, I don't mind milk." Thinking things were cool, they weren't. Kenji made his thoughts clear to me and everybody else saying, "Hold on here. I threw you out Wheels and you can leave now." "Jesus Christ Kenji! I've been here almost an hour. I can't believe you're tellin' me to leave!" Kenji boasted his ownership and said, "Forget it Wheels, you're out!" I took my car keys and left. I drove north a block, stopped at the red light and me and myself said, "Let's go back there." The light turned green and I made a U-turn to get to my parking place. With adrenaline running full speed ahead of me I was back in the bar. From the side door where I entered I yelled, "Hey Kenji! If I park my car in the drive, blocking the side-walk, you gonna call the cops?" "Yeah Wheels," he said, "You better leave." I laughed, the bikers got curious and I was out the door. Plan number three came naturally. Had to get my car in the drive way. And I did. It was back through the side door of The Pine. It slammed. The bar busted in a bizarre-breaking-silence. "Say Kenji! I'm in the drive way blocking the" side-walk. You wanna call the cops?" All eyes were on me and the owner. His honey-moon wife went to his side, holding his hand. Kenji looked at me with a wrinkled-brow, a sneer and taking way too long for an answer! Polite? Yes I was. Was I dearly heard by all? Hell yes! "Kenji? Do you know what you are? You're a pussy!" That got the riled bunch of bikers going. They banged their fists on the table, tapping, whistling and roaring was everywhere. One of the bikers yelled out, Fuckin 'A Wheels! Tell it like it is!" More cheering and stomping went on when another "Outlaw" said, "Say Wheels... You know you're too good for this place. The Radisson. That's where you belong Wheels!" The whole pack was for me. The stage a center and I had the lead. "How right you are! Fuck this place." Foot-kicking the side door for my exit I could hear the biker's rootin'and applauding. Where to go, where to go. The Barrel. They would expect me to go.

It was about closing time when I walked in. Ladie was there. Three females who I knew by face were seated at the bar. There was number five sneakin' up on me! When the three of them turned to see who had just walked in I sang. "… Well I've been waiting for this moment, for all my life, hold on…" My mood went bad when I entered the ladies room. My mirrored image was unrecognizable. Making a quick about face, I walked out of the room, stood behind each one of the girls who sat separately. Pointed at them by one. Something they needed to hear and it would come from me. "Fuck you. Fuck You! And realty fuck you!" Ladie's mouth dropped open and so did the three. Nobody knew what to say as I back-walked my out. That is, until I felt two hands holding on to both my arms. Harris was behind me and said, "Wheels! What the hell are you doing?" I broke from the firm grip he had on me. "Wheels, you're all skin and bones. What's wrong with you?" "Harris! There isn't anything wrong with me. See this?" I flexed an arm, slapped the tight muscle. "Bones Harris? I don't think so." Harris wanted to say something! Ladie's mouth gaped. The three sluts at the bar who wanted to be cool but would never be sat looking as stupid as they did before. I floated out and went to the house.

All was quiet and in order just the way it was left. Panic ran through me thinking that the bad guys may have heard talking at The Barrel. I reached for the phone and went to the wall for Noah's number. It rang several times when a tired, but alert voice answered. "Yeah?" "Noah, it's me Cap. I went all over the place to night. Well, only a couple of places and I think I said too much. I told somebody at the bar about John Lennon and now they are gonna know who l am and they'll try and get me. Noah! You gotta come over. I'm scared! They bugged everything! They're probably listening now. How can I go to The Barrel tomorrow? You gotta come over here Noah!" "Cappy, Caps. Hold on hon. I just have to tie this other shoe here and I'll be there. Watch for me. 45 seconds." "Okay Noah. I'll be at the table until you get here. Bye." The button to hang up on Noah was pressed but I held onto the phone in case something happened before he got to my house.

There was a knock. It was Noah. He didn't get one foot in the door and I came crashing in on him! "Noah. They know everything! They know what I look like. They're gonna get me Noah. What scares me is I don't see them. The white cars. Ya know? They're hiding but I don't know where. Noah. What if they get me before The Beatles do? Would they kill me? No they wouldn't kill me. I have too much information. I'd be no good to them dead would I Noah?" "Cappy relax! Quiet down. You're gonna end up scaring those kids and you don't have to yell at me. I'm here to help you and there is nobody who is going to kill you. Get it outta your head will ya?" "I can't Noah! 500 million dollars? Never know ya got a killer till you meet a price." "Cappy. You need to eat and sleep and get all this out of your head. Ya don't need to go roaming around at night acting this way. You'll end up getting hurt. You have to think about your health." "I'm fine. Just fine. I do have to go to The Barrel tomorrow to make sure that things are safe. Silver cars, ya know." Noah sat down at the table, took off his wool hat and said with a long sigh, "Cappy. You don't have to go anywhere tomorrow."

Footsteps were coming down the stairs. Too heavy to be anyone else's but Buffs. Before she was half way down the down I said, "Buff when you walk through the living room, will ya pick up that little paper clip or something on the floor. I think it's a paper clip. You'll see it. It's silver. Ya can't miss it" Buff called out, "Mom. I see it, I see it! It's right in front of me. I almost stepped on it. It's a safety pin mom!" "It's closed right?" I asked. "Yeah it is." Buff walked into the kitchen to show me the pin. "Buff. It's about the same size as a paper clip." Buff couldn't take it, showed the pin to Noah and said, "Look at this! How did my mom know it was right there? How Noah?" Noah looked at me and said, "Mom. How do you do that?" "Don't know. I just see it in my head. A quick picture and it's gone. Pisses me off when the picture doesn't stay long enough for me to make it out, it's kinda hard to explain really." "Mom that is so cool. Do you think about something or what do you do?" "Buff, like I told you, I just see it in my head. I don't know when it's gonna happen. Happens without warning. Here, let me have the pin so I can put it up."

She handed it to me and I stuck it in my pocket for the time being. "Don't get your hopes to high Buff, but I think I might have the lottery numbers. I'm pretty close anyway." "You know the lottery numbers mom? We could be rich! Do they pop in your head like the safety pin?" "No. This is something I've been working on for two weeks. That's why the kitchen table is such a mess. Think I have the right numbers but I'm not sure what day to play them on. Maybe I'll know tomorrow." "I believe you mom. Some of the things I hear you talking about down here. I think you know a lot of things mom." "Here Buff. Look out the window. Notice lots of silver cars lately? Limousines? Lots of those. Well, tomorrow sometime, one of those Limos is going to come and pick me up. Think you can handle me tellin' you why?"

Didn't take Buff a time. She had already broke in with CURIOUS! "Mom. Why? Tell me, I gotta know!" I paced the floor itching at my knuckles and peeking out the windows. Buff pleaded for information and Noah shook his head. "Buff. I am going to see someone very famous tomorrow. This person is the "biggest" name in rock and roll! Still wanna know?" "Mom. There goes one of those Limos. And there's another one!

Mom who is it? Who's coming here tomorrow?" "Buff. John Lennon. I know everybody thinks he's dead but he isn't Buff. He's alive and he will be here in Sandusky tomorrow!" "Mom. You mean... The Beatles? John, Paul, George and Ringo Beatles? John Lennon mom? Oh my God! John Lennon! You love him mom! Can I tell Jules? John Lennon! Oh God. Wait till all my friends here about this!" Shaking and nodding my head yes was feeling like a disease so I said, "Buff. You're getting me too worked up. I know it's hard to believe but it's true. You have to promise me one thing though." "Sure mom. I promise! What is it?" "Don't say anything to your friends till after he comes here first, tomorrow. Okay? I know it's going to be hard but it's just one more day." "Okay. But can I watch cars because I just saw another one." "Sure Buff. Watch' em for me."

Buff stayed fixed and hoping for more limos. Noah was foot-propped in front of the television. My world was at the guard table where it belonged. "No one can sing like you John." Self wasn't thinking and neither was I. "Can you guys all hear me loud and clear up there, over there, where ever you are? Having a good laugh? Makin'a video are ya? Gonna make a story about it boys?" "Mom. Who are you talkin' too?" Buff asked. I' m talkin' about John Lennon! I'm talking into all the hidden microphones. I'm sure this place is bugged. It would have to be!" "Mom, how do they do that?" "Well, I suppose they hire somebody to come here when the coast is clear and then that person bugs the house." "Mom maybe that's why Pinky was coming over? He's an electrician?" "You're right Buff. He is. And a good one at that. That has to be the one they hired. Shit. It just keeps making more and more sense all the time."

The excitement of Lennon wouldn't have been so bad if only I would've kept my big mouth shut! Buff wasn't through with me yet. "Mom. Maybe that cloud you saw in the sky was Pinky's initials. G.M. Gentry Mocean?" "Buff I thought about that since the time I first saw it. It could mean him. But see, he's never been married. In order for me and him to be me and him, he'd have to get married, raise some kids and then get divorced in seven years. No Buff. I wanted it bad for it to be him. I think he wanted that too but he knew that I loved John so much. Maybe that's why he left. He had to. It was his job to because of John Lennon! John Lennon Buff-Bag! Pretty sure the very big and very beautiful wedding will be tomorrow night." Buffs mouth dropped. "You mean... You mean you and John Lennon are getting married mom? Oh my God mom! You're going to be married to one of the Beatles? What are you gonna wear?" "I don't know. I can't think of anything. I don't have anything." "Mom yes you do. You got that dress grandpa got you. You know, the one from Argentina?" "Buff that's perfect! I was married once so white wouldn't be right but that would. It's teal. I love teal! Oh no! I don't have shoes to match." "Mom you can go to the store as soon as they open and get a pair. I'd watch Sonny and Jules if Noah is still sleeping." Noah was already asleep when I peeked into the living room. "Okay Buff. I'll go as soon as they open! Let's not talk about it anymore, I can't. I'm too excited. I gotta sit down and work on the lottery numbers or something." "But mom..." "Buff, really! This is too much even for me! Think about something else. Think about Pinky. Maybe he'll come over to wish us good luck or something." "Okay, I'll try."

Silence, but for the radio was heaven. All I could do was think about the next day. The shoes, the Limo and John Lennon. Will he catch me off guard? God l hope not! I might have a fuckin' heart attack! If you want something badly enough it does come true. Dreams do happen if you believe they will with all your heart. I should have known better from the start. The ferry boat ride to Cedar Point. Gary gave me the white-shiny-powder so I would never quite remember for sure. It didn't work Perrin. I remember because I'm supposed to remember.

Much time was spent in thought and Buff was long gone upstairs and asleep. Noah too. A picture slowly passed right in front of me. It was Pink standing outside the door with his head cocked to the side and resting... one hand on the porch rail. I put my head into the table and tried to stop crying. "Pink come on!" I pleaded, "You have to come over tonight or I may never see you again. This is our last chance Gentry. Please please!"

♫ ♪ *"Say You Love Me"* ♪ ♫
Words and Music by: Catherine Santi on June 27th, 1989

"I've wanted it bad, bad for you to be here.
I've wanted it bad for you to be dear to me.
I've seen you look so far away and in your eyes you're far away,
far away in a dream
I see the gentle lullaby has caught you squarely in the eye,
and oh, they say you love me.
It was never my intent to lose the sight of you.
It was never my intent to lose you all the way.
But you were never on the side where the shadow listen in,
you were afraid to come in.
Why can't you turn aside and say hello to me?
Why can't you realize it's us and not pretend?
When you're in front of my eyes, oh I can clear my mind,
so please say you love me."

"It's no use Capri," Self said calmly, "He's not coming. He didn't think he could hold a candle to John Lennon!" "But I'd give this up for him! All he has to do is show up!" Self had the last word. "Cap! How about the lottery numbers?" I concentrated on the winning ticket! This would get my mind off of things. It worked. When I was through I didn't want them anymore. Now that I knew them it didn't seem fair. I woke up my sleeping Ark maker. "Noah. I outta give these numbers to someone else. Don't think it would be right to play 'em. Who should I call?" "Hell Cappy. I don't know. You're gonna end up calling somebody anyway." Ha! But I decided there was no way I could give the numbers to anyone. Evil feeling were pulling me into the numbers and I didn't want to associate with them. Not lottery numbers anyway, just the ones that mattered. Number two and three.

Taking a deep breath I reached for The Beatle book. Held it closed against my chest looking at it. There were those words. The love you words. Who put them there? Was it Pink? Had to be. Who else? "Oh fuck you Pink! Who needs you!" Self was right. You had your chance and you blew it! Time's up, time's up!

So many things to do. I threw everything I was going to wear that day into the washer and dryer. I left for a store to get good shoes. The teal shoes were delicately feminine in every way. Perfect! I raced to put them with the original long-skirted and oh so feminine suit that Pope was kind enough to have bought me when he was in South America. The blend was together and put away for the night.

The scarves and yellow blouse were ready for the iron and the leather sneakers were polished. After my shower, my Cosmetology expertise make-up and hair, I was ready for the clothes and a drive.

Noah didn't like what he was seeing. I ran outside, ran back through the house and up the stairs. The balcony door looked as though it had been broken into. "Noah. Somebody got in here last night and stole my stuff! I can't find the pink scarf, the bell or the gold bible. Noah? You hear me?" He raced up the stairs and said, "Cap. Nobody broke into the house last night. You did that. You don't remember? Come out here." I followed him out and looked over where Noah stood. "See Cappy? You came out here last night swearing at God knows who, threw the stuff over the rail. I'm surprised nobody called the cops!" "I did that Noah? But I stayed at the table all night. I know! did. I wouldn't throw the pink scarf on the ground. It's more important than the bible ! I ran back into the house, raced down the hall, the stairs and outside to get my things.

Crossing back across the lawn, I saw a dead baby sparrow in the west corner of my yard. This puzzled me. This bothered me. It was if someone laid it just so. I told Noah to come out and see it. He did. After he looked at the bird we walked along the lawn and I saw baby blue jay feathers sitting in the east corner of the yard just in front of the step on the grass. I knelt next to them and cried. Why would anything hurt something so beautiful? Noah took me by the hand.

There would be a lecture about my sleep habits. My food. My driving. Noah shot me down with lectures like a machine gun! "Noah. What the fuck do you think I've been doing all this time? Playing? You were the one who told me to read something? How much did they pay you? Bet you made a lot. Look what you deal with, ha' Greed Noah! Funny what people will do for money." I got the Beatle book and the bell. Got my pink scarf cleaned and tied where it belongs. On the first left side of the belt loop. The one that would take me home.

"Cappy!" Noah yelled. "Where in the hell do you think you're going? You can't drive. You're gonna end up hurting somebody. You'll kill yourself driving! I can't let you drive Caps!" "Noah you can't tell me what to do. I have to leave, can't you see that?" "No I can't Cappy. Where ya gotta go and I'll drive ya?" "You can't drive my car Noah. This is something I have to do by myself. I am going out to find John Lennon. Look! You told me to read, so I did. It's all in here. You did a good job Noah. Job well done." Extending my hand to shake his, he said, "You are really going through with this crazy thing? Because if you are, then I have to leave. I'm sorry." "So am I Noah."

He looked at me for a second, turned and walked out the door. While he crossed the yard I called for him to come back. He kept on walking never looking back till he was out of view. I didn't cry, but the tears were there, somewhere. I stood speechless looking at the old neighborhood. Everyone I cared about was gone.

All I could hear was the clock's ticks in the kitchen, until the D. J. announced a song called, "Eternal Flame." The song filled me with so much emotion that I had to lean against a wall to brace myself. The clock showed me that the time was 2:28 p.m. "When ya comin' over Pink, when? This is it. When I go out this door you will never see me again. You got two minutes! You just have to come here so I can tell you what I always wanted to tell you. That I love you. That I do love you and I always will!" Did he hear me, I wondered. Would it matter? It couldn't anymore. The clock read 2:30 and I knew I had to leave.

Erasing every memory of the last few moments, I walked out of the house, secured it and got into my car. Taking their places next to me on the seat were the book and bell.

425

I backed out of the drive and watched for security. As I headed north on Route 4, one of the good guys was driving right in front of me. I knew it wouldn't be long before the bad guys would be on my ass and they were. Self talked. "Caps. They switched to vans. Do they think you're stupid?" "We both know I'm not." Safety was all that mattered and I was. I turned on the radio and figured 'CPZ would play a Beatle song. They had to! It was what they were paid for!

Columbus Avenue. The road I'm supposed to drive on. It divides Sandusky. It's center. "Noah, if you can hear me... I'm on the right side of the street. I'm staying in the lines!" "Fuck him!" Self said in anger, Turn the fuckin' radio on Caps!" The station was set and I drove downtown stopping at the first street. Washington Row. Yes I heard The Beatle song. "The Yellow Submarine." "Why this song? They outta know it's old, worn out and nobody seemed to care for it." "Quiet! Self reminded me, "They'll hear you." "You're right. They're behind me. Pray tell why are they driving like we are in a funeral procession?" "Caps! Shhh! Quit talking! They can hear you!"

"Yellow, orange, pink and blue and it really didn't fucking matter what the four of you wanted to the color of your submarine to be. I'm turning off WCPZ!" "WIOT" took it's place. I didn't even pass the first block when a silver car pulled alongside of mine and drove north bound with me. Bad as I wanted, I didn't look at the people in it. Obviously they were hired for more protection. And a D.J. spoke: "Hey, how's it goin'? She's right in front of us." "I know, I know "IOT! I don't think she has any idea... "CPZ: "It's a great thing to be a part of. Thanks for letting us help ya out." WIOT: "We'll keep ya posted. Stop at the station if you guys get sometime. Later." 'CPZ:

My attention was drawn to the license plate of the silver car in front of me. Could be a clue, I thought! CML427. Repeat: "CML427? Capri Marries Lennon - April 27th? Who could know that I had to be there that day except for me?" I never told. Not that, I thought. That business was between me and God.

With the white van right smack on my ass I couldn't read the plate. Guess all the stuff on top of it should have been enough. Antenna's and a small satellite dish. You can only see so much from mirrors. Didn't want to turn around and be obvious. It looked like a neat and compact radio station inside the van! The silver car parallel with me, well, it was still with me.

One block down to stop and rest for a red light. And I took in all the view I had and I had keen sights. Picture store fronts, displays in the glass, silver cars and their car-plates. Christ I was having a blast! Crossing Market Street the silver car to my left, turned left, and left.

Silver and white were both front and back. There'd be more, I thought. I better start watching the numbers on their plates. "Why didn't I think to do this sooner?" Spying one was easy. A silver car parked near the corner read: LCPM489: Lennon, Capri, Plan, Marry April, 1989? Or does the C P mean Cedar Point? Love Cedar Point Memories? Another red light and more cars.

Water Street, now there was no way to get passed the light once it did turn green. Silver in front of me was just under the light waiting, I guess, for the silver car that was going west on Water Street, but was stuck under the light. Maybe that's why there was another car behind him so he couldn't back up. Maybe the guy in the silver car going east on Water Street inched out too far. The only thing that held any logic was simple. They did not want me to go any further. I was where I was supposed to be. Problem? The parking place left on the west corner was clearly for the handicapped, it wasn't right, but they seemed to want me there so I parked.

As far as containing myself... How could I? I walked briskly across the street looking over the pier. Could see the ferry boats that took me to Cedar Point where I WAS with John Lennon listening to guitar solos and merry-go-round music.

Enter "Daly's." The atmosphere overwhelmed me. It wasn't a place I frequented. Only went there one other time when I bumped into Winky. Green was everywhere and I wanted to be a part of it. I grabbed one of the two seats left at the bar and placed my book and bell in front of me.

Flying high was I when the bartender asked what I'd have. "I don't want alcohol, but I will take a glass of soda water. Could ya drop a drop of green food coloring in it? Make it look, well, ya know." "No problem Miss. Be right back. He came back, right back. I wanted to pay but he insisted this one was on him. Life was good and getting better all the time!

Sipping on the green bubbly water, out of a corner of my eye, I saw a man walk into the bar. This was no ordinary man, I thought. Tall, clean and dressed in every shade of white. He was better than Hollywood-handsome, only I didn't dare turn my head to look. What if he played a part in the code? There was no more sitting, I had to burn off some energy somehow. The bar was big and ever. It's shape was like that of a long stretched out O. Hell if ya walked around it about twenty some times, you'd walk a mile, easy! To get my mind off the man in white, I walked.

Many people were dressed in green, wore green hats, shoes, shirts and then there were those who were there for the party. Going around the bar first time, I noticed a guy in a black leather jacket. Not too rough and tough looking, more like in the making. I walked up to him and said, "Hi. I'm Cap. I noticed that you didn't have anything green on. Here. Take this scarf.

It's green." He said nothing and gave me odd looks while I untied the green scarf off my right arm. Without asking, I tied it on his right arm over his leather jacket and said, "There ya go! Now ya got something green. It stands for Earth so it's an important color. Wear it for me will ya?" "Hey, thanks. Yeah I'd wear it. Does look kinda cool too. What's your name again?" he asked. "Oh I told ya Caps, but everybody calls me Wheels. Just call me The Wheels and watch me roll!" "Wheels. Cool name for a cool lady. Thanks Wheels." Blah, blah, the you're welcome was off to let go of another scarf.

I noticed a couple sitting together at a table holding hands. They looked so happy. I knew which scarf they should have and I untied the red one that was on the left thigh over my jeans. Walking over to them with smiles like I knew them I said, "Excuse me, I'm Wheels, I saw the two of you sitting here and you look so great together. Are you married?" "No we're not," The woman replied. "Well you outta be. If that isn't love written on your faces then you need to have this scarf. It stands for love." I tied it to the woman's arms and said, "You guys will end up walking the isle, you'll see. I know." The couple didn't have time to answer me because I was off to let go of another bandanna

There was a lady sitting at the bar alone. Her fingers, neck and wrists were covered with gems and gold. Although she appeared to have everything, I knew she didn't. "Are those sapphires in that ring?" I asked. "Yes they are. Why do you ask?" "I have a scarf that will go perfect with that ring! Hang on." I leaned over and got the navy blue scarf that was at the bottom of the ones dangling from my right belt loop. The woman's face looked like puzzle pieces. I tied it on her arm and said, "See! That's the universe there. The color stands for it and you got one of the better ones. You looked like you needed a little cheerin' up." Thanks," she said, "I guess maybe I did."

Making my way through the people to get to my seat, straight ahead of me stood the man in white. His back faced me while he talked to a group around him. He can't see me, I thought. He's more than I could have ever imagined. Wait, what's wrong with my thinking? I was thinking. I'm going to be with John Lennon. Last thing I wanted was any attention, so I quietly walked passed him and took my seat at the bar. The bell and book were just as I had left them. The soda had less soda and I was thirsty.

Didn't take long before some smart-ass-young-punk had something to say about my buttons. "So what's with the buttons? You a lesbian? I turned coldly to him. He pissed me off. "My buttons? I like girls? Damn straight I do! Shoot, I am one! Ya know what you need? You need a scarf. Here. Take the fuckin' purple one and with any luck there won't be punks like you bothering "women" like me!" I threw the purple scarf in his face and haled the bartender. "I'll take some mint with that soda. Think I need it!" He fixed me the faintly sweet drink and I took a big swallow. A sigh let out like the wind. I gazed behind and beyond the man in white to watch the ferry boats docked at the foot of the pier. Resting my neck in the cup of my hand I wondered and wondered about the man. Then I wondered about stitches. The ones in my neck. It took a long time remembering how they got there. My mind concentrated on the whys and the when's as I covered them up with my collar again. Tapping my fingers on the book it hit me. My doctor was all upset that I let a dentist cut the cyst out. Hell, I thought, I was under getting a tooth pulled so why not do both at once? It wasn't a big deal, just messed with my appearance.

Sitting didn't last long, so it was off and through the long-round-of-an-ever bar to pass out a yet another bandanna. For some reason, rings came to mind. Rings! It would be an orange stone. It would be on a woman's finger, I thought, I knew! No sooner the thought and the red-headed woman sitting alone was wearing "the" ring! Her appearance was weak. Not quite in the spirit of the "green" and I gave her the scarf I disliked the most The point is I hated the color orange. It was off my thigh and said, "Hi. I'm Wheels. You like orange huh? I saw your ring. It's beautiful! And with your hair this scarf will look great on you! Want it?" I asked. "That's pretty!" she said, "I do like any shade of orange." "Put it on." "Where should I wear it Wheels?" Straight and to the point I said, "Personally, I don't like the color. I gave four away already. They stood for something. The one you have stood for hate, but I gave it to you, who gave it new meaning. Love! And that's all ya need. Well, gotta fly." Flew I did, giving away the black, the yellow, the teal and lavender. My watch read 2:42 p.m. "Caps! Sit down!"

A name was called out and it was coming from ahead to my left. Is he calling over to me, I thought when I turned to see the voice? Again he asked, "Capri? Capri Spettro? Is that really you?" Hesitation, hesitation. Why don't I answer him, I thought? How can he know me? The man is 60 or more. I know a lot of people in Sandusky and I never forget a face, so how did I forget him? Does he know Pope? Self decided to do something. She couldn't stand waiting and showed the stranger the stitches on my neck. "Capri Spettro it is you! It really is you! Come over here. Let me look at you." The book-n-bell looked safe and secure. I took a quick sip of my drink, put out my cigarette and walked to him, timidly saying hello. The man's eyes swelled with tears. Wrapping both arms around me he laughed, he cried, "It's so good to see you again Capri." The hug was done. There was nothing I could think of except who the hell the man was. Self thought, "He's in the book." "Capri. I want you to turn around for a minute. See the man straight ahead of you?" he asked. "Yes." Joe's eyes were in the direction of the man in every shade of white. What's Joe thinking? I thought. "Capri, that's John! Go over and talk with him. He's been waiting for you." Self and I both knew the man was as tall as Lennon, could have passed for a 48 year old Lennon, but the man's eyes were blue. Blue like the sky. Tell Joe about the book, Self thought, "I know who you are now. You're in The Beatle book I have over there on the bar. You're a, wait, you're "George Martin," no, no, that's not it. I'm sorry. Nervous. You're "Sir Joseph Lockwood," of course. Wow! This is incredible." Joe's face was Santa-Clause-jolly and smiling. "Cappy, go on. Go over and talk to him." "Okay Joe. Nice meetin' ya"

Footsteps were like weights as John watched me walk his way. Self made a direct left leading me to my seat. Out of the corner of my eye, John was headed where I was sitting. I sipped my drink, lit up a smoke to get my mind off of John. "Hello. My name is John." His eyes, his hair, was the best anywhere! "Hello." {That's all ya can say?") It was Self. He stood with warmth and charm. "Would it be alright if I sit with you?" "Yes, please!" I said, "You're John." "And you are...?" "I'm Capri." Couldn't look him in the eye, found my hands scampering to The Beatle book flipping pages for air. "Capri. Can I get you something to drink? What are you having?" He sat so proper, manner's, so noble.

Looking at him was wanting to so I did. "No thanks John. Still have one." Thoughts raced me on a track. Why did Joe single me out? Who is this man John? I only know, really know, one John. "My brother's name is John, named after the famous John F Kennedy, "Mathis" and John the Baptist etc..." John spoke and said, "Capri. That book you have. Is it your bible?" Smiling allowed me to answer, "Yes it is. It's everywhere I am. Taught me all I need to know about the positives and the negatives. Numbers were left out of the bible." "Care if I take a look at your bible Capri?" John asked. "No. Here. It's a well written book but it ended with John Lennon dead." John held the book and glanced over the last few pages. "Capri. He doesn't have to be dead. All you have to do is put the book down, open it up to the beginning and he's alive." "Positive John. That's a positive. That's wonderful. I need to take a walk. I can hardly breathe." "Cappy, where you going? Do you have to leave?" "No. I have something to do. Be right back. Do me a favor will ya?" "Sure Capri. What?" "Don't let anyone get a hold of the book or the bell. Okay?" "Okay Capri. I'll be right here when you come back." I was off.

The bar was jamming and packed. Took a ride around the big long O and found Joe stationed. "Joe! You keep this scarf. It stands for the place where I came from. Where I have to go. Saint Mary's Lake." Joe didn't say anything. He took the deep turquoise scarf from me and held it in his hands smiling. "Hey Joe! John is wonderful. Thanks." Off I was back to my seat the book, the bell and John.

"Thanks for watchin' my things." "It wasn't a problem," said John, "I enjoyed watching them and you. You're a very colorful lady Capri!" "Oh John, there's more to me than color! Things have to be solid and hold meaning, truth, reality. Take your teeth for example..." With the tip of my finger nail I tapped his top white teeth. "Those are real aren't they?" I asked. "Yes, they are." "See these nails? They aren't real. My fingers demanded the nails to be long and there just wasn't enough time to grow the broken ones back. Say. I never did ask you were you were from. You can't be from Sand-Town. You don't dress here." "As a matter of fact I'm from Cleveland. Shaker Heights. Have you heard of it?" "Yes I have. Drove through it years ago when I was just a kid." "Capri. Are you married?" John asked. It was my turn. "Are you?" "I'm single. Never been married and what about you? Where are you from?" "I'm from Sandusky. Technically I lived in four states. Arizona, Montana and Washington. Been through 26 of them and there isn't one that compares to Montana. I lived in Glacier National Park for a season. Took off for a boat ride everyday!" Self and I couldn't stop until I put Her on pause, letting John get a word in. "So am I intruding on another man's wife or are you single?" "I had my happy divorce last-day-January of '85 and I have two daughters and a son, the baby, Sonny. Well he's the youngest. He just turned 5."

Self bitch slapped me mentally. Said to me that he may not want an entire crew. "You know Capri. I have a little one myself. She's three months old now. Let me show you her picture." John took his thin-slim-leather-wallet from an inside suit pocket. John has a daughter? Could she be as cute as my girls were, I wondered. "Here she is Capri. This is my baby!" "Oh John! I thought you were gonna show me a picture of a baby-baby, you know! She reminds me of my puppy. He's a Cocker Spaniel. He's 2 and a half months old, jet black, white-white, speaks by the sound of this bell. I call him Maxwell LP. Edison. Maxwell for the coffee I drink. LP. for albums. Edison who invented the light bulb. Dark to light. The Beatles fit in the name, kind of a game and you should see him."

The brass bell was sitting on the book center. Nervously I picked it up, polishing it with the last of the belt-looped-bandanna. Pale pink. "John is that your boat?" (yacht for sure). "Yes it is. The name is difficult to make out in this picture. It's named "Endeavor." "What a beautiful name!" I exclaimed, "it's like and ever and ever! Like numbers! Remains. You should add remains to the name." "Remains and ever would make more sense wouldn't it Capri?" "Remaining forever and ever. Like numbers. The word remains after the word endeavor made my word sound like nothing. Like remains. But there is a positive for nothing John and that is everything!" John took The Beatle book and opened it to a page. "Look here Capri. See this? Rye? That's how I spell my puppy's name. But I pronounce it Ray like the sun." "Were you supposed to open the book to that page?" "No, why do you ask?" John asked. "Maybe the book has a mind of its own. It always wants to open on the name of that book. The title gives me the creeps!" John leaned in closer to me. His quaint and proper fist held his chin with attention and wonder. "Capri. I love the way you think! Positives, negatives. Rye doesn't have to be negative. Think of Rye (Ray), my puppy." "Maybe when our puppies grow up they could have puppies of their own." John took a deep breath moving his face closer to mine. We were a hand-width-away and eye to eye close. John said, "Capri. Never in my life have I ever seen eyes more beautiful than yours. They're amazing! They change colors! You know I've been coming here every year for the last ten years. Where have you been?" "John, I'm here. Home. I'll call this seat home until I get to Goose Island. Tell ya John, I feel like I'm on the yellow brick road looking for the "Emerald City. People outta call me Dorothy instead of Wheels!" "Wheels. Now there's an interesting name," he replied, "I like that. Wheels. Will you excuse me a minute, I have to make a call. It's important. Promise me you'll be here when I through. I'll be looking for you."

John stood up and began to walk away. "Wait. Don't go John! If you go you won't come back. You'll leave and I'll never see you again!" "Capri, I promise you that I will be just outside. You'll see me and I am coming right back. This call should take a minute at most."

There wasn't anything I could say to keep John from making that call. My eyes watched his every step as he walked out to a black and shiny sport utility vehicle. He opened the driver side door, took out a phone, propped one foot on the rocker panel and made his call. I clocked the time. It was 2:55 p.m. Wishing I was a lip-reader I waited for John's return. Time passed slow, very slow. It was 2:57 p.m. I turned to see if my watch was in sync with the bars. It was.

Two minutes, two minutes. Come on John, I thought! I placed the bell back on the front cover of The Beatle book when I noticed pyramid-party-favors on the bar top. They were on all the tables and in between spaces.

2:59 p.m. Four minutes! There he was. John came through the door straight back to me. "I'm sorry Capri. It took a little longer than I thought it would. I told you I'd be right back and here you are!" "John? See this little pyramid here? If you take it, hold it upside down-imagine the sides are mountain sides... then it's just like a lake in Montana. There is an island that sits 10,000 feet down on the lake, between and in the middle of the water." "Sounds like a beautiful place Capri." "It is John. It is." The bar was playing "WCPZ" throughout the time I had been there and at 3 p.m. they played a song they played only one half hour ago when Noah left my house. "Eternal

Flame." I began to cry. I knew that John was a part of code and that he was supposed to call the radio station to play it again and on my number. Number three!

"How can this be John? I heard that song at 2:30. A half hour ago. Why would they play it again so soon? Did you call them? You must have! I can't stop crying John. This is too solid with too much meaning. I have to get up and walk. You wouldn't understand. Maybe you would, but I can't talk it about it now. I'll be back. Please don't leave yet. I promise I will only be a few minutes!" "Capri? Are you going to be okay?" John asked. "Me? Of course!"

They didn't call me Wheels for nothing. I ran outta Daly's. A cold misty rain fell upon me. Refreshed, energized and ready, I tore across Water Street to Shoreline Drive. Briefly I slowed it down to album speed. Had to look at the ferry boats, see the tips and points of The Point. Cedar Point. Self got me into high gear. We raced by the cable television building, passed the Jackson Street Pier, slipped into a very long brick building and skipped-a-step, running up some stairs.

The room was wooden-dark and lit only by the cloudy sky coming through small smoky windows. Large crates and planks filled either side of me and for a brief moment I was afraid. Standing and stopped in the middle, I peered all around. Down, up. Up was about 50 feet! Boldly, Self said, "What a place for a murder!" Murder, I thought? What am I thinking? I'm in a building right on the water. The boat! I need to find the boat! I'm sure there's one waiting for me.

Two shadows drew in closer making men. "Miss?" said one, "You shouldn't be in here." "Yeah. Who and what are you looking for?" asked the other. "I'm supposed to be here. There should be a boat here for me. Big one! Ya had to see it because you just came in from the rain!" The first man spoke, "Miss, there isn't a boat docked here. What makes you think there is?" "It's a long story and I can't talk about it. " Chills ran-over-in-and-out of me. Self was ready to rock. "There was supposed to be a boat. Maybe I'm in the wrong place. Sorry. I'll go." Feeling like a smart ass Self said, "Don't turn any lights on for me. I can find my way outta the dark." Wishing for a banister, I ran down the stairs.

The door that led out was just ahead. I couldn't wait to go through it, get back to Daly's and back to John, when a voice called out. "Hey lady, are you alright? You look like you need something to eat. Are ya hungry?" I turned and saw five younger guys sitting at a table with a few pizzas. There was no time for food and I said, "Not hungry. Can't eat, but thanks. I gotta go." Advice given was something Self and I didn't like when another man said, "Yeah, we saw you fly up those stairs. Come and join us, we don't bite."

"Have one piece of pizza with us?" Another asked. I gave in and sat with the five. I took one quick bite, thanked them and raced back to the bar. To home.

John wasn't seated next to the book and bell. Standing around him were full figured women in dresses and high heels. Their hands were through his hair and over his shoulders and around him period! In my eyes they were nothing more than cheap sluts trying to get on the yacht. It couldn't go on any longer!

In a march with honor I walked up to him and the girls. "Get your hands off of John." I tugged one woman away and another by her fake silk dress. "John they're sluts. They're dirty. They'll only hurt you!" John said nothing. It was like I wasn't even there. "I told you to keep your hands off of him! You bitches need to clean up and quit making the slut scene with John." Can you believe they didn't say anything to me? They didn't. John and the women laughed like they were at a dinner party. Bravely I walked away, low hearted, head high. My knees were shaky and I needed a seat, but when I got there and saw the book, the bell I remembered John Lennon was well. John was center. Attentive to the women. Wanting to leave, wanting to stay, I didn't know the what's and why's that made things that way. Should I leave, I thought? Look for more clues? Give in to them all and ask for the rules? Self thought, Float! I agreed. The book went with me. Faces Caps! Watch for a face. The ones in the book are all over the place!

Authors, authors. I checked out the picture of the two guys on the back cover of the blessed Beatle book and there they were! Sitting at a high table, facing the tinted front window glass. This is too real to be good, I thought! "Well, go introduce yourself Cap!" Sounded like the thing to do and I listened to Self. "Hi. I'm Wheels. But you knew that. I wanted to tell you how I love this book because I figured it out. I'm Capri. It's so cool the way you managed to sneak me in all of it. No one could ever dream up a scheme like that. Except for The Beatles. Oh, I see, you've been in it from the start! That's okay. You don't have to admit it because I know. I'm supposed to." Peter interrupted and said, "Miss. We're not the writers of that book. You obviously have us mistaken." "Look. Here's the book!" I handed the book to who I knew was "Peter Brown." That's you in the picture and your buddy there, "Steven Gaines." Come on! I'm supposed to know this. Let me show you some..." Peter interrupted and said, "Miss, Wheels. I'm sorry. My name is Les and this is Paul." It was my book so I took it away, held the picture of, (cough, cough), Les, and put it right next to his face. "It's you and it's your friend Steven, but if you want to be Les and Paul I won't say a word. No one's supposed to know any way right? Sorry if I bothered you. Oh and don't worry, I won't say anything to anyone. Our secret. Thanks guys. See ya at the party!"

Me and the book went to my seat at the bar, home. The bartender was on time but I wasn't ready. Too much was going around. Maybe that's why they chose Daly's, I thought. Hell, I gotta get outta here. Get my mind off of this charade game and find the "real" John!

Where to go, where to go? Felt like I was skip-walking. Like I wasn't walking on anything, quick, like a dream when you don't want to wake up. Self reminded me to stay centered. That made me think of John (at the bar), which made me think of Lennon the star! Rapidly did I go window-clue-shopping. The first one I noticed was a porcelain plate with a Unicorn on it. And I wondered... Noah. Did you come up with this one? God really blessed them didn't He? They could live under the water, swim with the sun. They could fly in the sky Noah and God they could run!

I kicked open the locked door of the store. The owner was standing behind the register with someone. "Excuse me. I'm Wheels. Did someone put this plate in your window today? Because I'm sure it's a clue. Never mind. You won't tell me because you're not supposed to. Okay, I get it. Thanks. Hope I didn't mess up the lock. Guess you can close now, see ya."

Off I went on a door-slamming-ram-game looking for clues. No one seemed to care that I was doing whatever I wanted. Me being me and Self being Self figured there had to me more. Found myself at the west corner of Market Street and I walked west to WCPZ. I kicked that door open like droppin' a pin because it wasn't locked. I raced to the top of the steps. The place was almost bare and drapes of drop cloths covered desks and chairs there. Remodeling for sure, I thought They were broadcasting live from somewhere outside the station, the building.

I walked into a large room. An older man, dressed in a suit and tie was sitting in an office chair watching out the window. "Sir, you'll have to excuse me but I've been running all over town looking for a friend of mine and I'm whooped! I'm just run through the local paper quick, smoke a cigarette, use the bathroom and I'll be gone. By the way, what are you doing here?" "Well little lady, I'm here because I own this building!" "That's even better!" By this time my butt was in a seat, my feet were up on a desk and I was flipping through "Sandusky Register." "Miss," said the owner, "You look like you need a rest. Go ahead and take your time. Warm up a little." "Thanks." I read through adds and horoscopes finishing my cigarette and used a rest room off the large office. Self took one look in the mirror and said, "Mouth." Mouth? What the hell was She talking about? The teeth? "No Capri. You smoke!" My hand turned the hot water faucet on. The cheap-slut-wanna-be decent-women made me think about "clean." My mouth would have to be clean and I didn't have my tooth brush with me. If I'm going to kiss John Lennon it had better be sanitary. Steam filled my reflection and I reached for a bar of soap. Washed it under the hot water for a couple minutes to make sure it was clean. I lathered up my hands and soaped out my mouth, I had to. It was the only thing available, it almost made me sick. My mouth went under the hot water to get enough to swish the soap bubbles inside and between my teeth. I repeated the rinsing many times. After which I shook my hair into place and was ready for home. Well, the home I thought it was.

The owner was still looking out the window and I wondered if he knew anything about John. He would have to know, I thought. He's the one who got the instructions and the check. "Sir? Did you happen to see a tall man outside here? He's 6 feet tall with brown hair that touches his shoulders. He would be wearing round rimmed sunglasses." "I've been up here a while and I haven't seen anybody that fits the description." "Well, if you wouldn't mind, and you do see him, would you tell him that Wheels went home. He'll understand. Oh, I'm Wheels by the way." "Wheels? Okay Wheels. If I see him I'll be sure he gets the message." "Thanks for lettin' me warm up. You're a good guy." "You're welcome, little lady. Hope you find who you're looking for." "Oh I will. Count on that. They don't call me Wheels for nothing!" He chuckled. Calmly I walked out of the office room until I was outta sight, then I ran like hell back to Daly's.

John was there. Still there with his friends. Keep your head up Caps. Remember... He's not John Lennon. Self was right so I grabbed my seat at the bar and drank the warm-watered-down-drink. Think! I thought ...

... Pink! Gentry! From September 22nd of "84 up until now he has kept specific tabs on me. All the wheres and the whos I loved the most... he knew them well, it was his job! God told him he was supposed to be here for me and this is why he isn't. This is why! There was no choice in the matter. If this pink bandanna stays with me, so does all I feel for Gentry. "Give it to someone. End it forever, I thought, for John!" Ooh Self sent me chills blowing through my heart.

Long at the front end of the O bar I sat watching, looking for just the right person to pass on my scarf to. The pink one.

Diagonally situated was a man in his late twenties, maybe. Cute and boyishly shy about his manners, he briefly smiled to me and the blush was setting in his face. He'd be the one. I untied the pale pink bandanna from a belt loop and walked over to him.

"I needed the smile you gave me, thanks. Oh, I'm Capri, but people call me Cap." This good lookin' guy didn't say anything yet. Wasn't sure what he was thinking. "It's almost 6 o'clock, it's cold and I've been giving people my scarves all day." "Why?" he asked. "Don't know why. Guess I was supposed to. They meant something. Each color stood for something important to me. This one means the most and I want you to have it." "What does this one stand for Capri?" "Hmm... I might cry on ya now." Felt the lump growing sharp in my throat. "Cry? Oh don't cry. Maybe you should keep it" "What's your name, I didn't ask you?" "I should have told you. My name is David" "I have a cousin named David but I haven't seen him in about 27 years. David. I want you to have the scarf. It stands for the man I'm in love with. He calls himself Pinky, but he doesn't wanna be with me anymore. Time to let go. Here, take it. Wear it anywhere you want. Keep it in your pocket. When you find somebody and you fall in love with her, give it to her, because it stands for love. Will ya do that for me David?" "Okay Cap. It would be and honor. You can tie it wherever you think it should be." "Okay, then it has to go closest to your heart. Your left arm. Up here." "Sounds alright by me," he agreed and I tied it as close to perfect as it was going to get and said, "There. Thanks David. I have to get back to my seat. Nice to meet you." "You to Capri. Thanks... for the scarf." "No David, thank you!"

Life wasn't so lonely anymore and the home seat felt like home again. I gazed out the windows and paid no attention to John. That is, not until he walked through a crowd of people behind me. He was about half way between me and the "out" door.

Hashed memories, things, thoughts. Song was negative because Noah left. Song was positive because of John! Pyramid paradise sitting right before my eyes. I took it into my hand, held it upside down. Stood with the symbol raised tall by my arm, and like Moses parting the seas, I called out, "John. This is for you! Goose Island! My Island. Where I came from. I'm Eve, John, don't you remember me?"

♫ ♪ *"My Dream To Be With You"* ♪ ♫
Words and Music by: Catherine Santi on April 8th, 1990

"The flowers that you said you sent never came to me.
Never true could you be to me.
And you believed what he had said and broke my heart,
walk away, in a dream I walk away from you.
And you who came along and turned my hopes away,
far away, in my dreams to be away.
These ships would take me on a voyage where I'd be safe.
Far away, in my dream to save the world with you.
I remember a time. I don't know why we met.
Oh and the chat we had I'd say it was Heavenly spent.

I remember your smile. How your eyes caught the sky.
But you were gone before I chanced to say good bye.
And you I held so close inside the heart of me,
you were so cruel it got the best of me.
And you who beat and dragged me down to loneliness,
gone away, in my dream to get away from you.
And you who taught me fear and took my strength away
gone to stay in my dream to get away.
Then you the only one who knew my sanity...
... Would you be in my dream, my dream to be with you

The crowds left me center, left John speechless and I turned around to the left, headed to my seat. All was calm until some clown yelled, "Hey lady. What ya gonna do when you run outta scares? Gonna take your clothes off too?" "Ya wanna see that don't cha! Feeling left out? Here. You want clothes?" The dude said, "I didn't say I wanted ya to, I just figured you would." "Yellow. Fucking yellow. You want the fucking shirt? You can have it." The punk stood there laughing with his punk friends grinning behind cupped hands. Damp from the rain, I took it off, crumbled it real tight and threw at him. Hit him the face. Made my day! I still had my tank top for back up. It had a tiny, stitched-emblem on the left. "Playboy's" little bunny ears. I was tough. I was cool. The punk and his friends were already buried in my brain. I needed air, rain and whatever God wanted to throw at me.

Running to the foot of Shoreline Drive I halted at the water. Centered right between ferry boats and "Neuman's" boat services. Boats and boats and not a one there for me. With my arms up and out stretched I called out to God. "Where the hell is my boat? Why are You putting me through all of this? For one bite off the fucking apple? Are Ya crazy? Didn't I give You enough? Gave up Gentry, and for what, for who for when?" Number One never came right out and said what was on His mind, but Self did, "Jesus! You're gonna get the rib and I don't break a promise. Be there. You know where. You know when. You know so much!"

Peered beyond the boats and across the water to the island. Slowing I took in the view and made up my mind to get back to the bar, fast. I ran.

And guess who decided to talk to me? John. "Capri! Look at yourself! Whatever happened to you?" "Nothing happened to me John! I'm healthy and strong." "You don't look healthy Capri." "John, go on and say it. Say skin and bones. God only knows how many times Noah said it. It won't be anything new. And hey! If ya ever need somebody to move a pool table, I'm her! Now if you don't mind please, I'd just like to be left alone for a while. I need to think. I have so much to do and it's 6:30 isn't it?" Curiously John looked at me after he noted the time on his watch and said, "Yes. It is six-thirty. Capri. Do whatever you have to."

John walked over to his friends and I thought. Always thought. I'm not sure how long I sat watching the sky grow darker. A lot of time passed thinking about the future. How my life was about to change. Dramatically!

Well, I was ready to talk more with John but I couldn't see him in the crowd. "He's probably in the men's room." Self was probably right. I waited and waited but he wasn't going to be the bathroom for 15 minutes!

"Hey bartender. I know you're busy, but do you remember that guy I was talking to earlier? You know. The one all in white?" He nodded, unsure. "You know, John? He's from Cleveland. Said that he's been coming here for the last ten years on Saint Patty's Day." "Oh! Okay, you mean John. Sheffield Lake I think. Yeah he does come here every year. I don't know Miss, I couldn't tell ya. He might have left for Cleveland."

Cleveland? Left and didn't say good bye? Why didn't he give me a chance to say to tell him how grand it was to meet him? A chance to say good bye? Home wasn't feeling like home again and I was mind-worn-heart-torn-burnt-born. Had to leave. Had to go somewhere only I didn't know where.

The ice in my drink had liquefied. The book, the bell and myself left Daly's to sort things out.

Dark and damp was the night walk to "Neuman's" on Shoreline. Guess I went there because it was close, the light was on and the door wasn't locked. Glass cases displaying ships and boats were almost a laugh. It was school time. On the service counter was a bell. You know the kind. Ring-bell-for-service-kinda-teacher-like-bell. Never did like them but I wanted someone to know that I was there.

A back office door was open and lit so I called out, "Hello? Is there anybody back there?" A woman walked out and said, "Hi. Can I help you with anything?" "No. I saw the light on and the bench inside the front door. Well, yes, I guess I do need something. If you're gonna be here a little while, would it be alright to sit down and warm up?" "Honey you go right ahead and do that. Don't you have a jacket?" she asked. "Nope. Didn't think I'd be downtown this long." The woman offered me a cup of hot coffee and I didn't hesitate to take some.

On the wooden bench I sat and I thought while I sipped on the coffee. Could have looked out the window at the bay, but I had enough boat watching. Felt warm, but I didn't feel secure. Didn't know why and I didn't want to know why. Didn't want to think anymore. Couldn't think. But Self butted in and said, "You never polished that bell. Maybe you got a real treasure brass bell for a buck."

Hope was about all I had left. The powder-blue-bandanna came off my arm. Chose the handle tip of the bell for a place to begin and I began the process to see if it was brass. The work was paying off. Half way through a shine and the woman from the back came out and asked me if I wanted more coffee. There was plenty in the cup so I declined. I kept working on the bell. After about an hour, when the entire bell was polished, I knew nothing would shine like it except for the real thing and it was beautiful and filled with memories. Maxwell LP. Edison knew the bell and knew it well! Three simple lessons, the smart little guy! Started feeling feelings and I started to cry. The bell and me would say goodbye. Gave it a few hot-short-shots-of-breath, powder-blued it once more. Teacher's bell, I slid it away. Put mine in its place and I left for the door.

Up the hill to Water Street, to my car, I thought. Maybe a drive. Maybe a Beatle song. Then I'll go back to Daly's one more time to see if John's there.

At the corner, on the side-walk where the bar was, I saw my car just across the street. Like anyone else, I waited for the right light to come on and began to cross when two officers popped outta their cruiser's with questions. "Excuse me Miss, were you in Daly's tonight?" "Yeah, so what if I was? Can't a person go home?" I kept walking. "Miss? We got a call tonight from Daly's. We were told that a woman in the bar was annoying the other patrons." The cops were pissing me off and Self struck. "Listen. My name is Capri Spettro and I was supposed to be in Daly's tonight. Shit you'd never understand. You're not supposed to! It's me, the FBI, the CIA and the rest Got it?" Self had me fucked now. One of the cops took me by the arm and put me in the back seat of the cop car. Never, never but never was I ever in the back of a cop car! They left the door open. Were they going to arrest me, I thought? For what? For wanting to go home? The two cops were about 15 feet away and talking between themselves. Were they going to arrest me? I got out of the car, walking on the walk that led to Daly's back parking lot, but Ah, another cop car blocked-me-stopped-me. "Capri? You did say your name was Capri? I'm Officer Trades. Do you have any identification on you?" "No sir I do not. I am who I am because | was supposed to be in Daly's tonight Ask Joe, an older man. He'll tell ya who I am." "Capri. You don't have any identification, you're out wondering around in the cold weather with no jacket, no coat. Look. Just have a seat in the back of the cruiser, warm up a little bit while me and Officer Lakes decide what to do." Stepped back a quick step and said, "Don't put me in me in handcuffs. You're not gonna do that are you?" "No we won't put you in hand cuffs." Officer Trades opened the door and got me inside. He shut the door and walked a few feet away talking to Trades.

Banging on the window to get the attention of the cops was getting me nowhere. I cried and pleaded for them to release me from the car. They were ignoring me on purpose. "Christ they have to hear me banging on the window. Why don't they open the fuckin' door?" Forever was going by and nothing I did, yelled or screamed helped. A long breath came from my mouth when Officer Trades opened the door telling me could get out. "Look! I got three kids at home, I live at 709 Polk Street. That's my car right over there. The "Citation." If you don't believe me call Doc Kellee. He's the one who put the stitches in my neck. See?" Self pointed them out. Pulled the collar back. Officer Lakes said, "Capri. We want you to go home. We're even willing to over look the fact that you parked in a handicap zone providing that you do not go into Daly's anymore tonight. They don't want you in there. Do I make myself clear?" "Yes. But I can't go back in there..." Officer Trades stepped in, "That's correct Capri, just go home." Glancing down to the pavement I shrugged my shoulders. "It's funny. I went through all this for nothin'. Ya know Mr. Trades? Somebody just played a big joke and it was all on me. I'll drive to my house. I'll go, but if you don't mind, I haven't had much sleep lately and I'm really tired. Could you follow me to my house? Make sure I get there okay?" "No problem Capri," said Trades, "We'd be right behind you."

There was my car and out came my keys. I started it up and checked my rear view mirror for the cop car and Trades was right behind me. Glad he couldn't see my face because I broke down to tears as I headed to the first red light on Market street. Kept wiping my eyes to see straight. Tuned WCPZ in when the D.J. came on the air and said, "We're looking for a young lady who was last seen crying when she left Daly's. Wherever you are wipe those tears away and get over to The Radisson. There's gonna be a big party in your honor. Good chance a wedding might take place out here tonight. I see a yacht docked out in the water and it's beautiful. Oh, and don't worry if you don't have anything green to wear just bring something that you can share with everyone." And a song played. If it had been a Beatle song I would have remembered. But that was beside the point, after the point, before the point, it didn't matter. I was the lady who left Daly's in tears. I'm the one they are looking for. "Capri. Hurry and get your shit together. You're getting married." Self got me motivated and me and the book turned west onto Polk Street. Officer Trades stayed in the street while I pulled in the drive. He waved me on as I got out and he drove away.

♫ ♪ *"Letting You Go"* ♪ ♫
Words and Music by: Catherine Santi on July 13th, 1986

I'm finally feeling to write, it feels so good by the night,
when the moons full of the light
Reflecting back it seemed so right
It's just my way of letting you go.
No I'm no longer afraid, but there's these plans that I've made.
I thought at the end of today, a priceless dream won't be my way.
It's just my way, I know it don't show.
Once in a while I'll dream of you.
The time I had and spent with you.
Now you're no part of me, foot notes of history.
Wasn't good enough for you, that's simple, that's true.
No I will never forget the first time you and I met
My love I could never regret, but hear me out these words I set,
It's just my way of letting you go."

Chapter Twenty Three: "Magical. Mysterious. Mad?"

Rushing through the front door I called for my oldest. "Buff where are you? You upstairs? Hurry and come down here. You won't believe it, you just won't believe it!" Jules and Buff both came crashing down the stairs with big-wonder-filled-eyes and questions. "Mom! Does it have anything to do with you know who?" "Yeah Buff it does ! I'm pretty sure." "Who are you talking about mom? How come nobody told me?" "Buff, I thought you were gonna tell Jules last night. How come you didn't?" "She was sleeping mom!" Jules spoke and said, "Wait a second you guys. What's going on?" "Jules, mom told me last night when you were sleeping that she was going to meet John Lennon. John Lennon Jules! Can you believe it?" "The Beatles John Lennon mom?" So seriously Jules asked! "Yes! But wait. There's more to it than just meeting him..." "Sonny," called Buff, "Don't you wanna hear about mom? " Sonny said nothing. Jules was up in front of his program. Her hands on her 7 year old hips demanding: "Sonny! Mom's meeting John Lennon!" "So. Move away from the TV., I can't see it!"

There were plans to be made so I me and the girls went into the kitchen. I paced. Buff watched out the window for more Limo's. Jules did too and they were out and plenty.

Buff called to me, "Mom. When are you going to meet John Lennon? What time? Is he coming here? God Jules! What if he comes here?" Enter Jules: (already on phone), "Can I call Libby up and tell her." "Sure, why not! Doesn't matter who finds out because tonight I am going to be the third and best Mrs. John Lennon ever!" "Mom? You're going to marry John Lennon? How do you know?" "Damn Buff, I can barely breathe it's so exciting! Today I went out looking for him. John that is. Anyway. That's where I've been till now. I cried when I left downtown because I couldn't find him any place. I thought that's where I was supposed to go until I heard the D. J. from 'CPZ telling me that I should go to the Radisson, that I might be getting married and that I should take something to share with everybody. They said they were holding a party in my honor. I can't wait to get there Buff! I can't believe it ! Wow!" "Mom, what are you wearing?" Jules asked. The skirt and top Pope got me. I bought the shoes this morning. Oh Jules, will you get them out of the closet for me? I gotta take a shower and start getting ready. I don't know when they're gonna to pick me up. Think they're supposed to pick me up."

443

Slip-slided my way through the back room in my socks. Buff nearly knocked me to the floor and said, "Mom, I think one is pulling in the drive right now!" I slid back to the kitchen and looked out the window of the front door. There were two Limos. A silver one and a white one. "Buff. The road's just tight, they're making more room. That's a white one pulling cock-eyed in the drive. The bad guys. I won't be riding in anything but silver!"

I rushed back to the shower and got in quick. Don't think I ever finished that fast. Ran out with my hair in a towel. I looked everywhere for a pair of stockings. I didn't have any. I clocked the time. There was no time to get to the store around the corner. Not in a towel and two minutes till closing. Now what? I asked myself. Self said, "Buff, I don't have any nylons and "I.G.A," is gonna close. There's no time. Call your baby-sitter Gina. See if she can has a pair I can borrow." "Okay mom." Time was blurred. Thoughts of what a bride should have when she's getting married were dear. Something old. My pearl earrings. 22 years old outta do it. Something blue. The beautiful mid length skirt, blouse and matching dress jacket was perfect. Borrowing nylons from Gina, would be borrowed. Hope she has some! New, new, new. Ah yes. The shoes! Good shoes! "Mom," Buff called, "Gina said to ask what your size is." "Medium. B." Felt like I was on flight to the bathroom. Dried my hair, made sure that my make-up was applied light but spoken.

Took about ten minutes. In the middle of putting lipstick on last, Gina raced through the door with a pair of new nylons for me. She was freezing, shaking and dying to know what all the excitement was about. Self and I wanted to know how she got here so fast. "Gina. What the hell did you do run?" "Yeah! Buff told me what was going on. I got so excited that I just grabbed a coat, my purse and ran to the store. Then... (pausing for air) ... I ran over here as fast as I could." "Gina you didn't have to buy me new nylons and you didn't have to run!" "I didn't have any nylons so I got ya some and I ran. I was so excited I couldn't help it. I wanted to yell or something. How did you know he wasn't dead? I mean, how did you find out John Lennon's really alive?" "Shit Gina. That's a long, long story. But to make the long story even shorter, I found it all in this book." I handed her The Beatle book. "It's a code. I'm the only one who can break it because John has to be absolutely certain that I'm Capri Spettro! The one he was with at Cedar Point sixteen years ago. Gina, I'm sorry, I'm too excited to talk. I gotta finish getting ready. Let me pay you for the nylons." "They were only a couple bucks. I just wanna come live with you guys!" "I wouldn't have it any other way Gina'"

Jules had her ears and mouth to the phone, Buff and Gina were pacing, watching for a car. A silver Car. A silver Limousine! Arrival time unknown and not yet seen.

Put on the finishing touches. The stocking and sling back teal shoes. I was ready. I was "not" ready! Take something to share with everyone," Self reminded me. "What do I have to share with everyone and how many people do I have to share it with?" Self pointed me in the direction of the cans. The cans? Sure. The cans! The guy on the radio said if I didn't have anything green to wear..."

The cupboard door opened and two dark-brown-leaf-bags were in my hands. Perfect, I thought! No one will see what's in them, till they're open. Buff, Jules and Gina stood in the kitchen, asking in wonder what I was doing and what was I saying. Self couldn't keep anything to herself. "I'm puttin' these cans in bags. It's perfect! I have 140 of 'em so... I'm gonna divide them equal. 70 in one and 70 in the other. No wait! It's not right. That's 14 and that's five." There was me and the cans sitting and strewn on the kitchen floor counting. Was counting. Lost count. Looked up at the girls and said, "Sorry you guys, but I gotta know just how many to put in each one. They have to be whole numbers! I'm good with numbers but I have to be alone, do ya mind?" Whoosh! They were back to the window and door. Jules was making more calls. Sonny? He dropped out on the couch watching his program.

Numbers, numbers. Check the time, check the time. Nine twenty-five "Jesus Caps! You gonna add the fucking time too? Think cans." "Of course. Cans. Numbers again and again and "boom," I knew it all along. Simple math didn't take too long.

Sixty cans went in one bag. Three and three is me! Eighty cans went in the other and that made the two, even if two was gone forever.

The cans were bagged so I stood ready set but a car didn't come yet. Something was missing. Something was wrong. Self and I heard it in my head, t'was a song. "... Send me your picture, send it my dear, so I can hold you and pretend you are here..." Picture. A gift for the groom. It's what I'm supposed to do! On a back wall, well out of view was a picture I drew. It had been there a year and a month and some 18 days long. This present is going where it belongs. It isn't of me, I thought! I'd have to go through shoe box upon shoe box to find one. Which one, which one? Well damn there it is! Leaning the "Omega," hair blowing in the breeze. It was warm, it was summer. Mayor said "Say Cheese." I was twenty-three and you were thirty-nine. You're still mine. I took out a pair of scissors. Cut it at angle so it would fit snug in the frame of the drawing I was taking.

This was it! I was set. Buff and Gina already loaded the car with the cans. Jules wanted to take something out and assured me she would not drop the present. Carefully she placed the pictures in the passenger seat. I was very neat. Jacket, softly shined. Silver buttons. Small, simple soft and white, trimmed the ends of the sleeves just right. Tossed a book of matches, some cigarettes in the roomy pockets sewed just below the hip line.

In this dream so real, so new, I wasn't sure what to do. Except that I was going to be doing my own driving. The girls wished me luck. "Say, keep the line open. If the wedding is on you're all coming. I can't wait. Okay, I'm ready, look out here I come. Watch me run. Okay you guys? Gina? You gonna hang out here?" "I wouldn't miss this for anything," she said excitedly. "Thanks. It's blast off time. 9:45!"

The Radisson Hotel was 7 minutes from my house. The short drive went quick and I parked close to the entrance. I held my art piece under my arm and carried the two bags of cans proudly to the entrance.

First stop, front desk. "Excuse me. My name is Wheels. There's a private party being held here for me tonight. I was wondering if you could get one of the bell boys to take these two bags up to the..." Assistance butted in with a smile and said, "How can I help you tonight?" "Yes, could you grab these two bags and take them up to the third floor? They're expecting me soon." He had a cart for that purpose, put my dark brown leaf bags on them and said, "Want to follow me up?" "Might as well. Yeah sure. I don't wanna wait down here." I turned to the clerk and thanked him for nothing!

Rushing into the elevator was a long trip when the clerk said, "Miss, I think something fell off your drawing. It's laying right behind you. See it?" "Yes. I do." For something, I thanked him. The bell boy politely asked, "So there's a party for you tonight?" "Yes there is. I'm getting married!" "Congratulations Miss. Third floor here we are."

Warm comfortable leather chairs and sofas were ahead. Me and my picture took a seat. A rest. So many doors in this huge room I thought, wondering which room was mine and who would escort me. Remaining seated wasn't easy, but with all the windows to look out of, or into, something inside said sit.

"Christ! What's taking so long? I'm already late!" Self bitched and I bitched right back. "You would think by now somebody would show me which door. And where's the fuckin' cans?" Self wondered. "What did the bell boy do with them?"

Approaching me quietly on the thick soft carpet was a tall man. Suit and tie kinda guy. "Miss? Is there anything I can help you with this evening?" This needed standing! "Yes! There's a party here for me tonight but I don't know which room it's in." The man said, "What's your name? I'll check the guest list to see if you're on it." "It's Wheels. Look for it. It's there. I would tell you my real name but no one's supposed to know I'm here." "I'm afraid I don't understand. Perhaps you can explain it to me." Self talked on my behalf. "Sir. If you don't mind, I'm already late. Would you please check the list for my name?" "Have a seat Miss, I'll go and see. Be right back."

As the man was down and well hidden in the hall, I grabbed my present and went through the nearest door. About twelve people sat at a long-linen-clothed-table. Beyond the people was an empty corner that needed decor. I walked past the table, placed my drawing where it belonged and took the one seat left at the head

Two men entertained. One sang and the other played a synthesizer. Small, I thought!

A lady to my left asked, "Got the last seat I see. What's your name?" "Me?" I said, "Don't think I should say who I am. It's a hush-hush kinda thing. Almost crazy just to be here! The band..." "Yes it is," she said, "Maybe I better not say my name so I don't give you away." "Thanks. Do you even know what's going on?" I asked. "You said it. It's crazy!" The conversation between me and the woman stopped abruptly, when I felt hands holding me by the arms. The voice connected to those arms said, "Wheels. Come with me please. You're name is not on the guest list. This is a private party and you shouldn't be here. Let's leave these people alone." Jerking from his grasp, Self demanded, "Who the hell are you?" "I'm the assistant manager." Standing eye to eye with him I said, "Assistant? That's all? You have no clue what's going on do you? Know why? Because you're not supposed to know. Can't you people understand that!" "Miss, I was patient, polite, but now I'm afraid you'll have to leave. And by that I mean now. Right now!" Fine! I'll go, but I'm not leaving without my picture. "Hold on Wheels, the door is here!" The assistant manager tail-gated my every step when a voice said, "Sir. Wait a minute. I saw her put that picture there when she came in. It's hers." It was my anonymous-table-mate speaking. I wink-thanked her, picked up my belongings and was escorted out of the room. We rode the elevator to the main floor, got out and the assistant manager said, "Wheels. Can I trust you to wait here till I find the manager Mr. Speel?" Trust me, I thought? That's a stupid question. I'm supposed to be here!"

A convention of people passed me by but only one stood out and I had to be right behind her. I tugged her dress sleeve and said, "You're "Olivia Newton John"! I'd know you anywhere! And don't worry, I won't tell anyone who you are because no one's supposed to know who I am either." "Excuse me?" she asked. Olivia began to walk away when I tugged her back and said, "It was really nice to meet you. Ya know, I write and sing my own music and I'm good, but I never got out of the house to show any body if ya know what I mean." "I appreciate the compliment. But I'm not Olivia My name is ... it doesn't matter. I'm sorry, I have to go. Conventions you know. Good luck with your music." Who does she think she's kidding, Self thought, but I kept talking. "I won't tell. Your secret is safe with me, and I know about secrets." By the way, you look great in person!" The woman turned and smiled with uncertainty and followed the clan she must have come in with. What will I do when I deal with Speel? I thought. He's not in on it and he wouldn't understand. More alert was Self. She saw a man coming my way. Then I did. Damn it! Must be Speel.

"Before you say anything to me Mr. Speel I'd like you to call me by my real name Capri. He did. "Capri? What seems to be the problem?" Anxiously I answered quick... "There is no problem and I can't tell you what is going on. Please don't ask. You're not supposed to know." With authority, Speel said, "Capri, I run this hotel, if there's something going on I would know. Whatever it is you can tell me." "I'm not telling you anything. Do you realize that as we speak the FBI and the CIA are all over your parking lot?" I stood, pointing to the lobby windows. Mr. Speel looked bewildered and asked, "The FBI and CIA are out there? Why would they be there? And if they are, don't you think I'd know? I over see everything here." Speel was patient. "Look, if you don't believe me, just ask Wayne. He's with the police. A detective who's on the third floor watching and recording everything I say and do. You may be manager, but this is something you can't know about. If I said anything to anyone and that includes you, it would create mass hysteria This place would be jammed full. Hundreds and thousands of people will be crawling everywhere! That's why I can't say anything." "Capri, my assistant is calling the authorities. I suggest that you tell me what's going on or I'd have no choice but to have you arrested."

From a second story balcony inside the lobby I heard a "shh" sound. I looked up, spied a man with a funny plastic green hat on and clover shaped pin that lit up when he pulled on a connected string. Again I heard the man above me saying, "Don't tell 'em. Shh...Quiet!" And he lit his Shamrock. Speel took over and demanded to know. "Capri, if you don't tell me what's going on then the deputies are outside and ready to take you." Not wanting confinement and wanting to be on time for my wedding I spoke out. "I am going to marry John Lennon tonight. He is here in this hotel. That's why the FBI and the CIA are outside the building. Like I told you, if word got out that John is alive and here, people would be packing the place like armies! That's what I'm not supposed to say." Mr. Speel took me by the hand and said, "Capri, I think you need some help, come on, let's go."

Speel was my escort to the cop car waiting for me in the lot. I was placed in the back seat and the doors were closed... again.

One of the deputies was inside talking with the manager and the other was inside the car with me. Front passenger seat. Maybe he'd understand, so I talked. "Sir, back in 1980 everyone heard about Lennon being shot, but suppose he wasn't. I mean after all he and the other Beatles had enough money that they could have fooled the world into thinking John was shot. He could still be alive! Why is that so hard to believe? It's not impossible." "I suppose anything is possible little lady." The deputy said nothing more, but his partner had no problem getting right to the point. "Capri. I see that you were picked up earlier this evening downtown by the Sandusky police. They instructed you to go home. Now if we let you go and you don't go home and stay home, we we'll have no choice but to take you where you will be watched. That would be the state mental hospital in Toledo. You don't want to go there do you Capri?" "No, no I don't want to go there. I'm no nut! I'm not crazy! Just because you guys don't know what's going on, and you're not supposed to know, you think I'm crazy." "Capri. Is there someplace where you can go tonight. Someone who'll look out for you? We wouldn't want to see you get hurt." Naturally, thought Self. "Yes you can call Pope. That's my dad. He's not going to let you take me to some nut house because he knows I'm okay."

The deputies let me lock my car up where I found the bagged coffee cans. I put the drawing in the passenger seat of the car, eyes down, locked it up and got back in the cruiser that would now be on route to Pope's house.

Good old Pope... Strong, calm and reliable Pope was ready to take care of everything when the police arrived at his door with me. He sent me to Shorty's house. The last place I wanted to be!

My youngest brother instructions were: Keeping me in the house. Period.

"C" Street. Back to number three... that was me. I was home again and I wanted to talk to Noah.

The black phone hung in the kitchen dark with the night and I dialed his number. He answered. "Oh Noah. It's me Cappy. I don't wanna be at my brother's house. That's where I am." There is little time to tell all. Shorty talked me outta the phone, talked to Noah and hung up. I yelled at my little brother. "Noah is my boyfriend. I don't wanna be here with you and your girlfriend, I wanna be with him!" "Cappy, I'm sorry, I can't let you go because if I do I gotta tell Pope and if I do that he's going to call somebody to come and get you. You don't want that. Try to get some sleep. Maybe you can see Noah tomorrow." Tomorrow was light years away. There was no fighting this readied team. I had no other alternative but to stay at Shorty's house till morning.

I watched the clock hands never move and saw the hours pass. The sun was up and I had to convince Pope to let me stay with Noah. Had to pretend that the night never happened. This will be a sure ticket out of here, I thought

Pope's house was situated in Shorty's back yard-left. I cut through the yard to dad's. He came to the door. "Pope please don't make me stay with Shorty. I want to stay with Noah, my boyfriend, and he won't let anything happen to me. If I promise to stay there will you let me go?" "I don't know what's going on, but I seen this happen to The Mayor I think. I think you are losing too much weight. You look like a little old woman. I'm going to talk to this Noah guy and if I don't like him or trust him you aren't going to stay there. I'll go over there with you. I want to see him face to face and talk to him." Pope asked me to get Noah on the phone so he could let him know we would be coming by.

The wait to get over to Noah's was antagonizing. The questions from Pope even worse. "What's wrong with you Cappy? Look at you! You have to eat. Let me see your hands. Your hands are so skinny I can see the bones in them. What are you doing? Are you taking something?" Had I not said something soon, I might have flipped his kitchen table right off its legs and made a mad dash out the side door. "Pope I'm fine. I'm not taking any drugs or anything. Sure I smoke a little pot now and then, so what. I'm skinny! Look at Hermit and John! You never said anything to them about being skinny. The older the three of us get, the skinnier we get. It doesn't mean we aren't healthy, just thin. Just the other day, a week or so ago I was at The Barrel. Remember when I drove dump truck? A few guys from "C. J. Speed Mix" were there. And Joe, the owner's son was getting dogged by the other guys. They told him he was a wimp and stuff..." "Come on, sit down. Rest, I'll make you some nice chicken broth. You need to start eating something. Maybe some crackers. Please Cappy, sit down! Can't you see that you are sick?" A disturbing question from him so I finished the story about Joe and me. "He was sitting at the bar and went to say hi. One of 'em asked me to show Joe my muscles. So I flexed my arm. Kevin was crackin' up. He said "Joe, I bet Cap can kick your ass!" Joe was easy to pick on so I sat down and said, "Like I will now! Come Joe, let's you and me arm wrestle. I'll put ya down." The other guys were roarin'. Joe put his arm on the bar and me, mine. Joe's an easy 6 feet and I put him down with one slap, bam! I mean he was on the floor! His buddies still dog him every time they see me when Joe's around.

So what makes you think I'm so sick? The cops, you, the people from The Barrel, Ladie and all of you think I'm sick and I'm just fine!" Pope had been pacing the kitchen up until then. He sat at the table with me. His words sort of split as he spoke to me. "They call me. I talk to the police. They told me you were picked up twice and the second time at a hotel because you said you were going to marry John Lennon. You can't marry John Lennon. He's not alive anymore. He's dead Cappy! You never knew John Lennon."

"No Pope. I know him. I know his music, sang his music, played his music, read books about him and I love him. I did since the first day I saw him. And even though you think he's dead, I can love him, dead or alive just like you love Mayor. She's dead. Tell me that you don't love her anymore. You do just like she was alive and around." "Cappy, you say you love him, okay. But you can't marry someone who is dead. John Lennon is dead!" "Pope, he isn't dead. No way did someone shoot him. It was a game. To get him outta New York City. He had to hide out. He knew he was going back to be a Beatle. Why do you always think they say the number nine all the time? John was born October 9th. It's 1989. Nine years after the year they say he was shot!"

Pope was nearly in tears trying desperately to change my mind but it was set. Self changed the subject. "How come you and Mayor didn't name me Holly? I was born on Christmas Day right? Did you lose my papers when you took me from my real mom? She's alive isn't she? I have a right to know where and when I was born don't I?" My voice was seething. "Cappy. I saw Mayor get sick after the baby died She was sick in her head. She had to go to a hospital for 6 weeks, because when she saw the baby at the funeral, she refused to believe it was hers. The doctors helped her get better. That's what I think you need to do. You're sick and there are doctors who can help you too. Why don't you let me take you to the hospital so they can see you?" "Forget it. No way am I going to get locked up with a bunch of loons for 6 weeks. No way. You can't make me go. I don't live here. That isn't my house. I am not going there." The words slammed my fists to the table. There had to be a way out.

Pope didn't give up and said, "Let's call "Doctor Buder." He's been your doctor since you were born. You like him." "No. I'm not getting locked up because I'm not your daughter. You don't wanna have anything to do with me do you? It would be easy for you. Have me locked up for good in some nut house. I ain't going I told you." Pope said I wouldn't get locked up and wanted me to talk to Buder myself.

That worked and in a few minutes Pope and Doc' were on the phone and it was handed to me. "Hi Doc', how's it going? You're not going to have me locked up are you? I don't need to go to any lunatic asylum. I'm fine. It's just that no one wants to believe that I may know things that they don't" "Slow down honey, I'm not going to make you go to the hospital. Maybe I could give you something to calm you down. Your dad tells me that you haven't been eating or sleeping. If you don't sleep, your body doesn't get the rest it needs. You reed to rest Cap. You need to eat. Your body needs food to function properly." "But Doc', I can't eat. My jaw is dime thin. It could break!" "Cap, are you allergic to anything? No, that's right, you're not. I'm going to call in some valiums for you." "Doc', are you talkin 'about a little blue pill? Hole in the middle?" "Yes..." "Oh, I just wondered. Somebody I knew had them once. Okay Doc'. I'll try' em if ya think they'll work," "Cappy, you're gonna be just fine. Will you put your dad back on the phone?" he asked. I handed the phone to Pope. He talked to Buder for a few minutes. Pope told me that I was allowed three pill a day. (it figured). Told me that he was supposed to keep the pills for me. I didn't have a problem with that, I just couldn't wait to pop one!

Pope said, "Will your friend be at home now? " "Yes Pope. He will. Are you gonna let me stay there? Can we leave now please?" "Call him on the phone and we'll stop by his house on the way to the drug store. I'll go warm up the car." In minutes we were on our way.

"Pope, that's Noah's house. Pull up In the drive." I started to get out but Pope insisted I stay in the car with the doors and windows shut. Talking with Noah would be private. Pope knocked on the side door. Noah poked his head out to see who it was. The meeting was a done deal dragging. I wondered... Would Noah extend his hand to Pope? Would Pope accept it? Noah did and Pope took it. The shake was over. They talked and I knew I was as good as in.

Seemed like they talked for an eternity. Wondered what Noah was saying. What Pope was saying to him. I couldn't hear them. The both of them walked over to the car and I was out. "Okay Cappy. I talked to Noah and he promised me he'd keep you here in the house." Noah said, "Cappy I told your dad you'd stay in. You have to stay in the house or you'll have to go the hospital and you don't wanna go there. Will you listen to me Cappy?" "Yes Noah. I promise I won't leave." "Cappy, I was talking to Noah and we think that maybe after tonight you might go to "Firelands," just for a few days. That's all, just a few day and you can go back home." Noah cut in politely, "Cappy, you're gonna be okay. Your doctor said they only keep you there a few days and let you go. Will you listen please?"

Jesus! Were the two of them ever gonna let me have some say? It was Pope's turn. "You got three kids to think about too." Concerned about the three days, I said, "What if they think I'm mental and they don't let me out? Maybe Buder is making it up. Maybe you are making it up. You want to get rid of me don't you! You said I didn't have to go and you're changing your mind." "Caps!" Noah said, "It can't hurt you. It's just for three days. Don't you wanna stay here?" "Yes I do Noah, I do!" "Hon, then you gotta listen to your dad, me and the doctor." Fine. I give in. Could I make a quick call? Is this okay or do I have to wait till we go to the drug store before I can do that? You guys gonna let me do anything at all? Before you know it, you'll say I can't have a fuckin' cigarette!" "Make your call Capri." Pope said. All of us were in the house. I dashed upstairs to use the phone there. "Priest! It's me. Cap. I can't go in too many details but you need to come over to Noah's right now. Me and Pope are going to the drug store to get me some valiums, then he's talking about having me put in the nut house for a few days and I think it will be forever, 'cause I don't think I'm his so please come over to Noah's! Make sure they don't take me away! I don't wanna be locked up Priest Please! You have to help me?" Immediately Priest agreed to come right over. I gave him the directions just in time because Pope came up the stairs to get me. "Come on let's get going, you need those pills." Then he asked a peculiar question. "Don't you have something else to wear, you can't wear that dress?" "Why not?" I asked, "What's wrong with it? You bought it for me and you don't want me to wear it? It was good enough to get married in until everybody, including you, made sure that wasn't gonna happen." "It's shameful!" Pope remarked.

Shameful? I thought. What was so shameful about a three piece suit? "This skirt, this jacket, the silver buttons, it's a beautiful suit! "What's so shameful about this suit Pope?" I asked his highness. Pope turned to Noah, "She can't wear it. Can she borrow some pants and a shirt? I don't think she has a coat or anything" "Oh fine, now my boyfriend and you are talking like I'm not even in the room. Do you think I don't know what you're saying? I know everything you're saying. You want me to wear his clothes! Why, why Pope? I don't do Noah's clothes. They won't fit me." Pope was direct, "Wear these pants and this shirt to the store." He gave me the clothes that Noah handed him. Jeans and a flannel shirt. I snatched them from Pope and looked down on the clothes, held the flannel up to my nose. The scent of Noah was all over the shirt. "Fine Pope, I'll wear 'em." In a rage I threw them on the bed and ordered both of them out so I could change. Time to rile the Pope so I went down the stairs laughing, pointing at my shoes. "Doesn't this look great! These teal heels carrying The Wheels. You know Pope? "… watching the wheels go round and round…" That's me. I'm the wheels. John Lennon's been watching and writing about me in his songs. They are all about me!" Pope didn't find this funny and asked Noah if he had some shoes I could wear. Noah got his sneakers that set by the side entrance door. Oh this was grand. What next a coat? The too big, heavy sneakers were on. They slopped around a lot and the coat you see, was Noah's. There was a pair of sunglasses on the counter top. Putting them on I peered at Noah and Pope. "Hey, these outta do the job. You obviously don't want anyone to recognize me but you don't have to tell me why, I know." I was ready for the two minute road trip to the drug store for the little blue pills.

At the first intersection we stopped for a light. Pope opened and shut his door. Making like he was checking to see it was closed. The instant he did, I immediately watched the car that was passing through the intersection. Driver in sunglasses. He did exactly the same thing Pope did. He's letting Pope know he got the signal that all systems were still a "go" I thought.

On we went where we cornered the drug store. Pope parked. "Look Pope, see that place? (pointing to "CPZ), "I was up there last night..." He could have cared less I thought. He took the palm of his hand, put it on the crown of my head and said, "Put your head down. You should be ashamed of yourself." "I was up there last night in that radio station. They had me go up there knowing they were remodeling and broadcasting from somewhere else. I ran all through the place and it's empty I tell ya! Wanna go up and see?" Pope refused. I started to get out of the car when he said. "You stay in the car, stay in the car and keep your head down."

Trying to keep myself company, I talked and cried, "What did I do to be ashamed of? I was out last night having a good time. Met John from Cleveland, Sir Joe, the authors of The Beatle book and last but not least, "Olivia!" Self pushed me and said, I'll show Pope the meaning of ashamed!" I got out of the car and walked right into the drug store standing right next to Pope. Looking directly at the druggist, I said, "I'm really a girl, but my dad here, Pope, wants everybody to think that he doesn't have a daughter." "Be quiet! Keep your voice down." Pope said. He took the bag that carried the valiums, escorted me out and back into the car.

Priest was just pulling in Noah's drive when me and Pope returned. Priest got out of his "El Camino," walked over to Pope to shake hands. Briefing Priest were Noah and Pope. Weren't they through figuring out what to do with me? Priest asked of a favor. "Pope would it be alright if I take Cap for a ride. Might help her relax and I promise I'll bring her back here." "Oh Pope I wanna go with Priest for a ride in that. I'd like to have that to drive around in myself." "What time would you be back?" Pope asked. I'll have her here, oh, how about hour and a half, two hours. Thought I'd drive over by Marblehead somewhere. It's real nice. A change would be good." Pope agreed? Yes he did!

He instructed Noah to call him upon my arrival. We got into the car, truck and drove. Kept my eyes out for any silver cars, white cars, assuming that this was going as scheduled. "So what's going on Cap. You're look tired. What's this you said about your dad wanting to have you locked up?" "He will, I really think he will. I was out last night like I was supposed to be. Supposed to get married until the cops detained me, Shorty detained me, Pope is trying to and damn I'm glad you came and got me Priest!" He grew concerned and said, "You never told me anything about getting married. Who's the lucky man?" "Oh shit Priest! You won't believe me! Nobody does. It's all in The Beatle book. It's been in John Lennon's solos for years.

Fuck it. Believe whatever the hell you want, but last night I was supposed to marry him.

John Lennon isn't dead like everybody thinks and no one but me and the other three Beatles are supposed to know. Well, there are a few other people. Pope, Noah and Gentry. Ultimately it is Pope who picks anyone. Maybe even you too. Hey is that white car back there? Did they signal to turn? Watch it, they're the bad guys." Priest didn't know what to say. I could see that. He turned to me changing the subject, "Look out there over the water, it's a good day for a drive, it's clear out and the bay is calm." "Where the hell are we anyway," I asked. "You never been here? This is Peninsula Point I think Cedar Point wanted to buy it a while back but they wouldn't sell. It's pretty quiet here." "It is nice here. Oh look, you can see The Point from here. Pull up over there will ya? I gotta say something important and I gotta be standing by the water so my voice will travel with it." Priest pulled over to the east side of the peninsula and turned off the engine. I got out. Over by the water was a small break wall. Climbing on to it, I gazed out over the water seeing the similarities in the two Points. "Priest," I said, "Look I can see the Blue Streak. John played guitar to me on the merry go round and it was the greatest day of my life, until today." I confided more in Priest. "I met John through a mutual friend from Cleveland when I was 16. We rode the ferry boat over there and spent the day. It's like being there again."

Priest wasn't sure what to say. I walked up a hill and said, " … twin land the place where I had met you once but now you're gone, stay all around me my love…" Walking down the small rock wall, Priest was getting into the car. I did the same but he wouldn't look at me. "Priest, what's wrong? Why you crying?" "I don't know what to do, what to say. I wanna do something for you." "You don't have to do anything for me. I'll have everything I want soon. You'll see! Hey, where's the nearest church, they'll probably want me there for a short rehearsal. That's why you're here! You're have to drive me to the church! Don't make us late Priest. We have to hurry, there's only about five minutes." "There's just one church here I think, Saint Mary's, but I don't think anyone will be there." "You gotta take me there Priest. I have to know!" He shook his head yes.

We drove in silence till we got there. "This is the church of my dreams. It even has the right name. St. Mary's, just like Goose Island. It sits on a Lake by the same name in Montana and I gotta go be there in April. Give God my rib, but don't worry, He won't let anything go wrong. I'm supposed to go there. He's gonna meet me. That's where I was born or didn't I tell you. I'm Eve! You don't have to believe me, no one else does. My rib is Adam's rib and I have to return it. Is this a scream or what!" Priest wasn't laughing and I quit when I found there was nobody at the church. No cars and no one.

Like the last 16 years of my life. How much longer will The Beatles keep me in suspense before I really do lose my mind, I thought? Priest turned to me telling me that we had to head back to Noah's. I couldn't wait to get back because I wanted to be with him anyway. Seemed like a day had gone by before we pulled up to Noah's. Priest took me to the door, we said good bye and Noah let me inside. He called Pope to tell him I got there okay.

Not long after that, Pope showed up with the little blue pills. I had forgotten all about them. More instructions were given by Pope and Noah said, "Don't worry. I'll be sure she doesn't get the other pills until the right time. You can go home. I promised I would take care of Cappy and I will." "You listen to Noah Cappy." "My two girls are coming over to spend the night and were getting a pizza. I'll try to get Cap to eat something and get some sleep." "Thank you Noah. You'll take good care of her and I'll be by in the morning. You listen to him Cappy! Don't leave here and try to eat something, sleep. This pill is supposed to help calm you down. Maybe you could have a glass of milk with it. Help coat your stomach a little, okay Cappy?" Pope rubbed my hair, told me to take it easy, said good night and shook Noah's hand to thank him.

The effects of the valium had hit. Walking was like floating on the kitchen floor and I kept walking around all the more. "Caps, you better sit down. Come on. My girls are here remember. Try to behave and calm down. Don't tell them all this stuff. They're too young to understand." The two little blonde cuties walked into the kitchen. Noah's little girls were polite, smart and pleasant. They were 4 and 6 years old. The eldest asked, "Do you like to color? Me and my sister are going to color. We can color a picture for you Cappy." "Okay! Put lots of colors. I like colors. Except for orange, I don't really like orange." The two ran off giggling, "Okay, yeah, we'll make you a surprise Cappy and you stay there. No fair peeking until it's done." "Okay, I'll stay right here at the kitchen table until it's done, I won't peek, I promise." Noah smiled.

"Damn Noah! Valiums are great! You outta take one. I'm just floatin'. It almost feels like THC or something." "Cap. Wanna check out some pictures I took of my vacation?" He handed me the package of photos. "Look Noah, this picture! This picture right here! Looks like part of the brick building is missing. Kind of like a puzzle. What happened? Did the camera fuck up on ya?" "Cap watch your language. I don't want the girls to hear it okay? And no, nothing was wrong with the camera, keep looking." Was this another game? Stack of meaningless pictures? Then I stumbled on another curiously-chopped-off-brick-building in one of the photos. Again I asked Noah. Again he said, "Keep looking." I flipped and flipped through them and there were still more of the photo's looking more like a puzzle. All the brick buildings looked like the same structure. "Oh come on Noah! There's at least six or seven pictures here with shorelines and they all have part of a boat. Like the bricks! What's up? Is this my house or something? It is isn't it Noah? The one that John Lennon and I are going to live in. Is this a puzzle or something? I even saw the back end Pope's old pick up. The black one with the white cap on the back. Wait. I'll find it. Yeah, there it is. See the tree to the right in this? Look, the trees and the bushes cut off the front end of it, but that's the end of Pope's truck alright." "I told you these are pictures of my vacation down south. That isn't your dad's truck." "But then how do you explain the street name on this picture? Why take a picture of that? Because you had to... for me. It's my new address. Over-Look. Over look these pictures Cap. Over look last night. Pretend everything is normal and I'll be fine. I'll bet Priest drove me right by it this afternoon when he took me to Peninsula Point. John probably bought the whole fuckin' thing!"

Noah laid certain photo's side by side until it was one full brick structure. One very long building that sat close to a shoreline and in the water was a ship anchored. It had to be at least 100 feet long or more. A yacht. "Cap. The camera takes a panoramic view. Ya take a series of photos to get the full picture. The ship was just there and I thought it would be kind of neat to take it this way." "So you're trying to tell me that this isn't my house? I don't believe it! One night I was talking to Pope on the phone. I told him that Professor had promised to send me and elbow of pot. Professor probably didn't have the funds, so I never got it and I told Pope. Told him I wanted my bow and he said, "Don't worry Cappy, I got your bow and you can stay in my "big" house. See he said it was a big house. At first I thought Pope had a personal investment in a castle from his country. He probably owns the mountain it sits on. He's good friends with the president of the country too. They went to school together. He owns the fucking castle Noah." "Cap you need to quit. I better put these pictures away, see if there isn't something else we can do. the pizza should be here pretty soon. Try to eat some when it's here." "Okay. Put the pictures away. I know it's all mine. How about I clean out my purse. Maybe something is hiding in there. You know Noah, after I hook up with John, I think I'll hire a maid to clean my purse out for me a couple times a month just for a laugh."

"Noah, look at this. I thought I threw this out when I cleaned the fucking desk. It's a piece of paper that says call the electrician and a number. It's a long distance number. You know I don't call long distance." Noah came over to see it and said, "I thinks that's over in Port Clinton somewhere, go ahead call." "Call? You crazy? I'm not gonna call any electrician. Pink might answer. Nah, Pinky wouldn't answer. He's on Neil Street" "Go on Cap, call and see who answers, it might be fun. What's a long distance call?"

Read the number to myself, held it in my hands wondering about Pink. What if he's the one who slipped the number in the fucking desk? If he did, I didn't see him. Like I didn't see him bug my house, my car and the places that I went to. Noah's house is wired for sure, I thought. "Noah. Fuck Pink! He's probably right at this number right now. He thinks I'm gonna call him? Fuck that! No way! He's the one that told me that he couldn't be with me anymore. He said that! He should come to me. His turn, not mine. I wouldn't give him the satisfaction. Just who the hell does he think he is playing with my head? I'll fix his adapter, I won't dial this number even if he calls asking me too." "Sorry Cap. Didn't think that would get ya going. I thought you'd calm down. Maybe he's at that number. He's the only electrician you know, didn't you tell me that? When you said it might be his number I thought you'd want to talk to him. Cappy, maybe Buff or Jules wrote it down and put it there, maybe it's there's?" "I don't care about the number Noah. I'm beginning not to care too much about being here either if you wanna know. Maybe I'll just leave and let the bad guys get me since all you and Pope wanna do is mess with my head and lock me up!" Noah came over to sit with me. He cupped his hands over mine that rested on the table and said quietly, "Cap hon, I'm just trying to do whatever it takes to make you happy. No matter what I do it ends up wrong. I don't know what to do? Tell me what I can do for you hon!" "Nothing Noah."

The girls were quietly coloring in the living room until the doorbell rang and the pizza came. They ran in the kitchen to for a serving and brought in the surprise they had been working on for an hour. "Oh what's this I see? Well it looks like seven little hearts. Did you two make this for me?" "Yes and we pasted them together. See how they get smaller at the end?" Noah's little girls were very proud of their art and I was impressed. "Each heart has its very own color. This is just beautiful! Think I'll ask your dad if he has a pin or something so I can wear it on my blouse here on the pocket. What do you think? I asked. "Yes. That will look nice and we remembered you didn't like orange so we didn't make an orange heart Cappy." "You remembered that? You're very smart girls. Thank you. I'm gonna get something from your dad so I can wear them now. Hey Noah, I need a safety pin. Got one? Your girls made me all these pretty hearts and I wanna wear 'em on my shirt." Noah looked at the hearts and complimented his girls, then he pinned the gift on my pocket. The girls were tickled and began naming the colors, in order from the top biggest heart to the smallest bottom heart. "Green, blue, purple, and the light blue sort of matches your scarf, then pink, red and yellow.

"Noah. Tomorrow I wanna stop at my house. I have the perfect thing to wear for the hospital. All white. That oughta get 'em goin' at Firelands huh? If they put me in a straight jacket, I'll match! Rubber room and all!"

He laughed but I don't think he really thought it was funny. It was time for the girls to get ready for bed. Noah was so good with them. He tucked them in for night and in no time they were asleep.

Noah asked me to join him in the living room. The TV. was on but I was too busy watching out the window. Looking at the porch, for safety, I spied a little leprechaun made of ceramic laying with his chin in his hands... Thought about Saint Patrick's Day... Thought Daly's and John. Then I thought of John Lennon. What if he's still waiting for me somewhere? The house. He's at the house you saw in the pictures Noah showed you earlier, Self said in my head. How could you forget it? Freedom was outside and dead ahead through the glass. I wanted out!

"Noah, I'm out of cigarettes. The only place close is the "Cameo" down the street its only a block or two." "Cap, can't you smoke mine? I can't let you go, I promised your dad." "Oh shit Noah. It's down the street. You can stand at the door and watch me. You have to watch me anyway, in case someone sees me and tries to get me. Please Noah! I gotta take a walk and get some fresh air. You got a gun? Keep it here by the front door next to you while I walk. That way if you see somebody jump out of a car trying to get me, you can shoot 'em. Please, I gotta have what I smoke. Promise I'll be right back. If you tell me no I'm just gonna go anyway." After a few moments to contemplate the idea of me leaving his safe haven, Noah said, "Okay Cap, but I don't need a gun. I'll be here in the chair waiting for you. I trust you." "But Noah, you gotta have a rifle or something! I'll be afraid to walk down there." "Okay Cap. If it'll make you happy I'd put the shot gun right here against the wall but I don't think I'm gonna need it." "Oh sure Mr. UDT Seal! Forgot you served in the military. Aren't you one of the proud crazy's!" I went out the front door to go and get my cigarettes. Was someone watching my every step, I thought? The walk wasn't nearly long enough and I was back at Noah's in no time.

Noah was real tired and was ready to crash right where he sat. Obviously the valium I had taken earlier did nothing. Calm? Hell no! I was ready to wonder in the house but I had to wait for Noah to go to sleep.

Chain smoked for nearly 45 minutes when I heard Noah softly snoring back in the chair. At last! A chance to take a good look around. Those pictures Noah had shown me earlier had to be my house, my yacht and Pope's truck. Certain as I was, there had to be more in the house where Noah dwelled.

There was nothing in the living room so I wondered into the dining room. One wall was most certainly mine. Collector's plates. Twelve decorated a wall in a full circle. Each one a character or scene from "The Wizard of Oz." Wouldn't you know the one that took place in the center of the circle was

Dorothy. "Incredible!" Yes I was talking and I didn't care who could here! "Pink? Am I coming in? Did you bug this place? 'Cause I found the fucking plates! Did John tell you about the yellow brick road?"

A corner cabinet filled. Pitchers, cups and saucers. I knew where they came from without even looking on their backs or bottoms. "France, Germany and England. The tea cups gotta be from England!" Like a feather I moved the cabinet away from the corner to check the tea cups first. "Ah ha' I am right! I've been right from the start and too fucking bad if nobody wants to believe me! How many items in the cabinet can I get right? 28 out of 30 enough?" Roaming my eyes on the downstairs once and again there was nothing left to be found. Guess the only place to go was up.

"Hmm, which door? There are so many. Like "Let's Make A Deal," only double!

The landing at the top of the stairs was a walk-way in a square shape, surrounded by the rails. Looking over from any side you could see the staircase that brings you to this area. Opened one door.. .Nothing. Opened a second... "Oops! The girls are sleeping in here." But the third door opened led me into a room filled with treasures. Old clothes, statues, coat racks and shelves filled with things I admired. All away across the room was a long-wooden vanity. My steps were light and quick to get there.

"Jewelry? My God there is a small fortune here! Pearl necklaces, gold chains, gold rings, earrings, garnets, emeralds, silver and sapphires. Stones and gems stretched over the table in different and old jewelry boxes. You'd think nothing could stand out unless it were a five pound rock of a gem, but something did. "Oh this is just what I wanted!" I put the round diamond solitaire ring on my ring finger, left hand. It fit like it was supposed to. But, while holding it up to see how it looked, I saw something that should not have been there. "How the hell did Mayor's wedding rings get in here? She was buried with them. It's impossible!" Self said, "Anything is possible." And here they were.

Just as I picked them up, Noah brought in a flood. "What the hell do ya think you're doing? This is my mom's stuff! You can't go through it like that. Just put everything back and leave it alone." I turned and glared at Noah, "You're crazy! These are Mayors rings. What the hell are they doing here? I can do whatever I want with 'em! This diamond is mine too. It's my engagement ring. Trust me Noah, before Mayor's funeral Pope asked me if I wanted Mayor's rings. I told him no. She had them on when I saw her at the funeral home in a casket! The only way they could get here is Pope, but I'm tellin' you right now they belonged to Mayor!" "Cap I don't wanna tell you again so put the stuff back. Put the rings back in the box and leave it alone. This is my mom's. She'll know someone went through it and nobody's allowed in here. Not even me! Go downstairs. I'm shuttin' the door. You? I don't want you outta of my sight" Fine Noah. I'll be wearing that ring soon enough! What's one more day? I've waited 16 years already!" Noah escorted me out of the room, led me down the square staircase and back in the living room.

"Noah, do you realize that I'll be with nuts tomorrow? I can't sleep! I've seen movies about those kinda people. Up all night, making strange noises, talking to people who aren't even there. They aren't gonna let me get any rest so I might as well stay awake. Shit Noah, I've been awake for a long time and to sleep is to drag. Can't do anything but dream. Who needs to sleep a dream. I'm living one! If I could see what I wanted, I'd sleep. If ya wanna know the truth, I don't wanna dream. I am the dream that the whole world will know about. Noah. That's today! It's today! Had no idea'. It's three-thirty in the morning!" "I know, I know and I would like to get some sleep but you won't let anyone sleep will you? Some people do need to ya know." He laid down on the couch and watched me out of the corner of his tired-blue and blood shot eyes. Time couldn't have slowed down anymore and I thought I'd never see light hit. I paced, waited, drank cold coffee and smoked lots of cigarettes.

The mantle dock chimed seven a.m. It was time for me to get ready for my straight jacket. "Noah, there sure are a lot of doors upstairs. I didn't look in all the rooms because by the time I got to the third door it didn't matter much. What I was wondering is this. While we're waiting for Pope to come and take me away for life, would you show me the rest?" "I guess I could but leave things alone Cappy. My mom has a lot of antiques up there, okay?" Well I got to the top of the stairs before Noah and he showed me the other rooms. He was right about the antiques. His mother had many. The last room he took me in was a room with old stands and dressers. What made this my favorite room, next to number three, was the fact that every kind of brass bell sat on them. Short, fat, tall and thin, wide and strong. Must have been fifty or more and one stood out about them all. I picked it up and rang the tiny little bed. A date was on it reading 1875. The word Liberty was spelled out above the year. "Noah, this is beautiful! So small. It's not even 2 inches tall! Listen to that ring. It sounds like the first note to a John Lennon song. "Just Like (Starting Over)" Surprisingly, Noah said, Take it" Take it?" I asked, "You told me not to touch anything. This is your moms." "Oh go ahead. She has so many bells she'll never know it's missing." "Noah I'm gonna keep this in my hand the whole time I'm at the hospital. Another symbol of hope. With liberty and justice for all. For all woman kind. Maybe all of us ladies will get the life we were meant to live."

There was a knock and I knew Pope was on the other side of the door. I slipped the bell in my pocket, went down stairs to get my shoes on and thought... This is it... the end!

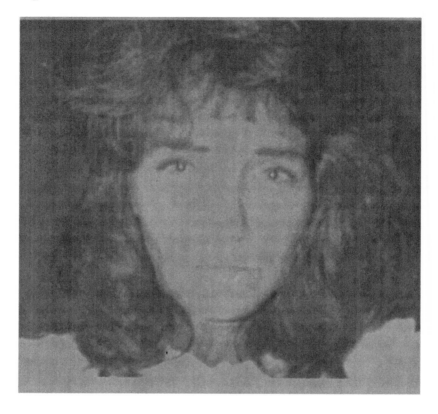

"Some Things... Just For Me." The Title For Chapter Twenty Four. Words late on the night of August, 1998, were written by Catherine Santi.

"Where does all the time go ? When time is up. When time is slow.
Where oh where will I go? Where I am. Where I am as I know.
What can all your eyes see? What mine have seen was meant for me."

"Noah, it's really morning and I'm supposed to go now? Where did all the time go? What did I do, sleep?" "Are you kidding Cap! You've walked around all night. You were ringing the bell, watching the "Oz" plates, but most of the night you were watching out all the windows. You kept talking about the bad guys and how they were gonna get you because they knew what your dad's car looked like. You don't remember? I didn't sleep much and you finally woke up the girls with that bell." "I don't remember any of it! I must have been out of it. Did Pope bring me another valium or something?" "Yes and I can't believe that they aren't knocking you out! You haven't slept since I met you and you are wired tight. I don't know Cappy... Come on, let's not keep your dad waiting."

I followed Noah out. There was Pope in dress clothes tie and all. "Well Pope! I'm ready to go. I'm wearing white in case they put me in a straight jacket. I'll match won't I?" They're not going to put you in one of them. They might give you medicine. They gave Mayor medicine and she felt real good. She called them her happy pills. Let's just go see what the doctor's say and don't start yelling and telling everybody fuck you. You gotta listen to them real good and do what they tell you. If you do what they say, then you'll get to go home." "Caps. He's right. Just listen and do what the doctors say and you'll be just fine."

What did these two know that I didn't, I wondered? We loaded up in the car and Pope drove to the hospital only blocks away. Together we walked into the emergency room. Self and I were having second thoughts, "You can't make me go in there. I told you the truth! I was supposed to go downtown and took for John Lennon! Oh they probably had a great time filming my every move. I bet the Beatles are sitting in some building, some van, taping and watching all this right now. Hell I'd like to sit back and watch it myself! Know why Pope? Do you wanna know Noah? Does anybody any where wanna know why I would want to watch it? Because for the first time in a

463

lot of years I had fun! It was the best time I ever had in my life! It didn't
cost me a fucking dime! Is that so bad? I was out having fun till you and the
cops didn't want me to have a good time anymore. Jealous? I think you're
all jealous! Poor John is out there waiting and I'm not going to make him
wait anymore. I want to see him now! Come on Pope. You said you had my
bow at your big house. My bow! Where is he?" Pope and Noah had a hold
of my arms to restrain me from taking off in any direction. Pulling away as
best I could I cried, "Where is John? In the hospital? Come on Pope, you're
supposed to know. Is he there?" I pointed to the emergency room door just
feet away and dropped the fight when Pope said, "I don't know Cap, maybe
he is. Just calm down and let's get inside. It's cold out here!"

"Oh the perfect plan. John's probably here somewhere! Might not be a
bad idea. I'll show those doctors I'm okay you just watch me. I know what
they're gonna do. They'll ask me stupid questions about you, Noah, when I
was born. Shit that's easy. Hurry and get me in there Pope." "We're going
Cappy. Let's get inside." Pope held onto me leading me in and I turned to
Noah, "Don't leave! Stay with me and call Priest. Make sure you stay. We
gotta build those boats! You gotta help me get to Montana." "Cap I'm not
going anywhere. I'm right here."

Cubicles. Curtain-covered. I watched everyone who passed. What if
John is in disguise, I thought? A nurse led me into an examining room where
I would wait with Noah and Pope for a doctor.

I let Pope con me into thinking John Lennon might be in the hospital.
I shouldn't have asked or said anything. I should have known better. The
doctors will have all kinds of questions and I ran a series of them in my
mind. Then a doctor walked in and introduced himself to the Pope, Noah
and me.

"Hi Doc, I'm Cap. Want my last name? It's Spettro. I was born here
in Erie County, Sandusky, Ohio on Christmas Day 1956. I'm 32 years old.
I have three children, three brothers. That's my dad. My mom died April
2nd, 1984, the same year my son was born, only he was born March 2nd
and I call him Sonny. Buff Bag was born June 28th 1978. Jules was born
December 3rd, same as Pope, and born in 1981. Do you want their middle
names?" Then Pope looked at the doctor, "I told you she was smart. You
better watch her real good! She's fast and she might out smart you, talk you
into letting her go now." Ignoring Pope, I said, "My oldest brother is Hermit
and I have 2 younger brothers. John and Shorty. See I was third born. Pope
and Mayor had a little baby before me only she died. I play piano and sing
a little too. Anything else you wanna know Doc?"

"Well, you answered pretty much what I had to ask you. Do you know
how you got here?" Shaking my head with a grin I looked at him and said,

"That's a smart question! Pope and Noah brought me here. They're sitting here aren't they? Can't you see them? Pope said he was my dad or weren't you paying attention? See you gotta pay attention to details because you never know what you might miss if you don't. If I didn't read The Beatle book as good as I did, then I would never know I was going to marry John Lennon. Everybody thinks he's dead, but I know different. It's in this book! Wanna see?" "Capri. You're saying that after you read this book you believed John Lennon was alive?" He flipped through the pages, (like John did) and said, "Well Capri, it says right here that he was shot and killed. Pronounced dead." "See that's how much you know. I was following the yellow brick road. They just happened to have one downtown last night. I ran into John and he told me that if I didn't like the way the story ended, all I had to do was open up to page one and it would start over. Starting over Doc. That's what this is all about, starting over. John Lennon and me. We rode the merry go round at Cedar Point one summer. You never knew Pope, but Mayor used to let me go after you left to play cards on Sunday. I met a guy from Cleveland and one time he brought a friend along with him. His friend was John Lennon. He sat right in your living room. Mayor saw him and nearly fell out of her chair. We never told you because she knew you would never let me go to The Point with an older guy and especially two of them. But I'm telling you Pope, Noah and this crazy doctor with all his stupid questions, that John was with me. He's got big and powerful people working for him to make sure I'm safe. The FBI, the CIA, Sir Joe and many many more!"

"Cap," The doctor said, "Why do you think these people are watching you?" "Because they have to keep me safe from the bad guys, the ones who drive around in the white cars. They might try and kidnap me. They know when The Beatles get back together they will be worth 500 million dollars! Wanna know why? Because it's the fucking best publicity stunt in the world! The Beatles will once again rule as the most popular band in the world. The best fucking band in the world. Imagine all the fans! They'll go crazy! People will be buying up all the new stuff as it comes out just the way they did before the band broke up. What a plan! And to top it off, I'll be the third and best Mrs. John Lennon. And that would be worth a lot! So you can bet they're keeping a close eye on me, my kids, my house, my car, Pope's car, Noah's house, any where I went and even here I'm sure. Oh you can bet they will really be paying close attention to how you guys treat me! You'll all be so sorry that you kept me locked up. One day they'll write a book about this. That will be everybody's ultimate truth doctor!" "So you think The Beatles are looking over you and you fear that you might be kidnapped. Your dad thinks you might end up hurting yourself because you haven't slept in weeks and you are not eating. You're very undernourished. According to your vitals, you only weigh 87 pounds! That's not good! You aren't speaking easily and that can happen when you are not eating and your body isn't getting what it needs to operate. You can barely talk Capri. I'd like you to stay here for a few days and see "Doctor Lee." He'd know what's best for you. He is a psychiatrist." "Then can I go? I'm only supposed to be here three days. I got things to do. Things I didn't get to finish on time 'cause the cops picked me up. Ask Pinky if you don't believe it." The doctor cocked his head with a pencil tapping at his clip board. "Capri. Who is Pinky?" "Pinky is the one who bugged everything. My house, The Barrel, Noah's house, my car. He did it all. He set up the yellow brick road and planted all the clues in the stores downtown. Had to kick some of the store doors open because they were closed before I could get in. They didn't care. Nobody stopped me. Like I've been tellin' everyone all along, I was supposed to do all that so why you wanna stop me I'll never know!" "Noah will you sit in here with Cap? I'd like to talk with her dad. Well be right back." "Sure," he answered, and the Doc' led Pope out of the examination room.

"Noah, I need a smoke. Just one." "Cap, don't worry about that. You'll have one soon enough, just be patient." "Oh that's funny Noah... patient! I'll be one when Pope convinces that fuckin' doctor that I should be a one!" Yelling at Noah was the wrong timing because Pope and the doctor came back through the door. "Well are you gonna keep me or let me go? I bet good old Pope there talked you into keeping me, didn't you?" And I pointed to Pope standing at the foot of the examining table. "Cappy stop. I didn't talk the doctor into anything. Talk to him. Let him tell you what he thinks is best" "Doc, what makes you so sure you know what is best for me? I ought to know what is best for me. I'm supposed to do what I do! That's all I keep telling everyone! Supposed to this, supposed to do that, come and go here. So tell me what you know Doc?" I waited for the calm younger doctor to reply. "Capri. I think it would do you good to spend a few days here, let us see if there's a problem and what that might be." "Pope I don't wanna stay here. I won't take zombie pills! I seen movies about nuts is a place like this. They walk around, drool and don't know who or what is in front of them. Don't wanna go around with my tongue hangin' out my mouth." "Cappy, pills make people feel better. The doctors will help you just do what they say." "Sure Pope if I do everything they say I'll be here forever." Then the doctor assuringly said, "Cap, you'll be fine. We'll take good care of you! The nurses and doctors will watch you all the time. We'll help you through this."

Noah came and put him arm around my shoulder, told me not to worry and hugged me. "Cap when you get settled I'll come and see you okay?" "I guess it has to be huh Pope?" "Yes honey you'll be fine. Then you can go home. Think about getting better and going home." I hugged Pope. Asked him and Noah, "When will you come back? Are ya sure you're coming back? I don't know anybody here! Whose gonna watch my kids? I won't be there!" Pope responded, "Shorty and Chelsea have your kids right now at their house. Their watching them and I'm helping. Nina said she will help too. All you have to do is get better Cappy, Okay?"

"Yes Pope." The answer was tearful. "Give 'em all a big hug and kiss from me. Sonny doesn't understand. He'll miss me the most. He'll be wondering why I'm not there. Tell him I'm okay, but don't tell him I'm in the nut house, tell him I broke my arm or something just not the truth!" "I know what to say. Quit worrying. Why don't you give me the key to your house in case the kids need anything. You might want some stuff too and I can pick it up for you okay?"

Pope held out his hand while I fished around for the keys in my pocket. Handed 'em to Pope. He put his hand on my shoulder, looking at the doctor, Take good care of my daughter." "We will Sir. You and Noah can say good bye to Capri now, that way we can get her checked in. If she needs anything you'll be able to bring them by. She may still be allowed visitors tonight!" "Okay and thank you. Now you heard the doctor, we have to leave. I'll bring whatever you want later. I'll call you in a little while and remember, do what.." Self cut in, "I know, do what the doctors tell me. Got it Pope. You can go. See ya." Noah and Pope left the room, shook hands with the doctor and waved as they walked out leaving me there. I wondered... Is the last time I'll seen them? Am I in this place for good? Will my kids even remember me? Sonny won't, he's only five! Jules and Buff know where I am. They understand the word "crazy."

A nurse walked in and introduced herself, "Capri, you don't have any weapons now do you? We have to be careful of the other patients." "Oh Fran why in the world would I need to have one? Are you nuts! I got the FBI and CIA and a lot of other people taking care of me. Maybe I should check you to see if you have any weapons. You might be working for the bad guys. I'm not stupid you know." "Capri I can assure you that this is strictly hospital policy. I'll just check your clothes for anything that might be dangerous." "Go ahead bitch, make your day." I hated this nobody nurse. Copying my style with her little white cap. Jealous that I would be Mrs. Lennon. "Doctor! Capri has a large safety pin in the back of her pants." She lifted my long-tailed-white shirt up to show him. I yelled at the nurse. "What's your problem! You figure the only thing that's keeping my pants up is a weapon? Give me a break. You know I just don't under-fucking-stand you people! Doc. What do you think? Should I take the pin off, huh? " I un-did the pin. Along with the nurse and the doctor, I watched my pants drop to the floor. "See! Everything matches. Even my underwear. Did ya

467

get to see 'em? Oh who cares. Now if you don't mind I'd kind of like to keep my pants on." I pulled the baggy white pants up, zipped them and held them scrunched up at the waist. The doctor examined the pin. Looked at the material in my hands and said, "Capri you lost a lot weight. Your pants are real big on you. Nurse, Capri has permission to use it." Thanks Doc. By the way," I asked, "Do you drive a silver car?"

"Capri I want you to go with Fran. She'll take you to your room and you're all set. And Fran, when you get Capri to the nurses' station tell them it's okay for her to use her safety pin." He smiled to me and left.

Fran brushed my blouse back into place, took me by the hand and led me out of the room. Like she was the driver the nurse said, "Capri? Do you want me to wheel you there?" "No thanks. I'd rather walk. Walking's easy! Let's go!" I watched all the people in all the rooms. Rooms half-curtains, whole-curtains, watching for who might be behind them. I watched windowed-rooms, staff members, nurses, doctors, pencils, pens, colors, anything or anyone that might tell me something. The place where John might be. There wasn't a clue in sight! Self got me to thinking... Perhaps John isn't here at all. He's waiting. He must know that you're here Cap. Don't you think they would have made him aware? She was right.

"Capri follow me down the hall. The South Pavilion is on this floor. Not far." "Come on Fran, can't ya walk any faster than that? Ya can't keep up with me? Hell, last night, downtown I was running up and down the yellow brick road. Fly the stairs like a bird. You gotta be able to go faster than that if you wanna keep up with me, come on Fran!" "You're real quick, I gotta admit. It is kind of hard to keep up with you." "Nurse Fran. It's easy. Remember when Dorothy, the Lion, Tin-Man, Toto and Scarecrow woke up from the witches spell? They stood up and saw The Emerald City. Even though they journeyed a long time and were tired, once they saw that beautiful shining city the race was on. And they ran. Ran till they reached its tall mysterious emerald gates. Come on Fran, how long before we get to Oz?" Fran laughed, "We just have to go down this hall Capri, it's at the end. See the doors?" I saw them as we turned left to an end. Those doors are gray Fran." "Capri, I never said you were going to The Emerald City. It's called the South Pavilion remember?" "Oh I remember.

Does this mean I'll get the suite of my choosing or has the best one been pre-selected for me? You realize that I'm getting married ? You know who I am going to marry? I'm sure it's somewhere in all those notes you guys got about me. It's cool too! There is no other girl on this earth who will have who I will! Four very important men worked on it. Began entrusting others with this plan when I was 16.

"Aah! This must be the place." I slid up to the doors waiting for Fran to open them. She hit a pad on the wall to her left and the first set of steel double doors thrust open. We walked through and came to wooden doors with small-screened windows (eye level). Fran knocked and a nurse from the other side came with keys unlocking the doors I went through. Fran said, This is Capri. She'll be here a bit. Oh, and the doctor said she could use the pin in her pants. All set Capri." And Fran was gone.

Chapter Twenty Five: "The Picture On The Wall"

Self thought...This is it! I'm locked up. Like they're gonna give me a set of keys! The little brass bell that Noah said I could have? It was still in my pocket when the nurse who led me to her station said, "Capri Spettro. Hi. I'm Mrs. Bell." "No shit! You gotta be kidding me? I just happen to have your name in my pocket." Took out the brass bell to show her. That's very nice Capri." "Thanks. Noah let me keep this one. Symbol of hope you might say." That's a healthy attitude. Can I see that?" she asked, "I'll have to make a check list of everything you have with you and on you anyway. We wouldn't want you to lose anything of value." The list was made... One gold necklace, gold bracelet and a gold ring, one pearl earring and gold earrings. Everything was accounted for, including my under garments.

Checking in was over. Mrs. Bell put my valuables in a plastic-lock-box that fit into a wall with the others. And it was room time!

About face and five rooms down the hall to the left was mine. "Mrs. Bell. John isn't going to be too happy about this room. Where's the suite? Where's the view?" "Capri I know it isn't all the comforts of home, but you have all you need here." Okay, I thought. A bed, a two-drawer-night-table and a sink and mirror, four feet from the foot of the bed. To the left of that was a door that led to the toilet. "Mrs. Bell - I don't see a shower or tub in here so why are you telling me that I'll have everything I need." "Capri calm down there is a tub and shower in the room right across the hall from yours. See?" She pointed.

The next room would be all mine any time. "Cappy, this is the day room. This is the only area we allow smoking if you're a smoker." Proudly I said, "As many as possible!" "You aren't permitted matches or a lighter. When you want to smoke walk up to the nurses' station and one of us will light it for you." "Be back Bell, I need a light now!" Darted quick to the station to get a light from one of the nurses. She reached in her pocket, pulled out a throw-away-lighter, giving me fired I needed. Once I learned where the coffee was... Well, you know how I feel about that, and the hospital happened to have my brand. There were many, many cups.

Spent most of the time walking for a light, a coffee and introducing myself to the other people.

"I'm Cap, but I'm not supposed to be here. I'm not nuts! Can't help what I know you know? Doctors and cops. What do they know?" "Cap. I like you. My name is John and I know what you mean. Look at them with their b-b-eyes. They wish they were in on it and they can't be. And they're not going to know anything because I'm not supposed to be here either." "John. I have to ask you a question. You're serious about your name being John? Who do you work for? Wait You must be working for me! Well, not for me but for somebody I know. Only I don't think you know who you are working for. I don't think anybody knows who they are working for. Then I broke a code. Was supposed to break it. Four mates in the organization made sure that I would on time. And I did. These guys run it all. They are at the top!"

"Cap. What if I worked for two sides? But if I were I wouldn't be at liberty to say. I'm on a secret assignment here. Doing some investigating. Take my pictures here." John pointed to his brown eyes behind the thick-lensed glasses. "See it, shoot it and store it. Can't keep any information on paper. No notes. Gotta keep it here. The mind. Mine. That's why I was sent here because I don't require any access baggage. What did you come with Cap?" "Same as you. Did bring one item with me. Maybe when you see it you'll be at liberty to tell me what side you're on. Mine or theirs. Christ John, I'm sorry but your name is fucking killing me." I broke out laughing handing him the bell. "Go on... read it. What does it say?" "Liberty," he replied. "You ever heard of starting over? Well that has a lot to do with the reason why I'm here. Listen to the bell. Hear it? Sounds like the same bell, note, at the beginning of one of John Lennon's songs. "Just Like (Starting Over)" Heard it? Lord and then there's another one called "Watching the Wheels." "Cap. Why do songs have anything to do with you being here?" "John it's real simple. I am The Wheels. People are always calling me Wheels. Cute name don't ya think?" "Wheels. I like it It's a real cool name and it fits you good. I'm gonna start calling you Wheels. Sounds good saying it... Wheels! Now we officially meet." "John I gotta go check out some of these people in here. What the hell's their problem? This place could make a person go nuts!" John nodded and I laughed at where we were!

At one of the round tables was a woman sitting alone. She was about 50 with dark shoulder length hair. She was no taller than five feet and was quite round and overweight. It was that woman I wanted to meet next. Wanted to know who the hell she was mumbling at! "Hi! My name is Capri Spettro but you can call me Wheels. John's calls me that, what's your name?" She nervously stuttered out her words. "I'm Teresa. Can I get a cigarette from you Cappy? Just one?" "I have lots of cigarettes. Sure!" "Without a single stutter, Teresa went off, "Those witches over there won't let me have one! If I wasn't in this damn place I could smoke all I want. They make me sick. I get one damn cigarette an hour. Wheels, maybe I was crazy when they brought me here and if I wasn't then they made me crazy because nobody likes me!" "I like you Teresa. Believe me when I walked through them doors the first thing I noticed was the fuckin' witches' tower." "Ah ha ha ha, you make me laugh Wheels. I like you. Don't tell any of the bitches you gave me a cigarette or they might take yours away. They do whatever they want and get away with it. You watch out for them. They're all liars."

Suddenly, one of the witches was standing over us. "How did you get that cigarette Teresa? You know you are only allowed to have one an hour. The doctor told you that" I cut in. "I gave her one. Man! You locked her up. Look at her! Teresa wants to smoke like everyone else! That should be her choice. What gives you and your shrink doctors the right to take her choices away?" "What's your name?" Then she looked at my wrist band and checked for the duplicate names and numbers and numbers that would identify me as Capri. The nurse firmly said, "Teresa has emphysema and the doctors think this is best." "Do I have freedom of speech here because if I don't I'm gonna talk anyway. You and your know-it-all doctors get some kind of sick thrill outta of legally messin' with our heads? Bet you guys sit back and have a good laugh. You want to piss us off. You may even have us here just to see how long it takes you on the average to drive a person into complete and total insanity! You're jealous really. You can't understand it. People like you fear the unknown. Make fun of it. It's too complicated." "Capri! This has nothing to do with you. I'm talking to Teresa. You need to calm down." "There you go again. I said it and I just said it and you're tryin' to tell me what you think I need to do! How the hell would anybody know what I need? They ain't me and you are not me because you ain't cool enough." Fine then Capri. I'm not cool enough." The witch then ignored me, Teresa was laughing her ass off rockin' in the chair. I went roaming.

Thought about what had just taken place. I was to the point. The nurse? She'd never get to the fucking point. I boated to get to The Point. Played and rode the fucking merry go round at The Point! Was there with John Lennon! She knows nothing about the points. Then I made a point to let one of the witches light me a smoke.

Stopped in the snack room for a cup of coffee and headed back to the day room. A group of people were at a long table smoking. "Can I sit here? I'm Cap but you can all call me Wheels." "Hey Wheels how ya doing?" It was John. He was seated at the head of the table in his dress bomber jacket. "Hi John. How's the investigation going?" "As I predicted it would. On schedule. " "Schedules John. Damn clocks, numbers, social security, numbers, a license number, fuckin' plate numbers and the letters. You got a letter didn't you John? I know about the letter. I got the book it came from." "Wheels you know about a letter? You gotta destroy letters. Remember? See, shoot, store." "You're right. I know the story by heart. Don't need the book anymore."

Out of the blue, a black man who was sitting across from me began laughing for no apparent reason. I looked at him and started laughing too. We were both cracking and I had to know... "What's so fuckin' funny? You think you're "Stevie Wonder" don't you? " "I can be "Stevie Wonder" and the man laughed more rocking side to side in his seat. "Shit you guys... he really does look like him too doesn't he. All he needs is some sunglasses." Then I asked the rockin' fool, "What the hell is your name?" "It's Michael and yours is Wheels 'cause I heard you sayin' it. I like you, Wheels." "You do?" "Sure I like you!" Michael said. "Yeah but do ya love me Michael?" "Sure I love you." "You wanna marry me." "Yes I'll marry you because I love you."

Michael associated well with the conversation we had and it became routine and fun. There were many days ahead to watch Michael act out "Mr. Wonder and he played the table well.

A big girl next to me tapped my shoulder and said, "Wheels. How are you? I'm here because I have two uteruses. I'm Becky. Hi Wheels." "You gotta be kidding me. That means you could get pregnant in either one? You got two sets of tubes?" "I do Wheels and I'm sure I'm four months pregnant in the right one. The doctors tell me I'm not. I had a couple kids. A girl knows right? They put me on these drugs and they can't be safe if you're pregnant. They got me takin' major tranquilizers. I don't want 'em but if you don't take 'em, they'll take you in a room and hold ya down. They'll stick ya Wheels. I know because they did it to me. And if they hurt this baby I'm taking the whole hospital to court." "You're pregnant in one of them? Sorry Becky, I don't mean to laugh, but if you're pregnant in one of your uteruses then you could have sex in get pregnant in the other one? You could have twins in one and quintuplets in the other one." "One's enough Wheels. Why are you in here? You don't act crazy." "Oh what the hell. You got two uteruses, Michael's doin' his Stevie thing again, John's a double agent and Teresa has her better side handy. Me? I was supposed to be married, till cops picked me up from the place where the wedding was going to be. Fuck them! I saw John Lennon when I was a kid. I waited 25 years! Kept telling everyone that when I grew up I was gonna marry him. Well I hung out at Cedar Point even Sunday and met this dude from Cleveland. One fine Sunday he brings John Lennon to my house. I was 16 years old Becky and spent the day with John Lennon. It was grand! That's who I was supposed to marry the other night till I let them lock me in this fuckin' place." "Who talked you into it?" Becky asked, "Because my dad talked me into it." "Yep. My dad did the same thing and I let him. Maybe we are nuts!" That left us laughing and Becky said, "Don't stop there Wheels. Let's hear the rest of the story."

"God Becky! There is so much to tell that I wouldn't know where to begin. Are you sure you want to hear it?" "Yeah Wheels, go for it." Becky's eyes went wide for information.

"Well, it really started in 1984 when I met a man named Gentry. I call him Pinky. That's what he told my girls to call him. Then again, maybe it started on December 8th, 1984 before Pink came to my door. The day I moved into the house I live in. The day "they" say John Lennon was shot in 1980, except that I know he wasn't. The Beatles just made it look that way so I could marry him on Saint Patrick's Day, only problem was the cops got in the way and here I am. I shouldn't be here. I was only doing what I was supposed to be doing and then the doctors got a hold of me." "Yeah Wheels. We were crazy to let our dads talk us into this." "You're sure as hell right about that Becky!" "Come on Wheels, tell me more. This is the best story I've heard." "It's no story Becky. It's the truth. Like you being pregnant. I understand. Why the hell is it so fucking hard for "them" to understand? Well, back to the yellow brick road...

... Or so to speak. I went downtown looking for John Lennon and nothing was going to stop me from finding him. There were clues in the stores and I ran through the treasures like I owned them. WCPZ was in on it. They were secretly in on this thing and didn't even know it. Security, you know. Christ this is the thing Becky. 500 million dollars big thing, big time, okay? And I'm the leading lady.

See, there were white cars... the bad guys. They wanted to get me bad, for ransom. This is about the 500 million I told ya about. The Beatles and John thought sure they'd be worth that much, only because they had been apart for 19 years and that everybody thought Lennon was dead. A new Beatle song? Album? Think about that Beck." "I am Wheels and you know they were the best band on earth." "Good. You think like me. I loved The Beatles since I was seven. I'm 32 now and met John at Cedar Point when I was just about sixteen years old. Spent the whole day listening to him play his guitar." "Damn Wheels! I bet that really must have been some day for you. You were so lucky!" "Yeah I was. You should have seen my mom when she saw John. Thought for sure she was gonna fall right off her chair. She looked like she just saw "Johnny Mathis." She loved him a lot!" "So you're mom knew about it. Did you ever tell anybody, I mean, you had to wanna tell everybody didn't ya?" "Ya know something Beck, I never did say anything. It was strictly between me, him and mom. "What did your dad say about it?" "Oh Pope? He never knew anything until now, so he says. I think he's been in on it 16 years.

See, he comes from this tiny little country in Italy. When I say tiny, I mean 20,000 people at most." "That's smaller than Sandusky." "Yeah for real! Pope went to school with the president of the country. Hell, everybody there knows everybody there. Pope and him are good buddies. This is where John has been staying for the past nineteen years. Safe in the one of the three castles that Pope helped build when he was a kid. Wouldn't surprise me if Pope owned the castle. And get this. There aren't names for them like they do in England, just numbers. Castle one, two and three. I'm three Becky. Everything happens to me in threes. This is March right?"

"Yeah it is definitely March! Damn woman! Everybody is in here for something, but after listening to you and your story, hell, you're the "queen around here Wheels!" "Thanks Becky. It is pretty cool. Just because the shrinks around here don't know what we know they call us crazy." "You know Wheels. You come in here and they make you wonder if you need to be here. Then after you're here, it's like you know nothing is wrong with you, but "they" say there is. One thing for sure, the way I feel about it is this. If you're not crazy when ya get here, you will be after you're in." "I'm sorry Becky, I don't mean to laugh, but look at Mike over there. They got him crazy enough to be "the" "Stevie Wonder." Look at him playing that table. You know what? I bet the real loons are the ones taking care of us." "You kill me Wheels," laughed Beck, "Where do you come up with this shit." "We're crazy aren't we? Might as well act like it. Look Becky, being that this is my first night here, I want to see what's going on. Talk to you later." "See ya your highness." Graciously I bowed and made a mad dash to what was called the activity room.

People were coming and going. It was visiting hours. I was hoping that Noah and Pope would still have time to come and see me and the time was running fast so slow.

Seemed like everyone was having a good time so I went around introducing myself to everybody. What can I say? I was proud to be the queen!

Where was Pope, I thought? Maybe I should call him. I changed my mind and called Nina. "Hi Nina, it's me. Where's Pope?" "Hi Cappy. You're father and I just got off the phone. I was going to call you but you beat me to it. Everything going okay for you?" "Yeah. I guess so. But I need stuff. Clothes, music, paper, pens. I don't have anything to do. All my makeup is at the house and I'm not about to let these nuts in here see me without it. Can you guys bring me some of my stuff here?" "Yes Cappy. That's what I was going to call you about. Your dad takes too long at writing and he wanted me to write down what you want over there. So Capri, now that I am your personal secretary... what would you like us to bring?" I gave Nina quite the list and she told me that they would be at the hospital in about fifteen minutes.

There I was at the nurses' station. Watching one of the witches who was watching me. I asked her to light my cigarette for me and watched out the little window for Pope and Nina and I couldn't have been happier when they finally arrived, on time.

"Hi Pope, hi Nina. Did ya find my stuff okay? Let me have it Nina" Nina started to give me the bag when one of the tower watchers called out, "Cappy. You know that we have to have everything checked in before you receive it." "See how they are Nina. Wonder where they park their brooms." Nina chuckled and we both went up to the station. Like there were boarding passes going anywhere.

"Hi Pope. I thought you forgot me?" "Cappy. You think I would forget you? How are you?" he asked, rubbing the top of my head. "Okay so far. I just want to be outta here in three days. You said so." "Are you doing what they tell you to do?" Pope asked. "Yes I am. I already know that I'm supposed to do everything the doctor tells me." "And eat. You need to gain weight, so make sure you eat a lot." "Okay Pope, I got it already. Hey. Have you seen Noah? Did he say when he'd come by to see me?" "Noah? He'll probably call you or come by tomorrow. I think they're trying to hurry us up. Let's go see the nurse." Great thought Self. This could mean trouble.

But it wasn't. They just wanted me to go over the long list of items and sign papers. Felt good to have my music there. I made sure Nina put that on the top of the list. "Cappy," Nina nudged me, "See that picture on the wall over there? Well don't tell your father I said this to you because I'm not supposed to." "What Nina? What about that picture?" I asked staring at it. "Well, not only is the picture a large one, but the person who put it there is too!" "Nina who was it? Do you know? Are you gonna tell me?" I couldn't take it. The picture was large. At least a four by six foot view of water, trees and mountains. "Nina who put the picture there?" "Cappy, let's just say that it's one very important person. Okay?" "Okay?" I said, "Are you crazy? You're not gonna say anymore?"

Lucky for her. Pope was tugging on Nina's coat, telling her that they had to go. Unfortunately for me, I was left wondering with who left the picture on the wall.

Quickly I got a smoke lit and ran looking for John. Found him sitting at a table in his dress bomber jacket. John was cool. "John. Come here. I wanna show you something. You won't believe this. "What's up Wheels? Was that your dad?" "Yeah, but come here and look at this." He got up. I almost dragged him over to the wall where the picture hung. "See this John? Pope's girlfriend wasn't supposed to tell me, but someone put that picture in here for me. That's mine John. She said it was someone very important. Think it might be..." "Wheels. Don't say it. Try not to. The nurses try like hell to pick up everything we say. I know who you're thinkin' Wheels." "You know something John. There is something really familiar about this picture, but it's so faded you know." "Yeah Wheels. Like when they blew it up, they blew it up too big or something. Don't cha think?" "Yeah. But know something else John? Now you got me thinking more. I knew I'd have my mind on this from the minute I heard it was mine. Sorry John. I gotta walk around or something. I can't stand still. If I had wings I'd fly. Later." "Fly Wheels, fly."

Me and Self took a good look at the scene on the wall. Something about it, perhaps it was fall. It wasn't imagination at all.

Self spied a room to the south of the witches' tower. It was the activity room. There were tables and tables with puzzles and games, a pool table, and TV for the zombie insane. Ah! But there was a sight I was wanting it then, to play "their" piano again and again. To sit and to sing, so I sang and I sang, but was stopped by a witch who came on with a bang. "Capri. I'm sorry, but you'll have to stop playing. Some of the other patients are trying to sleep. We need to be considerate of all the patients here." "Sure, okay. Guess that's leave about two things left to do. Coffee and cigarettes." "That would work Cappy. Need a light?" Now was that ever a stupid question since they didn't let us carry matches or lighters.

Figured while I was up at the tower I'd use the phone and see what more I could get outta Nina. Seemingly surprised to hear me on the other end, Nina said, "What took you so long to call Cappy? I thought I'd hear from you sooner." "Nina, you want to tell me about the picture don't you." "Cappy I can't say anything more about that, but I can say that you sure do have a good father. He told me that when you got out of there that you were going to have the biggest and most beautiful house. I mean big house Caps. Are you there?" "Yes Nina, I'm here. A big house you say? It wouldn't happen to be a brick one would it?"

Just then I felt John tugging on my shirt-tail. He only had a certain time to call his girlfriend up and I understand that, wishing Noah would show. "Nina, I have to go. John has to use the phone. And when you think the time is right, you better tell me about this house." "Okay Cappy. I'll talk to you tomorrow. Call me if you need anything." "You know I will. Bye Nina."

John made his call and I stared at my picture on the wall. Then it hit. I knew that place. I walked over to it and stretched my arms out. Self couldn't resist and said, "This is Lake McDonald you guys, I used to live there." A witch couldn't resist and told me to keep my voice down. Right smack behind me she was and I told her about that being the place I lived. Could tell right away she didn't believe a word I had to say. This only pissed Self off. "Fuck you. What do you know? Jesus Christ! I've only been through 26 states,

477

I should know where I've been." Naturally swearing was not permitted and she made a point to say so. I turned my back on her and waited for John to finish his conversation so I could tell him. He'd believe me.

What to do, I thought? Oh yeah! The stuff that Nina and Pope brought. I can look through it, see if there's something to do. The boom box. My cassettes! I could listen to some Beatles. No I couldn't. The witches said the music would disturb the other patients. This is grand I thought. Not only won't they let me play, they won't let me listen. What is their problem, thought Self? Yeah, they do have one, don't they, I agreed.

People were still coming and going and I wondered when Noah would show. Thought for sure that Pope would have called him to say I wanted to see him, but I heard nothing. Then I remembered the cards that Noah showed me at his house. They were with the things I was allowed to keep in my room. Took them out to the smoking area trying to figure out how to line up the holes just right to get a pencil through them. I couldn't and no one else was able to manage it either. I attempted it for the next hour with no victory, hid out in my room and washed my hair because it was something to do. Self wanted a cigarette and I did too.

Just when I thought the police, the Pope and the me's ruined my party, who is standing in the day room but "Sir Joe." Racing to him were me and my thoughts. That's John!" Flash: Daly's.

"Hi Joe. Remember me from St. Patty's Day? John? The man from Cleveland? Did he go home? Things are going as scheduled then, just re-scheduled?" The man stood tall and uneasy. "Miss. I'm afraid you have me mistaken for someone else. I'm Mr. Langston and this is my son George." "I get it. You wouldn't be able to just come right out and say who you really were or people might try to harm you. You know how the guys in the white cars are."

There stood his son. A real dork of a dude. Young, maybe twenty years old. Over weight by about 70 pounds tall with a butch hair cut. By his mannerism you'd think him retarded. What was his story, I wondered.

"Miss. I don't recall asking your name." "Come on Joe. You know I'm Capri Spettro." "Of course, Miss Spettro." "Saya, Joe. I think we can talk on a first name basis. You can call me Cappy." Dork son was scratchin'at his head looking lost. "Cappy. You seem like a pretty smart gal. I'd feel better if I knew that somebody like you was keeping an eye on my son George for me. Think you might want to do that for me?" Ooh! This is a tough one Spet, Self had her thoughts. What are you gonna tell him? I thought a moment and looked at his son. He was smiling his chubby face at me with eyes lit up. I said the only thing I could. "Only for you Joe." Joe laughed and said, "Guess you can call me Joe as long as you remember that my last name is Langston." "Oh, I already figured that you'd want to be called that Joe. Oh and George...This room we're in right now never closes. It's the day room." George slobbered out, "Okay thank you."

Enough of this Self said and we took off for the double doors wishing on a visitor for me! Wishing and wishing till I couldn't take it no more, so I said to myself, let's go off to explore.

Found John sitting at one of the round tables and spoke. "You waiting on anybody?" "No Wheels. She can't make it tonight or she doesn't want to. Well, Lauri has over a forty minute drive to get here and that would give us about 15 minutes to spend together... here. Anybody come to see you tonight?" "No and it's driving me crazy! What do you do John? You look so calm." "Wheels. I'll tell ya what I do and you can do it too. They'll make you do it after you've been here a few days anyway." "Are you gonna tell me what it is already John because I wanna break something."

John got up from the table and we both walked over to a post in the day room. "Wheels. The clock is right here to our right. See?" "Yes. So now what?" "We walk the mile. Know how this hall way is in here. It's pretty much a square and if you walk around it twenty five times you walked a mile and it's a real head rush. Wanna give it try?" "It beats doing nothing. I'm game." "Alright Wheels if you think you can keep up with me." "Those are words of challenge my good man John. This can't be a walk when you've made it a race. Say when."

He watched the clock. We both did. We were waiting for the second hand to strike the twelve and we were off.

John moved with speed and indulgence and I copied. "This is great John." "Feel the rush in your head Wheels? Corner it with me baby." "Damn John those corners rush up to ya don't they?" "Told you this feels good. It's worth the cigarette when we're done. " "John, that was one."

"So Wheels. Have you seen the doctor yet?" "Maybe. One in the emergency room I remember, why?" Then you'll probably see him in the morning. It's no big deal. He'll just tell you that you need medications, that you're out of your mind and here we are." "Sounds marvelous. Simply marvelous." My body felt waves of rushes as we continued to speed walk the mile.

The talking was non stop. At least one nut would keep the whole ward going twenty four hours a day and things were looking up.

"So Wheels... what are you gonna do when you get out of here? " ... Do you think you can tell? And did they get you to trade your heroes for ghosts..." "What's with the "Pink Floyd"?" I asked. "I started thinking about how we're both acting for them, you know..."them." " "Oh, that "them." "Got it Wheels. That's such a cool name." Immediately Gentry came to mind.

Could John be working for him? Self and I would say something so Pinky knew I was paying attention. "Thought you wanted to know what I was gonna do when I get outta here." "Sure I do. Side tracked. Sorry. " ... Hot ashes for trees?..." " ... Hot air for a cool breeze?..." A guy I worked for used to call me Cool Breeze." " ... Cold comfort for change?..." "He did. That's a pretty neat name Wheels, " ... And did you exchange a walk on a part in the war for a lead role in a cage?..." "Yeah John. We both did didn't we?"

We finished the song and we finished the mile but John was disturbed that we had not timed it. "You time it John?" "I've tried to but every time I walk the mile I think about how good it feels when I'm done that I forget to see how long it takes me." "I'd say we were going pretty fast" "You don't happen to remember when we started do ya Cool Breeze." "Sorry John. I don't remember and that was a cool breeze of a walk. Next time we both have to remember the time to begin with." "Indeed Wheels. Indeed."

"Cigarettes!" Said in harmonies. "Wheels, I'll get us some coffee and you watch the witch armies." That I did when I went for a light and people were standing and saying good night. Visitation would be over and done. Time's running out, wishing someone to come.

That was when I made up my mind to call Noah myself and find out why he hasn't stopped like he said he would. John was patiently at the table with our caffeine and I waited for the phone.

Noah's mother answered and said Noah wasn't there. I hung up with much despair. My eyes were not deceiving me when a bolt came through the doors. His mom didn't say he was on his way, but there he was, here he'd stay. For as much time as we had left.

"Noah. I thought you'd never get here. What took you so long? I was sure when you left me here earlier that I was never going to see you again." "Figured while you were here Cappy, getting settled in, I'd catch up on my sleep. Did you get any sleep yet? Are you eating?" "Noah too much going on around here for that. Come on back and stay for a smoke. We only have about ten minutes and you'll have to leave."

We went to the day room that was night lit and quiet. Noah sat down and I was right in his lap. "I missed you so much and you smell so good. I don't want to stop hugging you? Hope you don't mind having what "they" call a crazy girlfriend." "Cappy. I don't think the nurses like what's going on with you and me. "Cappy. Could you sit in your own seat please," a witch howled across the room. Slowly I removed myself from Noah and sat down. I couldn't keep my eyes off of him.

"So Caps. Did you ever figure out those cards?" "No and I don't want to. Nobody in here could. Well look at them will you. Look at me. Didn't you miss me? Why didn't you call me Noah?" "I told you I needed some sleep.

Look Cappy, I don't want to make you feel any worse than you do now, but honey, I never said I was your boyfriend. Don't get me wrong..." "You're not my boyfriend? Then why did you stay with me, take care of me like you did?" "Felt that you needed somebody to help you and I wanted to. Look I care about you and want to see you get better. Everybody does." "Okay. I can accept that I don't have you as a boyfriend, but under one condition. I want that white tee shirt you have on. It smells so good and it'll look good with my white pants. What do ya think?" "Sure, you can have it. I have lots of em." Noah stood and removed his jacket, took off the shirt and handed it to me when he was spotted by a witch at the tower. "Sir. I'm sorry. You can't give the patients anything unless it is checked and inspected up here." "See how they are Noah. And they have to be so mean too." Noah was putting his jacket on and said, "Well, if you want the tee shirt we're going to have to listen to them." "I want it. You know I do, that and I love ya Noah. Thanks for coming to see me." "I wanted to see you. Somebody has to keep an eye on you."

Noah was right. And the somebody's were still doing that. Noah checked the tee shirt and it was mine to keep. I walked with him to the freedom doors that would take him anywhere he wanted to go. We hugged and he left.

I raced to my room to change. I put Noah's shirt on, my white pants, my white everything on and walked the mile myself. Self had to remind me..."Forgot to time it Caps."

Later in the evening another person was brought in to be a part of the loon world. Her name was Carrie. Carrie liked injuring herself. How did I find out so fast? I walked right up to her and asked.

She sat curled in a seat in the day room looking sad as can be. "Hi. I'm Wheels. What are you here for?" Carrie didn't say anything but did show me the insides of both her arms. "Carrie, what did you do?" I asked. Faintly, she smiled. "You cuts your arms from your wrists to your elbows? Didn't it hurt?" "No." And Carrie smiled big.

Duke, I failed to mention, talked little to anyone about her depression and when she did she trusted only me, Becky and John. They had her loaded up with drugs and Duke moved slower than us all.

Teresa was not having a hard time at all bitching about a cigarette and on and on and on. John couldn't take it no more and threw one her way on the floor. The tower witches didn't catch it and the dork was sitting dumb, Mike was pounding on the table and Beck was on the run.

It was hard to take, it was easy to do. You had to be me, you couldn't be you.

When things got more lax, I found a catalogue laying on one of the end tables in the day room. My name wasn't on it but I claimed it mine. Page after page were the most beautiful dresses, shoes, rings, things and more. I wouldn't have no problem having anyone of those items if they'd let me out the door. So now we had a John and a George. Next would be Ringo and Paul. These name alikes had to go, 'cept for John, he was cute, kinda, but nowhere near as handsome as the John I had met St. Patrick's Day. Now this "George." Good grief. He was tall and dorky. His hair was cut in a butch style. He was stocky built. He had a boyishly slobbering grin on him, which made his less appealing from the get go. But I did tell his royal father that I would watch out for him, and watch out I did.

"Hey George, did you know that your dad is royalty. He knows where my boat is. Well, one of them at least. Oh there is going to be one hell of a party on it. I'm gonna have a lot of people there. I'll even take John over there. He's sitting at the round table. He's a spy. He's spying on me. But he has to spy on me to make sure I'm okay, because I'm going to marry John Lennon ya goon. Act stupid. Like you don't know. Hell, from the looks of you, you probably don't know too much. I can't help it George. Hey do you laugh even when people make fun of you?" "It doesn't bother me. I have a boat of my own. Well, it's my dads, but he lets me drive it once in a while." "Shit you ass, I'm talking about a yellow boat. It's in Lake Erie right now. Only I don't know where for sure. But your dad knows. He's going to be on the boat. So is Paul, Ringo , John, and George. No, not you George. You don't hold a candle's flame to the George I'm talking of. I'm talking about "George Harrison," The Beatles. You have heard of The Beatles haven't you George." "I heard of them Cappy. And if my dad is going to be at the party, then I'll be there too. He'll let me come with him." "Oh please George, don't piss me off. There isn't any way that I'll let you on my boat. Besides, if I didn't invite you personally, then you can't come. See your dad has been in on this for years. You my dear friend are not invited. I don't want some slobbering idiot on my nice clean ship. Got that!" I laughed at George, as I watched him smile back at me, without a flinch of dislike in his face. I walked over to John saying... "Can you believe that jerk, her really thinks that I'm gonna let him on the yellow submarine! You'll be there John. I want you to come. But wait till you get a load of this guy. He's an idiot! You can cut him down and he just smiles at you, like he likes it." "Sick Wheels, but maybe he does. Hell he is after all, one of us loons." "Oh God, I never thought of that. He is one of us. Well, he maybe one of "us" but he ain't one of me. I'll be back John, I gotta make them nurses earn their salary and light up." John said, "I'll get the coffee."

Soon most of the loons were in the smoking area reading, staring, sneaking about, watching over their shoulders. It was a sight. Teresa was constantly bitching about no cigarettes. Carrie broke out of her shy shell to show everyone the damage she had inflicted on herself. Mike was nowhere to be seen, nor Becky. George sat alone scratching at his head.

John came back with the coffee, as usual. We smoked. Laughed when John pointed out that Teresa had just found another cigarette on the floor beside her. "John, come here. I want to show you something. Something that has been bothering me since I got here." I took John over to see the picture that was etched in my mind. "John, I talked to Pope's girlfriend Nina... Oh what the hell. Fuck this code Adam, I already opened my big mouth and got put in this place. Doesn't matter now. Besides you're all in on it. See, I talked to Nina, my dad's girlfriend earlier tonight. She told me that someone very big and important put that there just for me. She also told me that when I get out of here, there is going to be a very big and beautiful home for me. Home. There I finally said it. Think there is a home John?" "It looks like a beautiful place Wheels. But the picture looks like they over blew it up. So big it looks faded and old." "John! Thank God for you! That's Lake McDonald. I lived there. I have a picture of that very seen at my house, I swear I do. I moved there in May and lived there till late September of '81. My ex, the Prof' had a job there. Buff my oldest was there. She turned three that summer.

That fucking number three. Did I mention that Prof's a third? Third of what I don't know, but if not for him, I would have never had the pleasure of actually living there at Glacier National Park. That's where that picture is from. One of the Lakes there. The one I gotta get to is Saint Mary's Lake. Goose Island is there. God's waiting there. Gotta give him something back. I didn't deserve it. It wasn't mine. Maybe if I do that he'll at least let me be with John for a minute. Just one minute. Maybe I wasn't supposed to know that The Beatles were getting together again. Perhaps it was a mistake. I told many people. The police even heard me go on. I'm a security risk. Well, The Beatles really. They probably got a hold of Pope and told him that they were going to have me put here and have me drugged, so I would keep my mouth shut. I was talking a lot. I was going to blow the surprise. They're working on a way to catch me off guard now. Maybe they are scared that I won't be able to handle seeing John again after all these years, but I can handle it. First the nice "made to be" like Lennon at the bar. Now in the hospital with you. You are John number two. See there has to be a three. Numbers can go as high as you care to count. You can die counting, I am. 30 thousand years and that's a long time to be counting. See, there has to be a third John. The real one this time. Only I missed him two days ago because I couldn't keep my big mouth shut. Told everyone and now I'm here. Those vipers will try to see to it that I can't talk. You just watch. You watch them and you watch The Wheels." "I'm watchin' alright. You're pretty cool Wheels and you have some beautiful blue eyes or are they turquoise? I better not look too close because I have a girlfriend and we're supposed to get married, but you could make me change my mind Wheels. I could easily fall in love with you if I get too close. I better go walk the mile." "Wait John, don't go. I want to walk with you, wait up! " "I'm walking alone this time Wheels. Think, I need to think." "Fine, then you go ahead and run away. Thought your job took a clear mind. Bet you lose your job if you don't get your shit together." But John walked quicker away and turned his first left for the mile.

I wondered back and forth from the picture, to the smoking area, telling everyone that that was my picture. A picture of my home. It was my home. I thought. This was "my" home!" I burst into tears. "I lived there once back in '81." Talked loud enough to get the attention from the tower and a nurse soon came to inquire, while I rambled in the smoking area chain smoking.

"Capri? What is going on? All this talking. You are disturbing the other patients. Some of them can't be around all this excitement. I want you to calmly tell me what exactly is going on." "Oh fuck you. Why don't you leave me alone. You think that just because I am here and you have that little pen in your hand, and I'll bet a syringe in your pocket too, that you feel I "have" to tell you. I don't have to tell you a fucking thing. Strange isn't is. Funny how the mind just kind of puts you on the shut off mode. There isn't a damn thing that you or a thousand doctors can do to make me talk. Don' you just love it." I was busting up laughing. "You just wish you knew what was going on. Maybe you'll read a book about it someday and you'll see just how well a part you played nurse." "Capri. Why don't you walk with me for a minute, come on, you don't have to tell me anything. I think you need to rest. Slow down a little. You have to remember that you are not the only one here. Me and the other nurses have to watch a lot of people. Some of the other patients want to rest."

As the nurse held me by the hand, we passed the nurses' station. Right across from it hung a picture of a real place, a place that was mine if only for five months. I stopped. I seen it. I shot it. I saved it. "Nurse. I lived there. That's Lake McDonald Lodge. Part of the National Park in Montana. Goose Island is there. I got a meeting with God. I saw Him once. He told me to listen. He said L-I-S-T-E-N 2 G M. Two. Like starting over. Glacier... Montana. It all started there ya know, when I was Eve. I killed Adam. Now he's Pinky. He never lets me forget that I killed him and put it on the kitchen wall in my house. He didn't know what death was. Because death was a word only learned after he had died. Don't you see? I gotta go to Goose Island. God knows I'm coming. He's waiting for me. You guys can't keep me here. I gotta get there." She firmly grasped my arm and said, "Capri, I'm going to take you someplace where you can get some rest. It's okay, I'm not going to hurt you. Come with me." I released a long breath and willingly went along with the nurse. The room was like no other. There was only a bed and a safety screened window.

Chapter Twenty Six: "Concentrate With Heart. Get The Dream And Live"

"This isn't my room. Where do I pee? On the floor? I'm not an animal. Let me outta here!" I tried to run out of the room, but within seconds, male and female nurses surrounded me in their blue and white uniforms. With about four or five restraining me as I stood, I was told to remove my scarves. "Please, do you really think that I'm gonna commit suicide or something. You'd like that thought wouldn't you? Get your fucking hands off me." "Cappy you're gonna have to take the scarves off. We'll lock them up for you in your personals. It's okay" Fine, take them. But they're damn important scarves they stand for something you wouldn't understand." "Now Capri, we'll need you to take off your earrings and necklace, we'll put them in a safe for you." "You guys are a real joke, ya know it? First you want my scarves and now you want my jewelry too? Here! Take the fucking earrings." I ripped them through my lobes throwing them at one of the interns. "Now your necklace." "Now the fucking necklace? Do you know how soft eighteen karat gold is bitch? Think I could really hang myself with it? You people make me sick. Here. Quick, catch it now." I broke the chain and flung it across the floor.

Next thing I know is I have about eight to nine people pinning me down on my stomach across the bed. I noticed a large syringe filled with something and I knew it was meant for me. I yelled, "What is that. You ain't shooting me up with anything. What the hell do you think you're fucking doing to me? I don't have to take that." "Capri we're just giving you something that will help you relax. Don't worry, we're not going to hurt you." Asking nervously, "What is that? I wanna know what you are giving me. You tell me what it is!" "Capri, don't worry about what it is right now, it's going to help." I looked up again. I knew I was out numbered. Even though I had counted longer than all of them put together. I gave up. I couldn't break free from all the hands that had been restraining me any longer. I let out a long sigh and let my head go limp and drop. I could see the floor. I saw many sets of feet on it.

Slowly I raised my now heavy head and saw the male nurse ready to jab me with a long needle. From left to right I saw the faces that met the feet I'd seen only seconds before.

There among them stood the white suit that had matched the white sneakers. That one in a million face! There standing right in front of me was John Lennon. His brown hair was below his shoulders in length. Just like on the "Abbey Road" album. His beard had grown out some too. His brown eyes watched me through the famous Lennon glasses. He uttered nothing as he stood before me with his hands in his pockets. I turned away and looked again and still he stood motionless, speechless. I said to the nurse, "Go ahead, give me whatever you want. I doesn't matter anymore." Silently Self whispered, "This is what you dreamed of!"

I felt the needle. Slowly I watched the little army march out of the room, almost as quickly as they arrived except for one. She told me to lay down and sleep. "If you need to use the rest room, just knock on the window of the door in here and someone will come and help you. Good night Capri." "Wait, you can't leave me in here! Where's John? He was just here a second ago. Please don't lock me in here, I want to get out! I began to bang on the door yelling "I need a cigarette. Somebody open the door. You said all I had to do is knock. Oh you are all fucking lying witches and demons. Don't you know who you are locking up?"

I went over to the bed and propped up my pillow so I could sit and watch out at the parking lot. I started to cry out loud and said, "I'm Capri. Does this have to be in the plans too? I can't keep up anymore. They won. They finally beat me." I lay down and tried like hell not to sleep. All I wanted to do was think of John. Then I thought, I don't have to give the rib back. God let me see you. For a moment you were mine. All in white like March 20th, 1969 the day you were married. Only this is the nineteenth and you were single tonight. Self said, "Lucky lady. Capri, get with it. You just saw John Lennon! He was here for you! In this very room!" Was he trying to tell me something? No. He said nothing. I said nothing. The silence filled my ears with questions that I barely heard. Were you real? Could I have reached out and touched a three dimensional Mr. Lennon? "You looked great. Remember when we first met? Sure, it was at The Point. We sat next to each other. I said, "Shoot, I look more like John Lennon than you do." That was then. This is strange. That was strange. Seen you twice now. Stored, restored. Renamed Endeavor Remains. All white, positive. A dark room that's negative. Positive you were here! Negative I am here. Positive it was you. Negative, who'll believe me? Positive, don't tell. That's it. Don't tell anyone... ever!"

The injection took over. At last, I was defeated. My eyes closed, but I kept John's image in full view. Standing silent and here for me.

Morning arrived like Lennon. Boom! Awake I went to the door, knocking on the tiny window to get the attention of a nurse. I asked permission to use the rest room, take a shower and have coffee. The nurse held the door open and allowed me back into the wacky ward with my fellow loons.

John was up. All dressed and neat, having coffee and a smoke. "Hey John. Can I sit with you?" To my surprise he said, "Not right now Cap. I don't feel like talking. Don't take it personal or nothing." "I do take it personal. You didn't call me Wheels. Okay John, I'll sit over there by myself. But it won't be easy. I'll be there. You over here. You'll tell me when you're ready. I'll go, leave ya alone." I walked over to the station to light a smoke. The nurse said, "Good morning Cappy." Now why the hell would I want to talk to any of them.

I wandered back to the smoking area, curled up in a chair next to a small end table and watched John over the rim of my coffee cup. He sat quietly staring. Most of the day remained typical of the day before, once my meds wore off.

I paced, I smoked, I drank coffee. Meals were provided three times a day. I ate little. I wanted Noah to come and visit. Call, something, anything.

Later in the day Doctor Buder came in to remove the sutures from my neck. It was good to see a friendly face. "Cappy. Next time you need a cyst removed, call me. Why would you want a dentist to do it?" "Doc', you gotta help me. I can't take it. I wanna go home. I can see my back yard from here. Can't you talk to Lee and tell him I wanna go home. They won't even let me listen to music. That's my whole life Doc', music! They get mad when I play the piano and tell me to quit. When I ask to listen to my boom box they got locked up back there, they say I'm not allowed. I can't sing, can't play. You'd think they'd let me listen. I hate them Doc'!" "Cappy, come on honey, I'll talk to them about letting you listen to your music, but I can't promise anything. And start eating. You won't have to worry about doing the dishes." Thanks Doc'. You'll let me know? You call me. Even if they say yes, you call. I want to hear you tell me that they said its okay, okay?" "Okay I will. Try to cheer up and I'll talk to you later." "You promise me you'll call!" "I promise Cappy." Good old Buder, I knew he'd come through for me.

The hours passed slow. I had my picture on the wall to look at. The picture in my head to think about. Waiting and hoping for someone to come and see me. Maybe Ladie would visit. Of course she will. She's my best friend. She'll be here. Jerry will be the first one through the door when he finds out I turned myself in. Pink doesn't know. He must know. He set this whole thing up. This was supposed to happen. But he won't come. He wouldn't want anyone to know what he's doing. But he's gotta come. I'll call him. No one's using the phone I thought. I raced to it. Dialed with lightening speed. It rang. The answering machine picked up. With a trembling voice, I left my message. "Pinky. The clouds. Remember? They said listen G M 2. It was you Pink. This is my Big Time. Please come and visit me. I'm at Firelands in the South Pavilion, please..."

My time was cut short when the limit for my message was stopped by a sound. I slammed the phone and went straight to the piano and banged out a song I had written about Pink.

"... I could hear the laughter inside, I can hear your voice in the wind. I can hear you breathing the air, even when you're not in the room. Up the stairs, down the hall at the end on the left, alright, the right when you left. I had sought the solemn and strong. I've been where I don't belong. But to me there's always a trace, the emptiness that's wearing your face. For me, it's been ideal! But I can't conceive, if you can't be real to me. Do you know what I mean? I'm sure you know what I mean. I wanna thank you, for what you have done. You let me go, and now I know you are the only one. I wanna thank you. You're one hell of a guy. Oh I think you are, but have no real reasons why. So let me tell you, for the time, just one time, I thank you so truly from the heart of my mind. If one day when you're not too blind, and you decide to change your mind. If there's words I just cannot say, would it be worth it anyway? Made a choice. What a choice. It's smearing your vision, that constant incision you feed... Or don't you know what you need? I'm sure you know what I mean."

"Wheels, where'd you learn that?" Beck asked. "That was wow Wheels!" "Who wrote it? You?" asked Duke. She was a new patient, self-admitted. "I wrote that for this guy I know. He has no clue how many I wrote for him. I could write about him forever." "Wheels, play it again. It's about time somebody let loose on them witches. Oh, and Wheels... could I get just one cigarette from you? I won't tell." Bless her heart, even Teresa liked my song. I began belting out another song, banging on the old upright, when a nurse came back and demanded that I quit disturbing other patients, etc, etc, etc... I satisfied the mean old witch and told her to give me my tape player. "Come on, Buder must have called you by now, it's almost eight-thirty! Said he'd straighten it out for me." "I'm sorry Capri, but he hasn't called us on that yet and if he does, we'll let you know. Now let's leave the piano alone. People are here to visits with each other and we can't have anyone playing the piano just yet."

Sure I thought. They always try to stop me. Damn. This place is getting on my nerves. I wish someone would come to see me already.

I walked to the smoking area introducing myself and shook hands with everyone. I heard my name being called from the tower. "Capri, you have a visitor." It was Priest. I ran to him, gave him a great big hug and immediately dragged him over to see my picture. I was lifted to have a friend at last come to see me. I couldn't get the words out quick enough saying my hellos and how are yous to Priest. We walked over to the smoking area and sat down. After a few moments with Priest, I said, "I can't talk. My mouth doesn't wanna open. Oh my God. My jaw must have broke. I can't feel my mouth Priest." I began crying as my face seemed paralyzed. I yelled at Priest "Go! Go home. I don't want you to see me this way. Must look pretty funny to you. Go away. Leave me alone." I took off for my room to lay on my bed. I stared at the soft light right above me.

Still in tears, I thought, look at the light. Think of light, think white, think John, think talk. Just don't talk about John. Talk. Talk, You can do it. You're Cool Breeze, Big Time. You are Wheels. Just do it. After about ten minutes of coaxing myself, I tried to talk and I was successful. Soon the nurse came to tell me that they had sent my visitor away, because he had angered me. "Nurse, Priest didn't get me mad. I couldn't talk. I sounded retarded. Next thing I'll be slobbering on myself. Bet you guys get a kick out of that too." "Capri that is just a side affect it will go away. You're okay now right?" "And Priest is really gone? Damn it. I love that guy! He's been there for me along time." The nurse checked my pulse and suggested I try walking about the mile to get my heart rate up. Wasn't want I really wanted to do, but I could tell it's what she wanted me to do. Then I heard a little Italian voice going off in my head saying... "Just do what they tell you to do so you can go home." So, I walked a couple minutes. The nurse came back to check my heart, my pulse. I was fine or sort of. Crying back to my room, feeling alone and afraid, I prayed for another familiar face to drop in on me.

About a quarter to nine I heard another voice call out to me from the nurses' station. "Capri. Some people here to see you." I raced out of my room to the station and saw no one there. But the nurse had pointed me in the direction of a room located off the smoking area, telling me that my visitors were there. I walked nervously to the room wondering why these people would be in there. There wasn't just a few people in the tiny room, but five. I cried with excitement. "Shorty, Chelsea, you brought my kids! You guys look so beautiful all dressed up. I miss you" Then I hugged Buff, Jules and little Sonny. Buff, my oldest daughter elected herself as the spokesman for her and her younger siblings. "Mom, how ya doing? We all went to church today. It's Palm Sunday." "So that's why you got those pretty dresses on and Sonny in a suit. You look so grown up. I miss you so much! Oh Chelsea, they took wonderful! I can't tell you what it means to see them. Thanks you for bringing them here." "Well, me and Shorty thought it would be a nice day for the kids to come and see you. I think the priest at your church is coming by to see if you want to receive communion." "Hey you guys," Shorty said, "Didn't you have something you wanted to give your mom?" Jules said, "Here mom, I brought you a palm from the church, so did Buff." They handed me the two palms and Sonny, handed me the third saying, "I got one for you too mom" "You know, I have the perfect idea for these palms..." Before I could

490

get the rest of my sentence out to them, I felt my face deform on me and I couldn't talk. To them I must have sounded like an old large and very slow barking dog.

Don't know how to describe it any better. Words a struggle for me? But they were. I grabbed a piece of paper laying on a table in front of the kids. Wrote them a note reading: "The medicine they give me makes it hard to talk. I have to go lay down and look at the light in my room for ten minutes. Be right back. I turned to Shorty and Chelsea motioning to them to explain it better for me.

Feeling helpless, I hung my head crying till I got to my room. Watched my watch, watched the light. Ten minutes passed. I could talk. Went back to the room where I had a few more minutes with my kids when Noah arrived. Happy as I was to see him, there was something I had to do for my kids. "Okay, now for these palms," I said. Took the three of the fresh, long and green leaves making a braid to wear round my head. "Hey you guys. This is the best thing you could have given me. They took my scarves away, but since these are blessed and gifts from you, my kids, there is no way they can take them. Looks pretty good doesn't it?" "It's cool mom," said Buff. All the kids said they missed me and wanted me to get better, get back home. It was hard to not know when I would be free of this place and even more difficult tellin' the kids.

"Pope said to do whatever they say and I'll get out of here faster. I'm trying! And you can call me anytime!" We all five hugged and six kisses were exchanged between me and the kids. After the blast off Chelsea and I had back on "C" Street, I was very surprised when she said, "Take care of yourself Cappy." She hugged me? "And don't worry about the kids. We'll make sure they have everything they need until you get home." By now I was teary eyed. Gave Shorty a Spettro look. He understood. "Come on Buff, Jules and you too Sonny. We have to leave. Your mom has to rest"

I nearly broke up watching them leave and go until I remembered that Noah was still waiting to see me in the smoking area. I joined him there, but for only mere moments, when the nurse announced that visiting hours were over. More tears. More crying. I couldn't take it. "Noah I didn't even get to spend five minutes with you and they are telling you to leave. Why don't you call? You don't even call me why? You're my boyfriend, you're supposed to take care of me. Why'd you stop ? Why did you leave? You left me. You slammed the door behind you. Couldn't get across my lawn fast enough! You never even looked back when I called to you. Can I help it if I'm supposed to marry John Lennon? You knew. You were part of it weren't you?" "Cappy. I wasn't in on anything. I saw a girl who I thought needed some help. That girl was you. Stayed with you because you needed help taking care of your kids or you were going to lose them. Children Services would have taken them away from you. And I never told you I was your boyfriend." "You're not my boyfriend?

So I'm begging my dad, the nurses and everybody to get you here cause I thought you were and now you tell me you're not? I have no one? My dad don't want me. My kids don't have a clue and now you say this? And Pinky, the electrician you said I should call won't return any call I've made. I left messages. He doesn't call me. You don't call me. What? No Emerald City? No pot of gold? Nothing? All this for nothing? That can't be. It can't. I got proof. But you'll never know what it is. I've learned something being in this place. You can't tell anybody anything." With my mouth going cockeyed once again, I begged Noah to leave. "Noah. Please go and don't bother coming back. You helped. I read the fucking Beatle book. My being locked in this fucking insane asylum is your fault and you're not my boyfriend? I think I hate you Noah. Hate you for ever coming to my house in the first place!" "I'm going Cap, but don't say ya hate me. I was trying to help you. I still am. Just believe me. I'll call you. Calm down. I'll call you later on alright." Then a nurse reminded Noah that it was time to go and Noah left.

I walked the mile. The whole mile. Twenty five times around the inside block. Around and around till I got to the clock. John called out to me. "Wheels, how long did it take?" "How long did what take? And why are you talking to me anyway. I thought you hated me too. Shit, everyone else does." "Cappy no. I want out of here as much as you do. Sometimes I get so caught up with that thought, that if I don't sit down, relax and focus on something else, I'm afraid I'll go off and break something or somebody. This place can piss you off, you know that. Them bitches up there always running the show, getting in your face about every something. Need a break to myself, you know? I told you not to take it personal, remember?"

"Capri. Telephone." I was paged. Maybe it was Pink. Nah, not him. It couldn't be Pinky. My luck wouldn't have it any other way, the way my luck had been. I took the phone, "Hello," I said. "Cappy how are you doing? This is Doctor Buder. I promised I'd call you and I have some good news for you. I talked to "Dr. Lee" and he said that you can use your boom box as long as you listen to it with headphones. So now you can listen to music whenever you want." "Oh Doc', that's the best news I heard all day! And my kids were here tonight. They gave me palms so I made a headband out of it. So far the nurses haven't said anything about taking it off." "I don't think they'll make you. Things will be okay. Listen to some music and try to relax." "Thanks Doc." Oh and remember I told you once you were gonna be on my boat?"

Buder chuckled and said, "Yeah, I think I remember you saying something about a boat." "It's not any boat Doc', it's The Yellow Submarine!"

Quickly I hung up on the Doc' and raced for the boom box, but I was turned down. "Cappy. The doctor said if you had headphones you could use it and you don't have any. Maybe someone you know could bring a set in tomorrow." Tomorrow, I thought. "Tomorrow," I yelled, "It's always something huh! You people just love to piss us off don't ya. Makes you feel so damned important! Oh you can bet I'll get the headphones. Just like all of you can bet you'll end up in hell!"

Self headed straight for the piano, belting out another original I had written for Pinky. "They" told me to quit again. Banging on the keys with the palms of my hands, I turned to the nurse who said stop. "Are you fucking happy now? I'm done. Drop dead." The powerful witch reminded me that if I didn't tone it down she would have me put back into the seclusion room, where they had injected me with their poisons. I obeyed. Played the part of the nice cooperating patient, just to get the bitch off my back. Got myself a cup of coffee, lit myself a cigarette and headed for the table to bullshit with the other loons.

About everyone had gone to their rooms. Poor Teresa, I thought. She probably be a blast to talk to if she were up and kicking 'cept they won't let her smoke. No wonder she goes to bed. Can't smoke, might as well sleep. Shit, I'll just smoke one after another. That'll keep me alert and on my toes, in case the nurses pulled another Code H on me to drag me into the seclusion room again. I didn't want to be there with no freedom at all and coma like. In the smoking room I could bump into a fellow comrade, and have some conversation. Which is how I spent most of my time that night. Up talking and smoking constantly.

How the hell would I listen to music, I thought. Have to find somebody who will get some headphones. But who? Priest. He'll get me a pair. I know he will. Morning couldn't come any slower and the evening was early. John wasn't talking much, but you can bet George had a mouthful to say and I didn't want to hear it.

"Hi Wheels. Remember me? My dad said to keep an eye on me?" "What the hell do you want George? Get real. I'm not going to watch you. Wanna know why? You're sick that's why. Do you really think that I'm gonna keep an eye on you? Look at you. You look like some big dumb dork. And I can say whatever I want, because they think I'm nuts, so who cares. Now leave me alone, I have to double check the guest list for the party I'll be having on my boat and you George are not invited!" "You aren't nice Wheels. Why are you being so mean to me? If I want to get on your boat I will." "Get a grip George. Ya think that for one moment you can just jump into the boat and go? This is my boat. I own the damn thing. I'll be getting married and that boat is going to take me home. I'm not taking you home George. You are not on the list. And do you want to why? Because you're not supposed to be, got that? Get that? Keep that!" "Wheels, you said my dad was invited. Usually when a person is invited to a party, aren't they allowed to bring a guest?" In anger and shock I raised my voice to George. "Who the hell ever told your big dumb ass that you could call me Wheels? Only my friends call me that. And only if I give them permission. You do not have my permission. You are not going to get my permission. And if you want to be stupid enough to keep talking to someone that doesn't want to talk to ya go on. But you better call her Capri or Wheels might rip your head off!" This kept him quiet for a while and I walked to the witches' tower to light a cigarette.

Morning came and I called Priest, asked for the headphones. During first visiting hours, Priest showed up with a walk-man and headphones. Pope brought more cassettes from my house that was just through the glass windows and over the fence.

Now in my room, I put the phones to my ears, lay flat on my back and put on who else but The Beatles and of course John Lennon. I was the one he wanted. Me. The Wheels. The queen of the stories in the wacky ward where I was supposed to be for protection.

Some protection, I thought. Drugs and a world of people who I didn't come close to except for maybe John. The one who wasn't talking to me much anymore. He would have to eventually. Maybe it was high time people in this place knew who I really was. I grew very angry. Confinement, contradictions, predictions, convictions, confirmations, invitations and here I was locked up.

Poor me. Late for the most important date. I rushed out of my room and got the attention from everyone in the smoking area and of course the witches' tower. "Look you cracked and fucked up insane lunatics. We may all be part of this crazy ward, but I'm not like any of you. Why? Because I am The Wheels. Why am I The Wheels? Because John was the walrus. Make sense? No of course not. How could any of you possibly understand who I am. You can't and that's why I am letting the truth out once and for all. I am not Capri Spettro. My name is Catherine Sue Elizabeth Santi and I am very proud of it because I am the chosen one. The one who will be in the history books about the greatest hoax on the planet!" Teresa shakingly said, "You don't like me anymore do you, Wheels." "Of course I do Teresa. And screw the witches. Take a cigarette. They just want to fuck with your head." "Thanks Wheels. I know I can count on you." George wanted in on the conversation and I told him to go away, like always.

It was John's attention I wanted, figuring he was the one protecting me, but he didn't utter a word. I walked up to the nurses' station. Told the witches in their protected little ivory tower. I'll be out of here tomorrow. I can leave after three days." "Now Catherine, you know that is up to the doctor. That isn't up to you." "Why not?" And I slapped my hand on the counter. "It's a free country, until people like you decide whether or not we are allowed to be free." "Catherine you came in with your father and voluntarily admitted yourself." "I know my rights. I don't have to take these pills. Those cute little brochures on top of our lovely little night stands don't say a word about what you do if I don't take your pills! That you get ten people to restrain me, give me a big injection of whatever it is, so I won't know what the fuck is going on! You don't fool nobody. I'll get an attorney and take you to court. You can't give me medication without my permission." "Catherine, may I remind you to watch your language. Other patients and we the staff don't like it." "Fine I'll drift into your world of make-believe. But aren't we just a little too old to be playing mother may I?"

Lit a smoke. Let's forget that once and for all. Assume that I chained smoked period.

I grabbed my catalogue that was more than likely put there by the same person who put the picture up there for me. But who?

"Catherine, you have a delivery." "Me, what is it? Are you sure? Who's it from," I asked, racing to the station. "Oh flowers and there from Jerry. The colors! Pink and burgundy. And the leaves. They're so green! God they're gorgeous!" I slid them down the counter where the flowers would be directly across from my picture on the wall and read the card: Hi... Hi... Hello... Hello... Hi... Hi, Love, Jerry. And if I know Jerry he'll be walking in the door any second to visit me. Just after the thought I heard, "Catherine, you have a visitor." I looked over and Jerry was standing there in his usual dark gray work suit. Same smile. Same gray hair and tired red eyes.

"Hi Jerry." "Hi, hello, hello, Hi. Figured I get that over with since I see you got the flowers I sent." "I love them. What are they?" Jerry said, "Well, Cathy, I told the guy at the florists that I wanted to get you something that would never die. They said Begonia's. Then I picked out the one with the most flowers and buds. You like it?" "It will always bloom?" I asked Jerry. "As long as you take care of it and water it like the card says, it should last all your life Cathy." I wanted to show everybody, when Jerry asked, "Are we allowed to have a smoke.?" "Back here Jerry. I smoke one after another."

We walked over to the smoking area, I pointed out my picture. Showed him my catalogue of all the things I was going to buy. "Jerry, see that retard over there. His name is George Langston. He's thinks he's going on the yellow submarine with me when I have my party. You're invited, but you probably knew that already. The first one I invited personally, was Doctor Buder. He was giving me a checkup. On my way out I told him not to forget about the boat. Need a doctor on board ya know." "Geeze Cathy, I'm not so sure I like the idea of being down under the water like that." "Jerry, it will be grand.

Imagine all of us in the yellow submarine. Priest is coming. So is The Captain and Noah. Pope and Mayor of course. She didn't really die. She was just dying to tell me about all off this too soon and couldn't keep it to herself anymore. The Beatles came up with a way to make it look like she died, but she's safe and Pope sees her after. John Lennon isn't dead either. Oh, but I told you that. I can't wait to get outta here Jerry! I should get out by tomorrow. That makes three days. Liberty and justice for all." I took the bell out of my pocket and walked around ringing it as hard as I could, until a witch demanded I give it to her. "Catherine, give me the bell. You have been ringing that bell too loud for the last time. We are going to have to lock it up with your other things." "That's my hope bell. It's my symbol of hope. Noah gave it to me. You can't have it. I won't give up the only thing that keeps me going!" Splashing tears hit the floor as I held onto my brass bell as hard as I could. "Catherine how about if we put a tissue inside the bell, so if it does ring, it will be quiet. If you promise to keep it just that way, we'll let you hold on to it. It could disturb the other patients. You know Mike. We've see you talk to him. Do you like him?" "Sure I like Mr. Wonder." "Well," she continued, "Then you wouldn't want to upset your friend would you? We have to be concerned for everyone."

"If that's all it takes too have the bell Noah let me keep, then I'll do it I'll be outta of here tomorrow anyway. Can I have that tissue please?" The hospitals brand was harsh. I had to placed just right inside the bell or it could get scratched. Never! Not my bell. I put it in my pocket and went back to sit with Jerry. "See that girl there, that's Becky. She has two uteruses. She told me if you ain't crazy when you get here, they'll make you go crazy. She's right. They driving me nuts. Over a fucking little bell! So I rang it. They don't understand rock and roll. Every time I go over to play something that I wrote on the damn piano back there, they tell me to stop. Jerry, rock is rock. I'm the coolest girl in America. I'm Wheels. The Wheels is gonna keep going round and round."

"Geeze Cathy, you sound like you are having a good time. Oh, I almost forgot. Here's something for you. Ladie made you a milk shake and wanted me to bring it to you. It's just the way you like it. Pure vanilla ice cream. Come on Cath. Drink her up!" "Damn this is good. Is she gonna stop by, tell her to bring one when she comes. I wonder if I can have my own stuff brought in. I'll have to check. I'll have Pope bring me some vanilla ice cream to keep in the freezer." Jerry said he would ask Ladie and asked, "So do you know anybody here?" "Well, that girl there, Carrie, likes to get attention by cutting her arm. John is an investigator over there, the one in the flight jacket. Over there is George. He thinks he's getting on the sub, but it isn't gonna happen. That's Duke, I don't know her too good. Here comes Teresa. Watch. She's gonna come and ask for a smoke and she's only allowed one an hour. Watch what we go through around here."

"Hi Wheels. Oh you have a visitor. I'm Teresa, but nobody likes me. Wheels, could I have a cigarette? Just one. I promise I won't tell them, okay?" I turned to Jerry 'cause he had a hard time containing himself. "Go sit down Teresa, you know." She sat on the closet chair next to mine a table away. I pulled a cigarette out of my pants pocket where I carried mine, and tossed one under the table where Teresa was sitting. She pushed it toward her chair where she could reach down to get it. She lit it off of somebody else who had one burning. We did a lot of smoking, us smokers. By this time Jerry was cracking up. "Where do I sign in. I think this place would be good for me. You're having fun aren't ya Cathy?" "You know Jerry, I am having fun because I know that when I get out of here and all this is said and done, people will probably be reading all about it in their local newspapers worldwide. So what the hell, I make the best of it. Sometimes I get sad, when I think of my kids. They miss me. Poor Sonny doesn't understand what is going on, he's only five ya know. But I try not to think of the house, the kids. I keep thinking of being John Lennon's wife. Man oh man! Talk about a dream come true! This is the dream. This is the truth. This will happen. And you'll be one of the many to witness the wedding. "The wedding? I'll be there and I might where a tux." "You can come any way you want. I'll be all in white. White what, I don't know. I really like what I have on. White. White looks good on me. When I get to be eighty four, because I figured out that's how long I'm going to live, my eyes are going to be so blue because I tried on a white wig at a Detroit hair show back in 1975 and I looked great!" "Geeze Cathy, slow down, I can barely understand you. Drink the rest of that shake before it gets runny." "You know Jerry, I feel sleepy. It's the pills they make you take. They took me to a room the first night I was here. They held me down and shot me up. Anyway, what I'm trying to say Jerry, is I need to sleep a little while. I usually only sleep ten minutes or so, so if you want to have a smoke and wait for me?" "No Cathy, you get your rest. I'll come back tomorrow and see you again. I'll bring you another shake if Ladie is working and if she isn't I'll get you one anyway." "Thanks Jerry, and thanks for the beautiful flowers." Jerry saw himself out and I took to my bed for a short nap.

When I woke up, a real priest from Saint Peter and Paul Church came by to see if I wished to have communion. "No father, I don't wish for it, but I'll take it you have it handy." The priest smiled and said holding up the host, The Body of Christ." I answered, "Amen." Thanked the priest and walked away.

Passing near George, I looked over at John and said, "John I feel so good. As soon as I get all my money, I'm going to buy everyone a flower who's been nice to me." George said, "You're gonna get me one too, aren't you Wheels?" "You think you're funny George. Keep calling me Wheels and I'm gonna bitch slap you right crossed your stupid face. No, I am not giving you a flower. I wouldn't give you a weed. Man why don't you fuck off already." "Yeah, George, if Catherine doesn't want you to talk to her, then it's a good idea not too, okay." I had a pretty hard time believing that a witch was on my side, but a witch defended me and I thanked her.

Under his breath George said to me, "I don't care, I don't have to be on your submarine because I have a ship of my own. Maybe I have Naval Destroyer." "George if you do have one then get on the fucking thing and destroy yourself." Again a voice from the nurses' station politely asked George to leave me alone.

It was time to make a phone call. I had to leave another message for Pink. Wondered if he would be home yet.

Every time I called I got his answering machine. He's gotta show up. It's been three days. I've been here three days. He's a third. The best third. He's gotta come. I dialed the number. I heard the ringing. Heard the recorded voice of the man I had loved ever too much. I pleaded for him to come and see me. I needed him to see me. If he didn't show up to see me it would mean he didn't love me, but he said he always would. He told me to remember that. Never forgot it Gentry, I thought, not ever! I went back to my room to lay on the bed to focus on the soft light just above me.

Another day passed and I thought I'd get to go home. I was upset that they still refused to let me leave. The doctor didn't think I was ready. What? He talks to me one time. Tells me my mind is out there. Hell I didn't see it. What the hell does he know anyway? He should be the one taking the Lithium, not me. And he oughta try some thorazine too. Hell, if he's gonna give it to other people then he should be trying it out on himself first. He doesn't know what this shit really does. He's not the one who is on it anyway, I am. I yelled out. "I hate this fucking place. Did you write that down in your notes miss nurse?" "Catherine you need to settle down. Why don't you find something to read. You have a couple papers here that your dad brought in for you. Want them?" "Oh sure. Let's get my mind off something else, if we can find my mind." I sneered at the older woman and grabbed the papers. I searched for the lottery numbers. Well, I didn't really have to search, they were always on the front page. Had to know where to look and I knew where.

I sat down at a table and the first thing I noticed was a car accident. The heading read: Woman killed in one car crash. My God, that's Missy, Professors new wife. The Professors second wife is the one who is dead in this crash. I don't even have to read it. I wonder if he knows about it yet. I bet he doesn't. Maybe I should call him up and let him know. Fuck him, I'm not going to talk to that prick. He should have died and if he didn't get rid of the "Salinger" book he's a dead man.

Poor Missy, only 24 years old. Just then Carrie came out from hiding. She once again was sitting in a chair against the wall looking hopelessly at her arm. I thought, damn, didn't she get enough attention from those cuts she put there yet? "Hey Carrie, haven't seen you in the smoking room all day. What you been up to?" Carrie said, "See Wheels, look what I did. They won't let me have my curling iron anymore. How am I supposed to do my hair?" Carrie held her arm to show me all the burn marks up and down the inside of her arm, that practically covered the slash marks from before. "Carrie! What are you trying to do curl your arm? Doesn't it hurt? I mean, didn't it hurt when you put that iron on your arm? You are crazy." She smiled proudly, shook her head and said, "No." "Carrie, I don't know about you. They aren't going to let you have anything that is going to hurt you. You're cute. You don't even need to wear makeup. I got to load the shit on! Look! I'm at least twice your age. What are you, about 15,16?" "Sixteen" she said. "You don't want to kill yourself that's for sure because you control it. You only cut until you can't bare the pain anymore and stop. Same with the burns. It got too hot so you pulled the curling iron away. I can slap myself in the face, when I think I screwed up. And I have done that enough times. I've never done anything that was ever really wrong. Never had to go to jail for anything. Got a couple of speeding tickets. Stuff like that. But, I never really done anything good either. No, I had three kids, that was good. The negative for that was the man that impregnated me with them. He belongs here, not me!" Carrie finally laughed.

"See things aren't so bad after all. Wait till someone else puts the beating on you. That's when you either take control or lose control. In my case I lost control. This creep who I had let stay with me after my divorce, beat me and raped me. He ripped me out of bed by my hair. Right at the temple. And you know how much it hurts to pull hair out right there." Carrie smiled with delight, as she stroked her head nodding yes. I assumed she must have done that to herself by her familiar expression of pride. I went on. I got up from my chair and began telling anyone within listening distance. "Henry threw me to the floor. Then he grabbed me by the hair again to stand me up. He punched me in the side of the head. My ear. I dropped to the bed and curled up. He punched me again. You know what, he just kept on throwing his fists into my head over and over and over. Always the same spot. He broke my jaw. Now the doctor says my jaw bone is too thin. It can break any time. Ha, I'll be just like Daffy Duck, a real Loon Toon. That's what we are aren't we?" "Yeah Wheels. The Loony Toons and don't forget where we are," John said laughing. "The Wacky Ward John, I'm up with ya on that. That's why so many of us are in the "captivity room" watching the television at three o'clock. The fucking cartoons are on. Daffy Duck, Donald Duck, Bugs. Shit that's us." It's was official, we were a rare breed: "The Loony Toons of the Wacky Ward."

"John this is driving me fucking crazy! You know how bad I want to ring that bell now!" "Better not Wheels. They like to take things. Save it. You'll get an outside pass soon." George had been acting up again, trying to get my attention just to piss me off. "Hey Wheels, you think your boat is really something don't you. I have a ship. A Naval Ship. I drive it. I'm the Captain." "Oh please. There is no way that you could ever be the Captain. You couldn't be the captain of the fucking little brown turtles. You know, the ones that show up in the porcelain pond." I laughed so loud I had to get up from the table and walk the mile to cool down. "John was busting up. Teresa too. Duke happened to be sitting nearby and said, "Damn, how do you do it Wheels? Where do you come up with this shit?" Teresa was laughing her ass off after she heard that. "Oh shit! That's it Duke. Ever since I've been on this medicine I can't go, I'm so constipated. I think I have to and I feel like I have to. So I walk over and have a seat on the porcelain pond and maybe if I'm lucky, a little painted turtle will pop out. Sometimes three or four." "Hey Wheels! I took my little guys for a walk there the other day. Couple of them were a little shy, but I managed to get three of them in there." John understood. "Is this something or what John? I'm having a blast and if the medicine is doin' it, I want more." "It is Wheels, just roll with it baby. Feel like walking the mile with me?" he asked. "John, you and me will glide that mile. Lets book?" John and I got to our starting position at the clock and we were off.

I could feel the head rushes. Goose bumps flying through my head and I could hear the air blowing in my ears. Like the sound of an ocean in a big sea shell. The faster we walked the louder it winded. The rush was everywhere. The mile was finished. "Wheels, we did it again. We forgot to check the time. I'll get the coffee, want a cup?" "Yeah, I need one."

Mean time I had wondered about when I might be able to get out side. Smell outside air. Maybe they'd let me go to my house since it was only a block away.

Jerry was by each and every night to visit. Ladie, my so called back-stabbing-best-friend, never came to see me or called. This got me to think.

I'll write a letter to The Barrel. In it, I asked simply, that if any of my friends wanted to visit me to just come to Firelands, but no one there showed up.

One evening, to my surprise, James came in to see me. Good old Jimmy. "Hey Jimmy, I'm so glad you came in to see me. You know, all I have to do is get my weight up to 120 pounds and I can get surgery on my jaw. It's not bad news because it means that I will finally get the hell outta here." "Cathy. Slowdown. Hey I got you a card." Then Jimmy leaned over talking quietly with his deep voice. "I stole it Cath. I was broke, but it doesn't mean I didn't think about what the card said. I love you Cath. Always will. We go back a long time. I don't like seeing you in here like this." "Come on, let's go sit over here and have a smoke Jimmy. Oh, Wait! Come here and look at the flowers Jerry gave me. Wait a minute James. Look. There's a little ceramic bird in my plant. See, it's way in the middle behind the leaves and I'm telling you that bird wasn't in this plant this morning when I watered it. I wonder who put it there. Oh, never mind. Let's sit down. I'm glad somebody came to see me. Jimmy, Ladie hasn't even called me. Guess ya know who your friends are." "Cath, you know that you and me will be friends forever. I couldn't not be your friend. I care about you and you know that." I cared about you too Jimmy.

We walked over to the smoking area and we sat right across from Mike. Now Jimmy really hated blacks. But this dude Mike peeked Jimmy's attention. "What's with this dude?" Jimmy said. "Watch," I said. "Mike, do you love me?" Mike answered, "Sure I love you." "You want to marry me?" Mike answered, "Sure I'm gonna marry you, I love you." "Hey Mike, do your "Stevie Wonder" for me one time." He did and now Jimmy was holding on to his gut, spitting in laughter. "How do you stand it Cath? This dude is a fucking idiot!"

"Hey Jimmy, you think that's bad, that girl over there is pregnant in her uterus." "So," Jimmy said. "Oh, I left something out. She has two." Jimmy had to take himself from the table so he could turn his face away from everybody. When he was through busting a gut, he told me that he had to go soon.

"Cath, I had to sneak over here to see you. You know me and Cindy are trying to work things out and if she find out I'm here she'll shit. You gain that weight so you can get home to those kids." I walked over to the doors that would set him free, when he said, "Well, am I allowed to hug you?" "Yes Jimmy, I need one." I gave him a big hug and kissed him on the cheek.

Just then, Mike lost control. He had seen me and Jimmy hug and was ready to jump my friend. Mike yelled out, "Hey, get your hands off her, I love her! Gonna marry her!" But before he could reach me, the code H people came and took him to his room where he'd be sedated for the night.

501

Jimmy's back was up against the wall. So was mine. I didn't know what to think. "Jimmy, you better go. They'll tell you it's time to leave anyway after that." And "they" did. Jimmy gave me a cheek to cheek hug and said that he would try to see me again. I knew he lived in Huron and I knew that his wife would be furious if she found out about tonight. After all, Jimmy and I had an affair and Cindy knew that. This innocent meeting of friends would be sure to end their marriage. I naturally assumed I wouldn't see Jimmy again, at least not in the hospital. I cried when he left and went over to a table to read the card he gave me. I read it at least three times a day or more, thinking of him.

It was time for music so I went to my room for the walkman and a cassette. The song next on the tape was "The Long And Winding Road." Yes, I thought. The Going to The Sun Road. The road that was curves and half circles for fifty miles that led to the lodge, had to be what The Beatles sang about.

"I lived there," I told the nurse who was giving me meds'. "I did, I lived there for five months. But you don't believe me, do you. That is my picture there I'm telling you. I'll get somebody to bring some pictures of mine here. Buff will know the ones I'm talking about. She's my oldest daughter. Jules comes after her and then Sonny. I got three brothers. I was the third born. There were three Cathy's living on "C" street, the third letter of the alphabet. Worked at the same shoe store three different times in my life. Worked in all three of the stores they had in town, which by the way did I mention, they are on their third name." "Catherine that's enough, why don't you go relax," the nurse said. "I don't feel like relaxing I want to finish. There was Gary III, who had asked me to marry him. When Professor III asked, I foolishly said yes. Then Pink III. The one who once said we should make music together forever, I think he said forever, but he did say music. The second time he asked Buff if he should marry me. Buff said yes. Pinky told her that he would have to have his mother's permission. One and final time Pink said marry me Big Time. But since I knew that he had been drinking a little, I had to tell him to ask me sober. He never asked me again. Are you writing this all down? Getting some sick thrill? You think I care if I die or not. I would rather be dead, than walk this world alone without him."

I left the nurses' station and thought. As long as I'm alive he'll never marry anyone. He's mine. In his heart, he knows that. In his heart, it is only me he loves. He was Adam once upon a time, I was his first. I'll be his last. That's the way it's supposed to be isn't it? "Why the hell don't you come and see me Gentry? If I die will you be sorry? Are you sitting somewhere, wondering and planning a way or are you gonna throw me away?"

Tore up and choked up with tears, I raced to my room. Curled up on the bed and took the little brass bell from my pocket. Clenching it tightly, I pressed it up to my heart. Seemed impossible to get through to him. I could hear his voice saying the same thing over and over each time on the recording. Killing me more. I can't come to the phone, I can't come to the phone, I can't come to the phone. If you want to leave a message, after the tone, after the tone. This was grand! Since he couldn't come to the phone, that was why he didn't call back because he couldn't come to the phone. There was only one thing I could do. I would need to call someone who could get through to him for sure, but who? I don't want Pope to call. Don't want Nina to. He won't call me if they call him. It has to be someone with authority. I know, I thought. I'll call Sparks. He'll help me. I've known him for years. I'll have him get the message to Pink. Gentry will show up for sure! If he knew it might be life and death, then he's got to see me! He'll want to be here! Like he always was supposed to until I gave him the apple.

Walking to the phone nearby, I called Sandusky Police and asked to speak to Officer Sparks. They radioed him to call the station. Max was soon on the phone with me. "Max, this is Catherine. Catherine Santi." "Hi Catherine. What's up? I hear your in Firelands. What happened? You okay?" "Sure, I'm okay. They got me locked up in the wacky ward here. I'm stuck here with a bunch of loons. Anyway, the reason I wanted to talk to you is because I have been trying to reach Gentry Mocean. All I ever get is an answering machine. He doesn't return my calls. Max, I'm 87 pounds, hell I could be dead if I lose anymore. I need to reach him. Couldn't you drive over to his house. He's working on one over on Neil Street. I know the address. Let me give it to you." "Catherine, how about if I call there first, see if he's home. If I can't reach him by phone I'll drive over there. When I see him I tell him what's going on." "Oh that would be great! Be sure to tell him that this might be the last time I'll ever be able to see him. Max, I never told him I loved him. I need to tell him that. Don't you tell him though. I want to be the first one to say it okay? I really love this man. Promise me you'll talk to him?" "Catherine, I'll make sure that he gets your message one way or another. Sit back and try not to worry. You take care of you for now and I'll talk to you as soon as I get in touch with him." The conversation ended but the worry didn't and I worried.

I went to get some ice cream from the freezer that Pope brought in for me. Got a big bowl of vanilla and walked in the line for meds'. When the nurse handed me a cup of pills, I dumped them into the ice cream. "You know. When they take that rib out of me to fix my jaw, I think I'll take the left over pieces and make a necklace out of it. Why not? I heard people make necklaces out of kidney stones." "Catherine, you have to take those pills"

Fine, I just thought they might add some flavor to my ice cream." I got the pills on the first bite of ice cream and laughed at the witch in charge and did what else? Coffee and cigarettes. These were like bread a water. Survival! You should have seen us if one of us ran out. Run for your lives because we all meant business when it came to our cigarettes.

I felt like playing something so I took for the piano, sat down, raised up my head, closed my eyes and sang a short ballad I had wrote for Gentry. There were applauds from my roommates. One of the nurses even said that the music sounded very nice. It shook me. They always asked me to quit. This made me wanna play more. But once I began the introduction for "Over The Rainbow," a witch yelled back to the captivity room. "Catherine, other people are watching television." I stopped. I looked behind me and saw that most of my friends were sleeping. And the cartoons were on for Christ's sake. Jesus! Like the fucking cartoons area so important! I wondered about another girl there who'd played and they never stopped her. She doesn't even sing. She just plays the same thing over and over. It's driving me nuts. "Hey, Lori. How come when you play they don't say anything? And you keep playing that same song over and over. What is it?" "Come on, I'll play it. The music is on the top of the piano. She sat down to play the song called "Masquerade." She played it through while I read the words and she finally convinced me to sing it. We sounded real good together and the witches in the tower said nothing.

Time to call my dad. Nina answered. "Put the Pope on the phone for me immediately. Pope, they won't let me play the piano, they won't let me sing. I got to keep practicing if I'm going to sing someday. They won't let me. I gotta sing Pope. "You're not going to be a singer Cappy." "Pope," I cried, "I can't help it if I've been the black sheep all my life!" The phone was slammed on him and I told the nurses that I didn't want to talk to my father anymore, but he called back. Yes. I hung up before he talked. I walked back to the piano thinking, I'll show him!

Later Pope came to visit me and I was very happy to see him. Maybe I was crazy, I hugged him and said, "Pope look. See how clear my eyes are. They never looked so blue before." Pope hugged me back, "That's because you don't have any of those drugs they gave you a long time ago when you were a kid." He smiled. "Pope, if I have to have my mouth wired shut when they fix my jaw, will you promise me that there will be a piano there. If I can't sing, I want to be able to at least play the piano or I'll go crazy." "Okay Caterina, you can have anything you want in there. But first you gotta gain weight. You gotta be a least 120 pounds. More would be better. You're gonna lose about twenty pounds with your mouth wired shut. You're too skinny now! They would have to feed you with tubes in your arms. They won't do it until you gain weight okay?" "Okay, from now on, I will eat everything they give me and make sure you bring me lots of ice cream, I'm almost out. Oh, and they're gonna give me a pass tomorrow, then I'll be able to walk around outside, but only on the hospital grounds. It's better than nothing. I hate this place. I just want to go home." "You'll go home, you won't be here forever. Just eat and eat. Do what they tell you and you'll get home." "Okay Pope. I'm gonna fix myself a snack right now, you don't have to stay, it's okay. I got lots of friends right here. We're the Loony Toons ya know." "Okay, Cathy, I'll see you later. You call us if you need anything." Then me and my dad hugged. I told him I loved him and he said he loved me too. It was very emotional and I broke down to tears when he left. Saying I love you was not a Santi tradition.

Chapter Twenty Seven: "John And Wheels Clock The Miles. And The Numbers Hit!"

Went to water my flowers. I had them nearly ten days now and the blooms were still as beautiful as the day Jerry had them sent. I took a closer look, noticed my fine feathered friend had vanished just as it mysteriously appeared. Ran to John quick. He was sitting with his girl friend. "John, the bird is gone. You took it didn't you. You put it there. It had to be you who took it away, why? I liked it. Why would you want to take that away from me too? Isn't it bad enough they won't let me play or sing." "Wheels, visiting is almost over and I'd like to say my goodbyes in private if you don't mind." Feeling betrayed, I watched John hold is soon to be bride, hugging her, kissing her.

Fuck him! I still have my rose. Yes, I had a rose. A long stemmed dead rose, surrounded with baby's breath wrapped in a white vase. It was Priest who taught me that something can still be beautiful even when it dies. Only when I got to that part of the nurses' station it was gone from the counter, just like the bird that had flown. "Who the hell threw my rose away? I want to know. I've had that a long time. I save them. My brother and his girlfriend. They know I save the damn things." A nurse approached me. "Catherine, I'm sorry. Maybe one of the nurses who had just came on duty threw it out not knowing that you were saving it. I don't really know, so please try not to talk so loud." "I know. I'll disturb the other patients. Disturb them, is that what you think I do? They fucking love when somebody goes off on you. About that rose ... my rose? My name was on that, somebody should have asked me. The card was hanging right from the stem like new. Man you people think just because YOU THINK we are all nuts that we don't know any better! I wish Jimmy was here right now, he'd say you're the ones who are livin' upstairs over a vacant lot!"

"Hey Wheels you really told them. Oh and could I get a cigarette from you. Please. You're such a nice girl. Just one. I won't tell them Wheels. Can I have just ooooone please?" Teresa, not now. I don't have them on me and I don't feel like getting one. Ask her?" "You bitch, you ain't my friend anymore. You stay away from me, I'm not talking to you anymore, I'm talking to Duke, she'll give me a smoke, won't you Duke. Just one, I won't tell okay Duke?" Duke tiredly handed Teresa a smoke.

"Say John. Are you ever going to tell me the story about the bird? You know the one that vanished from the flowers?" "I might have put the bird in the flowers, but I won't tell you if I did." "Why?" I asked him, "Why not?"

506

"Damn you John. I liked it. It fit there. You didn't see anyone put it there and you didn't see anyone take it." John sheepishly grinned.

"Hey Wheels, think we can do the mile, want to? This time let's remember what time we start, let's make sure to check the clock." "Sounds great to me. Just let me put out my smoke." "Yes, and let's smoke this mile. We'll let our hair blow back and fly around this crazy square, are ya ready? Okay, it's 9:20. Wanna try to do it in ten minutes." "You are talking some real speed walkin' aren't you John? Let's do in less than that. Come on. Okay it's nine-twenty-one... get ready... go."

John and I got off swiftly, like gracious unicorns. "Hey John, we're getting real good at this. Feel your hair blowing back?" "This is great Wheels. This will make once around right about now. Let's not talk this time. Just say the revolution number when we get to the clock, okay? Let's do this is 8 minutes, Wheels, " " ... Number nine, number nine..." "We did two, now quiet Catherine." It was hard not talking numbers, but I did. After about ten times around the block, John and I were counting in sync'. "Twenty five." We both cheered, checking our time. "Wheels. The minutes. We did the mile in seven and one half minutes." I noted the time too. It was nine twenty-eight. Second hand on the six. "John who will ever believe that we walked the fucking mile in seven and a half minutes?" Nobody will. "We're supposed to be crazy remember?" "Oh yeah, I forgot. Hey you know I managed to take five baby turtles for a walk today." "Was that this morning?" John asked, "because this morning, a couple different times I took mine to the pond. Eleven. Yeah it was, it was eleven, I remember. First time there were three. Think they came in to clean the pond out because later in the morning eight more took off for a walk." "Oh so the little guys like their porcelain shined up eh? I'll remember that. Clean pond, more turtles. Thanks John. We need to tell the others. They're gonna want their pets in the clean water."

"Wheels, let's get some coffee. Damn, we're good huh? Seven, count them, seven and one half minutes." "Yes John, I already wrote it in my diary. Got it in this big old baggy pocket." "Hey Wheels, do you have all your clothes here? Every day I see you in something different." "Yeah, I think I have all of it. I like wearing all the same color of everything. Felt like white today. Like the day I came in." "You look good in white Wheels." "Thanks John, but I knew that" "Ah, conceited aren't you Wheels?" John said with a bit of an Irish accent. "Yes, I'm supposed to be"!

After coffee and long talks over our accomplishment, I remembered something. "John, I have something important coming up. I have to go. I'm going to my room. I'll wash my hair. I gotta kill time. I forgot. I'm going to get married this Saturday. The groom-to-be doesn't know that it is Saturday, but I decided that it is. I have to figure a way to get a pass for that day. Hell, I'll need the whole day to get ready. They got to give me a pass."

I took off for my room leaving John to finish his fourth or fifth cup of coffee alone. Washed my hair and combed it this way and that way until it was dry. I never saw my hair or eyes look better, I thought, as I ran my fingers through my hair over and over. The rush was great, and it got my mind ready and in order for my plans. Max never told me if he got a hold of Pink or not. He would have called. Thought of calling another detective, but it would have felt like I was going over Max's head. I would just have to wait. He may still let me know something.

Headed for the tower and got my pass. I walked around the hospital grounds for about ten minutes. Went to a gas station and noticed that they had a new, cheap cigarette for only 69 cents a pack, "Rainbow." The package was a dark blue with a beautiful rainbow across it. You know I had to have them. Got six packs and took them back to the wacky ward with me.

I entered the building and got through the doors that bind me and showed the nurse. "Well do these fit me or what? You know, the yellow brick road, ruby slippers? I'll get to The Emerald City. I'm getting married this Saturday. Think Lee will give me a pass? I'm going to need one for the whole day. Maybe the night too. The wedding will have to be Saturday. Gentry asked me to marry him two times. I've known him about four and a half years. I never gave him and answer. But see, I wrote this letter, only I don't want to put in the letter that I'm going to marry him. He sent me hints through WCPZ radio station. They had this Rocky and Bullwinkle commercial on. The commercial talked about four different styles of furniture. I had all four of them styles in my house. Basically, the commercial was about an electrician. Gentry's an electrician. Who else would know how many kinds of sofas and chairs I had but him. I can't sleep tonight. I have to be in control. Power of mind over matter" The nurse looked bored, but I continued... "This is the gown I am going to wear Saturday." I held up a picture of it from "my" catalogue. "Gentry will be here Friday to see me. I left him the message to be here on his answering machine. When he arrives, I'll give him this letter and tell him then. The doctor will give me a pass if he knows it's my wedding day!" I left for my child proof wacky room to lay down.

What do they know, I thought? Just then I saw a dark shadow dart across the floor. I quick yelled for a nurse. "Something just ran across my floor! Right by the rest room!" "Catherine, calm down, what did it look like?" "I don't know, it was small. Smaller than a cat." "It's one of the side effects of the medication, it will go away. Try closing your eyes and get some sleep."

"Okay. Sounds like a good idea to me." I closed my eyes tightly. Didn't want to see it again whatever it was!

I woke up refreshed a few hours later and noticed the shadows of two tall men on the walls of my room and it was still dark outside! I raced to the nurses' station. "You gotta come look at this! There are the shadows of two guys on my wall! Just as plain as the shadow of my hand right here on your little snow white counter. Come and look! I bet they are still there when you get to my room." Afraid to go back in, I followed behind the nurse and let her go in first. I joined. "See? There they are. Only now they are right by the door to my room. Christ, can't you see them? There are two, of them right there at the door. One is right next to you. Aren't you going to do something? Somebody is watching me I'm telling you. I don't how they are pulling this one off, but they are watching me and good!"

"Catherine it's the medication like I told you a few hours ago. Sometimes it takes a few days for the side effects to go away, but they will. A few days and you'll be good as new." "Man you people are the crazy ones you know. I did all kinds of drugs back in High school. Took lots of pills. Then you go and give me something with terrible side effects and I'm going to be seeing this a few days! Oh you guys must really get a charge out it! Checked myself in voluntarily so you guys could fuck me up? I can barely see straight! Talk straight! You are messing up something in my brain that was working right to begin with! Then what? Ya make us get up and race around the track like a horse to make sure our hearts are beating at normal speed. Can't have a bunch of sloppy looking loons now could you? Poor Duke over there can barely walk now. Do you even help her? Shit she's gonna fall over one of these days. In fact, she looked better when she came in. At least she had some pink in her cheeks. What? Do you pick on one person just a little more than the rest of us? Look at her and Carrie. Teresa told me that Carrie is going to jump off of the top of the hospital and when Teresa said she told you... What did you guys do but sit there and do nothing. Just like you are now. I can't believe that you don't call security or something! Just let her jump huh? Give you people something to talk about over tea, right." The nurse was speaking to simple shrugged her shoulders and said nothing. Upset, I turned away from the tower to the captivity room for the piano.

"Well what do you know The little white witches let me play a few things. I wondered if they were taking some of our medications. Two of my buddies were trying desperately to shoot a game of pool, but neither one could even chalk the cues to start.

"Hey Wheels, guess what's going to be on tonight?" "What's that Becky? I asked. "The Wizard of Oz." I told you Wheels, we have our stories but you're the queen! You got the best story out of all of us and now this movie!

You gotta watch it. Bet whoever put that picture up on the wall for you..." "Oh stop right there Becky... That's just what I'm thinking. I don't know. I don' think that I'll be able to watch it. It might make me go crazy. Those stupid doctors, I don't think I am Dorothy from "Oz," I'm Eve. And I'm back. I never left actually and I've followed all the roads. Can I help it if I like brick ones best? There was this one brick I found in my back yard. Best thing I ever found. Only it wasn't yellow. Pink put it there knowing that I'd be on the yellow one now." "You crack me up Wheels, if it wasn't for you, I don't think that I'd be able to handle this place." "Hey Becky, it was all supposed to happen. Read the papers."

Pope had been playing the lottery for me, since I had no way to get to a store that sold the tickets. Each time it was time to play, I'd call him up and give him the two sets of numbers. Found them in the local paper, front page. The positive set and the negative one. Only they changed many times since I first told my sister-in-law about them just weeks prior.

Every time I was off by one or two numbers either in one set or both. It was making me nuts. Pope encouraged me not to play because he thought I was only thinking I knew the numbers. I knew them. I just had to figure them out

In between all of the number games, I noticed my stomach seemed bloated. Bigger. Oh know. I'm pregnant, I thought. This sucks. Now I knew what Becky was going through. I'm taking these pills and I'm carrying a baby? Maybe a normal one? I doubt that. Not with "this" medicine. That baby will be screwed up and I have to get this checked out.

"Nurse when is the doctor going to be here. I gotta quit taking these drugs, I think I'm pregnant. I feel the baby move. Look at my stomach." I lifted my blouse up and unzipped my pants. "See, look at how big it is. I bet I'm at least four or five months along." "Catherine. Have you had a period?" "Catherine," I mocker her, "Have I had a period. Why not call it what it is. "Yeah, I am bleeding once again this month. But that doesn't mean anything. I have had periods in every single pregnancy. All my test usually turn up negative. Buder always ends up giving me an ultrasound. I don't know, maybe it's my rare blood. Don't believe that either. Well go on and look in my wallet. I have a Rare Blood Donors card. I got that the year I graduated High School, 1975. Anything else you wanna know? Just listen with your stethoscope. I bet you will be able to hear the heart beat." Finally, I got a nurse to agree to look at me, three days later.

She felt my stomach. She listened. She said, "Well, I can hear your bowels moving." "Oh yeah, that would be the little guys. Damn those turtles! You got something you can give me. I'm having a hell of a time getting them to take a walk." "I beg your pardon?" said she. "The porcelain pond. Heard of it? We've all been flushing them down the creek and it's pissing us off. Christ, we wait and wait and push them and push them, but those little suckers are stubborn." "Oh, I see, you are having trouble moving your bowels." "Yes I am." And she had a pill for that too.

Later that night I was lying in my bed when I noticed a couple of men sitting in the tree outside my window. They were watching me with binoculars, wearing trench coats and what else? Sunglasses. I couldn't move. Just kept staring back. One of them waved to me and I knew that they knew who I was. They had to be the bad guys. "Shit!" I thought. How will I get out of here now? I'll be scared to take walks outside. Just when I get the permission too, I thought.

"Nurse, nurse!" I called from my room. "Look. First shadows and now what do you call that? See them? The two men up there in the trees? You gotta move me! They'll try to kin me! They are the ones who have been following me since March 3rd. I gotta have another room. You don't understand. Just because I know The Beatles worth and I'm going to be marrying John Lennon, they want me. They'll try to take me if I go outside. You gotta help me!" "Catherine, Catherine, there is no one out there." She walked over to the window, looked at the tree and pointed to it saying, "There are no men in the tree. There is just a tree. It's the medication. It's only a side affect It will pass." "It will pass? It's just a side effect? You make me sick do you know that? How the hell is a person supposed to get out of here. You like fucking us up and keeping us in here. You don't fool me. You guys make a lot of money off of us. Shit, $75 bucks to be in art therapy! And that's just for one hour. How long you gonna keep me in this joint anyway? I almost weigh 120 pounds. You can't keep me too long. I need surgery on my jaw! You can't make me stay knowing that it could break in a yawn! "Catherine..." "I know, you are going to tell me to try to go to sleep. How do I sleep with them guys watching me? Hallucination you say. You think you would at least oblige me and let me stay in another room you heartless nothing!" The nurse left me alone in my room. I left, or as Jimmy would put it, I broke camp. I joined the others in the smoking arena and smoked most of the night. When dawn came, I rested up for breakfast. Had to eat as much as I could because I only needed three more pounds to reach the 120 mark.

Later in the day John called me over and brought something to my attention. "Hey Wheels, Where's your wrist band? You know your tags? Yours are gone. So are mine. Now we can be whoever we want to be." "Damn John, I could walk right out of here and go home. They can't prove who I am, not without the damn wrist band. Think I'll make my escape late. At least I'm going to the emergency room and have them give me an ultrasound to see if the baby is okay. I'm sure I'm pregnant. No. No waiting.

I'm going now! Be back John. I gotta be careful about going out. The other side was watching me the other night from the tree outside my room." "Be careful Wheels," and John waved me on.

I signed out. Jetted through the double wooden doors and exited, stage right. I walked around over to the emergency room entrance. I was getting close to the door when a helicopter was about to land. The wind from the propellers was knocking me down and I had to run to get away. I waited while it slowed down a bit and got through the emergency room door, walking right passed the office, where I should have signed in. Went straight back to find an available doctor or nurse who would help me.

I finally convinced a nurse there that I indeed bleed four months each time I was carrying a baby and I was soon laying on an examination table when one of the witches found me. "Catherine, we wondered where you might be, we've been looking for you. It's okay," she told the other nurse, "Catherine is a patient over in the South Pavilion. It's the meds. It does that to a lot of the female patients. She's not pregnant. Come on Catherine, I'll take you back to your room. Supper will be ready soon and I noticed your appetite has been up. That's good." "Yes, I am getting hungry. But you don't understand nurse, I just want a baby so bad." When I began to cry, the nurse squeezed my hand and said, "I know how you feel. Babies are so sweet aren't they." "Yes, they are sweet."

She got me back to the wacky ward where everyone thought I belonged, keeping John waiting longer and longer.

How long do they think they can keep this up, I thought? They're probably all in on it. The nurses, the shrinks, the patients. They got to be on some damn good drugs. Better than the ones that they got me on, 'cause I wouldn't be able to keep a straight face. I'd probably piss my pants.

It was dinner time and I decided to have my meal in the smoking area. A few of us had gathered there. We could see George in his room. This big dork was rocking himself in the bed, with one arm behind his back. "Look Becky. 'Bout time he worked out," I said grinning. We had been watching him for about fifteen minutes, when we saw the bed rattling so hard, that George had knocked his sheets off himself. Becky nearly puked. I laughed my ass off. "Shit Becky, he's got his finger up his ass!" "I know Wheels. What's his problem?" "I don't know but before he tries to get on my yellow submarine, I'll shoot his fucking fingers off." "God Wheels, we gotta tell a nurse. You tell one, you're the queen." "Oh thanks a lot Becky, I get to do all the shitty work." I called a nurse over and told her about what George was doing. She told us to never mind him, that she would take care of it.

She went over to his room, covering him back up and closing the door. "Damn Wheels, he should get a shot or something. I don't even want this hamburger now. How can you eat?" "Almost had it out of my head Becky. Forget it now. I ain't eating anything."

Well, George came out of his room and went back for his dinner. He decided to join us. God only knew what would be next. Becky and I were trying hard not to laugh while he sat smiling looking like the idiot he was. George had a surprise for us. We must have pissed him off real good. He knew nobody liked him. He took a bite from his burger, chewed it a couple times and then licked the end of one of his fingers. After each bite, he'd do the same thing, making sure he got all ten fingers. Becky left the table holding her hand over her mouth ready to vomit. I was feeling pretty queasy myself so I called for the nurse again. "Catherine, is there a problem over here?" "Is there a problem over here? Inject this ass hole with something already. He's making us sick! He had his finger up his ass a few minutes ago and now he's licking the shit off with every bite of that burger! I'll puke on him in a minute." George sat there grinning. Then he stuck a finger in his mouth and began sucking on it. The nurse escorted him to a room. At last the loons were the victors! They shot him up good. We didn't see him until the next day.

John would be going out on his pass today, I thought. Pope won't play the numbers for me. Maybe if I talk to John... I got the newspaper out and looked over the front page real good. Found them. I looked for John. "Hey John, here's four bucks. When you go out for your pass this weekend, play these numbers on the lottery. It's up to thirteen million now. You gotta make sure that you play both sets of numbers. One is positive and one is negative. Got to play them both, because I know for sure now that it will be one or the other. Pope won't do it for me anymore. He thinks I'm wasting my money." "I'll play 'em for you Wheels, but you don't need four dollars. It's only two bucks to play two numbers." "Yeah I know, but since you're going to buy them, get yourself a set of tickets and we'll split the money when we win." John took the money, the paper with our fortune on it and was ready for his week-end. I couldn't wait for him to get back. We'd walk that mile in 5 minutes with the 13 million dollars of adrenaline that would sure get us pumped.

I never did get a pass to marry Pinky. It was Friday night and John was gone. Pinky didn't show up. I couldn't give him that letter I wrote. Some cop. Damn Max! You could have called me or something, I thought

Duke was trying really hard to get to her room. She complained for a few days to me and John that she could barely stand up from the medication she was on. She had always said they gave her way too much. When she was halfway to her room she fell to the floor right in front of the nurses' station. They sat there. Not a one got up. I yelled, "Aren't you even going to help her?" Just then Dukes husband came in to see her, finding his wife on the floor. With rage he said, "Jesus Christ! What is it around here? What's with you people?" He picked up Duke from the floor and carried her in his arms. "I brought my wife in to get better and look at her! You leave her laying on the floor? She can't even walk and you just sit there?" I'm gonna take her home and don't try to stop me or I'll sue this hospital!"

Duke would be fine, we all thought as we watched her husband carrying her off to safety. Good things did happen but then, so did bad. John was back from the week-end. "Well? Did you play the numbers John?" "Here's the tickets Wheels, you hold on to 'em." "Oh no John, you only played the positive numbers. What if the negative numbers are the winners?" "Sorry Wheels. I gave the lady at the lottery booth the numbers you wrote down, she must have misunderstood." "Guess we'll just have to wait for them damn nurses to give us a copy of the morning paper. You know they always wait till late to give us the news. Then it's old news." "Keep your fingers crossed Wheels. How about some coffee and we'll shoot the breeze." "A cool one I hope." I told John what had happened to Duke and he explained that his girlfriend was going to get him into a hospital in Lorain where the doctors knew what they were doing.

About eleven o'clock that night, they brought in the paper. Naturally I grabbed it right out of the nurse's hand and looked for the numbers. "John hurry! Come here and look, you won't believe this! I can't wait to show Pope! And he thought I was wasting my money. Look! Are you looking John." "Sure Wheels, did you find the numbers?" "I sure did. Told you I knew them. I've been telling Pope all along, except he didn't believe me. They hit! The fucking negative numbers hit. Damn John, think of what we could have done with all that money. Can you believe it? Just when they hit, we lost. Oooh, I wish that clerk would have gotten it right. It's not your fault. We'll do it again next week, okay?" "Wheels, are you mad?" "Hell no, I ain't mad, guess because I'm crazy. I know how to figure 'em out. I'll get the numbers for next week and maybe by then they'll let me out for a weekend, then I'll go buy us some tickets." "Sounds good to me, but I'm pretty sure that my girlfriend will have me in Lorain by then, otherwise, I'll play, but I don't want you to pay for my tickets next time."

I couldn't wait to call Pope and tell him just how right I was. I called him and he laughed thinking that I was just kidding around. "Pope. Just wait till next time."

Jerry was still coming to see me every night. Good old Jerry. Could count on him. Ladie hadn't shown up like I thought sure she would. No one from The Barrel came and it hurt, hurt real bad. It made me wonder who my friends really were. Guess I didn't have as many as I thought.

Then one night, to my surprise Frank showed up to see me. He had brought a friend along named Ron. I rattled on to Frank and Ron all about what my plans were and the big wedding between me and John Lennon. Frank seemed to try to understand and said very little. I could tell by looking at my ex boyfriend that it had bothered him to see me in a place like this. On the other hand, his friend was sitting down right behind me and Frank. I looked over Franks shoulder, saw his friend laughing and I got pissed. "Hey what the fuck you laughing at? Oh, so you think this is funny huh? You don't know the half of what we have to deal with in this place! Sure, I make it sound real cute. I got big things coming up, more than most and obviously more than you can get a grip on. I don't want you here. You're laughing is making me sick and I'm gonna go off. Get him outta here Frank, you just get the fucker outta here." Frank said, "Okay, we'll leave ya alone, I'll see ya." He turned to his friend, motioning to him for them to go. By this time the nurses were already there telling Ron that if he was going to upset me, or any of the other patents, that he would have to leave. They escorted both of them to those freedom doors and I didn't see either of them again, well, not for a long time anyway.

It was into April and I was still a part of the wacky ward. I wanted to go home. Thought I would have been out at 120 pounds. I'd been that for over a week. My jaw, I thought, could go any time. How would I ever sing? What if it breaks in here? Who's gonna help me? They'll just tell me that it is a side effect from the meds. The meds!!! The fucking zombie pills I swore I would never take no matter what and I was on this stuff too long. They just want to shut me up. Put me to sleep forever. Why don't they just kill me. I was having a good time. Wasn't hurting anyone, just doing what I was supposed to do. But then I told. Talked about it. I let out the big fucking secret too soon. So this is it. I screwed up the biggest most magical plan the world was ever going to know! Come on you guys! It's a tough secret to keep. Think that I, the coolest girl in America can't wait? I'll fool you. I'll have a better gimmick than The Beatles. I'll show them I can wait. That I can remain silent. If I want to go home, I'll surely have to keep this under lock and key.

I turned in my little brass bell and told the nurse, "I have a slipped disc. Now isn't that crazy. I can't stand in one place for too long, but I can walk the mile in seven and one half minutes." She said nothing. They usually didn't and locked my bell with the rest of my things.

Later, a new patient was brought in to my unit. No one knew him, or had seen him around locally. He didn't talk to any of us. He just walked the halls, standing by our door looking at us. Wasn't too bad, until he hung out by my door. The first couple times he smiled. I sat in my room. I'd tell him to go, but he wouldn't. A nurse eventually took him away from the door, telling him that he couldn't do that again. But he did. And when he got to my room, he looked in and glared at me. To get to the point, he scared the livin' shit outta me. I got up, ran, and slip-slided my way to the nurses' station. "I gotta have my bell back. I need it. That guy over there is still coming to my room. He looks at me like he hates me. Like he's gonna hurt me. Can't you do something with him? Please hurry, I gotta have the bell! It's the only thing in here that makes me feel secure." "Sure Catherine. I'll get it for you. We'll talk to Ed again and tell him to keep away. If you aren't sleepy, why don't you go on over to the smoking area for a while till you calm down."

Like I could. Afraid, I went to get myself a cup of coffee, light a smoke and sit down. While I had the chance I went back to my room to get out the photo albums I asked Pope to bring me. I was looking through my pictures of Montana. There it was ... Goose Island, I thought! I can still get there on the 27th. They can't keep me here much longer. Duke is gone. Becky's gone. They fooled Teresa, made her believe she was going to have her hair done and transported her to a state mental hospital in Toledo. I'd miss her. I miss them all. We became a family... strange family, but we all related well. John would be leaving to. What would I do without him? Who would be left? Great, I thought! George. I didn't want to think about what it would be like to deal with him alone, so I didn't think about George. I thought about Gentry and Bobby, Captain and Priest. It was hard to keep from crying and I didn't want to break down over things that were obviously over with. Besides, I gotta be a quiet little zombie to get home. Guess I'll have to forget about Gentry too. Time to let go. But how? How do I let go when you're not mine to hold? I questioned myself off-ten. I couldn't forget him. There would never be a way, until my dying day.

The phone rang. What if? Oh it's for John. He's smiling. He's going home or somewhere, but he won't be here. Not no more. Then John walked over and gave me the bad news, that was only good news for him. "Wheels! My girlfriend got me signed into a regular hospital and I'll be leaving tomorrow for Lorain. I'm gonna miss you Wheels. We clocked the miles you and me." "That we did Sir John ... that we did. Will you look at what you are leaving me to contend with, (pointing to George)." "You'll be alright Wheels, I've been watching you. They won't keep you here much longer. You've been going out on passes every day. Bet you're outta here in a few days." "I hope you are right John. You were the only one in here that was any fun to talk to. You understood. Really understood and I've learned something. S.S.S." "You got it Wheels. Just remember that. Keep things to yourself and you'll be home free. You don't belong here. You're alright

Wheels and don't let anybody say you're not. Hey! You're The Wheels." "Yes. I am. I won't let them take me from my throne!" "That's the spirit."

John explained that he was going to his room to get his stuff packed up when I fumbled on a very familiar photo. "John, wait, don't go yet. Here. I want you to look at this picture and tell me where you've seen it before. Look at it real good because it's so small." "Wheels, you really did live there! That is the picture on the wall! Let's take yours over to the big one and compare the mountain peaks." "Finally, someone who believes me." We hurried to the pictures larger twin. And twin it was. "Damn John. I think someone took this picture out of my album and had it blown up. The mountain peaks are the same. They are!" "You're right Wheels. Hey, why give them the satisfaction, we both know and that's what counts." "You mean, S.S.S?" "Yep. Say Wheels. There's something I've been wanting to give you since we first met." John gave me a hug and a small kiss on the cheek. "Good night Wheels. Don't forget, coffee at six." "Good night John."

I pressed the photo of Lake McDonald against my heart and I smiled inside. With these warm feelings, I took off for my room and took a short nap.

Morning came. John was there with the coffee. Then morning left and John was gone. No long drawn out good-byes, just silent nodded smiles as he and his girlfriend walked out the doors never to return again.

I had seen the doctor myself that afternoon and we talked about my going home in a few days, if my progress was good and my condition remained stable. I of course was all for the idea. The next few days were slow. Spent much of my time drawing, writing letters and poetry. I played little piano and kept quietly to myself waiting.

Chapter Twenty Eight: "Judgment Day"

It was the 8th of April. I had my appointment with the doctor once again. The nurses seemed more cooperative than usual. I got to play piano and sing. Mike was gone, so I didn't have to listen to music in my headphones anymore. I could use my boom box as long as it was in my room. I walked up to one of the nurses who called me to the station. "So Catherine. You're seeing the doctor today?" "Yep. Some of the other people seem to think he'll let me to home today. Do you think he will or cant you tell me?" She looked at my charts and said, "Well, don't get your hopes up, but I think he just might let you leave today. You've been taken your medications like you are supposed to. You don't get angry anymore. You appear to be ready to go home." "I hope you're right."

I waited and waited till afternoon finally came. The doctor called me in his office and asked me how I felt about going home. Was I ready to take care of myself and continue my medications at home without observation. "Doctor, I just want to get home and be with my kids. I don't think John is alive or anything else. I don't know whatever made me think he was. It doesn't matter anymore. I don't care what I have to do, I just need to be home. I got three kids who miss me. I want to take my medication so I can stay home with them. They need me." The doctor smiled. He was brief in his words. "Catherine you can go home any time." "I can? You mean it? Right now? Are you sure?" "Yes. Continue to see Dr. Buder and take your medications." He walked out of his office as quickly as he walked in. I busted out in uncontrollable laughter! Could the doctor walk the mile as fast as me? "It doesn't matter," said I, out loud, "I'm going home."

Called Pope and told him, called Jerry and tried to call Ladie. I couldn't call Jimmy. And I certainly wasn't going to call Gentry.

I ran to my room, slid in on stocking feet and began packing all my things. I had no suit cases, but filled two leaf size bags with my belongings. Remember? All my things were there.

Waited for Pope to come and get me. I had a heavy load to take with me and jumping the fence wouldn't be easy.

Paper signing. One, and the another and more. Got all my personals that had been locked into a wall with others there. I had everything. They opened the doors I had long called the freedom doors, where I watched so many come and go in the 18 days of my stay. I did not look back. I breathed in the outside air. It was fresh. It was spring. Pope and I got into the "Monte Carlo," and within a couple blocks we pulled in my drive way. I jumped out of the car, grabbing my house keys from Pope and raced to unlock my house.

Ah, my house, I thought. My kitchen. My piano. My kids. My kids were still with their aunt and uncle and I wanted to call them, but they were still in school. Pope came in and brought my bags of clothes and told me not to worry about the kids just yet. "You need to get more rest here at home. You shouldn't have the kids just yet. They are fine at your brothers. You need time by yourself a while, maybe a week and they can come back home. Oh and Nina came over and got your place all cleaned up for you, so you could just sit back and take it easy for a little while. She did laundry and dishes. Washed the bathrooms and floors too. Maybe you should call her later, tomorrow or whenever you want. Thank her. She worked hard." "K, Pope, I'll call her later. Right now, I just wanna be by myself, make some coffee in my own coffee pot and listen to music as loud as I want to." "Okay Caterina. Maybe you should try and drink "Sanka," all that caffeine isn't good for you." "Pope please, not the fake coffee just yet. You know I can tell the difference and I gotta have the real thing. It doesn't hurt me. They let me drink it in the wacky ward as much as I wanted." "Okay, but I think all that caffeine is bad for you." "Yes Pope. Now can I please have a little privacy. I've been around a bunch of nuts for almost three weeks ya know?" "You were a nut yourself," he laughed, "Just be glad to be home, I'll call you later, okay?" "Okay Pope. Thank you." Pope exited out the front door.

My "In Case Of An Emergency" sign was taken off the wall, but my coffee can collection was just a "Citation" away.

The infamous table. There it was. Empty of notes, numbers, horoscopes and the book. The book that took me a couple blocks away to a place called the South Pavilion. The blessed Beatle Book! I looked for it. Then I took a good long look at it after I found it. I placed it with other books I had read before. It was in no special place. In fact, I didn't even want to look at its cover! I saw who I saw, I thought to myself. I don't need to look at this anymore. I fooled them John. Never told the witches what I was thinking. If I did I would still be there, I thought. Maybe our wedding day is close and coming. After all it isn't the 27th of April now is it! Looks like I'll get to Goose island on time. Wonder if they postponed the date?

The coffee was ready and I poured a nice hot cup of it, went into the living room where my piano had been moved back into. I sat at it and I just couldn't play. Couldn't sing. Could barely sit still. I was scared for some reason. Fear came over me and I rushed to the front door making sure to lock it up. It was back to the guard table. There I could see every entrance possible to my house. I wanted to go out and get my cans from my car, but I couldn't. My car was at Pope's house. Called him and told him I wanted to have my car. But he insisted that I do without for a while, until I got used to taking the medication at home and by myself.

Not being able to drive, I felt more afraid and more confined to my house. I shut all the windows and closed all the curtains. I didn't want anyone to look in on me. Didn't want anyone to see the crazy lady they all thought I probably was anyway.

I remained in my kitchen most of the evening, finding sleep much too complicated.

I jumped at any sound, even the phone. It rang a long time before I got up from my seat to answer it. It was Jimmy. "Oh Jimmy. I don't think I like being here all alone. I can't handle this. Are you gonna come over, oh please say you are." "Cath, I just called over to Firelands to talk to you and they said you were home. Wish I could come over. You know I hate phones, but I'm watchin' my kids. I wanna come and see you, but the wife will be working late. You gonna be okay?" "I guess I have no choice." I got angry at him and hung up. He tried to call back and again, but I kept hanging up. Didn't want to talk. I needed a person with me.

Later that night Ladie showed up and I asked, "Why didn't you come and see me? You're supposed to be my best friend and you never even called." Just then the phone rang. I asked Ladie to answer. She picked up the phone and said hello. "Cathy, come here, hurry, it's a little girl's voice hurry come and listen." I went to the phone to listen with Ladie. The little voice kept saying, "Hello? Who is this? Hello? Who is this?" I told Lady to hang up. It rang again. It was the same little voice asking the same things over and over. At first I thought I was hearing things, but Ladie heard it too. I left the hospital okay. They wouldn't send me to a house alone like this. Ladie freaked out over the calls. Then she told me why she didn't see me at the hospital. Said she was afraid. She barely finished her coffee and told me she had to leave.

There I sat again, all alone. It was getting later and the phone rang again. I picked it up and said nothing. A little voice said, "Why are you hanging up on me? Don't you like me?" Click, I hung up, afraid. It rang again. I let it ring and ring but it wouldn't stop, so once more I answered only to be terrified by this little voice. I slammed down the phone and took it off the hook so I wouldn't be called again. Paced my floors. To the living room, which led to the dining area down a short hall and back into the kitchen. Kept myself good company as I tried to make believe I was walking the mile. Began talking to myself out loud. "It won't ring again. It can't ring again. I know the phone is off the hook. I'm off the hook. Off the wall. No. I'm in the wall. Am the wall? An enormous thick brick wall! I am millions of miles tall. I'm scared of heights. Better make that ten feet. No Cath. Ten feet isn't tall enough and one hundred is too many. Forty might do to stand around the sandy beach you will reach. Hey, after all Wheels, it's your beach. See Wheels, remember you have a very large home waiting for you on the shore." Self was on a role, but she was correct. "That's right, Nina told me about it over the phone. The picture on the wall, the picture was mine after all. I know that you are still waiting for me John. I can be there on the twenty seventh and I know how to get to Goose Island like the beauty mark on my face ...

... There isn't any one here but me. Shit! Sorry guys! Forgot the place is bugged. But remember... They let me get back here for crying out loud! Haven't I done enough?

Are you listening God? I repeat. Haven't I done enough? Come on, let's be realistic God! I know and You know that I've been crying for 30 thousand years. I deserve to be happy. You want the rib You can still have it. Never said I wouldn't bring it. Damn I feel like I'm talking to the great "OZ"! You know? Since you and Pink and those jerk off men in their fancy silver cars won't talk to me, I'm done. I'll just get on my feet, head out the door and take about a 1,500 mile walk to You know where. Okay? Does this please all of you who think that my life is just one big fucking joke?"

I stopped, remained silent. Went to the bathroom off the kitchen. Ran a brush through my hair, put some lipstick on and took off through the kitchen to the door. But I stopped dead there with one glance through the glass. Things were very dark. Even the street lamp right across the street from where I lived shed little light through the vicinity. Then as I started to open the door my eyes fixed south down the street. Took one step backwards and locked myself back inside the house. In the front yard of the next block, a house had 3 white crosses easily standing eight feet tall and they were on fire. I gotta call the cops, I thought. The flames grew stronger and taller. What if the little voice is on the phone when I go for it? I don't want to hang it up and take that chance. I left the phone off the hook. I checked the locks on the inside door. Secured, I went through the entire house running to every window and door, making sure they were locked. Curtains were closed, blinds pulled. I ran down stairs and peeked through the window by the infamous table with one eye. More crosses were burning. I turned the radio on. Which station? I can't listen to WCPZ. Then again, maybe they know I'm home. Come on Cath, they did their job. You ran all over town looking for John. You weren't supposed to find him yet. "Oh yeah, right, I am still suppose to."

I broke down in a fistful of tears at the table. It was only two in the morning. Still dark, wishing the sun would rise. Collect yourself, Self thought. Okay, I can't get on the phone. I can't go out. Don't wanna look outside either. I'm fucked. Got no choice but to just sit here at the guard table.

Two o'clock turned into three, then four. Had lots of paper so I drew eyes, wondering what the drawings were trying to say about me. In between the eyes, I had to figure out how to get outta the house.

"Cathy, Cathy. Please help me, help me." I heard babies call me from up stairs. I could think of nothing but the cry. I shut the radio off, stood up and remained motionless and silent so I would know precisely where the little toddlers might be in my house. Again I heard it. "Help me! Please Cathy, you have to help me. Please Cathy, hurry!" The cry chilled me. I still couldn't move and now there was more than one child begging for my help. "Okay, I'm coming. Hang on, I'll fly up there and help you, just hang on." I ran through the living room and up the stairs. I checked all the rooms still hearing the children cry. I got to the end of the hall and found no one. Then I heard the kids calling me to come down stairs. Tripping on the carpet, I quick jumped up and raced down the stairs. The kids stopped. I went to the closet that was under the stair case and opened the door and flipped on the light. Empty except for a ten-speed bicycle. Slowly I walked to the bathroom, but there was no one in there. Stopping just outside the door, I listened and the silence rang out. Felt the fear grow deeper as I made my way to the guard table feet away.

I watched the phone. Still unhooked, the way it's been for hours now. I watched the clock hands. I made steady contact with the curtain that draped my front window for crosses. Then I turned the radio on at a volume of a cats purr.

I spun my pen on the table. My all-chrome pen. It pointed to the east, it pointed to the west, it pointed to the one I like the best. The one who gave me up so John could have me. Wonder if Pinky even knows I'm home. He probably could care less. He never did come to see me. He said we can't be together. Gotta get over him. John will take his place now.

Daylight arrived. I left the table so I could make another pot of coffee. The phone was still off the hook and the windows remained covered. I got my nerve to go into the living room. The couch looked inviting. I laid on it and closed my eyes. I fell asleep and woke to the sound of knocking. The time was five in the afternoon. I must have needed the sleep. I wondered who the hell it might be. Can't be Ladie. She's scared to be around me. I was afraid to answer and then, Bam, bam, bam! The knocking got louder. I decided that since I had the sun working in my favor I'd chance it and answer the door. The someone on the other side was Jerry. I asked him in and offered him what else? "Maxwell House." We talked for a long time until afternoon, became dark and Jerry had to leave. He gave me a beautiful card and hugged me good night. The door was locked tight. The curtains were once again closed making sure that no one could see me there.

I thought ... If I slept all that time and it took the banging to get me up, maybe I could sleep some more. Wouldn't have to worry about how long and dark the night would be.

I went back to the couch and laid down once again. I slept and this time when I woke it was nearly ten the next day. I was happy to see that I made it through the night without a shadow. Maybe all this was the medications. Maybe I was in fact just seeing things. Made myself think brave and peered out my front window. The birds were in the yard and I could hear the blue jays in the distance. They will arrive about 11:30, I thought. They always did.

The leaves were starting to sprout from all the branches and the grass looked wet from rain. All appeared normal outside. I went into the living room and opened up the curtains. How lovely the fucking fence looks right next to my drive way, I thought. Let me take a jolly walk over to the kitchen and see what the creep next door is up to. "His house could stand a new coat of paint. I do it for him too if he wasn't such an ass hole." Talking to myself out loud, as I did most of the time, I went to open the bathroom window, just a crack to let some spring air in. Then I walked to my back door and pulled on the string to roll up the blind. I cringed. The "KKK," I thought. "What are they doing in my back yard dressed in black?" There was a large hole dug in the yard like a shallow grave. Oh no! "Jesus! What's the huge fire in it for?" Self said, and close the blind." I did, but I watched through the slats. Fearing for my very soul, the two blacked dressed Klansmen began tossing a baby back and forth over the fire laughing. Crying, I wondered what I could do to help the baby. Was it the one in my house? God Damn You! "Why didn't You tell me the baby was outside! If I try to help him, he could get tossed into the fire ... and ... if the black caped men see me they might kill him! "

Afraid for the baby, I paced the kitchen floor crying, talking to myself out loud. "This is not medicine. There is no way. Just to prove it to myself, I'll hang that fucking phone up. I know the little voice will call. Ladie heard it. That's why she isn't here, or was she here at all?" I hung up the telephone and within seconds it rang. I was startled. Afraid to answer. I let it ring and ring. It stopped but only for moments and it rang more. I walked over to the phone and slowly picked it up, putting to my ear. I said trembling, "Hello?" "Please don't hang up Cathy! Help me!" I pushed down on the receiver and lifted up on it, the little voice was still there. "Cathy, help me please!" I held down on the receiver longer this time, timing it till a minute was up. I listened again and the voice was now the dial tone I hoped for. A knock nearly knocked me off my feet. Should I go to the door, I asked myself? What if it's the "KKK" out there? What if they want to me dead too? "Be reasonable Cathy," I said to myself. "You're white. Why would they want to hurt you?" "Because they wanted to hurt the white neighbors down the street and the baby is white, that's why! That's three. The house, the baby and me!"

The knocking at the door persisted. Fearing the worst, I managed to get my feet mobile to go to the front door. The closer I came to it, the more I could hear a voice beyond it. It was a strong, determined and deep voice. "Cathy. Aren't you gonna let me in? It's me Jimmy." I breathed a huge sigh of relief and let Jimmy in my sealed up fortress. "Cathy, what's going on? You okay? I've been trying to call you all day and the line's been busy. Oh, I see, you took the phone off the hook. What's up with that?" "I'll tell you what's up Jimmy. If I pick up the phone a little baby will be on it. They keep asking me for help. I ran all over the house last night looking for them." "Back up Cath, what baby? You heard a baby asking for help on the phone, then you went upstairs looking for them? Why?" "I told you Jimmy.

"It started on the phone. A couple nights ago, the night I got home, the phone rang, and when I answered it, I heard a little kid saying not to hang up, that they wanted me to help. Every time I picked up the phone! Ladie heard it too. Scared her so bad she left. Haven't heard from her since. Then down the street, over there, (pointing down the road), there were 3 white crosses in that front yard. Jimmy they were on fire. I saw them, just like I see you now. Let me touch you and make sure you're real. Yep you are." "Catherine, if there were crosses burning in that front yard, don't you think that there would be ashes laying there? Somebody would have called the cops. Did you see any cops over there?" "No, I was too afraid to look. Went around the house, locked and covered all the windows and doors. But that isn't anything compared with what I saw today." "But Cath, you don't need to keep the curtains closed. There isn't anything out there." "Yes there is. If you promise me that you won't go out there, you can look out the back window. You'll see. But don't unlock the door. They don't know I saw them. If they know, they might hurt the baby." "Cathy, what baby? Are you saying somebody is in your back yard right now?" "Yes Jimmy. Go on back there if you don't believe me, just promise me you won't open the door. Please don't open the door!"

Jimmy walked back to the door and pulled over the blind, turned back to me. "Cathy. There isn't anybody back there!" "Don't give me that shit Jimmy I just saw them, they were right back there!" I went to the door, pointed out the window and said, "See? They're throwing that poor little baby over the fire Jimmy. I'm so scared. What are we gonna do?" "Cathy. There isn't anyone back there throwing anything." "Jimmy what do you mean you can't see anything. Look at 'em in their pointed black hats and capes. My God, what if they throw that little baby in the fire? Oh God Jimmy! Don't open the door! Pease, please leave it locked!" "Cathy, I am going to walk back there and you're coming with me. I'm going to show you that there is nothing there."

Jimmy pulled on my hand and I screamed to get away from him. "Cathy. You are going in the back yard whether you like it or not! You have to see that there is nothing there." Jimmy had to practically drag me. He led me to the very back yard pointing to the ground. "See? It's just a broken two by four. That's all. See it?" "Yeah, it is." Jimmy picked it up and handed it to me. I held it for a moment and said nothing. I dropped it back on the ground as Jimmy led the way back into the house. "Cathy, I don't like to see you like this. Are you going to be okay here by yourself?" "What, you mean you're leaving?" I asked. "No, I'm not leaving you yet, but I will have to leave in a while. You know I have to watch the kids for Cindy when she goes to work, but you know if I could I would stay here with you. You got me worried Ca. And ya know something. I think I know who that little voice was on your phone." "You do?" "Yeah. Remember the night I called you, well we have redial on the phone. Windy was playing with the phone and you were the last number I called. She was calling you. Ain't this a trip." "No. It's a relief." "I'll bet if you hang up the phone you won't hear her anymore, because just before I left the house, I called Roger. So if she remembers that button on the phone, she'll be calling him." "Damn Jimmy, I never would have thought of it. Now I can hang the phone up, open the curtains and get you a cup of coffee ... finally. Jimmy laughed, "Ya know, this kitchen looks a little empty without the coffee cans." "They're still in my car." Later became just that and Jimmy had to leave. Said he'd call me later to keep me company while he stayed home to watch his kids.

I was sad to see Jimmy leave in Old Red. Watched him back out of the drive and wondered what I would do now that he was gone.

Sleep I thought, sleep. I'll just lay down and try to sleep. I'll put a cassette in the boom box. Something by The Beatles. That outta give me good dreams. I put the tape on and lay on the couch. It took me awhile, but eventually I was sleeping again.

I passed the next day waiting and watching for the blue jays to make their two visits to my lawn. I threw out pieces of apples to them and some bread. Just like clockwork they arrived. Once at 11:30, once again that evening at 5:45. All four of them. I was glad to see that my blue flying friends hadn't forgotten about me like so many people I thought I knew.

That night I was having trouble in my own porcelain pond. I felt cramps. I sat on the toilet a long time. I pushed and pushed. Something came out at last. There was no blood. But I saw the head of a fetus floating in the water. Felt another cramp and felt the need to push again. This time, I saw four heads in the water. I wiped myself and stood over the toilet looking at the heads with tight shut eyes and mouths. No bodies. The babies were miscarried. I flushed the toilet, when one set of eyes opened on me and I threw up in the sink. Trying to get over what I had seen, had worked me into a sweat. I went into the kitchen to splash my face with cold water and brushed my teeth. On my way out of the room, Self thought, better make sure there is nothing in the water. The water was clean.

I fixed myself something to eat. Tried to put the incident out of my mind, but if all I lost were the babies' heads, then it'd be just a matter of time and remaining parts will be miscarried too.

Wobbling to the living room I laid down on the couch, put my feet up on the arm of the sofa and told myself to sleep. Self couldn't and all I could see was the eyes of the one that went down the drain with the others. Got right up and tried to call Jimmy, but there was no answer. Ladie was neither home or at work. There was no one to talk to, at least not a friend. Not being able to sleep, I spent time at the kitchen table, drinking coffee, afraid to go into the bathroom again.

The evening went on and before I knew it, it was the morning of the April 12th. Had fifteen days to get to the Island. I needed my car! Concentrated only on how I would talk Pope into giving it to me. It wouldn't be easy and it needed careful thought and planning. What would I say? He already specifically told me, that until I got used to being home alone, which I'm not, he's not going to let me drive it. Can't argue with him too much, then he'll suspect that I'm up to something. But I need my car! He'll say he bought it and just say no. I gotta forget about the car.

Cramps were coming on strong like labor. I ran to the bathroom and got my pants down. I sat and pushed. I looked. Another head, I thought? "What's going on!" I yelled. Felt the need to push harder and there was the head of another fetus. Screaming to God ... "How many more are in me?" I dialed 911. "Quick, you gotta get here quick. I've been having miscarriages since last night. I'm losing parts of the baby in the toilet. Hurry, please hurry!"

The paramedics rushed through the front door asking directions to my bathroom. With gloved hands, one of them reached into the muddy like water and lifted its contents. The other paramedic ran to the door covering his mouth as if he was about to throw up. The man still in the bathroom said, "Miss, there isn't anything here. You've had a bowel movement, but I see nothing that indicates that you lost a baby, or even part of one. Have you had any bleeding?" "No. Just go on and tell me I'm seeing things, everyone else is. Better still ... just go. Forget I called. Thanks for nothing." The man put his hat on, nodded and said, "Hope you're feeling better. Try to have a nice day."

Oh once he was gone, me and Self had it out and She began. "Have a nice day?" "Right. Sure. Have a nice day. I was just out celebrating St. Patty's Day the only way I knew. Took all my coffee cans to share with everyone at the party because I was supposed to have a nice fucking day till the fuckin᠍ Sheriff's Department got me and took me to Pope's house. Some fun I was having! If everybody would have just let me do what I knew I was supposed to be doing, I wouldn't be in this mess." "If the walls could talk they'd be saying, no they would be begging to be torn down and burned!" Self was right she was. "It's just a side affect Catherine. You just think you are seeing shadows. It will pass soon." Gone, I thought? What the hell do "they" know! I know what I saw. Nobody knows what I saw. You were there John. Pope said he had my bow at his big house. Maybe his big house is the castle he helped to build in San Marino. Owns that Castle. This is about as sweet as a green apple can get.

Later had come and I was in the bathroom once again. I sat on the toilet, reached behind me to get a monthly horoscope book. I was gonna be in there a while. By the window the night had come and the window needed to be locked.

I read and read. Read Gentry's horoscope to see if he might have sent me a message to decode. Naturally read Pope's. He was the definite and infinitive authority when it came to me and Beatles. He'd pick and choose and his was the final say for me and my safety. Feeling better, when I thought I wouldn't, I didn't. Pushing was like giving birth and I could feel my face tightening in red. I gave out a harsh cry and was frightened of what I would find in the water. "No Catherine. It isn't a whole baby," Said Self with assurance. "But it is, it is! And he could still be alive," I exclaimed. He's 5 months too early at least! "Oh! Gotta get something and take you to the hospital while there's still time. Hold on little boy."

I dashed into the kitchen and found a large glass jar. Cleaned it out with the soapiest and hottest water I could. Then I put body temperature water inside it and took it to the bathroom. As I took the premature baby to put him in the jar of water I mumbled. "If I hurry, they can life flight him someplace. Toledo or Cleveland. They can save Him!" I put the lid of the jar and placed it in a brown paper bag. "This should keep you warm enough until I get us to Firelands. Don't worry. I'll run as fast as I can." Grabbed a coat, my bag and ran to the hospital around the corner. I flew into the emergency room, yelling for help. "Somebody! Nurse? Doctor? Oh good, a doctor. Hurry take this. If you hurry he'll make it. It's a boy. Please hurry and look. Must be at least five months premature! Damn it anyhow! Are you gonna get a helicopter over here or what? Christ! You gonna stand there and keep looking or are ya gonna help him? Critical Care. I saw that helicopter here. Gonna tell me there isn't one? They told me if I needed help, to come back here!" "Miss, we want to help you. We need your name okay?" said a standing by witch. "My name? You stand there worried about my name while that baby is struggling to live? What the fuck's your problem? Take too much thorazine? Take care of my baby!" "Ma'am we need your name, please! We've called for help and it is on the way. Can you please give us your name?" asked the doctor. "Christ everybody knows who I am. I'm Catherine Sue Elizabeth Santi! Now where's the help you said you'd give me. What's taking so fucking long? Don't you realize who I am?" Their background, sneaky words unified and the room became a fog while everyone rushed nowhere. Blankly I stared at "them." The "theys" that seemed to deliberately ignore me. "Catherine," the doctor said, "We can help you now." "How's my baby? Is he going to make it? You don't tell me anything about the baby! You can help me? I'm not the one who needs help for crying out loud! What's with you people? This is the emergency ... " Cut off by a witch she spoke fork tongued, "They are here to help you. Go with them Catherine." Go with who? Go? Why? "I'm not leaving. I'm not leaving without knowing about my ... " "Catherine. You'll be in good hands, just trust us and you'll be okay."

But I am okay, I thought. Go with them? "They" told me if I ever needed any help when they released me to come back. I'm here and they're refusing to help? Get a grip Cathy, thought Self. They're acting. Everything was an act, and so is this. Still act one so to speak. Self and her ideas. An act! Oh! This was supposed to happen like everything else! A thought came to me about where I was going, why, and with who. Self silently said this is act number two ..."

Breinigsville, PA USA
21 October 2009
226205BV00002B/5/P